Lecture Notes in Computer Sci

Edited by G. Goos, J. Hartmanis and J. van Leeuwen

Springer
Berlin
Heidelberg
New York
Barcelona
Hong Kong
London
Milan
Paris
Singapore
Tokyo

Victor Malyshkin (Ed.)

Parallel Computing Technologies

5th International Conference, PaCT-99
St. Petersburg, Russia, September 6-10, 1999
Proceedings

Springer

Series Editors

Gerhard Goos, Karlsruhe University, Germany
Juris Hartmanis, Cornell University, NY, USA
Jan van Leeuwen, Utrecht University, The Netherlands

Volume Editor

Victor Malyshkin
Computing Center
6 Lavrentiev Avenue, Novosibirsk, 630090, Russia
E-mail: malysh@ssd.sscc.ru

Cataloging-in-Publication data applied for

Die Deutsche Bibliothek - CIP-Einheitsaufnahme

Parallel computing technologies : 5th international conference ;
proceedings / PaCT-99, St. Petersburg, Russia, September 6 - 10,
1999. Victor Malyshkin (ed.). - Berlin ; Heidelberg ; New York ;
Barcelona ; Hong Kong ; London ; Milan ; Paris ; Singapore ; Tokyo
: Springer, 1999
(Lecture notes in computer science ; Vol. 1662)
ISBN 3-540-66363-0

CR Subject Classification (1998): D, F.1-2, C, I.6

ISSN 0302-9743
ISBN 3-540-66363-0 Springer-Verlag Berlin Heidelberg New York

This work is subject to copyright. All rights are reserved, whether the whole or part of the material is
concerned, specifically the rights of translation, reprinting, re-use of illustrations, recitation, broadcasting,
reproduction on microfilms or in any other way, and storage in data banks. Duplication of this publication
or parts thereof is permitted only under the provisions of the German Copyright Law of September 9, 1965,
in its current version, and permission for use must always be obtained from Springer-Verlag. Violations are
liable for prosecution under the German Copyright Law.

© Springer-Verlag Berlin Heidelberg 1999
Printed in Germany

Typesetting: Camera-ready by author
SPIN: 10704177   06/3142 – 5 4 3 2 1 0   Printed on acid-free paper

Preface

PaCT-99 (Parallel Computing Technologies) was a four-day conference held in St. Petersburg on 6–10 September 1999. This represented the fifth international conference in PaCT series, which take place in Russia every odd year. The first, PaCT-91, was held in Novosibirsk (Academgorodok), 7–11 September, 1991. The second PaCT-93 was held in Obninsk (near Moscow), 30 August – 4 September, 1993. The third, PaCT-95, was organized in St.Petersburg, 12–15 September, 1995 and the last fourth PaCT-97 was held in Yaroslavl 9-12 September, 1997.

PaCT-99 was jointly organized by the Institute of Computational Mathematics and Mathematical Geophysics of the Russian Academy of Sciences (Novosibirsk) and by the Electrotechnical University of St.Petersburg. The purpose of the conference was to bring together scientists working with theory, architecture, software, hardware and solution of large-scale problems in order to provide integrated discussions on Parallel Computing Technologies.

The Conference attracted more than 100 participants from around the world. Authors from over 23 countries submitted 103 papers and there were 2 invited papers. Of those submitted, 47 papers were selected for the conference; in addition there were a number of posters presented. All the papers were internationally reviewed by at least three referees.

As usual a demo session was organized for the participants. Three different tools were submitted (demonstration and tutorial) under the condition that the tools would be free for noncommercial use. One of them is WinALT (Russian Academy of Sciences, Novosibirsk), a software tool for fine-grain algorithm simulation. Another one is DEALed (State Technical University of St.-Petersburg), a tool for the development of real-time systems. The third is PLATINUM, a tool for workload construction on a workstation network run under UNIX.

Many thanks to our sponsors: the Russian Academy of Sciences, the Russian Fund of Basic Research, the Russian State Committee for Higher Education, PARSYTEC (Germany) and the Institute of Computer Based Software Methodology and Technology (Japan) for their financial support. Organizers highly appreciate the help of the Association Antenne-Provence (France).

June 1999

Victor Malyshkin
Novosibirsk, Academgorodok

A. Alekseev   General Chairman,
                     Russian Academy of Sciences, Novosibirsk, Russia

Program Committee

V. Malyshkin	Chairman,
	Russian Academy of Sciences, Novosibirsk, Russia
O. Bandman	Russian Academy of Sciences, Novosibirsk, Russia
A. Bode	State Technical University of Munich, Germany
H. Burkhart	University of Basel, Switzerland
P. Ciancarini	University of Bologna, Italy
M. Cosnard	Ecole Normale Superieure de Lyon, France
P. Degano	State University of Pisa, Italy
A. Doroshenko	Academy of Sciences, Ukraine
D. Etiemble	University Paris-Sud, France
A. Hurson	Pennsylvania State University, USA
V. Ivannikov	Russian Academy of Sciences, Moscow, Russia
P. Jorrand	LEIBNIZ Laboratory, IMAG, France
Y. Karpov	State Technical University, St. Petersburg
V. Kotov	Hewlett-Packard, Palo Alto, California, USA
B. Lecussan	ONERA/CERT, France
C. Lengauer	State University of Passau, Germany
T. Ludwig	State Technical University of Munich, Germany
G. Mauri	University of Milano, Italy
N. Mirenkov	The University of Aizu, Japan
I. Pottosin	Russian Academy of Sciences, Novosibirsk, Russia
B. Roux	IRPHE-IMT, France
G. Silberman	IBM, Canada
J. Smith	Drexel University, Philadelphia, USA
V. Val'kovskii	Academy of Sciences, Ukraine
D. Walker	University of Wales, Cardiff, UK
A. Wendelborn	University of Adelaide, Australia

Organizing Committee

V. Malyshkin	Co-chairman
D. Puzankov	Co-chairman
A. Krainikov	Vice-Chairman
O. Bandman	Publications
V. Ryabov	Financial Director
N. Kuchin	
V. Plusnin	
O. Repin	
A. Selikhov	Secretariat (Novosibirsk)
S. Semenova	
S. Shaposhnikov	

List of Referees

B. Alexander	A. Hurson	Yu. Pogudin
E. Angel	V. Il'in	I. Pottosin
O. Bandman	P. Jorrand	T. Priol
A. Bode	B. Kargin	S. Pudov
F. Capello	Yu. Karpov	O. Repin
M. Carro	K. Kerry	C. Robach
C. Cerin	G. Kèryvel	V. Samofalov
R. Chevance	A. Konovalov	E. Shurina
P. Ciancarini	V. Kotov	I. Shvetsov
P. Coddington	M. Kraeva	V. Semenov
M. Cole	Yu. Laevskii	G. Silberman
V. Debelov	B. Lecussan	J. Smith
P. Degano	C. Lengauer	P. Stenstrom
A. Doroshenko	T. Ludwig	P. Thanish
J. Esparza	V. Manca	V. Valkovskii
D. Etiemble	F. Martinelli	A. Vazhenin
V. Evstigneev	G. Mauri	G. Vesselovskii
Ya. Fet	N. Mirenkov	I. Virbitskaite
M. Furer	O. Monakhov	V. Vshivkov
S. Gaissarian	V. Morozov	D. Walker
J.-L. Giavitto	V. Narayanan	A. Wendelborn
B. Goossens	E. Okunishnikova	R. Yves
G. Hains	A. Peron	
C. Herrmann	T. Plaks	

Contents

Theory

Software

Architecture

Applications

Posters

Tool

WOLFGANG HÄNDLER

(11 December 1920 – 19 February 1998)

Wolfgang Händler (from a portrait by Konrad Zuse, 1995)

Wolfgang Händler, the talented scholar and engineer, and one of German computer pioneers, was born in Potsdam, Germany. He studied naval engineering from 1941 to 1944 at the Technical University of Danzig. Then he served in the German Navy.

After the War, he studied mathematics and physics at the University of Kiel from 1945 to 1948 and was awarded a degree in Mathematics. In his thesis "Nomographische Darstellung einer erweiterten Thiele-Transformation" Händler had his first encounter with astronomy. Perhaps this was the origin of his interest in the history of mathematical machines, and the background for his highly interesting lectures on the astrolabe, astronomic chronometers, and ancient calculating devices. (Note that in 1993 Professor Händler prepared a special course and a monograph entitled "Instrumental Mathematics: 2000 Years of Computers").

In 1958 Wolfgang Händler earned his doctorate from the Technical University of Darmstadt with a dissertation entitled "Ein Minimisierungsverfahren zur Synthese von Schaltkreisen Minimisierungsgraphen."

From 1948 to 1956 he was employed by the German North-Western Broadcasting Corporation (Research Division Hamburg) working on the theory of communications and the use of computers for improvement of TV pictures. Here, while designing filters, he met up with computers for the first time: BESK in Stockholm and G1 in Göttingen. The young engineer was fascinated, he understood the epoch-making significance of computers, and subsequently devoted to them the whole of his scientific life.

From 1956 to 1959 Wolfgang Händler was with the Telefunken Corporation. He was one of the leading architects of the first transistorized Telefunken computer TR4, the fastest European computer of its time.

From 1959 to 1963 he was Assistant Professor at the University of Saarland, then Professor of Computer Science at the Technical University of Hannover.

Beginning in 1966 he was Professor of Computer Science at the University of Erlangen-Nürnberg, where he founded in 1966 the "Institut für Mathematische Maschinen und Datenverarbeitung (Informatik)."

Professor Wolfgang Händler's main scientific interests were in computer architectures, especially of a non-traditional type, the organization of parallel computing, microprogramming, and the history of mathematical instruments and machines. He was interested not just in the design and implementation of computers but also in the development of corresponding principles. Brilliant evidence of this was the creation in 1974 of the "Erlangen Classification System, ECS," later named after him.

The next area that attracted Professor Händler strongly was visualization. The first of Händler's achievements in this field was related to the minimization graphs explored in his doctoral dissertation. In one of his U.S. patents he described the techniques for presentation and debugging of computer programs by means of an oscillograph. At the end of the 1960s and the beginning of the 1970s Händler began his work in computer graphics and organized Workshops on the man-computer interface.

At the end of the 1970s Professor Händler launched, together with his colleague, physiologist Professor Keidel, a new project on "Data Processing in Computing Devices and Organisms" in which the problems of bionics were examined by a new approach combining the methods and findings from both computer science and the physiology of cognition.

Professor Händler is the author of more than a hundred scientific publications, books and patents. One of his works should be especially noted, namely the paper "Innovative Computer Architecture - How to Increase Parallelism But Not Complexity." It was the first, introductory chapter of the well-known multiauthor volume *Parallel Processing Systems,* written by world authorities on methods and tools of parallel data processing. Professor Händler offered in this work a brilliant analysis of modern computer architectures based on his elegant and effective Classification System. Works by Professor Händler laid the foundation for a new trend in computer science related to the idea of combining various computer models within a single structure. A good example of such an approach is the associative model embedded in the universal architecture of the von Neumann type.

Wolfgang Händler was the leader and active participant in several famous projects of parallel computing systems realized in Erlangen: EGPA (Erlangen General Purpose Array), DIRMU (Distributed Reconfigurable Multiprocessor Kit), SUPRENUM (Supercomputer for Numerical Application), and MEMSY (Modular Expandable Multiprocessor System).

Professor Händler was awarded the Distinguished Service Cross (1st class) in 1982 by the President of the Federal Republic of Germany for his contribution to the development of informatics, particularly at the University of Erlangen-Nürnberg. In 1991 he received honorary doctorates from the Universities of Karlsruhe (Germany) and Novosibirsk (Russia).

Professor Händler was one of a glorious cohort of computer pioneers, which included John Atanassov, Arthur Burks, Moris Wilkes, and Konrad Zuse. These talented and noble people saw the purpose of their life and their creative work not simply in building computing machines of enormous power but above all in using this technology for the benefit of mankind.

Wolfgang Händler and International Scientific Cooperation in the Field of Computer Architecture

Professor Wolfgang Händler is well-known as one of the computer pioneers. Being a contemporary and a friend of Arthur Burks and Konrad Zuse, he made a significant contribution to the theory and applications of computing. He was an eminent authority on the architecture of parallel computing systems.

At the same time, Händler was a distinguished organizer of scientific cooperation between different countries. For these activities, professional skill and great erudition are not enough. In addition, one should have highly developed human qualities and possess the art of personal contacts. Händler was generously endowed with these traits.

Professor Händler was the founder of the European Conferences CONPAR devoted to the problems of parallelism. The first Conference of this series was held in his native city of Erlangen in 1981, the second - in Aachen (1986), the third - in Manchester (1988), the fourth - in Zürich (1991), and the fifth - in Lyon (1992).

For the exploration of computer architectures as well as for the development of international cooperation, the Workshops on Parallel Processing by Cellular Automata and Arrays (PARCELLA) were of special importance. W. Händler was one of the founders of this Workshop series.

The PARCELLA Workshops have been focused mainly on parallel computing in regular structures, a subject which was very close to Händler's interests (it suffices to remember his famous "Horizontal-Vertical Computer"). Moreover, these Workshops were, perhaps, one of the earliest "bridges" between scientists from Western Europe, on the one hand, and from Central and Eastern Europe, on the other. It was an obvious outline of the future cooperation within the framework of united Europe.

Together with Professor Händler, many efforts in the organization of PARCELLA were made by his colleagues from the FRG (R. Vollmar, U. Schendel), the GDR (G. Wolf, W. Wilhelmi), Hungary (T. Legendi), and England (D. Parkinson), among others.

Händler was a constant participant at all PARCELLA Workshops (except the last, the Seventh). And not just a participant! In the Preface to the Sixth PARCELLA (1994) we read: "He didn't restrict his engagement to the program committee's activities and as a honorary lecturer, he also provided participants from East Europe with recent results from the Erlangen IMMD and supported their scientific visits there. It is a good opportunity here to thank him for his valuable gifts of computer journals and computer science literature to the former Academy of Sciences and to the University of Potsdam. We were proud to welcome Professor Wolfgang Händler as an honorable member of the Program Committee."

Recalling the history of the establishment of our PaCT Conference series, we feel a deep gratitude to and a profound respect for Professor Händler. It may be supposed that the PaCT series founded by Professor Nikolay Mirenkov in 1991 was, in a sense, a further elaboration of basic ideas brought by Händler to the COMPAR and PARCELLA Conferences. Actually, the PaCT Conferences continue and extend the subject of parallel methods and architectures. Special attention in PaCT is paid to the cooperation between East and West. Remember that all the PaCT Conferences were held in Russia, but that each of them receives 50% of its participants from a dozen countries of Western Europe and other regions.

The very beginning of the PaCT Conferences, the first Keynote Lecture, was Professor Händler's brilliant lecture "Nature Needed Billions of Years ... " presented on 7 September 1991 at the opening of PaCT-91. Concluding this lecture, Professor Händler said:

"The teraflop-computer will come in a remarkable number at the end of this century. There is no doubt about it. The teraflop-multiprocessors will represent a means to an end - to numerical simulation, to huge data bases, to artificial intelligence, to expert systems and to many things else. The mail question will nevertheless be whether we will wisely utilize these tools to preserve our world and its natural sources from destruction and to prevent the humanity from serious conflicts or wars."

Returning to Erlangen after PaCT-91, Händler prepared a "Report on a Professional Business Trip," a quite interesting document reflecting all the important features of his visit to Russia. First of all, Professor Händler describes in detail the main reports of the Conference. But not just the reports! He also paid sufficient attention to the cordial atmosphere of the meeting, stimulating creative contacts between scientists from different countries. Moreover, the Report was adorned by numerous photos.

Thus, Händler describes in his Report the steamer excursion along the Ob Sea (an artificial reservoir near the Academic Village) organized for the participants on the last day of their stay in Novosibirsk. It was a marvelous "velvet" September day. The ship moored in one of the bays, where the hosts had built a kind of an improvised restaurant, right on the clean sandbar. The ordinary self-made wooden tables were served with a lot of delicacies. The durable Armenian cognac and the fresh shashlik (being prepared "on-line," right here, on the beach) represented only a minor part of the menu. This picnic appears in one of Händler's photos. One can see the crowd of scientists sitting around long tables and the ship waiting at a distance to bring them to the city in the evening ... "Undoubtedly, this excursion will always remain in the memory of all participants" – concludes Professor Händler.

The next of Professor Händler's visits to Russia was connected with an outstanding event. On 10 February 1992, he received an Honorary Doctorate from the University of Novosibirsk. It should be emphasized that Wolfgang Händler was *the first* scientist awarded this newly established honorary title. In a special resolution of the Academic Council of the University of Novosibirsk it was stated:

" ... to award the degree of Honorary Doctorate from the University of Novosibirsk to W. Händler, Professor of the Erlangen-Nürnberg University, for his outstanding contribution in studying informatics problems, development of methods of parallel data processing, study and comparative analysis of multiprocessor system architectures, for his great success in spreading scientific knowledge, and enduring efforts in development of scientific cooperation between people of different countries."

To join the Ceremony of Conferment, the Rector of the Erlangen-Nürnberg

University, Professor Gotthard Jasper, and the Head of the AI Department, Dr. Herbert Stoyan, accompanied Professor Händler to Novosibirsk. The festive Ceremony was held in the Assembly Hall of the House of Scientists (Novosibirsk, Academic Village). After the addresses of Novosibirsk scientists and the presenting of the diploma, Professor Händler delivered a remarkable Inaugural Lecture "History of Computing - A Taxonomic Approach." During intermissions in the ceremony, the Hall resounded with classical music performed by a symphonic orchestra.

At the PaCT-91 Conference, aside from the aforementioned Keynote Lecture, Professor Händler presented a regular paper "Vertical Processing in Parallel Computing Systems" (with Ya.I. Fet). At the next PaCT Conference (Obninsk, Russia, 1993) he presented a paper "Why We Favour Pyramids" (with N.N. Mirenkov). Professor Händler's report to the PaCT-95 (St. Petersburg, Russia, 1995) "Parallel Processing: Increasing Performance and Dependability," was presented, on his behalf, by the author of these lines. The PaCT-97 Conference (Yaroslavl, Russia, 1997) found Professor Händler unable to attend.

Wolfgang Händler was an active organizer and a permanent member of the Program Committees of all previous PaCT Conferences. Today, Professor Händler is no longer with us. However, the participants of the PaCT-99 Conference as well as of future PaCTs (already in the twenty-first century) will keep alive the memory of Wolfgang Händler, one of the prominent scientists of the twentieth century, who has been and remains our true friend.

Yakov Fet
Institute of Computational Mathematics and
Mathematical Geophysics, Siberian Division of RAS,
Novosibirsk, Russia

Analytical Modeling of Parallel Applications in Heterogeneous Computing Environments: A Study of Choesky Factorization

R. Aversa[1], N. Mazzocca[1], and U. Villano[2]

[1]DII, Seconda Universita' di Napoli, via Roma 29, 81031 Aversa (CE), Italy
aversa@grid.unina.it , n.mazzocca@unina.it
[2]Universita' del Sannio, Facolta' di Ingegneria, C.so Garibaldi 107, 82100 Benevento, Italy
villano@unina.it

Abstract. Achieving satisfactory performance results in heterogeneous computing environments requires a careful workload assignment. The use of approximate analytical models can help to understand which are the parameters that mostly affect performance. In this paper we will show how to study analytically the behavior of a Cholesky factorization code running in a heterogeneous NOW under the PVM run-time system. Firstly the Cholesky factorization algorithm is introduced, and an analysis of the load distribution is performed. Then the construction of the analytic model of the application is described. Finally, the obtained results are compared to the performance figures obtained by executing the program in the real computing environment.

1 Introduction

During the last decade there has been a widespread diffusion of parallel computing culture. Also thanks to the availability of simple programming environments such as the PVM run-time system [1], now teaching a class of undergraduate students how to develop simple parallel programs requires just few hours. Unfortunately, for inexperienced developers it is not easy to understand why the obtained performance results are so far (this is almost always the case) from the expected ones. Paradoxically, the latest performance developments of personal workstations and interconnection networks have made things worse. The availability of cheap distributed computing power over fast networks has made particularly convenient the use of networks of variously-assorted workstations (NOW) [2] for parallel program execution. Therefore, most of the times the environment of choice is characterized by computing resource heterogeneity.

All heterogeneous computing environments present a problem that is not encountered in the development of parallel software for homogeneous machines, namely the necessity to choose carefully the workload to be assigned to each target machine. In NOWs, the issue is to assign each processor with an amount of workload proportional to its processing speed, so as to reduce idle times and attain high computing efficiency [3]. Sometimes, also the interconnection networks involved are heterogeneous. However, we will not deal with this problem here, assuming that the processing nodes are connected by a single homogeneous network.

The sometimes subtle effects of computer resource heterogeneity further complicate the difficult task of program performance evaluation and tuning. Therefore, sophisticated and cost-effective performance evaluation techniques are needed. At the state of the art, no general and completely satisfactory solution seems to exist for analyzing and improving the performance of parallel applications developed in heterogeneous computing environments. Our research group has been involved in the last few years in the development of a simulator of parallel programs [4]. Simulation has been proven to be a simple and effective technique to predict and to analyze parallel program performance behavior. Simulation in modern high-performance simulators is essentially a "black box" technique: the developer submits the program as a whole and gets in an automatic way the performance figures corresponding to its execution on the target hardware. This characteristic is at the same time the best advantage and the main drawback of simulation environments. Since obtaining global indexes related to program execution is fairly easy, the developer may not be sufficiently stimulated to gain insight on program behavior by an in-depth analysis of simulation output.

In fact, abstracting from simulated performance results the inner behavior of software and computing environment is only for skilled developers. The use of approximate, perhaps oversimplified, analytical models can help to understand which are the parameters that mostly affect performance, and to reduce the number of simulated runs required to obtain satisfactory performance results. While several simulation or monitoring environments are currently available [4,5,6,7], no tool is able to construct automatically an analytical model of a given application. Things are worse if the application is to be executed in a heterogeneous environment. As a matter of fact, analytically modeling is still a task with intellectual challenge.

In this paper we will show how to study analytically the behavior of a Cholesky factorization code running in a heterogeneous NOW under the PVM run-time system. The techniques that will be used are not completely general, in that they cannot be used for the totality of parallel programs. However, in the absence of any consolidated methodology for the construction of analytical models of parallel code, we think that showing in detail how to study a rather customary application can be useful. To our knowledge, no detailed example of the construction of an analytic model of a message-passing application executed in heterogeneous environments is currently available in the literature. Most of existing work can be applied only to systems that are homogeneous both in the computing nodes and in the network connections between them [8,9]. We think that, after reading the following example, a developer should be able to model (with some effort) the majority of message-passing programs, even in the presence of computing resource heterogeneity.

This paper is structured as follows. Firstly the Cholesky factorization algorithm is introduced. An analysis of the load distribution is performed, describing several techniques that can be adopted to balance suitably the number of data elements assigned to each processor. Then the construction of the analytic model of the application is thoroughly described. Finally, the obtained results are compared to the performance figures obtained by executing the program in the real computing environment and the conclusions are drawn.

2   Cholesky Factorization in a Heterogeneous NOW

The example chosen to show how to tackle analytical modeling of a parallel application is the study of a program that computes the solution of a positive definite symmetric system of linear algebraic equations $A \cdot x = b$ by Cholesky factorization. The matrix A is firstly written as $L \cdot L^T$, where L is lower triangular. Then the system $L \cdot y = b$ is solved, from which it is obtained the solution vector x by solving the system $L^T \cdot x = y$. Cholesky factorization is a classical test application, and one that lends itself well to non-trivial performance considerations if the target computing system is heterogeneous. We will assume that the program is executed in a heterogeneous NOW made up of N variously-assorted workstations under the PVM run-time system. We will not consider instead heterogeneity at the network level. The diagrams and performance figures that will be presented are relative to the use of a 10 Mb/s Ethernet LAN. However, the analysis is valid for different networks as well.

The algorithm adopted to perform the above-mentioned computation steps is made up of the following phases:

1. submatrix Cholesky factorization using synchronous fan-out broadcast communication;
2. forward substitution for the lower triangular matrix;
3. backward substitution for the upper triangular matrix.

Let the $dim * dim$ input data matrix be distributed in vertical strips of b (blocksize) columns among the N component tasks, which are allocated one per processor (see Fig. 1, where $N = 4$). The three algorithm phases can be schematized by the pseudo-code shown in Fig. 2, 3 and 4, respectively.

2.1   Load Distribution Analysis

The Gantt diagram in Fig. 5 was obtained from a first execution on a heterogeneous cluster of four dedicated workstations interconnected through a *silent* 10Mb/s Ethernet[1]. The chart shows long CPU idle phases, which are due to a very uneven workload sharing (see the central part of the diagram, where processor 2 is busy and the others are waiting for it to finish). In fact, as the computational load of each task is an increasing function of the number of elements assigned to it, a decomposition as the one shown in Fig. 1 fails to distribute evenly the workload among processors.

---

[1] This and the following diagrams are in fact obtained from simulated program executions. In [4], it is shown that the simulated performance results presented here are representative of real program executions apart from an error typically less than 5%.

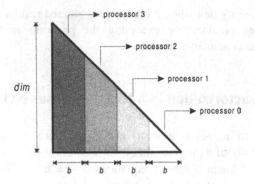

Fig. 1. Basic distribution of the data matrix to processors (fixed blocksize)

```
for (k = 0; k < dim; k++)  {
     if (column k is mine) {
          modify column k;
          send column k to all other tasks;
     }
     else
          receive the modified column k;
     for (all columns of mine > k)
          update it using the new values of column k;
}
```

Fig. 2. Code skeleton for the Cholesky factorization phase

```
for (k = 0; k < dim; k++)  {
     t=0;
     compute t = Σ a[k,j]*y[j] for each local column j;
     if (column k is mine) {
          receive t from all other tasks;
          compute y[k];
     }
     else
          send t to the owner of column k;
}
```

Fig. 3. Code skeleton for the forward substitution phase

```
for (k = dim-1; k >= 0; k--)  {
     if (row k is mine) {
          compute x[k];
          send x[k] to all other tasks;
     }
     else {
          receive x[k] from the owner of row k;
          substitute x[k] in all rows;
     }
}
```

Fig. 4. Code skeleton for the backward substitution phase

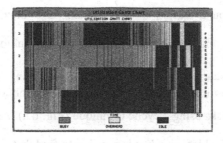

Fig. 5. Program execution Gantt chart ($N = 4$, $dim = 600$, $b = 150$)

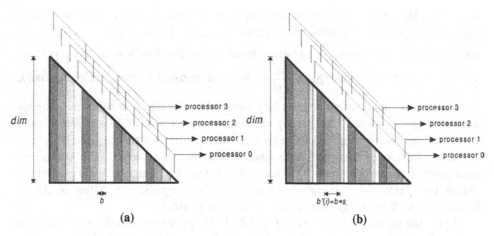

(a)   (b)

Fig. 6. Alternative distributions of the data matrix to processors: fixed blocksize with interleaving (a), variable blocksize with interleaving (b)

The problem of load distribution can be tackled analytically as follows. Let processor number 0 be assigned the rightmost strip, and processor $N - 1$ the leftmost one. Let us also assume for simplicity's sake that dim is an integer multiple of N. In the above hypotheses, processor 0 gets $1 + 2 + ... + \dfrac{dim}{N}$ elements. In its turn, processor 1 gets $\left(\dfrac{dim}{N} + 1\right) + \left(\dfrac{dim}{N} + 2\right) + ... + 2 \cdot \dfrac{dim}{N}$ elements. In general, the i-th processor ($i = 0..N - 1$) gets $elem(i)$ matrix elements, where

$$elem(i) = \frac{dim}{2N} \cdot \left[\frac{dim}{N} \cdot (2i + 1) + 1\right] . \tag{1}$$

From the equation above it can be easily seen that $elem(i)$ is an increasing function of i. If we define Δe as the difference in the number of elements assigned to two consecutive processors (i.e., $elem(i+1) - elem(i)$, $i = 0..N - 2$), we find that the number of assigned elements grows with processor number in steps of Δe. Hence Δe must be minimized in order to attain an even workload distribution. From equation

(1) it can be readily found that $\Delta e = \dfrac{dim^2}{N^2}$. In the case of the program execution leading to the results of Fig. 5 ($dim = 600$, $N = 4$), Δe is equal to 22,500, on a total of 180,300 elements making up the whole data matrix.

A more even load sharing can be attained by interleaving the strips assigned to every processor. In order to do so, it is necessary to reduce the width of the strips, and to assign them to the tasks using a cyclic technique (Fig. 6.a). Assuming that $\dfrac{dim}{N}$ is an integer multiple of the blocksize b, it is possible to find that

$$elem(i) = \frac{dim}{2N} \cdot \left[b \cdot (2i+1) + 1 + dim - b \cdot N \right] \cdot \qquad (2)$$

This formula, whose derivation is omitted here for brevity, can be obtained fairly easily by recurrence, examining the expressions of $elem(i)$ for $b = 1, 2, \ldots$. As in the previous case, the number of elements is an increasing function of the processor number. Now we find that $\Delta e = \dfrac{dim \cdot b}{N}$; if the dimension of the problem is fixed, smoother workload distributions can be obtained by reducing b or by using a higher number of processors. In the already mentioned case of $dim = 600$ and $N = 4$, even with a not particularly fine blocksize ($b = 25$) it is possible to reduce from 22,500 to 3,750 the difference between the number of elements assigned to two successive processors. A second program execution with this load assignment made it possible to obtain the Gantt chart in Fig. 7.a, which shows a significantly better workload balancing, and the consequent reduction of the idle phases.

In fact, the utilization summary in Fig. 7.b clearly points out that the load is not yet evenly shared, due to processor heterogeneity (the processing speed of processors 0, 1, 2, 3 scales approximately as 2:4:1:1). A reasonable solution for obtaining a better workload distribution is to assign each processor with a number of columns proportional to its *relative power index*. Relative power indexes, which have been formally defined in [3], are a relative measure of the peak processor speed to the speed of a reference processor for a given problem. They can be found by executing a suitable benchmark and comparing the completion times measured on each processor.

Let $\overline{s}$ be the vector whose components are the relative power indexes of the N involved processors, normalized to index of the slowest processor and rounded to the nearest integer. An interleaved strip assignment with variable blocksize (Fig. 6.b) can be derived from a fixed blocksize assignment with blocksize b such as the one in Fig. 6.a, using the usual cyclic technique and assigning to each processor i a strip of width $b(i) = b \cdot s_i$ at every turn. Given the vector $\overline{s}$, the expression of $elem(i)$ can be obtained trivially from (2). It should be pointed out that Δe is not constant as in the two previously considered assignments. However, $elem(i)$ is still a growing function of i, so that processors with higher numbers (i.e., higher values of i) get an excess of matrix elements as compared to processors with lower numbers. Whenever the load unbalance due to the excess elements is not negligible, it is useful to adopt a processor numbering in increasing order of processing speed, in such a way that

$s_i \le s_j$ if $i < j$. This clearly minimizes the time penalty due to the processing of the excess elements, and therefore helps keeping the load well balanced.

A variable blocksize assignment led to the results represented in Fig. 8 a,b, which show a substantially even workload distribution.

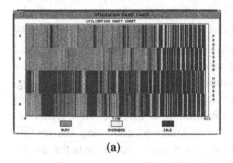
(a)

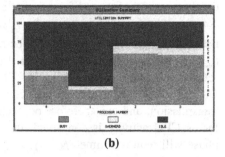
(b)

Fig. 7. Program execution Gantt chart (a) and utilization summary (b), fixed blocksize with interleaving ($N = 4$, $dim = 600$, $b = 25$)

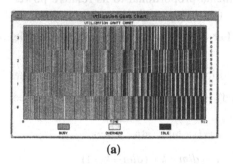
(a)

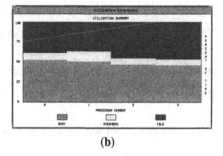
(b)

Fig. 8. Program execution Gantt chart (a) and utilization summary (b), variable blocksize with interleaving($N = 4$, $dim = 600$, $b' = [20;40;10;10]$))

2.2 Analytical Modeling

The Cholesky code chosen as an example is fairly complex, and in general it does not lend itself to straightforward analytical modeling, especially when it is executed in a heterogeneous environment. However, in light of the results of the previous subsection it is reasonable to assume that the workload is perfectly balanced. Under this assumption, it is possible to construct a model of program execution of tractable complexity. This model describes an ideal system behavior, and, as such, it only gives lower bounds for program execution time. These, though useful to help understand how far a given solution is from the ideal one, may be close to real execution times only in the case of very optimized programs. Alternative methods (see [10]) are to be used for the prediction of program performance under different operating conditions.

According to the code skeleton shown in Fig. 2, Cholesky factorization (which is an O(dim^3) process, and is the more computation-intensive of the three phases making up the program) consists of *dim* elementary steps. At the k-th step ($k = 0..dim - 1$), a column of *dim - k* elements is modified by its "owner", and transmitted to the other $N - 1$ processors. Then each of the N processors updates the portion of the columns from $k + 1$ to *dim - 1* it owns. Let processor o be the owner of the column to be modified and s_o its relative power index, normalized to the slowest processor. If t_m is the time required for modifying a single matrix element *on the slowest processor*, the column modify time is given by $1/s_o \cdot t_m \cdot (dim - k)$. In shared media local area networks, communication time can be modeled by the sum of a constant component $t_{comm,setup}$ plus a component proportional to the amount of data transmitted [11]. The setup component is mainly spent in CPU activities, such as data packing and copying. On the other hand, the second component takes into account the actual data transmission, and can therefore be overlapped in time with CPU activity. Hence, as far as CPU activity is concerned, the $N - 1$ communications following the modify phase will require a time $(N - 1) \cdot t_{comm,setup}$ from processor o. As regards the update phase, it should be noted that the total number of elements to be updated is $(dim - k)(dim - k - 1)/2$. In the hypothesis of ideal workload sharing, each processor will be the owner of a number of matrix elements proportional to its relative power index. Hence the generic processor i ($i = 1..N$) will be the owner of $\dfrac{s_i \cdot (dim - k) \cdot (dim - k - 1)}{2 \cdot \sum_i s_i}$ matrix elements. Let t_u be the update time for a single

matrix element on the slowest processor. It follows that the duration of the update phase in each processor (processor o included) is $\dfrac{t_u \cdot (dim - k) \cdot (dim - k - 1)}{2 \cdot \sum_i s_i}$. Hence

the owner processor will be able to process the next column after a time

$$T_{owner}(k) = \frac{t_m}{s_o} \cdot (dim - k) + (N - 1) \cdot t_{comm,\,setup} + \frac{t_u \cdot (dim - k) \cdot (dim - k - 1)}{2 \cdot \sum_i s_i} \ . \qquad (3)$$

Commutations from one owner processor to the next one may be advantageous or introduce further delays, depending on the relative length of communication setup and transmission phases. In Fig. 9.a, $t_{comm,setup}$ dwarfs the times t_{comm} required for actual message transmissions (transmissions are represented by cross-processor arrows in the diagram). This is the most likely case for small values of *dim*. The commutation from processor 0 (the owner for the first two steps in the figure) to processor 1 leads therefore to a reduction of idle phases for the involved processors. This is evident by observing that the update phases are closer to one another astride the owner commutation. On the other hand, in Fig 8.b, actual message transmission are much longer than setup times. As a result, the owner commutation after the first two steps introduces additional idle time. The commutation penalty can be minimized by structuring the code in such a way that the first packet transmitted by the owner processor is always sent to the next owner. This is the case depicted in Fig. 9.b, where processor 1 sends the first packet to processor 2, which will be the next owner.

9

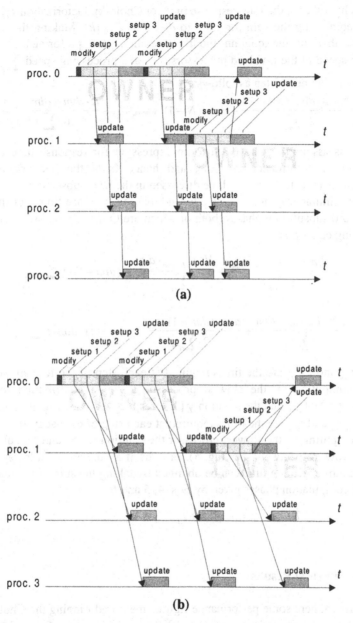

Fig. 9. Commutation of the "owner" processor. $t_{comm,setup} \gg t_{comm}$ (a); $t_{comm,setup} \ll t_{comm}$ (b)

The overall effect of commutations cannot be easily taken into account, since the length of the data packets sent, and hence the duration of message transmission times, varies as the reduction completes. Anyway, in Ethernet networks $t_{comm,setup}$ is three orders of magnitude higher than the communication time per byte [12]. Therefore, owner commutations are likely to be advantageous unless very large matrices are processed. In what follows, we will simply neglect the effect of owner commutations.

Under this hypothesis, the total response time for Cholesky factorization $T_{Cholesky}$ can be found by computing the sum for $k = 0$ to dim-1 of $T_{owner}(k)$. Making the simplifying assumption that all the column modify operations are performed at the mean processing speed of the involved processors (i.e., at a processing speed $\sum_i s_i / N$), the response time can be written as follows:

$$T_{Cholesky} = \frac{N \cdot t_m \cdot dim \cdot (dim + 1)}{2 \cdot \sum_i s_i} + dim \cdot (N - 1) \cdot t_{comm,\,setup} + \frac{t_u \cdot dim \cdot (dim^2 - 1)}{6 \cdot \sum_i s_i} \quad . \tag{4}$$

Our previous assumptions have led to an expression for response time completely independent of communication time, and hence from the network bandwidth. Whether this is realistic or not, will be discussed in the next subsection.

In a very similar way, it is possible to find that the response times for the forward and backward substitution phases (both of which are O(dim^2) processes) are given by the following equations:

$$T_{forward} = \frac{dim \cdot (dim - 1) \cdot t_{sum}}{2 \cdot \sum_i s_i} + \frac{N \cdot t_{sol,forw} \cdot dim}{\sum_i s_i} + (dim - 1) \cdot t_{comm,setup} \quad , \tag{5}$$

$$T_{backward} = \frac{N \cdot t_{sol,backw} \cdot dim}{\sum_i s_i} + \frac{dim \cdot (dim - 1) \cdot t_{subst}}{2 \cdot \sum_i s_i} + (N - 1) \cdot dim \cdot t_{comm,setup} \quad . \tag{6}$$

In Eq. 5, t_{sum} and $t_{sol,forw}$ are the times required at each step of the forward substitution loop for computing on the slowest processor a single contribution to the sum t=Σ a[k,j]*y[j] and the solution y[k], respectively (see Fig. 3). Analogously, in Eq. 6 $t_{sol,backw}$ and t_{subst} are the times required at each step of the backward substitution loop for computing on the slowest processor the solution x[k] and for substituting it in a single row, respectively (see Fig. 4). In light of all the above, a lower bound for actual program execution time can be obtained by taking the sum of the length of the individual computation phases given by Eqs. 4, 5 and 6:

$$T_{response,ideal} = T_{Cholesky} + T_{forward} + T_{backward} \quad . \tag{7}$$

2.3   Experimental Results

We will present here some performance figures measured running the Cholesky code on the real computing environment. Fig. 10 shows the response times obtained with fixed and variable blocksize assignment with interleaving in the range of values of dim from 100 to 1200. These are compared against the lower bound obtained through the analytical model valid for perfectly-even workload sharing. The diagram shows clearly the performance advantage due to the adoption of variable blocksize over fixed blocksize. In fact, the response times found by means of the model presented in the previous subsection are a reasonable approximation of the actual ones if a variable blocksize assignment is used. The difference between the model results and the response times measured on the real system (typically contained between 20 and 30%) is essentially due to the non perfectly-even load sharing, to transmission collisions over the shared Ethernet medium and to the presence of a light background load (the activity of system daemons) in the workstations used for the tests.

An interesting result can be found by fitting the two curves giving actual response times with polynomials of degree 3, and comparing their coefficients to those that can be obtained by substituting the actual service times in Eq. 7. The effect of uneven workload sharing is the rise of the quadratic and cubic coefficient as compared to the coefficient of the lower-bound curve. Whereas, the coefficient of the linear term, which dominates the curve for small values of *dim*, is unaffected by workload sharing policy, since it is at a great extent determined by communication setup times.

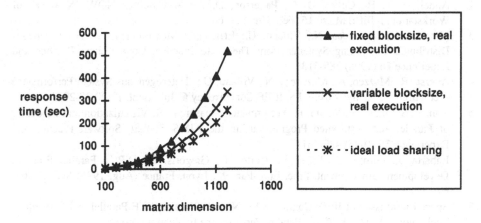

Fig. 10. Response time with fixed and variable blocksize, ideal and real program execution, *dim* = 100-1200

3 Conclusions

Performance evaluation of parallel and distributed systems can be approached from three major directions: direct measurement, analytic models and simulation. The relaxation of the need for the target computing platform is perhaps the most useful characteristic of analytic and simulation approaches. Simulation on high-performance simulators appears to be the simplest and most promising technique for fast application development and tuning. However, it is a fact that even over-simplified analytical models can be useful to gain insight on the behavior of complex programs executed in heterogeneous environments.

Since consolidated and general techniques for the construction of analytic models are still lacking, we have thoroughly presented in this paper a model of a Cholesky factorization code running in a heterogeneous NOW. The objective of the exposition has not been to propose completely general techniques, but simply to show an example that could allow the reader to understand how models can be developed, even if targeted to different environments. Notwithstanding the assumptions made to obtain a model of tractable complexity, the performance figures predicted by means of the proposed model have turned out to be very close to the ones measured by running the real program on the target computing environment.

References

1. Geist, A., Beguelin, A., Dongarra, J., Jiang, W., Manchek, R., Sunderam, V.: PVM: Parallel Virtual Machine. MIT Press, Cambridge, MA (1994)
2. Anderson, T. E., Culler, D. E., Patterson, D. A.: A Case for NOW (Networks of Workstations). IEEE Micro **15** (Feb. 1995) 54-64
3. Mazzeo, A., Mazzocca, N., Villano, U.: Efficiency Measurements in Heterogeneous Distributed Computing Systems: from Theory to Practice. Concurrency: Practice and Experience **10** (1998) 285-313
4. Aversa, R., Mazzeo, A., Mazzocca, N., Villano, U.: Heterogeneous System Performance Prediction and Analysis using PS. IEEE Concurrency **6** (July-Sept. 1998) 20-29
5. Yan, J., Sarukkai, S., Mehra, P.: Performance Measurement, Visualization and Modeling of Parallel and Distributed Programs using the AIMS Toolkit. Software-Practice and Experience **25** (1995) 429-461
6. Labarta, J., Girona, S., Pillet, V., Cortes T., Gregoris, L.: DiP: a Parallel Program Development Environment. Proc. Euro-Par '96, Lyon, France (Aug. 1996) Vol. II 665-674
7. Special joint issue of IEEE Computer **28** (Nov. 1995) and IEEE Parallel and Distributed Technology (Winter 1995) on Parallel Performance Evaluation Tools.
8. Qin, B., Sholl, H. A., Ammar, R. A.: Micro Time Cost Analysis of Parallel Computations. IEEE Trans. On Comp. **40** (1991) 613-628
9. Steed, M. R., Clement, M. J.: Performance Prediction of PVM Programs. Proc. 10th Int. Par. Proc. Symp., Honolulu, USA (April 1996) 803-807
10. Aversa, R., Mazzeo, A., Mazzocca, N., Villano, U.: Developing Applications for Heterogeneous Computing Environments using Simulation: a Case Study. Parallel Computing **24** (1998) 741-761
11. Hockney, R. W., Jesshope, C. R.: Parallel Computers 2, Adam Hilger, Philadelphia, USA (1988)
12. Dongarra, J., Dunigan, T.: Message-Passing Performance of Various Computers. University of Tennessee Comp. Sc. Tech. Rep. UT-CS-95-299 (May 1996)

Skeletons and Transformations in an Integrated Parallel Programming Environment*

Bruno Bacci[1], Sergei Gorlatch[2], Christian Lengauer[2], and Susanna Pelagatti[3]

[1] Quadrics Supercomputers World Ltd., Via S. Maria 83, I-56125 Pisa, Italy
[2] Universität Passau, D-94030 Passau, Germany
[3] Universitá di Pisa, Corso Italia 40, I-56125 Pisa, Italy

Abstract. We present an integrated environment for the systematic development of parallel and distributed programs. Our approach allows the user to construct complex applications by composing and transforming *skeletons*, i.e., recurring patterns of task and data parallelism. First academic and commercial experience with skeleton-based systems has demonstrated the benefits of the approach but also the lack of a dedicated set of methods for algorithm design and performance prediction. We take a first step towards such a set of methods by proposing an environment which integrates a framework for algorithm transformation, called FAN, with two existing skeleton-based programming systems: the academic system P3L and its commercial counterpart SkIE.

1 Introduction

Current difficulties in low-level parallel and distributed programming using, e.g., the MPI (Message Passing Interface) standard [16] can be addressed by high-level programming models together with convenient programming environments.

A number of parallel programming environments are already available. For instance, in HeNCE (Heterogeneous Network Computing Environment) [5,6], applications are written in C or Fortran77 and run on top of PVM. The HeNCE programmer writes parallel applications by graphically drawing the interrelationships between the different (sequential) process components of the parallel application. The Annai project [10] led to the development of a set of tools including PST (a parallelization support tool), PMA (a performance monitor and analyzer) and PDT (a parallel debugging tool). The kinds of code restructuring and optimization that can be carried out by these environments are rather limited. Decisions concerning difficult problems such as scheduling, mapping, load balancing and data distribution are made on the basis of a few weak heuristics, since there is little knowledge about the parallel structure being defined. This forces the user to restructure the code by hand both when tuning performance on a particular machine and when porting an application to a different machine.

---

* *Contact author:* Sergei Gorlatch, University of Passau, D-94030 Passau, Germany. Tel: +49 851 509-3074, Fax: +49 851 509-3092, Email: gorlatch@fmi.uni-passau.de

An alternative, higher-level approach is based on so-called *skeletons* [11], which can be viewed as recurring algorithmic and communication patterns, expressed in a rigorous way [17]. Representatives of skeleton-based systems are the P3L system at the University of Pisa [4], its commercial analogue SkIE at QSW Ltd. [2,3], SKIL at RWTH Aachen [8], and SCL at Imperial College [12]. These systems provide the user with a number of higher-order skeletons, which can be customized and combined for a particular application. A skeletal program is then translated (semi)automatically to some target language, e.g., C plus MPI, using prepackaged parallel implementations of skeletons. The abstraction from communication and other details gives skeletal programs a considerably better structure and makes them less error-prone than their low-level counterparts.

In the long run, the *approach of skeleton-based programming* should include methods and support tools for choosing suitable skeletons, composing them to a program, estimating its expected performance, and making changes to improve efficiency. Our present proposal has grown out of experience in transformational programming [1, 15], compiler optimization [9] and efficiency analysis [13]. In particular, we have proposed a framework, called FAN (for Formal Abstract Notation), for the description and transformation of parallel algorithms, which is at a higher level of abstraction than existing skeleton systems [14].

Here, we present an integrated environment which provides the user with specific methods and tools for skeleton-based program development. The environment extends the existing versions of the systems P3L and SkIE by transformation methods for application algorithms which are composed of skeletons.

The paper is organized as follows. After a brief overview of the environment, we present the basic skeletons available in P3L and SkIE, and their higher-level counterparts in FAN. We describe how the user interacts with the programming environment under visual support at the main stages of the design and implementation of a parallel algorithm. Finally, we present transformation rules for skeletons, and illustrate the entire approach with a small case study.

2   System Structure Overview

In this section, we take the P3L system [4] as a representative of skeleton-based systems, and outline how it is augmented by the FAN transformational framework. The overall structure of the resulting environment is presented in Figure 1.

The figure shows how the user communicates via the visual support system (Visual SkIE, described in Section 4) with the programming environment. The latter is partitioned by horizontal, solid lines into three parts – from top to bottom: the transformational framework, the P3L system, and the target machines. Solid arrows show the connections between the parts of the system, dashed arrows depict the user's interaction with the system, with bold, dashed arrows for the new interactions added by the transformational framework.

In the P3L system, the user starts the development by writing a complete skeletal P3L program (in the middle of Figure 1). The user must provide a skeleton-based algorithm and also supply all necessary sequential modules, input and output files. The program is optimized and translated by the P3L compiler, which provides the user with preliminary cost estimates, i.e., computation and communication time, for the program. If the user is satisfied with the cost, the C plus MPI code produced by the compiler can be run on an available target machine; some current platforms targeted by the P3L compiler are shown in the figure.

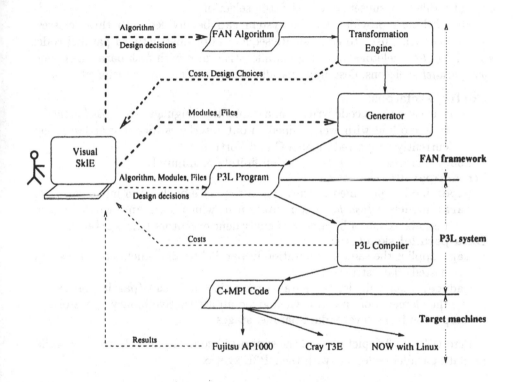

Fig. 1. FAN on top of P3L

The transformational framework **FAN**, shown in the upper part of Figure 1, offers the user additional support in designing a skeletal program. Using **FAN**, the design process starts by writing a functional version of the parallel algorithm, without providing concrete sequential modules and files. The algorithm is analyzed by the transformation engine, which attempts to apply transformations from its repository of rules and suggest a choice of design alternatives to the user, with a cost estimate for each alternative. After, possibly, several iterations of design choices, the user may decide to generate a P3L program, which is then compiled and executed as described above.

3 Skeletons and Transformations

3.1 Skeletons

In this section, we describe algorithmic patterns, called *skeletons*, which are available in our integrated environment. These skeletons are implemented currently in two programming systems which we use as testbeds in our work: P3L, developed at the University of Pisa, and the SkIE system with coordination language SkIECL [3], developed at QSW Ltd. We use both since they implement currently different subsets of our skeleton selection.

The skeletons provided by the system can be divided into three classes: *control* skeletons, used to encapsulate sequential or unstructured parallel code; *stream-parallel* skeletons, modeling parallel structures with task parallelism; and *data-parallel* skeletons, describing parallel computations on partitioned data.

Control skeletons:
  seq: encapsulates code written in a sequential language (the *host language*) in a module with well defined in-out interfaces. Sequential languages currently supported include C and Fortran.
  loop: iterates skeleton composition finitely or infinitely.
Stream-parallel skeletons:
  pipe: models pipelined execution of a sequence of skeleton instances.
  farm: models a *task farm* computation in which a stream of independent tasks is executed by a pool of equivalent executors (the *workers*).
Data-parallel skeletons:
  map: applies the same computation in parallel to all elements of a (possibly nested) data structure.
  reduce, scan: model the parallel reduction and scan (parallel prefix) on the elements of an array when given an associative binary operator.
  comp: combines several data-parallel stages.

Figures 2 and 3 depict some of the supported control-parallel, stream-parallel and data-parallel skeletons, with their P3L syntax.

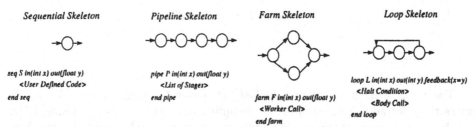

Fig. 2. Control-parallel and stream-parallel skeletons

All P3L skeleton definitions are opened and closed by the skeleton name (e.g., *farm ... end farm*). Each skeleton instance requires a name for subsequent use (e.g., *F* in the farm skeleton) and the specification of input and output parameters (*in()* and *out()* lists). The *body*, denoted by < ... >, is skeleton-specific. A seq body specifies pure functional host language code (without side effects).

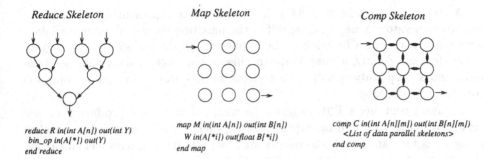

Fig. 3. Data parallel skeletons

Libraries, objects and sources can be imported to the body by simply including them with special pragmas. A `pipe` body calls a sequence of skeleton instances which represent the stages of the pipe. A `farm` body calls a skeleton representing the generic executor function (the number of executors to be spawned is decided by the compiler or prescribed by a user directive).

```
#define N 400
#define NW 4
seq prod in(int x, int s) out(int y)
${  y = x*s; }$
end seq

seq sum in(int x, int s) out(int y)
${ y = x+s; }$
end seq

map m1 in(int a[N], int b[N]) out(int c[N])
nworker NW
    prod in(a[*i],b[*i]) out(c[*i])
end map

reduce r1 in(int c[N]) out(int z)
nworker NW
    sum in(c[*]) out(z)
end reduce

comp main in(int a[N], int b[N]) out(int z)
    m1 in(a, b) out(int c[N])
    r1 in(c) out(z)
end comp
```

Fig. 4. A P3L program computing the inner product of two arrays.

A **reduce** or **scan** body calls a skeleton instance representing a binary associative operator. A **map** body specifies the partitioning and alignment of data across an array and a function to be applied to all data aligned with a given array element. Finally, a **comp** body specifies a sequence of data-parallel skeletons, and a **loop** body specifies the skeleton to be iterated and the termination condition for the loop.

Figure 4 contains a P3L program to compute the inner product z of two vectors a and b. The pointwise products $a[i] * b[i]$ are all computed in parallel, using a map instance (**m1**). the results are stored in array c, whose elements are then summed up using a reduce skeleton (**r1**). The composition of **m1** and **r1** is specified by the **main** function of the program. The directive **nworker** states the number of available processors. P3L types are similar to C types, except that pointers are not allowed.

3.2 FAN notation

As illustrated by Figure 1, the algorithm design process in our environment is based on a more abstract representation of the skeleton program than is provided by P3L. It emphasizes the information relevant to skeleton manipulation, and allows the designer to abstract from details which are irrelevant at this stage of the program development.

This representation is given in a notation, called **FAN**, which we use in the rest of the paper to describe transformations and to illustrate the kind of support the development system provides.

A **FAN** program consists of a *header* and a *body*. The header specifies the program name and the list of variables taken as input (in) and produced as output (out):

prog.name (in *invars* out *outvars*)

Input/output variables are specified by name and type: $v : T$ states that the variable named v has type T. Types can be scalars (scalar) or arrays (arr[n], arr[n][m], etc.). Bodies define the parallel computation in functional notation with single-assignment variables. The parallel structure is defined by skeleton instances in the body. FAN skeletons are second-order functions defined on arrays and scalars. We describe here only FAN skeletons which we use in the rest of the paper.

The reduce and scan skeletons in P3L are modeled by the following **FAN** skeletons:

reduce $(\oplus)$ $[x_1, \ldots, x_n] = x_1 \oplus \ldots \oplus x_n$
scanL $(\oplus)$ $[x_1, \ldots, x_n] = [x_1, x_1 \oplus x_2, \ldots, x_1 \oplus \ldots \oplus x_n]$
scanR $(\oplus)$ $[x_1, \ldots, x_n] = [x_1 \oplus \ldots \oplus x_n, \ldots, x_{n-1} \oplus x_n, x_n]$

where $[x_1, \ldots, x_n]$ denotes a vector of length n and $\oplus$ is an associative operator.

The map skeleton in FAN applies a function f to all elements of an array and arranges the results in an array with the same shape, for instance:

$$\text{map } f \ [x_1, \ldots, x_n] = [f \ x_1, \ldots, f \ x_n]$$

applies f to a vector of n elements.

Note that a map skeleton in P3L is a combination of two or more simpler skeletons in FAN. These skeletons take care of either the computation (map skeleton) or the data arrangement (replication, alignment, etc.) – two distinct aspects which are merged in the P3L map skeleton.

Skeletons for data arrangements take care of data replication, alignment and distribution to arrange data properly for a subsequent application of computational skeletons like map, reduce, etc. The arrangement skeletons used in this paper are:

$$(x,y) = [(x_1, y_1), \ldots, (x_n, y_n)]$$

which pairs two arrays x and y of the same length,

$$\text{proj } 1 \ x = [x_1^1, \ldots, x_n^1]$$

which extracts the first element from an array of tuples x, (x_i^1 is the first element of tuple i), where the array may be nulldimensional, i.e., just one tuple, and

$$\text{copy } n \ s = [s, \ldots, s]$$

which creates an one-dimensional array of length n, filled with copies of s.

```
inner.product (in a, b : arr[n], out c : scalar);
t = map (*) (a,b);
c = reduce (+) t;
```

Fig. 5. A FAN program to compute the inner product of two vectors

As an example, Figure 5 shows the FAN code for the P3L code in Figure 4. Here, the input data are described more abstractly, without reference to the concrete element types. Program inner.product takes as input two vectors a and b of length n and returns a scalar c. The body describes how the parallel computation takes place. First, the elements of a and b are paired using the (a,b) skeleton, which creates a vector s of length n, $s[i] = (a[i], b[i])$. Then, the map skeleton multiplies all the pairs in s and stores the results in array t. Finally, elements of t are summed up using the reduce skeleton.

4 Visual Support

The development of parallel applications in our integrated environment is carried out using VisualSkIE (VSkIE), the SkIE graphical working window. Figure 6 shows the VSkIE main window. The horizontal toolbar provides easy access to all main functions and tools. For instance, the user can start a new program, load a previously defined one, cut and paste skeletons from one part of the program to another, make copies, invoke compilation, execution, debugging. Moreover, he/she can invoke performance analysis tools and transform the program structure interactively by invoking the skeleton transformation engine.

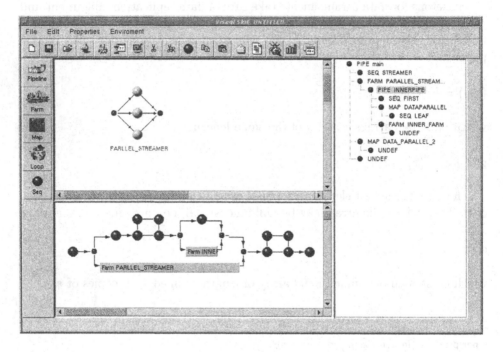

Fig. 6. VSkIE, the graphical working environment for SkIE

The user can define the global structure of his/her application interactively both by encapsulating already developed sequential/parallel software and by editing new sequential parts of the application, using an integrated editor. The parallel structure of the application can be defined either *explicitly*, in C or Fortran plus MPI, or by using the built-in skeletons. The available skeletons are shown in the vertical toolbar on the left.

The three sub-windows provide three different views of the application under development. The upper window shows the logical structure of the skeleton – in this case, a farm skeleton. The lower window shows the corresponding global process network. The tall window on the right describes how the skeletons are nested in the application (this nesting is called the *skeleton tree*).

Figure 7 illustrates how a new instance of a predefined skeleton structure can be created interactively. Using the dialog box, the user can choose or change the skeleton being defined, specify its input and output parameters, and set skeleton-dependent parameters such as the number of stages in a pipeline or the number of workers in a task farm or in a map skeleton.

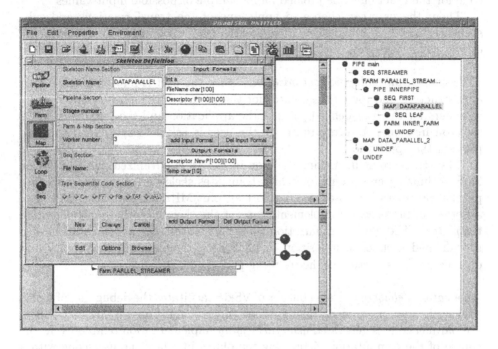

Fig. 7. Specifying the characteristics of a map skeleton instance in VSkIE

After having defined the structure of a parallel application, the VSkIE upper toolbar provides access to the integrated environment functions and tools. In particular, it facilitates the following activities: *transformation and cost estimation* of a skeleton program, *code generation and global optimization* of the application structure, *application debugging*, and *performance analysis*.

Program transformation and costing. The support for transformation and cost estimation allows for the analysis of the parallel structure of a skeletal program and its (semi)automatic transformation using predefined rules of proven equivalences of skeleton compositions. Program transformation is applied to a "partial" description of the skeletal program, in which only the details relevant to the transformation engine are specified (the FAN code for the program). This does not include, for instance, concrete modules and files for sequential modules or all aspects of the data types. Once the program has been specified graphically, it is automatically transformed into an internal representation for the transformation engine, which tries to apply transformations from the repository of predefined rules. Possible transformations are then suggested to the user, along with a performance estimate of the expected gain.

For an accurate cost prediction, the user is asked to supply a cost estimate for each sequential function. This can also be done automatically by invoking a profiling tool via the visual interface. In this case, the user must provide the code for the function to be profiled and a sample of possible input values.

Then, the user can choose to apply one of the transformations and subsequently iterate the transformation process until program structure and cost estimates are satisfactory.

Code generation and global optimization. Once the user is happy with the parallel structure and the cost estimates for the program, this phase generates the wrappers for the user-defined parts of the application and the parallel code for skeleton instances. In order to do so, the user is asked to specify all concrete parts of the application.

The structure defined using skeleton instances is optimized globally by the SkIE optimizing cross-compiler, which translates skeletons of the program into parallel processes expressed in C or Fortran plus MPI. In this phase, SkIE uses a library of prepackaged implementations of the skeletons (the *implementation templates*). The global optimization phase generates the implementation of a user-defined skeleton composition, instantiating templates in the library and optimizing the structure of the resulting process graph.

Application debugging. The debugger of VSkIE facilitates the debugging of a parallel application program as follows. When the debugging option (-g) is specified, the parallel code is generated using *debugging* implementation templates. In the course of the computation, debugging templates interface the user code with a sequential or parallel debugging tool, which supports the interactive placement of breakpoints, the inspection of variables and other usual debugging activities in a transparent way. Only the (sequential or parallel) code produced by the user need be debugged. The code in the template library is supposed to have already been verified and tested by the system implementers. If the user has specified a fragment of sequential code using a seq skeleton, the execution of the parallel process in which this code is wrapped will stop when the first instruction of the user-defined code is executed. Then, a graphical debugging window is displayed showing the user's source code and highlighting the point at which the execution has stopped. The user can continue the program execution step by step, inspect the values of variables and set new breakpoints in the code, just like in the debugging of a sequential program. User codes belonging to different, running processes (e.g., different executors in a farm skeleton) are displayed in separate debugging windows. The parallel code generated by the compiler is not displayed in the debugging windows. This allows the user to concentrate on the deterministic execution of the sequential code on different input data.

If the user code is parallel (C or Fortran plus MPI), the debugging facilities still hide the compiler-generated code and support the debugging of the user code using a parallel debugging tool.

Performance analysis. The performance analysis support facilitates a transparent inspection of the actual performance achieved when running a SkIE application. To this end, the user specifies the performance analysis option (-p), and SkIE-generated code is automatically augmented with additional code to detect and keep track of the execution of performance analysis activities. For instance, the system automatically keeps track of the time at which all messages are sent/received and of the time spent in executing both the user-defined code and the system-generated code. When the program terminates, all time values traced are collected in a single table and can be visualized by invoking the visualization tool via the interface. If needed, the user can define new activities to be monitored (for instance a call to a specific user-defined function) and specify how these activities should be assessed and visualized.

5 Transformations in Algorithm Design

The design of a skeleton program consists of transformation and cost estimation steps. The goal of the transformations is to arrive at a program with the best performance estimate, which very often requires a reduction of the number of communications. As a non-trivial demonstration that this can improve performance substantially, consider the scan-reduce fusion:

Rule SR-ARA

$b = \text{scanL } Op1\ a$
$c = \text{reduce } Op2\ b$
$b = \text{reduce } (New\ (Op1, Op2))\ (a,a)$
$c = \text{proj } 1\ b$
If $Op1$ distributes forward over $Op2$
$(a_1, b_1)\ New(Op1, Op2)\ (a_2, b_2)\ =\ (a_1\ Op2\ (b_1\ Op1\ a_2),\ b_1\ Op2\ b_2)$

The name of the rule, SR-ARA, hints on the transformation it specifies: "Scan;Reduce → Arrange;Reduce;Arrange", where arrange stands for any FAN skeleton performing only data arrangement. The rule transforms a sequence of two relatively costly skeletons – a scan followed by a reduction – into one reduction, with pre- and postarrangement of data. The prearrangement is pairing and the postarrangement is projection. Both are simple actions requiring no communication. Thus, the SR-ARA rule usually saves communication and improves performance.

We present transformation rules in a format which consists of four boxes; from top to bottom: (1) the FAN program fragment before the transformation (the "left-hand side" of the rule), (2) the fragment after the transformation (the "right-hand side"), (3) optional: a precondition stating when the rule is applicable, (4) optional: local definition(s) of function(s) used in the rule. Rule SR-ARA expects two operators as parameters: $Op1$ and $Op2$, and makes use of a local operation $New(Op1, Op2)$ composed of them.

Another transformation, rule CS-CM, states that a copy operation followed by a scanL with operator $Op1$ can always be transformed into a copy followed by some local computation, in which the operator $Op1$ is iterated using *repeat*:

Rule CS-CM

$b = $ copy n a
$c = $ scanL $Op1$ b
$b = $ copy n a
$c = $ map$_\#$ f b
f k $x = $ proj 1 (map (*repeat* (e, o) k) (x,x))
where
$repeat(e, o)$ k $b = $ if $k = 0$ then b else
$\qquad\qquad repeat(e, o)$ $(k$ div $2)$ (if $(k$ mod $2 = 0)$ then e b else o $b)$
with
$e(t, u) = (t, u$ $Op1$ $u)$ and $o(t, u) = (t$ $Op1$ u, u $Op1$ $u)$

The *repeat* function [18] performs the local computation of g^k using a logarithmic-time algorithm. It traverses the binary digits number k from the least significant to the most significant. If the digit is 0, it applies function e, if the digit is 1 it applies function o. Since the binary digits of a number k are $\lceil \log k \rceil$, the cost of $repeat(e, o)$ k b is logarithmic in k.

Function map$_\#$ is an extended version of map, which allows the argument function to have the element index as an additional parameter:

$$\text{map}_\# f[x_0, \ldots, x_k] = [f\ 0\ x_0, \ldots, f\ k\ x_k]$$

A rich set of transformation rules for various skeletons has been developed recently [1, 13, 15, 18]. These rules transform compositions of two to three skeletons, like copy, reduce, scan, etc., into more efficient combinations. Some of these transformations, e.g., scan-reduce fusion, originated in the functional Bird-Meertens formalism [7] for sequential algorithms, some are new.

6 Case Study: Polynomial Evaluation

In this section, we illustrate a typical application development cycle in our framework, using a small example. We take a previously proposed derivation, done by hand in [15], and demonstrate how it can be reproduced using the FAN support for program transformation.

Consider the problem of evaluating a polynomial

$$a_1 x + a_2 x^2 + \ldots + a_n x^n$$

on m points $y_1, \ldots, y_m$ in parallel.

We start the design process by determining how the parallelism inherent to polynomial evaluation can be expressed using the skeletons provided by the FAN notation. The direct way of computing a polynomial on points given as vector $ys = y_1, \ldots, y_m$ is to compute the vectors of powers, $ys^i = [y_1^i, \ldots, y_m^i]$, $i = 1, \ldots, n$, then multiply all values in ys^i by the polynomial coefficient a_i and, finally, sum up all intermediate results.

This simple idea can be expressed by the following FAN algorithm:

```
pol-eval1 (in ys : arr[m], as : arr[n], out  zs :  arr[m]);
  ts = scanL (*) (copy n ys);
  ds = map (*sa) (as,ts);
  zs = reduce (+) ds;
```

The algorithm takes as input vectors as and ys (represented as arrays) and proceeds as follows:

- copy n ys returns an array of n copies of vector ys,

- scanL (*) computes ts : arr[n][m], where $ts[i] = ys^i$ for all i,

- map $+_{sa}$ (as,ts) computes ds : arr[n][m], such that $ds[i] = [a_i * y_1^i, \ldots, a_i * y_m^i]$,

- reduce (+) ds sums up all rows of ds elementwise and puts the results in zs, such that: $zs = [(\sum_{i=1}^n a_i * y_1^i), \ldots, (\sum_{i=1}^n a_i * y_m^i)]$.

Note that operator $*$ in the scan skeleton and operator $+$ in the reduction skeleton are overloaded to work both on scalars and on arrays of equal shape; in the latter case an operator is applied elementwise. Operator $*_{sa}$ takes a scalar and an array (subscript sa) and multiplies each array element by the scalar:

$$x *_{sa} [y_1, \ldots, y_k] = [x * y_1, \ldots, x * y_k]$$

Algorithm pol-eval1 is rather communication-intensive: it broadcasts all copies of ys, and then it applies two skeletons, scanL and reduce, both communicating m-sized vectors. We can improve the program by applying rule CS-CM introduced in the previous section.

According to the cost estimates of [15], every application of rule CS-CM will result in a performance improvement, so the system will suggest to apply it by instantiating the operator $Op1$ with $*$. In this case, functions e and o are of type

$$e, o : (\text{arr}[m], \text{arr}[m]) \rightarrow (\text{arr}[m], \text{arr}[m])$$

and are instantiated by the system as follows:

$$e'(t, u) = (t, u * u) \quad o'(t, u) = (t * u, u * u)$$

The result version of polynomial evaluation is as follows:

pol-eval2 (in ys : arr[m], as : arr[n], out zs : arr[m]);
ts = map$_\#$ (f) (copy n ys);
ds = map ($*_{sa}$) (as,ts);
zs = reduce (+) ds;

where f is defined by: f k x = proj 1 (map ($repeat$ (e',o') k) (x,x)).

The P3L program generated from the FAN algorithm pol-eval2 can automatically be translated into a C plus MPI program working on distributed data. In particular, the block distribution of the data implies that, for all i, element $as[i]$ and the ith row of ds and ts are located on the same processor, so that the computation in map$_\#$ and map and the data arrangement (as, ts) can be performed without communication. The implemented program pol-eval2 runs indeed faster than pol-eval1 on different target platforms [18].

7 Conclusion

We argue that the implementations of high-level languages should be augmented by specialized programming environments to support the development of efficient, high-level parallel programs. We have sketched an integrated environment, which combines the transformational framework FAN with the programming systems P3L and SkIE, and have demonstrated the use of the environment. The environment provides the user with a rapid-prototyping tool which will automatically produce executable code in C or Fortran plus MPI, together with expected performance estimates. The current implementation of the environment includes the visual support system, the compiler and the performance estimation tools. We are presently working on the implementation of the transformation engine and on the finalization of the FAN syntax and semantics.

The main novelty of our work is the intensive use of program transformations in the early stages of the programming process, supported by corresponding cost models and programming tools. The framework is language-independent and can be integrated with existing high-level parallel programming environments, as our experience with P3L and SkIE demonstrates.

Acknowledgements

This work is being supported by a travel grant from the German-Italian academic exchange programme VIGONI.

References

1. M. Aldinucci, M. Coppola, and M. Danelutto. Rewriting skeleton programs: How to evaluate the data-parallel stream-parallel tradeoff. In S. Gorlatch, editor, *Proc. 1st Int. Workshop on Constructive Methods for Parallel Programming (CMPP'98)*, pages 48–58. Universität Passau, May 1998. Technical Report MIP-9805.

2. B. Bacci, B. Cantalupo, P. Pesciullesi, R. Ravazzolo, A. Riaudo, and M. Vanneschi. SkIE user guide (Version 2.0). Technical Report, QSW Ltd., Dec. 1998.
3. B. Bacci, M. Danelutto, S. Pelagatti, and M. Vanneschi. SkIE: a heterogeneous environment for HPC applications. To appear in *Parallel Computing*, 1999.
4. B. Bacci, M. Danelutto, S. Orlando, S. Pelagatti, and M. Vanneschi. P^{3}L: A structured high level programming language and its structured support. *Concurrency: Practice and Experience*, 7(3):225–255, 1995.
5. A. Beguelin, J. Dongarra, G. A. Geist, R. Manchek, and V. S. Sunderam. HeNCE: A users' guide. Available at http://www.netlib.org/hence/.
6. A. Beguelin, J. Dongarra, G. A. Geist, R. Manchek, and V. S. Sunderam. Graphical development tools for network-based concurrent supercomputing. In *Proc. Supercomputing '91*, pages 435–444. IEEE Computer Society Press, 1991.
7. R. Bird. Lectures on constructive functional programming. In M. Broy, editor, *Constructive Methods in Computing Science*, NATO ASI Series F: Computer and Systems Sciences. Vol. 55, pages 151–216. Springer Verlag, 1988.
8. G. H. Botorog and H. Kuchen. Skil: An imperative language with algorithmic skeletons for efficient distributed programming. In *Proc. Fifth Int. Symp. on High Performance Distributed Computing (HPDC-5)*, pages 243–252. IEEE Computer Society Press, 1996.
9. S. Ciarpaglini, M. Danelutto, L. Folchi, C. Manconi, and S. Pelagatti. ANACLETO: A template-based p3l compiler. In *Proc. 7th Parallel Computing Workshop (PCW'97)*, pages P2-F-1–7. Australian National University, 1997.
10. C. Clèmençon, A. Endo, J. Fritscher, A. Müller, R. Rühl, and B. J. N. Wylie. Annai: An integrated parallel programming environment for multicomputers. In A. Zaky and T. Lewis, editors, *Tools and Environments for Parallel and Distributed Systems*, chapter 2, pages 33–59. Kluwer, 1996.
11. M. I. Cole. *Algorithmic Skeletons: Structured Management of Parallel Computation*. Research Monographs in Parallel and Distributed Computing. Pitman, 1989.
12. J. Darlington, Y. ke Guo, H. W. To, and J. Yang. Skeletons for structured parallel composition. In *Proc. 15th ACM SIGPLAN Symposium on Principles and Practice of Parallel Programming (PPoPP'95)*, pages 19–28. ACM Press, 1995.
13. S. Gorlatch and C. Lengauer. (De)Compositions for parallel scan and reduction. In *Proc. 3rd Working Conf. on Massively Parallel Programming Models (MPPM'97)*, pages 23–32. IEEE Computer Society Press, 1998.
14. S. Gorlatch and S. Pelagatti. A transformational framework for skeletal programs: Overview and case study. In J. D. P. Rolim et al., editors, *Parallel and Distributed Processing*, LNCS 1586, pages 123–137. Springer-Verlag, 1999. IPPS/SPDP'99 Workshops.
15. S. Gorlatch, C. Wedler, and C. Lengauer. Optimization rules for programming with collective operations. In *Proc. 13th Int. Parallel Processing Symp. & 10th Symp. on Parallel and Distributed Processing (IPPS/SPDP'99)*, pages 492–499. IEEE Computer Society Press, 1999.
16. W. Gropp, E. Lusk, and A. Skjellum. *Using MPI: Portable Parallel Programming with the Message-Passing Interface*. Scientific and Engineering Computation Series. MIT Press, 1994.
17. S. Pelagatti. *Structured Development of Parallel Programs*. Taylor & Francis, 1998.
18. C. Wedler and C. Lengauer. On linear list recursion in parallel. *Acta Informatica*, 35(10):875–909, 1998.

Sequential Unification and Aggressive Lookahead Mechanisms for Data Memory Accesses

Chi-Hung Chi, Jun-Li Yuan

School of Computing
National University of Singapore
Singapore 119260

E-mail:chich@comp.nus.edu.sg

Abstract. Recent work in hybrid data address and value prediction has successfully increased the accuracy of data prefetching. However, many predictable data are still found to be missing from cache. Detail investigation showed that this is mainly due to two reasons: (i) partial cache hit for data being prefetched, and (ii) abortion of highly accurate prefetch requests by demand fetch requests. To improve this situation, we propose two mechanisms to reduce the startup latency of prefetch requests. They are the sequential unification of prefetch and demand requests and the aggressive lookahead mechanisms. The basic idea behind these two mechanisms is to combine accurate data prefetching with current demand fetching whenever the prefetch accuracy is expected to be high. Simulation of these two mechanisms on RPT (Reference Prediction Table - one of the most cited selective data prefetching schemes [2,3]) using SPEC95 showed that significant reduction in the data reference latency, ranging from a few percent to 60%, can be obtained. Furthermore, the additional hardware support for this scheme is very simple, thus making the mechanisms attractive for practical cache implementation.

1 Introduction

Memory latency is the well-known performance bottleneck in modern microprocessors. The sharp increase in the processor clock speed causes a relatively longer memory access latency; the improvement in the VLSI chip density allows more functional units to be put on-chip; the wider-issue superscalar parallelism results in a higher demand for instructions and data. All these make the data reference latency to be more visible to the program execution. To overcome this memory latency problem, caches are used to bridge this increasing speed gap. Furthermore, cache prefetching is often employed to overlap the memory latency time with the program execution [21].

Current research on cache prefetching often focuses on accuracy and coverage. With a higher prefetch accuracy, the chance for cache pollution is reduced. A larger coverage also allows more data/instruction references to be handled by the cache prefetch unit. To achieve these goals, recent work in data prefetching emphasizes on the exploration of hybrid data address and value prediction. Data accesses in a program are partitioned into distinct reference classes. Members in each class are usually generated by a unique data structure in a program and are handled exclusively by one predictor and prefetch unit. Good examples of these predictors include linear memory references.

Table 1. Distribution of Reference Types for Cache Misses Under RPT Mechanism

Benchmark	Cache Misses Due	Cache Misses Due to RPT References		
Program	to Non-RPT Ref.	Same Block	Consecutive Block	Non-Consecutive Blk
099.go	44.4%	44.4%	11.1%	0.0%
124.m88ksim	12.6%	49.9%	37.3%	0.1%
126.gcc	82.1%	13.9%	2.1%	1.8%
129.compress	99.0%	0.9%	0.0%	0.1%
130.li	84.8%	4.5%	7.8%	2.8%
101.tomcatv	11.9%	85.3%	2.8%	0.0%
103.su2cor	2.9%	94.3%	1.4%	1.4%
104.hydro2d	26.0%	70.7%	3.3%	0.0%
107.mgrid	11.3%	31.6%	33.8%	23.3%
110.applu	66.2%	7.9%	9.3%	16.6%
145.fpppp	94.9%	4.8%	0.0%	0.3%
141.apsi	15.2%	49.3%	34.8%	0.6%
Average:	46.0%	38.1%	12.0%	3.9%

Same Blk: Demand Fetch & RPT Prefetch from a Memory Access Instruction (MAI) are in Same Cache Block
Consecutive Blk: Demand Fetch and RPT Prefetch from the same MAI are in Consecutive Cache Blocks
Non-Consecutive Blk: Demand Fetch & RPT Prefetch from the same MAI are in Non-Consecutive Cache Blocks

With an accurate predictor and its supporting hardware, good cache performance is expected. In particular, references that are covered by the predictors should be prefetched in time for consumption and most cache misses should be due to non-predictable references. However, experiment showed that it might not be the case. Table 1 gives the result of the Reference Prediction Table (RPT) mechanism on SPEC95. RPT is an address predictor proposed by Chen and Baer [2,3] for the prediction and prefetching of memory reference sequences with linear address sequences. The baseline architecture used in the simulation is an UltraSPARC ISA (instruction set architecture) compatible, superscalar processor described in Table 2 (in Section 1.2 below). Even though the overall cache performance is improved, the table shows that there are still many data references that are predicted accurately by the RPT but are missing from the cache. This percentage ranges from a few percents to over 95%, with an average of 54%. In other words, over half of the cache misses are actually due to data references that can be predicted accurately!

Further investigation reveals that this performance loss is mainly due to two characteristics, which are shared among different predictors and prefetch mechanisms. The first characteristic is about the bus usage priority. In the traditional memory system, a demand fetch always has higher priority over a prefetch request to use the bus. If a demand fetch occurs while a prefetch request is being served, the prefetch request will likely be aborted and the demand fetch will then be served as soon as possible. The argument behind this decision is that any delay to a demand fetch is supposed to be visible to the program execution. However, the same argument does not apply to a prefetch request. Furthermore, the accuracy of prefetching is usually not high enough to justify for an increase in the bus usage priority.

Due to the advance in processor architecture, the above argument needs to be re-evaluated. With the out-of-order execution and the non-blocking cache, small delay of a demand memory access might not necessarily be seen by the program execution. At the same time, the high accuracy in recent data prefetching results in a higher chance for the aborted prefetch request to be referenced (or re-issued) later. This not only wastes the bandwidth consumed by the "partial", aborted prefetch requests, but also increases the total number of cache misses caused by data references associated to the aborted, accurate prefetch requests.

The second characteristic is about the collaboration between demand fetch and prefetch requests. Once a prefetch request is triggered by a memory access instruction, there is very little (if any) collaboration between the demand fetch of the memory access instruction and its corresponding prefetch request. Each of them is handled separately as an independent request. This approach of handling memory requests is simple, but might not give very good performance. Despite the prefetch accuracy, the startup overhead of each prefetch or demand fetch is fully visible to the bus. As the bus bandwidth between the first and second level caches increases, the cache miss penalty will mainly be determined by the transfer time of the first byte of data. The time required for the transfer of additional bytes of memory data is relatively much smaller. As an example, to transfer a 32 bytes of data from the 2nd level cache to its 1st level cache, the startup time can be 6-10 cycles while the additional time to finish the transfer is only 3 cycles for a 8-byte wide bus. Thus, if the chance to reference the additional information is reasonably high, it might be good to combine the accurate prefetch action with the unavoidable demand fetch. In this way, the startup cost of the prefetch action is eliminated and only the actual data transfer time is visible to the bus. Since the prefetch action is "upgraded" to have the priority of a demand fetch, it will not be aborted by other memory requests.

In this paper, we propose two mechanisms to make up for the discrepancy between the ideal and the observable performance of accurate prefetching. They are (i) intelligent sequential unification of demand and prefetch requests, and (ii) aggressive lookahead prefetching. The basic idea of these mechanisms is to avoid paying the startup overhead of a prefetch request by integrating it into an unavoidable demand fetch whenever the prefetch accuracy is expected to be high. In the sequential unification of demand and prefetch requests, simple hardware will be used to check for the consecution of blocks corresponding to these two types of requests and combine them if found. In the aggressive lookahead prefetching, an additional multiple iterations lookahead prefetching will be triggered on top of the existing prefetching mechanism if both the demand fetch and the prefetch data fall into the same memory block. An indirect effect of these two mechanisms is that once a prefetch request is integrated into a demand fetch, its priority will be raised to the level of a demand fetch. The integrated request will not be aborted once it is started. Of course, the integrated request will also take longer time to complete. To ensure the performance gain, the two mechanisms will only be triggered selectively, based on the level of confidence for the urgency and accuracy of the prefetched data. Experimental result on SPEC95 shows that with these two mechanisms working collaboratively with each other, the memory latency due to data accesses can be reduced significantly, ranging from a few percents to about 60%. Another nice feature of the mechanisms is the simple hardware required for the implementation, thus making them attractive for practical cache implementation in high-end microprocessors.

The outline for the rest of the paper is as follows. Section 2 will briefly summarize previous work related to the accurate data prefetching and data predictors. Then, the two proposed mechanisms, the sequential unification of prefetch and demand requests and the aggressive lookahead prefetching, will be proposed in Section 3. Simulation result for these two mechanisms, together with the analysis, will be given in Section 4. Finally, the paper will be concluded in Section 5.

To help understand the discussion in the rest of the paper, the reference prediction table (RPT) prefetching will be chosen as the basic accurate data prefetch scheme, on which our mechanisms will be added on. RPT is chosen because it is one of the most cited schemes for accurate data prefetching. It has also been agreed to be one of the most efficient schemes to prefetch memory references with linear address sequences. Note that the *two mechanisms proposed here are not limited to RPT. They can be applied to other accurate prefetch schemes with very little (if any) modification.*

Before we proceed, it will be helpful to give precise definition for the following terms used in the rest of the paper:

- A *partial hit (or partial miss)* for a cache block *I* is said to occur if, while the block *I* is being prefetched from the next level of the memory hierarchy, a demand fetch for block *I* occurs.
- The *memory latency due to data references* for a cache design *D* is defined as the difference between the total execution time of the system with the cache design *D* and the total execution time of the system with a perfect data cache (i.e. no data cache miss).

Note that this paper only focuses on data cache prefetching. A default prefetch-on-miss mechanism is assumed for the instruction cache.

1.1 Basic Simulation Environment

The baseline architecture together with its parameters used in the simulation study is given in Table 2. It is an UltraSPARC ISA compatible superscalar processor with rich details on its architectural features, including the pipeline, register renaming, reorder buffer, branch prediction, and multi-level memory hierarchy. In our study, SPEC95 was chosen as the benchmark suite for experimentation (see Table 3). These programs were compiled on the UltraSPARC platform with the optimization flag on. Then, each of them was traced and simulated cycle-by-cycle for 100 million instructions.

Table 2. Simulation Parameters for the Baseline Architecture

Processor Specification:
UltraSPARC ISA compatiable
Superscalar architecture with 3 integer units, 3 floating pt. units, 1 branch unit, 1 LOAD/STORE unit
Out-of-order execution, register renaming, 2-bit branch predictor, reorder-buffer with 64 entries.

1st Level Instruction Cache:	1st Level Data Cache
Cache Size: 32 Kbytes	Cache Size: 32 Kbytes
Block Size: 32 bytes	Block Size: 32 bytes
Associativity: direct-mapped	Associativity: direct-mapped
Replacement: LRU	Replacement: LRU
Placement: write-back	Placement: write-back
Mem. AccessTime to 2nd Level Cache: 6 cycles	Mem. Access Time to 2nd Level Cache: 6 cycles
Bandwidth to 2nd Level Cache: 8 bytes	Bandwidth to 2nd Level Cache: 8 bytes
Memory queue: 8 entries	Memory queue: 8 queue
Basic prefetch-on-miss scheme	Store buffer: 8 entries
	Non-blocking cache
	Prefetching using Chen's RPT (i.e. linear memory access prefetching) with 512 entries and lookahead iteration of 3

2nd Level Unified Cache:
Cache Size: 256 Kbytes
Block Size: 64 bytes
Associativity: direct-mapped
Replacement: LRU
Placement: write-back
Mem. Access Time: 60 cycles
Bandwidth to Main Memory: 8 bytes

Table 3. Description of SPEC95 Benchmark Programs Used in Simulation Study

Integer Benchmark	Description	Floating Pt. Benchmark	Description
124.m88ksim	Motorola 88K chip simulator	101.tomcatv	A mesh generation program
126.gcc	GNU C compiler for SPARC	104.hydro2d	Hydrodynamic Naiver Stokes equations
129.compress	Compression of files in memory	110.applu	Parabolic/elliptic partial differential eqn.
		141.apsi	Problem solving related to temperature, wind velocity, & distribution of pollutant
		145.fpppp	Quantum chemistry

2 Previous Research

Prefetching is always an important issue in cache design [21]. Recent work in data prefetching concentrates on the predictability of references and the accuracy of prefetching. A direct consequence of this research direction is the introduction of hybrid address and value predictors [1,6,7,9,13,15,18-20,22]. Multiple predictors are implemented, each of which will be designed, optimized, and responsible for one type of references. Examples of typical predictors include stride predictors [2,3,17] and linked list predictors predictors [8,10,12,14,16]. Most of them give very good prefetch accuracy. Another research direction in data prefetching is to implement multiple prefetch schemes in a cache system [4] [5] [11]. Usually, in additional to the selective, accurate prefetch schemes (such as stride or linked-list predictors) used in the prefetch controller, the prefetch-on-miss mechanism will be employed as the default prefetch scheme in case the references do not fall into the coverage of accurate prefetch group. Both directions give good potentials to improve the cache performance. However, they all depend on the availability of the bus bandwidth, which is often not enough to support their memory activities.

3 Collaboration Between Prefetch and Demand Fetch

Due to the limited bus bandwidth for (pre-)fetching and the increasing memory access latency, the observed performance for accurate data prefetching often differs significantly from its ideal one. Either the correctly predicted data cannot be prefetched in time for consumption or the accurate prefetch requests are aborted while they are being served. The observation is generally true, independent of the accuracy of the prefetch mechanism. To make up for this performance gap, two mechanisms are proposed in this section. They are: (i) the sequential unification of prefetch request and demand fetch to reduce the average memory access latency, and (ii) the aggressive lookahead prefetching when the bus is expected to be free.

Before we go into the discussion of the mechanisms, let us investigate closely on how cache misses in RPT occur using the sequential relationship between the demand fetch of a MAI and the prefetch of RPT. Table 1 gives the distribution of cache misses according to the following four types of references:

[1] *Non-RPT References:*
These references are not covered by the RPT mechanism.
[2] *Same Block / RPT References:*
For a given memory access instruction, both the demand fetch and the RPT prefetch are mapped to the same memory block.
[3] *Consecutive Blocks / RPT References:*
For a given memory access instruction, the memory block containing the demand fetch and that containing the RPT prefetch are consecutive to each other.
[4] *Non-Consecutive Blocks / RPT References:*
For a given memory access instruction, the memory block containing the demand fetch and that containing the RPT prefetch are not consecutive to each other.

Potential prefetching improvement for group 1 (i.e. non-RPT) and group 4 (i.e. non-consecutive RPT) references are difficult. They are either not covered by the prefetch scheme or too far to find useful correlation between the demand fetch and prefetch requests. For the rest two groups, however, the situation is difficult. For group 2 (i.e. same block) references, since they fall into the same memory block, their demand for bus bandwidth is relatively low. As a result, more aggressive prefetching might be possible at the point of their references. For group 3 (i.e. consecutive blocks) references, since their corresponding memory blocks are consecutive to each other, the demand fetch and prefetch requests of a MAI might possibly be integrated into a single request, thus removing the startup overhead of the prefetch request. They are important because about 50% (38% and 12% respectively) of cache misses are due to these two groups of references.

3.1 Consecutive Unification

There are at least two approaches to reduce the effect of a memory system to the overall system performance. The first approach is data prefetching - overlapping the data fetch time with the program execution. Its effectiveness is often determined by the prefetch accuracy and by the bus bandwidth availability. An alternative approach is to reduce the average memory latency for fetching data. Besides the effect of the VLSI hardware implementation, there is an architecture consideration that can serve similar purpose.

In current memory hierarchy systems, the basic unit of data transfer between two successive levels is a block, which is made up of multiple bytes. For example, the typical cache block size in the latest microprocessors is about 32 bytes. The time required to transfer a block of data can roughly be divided into two components: (i) the memory startup latency between the sending out of the request and the receiving of the first byte of data, and (ii) the actual transfer time for the subsequent data. As the bus bandwidth between successive memory levels is getting bigger, the overall fetch time for a block of data is mainly dominated by the memory startup latency and the subsequent transfer time is relatively small. Given a typical bus width of 8 bytes, the fetch time for a 32 bytes data block can be 8 cycles for the startup time plus 3 (or 4) cycles for the subsequent transfer time. In other words, the block transfer time is only about half of its startup time. Thus, it will be significant to the system performance if the startup time of some memory requests can be eliminated.

Given a memory access instruction, two possible types of memory references can occur. They are the demand fetch and prefetch requests. Thus, one good way to eliminate the startup overhead of memory requests is to combine these two types of requests for the same MAI aggressively. Whenever the memory blocks containing the demand fetch and prefetch data are consecutive to each other, they will be combined to form a single request with double blocks access and with higher bus usage priority. Table 1 shows that this situation contributes to a non-negligible portion of the cache misses, ranging from a few percents to about 40%, with an average of 12%. As an example, executing an instruction I might result in a demand fetch for data in block 1000 and a RPT prefetch for data in block 1001. Current memory system will send out two independent requests, the demand one with higher priority and the prefetch one with lower priority. To combine these two requests in case of the cache misses, a single memory request with starting block address 1000 for two blocks of data will be issued instead. Furthermore, this request will have the bus usage priority of the demand fetch. The sequential unification technique can be summarized as follows:

Mechanism for Sequential Unification:
Given a memory access instruction I with data reference D_I in memory block M_D and its corresponding prefetch request P_I in memory block M_P. If M_D and M_P are consecutive to each other (i.e. ([address of M_D] - [address of M_P]) = ±1) and they are both missed from cache, these two requests will be combined to form a single memory request with twice the original size and with the bus usage priority of a demand fetch.

Note that in the sequential unification mechanism, we only combine demand fetch and prefetch requests from the same MAI instruction. There is no unification of memory requests from different instructions in the memory pending queue. Our argument towards this decision is that the hardware involved is much more complicated (such as associative comparators) and the additional benefit is not high.

There are two side-effects of the sequential unification mechanism that one needs to be careful. The first one is the bus usage priority. High priority is good to prefetch requests with high accuracy, but is bad to incorrect prefetch requests. The additional time for the transfer of the prefetch data is likely to be seen by the processor. If the benefit for prefetching it is not high (again related to accuracy), it will not be good to do it. Consequently, the mechanism is triggered only when both requests are missed from cache. We choose this situation because the startup overhead of the unified request will be the same as the unavoidable demand fetch, thus making the prefetch time to be the actual, small transfer time of the additional data. This is important because it provides a higher chance for performance improvement.

3.2 Aggressive Lookahead

Current data prefetch schemes, independent of hardware driven, or software assisted, try to prefetch the next iteration datum while the current iteration datum is being referenced. In case of a cache hit, no prefetch request will actually be issued, regardless of whether the current reference and the prefetch data are mapped to the same cache block. Under this situation, partial cache misses are found to occur quite often, especially in the situation of small stride linear memory accesses. This is not difficult to understand. The next block is prefetched only when the current referenced block is about to be used up. Thus, the memory latency of 1 to (*Cache_Miss_Penalty* - 1) cycles might potentially be visible to the program execution. This is true even if the prefetch accuracy were 100% correct. The second one is the abortion of the accurate prefetch requests by some demand fetch requests after the prefetch requests are triggered. As was said before, a cache miss for the prefetched but aborted block is likely to occur because of the high accuracy of current data prefetch schemes. From our simulation, we found that these two situations can occur quite often.

As an example, suppose an array of data is referenced using a constant stride value of 1 in a loop and the cache block size is 8 words. When *a[1]* is referenced, *a[2]* will be prefetched. Since *a[1]* and *a[2]* are in the same cache block *i*, no prefetch request will be issued. This situation will go on until datum $a[7]$ is referenced. At this time, the next cache block $i+1$ that contains $a[8]$ will be prefetched. The potential danger of this approach is that there might not have enough free bus cycles between the accesses of $a[7]$ and $a[8]$ for the prefetching of block $i+1$ to finish. A partial hit will then occur and additional processor stall time will be introduced. In the similar way, the prefetch request for block $i+1$ might be killed by a demand fetch, and this also results in additional processor stall time.

It is observed that during the time period of accessing $a[0]$ to $a[7]$, the chance to have some free bus cycles is very high. Hence, in order to improve this situation, it would be useful to perform more aggressive, yet accurate prefetching for the selected references when some free bus cycles are expected. This happens when the linear array references with small stride sizes are referenced. Since one single cache block contains multiple data references, free bus cycles are expected when the block is referenced for the second time and onwards. As a result, more aggressive prefetching can be achieved easily by dynamical adjustment of the prefetch block address. When the current selected reference and the prefetch data are mapped to the same cache block address i, the prefetch block address will be adjusted to the next sequential one. That is, the block with address either $i+1$ or $i-1$ will be prefetched, depending on whether the prefetch address is greater or smaller than the current reference address. This kind of additional prefetching has similar accuracy as the original schemes do because they all target to array accesses with constant strides with similar kind of confirmation test.

Using the above example, when $a[1]$ in cache block i is referenced, the prefetch block address will be adjusted to $i+1$ because both $a[1]$ and $a[2]$ map to the same block i. In this way, there are more time to prefetch block $i+1$. Furthermore, in case where this prefetch request for block $i+1$ is killed by some demand fetch, the same prefetch request can be issued again when $a[2]$, $a[3]$, and up to $a[7]$ are referenced. This aggressive lookahead mechanism is summarized below. Note that unlike the sequential unification, its triggering will be independent of the cache miss or hit for the reference.

Mechanism for Aggressive Lookahead Prefetching
Given a memory access instruction, if the cache block j containing the prefetch candidate is not the same as the cache block i containing the current data reference, a prefetch request for block j will be issued. On the other hand, if cache block j and block i are the same (i.e. $i = j$), the cache block to be prefetched will be adjusted to either $i+1$ or $i-1$, depending on whether $i < j$ or $i > j$.

From Table 1, almost 40% of the cache misses occur under this situation, either as complete misses or partial misses. This gives an estimate of its significance.

The sequential unification and aggressive lookahead mechanisms are orthogonal to each other. Hence, they can work collaboratively to improve cache performance further. In this case, the sequential unification will work on the aggressive lookahead prefetch request whenever it occurs.

3.3 Comparison with Existing Techniques

Up to now, we have introduced two mechanisms either to reduce the memory startup time or to perform aggressive prefetching. Compared to the existing caching techniques, it seems that there are mechanisms that perform similar functions as they do. In this section, we would like to take a detail look at these techniques and identify their difference. In particular, the following three techniques will be investigated: block size, bus usage priority, and lookahead distance.

3.3.1 Block Size

Block size is the basic unit of data transfer between two successive levels in a cache/memory hierarchy. Currently, the typical block size ranges from 16 to 64 bytes. This block size is used mainly for prefetching purpose. Compared to our two proposed mechanisms, all of them try to prefetch data and to avoid paying the memory startup overhead of transferring additional data. This argument is correct. However, there is an important distinction on how this will be done. Block size is a basic parameter in the cache configuration and it applies to all memory references. It is independent of what type of references (referred to the four reference types mentioned above) it belongs to and whether it is a RPT reference or a scalar reference. As a result, it is a threshold value beyond which the benefit in prefetching cannot tradeoff the performance degradation due to pollution. However, for our sequential unification mechanism, we only try to eliminate the startup overhead of some accurate, prefetch requests. There is no significant change to the amount of data content that will be fetched into the cache. Hence, the chance of additional cache pollution will be very lower. For aggressive lookahead prefetching, it is done only when the bus utilization is low. The cache pollution problem is also not serious in this case because it is triggered for highly confident cases. Furthermore, in both cases, they are only applied selectively - when the level of confidence for performance gain is high. Instead of competing with the block size concept, they should be viewed as orthogonal techniques that can work collaboratively for good cache performance.

3.3.2 Usage Priority

With the improvement of prefetch accuracy, there is always a tendency to improve cache performance by increasing its bus usage priority. In this way, these accurate prefetch requests will not be aborted and can be completed on schedule. To a certain extent, our two mechanisms also do the same. However, there is a big distinction among them. As we pointed out previously, the overhead of raising the bus usage priority of a prefetch request is the additional delay time to the demand fetch. Separate study showed that simply increasing the bus usage priority of all accurate prefetch requests might actually degrade the system performance instead of improving it. In our proposed mechanisms, the bus usage priority of a prefetch request is increased only if two conditions are satisfied: the prefetch accuracy is high and the time to complete the prefetch request is short. This is the reason why it is triggered only when the prefetch request is successfully unified into a demand fetch.

3.3.3 Lookahead Distance

In accurate data prefetching such as RPT, it was proposed that multiple iteration lookahead can provide better cache performance. It is because more time is given to complete a prefetch request. Compared to the N-iteration lookahead prefetching, our aggressive lookahead mechanism is unique in the following ways. First, our technique performs aggressive and accurate prefetching without the need to consider the actual value of the physical block size in the cache hardware implementation. To achieve this same effect using the N-iteration lookahead mechanism, the exact value of the cache block size is needed to determine N. Second and more important, our lookahead mechanism carries out aggressive, yet very accurate prefetching only when the stride size is small and the bus is expected to be idle. For references with large stride size, no aggressive prefetching will be triggered because the chance for the bus to be free is low. However, under the N-iteration lookahead prefetching, the lookahead operation will be applied to every reference, independently of the stride size and of the chance for free bus cycles. If the selected reference has small stride size, the N-iteration lookahead process will have similar positive effect as our aggressive prefetching. On the other hand, for selected references with large stride sizes, the N iteration lookahead mechanism will decrease the cache performance. Since there are not many free bus cycles available in this case, whether the scheme is N iterations lookahead or one iteration lookahead will not make a lot of difference. However, with larger value of N, higher penalty needs to be paid to go to the steady loop prefetch process. Cache misses will occur in the first N-1 iterations and more useless data will be prefetched into the cache at the exit of the loop. These do not happen in our case.

4 Experimental Result

To study the performance of our proposed mechanisms in Section 3, cycle-by-cycle simulation on the baseline architecture given in Table 1 was conducted for various cache configurations and control designs. In particular, the following cache designs were simulated and analyzed:
1. Perfect data cache (i.e. no cache misses).
2. Normal data cache without prefetching.
3. Data cache with RPT.
4. Data cache with RPT and sequential unification.
5. Data cache with RPT and aggressive lookahead.
6. Data cache with both sequential unification and aggressive lookahead.

In the study, the normal data cache without prefetching was used as the reference standard. The primary measurement parameters were the execution time and the memory latency reduction. The memory latency reduction is given by the following formula:

$$Mem\_latency\_reduction = \frac{Execution\_Time(Normal\_Cache\_No\_Pr\,efetch) - Execution\_Time(New\_Design)}{Execution\_Time(Normal\_Cache\_No\_Pr\,efetch) - Execution\_Time(Perfect\_Cache)} *100\%$$

4.1 General Result

The overall result of the four cache designs with the basic configuration parameters (in Table 1) for SPEC95 is summarized in Figure 1. The x-axis is the SPEC95 program name and the y-axis is the percentage of memory latency reduction, as compared to the performance of the normal data cache without prefetching.

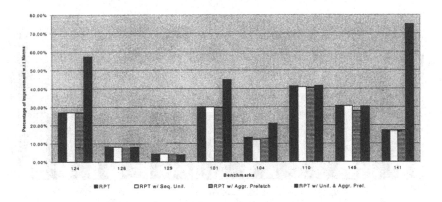

Fig. 1. Performance of RPT and Our Proposed Mechanisms on SPEC95

Figure 1 shows that when the two mechanisms are used collaboratively, significant improvement in cache performance is obtained. Based on SPEC95, the memory latency due to data references was greatly reduced for half of the benchmark programs. The reduction percentage ranges from about 9% to over 50%. For the other half of the benchmark programs, their performance is similar to the original RPT. This illustrates the potentials of the mechanisms. They try to improve the prefetch performance aggressively only when the level of confidence for performance gain is high. For other situations, they choose to remain passive; it is better to have similar performance as the original RPT than to perform wrong prefetch decisions. This is also the reason why the two techniques are more effective in floating point benchmarks than in the integer ones. The chosen RPT scheme is supposed to be more effective in floating point applications than in integer applications.

One very interesting observation in Figure 1 is that while the combined effect of the two mechanisms is very impressive, their individual effects are negligible. It is surprising because this means that the overall performance gain is not accumulated from individual results. Careful investigation found that they enforce the effect of each other instead. Sequential unification helps to improve the bus usage. However, it does not perform aggressive prefetching. As a result, simply squeezing free bus cycles cannot provide good performance improvement. On the other hand, aggressive lookahead mechanism issues more accurate prefetch requests, but there is not enough free bus cycles for these requests to complete. As a result, when these two mechanisms put together, they form a perfect match and give an enforcement effect to cache performance.

To confirm our argument, Figure 2 gives the amount of prefetch requests returned successfully by our mechanisms, as compared to that by the original RPT scheme. The result is exactly what we expect. For those benchmarks that can be improved by our combined mechanism, the amount of successful prefetch requests is significantly larger than that from RPT. Furthermore, this extra amount of successful prefetch requests is directly translated into performance performance. For those benchmarks with negligible performance improvement, the amount of successful prefetch

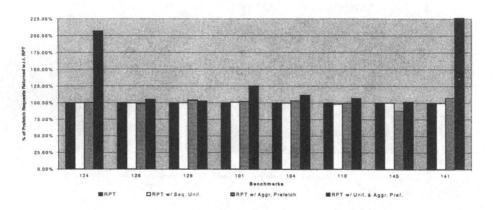

Fig. 2. Prefetch Requests Successfully Returned w.r.t. RPT Scheme

requests by our new mechanisms is about the same as that from the RPT. Figure 3 shows that the accuracy of prefetch requests. Basically, the prefetch accuracy of the proposed mechanisms is about the same as that of the RPT. This is reasonable because the basic reference predictor of all schemes under study is still linear memory reference detection. The only exception is in benchmark 141.apsi, where the prefetch accuracy of our combined mechanism drops significantly. This is due to the most aggressive prefetching that the combined mechanism implies. Figure 3 shows that the amount of successful prefetch requests is about 225% of that from RPT. Despite the low accuracy, the performance improvement obtained in this case is still the largest.

5   Conclusion

Recent work in data prefetching has successfully improved its accuracy and coverage. However, it is found that more than half of the cache misses are actually due to this predicted group of data references. Investigation shows that this is mainly due to the partial hit effect and the abortion of the accurate prefetch requests. To make up for this situation, we propose two new mechanisms to improve the use of the limited bus bandwidth. By integrating a prefetch request into an unavoidable demand fetch request, the startup memory latency is eliminated and the bus priority of the prefetch request is increased. More aggressive prefetching is also carried out whenever the bus is expected to be relatively idle. Simulation shows that these two mechanisms enforce each other and provide significant performance improvement

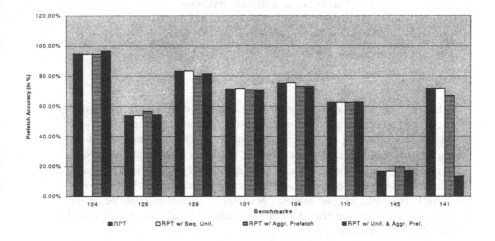

Fig. 3. Prefetch Accuracy of Proposed Mechanisms and RPT

over current prefetch schemes such as RPT. These mechanisms are very attractive to memory system designs because the additional hardware support is very simple.

References

1. Black, B., Mueller, B., Postal, S., Rakvic, R., "Load Execution Latency Reduction," Proceedings of the ACM International Conference on Supercomputing, July 1998.
2. Chen, T.F., Baer, J.L., "Reducing Memory Latency via Non-Blocking and Prefetching Caches," Proceedings of the Fifth International Conference on Architectural Support for Programming Languages and Operating Systems, October 1992, pp. 51-61.
3. Chen, T.F., Baer, J.L., "Effective Hardware-Based Prefetching for High Performance Processors," IEEE Transactions on Computers, Vol. 44, No. 5, May 1995, pp. 609-623.
4. Dahlgren F., Dubois, M., Stenstrom, P., "Fixed and Adaptive Sequential Prefetching in Shared Memory Multiprocessors," Proceedings of the 1993 International Conference on Parallel Processing, August 1993, pp. 156-163.
5. Dahlgren F., Stenstrom, P., "Sequential Hardware Prefetching in Shared Memory Multiprocessors," IEEE Transactions on Parallel and Distributed Systems, Vol. 6, No. 7, July 1995, pp. 733-745.

A Coordination Model and Facilities for Efficient Parallel Computation

A.E. Doroshenko, I.S. Kononenko, A.Y. Korotun

Institute of Software Systems
National Academy of Sciences of Ukraine
Glushkov prosp., 40, Kiev 252187, Ukraine
e-mail: dor@isofts.kiev.ua

Abstract. In this paper we propose to enhance concurrency of computation and communication by means of a coordination model we develop on the base of orthogonal parallel programming abstractions called forcing expressions. It is shown that besides efficient synchronization forcing expressions can facilitate formal development of dedicated schemes of efficient data exchanges in multilevel memory environment yielding systematic reduction of slow memory accesses. The coordination programming facilities are illustrated by a case study to enhance data parallel paradigm of computation.

1 Introduction

Recently coordination models and languages have attracted attention of scientific communities in many fields including design of distributed and parallel computer systems [5, 6]. This is due to promises that coordination facilities can contribute to reduction of complexity of managing dependencies of parallel computation activities. Coordination models and facilities are commonly considered as software integrators [2]. In this paper we use coordination model to improve performance of parallel programs by means of enhancing communication and synchronization features of programs.

Our approach is based on algebraic treatment of parallel programs composed as sets of communicating regular sequential programs [3] and the notion of forcing expression previously introduced in [4]. We follow the principle of orthogonality of computation and coordination models [5]. There is considered a class of coarse-grained parallel programs with distributed primary (local) memory and shared secondary (global) one that have static, race free structure of accesses to shared memory. Our objective is to capture this structure with a kind of formal regular expressions (forcing expressions) and to use them as synchronization and communication tools.

The very idea of regular control for synchronization of parallel processes was pioneered in [1] in the form of path expressions. We use it in context of determinism of shared data accesses order that can often be known a priori. A user can exploit this knowledge to enhance data parallel style of programming by capturing this order in user-based orthogonal specification of shared memory accesses. Moreover, using these expressions we show how to produce simple user-based forms of governing data exchanges to improve also communication part of parallel programs efficiency for multilevel memory environment via formal program transformations and systematic elimination of slow memory accesses.

2 A Model of Parallel Programs

Our model of parallel programs consists of two orthogonal parts: computation and coordination models.

Basic Computation Model. We consider parallel programs to be tuples of the form $p = (P, K, t, E)$ where $P = \{P_i\}$ is a finite set of sequential component programs (modules), K is a set of components — logical names of parallel processes, $t : K \to P$ is a (partial) initialisation map providing initial program configuration, E is a set of outer array names. Modules are composed as regular programs in the following manner of algebra of algorithms [3].

Let V be a variable set and D a data domain for these variables. A set of partial mappings $B = \{b : V \to D\}$ is called a set of memory states. Assume being known a set of basic statements $Op = \{y : B \to B\}$ of modules with unit statement ε and a set of basic conditions $Co = \{u : B \to \{0, 1\}\}$ that also includes boolean constants 0 and bf 1. An algebra of partial transformations Y, generated on Op by means of three operations: $P; Q$ — concatenation ";", $u \to (P \ else \ Q)$ — branch operation and $while(u, P)$ — iteration, where P, Q are statements and u is condition, is called algebra of statements. An algebra U, generated on Co by means of boolean operations and operation of multiplication by condition Pu that stands for "u after P", is called algebra of conditions. The two-set algebra $A(Y, U)$ considered as set of statements and conditions closed under operations above is called algebra of algorithms. Each element of algebra $A(Y, U)$ can be represented as regular expression of elements basic operators and basic conditions sets and operations of algebra of algorithms. Regular expressions of algebra of statements Y are called regular programs.

So we consider modules as sequential regular programs where the set of basic statements includes a parallel procedure call of the form Pcall F(x), and data exchanges statements. The last are of two kinds: direct pairwise exchanges with statements of sending and receiving, x -> k1 and y <- k2 that are executed at components $k2$ and $k1$ respectively, and external exchanges through shared memory with statements of reading and writing x:<- A and y:-> A), where x, y are inner and A is outer array name. Performing a pair of send/receive statements x -> k1 and y <- k2 which correspond one another is semantically equivalent to assignment y:=x.

Program computation begins with simultaneous starting its initialised modules and finishes on completing all of them. Input and output data of a program are supposed to be in external memory.

Coordination Model. We introduce the concept of forcing expressions as an alternative to standard semaphore-like and barrier-like facilities for specific case of race free parallel programs. The last feature means that any pair of data dependent statements, at least one of them modifying shared value, should be always performed in the same order. This class is fairly broad and includes, for instance, all direct and many iterative methods for solution of linear algebraic equation systems. We formalise forcing expressions in general terms of algebra of algorithms [3].

Let (P, K, t, E) is a parallel program satisfied definition above. For every $k \in K$ designate R_k to be symbol of reading and W_k to be symbol of writing. Assume to be defined the binary operation of parallel reading (P, Q) to be commutative and associative operation constructed with regular expressions P and Q that use the reading symbols only. Let $K(A)$ be a set of components of a race free program that are communicated via outer name A. Then the *forcing expression* (FE) is a regular expression $f(A)$, constructed with symbols R_k and W_k , $k \in K(A)$, unit statement and memory conditions by means of regular operations and operation of parallel reading.

Now we extend the notion of parallel program to be (P, K, t, E, F) where F is a set of forcing expressions. Execution of race free program where external exchanges are governed by FEs from F consists in joint execution of modules and forcing expressions. Read (write) statement execution initialised in module k must correspond to interpretation of R_k (W_k) as current symbol of the FE otherwise synchronization delay in this module occurs until needed read (write) operation will happen. Of course, it doesn't matter FEs being defined in terms of regular programs. What is essential is that FEs are to be agreed with module programs. In this context a FE is an significant and inalienable part of the parallel program that provides expected behaviour of the program computation.

3 Enhancing Data Parallel Style: A Case Study

The main idea of FE introduction is to enforce the order of parallel component accesses to shared memory, that may be known a priory in the case of race free program, and to eliminate redundant nondeterminism for the purpose of increasing parallel program performance. In this respect FEs are thinner tools than standard synchronization facilities. We will show advantages of FEs application for efficient synchronization of external data exchanges in data parallel computation by example of well-known Cholesky factorisation computational problem.

Let input matrix $A = (a_{ij})$ and Cholesky factor $L = (l_{ij})$ are assumed to be, for simplicity, dense full $N * N$ symmetrical positive definite matrices broken into square blocks $B * B$ so that $n = N/B$ is integer. Define component set as $\{K(i, j) : 1 \leq j < i \leq n\}$ and assume that factorisation of (i, j)-block is performed by component $K(i, j)$. Designate r_{ij}^{jk} a moment of reading the block produced by component $K(j, k)$ in component $K(i, j)$ and w_{ij} — a moment of writing result block into outer array by component $K(i, j)$. Then conditions for correct synchronization can be presented as $w_{ij} < r_{il}^{ij}$, $j < l \leq i$, and $w_{jk} < r_{ij}^{jk}$, $1 \leq k \leq j$. These inequalities (call them specifications) can be implemented in different policies. If wavefronts are defined as $Q_k = \{(i,j) : i + j = const, 1 < i + j \le 2n\}$, $1 \le k \le 2n - 1$ (Fig. 1a) then only $PARDO \ldots PAREND$ synchronization is sufficient. To give an estimation it is convenient to assume the time needed to factorisation of a block of the first column as a time unit. Then $T_1 = n^3/6 + O(n^2)$ and $T_{n/2} = n^2 + O(n)$. Therefore the efficiency $e(p) = T_1/pT_p$ is of order $1/3 + O(1/n)$ in this case.

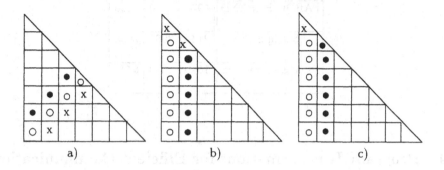

a)   b)   c)

Fig. 1. Cholesky factorisation: outlook of wavefronts

If wavefronts are organised along columns of components matrix and semaphore-like statements are used for synchronization then the wavefront Q_k, $1 \le k \le 2n - 1$ includes diagonal component given k is odd and consists of components of the same column but the diagonal one if k is even (Fig. 1b). In spite of increasing the front width from $n/2$ to n this does not improve the order of computation time $T_n = n^2 + O(n)$ and even decrease the order of efficiency to $1/6 + O(1/n)$ due to extreme workload dispersion for different points of the same front. Diagonal blocks play the role of barrier for synchronising computations of blocks of the same column.

Forcing expressions for this race free program are:

$$f(A)) = R_{ij};$$

$$f(L_{ij}) = W_{ij}; (while(u, R_{ij+k}), \; while(v, R_{li}));$$

where $0 < j < i \le n$, $u = (1 \le k \le i - j), v = (i \le l \le n)$. It may be shown that these expressions provide correct access of components to blocks of outer arrays and allow partial overlapping the computations of diagonal and column fronts (likely designated wavefronts in Fig. 1c are overlapped). Forcing expressions leave efficiency at the level of order $1/3 + O(1/n)$ but allows to obtain a variant of program that is roughly two times faster than previous ones: $T_n = n^2/2 + O(n)$. These results are confirmed in experimental implementation in Java (Sun's JDK 1.1.5, Pentium 60 MHz) where the three polices above are modelled by threads. Following Table 1 gives running times for these polices for the Cholesky factorisation problem of size $N = 200$ equations and different block size T (10, 20 and 50) assuming unrestricted parallelism of computation.

Table 1. Java running times for different synchronization policies (in msec)

Policy	T=10	T=20	T=50
PARDO-PAREND	1970	4170	7850
Semaphors	2143	3907	7638
Forcing expressions	1610	2580	5440

4 Program Transformations for Efficient Communications

Exchanges speedup in multilevel memory environment by means of hiding latency and spatial/temporal locality improvement of memory accesses is an important source to increase parallel programs efficiency. We use a method that instead of general purpose buffering algorithms takes into account some knowledge of special case caught in forcing expressions. In many important cases transformations are very simple and buffering is of low cost. We illustrate below such an application of our coordination model with following example of matrix multiplication.

We assume coarse-grained parallelization with two input and one result $nm * nm$ matrices divided into square blocks of elements to be placed in two-dimensional $n * n$ outer arrays of two-dimensional $m * m$ data blocks, respectively, A, B and C. The algorithm computes the result sum of products $C(i,j) = \sum_{k=1}^{n} A(i,k) * B(k,j)$, $1 \leq i, \leq n$, at the level of blocks of matrix elements, where $+$ and $*$ are ordinary sum and product matrix operations on blocks. A component of this program that computes (i,j)-block of result matrix is shown below in two facets: the initial and transformed component program.

```
                              Z:= 0;
                              for k:=1 to n do{
                                if q2=1 then {U:<-A(i,k);U->K(q1,q2+1)};
Z:= 0;                          else {U<-K(q1,q2-1);
  for k:=1 to n do{                  if q2<n then U->K(q1,q2+1)};
    U:<- A(i,k);                 if q1=1 then {V:<-B(k,j);V->K(q1+1,q2)};
    V:<- B(k,j);                 else {V<-K(q1-1,q2);
    Z:=Z+U*V;                        if q1<n  then V->K(q1+1,q2)};
  }                               Z:=Z + U * V
Z:->C(i,j);                     }
                              Z:->C(i,j);
```

The right facet represents a FE-driven algorithm for this problem (given the component coordinates are saved in pair of variables $(q1, q2)$ in every component). Given (i,j)-element of result matrix is computed by component named (i,j), forcing expressions for outer arrays are:

$$f(A_{ij}) = while(u, R_{ik}), \quad f(B_{ij}) = while(u, R_{kj}),$$

$$f(C_{ij}) = W_{ij}, \quad u = (1 \le k \le n), 1 \le i, j \le n$$

It is clear from these expressions that C array exchanges buffering is unnecessary because of once being written a block of C matrix then never be read. But A and B arrays exchanges are multiple and therefore need to be buffered by means of single reading an element to one component and propagating it then to another ones. As a result, almost all of nonlocal exchanges, namely $2n^2(n-1)$, will be replaced by fast direct exchanges between components. Note that because of the buffer migrates there no auxiliary memory is needed but only the one provided by compiler.

5 Conclusion

Coordination models can give more insight in tractability of parallel computation problems including parallel systems intelligence and performance. The coordination model of forcing expressions is orthogonal to computation model [5]. The main idea of forcing expressions introduction is to enforce the order of component accesses to shared memory that may be known a priory for race free program, and to eliminate nondeterminism in order to increase parallel program performance. Due to the same idea forcing expressions can facilitate development of dedicated schemes of efficient data exchanges in multilevel memory environment and yield systematic reduction of slow memory accesses. As a result they can provide nontrivial program development techniques.

References

1. R.H. Campbell, N.A. Habermann, The specification of process synchronization by path expressions, in: *Lect. Notes Comput. Sci.* (Springer Verlag, New-York, 1974), vol.16, p. 89-102.
2. P. Ciancarini, Coordination Models and Languages as Software Integrators, *ACM Computing Surveys*, June, 1996, 28(2), pp. 300-302.
3. A.E. Doroshenko, Modeling synchronization and communication abstractions for dynamical parallelization, *High-Performance Computing and Networking, Vienna, Austria, Apr.1997*, Proc.Int. Conf., Springer Verlag, Lect. Notes in Computer Sci.,vol. 1225, 1997, pp.752-761.
4. A. E. Doroshenko, Programming Abstracts for Synchronization and Communication in Parallel Programs, *Parallel Computing Technologies, Proc. Third Int. Conf. PaCT'95*, Lect. Notes Comput. Sci.,vol. 964, 1995, pp.157-162.
5. D. Gelernter, N. Carriero, Coordination Languages and Their Significance, *Commun. ACM 35*, No. 2 (1992) 97-107.
6. T.W. Malone, K. Crowston, The Interdisciplinary Study of Coordination, *ACM Computing Surveys*, **26**, No. 1 (1995), pp. 87-120.

Parallelizing of Sequential Programs on the Basis of Pipeline and Speculative Features of the Operators *

Alexander Godlevsky, Martin Gažák, and Ladislav Hluchý

Institute of Informatics, Slovak Academy of Sciences
Dúbravská cesta 9, 842 37 Bratislava, Slovakia
{upsygod, upsyhluc}@savba.sk

Abstract. An approach to dynamic parallelizing of coarse grained program where the parallelization sources are both dataflow analysis and the features pointed out in the program by annotating is proposed. Program annotating enables to hold two additional types of parallel computations which cannot be found out only from the analysis of dataflow dependences. Firstly, there are speculative computations based on anticipating alternative branches of the program's computational process. Secondly, there are pipeline computations that sometimes may be initialised for operators at the moment when their input data are not complete. Automated program analysis of this type of concurrency is either very hard or it generates a lot of surplus computation, thus absorbing the effect of program parallelization.

The implementation of the system of dynamic program parallelization for clusters of PCs and results of some experiments performed on it are described.

1 Introduction

An analysis of dataflow dependencies is the main source for parallelizing procedural programs. The approach based on it is the most productive for data processing programs whose bulky volume of computation relates to nested loops. The similar parallelizing is applied in compilers for parallel computers and is known as data parallelism. However, the dataflow analysis regarded as the unique source of parallelization is not enough to parallelize irregular programs. These are usual for other programming paradigms, logic and functional ones, where ideas of speculative [5] and pipeline [2] computations for program parallelization are developed. In short, the idea of former computations is to compute simultaneously both a function and some of its arguments in the manner when only the function body computation is mandatory. This process determines what to do with each of other processes - to delete it or to make it mandatory. When it is deleted the computation's overhead is increased; when it is made mandatory

---

* This work was supported by the Slovak Scientific Grant Agency within Research Project No.2/4102/98

then the computation of whole function is speeded up. For function composition $F(..., G(...), ...)$, the idea of pipeline computations is realized by a stepwise and simultaneous execution of both functions F and G. For each execution step only the partial result of G computation is passed to F function to process.

In this paper, combined use of both dataflow analysis and the features of the speculative and pipeline computations is proposed. Programs are supposed to be written in a simple programming language in which there are only three constructions to compose operators: sequential composition, *if* and *while* constructions. The characteristic feature of this language is the possibility to annotate some operators of parallelized programs by *spec* and *pipeln* marks. Our system for dynamical parallelization of annotated sequential programs is based on *PDS* semantic proposed in [4]. It guarantees that results of sequential and parallel computations of the same program are equal to each other. The idea of such program parallelization was to reduce the process of parallel programs development to the process of annotating sequential ones. The main result of this paper is to describe the implementation of dynamical program parallelization.

2 Parallel Dynamical Semantic

In this section the sketch of *PDS* semantic is given. It is represented by finite system S of transition rules which act on the states - abstractions of the available states of programs during their parallel execution. A state of S system is 4-tuple $(b, heap, pheap, P)$ where b is a current state of the program environment, P is a residual program, *heap* and *pheap* are sets of unstructured operators extracted earlier from P. Operator y is transferred from P into *heap* or *pheap* if it is dataflow independent to all operators which are in *heap* or *pheap* sets or precede y in P. *heap* and *pheap* differ by the feature that operators from *pheap* can be executed in the pipeline mode. The notion of dataflow independence is modified for them: operators R and Q, where R precedes Q and Q is annotated by mark *pipeln(x)*, are independent if the set intersection of output variables of R and input ones of Q contains the variable x whose value is step by step transferred from R into Q. The environment b is interpreted as functional $X \to D$ where X is the set of all variables of parallelized program and D is their data domain. Beside S system rules for transferring unstructured operators from P into *heap* or *pheap* there are rules both for transforming P residual program and for executing operators from *heap* and *pheap*. The former ones are the reduction rules of *if* operators, the unfolding or deletion rules of *while* operators. When the execution rule is applied to unstructured operator y from *heap*, y is deleted from *heap* and b is transformed according to the semantical interpretation of y. The similar rule for pipelined y operator from *pheap* differs in that y may be deleted from *pheap* or not. A speculatively executed y operator differs from that with mandatory execution by executing in b environment extended by local variables. If y's speculation, for some y from *heap*, is found to be useless, then its environment extension is deleted. If it is turned to be mandatory then the b environment is changed by decreasing localisation level of its local variables.

Being limited by the paper volume we cannot demonstrate accurately any of the transition rule. We only note that the correctness of their system was proved in [4]. The order of rules' application is limited only by conditions of their applicability. The potential differences in the order can affect computation speed-up but not correctness.

3 Implementation

Although the system for dynamic parallelization of programs (SDP) is implemented in C++/PVM [6] and uses features like object-oriented programming, remote procedure call based on PVM messages and multithreading, it is suitable for other implementation languages (Java).

Current version assumes a distributed memory homogenous message passing machine. The target machine for SDP implementation is a cluster of PCs running Linux using fast ethernet hub.

Parallel program execution consists of two steps:

1. Compilation: the source program consists of skeleton of algorithm written in a modified subset of C language enriched with keywords for *pipeln* and *spec* annotations and of implementation of unstructured operators. During the compilation phase two pairs of C++ files are generated : resolver.cxx, resolver.h implements remote procedure call via PVM, and dpc_program.cxx, dpc_program.h initializes representation of program in a form of linked lists of statements (unstructured operators, while, etc.).
2. Interpretation and parallel execution: the input for dynamic paralleliser consists of object of the Program class and of the initial memory state. Program is interpreted according to *PDS* rules presented in section 2.

SDP has a star topology. It consists of:

1. Master process running on the main processor and consisting of two threads - the *analyzer* and the *scheduler*; within this process the interpretation and parallelization of sequential program take place. Analyzer and scheduler run concurrently and share data structures. An access to those data structures is synchronized by synchronization mechanisms - monitors and synchronized methods.
2. Slave processes on the slave processors. Slave processes communicate with the scheduler, manage the task threads (a *task* is an unstructured operator under execution) and the local memory of variables shared among the tasks (an example of shared variable is a list used for pipeline parallelism).

During the interpretation the analyzer analyzes dependencies among operators and gradually transforms program into directed acyclic graph (DAG), where nodes correspond to unstructured operators and edges correspond to dataflow dependencies. As soon as for any node the number of incoming edges is 0 (or 1 for nodes representing pipeline operators), the operator is moved to corresponding task queue (priority of mandatory operators is higher than that of speculative ones, etc.). *DAG* is generated from sequential program in run-time, programs with conditional statements (*if-then-else, while*) cannot be transformed into *DAG* during one pass. The analysis starts at the beginning of program, then links between operators from *DAG* and conditional statements, which depend on the values of output variables, are established, so that after the execution of an operator the analysis need not start at the beginning. The analyzer also manages the memory and takes care of variable localization and garbage collecting of unnecessary copies of variables.

The scheduler manages the whole system. During the initialization it establishes connections to slave processes, launches an analyzer and then manages the tasks. The tasks wait for execution in several queues with different priority. The scheduler does not have information about task granularity, and simple FIFO scheduling algorithm is used. The scheduler maps the task on the first free processor (with respect to load). Since values of output variables of operators are necessary for further analysis, and tasks which became useless (e.g. during speculative parallelization) are destroyed, all communication is between task and scheduler, not between the tasks themselves.

4 Buchberger's Algorithm

The Buchberger's algorithm for the computation of Gröbner bases is one of the fundamental algortihms to solve polynomial system. From the perspective of computational complexity the algortihm is intractable, but in practice it can solve a considerable number of interesting problems and there are indications that problems arising from real situations are far from the worst case of algorithm.

Let K be a field, and assume we have a term-ordering in polynomial ring $K[x_1, \ldots, x_n]$; a power-product in this ring is the product of variables, a monomial is a product of non-zero constant from K and a power-product. The leading power product $Lpp(p)$, the leading monomial $Lm(p)$ and the leading coefficient $Lc(p)$ of polynomial p are defined w.r.t. the term-ordering. We say that p reduces to p' by q at τ, and write $p \to_q^\tau p'$ if $p = a\tau + \rho$ and $q = b\upsilon + \eta$, with $a, b \in k$ constants, τ and υ power-products such that $\upsilon = Lpp(q)$ and $\upsilon\mu = \tau$, then $p' = b\rho - a\mu\eta$.

The polynomial p had reduced relatively to the polynomial set P if any its polynomial does not reduce it. In this case it is also said that polynomial p has the irreducible form w.r.t. to P. Let P be a polynomial set, $Id(P)$ be the ideal generated by P over the polynomial ring $K[x_1, \ldots, x_n]$; then a polynomial set G such that $Id(G) = Id(P)$ and irreducible form of each polynomial from P is 0 will be named Gröbner's basis of P. Buchberger's algorithm for construction of Gröbner's basis is based on the notion of S-polynomial. In [3] it was proved the basis G is Gröbner's basis if and only if for each pair of polynomials from G its S-polynomial is reduced to 0 relatively to G.

```
Program Grobner (inout S: set of poly);
  Pairs:={(f,g)|f,g ∈ S, f < g};
  while not isempty(Pairs) do
    Var f,g,p:poly;
    (f,g):=Select(from Pairs);
    Pairs:=Pairs \ {f,g};
    p:=Red(Spol(f,g),S);
      if not eq(p,0) then S:=S∪{p}; Update({p}*S to Pairs); fi;
  end_while;
  S:=Reduce(S);
end program
```

The algorithm contains the calls of operators (procedures) *Select, Red, Reduce, Update* and *Spol* which have the following meaning. The *Select* selects an element from *Pairs* set. The *Red* reduces polynomial *p* relatively to the current value of the *S* basis. The *Reduce* interreduces the *S* basis and transforms it to reduced. The *Update* completes the *Pairs* set by new elements applying the B-criterium. The *Spol* constructs *S*-polynomial for its two arguments. Only *Spol, Red, Reduce* are marked as unstructured operators.

Because of data dependencies among the loop iterations this algorithm cannot be parallelized in the framework of the conservative approach. Annotating this loop by *spec(Pairs)* mark we open the possibilities to initiate speculative parallel computing of certain iterations. If for some element of *Pairs* speculative computing is initiated and after this moment according to B-criterion [1] for current completing of *Pairs* this element is eleminated, then speculative process initiated by it will also be killed by corresponding mechanism of *SDP*.

It is evident that the following relationships for *Red* and *Reduce* operators,

$$Red(p, M \cup N) \cong Red(Red(p, M), M \cup N)$$

$$Reduce(M \cup N) \cong Reduce(Reduce(M) \cup N)$$

where the sign $\cong$ is understood as equivalence, are true. Thus, these operators are pipeline computing.

5   Experimental Results

In this section the results from Buchberger's algorithm running on PC cluster are presented. During the parallel execution one processor interpreted the program and the rest of processors computed unstructured operators. Time for one processor is the time of execution of sequential version (without overhead caused by interpretation). The benchmarks *Quad* consisted of 11 polynomials of 7 variables (degree 2, 435 pairs of polynomials), *Symm 2* of 3 symmetric polynomials of 4 variables (degree ≤ 3, 36 pairs), *Nonsymm* of 3 polynomials of 3 variables (degree ≤ 3, 120 pairs).

Number of processors	Quad(time / speedup)	Symm 2	Nonsymm
1	44.8 / 1	8.041/1	223/1
4	16.47 / 2.72	3.1 / 2.59	78.4 / 2.84
8	7.1 / 6.31	1.82 / 4.45	32.84 / 6.79

Configuration of slave processors permited concurrent computation of several tasks (in separate threads) on one processor. With increasing number of threads per processor the behaviour of simulation became more nondeterministic because of communication collisions; in general the speedup was the same.

Granularity of tasks of the *Quad* example is the lowest, that of *Nonsymm* is the highest. *Symm2* shows how efficiency is affected not only by granularity of tasks, but also by their number.

6 Conclusion

SPD system for automatical parallelization of annotated sequential programs is represented. Its dynamical manner of processing enables to adapt the parallelization process not only to parallelized programs but to their input data as well. As a consequence, the system can take its place for parallelization of irregular programs for which the developped methods of data parallelization are not applied. The results of experiments with Buchberger's algorithm demonstrated a significant parallelization level supported by the system.

References

1. Attardi G., Traverso C.: *A Strategy-accurate Parallel Buchberger Algorithm* // J. Symbolic Computation (1996), 21, P.411-426
2. Guy E.Blelloch, Margaret Reid-Miller, *Pipelining with Futures*, in Ninth Annual ACM Symposium on Parallel Algorithms and Architectures (SPAA'97), 22-25 June, Newport, Rhode Island
3. Buchberger B.: *An Algorithm for Finding a Basis for the Residue Class Ring of Zero-Dimensional Polynomial Ideal.* Ph.D.Thesis, Math.Inst., Univ. of Insbruck, Austria, 1965.
4. Godlevsky A.B.: *The Parallel Dynamical Semantics of Sequential Program that Allows Speculative and Incremental Computation.* Kibernetika i sistemny analiz , 1996, No. 2, pp.131-153 (in Russian).
5. M.Hermenegildo.: *Automatic Parallelization of Irregular and Pointer-Based Computation: Perspectives from Logic and Constraint Programming*, in Euro-Par'97 Parallel Processing, number 1300 in LNCS, pages 31-45, Passau, Germany, August 26-29, 1997. Springer-Verlag
6. Geist A., Beguelin A. Dongarra J., Jiang W., Manchek R. and Sunderam V.:*PVM: Parallel Virtual Machine, A User's Guide and Tutorial for Networked Parallel Computing.* The MIT Press, 1994.

Kinetic Model of Parallel Data Processing

Katya O. Gorbunova

Institute of Computational Modelling of SB RAS, Krasnoyarsk, Russia, 660036

Abstract. A new formal model of parallel computations — the Kirdin kinetic machine — is studied. It is expected that this model will play the role for parallel computations similar to Markov normal algorithms, Kolmogorov and Turing machine or Post schemes for sequential computations. The basic ways in which computations are realized are described, correctness of the elementary programs for the Kirdin kinetic machine is investigated. It is proved that the determined Kirdin kinetic machine is an effective calculator. A simple application of the Kirdin kinetic machine — heap encoding — is suggested.

1 Introduction

The problem of effective programming with fine-grained parallelism is far from being solved. It seems that, despite numerous efforts, we have not yet understood parallel computations, considering them mainly as result of usual algorithms parallelization. There are some promising approaches based on models of computing environments constructed from large number of elementary calculators of the same type (neural networks, cellular automata etc.). If it is possible to implement a problem in such environment (for example, by methods of neural networks training [7]), further realization with parallel computers can be easily constructed within the framework of the ideas "similar tasks for different elements". There are other perspective ideas and approaches to construction of models of fine-grained parallelism besides neural networks.

Parallel Substitution Algorithms (PSA) [9] conceptually go back to von Neumann cellular automata, but have more powerful expressive capabilities. PSA are capable of processing multidimensional data arrays that are represented as a set of cells. Based on PSA concepts a theory has been developed which comprises the correctness conditions, equivalent transformations and a number of methods for algorithm and architecture synthesis. A computer simulation system allows to construct cellular algorithms and observe computation processes in dynamics.

The chemical computer (SCAM — *Statistic Cellular Automata Machine*) is offered in [8] in development of the cellular automata theory. SCAM is based on imitation simulation by Monte-Carlo methods of a class of heterogeneous chemical reactions occurring in a very thin layer of molecules adsorbed on the surface of a crystal catalyst. Algorithmic universality for SCAM has been proved.

Artificial Immune Systems seem to be closest to our model [10]. Artificial Immune Systems are highly distributed systems based on the principles of natural system. This is a new and rapidly growing field offering powerful and robust information processing capabilities for solving complex problems. Like artificial neural networks, artificial immune systems can learn new information, recall previously learned information, and perform pattern recognition in a highly decentralized fashion.

A new abstract model of computations — *the Kirdin kinetic machine* — is investigated in this paper. This model is expected to play the same role for parallel computations as the Turing machine and other abstract algorithmic calculators for sequential computations.

The Kirdin kinetic machine is based on chemical reactions in liquids or gases. Our optimistic expectations go back to the theorem of M.D.Korzuhin [12] on chemical reactions ability to imitate any dynamic system for finite times and to the theorem of A.N.Gorban [13] on chemical systems approximating any dynamic systems.

2   The Kirdin Kinetic Machine

Processable unit for the Kirdin kinetic machine is *an ensemble* of words M from the alphabet L, which is identified with a function F_M taking non-negative integer values: $F_M : L^* \to N \bigcup \{0\}$. The value of $F_M(s)$ is interpreted as a number of copies of a word s in the ensemble M.

The processing consists of an aggregate of *elementary events*, which occur non deterministically and in parallel. An elementary event $S : M \to M'$ means that from the ensemble M an ensemble K^- is removed and an ensemble K^+ is added. The ensembles K^- and K^+ are unambiguously set by *rules* or *commands*, which are combined in a *program*. The commands can be of only three kinds (u, w - arbitrary, v, f, g, k, q, s are fixed):

1. Disintegration $uvw \to uf + gw$
2. Synthesis $uk + qw \to usw$
3. Replacement $uvw \to usw$

The program P *is applicable* to an ensemble M, if any command of P is applicable to M. Elementary event S is unambiguously determined by a rule p from the list of commands of the program P, and by an ensemble K^- determined by this rule and such that $F_K^-(s) \le F_M(s)$ for any s. An elementary event S *is allowable* for an ensemble M and a program P if there is a rule p in the list of commands of the program P and the values of function F_M for words in the left part of this rule are positive.

Let's say that N of allowable events *are compatible*, if

$$F_M - \sum_{i=1}^{n} F_i^- \ge 0$$

where F_i^- is a removed ensemble for i-th event.

Ensemble M is called *a final ensemble* if no command of the program P is applicable to it. P is refered to as *a finite program* if application of commands of the program to the initial ensemble always leads to a final ensemble. If all final ensembles coincide, the program P is named *deterministic* for the ensemble M.

The Kirdin kinetic machine can be informally described as a jar with words. We add rules-catalysts to this jar, some of them, colliding with the words, promote their disintegration, others, meeting a pair of suitable words, promote their synthesis, and the third replace some subchains in the words.

3 Correctness of the Programs Consisting of One Command

The commands of disintegration and replacement are undetermined, if conditions 1& 2 or 1& 3 of the following list are fulfilled.

1. The chain v being replaced can be decomposed as aba, i.e. its beginning and end coincide.
2. In words, to which these commands are applicable, there are the chains of the kind $ababa$, i.e. the chain v can be chosen in two ways.
3. In the words obtained after application of these commands there are chains of the kind $ababa$, i.e. the chain v can be chosen in two ways.

For the programs consisting of any number of commands of disintegration and replacement, these criteria are easily generalized. A program consisting of commands of synthesis is always finite, and in general case undetermined.

4 Algorithmic Universality of the Kirdin Kinetic Machine

We assume that the Kirdin kinetic machine will be of a universal character. Thus a question arises: how the Kirdin kinetic machine correlates with consecutive standard algorithmic formal models.

Theorem 1. *The determined Kirdin kinetic machine is equivalent to any consecutive standard algorithmic formal model, such as the Turing machine or Markov normal algorithms. Hence, it is an effective calculator.*

The halting problem for the Turing machine is unsolvable in the general case, *hence finiteness the Kirdin kinetic machine for the programs consisting of commands of replacement is also unsolvable.*

The Kirdin kinetic machine is undetermined in the general case. It is natural that it cannot be completely equivalent to the determined calculator. Nevertheless, we have seen that it completely includes all determined universal calculators. What can be said about the Kirdin kinetic machine in the undetermined case? Let's distinguish another class of the Kirdin kinetic machine.

We will call the Kirdin kinetic machine *partially determined*, if its program consists of determined commands of replacement and disintegration and any commands of synthesis.

A partially determined Kirdin kinetic machine can be modelled by a specially arranged system of algorithmic calculators, for instance, let them be the Turing machines. Consider a partially determined Kirdin kinetic machine, $|M|$ is the number of words in its ensemble. From the beginning $|M|$ Turing machines are initialized, each of them processes its own word. The program for each machine consists of commands of replacement and disintegration. The application of a command of disintegration means initiation of a new Turing machine, and the configuration of the first of them corresponds to the word uf, and the configuration of the second — to the word gw.

At the same time, *an over-calculator* is functioning, with a program consisting of all commands of synthesis of the initial program. It compares configurations of Turing machines with words uk and qw. If both are present in the configurations, it "switches off" one of these machines, and the configuration of the another turns into usw.

5   Unstructured Memory

Unstructured memory is an organic elementary application of the Kirdin kinetic machine. Its basic idea is to store the information about a long text by means of a special dictionary, consisting of words which length is much shorter than the length of the initial text. The list of all words of length q, included in the given text, referred to as q-carrier of the given text. Words starting from any place in the text are considered. For a text of the length N there are $N - q + 1$ of such words [11]. If each word of the q-carrier is put into correspondence to the frequency of its occurrence in the text, we obtain the frequency dictionary of length q.

Transition from the text to its frequency dictionary is a useful technique which allows to compare texts of different lengths and perform their information analysis, which was successfully made for genetic texts in [11]. Besides, the frequency dictionary fixes the information about the text in a set of small objects — words with their frequencies, which can be stored separately, "in a heap". There exist probabilistic estimations of the length of the dictionary, sufficient for the text unambiguous reconstruction.

If a dictionary of the length k contains words which occur uniquely, then for the dictionary of the length $k + 1$ and larger the text is restored unambiguously. This very case will be considered. The following program for the Kirdin kinetic machine constructs the dictionary of the length k from an initial (long) text. This program is finite and determined. The obtained dictionary does not contain complete information about the initial text if the final ensemble will consist of an unique word — !. It means, that such length of the dictionary is insufficient for the unambiguous reconstruction of the initial text. Hence, the given procedure should be started anew for the initial text, but with k increased by 1. And so on, until we obtain a dictionary of length k as a final ensemble , and now it is necessary to start the program for the last time, to construct the dictionary of length $k + 1$, from which the initial text can be reconstructed unambiguously.

Introduce a new designation: v^k in the left part of a rule denotes an arbitrary word of the length k in the initial alphabet. All entries of v^k in one rule denote the same word. Entries of the symbol v^k in different rules are not connected.

$$uv^1 v^{k-1} v_1^1 w \to uv^1 v^{k-1} + v^{k-1} v_1^1 w$$

$$v^k + v^k \to !$$

$$! + v^k \to !$$

Now, storing and, probably, transferring the initial text through communication channels as the dictionary, we can always unambiguously reconstruct it from this dictionary. The following program of the Kirdin kinetic machine is intended for this purpose.

$$uv^k + v^k w \to uv^k w$$

6 Conclusions

The Kirdin kinetic machine is based on two paradigms:

- fine-grained parallelism
- structureless parallelism

These seem to be the most perspective directions of the development of computer science.

We have seen that the Kirdin kinetic machine is a universal calculator. The ways of solution of the problem of programs execution correctness for the Kirdin kinetic machine are offered. Determination of finiteness for the Kirdin kinetic machine is very complicated and, in the general case, unsolvable. But the same is known about the Turing machine.

Determinacy means definiteness of the result. Most likely, for some range of problems we will not be interested in strict determinacy, but in near determinacy or even simply probabilistic distributions of the final ensemble.

According to the well-known "Minsky hypothesis" the efficiency of a parallel system increase proportionally to logarithm of processor number. To overcome this restriction the following approach often applied. Extremely parallel algorithms of solutions are built for different types of problems. The algorithms use some abstract paradigm of fine-grained parallelism, for example, structureless parallelism. For particular parallel computers means of parallel processes realization with a given abstract architecture are created. As a result an effective tool for parallel programs production appears.

References

1. Kirdin A.N. Ideal ensemble model of parallel computations // Neural informatics and its applications. Abstracts of V all–Russia seminar. — Krasnoyarsk, KGTU, 1997. —p.101: in Russian.

2. Gorbunova E.O. The analysis of elementary programs for ideal ensemble model of parallel computations // Abstracts of INPRIM–98. — Novosibirsk: izd-vo Instituta matematiki, 1998. — p.77: in Russian.

3. Gorbunova E.O. Finiteness and determinacy of simple programs for the Kirdin kinetic machine // Methods of neuroinformatics. / A.N.Gorban (ed.). Krasnoyarsk; KGTU. — 1998. -p. 23–40: in Russian.

4. Gorbunova E.O. To the question of algorithmic universality of the Kirdin kinetic machine// Neuroinformatics and its applications. Abstracts of VI all-Russia seminar. — Krasnoyarsk, KGTU, 1998. p.147–48: in Russian.

5. Markov A.A., Nagorny N.M. The theory of algorithms. — M.: Nauka, 1984. 432p.: in Russian.

6. Uspensky V.A., Semenov A.L. The theory of algorithms: basic discoveries and applications. —M.: Nauka. 1987.— 288 p.: in Russian.

7. Gorban A.N., Rossiev D.A. Neural networks for personal computer. — Novosibirsk: Nauka, 1996. 276 p.: in Russian.

8. Latkin E.I. SCAM: chemical computer // The theory of computations and languages of specifications. — Novosibirsk, 1995.— V. 152: Computing System. — p.140–151: in Russian.

9. Achasova S., Bandman O., Markova V. and Piskunov S. Parallel substitution algorithm. Theory and Application.— WORD SCIENTIFIC, 1994.

10. D.Dasgupta (Ed.). Artificial immune systems and their applications.— SPRINGER, 1998. XIV, 310 pp.

11. N.N.Bugaenko, A.N.Gorban and M.G.Sadovsky. Maximum entropy method in analysis of genetic text and measurement of its information content — Open Sys. And Information Dyn. 5, 1998. —p.265-278.

12. A.M.Jabotinskii Concentration selfoscillations. — Moscow: Nauka, 1974: in Russian.

13. A.N.Gorban, V.I.Bykov, G.S.Yablonsky. Essays about chemical relaxation. — Novosibirsk: Nauka, 1986: in Russian.

PSA Approach to Population Models for Parallel Genetic Algorithms

Peter Hartmann

Cordsen Engineering GmbH
Ostring 5, D-63533 Mainhausen, Germany
Tel.: [+49] 6182 / 9294-0   Fax: [+49] 6182 / 9294-45
E.-Mail: hartmann@cordsen.com

Abstract. A universal approach for describing the *population model* of genetic algorithms is developed which is based on the *Parallel Substitution Algorithm* (PSA) theory. Genetic algorithms (GA) are a suitable method if good approximations for problems are required which were otherwise not solvable in practical environments. Optimisation of GAs can be done on several levels, in this work we concentrate on the *population model*. Most prominent population models are the classical *global* model, the *island model* and it's extreme variant, the *cellular model*. The PSA theory supports us with a general approach which is essential for systematically studying convergence behaviour of GA population model variants and consequently for their optimisation.

1   Introduction

Genetic Algorithms (GA) [4, 7] are a general principle for solving difficult problems, and the main task when finding an optimised implementation of a GA is to make selections from a possibly large variety of variants. This contribution will deal with variants on level of the *population model*.

We introduce the term *population model* to describe how the individuals from a GA population are interacting. Our studies on *cellular genetic algorithms* have shown that the choice of the right population model has an impact on convergence behaviour of the GA. First investigations in GA use a *global* population model where all individuals of the population are kept in a global "container" and competition and mating between each pair of them is not depending on individual's coordinates. Other approaches are known from literature, i.e. the *island model* [3] where small sub-populations of the global type are interconnected by a network with lower probability for exchange of genetic information.

Our *cellular* population model [6] can be seen as an extreme case of the island model where the individuals occupy nodes on an orthogonal grid such we have islands occupied by at most one individual at a time. This model is inherently massive-parallel and it can be described using a cellular automaton (CA) model. The *local transition function* of the CA then describes all genetic operators like *selection*, *mutation* and *crossing over*. Advantageous behaviour of cellular genetic algorithms comes from the fact that sub-populations are enabled to populate niches, hence yielding a larger variety of genotypes [5]. Further focusing on this we developed a general concept for *architectures* and *textures* of a cellular GA which is used to control behaviour of individuals and sub-populations [2].

Conclusions from these studies are that the population model influences the behaviour of the GA significantly and a general model of population models will be required for optimisation of GAs. We choose the *Parallel Substitution Algorithm* (PSA) [1] for describing population models, because

- PSA covers all relevant cases of population models,
- the PSA theory allows construction of equivalent CA or other parallel paradigms for the practical implementation,
- population models can be described unambiguously with a PSA which is essential for documentation and scientific discussions,
- PSA simplifies to identify parts of the algorithm that can be executed in parallel, and
- it even allows extensions for growing populations (future work).

In the next section we describe principle population models including our massively-parallel cellular model. We represent these basic population models based on a PSA. Then we introduce the concepts of *textures* and *architectures* imprinted into the cellular population model and the corresponding PSA. Finally we discuss results from the implementation of the cellular population model.

2 Population Models of Genetic Algorithms

Coming from the general idea of genetic algorithms we develop the massively-parallel *cellular* population model for GA.

Principle task when using GA is to find optimal solutions for a given problem domain $\mathcal{X}$ on which a certain function $w : \mathcal{X} \to \mathbb{R}$ into real value space is defined. We call w the *fitness function* which directly expresses quality of a certain solution $x \in \mathcal{X}$. In a GA we deal with a population $\mathcal{P}$ of individuals $p \in \mathcal{P}$ each having a certain genome $x(p) \in \mathcal{X}$ representing a specific solution from $\mathcal{X}$. Ergo we search for individuals $p \in \mathcal{P}$ with as high as possible $w(x(p))$. The GA search method has been derived from biological observations; new and better individuals are generated by selection, mating and mutation. Design of a specialised GA incorporates the following steps:

1. Find suitable representation for solutions $x \in \mathcal{X}$, we call this coding of a solution the *genes* of an individual.
2. Define genetic operators on the genes.
3. Define a suitable population model for the individuals which describes interactions between individuals.
4. Run the GA, measure convergence properties and re-assess steps 1-3 from above iteratively until desired behaviour is achieved.

The genetic operators describe how a certain subset of individuals will generate offspring by mating and mutation:

Selection: how to select individuals for further processing. Selection operator $S : \mathcal{P}^* \to \mathcal{P} \times \mathcal{P}$ yields two individuals taken from a sub-population $p_1, p_2, \ldots$, we write $(p_a, p_b) = S(p_1, p_2, \ldots)$.

Crossing-Over: how to combine two individuals to form a new individual. Crossing-over $X : \mathcal{P} \times \mathcal{P} \to \mathcal{P}$ gives us one individual from the two input individuals, we write $p = X(p_a, p_b)$.

Mutation: how to perform random changes on the individuals. Mutation $M : \mathcal{P} \to \mathcal{P}$ is an operator acting on the genome of a single individual, we write $p' = M(p)$.

Based on these three operators we derive new organisms according to the formula $p' = M(X(S(p_1, p_2, \ldots)))$. The task of population models (ergo the task of PSA productions developed subsequently) is to describe how to choose individuals p_a and p_b from a certain sub-population $p_1, p_2, \ldots$ and where to store the result p'.

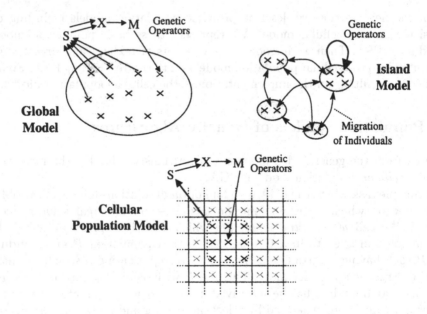

Fig. 1. Sketch of selected GA population models.

Figure 1 illustrates frequently used population models, namely the *global*, *island* and *cellular* models. In the global model all individual selection is based on the whole population, hence individuals are not associated with certain spatial positions. The island model can be seen as an aggregate of a number of smaller and mostly autonomous global populations, between which migration of individuals takes place sporadically. In the cellular variant the individuals are localised in a regular grid, and the scope of the selection operator is restricted to the local environment of an individual (the *neighbourhood index* of the underlying CA).

3 PSA of Population Models

A parallel substitution algorithm (PSA) $\Pi = < \Phi, K(A, M) >$ is a parallel replacement system on cellular systems [1]. $K(A, M)$ describes the configuration space based on the alphabet A and the cell naming space M. The dynamical behaviour of such a PSA is described in terms of the set of productions $\Phi = \{\Theta_1, \Theta_2, \ldots\}$. Each production has the form $\Theta_i : \{base\} * \{context\} \rightarrow \{right-hand\ side\}$ describing how cells from the left-hand side (base and context) can be replaced by the right-hand side.

The application of productions is done in parallel, consequently a PSA might be non-deterministic. A GA is in principle non-deterministic, but the probability of application of productions must be made dependent on the fitness of the individuals that are associated with the modified cells. For this we introduce an extended version of productions which allows us to note the weight like:
$\Theta_i : \{base\} * \{context\} \rightarrow_{weight} \{right-hand\ side\}$. The interpretation of this weight is, that we sum up all weights of conflicting substitutions and chooses one of the substitutions to be applied to the cellular array randomly, such that the probability for choosing one production is proportional to its weight.

For formulation of the population models from above we use *stationary* PSA, because size of the population stays fixed [1]. Furthermore we use *functional* type of productions [1]. The alphabet of the PSA is taken from problem domain (typically $A = \mathcal{X}$). The name set of cells depends on the population model.

Most general are the following rules Θ_1 and Θ'_1 for the global population model, where any two individuals from the populations are allowed to mate. Using our extended version of productions, the global population has productions

$$\Theta_1 = \{(c, -)\} * \{(a, x_a), (b, x_b)\} \rightarrow_{w(x_a) \cdot w(x_b)} \{(c, M(X(x_a, x_b)))\}$$
$$\Theta'_1 = \{(c, x_c)\} * \{(a, x_a)\} \rightarrow_{w(x_a) \cdot w(x_c)} \{(c, M(X(x_a, x_c)))\}$$

Production Θ_1 assigns a new genome to the cell with name c, this cell can initially contain any genome (don't care symbol "-"). The resulting genome is constructed from the two input genomes x_a and x_b (by crossing-over $X(\ldots)$ and mutation $M(\ldots)$), both taken from the context cells a and b. Θ'_1 acts similarly with the exception, that the cell c, to which the genome is assigned, contributes its genome to the result.

It is important to note that we do not necessarily need to deal with two generations like in other pseudo-parallel implementations of GA: since the PSA formulates the implicit parallelism in the model, we regard only one generation of the GA that is synchronously replaced by the next generation in each step. Note furthermore that the selection operator is completely covered by the PSA rule, while we abstract from crossing over and mutation by using operators $X(\ldots)$ and $M(\ldots)$ which are application specific.

For the island model we use two rules similar to those of the global model (extended by identifiers for certain islands) plus a rule for exchange of individuals

---

[1] Interesting future extensions might introduce non-stationary variants were size of the population is allowed to adapt to global state (convergence) of the GA calculations.

between separate islands. We use a name space $M \subset I\!N \times I\!N$ where the first entry is the index $(i, j, \ldots)$ of the island and the second $(a, b, c, \ldots)$ is the name of cells within the concrete island. Rules Θ_{2a} Θ'_{2a} describe generation of new individuals, Θ_{2b} stands for exchange between islands, with probability $p(exg)$:

$$\Theta_{2a} = \{(<i,c>,-)\} * \{(<i,a>,x_a),(<i,b>,x_b)\}$$
$$\rightarrow_{w(x_a) \cdot w(x_b)} \{(<i,c>, M(X(x_a,x_b)))\}$$

$$\Theta'_{2a} = \{(<i,c>,x_c)\} * \{(<i,a>,x_a)\}$$
$$\rightarrow_{w(x_a) \cdot w(x_c)} \{(<i,c>, M(X(x_a,x_c)))\}$$

$$\Theta_{2b} = \{(<i,a>,x_a),(<j,b>,x_b)\} * \{\} \rightarrow_{p(exg)} \{(<i,a>,x_b),(<j,b>,x_a)\}$$

Θ_3 and Θ'_3 are examples for a cellular-type population model based on the Moore-neighbourhood index. For this model we use a two-dimensional name space $<r,s> \in I\!N \times I\!N$ in which we allow relative addressing with offsets $<\Delta r, \Delta s> \in \{-1,0,1\} \times \{-1,0,1\}$:

$$\Theta_3 = \{(<r,s>,-)\} * \{(<r+\Delta r_a, s+\Delta s_a>, x_a),(<r+\Delta r_b, s+\Delta s_b>, x_b)\}$$
$$\rightarrow_{w(x_a) \cdot w(x_b)} \{(<r,s>, M(X(x_a,x_b)))\}$$

$$\Theta'_3 = \{(<r,s>,x_c)\} * \{(<r+\Delta r_a, s+\Delta s_a>, x_a)\}$$
$$\rightarrow_{w(x_a) \cdot w(x_c)} \{(<r,s>, M(X(x_a,x_c)))\}$$

4 Architecture and Textures

Experiments with GA [2] have shown that the convergence of the GA can profit from increasing the mutation rate for a short period of time, in case the GA has got stuck in a local minimum. Our motivation for introducing *architectures* in our cellular GA was to spatially embed this temporal change of the GA's environment into the cellular array: the individuals are forced to migrate through spatial structures with different properties (size, mutation rate, ...). In addition to this, separation of sub-population increases genetical heterogeneity which reduces risk to get stuck in local minima, but for the costs of slower speed of convergence.

We use a simple while universal scheme to describe these structures. Every cell incorporates relative weight factors f for each of the neighbour cells that multiplies with the probability that a neighbour from the certain direction is chosen for crossing over with the regarded cell. For these weight factors we introduce another alphabet for the PSA which is $A = X \times I\!N_0^{3 \times 3}$. The second component of the alphabet will be used to store the weight factors f in form of a two-dimensional array of integers. Please note coincidence between these weight factors and the neighbourhood index of the underlying CA. This population model is expressed by a PSA with productions Θ_4 and Θ'_4:

$$\Theta_4 = \{(<r,s>,<-,f>)\}*$$
$$\{(<r+\Delta r_a, s+\Delta s_a>, <x_a,->),(<r+\Delta r_b, s+\Delta s_b>, <x_b,->)\}$$
$$\rightarrow_{(f_{\Delta r_a, \Delta s_a} \cdot w(x_a))(f_{\Delta r_b, \Delta s_b} \cdot w(x_b))} \{(<r,s>, M(X(x_a,x_b)))\}$$

$$\Theta'_4 = \{(<r,s>,<x_c,f>)\}*$$
$$\{(<r+\Delta r_a, s+\Delta s_a>, <x_a,->)\}$$
$$\rightarrow_{(f_{\Delta r_a, \Delta s_a} \cdot w(x_a))(f_{0,0} \cdot w(x_c))} \{(<r,s>, M(X(x_a,x_c)))\}$$

The main difference compared with Θ_3 is, that probability is influenced by the weight factors $f_{\Delta r_a, \Delta s_a}$ and $f_{\Delta r_b, \Delta s_b}$. We address the correct weight factor by referring to the index that was used pointing to the neighbour cells of the Moore neighbourhood.

Based on this extension a new quality of the cellular population model arises for which we introduce the following terms:

Architecture: An imprinted coarse-grained structure is interpreted as the *architecture* of our GA, i.e. we can construct containers, barriers, migration paths with certain direction, ...

Texture. Fine-grained structures have the meaning of a *texture* which gives us a certain mixture of cellular behaviour optimised for a certain application.

5 Experiments and Results

Using this mechanism of directed propagation of organisms, we construct three sample architectures for performance comparison. Aim is to investigate only the impact coming from certain architecture variants of the cellular population model: (1) the flat cellular architecture, (2) a cellular architecture with 4 separated islands, and (3) with a separated channel with higher mutation rate. Images of variants (2) and (3) which were produced with our GA simulation system are shown in figure 2.

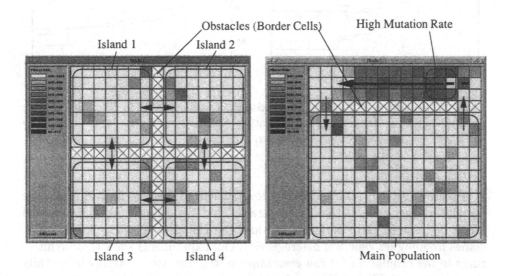

Fig. 2. Two variants of architectures: Left-hand side is the *Island Model* (2) and right-hand side a *Channel with high mutation rate* (3); results of fitness values in the simulation system: dark is low fitness, bright is high fitness.

A TSP with 50 cities has been run on the implementation of these three architecture variants. For the 10 runs we defined different initial populations which were input to each of these architectures. Global mutation rate, problem domain and genetical operators are identical for all cells of the automaton. Genetic operators were chosen as in [2].

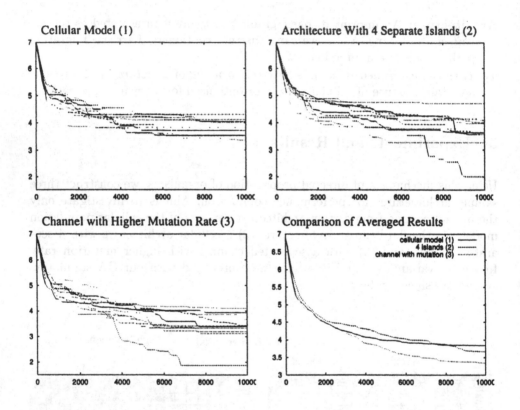

Fig. 3. Comparison of Performance statistics of variants (1)-(3) from the cellular population model. Diagrams show deviation from best value in logarithmic scale $(ln(w_{min} - w_{opt}))$ over generation number.

Figure 3 displays graphs showing development of the best individuals in the population over time. [5] has demonstrated that the cellular population model has a better long term performance than the global population model, which comes from higher genetical heterogeneity. Our experiments show that architectures in the cellular model can even improve this genetical heterogeneity: Only the architectures (2) and (3) investigated the near optimal solution. The average diagram shows that in the beginning the island architecture (2) develops slower than (1), but can achieve better results in a latter stage. In general, architecture (3) develops significantly faster.

6 Conclusions

We have introduced the concept of population models motivated by the observation that interactions between the individual solutions of a GA have impact on convergence behaviour of the GA. Our research concentrates especially on the cellular variant of population models where we can imprint textures and an architecture into the cellular array.

The PSA concept has proved to give us a valuable method at hand for formulating population models for all our parallel genetic algorithms. This is elementary for the systematic optimisation of GAs, since population models are one main direction in which we must investigate variants of our algorithms.

Our assessment of different architectures to be used in a cellular GA can yet only cover some examples. Our research has shown that the principle cellular implementation can be further enhanced by simple architectures. Future work will concentrate on architectures where areas with different mutation rate force the forming of new solutions, preservation of existing good solutions and fusion of solutions with different origin.

References

1. S. Achasova, O. Bandman, V. Markova, and S. Piskunov. *Parallel Substitution Algorithm - Theory and Application.* World-Scientific, 1994.
2. A. Becher. *Konvergenzverhalten Zellularer Genetischer Algorithmen bei kombinatorischen Optimierungsproblemen.* Diploma thesis at the University of Technology, Darmstadt. 1998.
3. D. Eichberg, U. Kohlmorgen, and H. Schmeck. Feinkörnig parallele Varianten des Insel-Modells Genetischer Algorithmen. *Mitteilungen - Gesellschaft für Informatik e.V.*, Parallel-Algorithmen und Rechnerstrukturen, PARS Workshop Stuttgart, 1995.
4. David E. Goldberg. *Genetic Algorithms in Search, Optimization and Machine Learning.* Addison Wessley, 1989.
5. J. Liebich. *Zellulare Genetische Algorithmen mit Anwendung auf die Simulation von Ökosystemen.* Diploma thesis at the University of Technology, Darmstadt. 1997.
6. J. Liebich and P. Hartmann. Zellulare Genetische Algorithmen mit Anwendungen bei der Simulation von Ökosystemen. *Second German Workshop on Artificial Life (GWAL97)*, April 1997.
7. M. Mitchell. *An Introduction to Genetic Algorithms.* The MIT Press, 1996.

Highly Accurate Numerical Methods for Incompressible 3D Fluid Flows on Parallel Architectures

Vladimir N. Konshin and Vladimir A. Garanzha

Computing Center RAS, Vavilov str. 40, 117967 Moscow, Russia
garan@ccas.ru , konshin@ccas.ru

Abstract. We consider an approach to efficient parallel implementation of the high order Control Volume Padé-type Differences (CVPD) applied to spatial time-dependent flow in the mixing tanks. This numerical technology allows to obtain very high quality solutions on the block-structured curvilinear grids with sliding grid capability. In some sense it combines the flexibility of the finite volume methods with the accuracy of the spectral methods. However, the payoff for the high accuracy is that the parallel implementation issues become more complicated as compared to conventional low order approximation methods.

Our objective is to demonstrate that reasonable parallel efficiency can be attained on the parallel computer platforms without compromising the high accuracy, when the highly accurate non-local discrete operators and implicit time-steppings are used as the building blocks of the numerical methods. We present numerical results obtained on CRAY C90, CRAY T3D and IBM SP2.

1 Introduction

The problem which is encountered in most CFD applications is how to obtain the accurate enough numerical solutions in the most efficient way. The criteria of accuracy can vary, however they are becoming more and more strict since the CFD become widely used in the industry. In the small, the objective of the parallel computing is to construct and implement scalable and efficient parallel versions of the specified numerical methods. However, in the large the main problem is to reduce the solution wall-clock times for a given simulation accuracy. The use of the latter approach typically shifts the comparison criterion from "minimal wall-clock time per iteration per grid cell" to "minimal wall-clock time for a given accuracy estimates" . The last criterion while being the most fair one, is the most difficult to implement. The closest simple guess to this criterion is to include into the benchmarking of the parallel methods the solution quality indicators along with the wall-clock times, performance and scalability data.

2 Description of the Numerical Technology

We present the numerical technology designed for development of the highly accurate and reliable CFD tool for the chemical process industry. Since this problem requires substantial computational resources we have developed the tool for scalable parallel architectures. The ability to support an efficient parallel implementation on scalable parallel platforms is the key to progress in certifying, incorporating, and evaluating new advanced physical models.

The crucial component of our numerical method is the highly accurate discretization based on the non-centered Control Volume Pade-type Differences. As compared to the conventional finite difference or finite volume methods which can be interpreted as some kind of polynomial operator approximations, the Pade-type differences can be considered as operator rational approximations to the systems of the conservation laws. The conservative Pade-type approximations are close to finite volume methods from the implementation point of view and approach the spectral methods from the point of view of accuracy. When developing the CVPD technique we were interested in preserving the very favorable spectral properties of the Pade-approximations in the case of complex geometries and complicated physics. The basic features of the resulting scheme are presented below:

- high order truncation error $(O(h^4), O(h^6), ...)$;

- spectral-like resolution, i.e., extremely low phase errors and a dissipative mechanism which suppresses or filters only spurious solution modes;

- positive definiteness and compatibility of the resulting discrete systems;

- discrete conservation, i.e., the approximation is based on the integral form of the system of the conservation laws;

- geometric conservation;

- high accuracy and stability on block-structured curvilinear meshes; a stable incompressible cell-centered formulation based on the high order Pade-type pressure stabilization;

- a highly accurate non-matching sliding grid interface capability;

- fully implicit time stepping with Newton's method for the solution of resulting nonlinear systems;

- a fully coupled solution strategy for the incompressible Navier-Stokes equations.

Since our goal is to retain all of the favorable properties of CVPD for the case of very complicated geometries, we consider the non-matching sliding mesh interface quality as a crucial contribution to our method's overall accuracy. At present we use partially non-matching meshes for different subdomains, i.e., the boundaries of the subdomains coincide with the curvilinear coordinates isosurfaces.

The basic advantages of CVPD are based not only on the higher order truncation error (e.g.$O(h^4)$), but also on the fundamental properties of rational approximations which are much more accurate and stable than polynomial ones with the same order of the truncation error. The authors experience with CVPD revealed drastic improvement in accuracy over conventional finite volume methods on curvilinear structured grids. The basic disadvantage of CVPD is the non-local nature of the discrete operators, i.e., in order to compute the residual of the discrete system it is necessary to solve the set of linear systems with tridiagonal matrices.

3 Building Blocks of the Numerical Methods and Parallel Implementation Issues

Consider the nonlinear problem described by the incompressible Navier-Stokes equations. In the operator form the discrete problem can be written as follows

$$Lu = f, \tag{1}$$

where the nonlinear discrete operator L corresponds to the approximation of the Navier-Stokes equations.

The solution method for the system (1) is the Newton-like method which can be written in the following form

$$L_f(u^{k+1} - u^k) + Lu^k = f, \tag{2}$$

where k is the iteration number and the linear operator L_f is a suitable linearization of L. In order to compute the iterate u^{k+1} from (2) it is necessary to solve the pre- or post- conditioned linear system of equations

$$L_f B^{-1} y = r, \tag{3}$$

where B is an easily invertible operator, $y = Bu^{k+1}, r = f + L_f u^k - Lu^k$.

¿From the algorithmical point of view, the solution method is split into three major blocks:

1) the computation of residuals, i.e., the computations of vectors Lu^k and $L_f u^k$;
2) generation of matrices which are needed to construct B;
3) iterative solution of linear system (3).

The first block is in fact the kernel of the flow solver. In the case of using the Padé approximations the discrete operators L and L_f are nonlocal, but the computation of the vectors Lu^k and $L_f u^k$ requires only $O(N)$ operations, where N is the number of grid cells times the number of unknowns per grid cell. This stage is totally independent of the iterative solution stage which is "external" part of the flow solver which can be easily changed and substituted. In order to achieve this independence the second block is split into "high-level" part which depend on the approximation scheme and into "low-level" part which depends on the storage format for the sparse matrices and on the choice of the linear solver.

The property which is very important for the efficient parallel implementation is the uniformity of the computations. The main obstacle for nonuniformity is the complicated computational domain topology, the presence of different boundary conditions, cutouts, *etc.* In order to represent the topology we use a set of index arrays, where in each grid cell the coefficients of the discrete operators are chosen from a relatively small set (10 – 50 elements for the high order schemes). As the result, the computation of discrete operators reduces to the scatter operations which can be done very efficiently in the background of the floating-point computations. This approach does allows to "hide" all the information about the flow domain topology into an index array which are generated at the preprocessing stage and to implement the high-order method using uniform computations.

4 Parallel Implementation of Technology

In order to construct the parallel version of the algorithm we have used the geometrical partitioning of the computational domain and the message-passing programming model. In this case it was sufficient to split the above index array between the processors and to implement elementary low-level block for parallel computation of the discrete operators. When possible, the equal number of the control volumes was assigned to each processor.

Consider the main factors which influence the parallel efficiency.

Load balancing problems. Even efficient matrix-vector product computation is very difficult problem, since optimal partitioning for the computational cell number and for non-zero elements of the matrix are quite different and both result in non-uniform load balancing.

Serial part of the code. We do not have serial part in our code. We have some global operations e.g., global sums or solution of systems with banded (e.g., tridiagonal) matrices.

Communication costs. The above mathematical technologies were implemented in a portable software written in a message-passing style using the MPI-like interface to the low-level communication library. When possible we extensively use the overlap of communications and computations, which results in better portability and reasonable communication costs.

5 Parallel Tridiagonal Solves

The potential bottleneck in parallel implementation of the CVPD approximation scheme is the solution of the linear systems with the tridiagonal matrices. Generally the data for the tridiagonal solves are split over different processors and it is necessary to solve these systems "across" the processors. The serial tridiagonal solves are accessible in LAPACK package, but the parallel version of SCALAPACK package does not contain the parallel solves of tridiagonal systems "across" the processors. This fact is the main motivation for investigation of the parallel tridiagonal solves which is presented below.

It is well known that 100% parallel efficiency for such algorithms is attainable only in the case of 2 processors when the pipeline twisted factorization or the so-called burn from both ends algorithm is used. When the number of processors is more than 2 the problem becomes very complicated. However in our case the 1D tridiagonal solves are used in the 3D domain, i.e., $O(N^{\frac{2}{3}})$ independent linear systems of the size $O(N^{\frac{1}{3}})$ should be solved. This allows for additional pipelining.

There exist various approaches for parallel solution of linear systems with tridiagonal matrices: cyclic elimination, pipeline elimination, pipeline twisted elimination, domain decomposition methods.

The idea of the cyclic method is to impose fictitious periodicity boundary conditions for the tridiagonal system. The formulae for the cyclic elimination are well-known and we show in Fig. 1 the global structure of the algorithm only using the cyclograms which demonstrate the data partitioning and the algorithm steps.

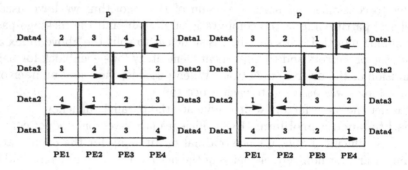

Fig. 1. The cyclogram of the cyclic tridiagonal solve

The cyclic algorithm ensure ideal load balancing, however it requires more arithmetic costs that the original algorithm. As a result the theoretical parallel efficiency of this algorithm is about 60%. However, for the mixed tank simulation it is necessary to use the periodicity or quasi-periodicity boundary conditions. In this case the parallel efficiency becomes about 100%. The pipeline and cyclic methods require low latency and high communication bandwidth. It is possible to use the domain decomposition methods which are more tolerant to the latency time.

The pipelined twisted factorization is illustrated on Fig. 2 for the case of two processors. **Data 1** and **Data 2** are two independent groups of linear systems.

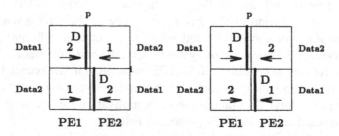

Fig. 2. The cyclogram of the pipeline twisted factorization

This algorithm ensures perfect load balancing, moreover if the nonblocking communications are supported by the hardware and the operating system, then this algorithm allows the overlap between computations and communications. It is possible to use the same approach for the larger number of processors. However in this case the additional cost includes the pipeline start-up phase. The speedups (SPEEDUP) and the wall clock times (TIME) in seconds of the test runs on the IBM SP2 are presented in Table 1 for various number of processor elements (PE).

Table 1. Parallel efficiency of pipeline twisted elimination algorithm on IBM SP2

PE	Domain	Subdomain	TIME	SPEEDUP
1	600×601	600×601	0.2190	1.00
2	600×601	300×601	0.1280	1.71
4	600×601	150×601	0.0638	3.43
1	$80 \times 80 \times 161$	$80 \times 80 \times 161$	0.7800	1.00
8	$80 \times 80 \times 161$	$80 \times 80 \times 161$	0.0885	8.81

Scalability of an algorithm can be defined by considering its performance for either a fixed problem size per processor or a fixed total problem size. In Table 1 we consider the approach, when the total size of the problem is kept fixed while the size of each subdomain becomes smaller as the number of processors increases. In this case the superlinear scalability arises which is attributed to the cache size effect on the RISC architecture.

6 Description of Results

A set of numerical experiments was performed with a special emphasize on the accuracy of the computed solution [1]. These experiments include 2D and 3D lid-driven cavity flow and Couette flow. The set of numerical experiments with grid refinement shows the errors behavior close to $O(h^4)$, moreover on the good quality grids for a given solution accuracy this technique allows almost ten-fold decrease in the number of grid cells in each grid direction as compared to the conventional second order methods.

2D lid-driven cavity flow. This model problem was chosen to investigate the influence of corner singularities on the accuracy of computed solutions. The computational domain of this problem is the unit square $\{(x_1, x_2), 0 \leq x_1 \leq 1, 0 \leq x_2 \leq 1\}$ and boundary conditions are defined by $u = (1,0)^T$ for $x_2 = 1, u = 0$ elsewhere. We used mesh refinement and computed solution to the problem for the Reynolds number **RE** $= 100, 1000$. Table 2 shows the results of numerical experiments for 2D lid-driven cavity flow as well as the comparison with known numerical data.

Table 2. Velocities and positions of local extremum for 2D lid-driven cavity flow

mesh	Re=100			Re=1000	
	$u_1(\frac{1}{2},\frac{1}{2})$	$\min u_1(\frac{1}{2},x_2)$	$(x_2)_{\min}$	$\min u_1(\frac{1}{2},x_2)$	$(x_2)_{\min}$
10×10	-0.21030	-0.21441	0.45912	-0.3648	0.16189
20×20	-0.208963	-0.21387	0.45772	-0.3805	0.17872
40×40	-0.2091454	-0.2140241	0.45816	-0.38826	0.17229
80×80	-0.2091490	-0.2140415	0.458098	-0.388557	0.171671
160×160	-0.20914915	-0.2140423	0.458089	-0.388569	0.171698
129×129 [5]	-0.20581	-0.21090	0.4531	-0.38289	0.1719
161×161 [6]		-0.212	0.4594	-0.381	0.1719
321×321 [6]		-0.213	0.4578	-0.387	0.1734

The velocity values and positions of local extremum presented in Table 2 were calculated using smooth interpolation with the error $O(h^4)$. From the Table 2 one can to conclude that the results from [5] and [6] are less accurate than ours.

3D lid-driven cavity flow. In this case the computational domain is a unit cube $\{(x_1, x_2, x_3), 0 \leq x_i \leq 1, i = 1, 2, 3\}$ and boundary conditions are defined by $u = (1, 0, 0)^T$ for $x_3 = 1, u = 0$ elsewhere. We have used mesh refinement and computed solution the problem for the Reynolds number $\mathbf{RE} = 100, 1000$. In Table 3 the control parameters, viz the negative horizontal velocity values and the positions of local extremum on the line $x_1 = \frac{1}{2}, x_2 = \frac{1}{2}$ are presented.

Table 3. Velocities and positions of local extremum for 3D lid-driven cavity flow

mesh	Re=100		Re=1000	
	$\min u_1(\frac{1}{2},\frac{1}{2},x_3)$	$(x_3)_{\min}$	$\min u_1(\frac{1}{2},\frac{1}{2},x_3)$	$(x_3)_{\min}$
$10 \times 10 \times 10$	-0.2185	0.4697		
$20 \times 20 \times 20$	-0.21528	0.4691	-0.2738	0.1259
$30 \times 30 \times 30$	-0.21555	0.46895	-0.27904	0.12411
$42 \times 42 \times 42$	-0.21557	0.46908	-0.28015	0.12417

3D laminar stirred tank flow. The CVPD technique has been successfully used for a numerical simulation of a time-dependent flow in a Dow Chemical experimental stirred tank reactor. This experiment used two structured grid blocks, one of them was fixed and the other was rotating with the axial pitched blade turbine (PBT) impeller [2]. The coupling between subdomains was implemented via the sliding interface surface around the impeller [3]. The simulation was performed on both a single CPU of Cray YMP-C90 and the massively parallel Cray T3D computer system (up to 128PE's). Both experiments used a "black box" approach, when the parallel or vectorized linear solver using spectrally equivalent 7-point discrete operator as a preconditioner was unaware that non-local

Padé approximations were employed to compute exact matrix-vector product. As a result 318 MFlops performance on CRAY YMP-C90 was achieved while 1 GFlops performance was achieved on 128 PEs of CRAY T3D.

Table 4. Timing and performance characteristics on CRAY T3D

	T3D				C90
PE	16	32	64	128	1
TIME	3220	1623	867	444	1320
PERF	129	249	485	938	318
SPEEDUP	**0.41**	**0.78**	**1.53**	**2.95**	**1.00**

Table 4 contains the timing and the performance results when solving the sample problem on T3D and C90. Table 4 adopts the following notation: TIME stands for the total wall clock time in seconds for solving the sample stirred tank reactor problem, PERF denotes the sustained performance in MFLOPS, and SPEEDUP denotes the actual speedup obtained using multiple CPUs of T3D as compared with a single CPU of C90.

Table 5. Parallel efficiency of algorithm on CRAY T3D

PE	Domain	Subdomain	TIME, sec	PERF, MFlops	SPEEDUP (CRAY C90)	Parallel Efficiency
16	41×41×40	11×11×40	805	129	0.41	≈100%
32	81×41×40	11×11×40	812	249	0.78	99%
64	81×81×40	11×11×40	867	485	1.53	93%
128	161×81×40	11×11×40	888	938	2.95	90%

The results of numerical experiments which demonstrate the parallel efficiency of the computational technique on CRAY T3D computer are presented in Table 5. It is possible to achieve the parallel efficiency in industrial applications no smaller than 90%.

It is easy to see from the Fig. 3 that the results of numerical experiments on the parallel computer CRAY T3D with the CVPD approximation schemes demonstrate quite reasonable scalability when solving large scale 3D CFD problems.

7 Conclusions

We have demonstrated that reasonable parallel efficiency can be attained on the parallel computer platforms without compromising the high accuracy of the

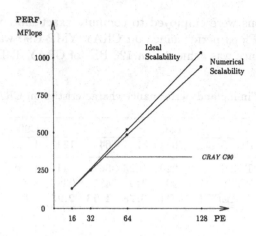

Fig. 3. The cyclogram of the pipeline twisted factorization

simulation, when the highly accurate non-local discrete operators and implicit time-steppings are used as the building blocks of the numerical method. The presented numerical technology has been shown to be very accurate and reliable when solving industrial problems on parallel computer platforms [4].

References

1. Garanzha, V.A., Konshin, V.N.: Highly accurate upwind Padé-Type Approximations for the Systems of the Conservations Laws. I: Application to the Incompressible Navier-Stokes Equations on a Single-Zone Structured Meshes. Computing Center RAS (1996).
2. Garanzha, V.A., Ibragimov, I.V., Konshin, I.N., Konshin, V.N., Yeremin, A.Yu.: High Order Padé-Type Approximation Methods for Incompressible 3D CFD Problems on Massively Parallel Computers. In: Parallel Computational Fluid Dynamics: Implementations and Results Using Parallel Computers. Elsevier Science B.V., (1995) 199-205
3. Garanzha, V.A.: Nonmatching Grid Technique for Highly Accurate Control Volume Padé-type Differences (CVPD), In: Proceedings of 5 Int. Conference on Grid Generation in CFS, Starkville, USA (1996) 647-656
4. Garanzha, V.A., Kaporin, I.E., Konshin, V.N.: Reliable Flow Solver Based on the High Order Control Volume Padé-Type Differences. In: Lecture Notes in Physics, Springer, Vol.515, (1998) 278-283
5. Ghia, U., Ghia, K.N., Shin, S.T.: High-Re Solutions for Incompressible Flow Using the Navier-Stokes Equations and a Multigrid Method. J. Comput. Phys. Vol.48 (1982) 387-411
6. Vanka, S.P.: Block-Implicit Multigrid Solution of Navier-Stokes Equations in Primite Variables. J. Comput. Phys. Vol.65, (1986) 138-158

Dynamic Task Scheduling with Precedence Constraints and Communication Delays

Slavko Marić [1] and Zoran Jovanović [2]

[1] School of Electrical Engineering, University of Banja Luka,
Republic of Srpska, Bosnia and Herzegovina
ms@etf-bl.rstel.net
[2] School of Electrical Engineering, University of Belgrade, Yugoslavia
zoran@rcub.bg.ac.yu

Abstract. In this paper we have introduced the K1 heuristic algorithm for dynamic task scheduling with precedence constraints and communication delays. The execution of a task set repeats in cycles, while the execution and communication profile of a task set changes in time. During a task set execution, a new schedule is generated by tuning the previous schedule. The scheduling is distributed - performed on the processors of a highly parallel computer architecture. The goal is to reduce a dominant sequence of a task set during run-time. Only the tasks that can have an influence on dominant sequence reduction are considered for reordering/migration. The applied techniques are load balancing, task reordering, and data-wait reduction. Simulation is used for the algorithm validation and evaluation.

1 Introduction

Remarkable expansion of highly parallel and distributed computing systems has been accompanied with efforts to efficiently exploit their processing power. One of the main problems is how to schedule a set of tasks that need processing onto the available processor resources. The scheduling includes an assignment of tasks to processors and a sequencing of task executions. In *static scheduling*, a decision is made during the compile time, with the assumption that task execution times and intertask communication characteristics are known prior to the execution. While these scheduling techniques are satisfactory for some application classes (e.g. digital signal processing), in many others this is not the case. In such systems the task, communication, and processor structure and characteristics can change during run-time. These dynamic changes can result in overloading some processors and idling others at the same time, with a much longer total execution time of a task set than the optimal. To resolve this problem, efficient *dynamic scheduling*, providing a possibility for task reordering and re-assignment during the run-time is required.

Most of the scheduling problem instances have been proven to be NP-complete, i.e. no polynomial-time solution has been found. Optimal algorithms in polynomial time are devised only for some special classes of the problem. This directs the scheduling solutions to the *heuristic* and *approximative* approaches, which should provide satisfactory results at a reasonable cost. Many of them have been proposed, considering different application and computer system characteristics.

Dynamic *load balancing* schemes try to provide an even processor load that results in efficient processor resources utilization and/or minimization of the average task response time. Well known strategies, among others, are *Gradient Model, Receiver Initiated, Sender Initiated, Hierarchical Balancing Method and Prediction-Based strategy* [16], [8]. The targets are usually general-purpose distributed computer systems, such as interconnected Local Area Networks, for example. In *distributed real-time systems*, tasks are scheduled in order to guarantee their completion before the corresponding deadlines or to minimize the *probability of dynamic failure* [12].

The above mentioned approach in general, assumes that tasks arrive dynamically at a processor node, with some probability distribution (usually Poisson) of their interarrival times. Tasks are considered to be mutually independent, so neither intertask communication times nor precedence constraints should be taken into account.

Dynamic scheduling algorithms generally include: mechanisms and strategies for information evaluation and distribution (*information policy*), making decisions about when to transfer the tasks (*transfer policy*), determining where to transfer the tasks (*location policy*) and which tasks to transfer (*task selection policy*) [18]. Either the *sender (source)* or *receiver (server)* can initiate the transfer with a different knowledge level of the state of nodes which are receiving/sending the overload. At the lowest level is "blind" fixed scheduling, where no run-time information is required [15], but more or less complex information is usually required and collected through different techniques e.g. *state broadcasting, probing or bidding*. An increase of the information level can incur high communication overhead and thus some task execution delays and state information aging, so a compromise needs to be achieved. *Transfer policy* determines, according to the goal function and established criteria, whether to transfer the load/tasks from the source to the server node or not. For example, in dynamic load balancing, the benefit of load distribution must be greater than the communication cost of the task transfer. In distributed real-time systems, a task should be transferred if its execution can't be guaranteed on a current processor node. Selecting the location of the task transfer can be done in a deterministic, probabilistic or adaptive way. A deterministic location policy uses a fixed pattern for selection, while a probabilistic policy selects a destination node of transfer based on some probability distribution (e.g. random selection). Adaptive schemes use state information to make the selection (e.g. focused addressing).

This paper addresses *fully dynamic scheduling* [4] of a task set to be executed on a highly parallel computer system. The execution of a task set is repeated in successive cycles. Precedence constraints and data communications exist among the tasks that incur a synchronization and communication overhead. The structure of the task graph is fixed, however, the task execution time and amount of intertask communication data change in time. This non-uniform time behavior can originate from varying characteristics of the input data, different operational processing modes conditions, and the like. Similar problem presentation is given in [4], where data dependent iterations are considered, however, a fully static schedule construction is proposed based on the assumed execution time of the iteration actor.

Embedded computer systems usually have this kind of application characteristics as well as many other applications e.g.: complex simulation systems, image processing and animation, all with weaker real-time requirements than in embedded systems. Real-time requirements for an application that processes continuous media streams can be specified by the required time for processing resources within a specific time window [7]. The processing consists of repeated executions of the task set continuously transforming input data streams into output streams. The task execution times and intertask communications depend on input data stream characteristics and application operational mode. The ability to dynamically tune assignments of tasks can provide better average response time per cycle than fixed assignments, and consequently, better quality of service. Since multithread concept will dominate in near future [2], dynamic adjustment of the assignments and sequencing of thread/task executions is of primary interest for efficient parallel processing.

In Section II of this paper, the definitions and assumptions of the system and the approach overview of the dynamic task scheduling with precedence constraints and communication delays, are described. The K1 heuristic algorithm for dynamic task scheduling is given in Section III and in Section IV the simulation results are presented. The conclusions are given in Section V.

2 The System Model

2.1 Definitions and Assumptions

1. A task set is represented by a directed acyclic graph (DAG) $G = \{T, A\}$, where $T = \{T_i\}$, $i = 1 \ldots m$ is the set of tasks, representing program computations, and $A = \{A_{ij}\}$ is the set of directed arcs, which represent both, precedence constraints and data paths among the tasks. Every $A_{ij} \in A$ has a weight D_{ij} which denotes the amount of data that T_i passes to the T_j after it has finished the execution. We assume that all data produced by T_i is communicated to the corresponding successors in parallel, just after T_i has finished the execution. Tasks receive data in parallel, and task T_j can't start execution until all of it's immediate predecessors have finished their execution and all data D_{ij} from these tasks are completely available at T_j.

2. Tasks execute on a set $P = \{P_j\}$, $j = 1 \ldots n$ of n homogenous processors interconnected by some interconnection network. We assume that the communication cost of a data unit transfer between two processors P_i and P_j is fixed.

3. A set of m tasks is executed repeatedly on (up to) n processors in successive cycles. Every processor can measure start and end execution times of the tasks assigned to it. The period from the beginning of the cycle c_i, to the point when processor P_p finishes the execution of all of the tasks assigned to it in that cycle is $FT_p(c_i)$. Actually, it is the finish time of the processor P_p in cycle c_i. The system response time in cycle c_i is $RT_i = MFT_i + T_{ov}$ where $MFT_i = \max \{FT_p(c_i)\}$, $p = 1, \ldots n$ and T_{ov} is the system overhead. $D_{ij}(c_i)$ denotes the amount of data that T_i passes to the T_j in cycle c_i and $\tau_i(c_i) \geq 0$ is the execution time of T_i in cycle c_i. Processors are synchronized between the successive cycles by passing the barrier, so that they can identify the beginning of the next cycle. An example of an efficient and scalable

barrier synchronization scheme is given in [11]. In this paper, we have assumed, like in [4], sequential execution of cycles instead of overlapped execution.

4. It is reasonable to assume for the application classes we have considered, that the task execution times and intertask communications don't change abruptly in successive cycles, i.e. the probability of a significant change between successive cycles is low.

5. Tasks exchange data via asynchronous message passing. Besides data, a message contains information about the sending and receiving processors and tasks, and time stamps of the important events (sending task start/end execution time, message sending and receiving times) are also added to the message. Passing messages between tasks on different processors incur communication overhead, while the communication cost is zero if the communicating tasks are on the same processor.

6. Execution of tasks is non-preemptive, and depends only on the state of the memory and communication context just before the execution starts. So, if a task is migrated between successive cycles from one processor to another, it is necessary to transfer both, its memory context and control information for the task re-assignment and communication redirection.

2.2 Approach Overview

Scheduling which considers only available parallelism between tasks, without regard to the corresponding communication cost, can results in poor and inefficient execution. Tasks should be grouped in a way that make a good balance between parallel execution and communication costs [3], [6]. So, the problem of finding an appropriate set of clusters and mapping those clusters to processors is closely related to the scheduling problem. In addition, the proper sequence of the task executions within each cluster should be determined. In the applications with repeated executions of the task set, where the task set characteristics change in time, it is natural to suppose that the granularity of the clusters allocated to processors can change signifi-cantly, degrading the system response time as a consequence. A reasonable approach to resolve the problem is to provide appropriate scheduling mechanisms for dynamic cluster tuning.

Dynamic scheduling should be applied only if its average cycle response time (taking into account scheduling and task migration cost) is shorter than the fixed task assignment. Because of that, scheduling should be efficient with the lowest possible number of task migrations. This implies that:

- The information policy of the scheduler should provide limited but essential information necessary for transfer decisions.
- Transfer decisions should rely on heuristics and prevent forward and backward task migration between clusters.
- The scheduler should try to adjust existing clusters by moving appropriate tasks between them instead of making a new schedule from the beginning, like in static scheduling.

The above requirements impose the scheduling process to be heuristic, to attack a dominant sequence (DS) [17], and to be distributed and cooperative. This means that only the tasks that have influence on a dominant sequence are considered for migration/reordering.

3 K1 Algorithm for Dynamic Task Scheduling

For the considered application classes, it is realistic to assume that the probability of significant change in task execution and communication characteristics between successive cycles is low. The K1 algorithm determines the schedule for the next cycle on the basis of the run-time information of the current cycle. A scheduler on each of n processors starts its execution, after all application tasks assigned to it have been finished in a cycle c_i. In the scheduler INIT state (Fig. 2), a processor registers on the barrier, where it gets its sequence number of arrival. K processors, which first arrive to the barrier in a cycle c_i (processors with the shortest execution time in c_i, called 'underloaded' processors), send information about their state (ULOAD message) to one predefined processor. The processor which last arrives to the barrier in cycle c_i (we shall call it the 'overloaded' processor), requests data about K underloaded processors from the predefined processor (Fig. 1).

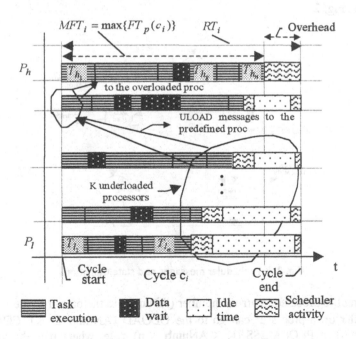

Fig. 1. Execution of the task set in the ith cycle

The basic idea is to attack a dominant sequence by applying different techniques to shorten it. By definition [17], a task T_x belongs to a dominant sequence if the sum of its top and bottom level is the highest. The top level *tlevel* (T_x) is the longest path from a start task (task that has no predecessors) up to the task T_x in the scheduled graph (taking into account the task executions as well as the communication delays on the path). *blevel* (T_x) is the longest path from the start of T_x to a terminal task. In our notation

$$\text{MFT} = \max_{T_x \in T}\{tlevel(T_x) + blevel(T_x)\}. \tag{1}$$

It's clear that the overloaded processor P_h, with the current cycle finish time $FT_h = $ MFT, partly or completely contains a dominant sequence since the last task executed on processor P_h evidently belongs to it.

Thus, the scheduler on the overloaded processor initiates activities for dominant sequence reduction if an imbalance between overloaded and underloaded processor finish times is over the threshold. If a scheduler decides to tune some clusters, it is done at the end of the current cycle, and the tuned schedule is applied in the next cycle. During these cooperative activities a scheduler can be in one of the states as described in the following text.

3.1 Scheduler States

The scheduler states, transitions from one state to another and passed messages are presented in Fig. 2.

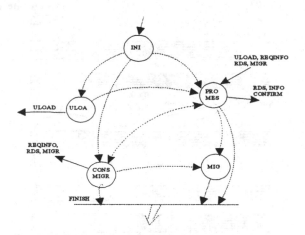

Fig. 2. K1 scheduler messages and state transitions

After getting the processor's arrival number (ANumb) to the barrier in the INIT state, the scheduler on a processor can go to the ULOAD (ANumb $\leq$ K), CONSMIGR (ANumb = n) or PROCMESS (K < ANumb < n) state, where n is the number of processors. The schedulers on processors with Anumb $\leq$ K send ULOAD (underload) messages to the predefined processor and then go to the PROCMESS state. The scheduler on the overloaded processor enters CONSMIGR state, where it gets ULOAD messages from the predefined processor and starts considering the way to reduce a dominant sequence. If this scheduler doesn't succeed to reduce a DS, it identifies the critical task on another processor, and sends a RDS (reduce dominant sequence) message to the scheduler on that processor with appropriate data. After that, the scheduler that has sent a RDS goes to the PROCMESS state. If the second scheduler fails to reduce a DS, it sends a RDS message to the next scheduler containing the next critical task on a dominant sequence, and so on. If a scheduler concludes that it can reduce a DS by the migration of some tasks to another processor, it enters MIGR state to execute the migration process.

When a local scheduler considers reducing a DS it uses:

1. a local copy of communication costs between processors and the DAG task structure,
2. the data gathered by the local control system such as processor wait intervals, task start/end times, and data communication characteristics. This data acquisition is cheap, because it is produced locally as a by-product of the control system,
3. limited information about task execution and communication characteristics on other processors through data communication and scheduler messages.

Run-time measurements and observations acquire data values which the K1 algorithm uses as basic information to make decisions. This is unlike the static algorithms, which rely on assumed values. Information gathered in the current cycle is used to determine a schedule in the next cycle. While the calculation of the makespan for a given DAG is of NP-complete complexity, the K1 algorithm easily gets maximum finish time for the current cycle, by measuring. The execution of the K1 algorithm doesn't produce a completely new schedule; instead, it makes an adjustment of the previous schedule. By careful implementation, the K1 algorithm can spread the analysis of a DS reduction to several cycles (incremental scheduling), and adapt the rate of a DS reduction consideration based on the system behavior. This can also limit maximum scheduling overhead per cycle and decrease the total overhead time.

3.2 DS Reducing Techniques

The scheduler on the overloaded processor starts considering the possibility of reducing dominant sequence if $FT_h >= kUB * FT_l$, where FT_h is the finish time of the overloaded processor and FT_l is the finish time of the underloaded processor (kUB is the coefficient of imbalance; we used the value of 1.1). The overloaded processor gets FT_l through the ULOAD message from the underloaded processor. The scheduler initially considers the possibility to reduce a dominant sequence by:

1. load balancing,
2. task reordering within a cluster,
3. reducing a communication delay on a DS by task migration.

Load Balancing. If a cluster is characterized as a coarse grain, then there should be an attempt to perform load balancing. This technique tries migration of the excess load from the overloaded processor to the underloaded one. The right amount of load on the overloaded processor must be chosen for transfer. Migrating excessive load can produce overload on the destination processor and possibly longer system response time in the following cycle. This can cause oscillating - migration of the load back and forward in the next migration considerations. To prevent such undesired behavior, the proposed heuristic algorithm works as follows:

The algorithm analyzes the benefit of the migration of a subset of tasks that belong to a dominant sequence on the overloaded processor P_h. The tasks that are considered start from the last task T_{h_n} in a dominant sequence and end up with the first task T_{h_g} waiting for data (there is a data wait interval just before that task) (Fig. 1).

The subset of tasks that are considered are *strongly linear clusters*. Tasks $\ldots T_x, T_y$ $\ldots$ belong to a strongly linear cluster, if $T_x \in PRED(T_y)$. $PRED(T_y)$ denotes the set of all immediate predecessors of a task T_y. The reasons for analyzing only strongly linear clusters are:

1. simplicity and efficiency of extraction and benefit evaluation,
2. simplicity of positioning in a new cluster,
3. good parallelism exploitation can be achieved by parallel execution of the linear clusters.

We also characterize a strongly linear cluster by it's type. Specific types are evaluated for migration in a slightly different way. Based on the characteristics and type of the cluster, the algorithm evaluates the benefit of migration and makes a record in a priority list (PL). The strongly linear cluster with highest positive benefit value exceeding the threshold is chosen for migration. For example, let's describe the benefit calculation if the cluster type is the 'last linear cluster' (LLC): the strongly linear cluster on the overloaded processor containing the last executed task T_{h_n}.

Let P_h denote the overloaded and P_l the underloaded processor and let $\{T_{h_i}, \ldots ,T_{h_n}\}$ be LLC on P_h. Denote $T_{load} = \sum \tau_{h_j}$, where τ_{h_j} is the execution time of the T_{h_j} in the current cycle, $T_{h_j} \in LLC$. The scheduler on the overloaded processor knows the following in the cycle for which it is considering load balancing:

1. start/end execution times of tasks on P_h (gathered by local control system data acquisition),
2. receiving data volume, data source (task and processor), sending/receiving time moments,
3. cost of data unit transfer between processors.

Based on that data, it can calculate data availability of the leading task (T_{h_i}) of the LLC on the processor P_l, $DA(T_{h_i}, P_l)$. Let $ET_{h_{i-1}}$ denote the ending time of the task executing before T_{h_i} on P_h. The benefit of LLC cluster migration is calculated by the following heuristic function:

$$B = FT_h - \max(ET_{h_{i-1}}, \max(FT_l, DA(T_{h_i}, P_l)) + T_{load}) \qquad (2)$$

Benefit function is equal to the shortening of the maximum finish time of the processors involved in migration. FT_h is the finish time of the overloaded processor P_h in the current cycle. The *max* term represents the evaluated maximum finish time on processors P_h and P_l in the next cycle, after migration. The negative value of B indicates that the finish time would be longer after LLC migration. Recall that we have assumed that the task execution profile wouldn't significantly change in the next operation cycle. Let's note that breaking LLC and migrating the right part would introduce a new communication delay at the break and thus, the response time would be prolonged. A similar consideration is applied in case of the middle linear clusters (MLC) that could be in front of LLC (MLC_LEAF, MLC_NOLEAF – middle linear cluster with an ending task as leaf/no-leaf task node in DAG). Unlike the LLC, the K1 algorithm considers the breaking of MLC for load balancing. It calculates benefit function for the subclusters, and makes a record in PL. The subcluster with the highest benefit value is selected for migration, providing that it exceeds the threshold value. Subclusters are formed in a way that if $\{T_{h_i}, \ldots, T_{h_m}\}$ is a MLC subcluster, the next subcluster is $\{T_{h_{i-1}}, T_{h_i}, \ldots, T_{h_m}\}$, $T_{h_{i-1}} \in$ MLC. The breaking of MLC's allows the finding of the best break point with a balanced amount of migration load and communication costs. Migration considers the best place/ordering of the migrated subcluster on the destination processor. A late scheduling delays the successors of the migrated tasks, but premature scheduling delays the start of the execution of tasks scheduled after the migrated group on the destination processor, and very probably of it's successors too. The estimated migrated cluster head data available time on the processor P_l will be denoted with $CIDA_l$, and the cluster start time on processor P_h with $CIST_h$. Then, the migrated cluster is placed on P_l so that the estimated start time on P_l is $CIDA_l$ if $CIDA_l >= CIST_h$, and $(CIDA_l + CIST_h) / 2$ otherwise.

Task reordering. If the load balancing fails to make a better schedule, task reordering is considered. This method attempts to reorder the execution of tasks within a cluster, so that a task laying on a dominant sequence is executed earlier. As an illustration, let's consider Gant's chart of the overloaded processor in Fig. 3.

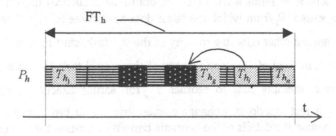

Fig. 3. Task reordering on the overloaded processor

A dominant sequence reduction by reordering, can be done by:

1. moving some of the tasks from the subset $\{T_{h_{g+1}}, \ldots, T_{h_i}, \ldots, T_{h_n}\}$ to be executed in some of the wait intervals,
2. reordering the task on another processor, from which the latest data come to the task T_{h_g}, for earlier execution.

If the task T_{h_i} is moved in front of T_{h_g} then, probably, the tasks following T_{h_i} will be executed earlier in the next cycle, with a possible new wait interval, revealing a new dominant sequence (that could be attacked in the following cycles). If the task T_{h_i}, because of data availability, partly fills the wait interval after reordering, some care must be taken. If it's execution is long, and if the overlapping with the wait interval is small, then it's reordering will force later execution of the tasks $\{T_{h_g}, T_{h_{g+1}}, \dots, T_{h_{i-1}}\}$ and also of their successors on other processors. Thus, we limit the pushing of the subset $\{T_{h_g}, T_{h_{g+1}}, \dots, T_{h_{i-1}}\}$ for later execution by defining the benefit function as

$$B = B1 - G1, \tag{3}$$

where B1 = WI_TimeReduction; G1 = max ($0, \tau_{h_i}$ – WI_TimeReduction – (FT$_h$ – $\overline{FT_l}$)*2/3).

The WI_TimeReduction is calculated by the scheduler and represents shortening of the wait interval after reordering, τ_{h_i} is the execution time of the reordering task T_{h_i}, FT$_h$ is the overloaded processor finish time, and $\overline{FT_l}$ is the average finish time of the underloaded processors in the current cycle. The G1 term represents the loss of benefit for the amount of the pushed subset $\{T_{h_g}, T_{h_{g+1}}, \dots, T_{h_{i-1}}\}$ over the threshold (FT$_h$ – $\overline{FT_l}$) *2/3.

If a dominant sequence couldn't be shortened by the previous steps, the scheduler on the P$_h$ processor, when the data wait interval in front of T_{h_g} is significant, considers migration of the subcluster $\{T_{h_g}, \dots, T_{h_i}\}$, i=g, ... ,n to another processor. This is done in order to eliminate the data-wait interval in front of T_{h_g} (data wait reduction). If that fails, the scheduler sends a RDS (reduce dominant sequence) message to the sched-uler on processor P$_j$ from which the latest data have come to T_{h_g} . The RDS message contains (among other data) the identity of the T_{h_g} task, start time and duration of the wait interval in front of T_{h_g} , and identity of the critical task T_{j_m} on processor P$_j$. The P$_j$ processor attempts first to reorder T_{j_m} for earlier execution, considering that reordering is fast and doesn't change cluster structure or task assignments. Here, we shall not explain the details of the heuristic benefit evaluation for that case.

Data-wait reduction. If the previous attempts have failed and if there is a signifi-cant data-wait interval on a dominant sequence, then data-wait reduction is to be tried. There are two alternatives for this:

1. the migration of the task that sends data which comes the latest,
2. the migration of the task that waits for data to the cluster from which the latest data come.

As an illustration, lets consider the first case in Fig.4. The waiting of task T_{i_g} on processor P_i can be reduced by moving the task T_{j_m} from processor P_j to processor P_i, since communication between T_{j_m} and T_{i_g} becomes cheap. However the migration should take into account the following:

- If T_{j_m} migrates to the processor P_i, its finish time should be as close to the beginning of the wait interval as possible. But, if data communication between $T_{j_{m-1}}$, and T_{j_m} is high, it becomes expensive when T_{j_m} migrates to the P_i. Thus, if the subset $\{T_{j_h}, \dots, T_{j_i}, \dots, T_{j_m}\}$ on P_j is a strongly linear cluster, the migration strategy will consider the best subcluster $\{T_{j_i}, \dots, T_{j_m}\}$, i=h, ... ,m to move to P_i.
- The break point should provide that the migrated subcluster should start on P_i within the wait interval, and finish as soon as possible.
- Possible later execution of the successors of the migrated tasks should be minimal.

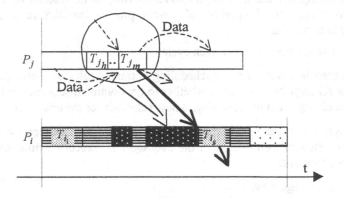

Fig. 4. Data-wait reduction

The benefit function for every considered subcluster is defined as:

$$B = WIET_i - CIET_i - \max(0, G_1), \tag{4}$$

where $WIET_i$ is the end time of the wait interval, obtained through RDS message from the scheduler on P_i; $CIET_i$ is the calculated end time of the considered subcluster after migration on P_i; G_1 is the calculated maximal increase of data communication delay from the tasks in the migrated cluster to their successors, compared to data communication from processor P_j. Similar consideration is applied for the second case.

4. Simulation Results

We have used simulation to validate the K1 algorithm. The simulation was performed on Simulation Environment for Parallel Program Execution (SEPPE) that was developed using C++ programming language. For each simulation experiment we have to:

- Generate a DAG, that represents a task set, by the random graph generator. A number of parameters can be set to generate a DAG with characteristics within desired ranges.
- Generate a profile of the task set dynamic behavior, by varying randomly task execution times and data communication volumes in successive iterations (cycles).
- Choose parameters of the simulated computer architecture and dynamic scheduling algorithms for the simulation run. To evaluate the K1 algorithm, we compared it with the:

  1. fixed schedule (FSTAT), that was determined by a static scheduling algorithm applied to the task set characteristics in the first cycle. In the presented results, we have used the HDLFET algorithm [13] to determine the fixed schedule,
  2. unreal quasi-optimal (DLS_DYN) scheduling. This scheduling applies static scheduling algorithm in every cycle, but it doesn't take into account neither the scheduling nor the task migration/reordering costs. Instead of using the time consuming optimal algorithm of NP-complexity, the DLS static algorithm [13] has been applied.

- Run the simulation, where in each cycle:

  1. the response time for every scheduling variant is calculated and recorded,
  2. The K1 algorithm considers whether to try dominant sequence reduction, and in case of migration or reordering, a new schedule for the next cycle is determined.

For the overhead calculation in the K1 algorithm, we have assumed the values used in [12]. The following percentages of the average task execution time are used for the overhead estimation:

1. for each message delay 1%,
2. for scheduling heuristic calculations 2%.

The delay associated with each task transfer is assumed to be 10% of the execution time of the task being transferred. To simplify, we assumed that the transfer of D_{ij} units of data between the tasks T_i and T_j, which are being executed on two different processors, takes D_{ij} units of time.

For the purpose of graphical presentation and for statistic analysis of the simulation results, we have used the STATISTICA package.

An example of a simulation run result, for the task set consisting of 9 tasks and running on two homogenous processors, is given in Fig. 5. The average response time is 80.02, 60.45 and 59.52 time units for FSTAT, K1, and DLS_DYN, respectively.

The response time of the K1 algorithm for the presented example is near the quasi-optimal algorithm (96.9%). Note that in some segments, the K1 algorithm performs slightly better than the DLS_DYN. The reason is that K1 makes cluster tuning by attacking directly on a dominant sequence, while the static algorithm doesn't know the ultimate effect during the scheduling steps. The K1 algorithm performs in some segments even worse than FSTAT. The reason is that in some situations the K1 algorithm couldn't make a better schedule because it doesn't analyze the complex inter-relation between different phenomenon. Instead, it makes decisions on the basis of simple heuristic rules. It also doesn't perform tuning, if the calculated benefit is below the threshold.

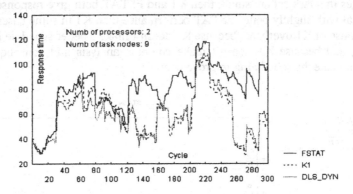

Fig. 5. System response time for K1, fixed (FSTAT) and quasi-optimal (DLS_DYN) scheduling (simulation results for a simulation run)

To evaluate K1 algorithm, we have generated 3 groups of 5 task sets (and the corresponding dynamic behavior profiles), with a task set in each group consisting of 10, 25 and 40 tasks respectively. The execution on a 2 and 4 processor system has been simulated for the first group and on a 4 and 8 processor system for the other two groups. The average overall response time is 438.5, 353.3 and 331.6 time units for FSTAT, K1, and DLS_DYN, respectively.

Fig. 6 and Fig. 7 give a comparison of the K1 and FSTAT, taking quasi-optimal DLS_DYN algorithm as a reference.

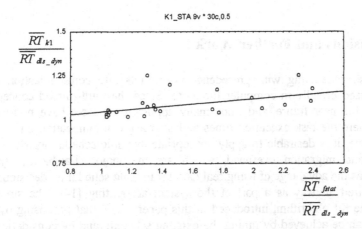

Fig. 6. Comparison of the average response times for K1/FSTAT algorithm. $\overline{RT}_{alg}$ is the average response time of an *alg* for a particular simulation run

Those figures show that K1 algorithm performs much better than FSTAT, if non-uniform dynamic changes in a task set are high, causing FSTAT to produce poor response time. While in some simulation runs FSTAT produced an average response time 2.4 times longer than the DLS_DYN, the maximal deviation of the average response time from quasi-optimal algorithm for K1 was 25% (Fig. 6). If the dynamic changes in a task set are small, then K1 and FSTAT both give response time near the optimal with slightly better FSTAT performance than K1 in some cases (Fig. 7). This is because of K1 overhead, because K1 doesn't make a better schedule if the benefit is small, and because K1 doesn't make complex analysis and consenquently it can't always make the scheduling improvement.

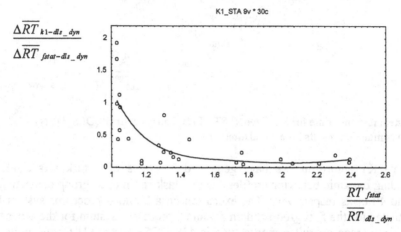

Fig. 7. The ratio of deviations from quasi-optimal response time for K1 and FSTAT. $\overline{\Delta RT}_{k1-dls\_dyn}$ ($\overline{\Delta RT}_{fstat-dls\_dyn}$) is the deviation of the average response time of K1 (FSTAT) from the average response time of the quasi-optimal DLS_DYN algorithm for a particular simulation run

5. Conclusions and Further Work

Dynamic task scheduling with precedence constraints and communication delays wasn't analyzed broadly in computer literature. Since the multi-thread concept will dominate in the near future, and since many application classes have non-uniform behavior, where the task execution times and intertask communication data volume change in time, it is desirable to apply appropriate dynamic scheduling. Besides the scheduling and migration overhead, which are the major drawbacks, dynamic scheduling has the advantage of using real data for making scheduling decisions. This data is acquired anyway as a part of the system accounting [14]. The simulation results for the K1 algorithm, introduced in this paper, show that promising dynamic scheduling can be achieved by tuning the existing schedule and by considering only those tasks that have influence on a dominant sequence.

Future work will be directed towards implementation and evaluation of the algorithm in a real system, and in bringing more flexibility into the algorithm through the concept of incremental scheduling. An interesting research area is also adaptive activation of the algorithm based on the system behavior.

References

1. Chang, H.W.D., Oldham, W.J.B.: Dynamic Task Allocation Models for Large Distributed Computing Systems. IEEE Trans. on Parallel and Distr. Systems, Vol. 6, No. 12 (1995) 1301-1315
2. Dennis, J.B.: Machines and Models for Parallel Computing. International Journal of Parallel Programming, Vol. 22, No. 1 (1994) 47-77
3. Gerasoulis, A., Yang, T.: On the Granularity and Clustering of Directed Acyclic Task Graphs. IEEE Trans. on Parallel and Distr. Systems, Vol. 4, No. 6 (1993) 686-701
4. Ha, S., Lee, E.A.: Compile-Time Scheduling and Assignment of Data-Flow Program Graphs with Data-Dependent Iteration. IEEE Trans. on Comp., Vol. 40, No. 11 (1991) 1225-1238
5. KaoH, B., Molina, H.G.: Scheduling Soft Real-Time Jobs Over Dual Non-Real-Time Servers. IEEE Trans. on Parallel and Distr. Systems. Vol. 7, No. 1 (1996) 56-68
6. Kruatrauche, B., Lewis, T.: Grain Size Determination for Parallel Processing. IEEE Software, Vol. 5, No. 1 (1988) 23-32
7. Leslie, I.M. et al.: The Design and Implementation of an Operating System to Support Distributed Multimedia Application. IEEE Journal on Selected Areas in Communications, Vol. 14, No. 7 (1996) 1280-1297
8. Loh, P.-K., Hsu, W.J., Wentong, C., Sriskanthan, N.: How Network Topology Affects Dynamic Load Balancing. IEEE Parallel&Distributed Technology, Fall 1996 25-32
9. Palis, M.A., Liou, J.-C., Wei, D.S.L.: Task Clustering and Scheduling for Distributed Memory Parallel Architecture. IEEE Trans. on Parallel and Distr. Systems, Vol. 7, No. 1 (1996) 46-55
10. Ramamritham, K., Stankovic, J.A., Shiah, P.-F.: Efficient Scheduling Algorithms for Real-Time Multiprocessor Systems. IEEE Trans. on Parallel and Distr. Systems, Vol. 1, No. 2 (1990) 184-194
11. Shang, S., Hwang, K.: Distributed Hardwired Barrier Synchronization for Scalable Multiprocessors Clusters. IEEE Trans.on Parallel and Distributed Systems, vol.6, No.6 (1995) 591-605
12. Shin, K.G., Hou, C.-J.: Design and Evaluation of Effective Load Sharing in Distributed Real-Time Systems. IEEE Trans. on Parrallel and Distr. Systems, Vol. 5, No. 7 (1994) 704-719
13. Sih, G.C.: Multiprocessor Scheduling to Account for Interprocessor Communication. P.H.D Theses, U.C. Berkley (1991)
14. Stone, H.S.: Multiprocessor Scheduling with the Aid of Network Flow Algorithms. IEEE Trans. on Softw. Eng.., Vol. SE - 3, No. 1 (1977) 85-93
15. Wang, Y.-T., Morris, R.J.T.: Load Sharing in Distributed Systems. IEEE Trans. on Computers, Vol. C-34, No. 3 (1985) 204-217
16. Willebeek-LeMair, M.H., Reeves, A.P.: Strategies for Dynamic Load Balancing on Highly Parallel Computers. IEEE Trans. on Parallel and Distr. Systems, Vol. 4, No. 9 (1993), 979-993
17. Yang, T., Gerasoulis, A.: DSC: Scheduling Parallel Tasks on an Unbounded Number of Processors. IEEE Trans. on Parallel. and Distr. Systems, Vol. 5, No. 9 (1994) 951-967
18. Zhou, S.: A Trace-Driven Simulation Study of Dynamic Load Balancing. IEEE Trans. on Softw. Eng.., Vol. 14, No. 11 (1988) 1327-1341

Two-Dimensional Scheduling of Algorithms with Uniform Dependencies

N.A. Likhoded

National Academy of Sciences of Belarus, Institute of Mathematics,
Surganov str., 11 , Minsk 220072 BELARUS
Phone: 375 17 284 26 43   Fax: 375 17 284 09 15
E-mail: likhoded@im.bas-net.by

Abstract. A formal method to schedule algorithms for the special case of 3D → 1D spatial mapping is proposed. The method is based on a technique of two-dimensional scheduling. Initial 3D algorithms should be represented as a system of uniform recurrence equations or as a uniform loop nest. The method can be generalized for the case of 4D → 2D, 5D → 3D spatial mapping or for the case of affine scheduling with the same linear part.

1 Introduction

Many algorithms from numerical analysis, signal and image processing may be represented as algorithms with uniform dependencies (UDAs, uniform dependence algorithms). We say that an algorithm has uniform dependencies if the dependencies between informatively connected points of index domain are determined by a set of several vectors. Two points are informatively connected if they share a common datum. The UDAs can be written in the form of uniform recurrence equations [1] or uniform loop nests [2].

One of the most important problem for the space-time mapping UDAs onto VLSI array processors and distributed memory parallel computers is the problem of the obtaining scheduling function. The problem is well developed for the case when the dimension of the algorithm exceeds the dimension of the target parallel architecture by one (see, for instance, [3]). In papers [4-7] the much more complicated case when the dimension of the algorithm exceeds the dimension of the target parallel architecture by two or more is considered. In those papers the methods to search one-dimensional scheduling vectors are proposed. The new method of the present paper is based on a technique of two-dimensional scheduling [8,9]. The main theoretical contribution of this paper is the obtaining and analysis of the restrictions to two-dimensional scheduling functions suited for 3D → 1D spatial mapping. The study of two-dimensional scheduling can result in more efficient procedures of space-time mapping UDAs onto parallel computers.

2 One-Dimensional Scheduling Function

Let an algorithm with uniform dependencies be represented by uniform loop nests:

$$
\begin{aligned}
&\text{for } i_1 = l_1 \text{ to } u_1 \text{ do} \\
&\quad \text{for } i_2 = l_2(i_1) \text{ to } u_2(i_1) \text{ do} \\
&\qquad \text{for } i_3 = l_3(i_1, i_2) \text{ to } u_3(i_1, i_2) \text{ do} \\
&\qquad\quad \text{Program composed of } K \text{ statements } S_1(i_1, i_2, i_3), \\
&\qquad\qquad\qquad\qquad\qquad\qquad\qquad\qquad S_2(i_1, i_2, i_3), \\
&\qquad\qquad\qquad\qquad\qquad\qquad\qquad\qquad \ldots \\
&\qquad\qquad\qquad\qquad\qquad\qquad\qquad\qquad S_K(i_1, i_2, i_3) \\
&\qquad \text{endfor} \\
&\quad \text{endfor} \\
&\text{endfor}
\end{aligned}
\tag{1}
$$

Here l_1, u_1 are constants, l_2, u_2 are functions of i_1, l_3, u_3 are functions of i_1, i_2.

Let there be a dependence between iterations $S_i(I)$ and $S_j(J)$. The dependence vector between them is $\varphi^{(i,j)} = J - I$. As far as we consider only uniform algorithms, vector $\varphi^{(i,j)}$ is the same for all permissible I and J. We denote the set of dependence vectors by Φ.

We call the set $V = \{v(i_1, i_2, i_3) \in \mathbf{Z}^3 \mid l_1 \leq i_1 \leq u_1, \ l_2(i_1) \leq i_2 \leq u_2(i_1), \ l_3(i_1, i_2) \leq i_3 \leq u_3(i_1, i_2)\}$ an index domain of algorithm (1).

Let $\pi : V \to \mathbf{Z}$ be a linear allocation function defined by a vector $\bar{\pi}$. Allocation function establishes the correspondence between any point $v \in V$ and location of processor that implements the computations assigned to v.

Consider scheduling function $t : V \to \mathbf{Z}_+$. Scheduling function determines nonnegative integer $t(v)$ for each block of statements assigned to the point $v \in V$. Scheduling function is to satisfy two constraints:

a) condition for preservation of dependencies:

$$
t(v + \varphi) - t(v) \geq 1, \quad v, \ v + \varphi \in V, \quad \varphi \in \Phi
\tag{2}
$$

(computations at point v should precede the computations at point $v + \varphi$);

b) condition of compatibility of scheduling and allocation functions:

$$
t(v') \neq t(v'') \text{ if } \pi(v') = \pi(v''), \ v', v'' \in V, \ v' \neq v''
\tag{3}
$$

(there are different values of the scheduling function for all points having the same value of the allocation function; this constraint appears because each processor of the target parallel architecture can perform concurrently only one block of iterations of the algorithm).

Let the scheduling function be defined as $t(v) = \lfloor \tau \cdot v + a \rfloor$, $v \in V$, $\tau \in \mathbf{Q}^3$, $a \in \mathbf{Q}$.

Lemma 1 *Constraint (2) on scheduling function t is valid if (iff for the case $\tau \in \mathbf{Z}^3$, $a \in \mathbf{Z}$) $\tau \cdot \varphi \geq 1$, $\varphi \in \Phi$.*

Lemma 2 *Constraint (3) on scheduling function t is valid if (iff for the case $\tau \in \mathbf{Z}^3$, $a \in \mathbf{Z}$) $|\tau \cdot s| \geq 1$, $s \in S = \{s \in V \ominus V \mid \pi(s) = 0, \ s \neq 0\}$, $V \ominus V = \{v \in \mathbf{Z}^3 \mid v = v' - v'', \ v', v'' \in V\}$.*

A proof of these statements is based on the equality

$$t(v') - t(v'') = \lfloor \tau \cdot (v' - v'') + \tau \cdot v'' + a - \lfloor \tau \cdot v'' + a \rfloor \rfloor, \quad v', v'' \in V. \quad (4)$$

3 Two-Dimensional Scheduling Function

We shall use a two-dimensional scheduling function [8, 9] of the form

$$\bar{t} = (t_1, t_2), \ t_i(v) = \lfloor \tau^{(i)} \cdot v + a_i \rfloor, v \in V, \ \tau^{(i)}(\tau_1^{(i)}, \tau_2^{(i)}, \tau_3^{(i)}) \in \mathbf{Q}^3, \ a_i \in \mathbf{Q}, i = 1, 2.$$

The scheduling function is to satisfy two constraints:

$$\begin{bmatrix} t_1(v + \varphi) > t_1(v), \ \text{or} \\ t_1(v + \varphi) = t_1(v), \ t_2(v + \varphi) > t_2(v) \end{bmatrix} \quad \text{for } v, v + \varphi \in V, \ \varphi \in \Phi. \quad (5)$$

(condition for preservation of dependencies),

$$\bar{t}(v') \neq \bar{t}(v'') \ \text{if} \ \pi(v') = \pi(v''), \ v', v'' \in V, \ v' \neq v'' \quad (6)$$

(condition for compatibility of scheduling and allocation functions).

Theorem 3 *Constraint (5) on scheduling function $\bar{t}$ is valid if*

$$\begin{bmatrix} \tau^{(1)} \cdot \varphi \geq 1, \ \text{or} \\ 0 \leq \tau^{(1)} \cdot \varphi < 1, \ \tau^{(2)} \cdot \varphi \geq 1 \end{bmatrix} \quad \text{for } \varphi \in \Phi. \quad (7)$$

If $\tau^{(1)}, \tau^{(2)} \in \mathbf{Z}^3$, $a_1, a_2 \in \mathbf{Z}$, then (7) is necessary and sufficient condition.
Proof. Let $\tau^{(1)} \cdot \varphi \geq 1$. Then $t_1(v + \varphi) - t_1(v) \geq 1$ by Lemma 1. Let $0 \leq \tau^{(1)} \cdot \varphi < 1$.
Then $t_1(v + \varphi) - t_1(v) \geq 0$ by equality (4) (where $v' = v + \varphi$, $v'' = v$). Let
$\tau^{(2)} \cdot \varphi \geq 1$. Then $t_2(v + \varphi) - t_2(v) \geq 1$ by Lemma 1. Thus, it follows from
Lemma 1 and equality (4) that condition (7) is sufficient (necessary and sufficient
if $\tau^{(1)}, \tau^{(2)} \in \mathbf{Z}^3$, $a_1, a_2 \in \mathbf{Z}$) to guarantee the following conditions

$$\begin{bmatrix} t_1(v + \varphi) - t_1(v) \geq 1, \ \text{or} \\ t_1(v + \varphi) - t_1(v) = 0, \ t_2(v + \varphi) - t_2(v) \geq 1 \end{bmatrix} \quad \text{for } v, v + \varphi \in V, \ \varphi \in \Phi. \quad (8)$$

These conditions mean that constraints (5) are fulfilled. □
Theorem 4 *Constraint (6) on scheduling function $\bar{t}$ is valid if $\overline{S} = \{s \in V \ominus V \mid \pi(s) = 0, |\tau^{(1)} \cdot s| < 1, |\tau^{(2)} \cdot s| < 1, s \neq 0\}$ is empty set.*
Constraint (6) on scheduling function $\bar{t}$ is valid if $\tau^{(1)}$ and $\bar{\pi}$ are linearly independent vectors, components of vector $\tau^{(1)}$ are integers, and

$$|\tau^{(2)} \cdot s^{(0)}| \geq 1 \quad (9)$$

where $s^{(0)}$ is the basis vector of the set $S_0 = \{s \in V \ominus V \mid \pi(s) = 0, \tau^{(1)} \cdot s = 0, s \neq 0\}$ ($s^{(0)}$ is such that any vector of S_0 has the form $s = \alpha s^{(0)}, |\alpha| \geq 1$).
If $\tau^{(1)}, \tau^{(2)} \in \mathbf{Z}^3$, $a_1, a_2 \in \mathbf{Z}$, then condition $\overline{S} = \emptyset$ (and condition (9)) is necessary and sufficient condition.

Proof. Let $\overline{S}$ be empty set. Then

$$\begin{bmatrix} |\tau^{(1)} \cdot s| \geq 1, & \text{or} \\ |\tau^{(2)} \cdot s| \geq 1 \end{bmatrix} \quad \text{for } s \in S. \tag{10}$$

By Lemma 2 these conditions are sufficient (necessary and sufficient if $\tau^{(1)}, \tau^{(2)} \in \mathbf{Z}^3$, $a_1, a_2 \in \mathbf{Z}$) to guarantee the conditions

$$\begin{bmatrix} t_1(v') \neq t_1(v''), & \text{or} \\ t_2(v') \neq t_2(v'') \end{bmatrix} \quad \text{for } \pi(v') = \pi(v''), \ v', v'' \in V, \ v' \neq v''. \tag{11}$$

These conditions mean that constraints (6) are fulfilled. Let $\tau^{(1)}$ and $\overline{\pi}$ be linearly independent vectors, components of vector $\tau^{(1)}$ be integers. In this case the set S_0 is one-dimensional, $\overline{S} = \{s \in V \ominus V \mid \pi(s) = 0, \ \tau^{(1)} \cdot s = 0, \ |\tau^{(2)} \cdot s| < 1, \ s \neq 0\}$. Any vector $s \in S_0$ has the form $s = \alpha s^{(0)}$, $|\alpha| \geq 1$. Therefore, if condition (9) is valid, then $|\alpha||\tau^{(2)} \cdot s^{(0)}| \geq 1$, $|\tau^{(2)} \cdot s| \geq 1$ for $s \in S_0$. It is clear that $\overline{S} = \emptyset$, constraint (6) is valid. □

4 One-Dimensional Scheduling Function Generated by Two-Dimensional Scheduling Function

Since time is one-dimensional, we put a 1D scheduling function into correspondence to a 2D one:

$$t(v) = Pt_1(v) + t_2(v), \quad v \in V \tag{12}$$

where $P \in \mathbf{Z}$, $P \geq 1$, P does not depend on v.

Scheduling function of form (12) is to satisfy constraints (2) and (3):

$$P(t_1(v + \varphi) - t_1(v)) + t_2(v + \varphi) - t_2(v) \geq 1, \quad v, v + \varphi \in V, \ \varphi \in \Phi, \tag{13}$$

$$P(t_1(v') - t_1(v'')) + t_2(v') - t_2(v'') \neq 0 \text{ if } \pi(v') = \pi(v''), \ v', v'' \in V, \ v' \neq v''. \tag{14}$$

Theorem 5 *Constraints (13), (14) are valid if conditions (7), $\overline{S} = \emptyset$ (or (9)) are valid and*

$$P \geq \max(\max_{\varphi \in \Phi} \lceil \tau^{(2)} \cdot \varphi \rceil, \ \max_{m \in \mathbf{Z}_+} (\frac{1}{m} \max_{s \in S_m} |\lceil \tau^{(2)} \cdot s \rceil|)) + 1$$

where $S_m = \{s \in V \ominus V \mid \pi(s) = 0, \ m - 1 < |\tau^{(1)} \cdot s| < m + 1, \ s \neq 0\}$.
Proof. It follows easily from equality (4) that $\lceil \tau^{(2)} \cdot \varphi \rceil + 1 > t_2(v + \varphi) - t_2(v)$ and $\lceil \tau^{(2)} \cdot (v' - v'') \rceil + 1 > t_2(v') - t_2(v'')$. From (4) it follows also that $\{v', v'' \mid |t_1(v') - t_1(v'')| = m\} \subseteq \{v', v'' \mid m - 1 < |\tau^{(1)} \cdot (v' - v'')| < m + 1\}$, $m \in \mathbf{Z}_+$. Since (7) is valid, we see that (8) is valid; hence (13) is valid for the case of $t_1(v + \varphi) - t_1(v) = 0$. If $t_1(v + \varphi) - t_1(v) \geq 1$, then $P(t_1(v + \varphi) - t_1(v)) \geq P \geq \max_{\varphi \in \Phi} \lceil \tau^{(2)} \cdot \varphi \rceil + 1 > t_2(v + \varphi) - t_2(v)$. It follows from here that (13) is valid.
Since $\overline{S} = \emptyset$ is valid, we have that (11) is valid; hence (14) is valid for the case of

$t_1(v') - t_1(v'') = 0$. If $|t_1(v') - t_1(v'')| = m$, $m \in \mathbf{Z}_+$, then $|P \cdot (t_1(v') - t_1(v''))| = mP \geq \max\limits_{s \in S_m} |\lceil \tau^{(2)} \cdot s \rceil| + 1 \geq \max\limits_{v', v''} |\lceil \tau^{(2)} \cdot (v' - v'') \rceil| + 1 > t_2(v') - t_2(v'')$,

where we consider in $\max\limits_{v', v''}$ the points $v', v'' \in V$ such that $\pi(v') - \pi(v'') = 0$, $|t_1(v') - t_1(v'')| = m$, $v' \neq v''$. It follows from here that (14) is valid. $\qquad\square$

The total execution time of a schedule $t(v)$ is $T = \max\limits_{v \in V} t(v) - \min\limits_{v \in V} t(v) + 1$.
Since

$$T = P(\max\limits_{v \in V} t_1(v) - \min\limits_{v \in V} t_1(v)) + \max\limits_{v \in V} t_2(v) - \min\limits_{v \in V} t_2(v) + 1,$$

T is directly proportional to P, we set

$$P = \max(\max\limits_{\varphi \in \Phi} \lceil \tau^{(2)} \cdot \varphi \rceil, \max\limits_{m \in \mathbf{Z}_+} (\frac{1}{m} \max\limits_{s \in S_m} |\lceil \tau^{(2)} \cdot s \rceil|)) + 1. \qquad (15)$$

5 Procedure for Obtaining 2D Scheduling Function

We assume that components of vector $\tau^{(1)}$ are integer. If it is not so, $\tau^{(1)} = \frac{1}{\beta} \tilde{\tau}^{(1)}$, where $\beta \in \mathbf{Z}$, $\tilde{\tau}^{(1)}$ is the vector with integer components, then we consider $t_1(v) = \lfloor \tilde{\tau}^{(1)} \cdot v + a_i \rfloor$ instead of $t_1(v) = \lfloor \tau^{(1)} \cdot v + a_i \rfloor$. Usually, the replacement of $\tau^{(1)}$ by $\tilde{\tau}^{(1)}$ does not change the value of T considerably in view of the fact that P decreases because domains $\overline{S}$ and S_m are contracted, constraints (7) and $\overline{S} = \emptyset$ (or condition (9)) for vector $\tau^{(2)}$ become weaker.

By $\overline{\Phi}$ denote the set $\{\varphi^{(1)}, \varphi^{(2)}, \cdots, \varphi^{(Q)}\}$ of $\varphi^{(q)} \in \Phi$ such that the validity of condition (7) for the vectors $\varphi^{(q)} \in \overline{\Phi}$ guarantees that of (7) for the vectors $\varphi \in \Phi$. Suppose $\tau^{(1)} \cdot \varphi^{(q)} \geq 1$ for one vector $\varphi^{(q)} \in \overline{\Phi}$ at least. Otherwise the values of $t_1(v)$ are the same for any point $v \in V$, 2D scheduling degenerates into 1D scheduling: all constraints on $\tau^{(2)}$ are the constraints on τ for the case of the one-dimensional scheduling. Suppose moreover that $\tau^{(1)}$ and $\overline{\pi}$ are linearly independent. Otherwise the set S_0 is not 1D ($S_0 = S$), conditions of compatibility for $\overline{t}$ and π are conditions of compatibility for t_2 and π; 2D scheduling degenerates into 1D one.

Taking into account theorems and assumptions stated above, we have the following procedure for obtaining vectors $\tau^{(1)}$ and $\tau^{(2)}$.

At the beginning put $q = 1$.

Step 1. Put $\overline{\varphi} = \varphi^{(q)}$ and solve optimization problem

$$\min\{|\tau_1^{(1)}| + |\tau_2^{(1)}| + |\tau_3^{(1)}| \mid \tau^{(1)} \cdot \overline{\varphi} \geq 1, \tau^{(1)} \cdot \varphi \geq 0, \varphi \neq \overline{\varphi}\}. \qquad (16)$$

Step 2. Check linearly independence of $\tau^{(1)}$ and $\overline{\pi}$. If $\tau^{(1)}$ and $\overline{\pi}$ are linearly dependent then go to Step 4. If $\tau^{(1)}$ and $\overline{\pi}$ are linearly independent, then go to Step 3.

Step 3. If the components of the vector $\tau^{(1)}$ are integer, then find the vector $\tau^{(2)}$ by a solution of the optimization problem

$$\min\{|\tau_1^{(2)}| + |\tau_2^{(2)}| + |\tau_3^{(2)}| \mid \tau^{(2)} \cdot \varphi \geq 1, \varphi \in \Phi_1, |\tau^{(2)} \cdot s^{(0)}| \geq 1\} \qquad (17)$$

where $\Phi_1 = \{\varphi \in \Phi \mid \tau^{(1)} \cdot \varphi = 0\}$. If the components of the vector $\tau^{(1)}$ are not integer, $\tau^{(1)} = \frac{1}{\beta}\tilde{\tau}^{(1)}$, $\beta \in \mathbf{Z}$, $\tilde{\tau}^{(1)}$ are vectors with integer components, then replace $\tau^{(1)}$ by $\tilde{\tau}^{(1)}$ in the problem (17). Find P for obtained pair $(\tau^{(1)}, \tau^{(2)})$ (by formula (15)); compute T.

Step 4. Increase q by 1. If $q \leq Q$, then go to step 1. If $q > Q$, then choose $(\tau^{(1)}, \tau^{(2)})$ such that T is minimal.

Note that we minimize the functions $|\tau_1^{(i)}| + |\tau_2^{(i)}| + |\tau_3^{(i)}|$, i=1,2. One can suppose to minimize the other functions taking into account the shape of the domain V.

6 Conclusion

Thus, a new method to obtain schedules for the special case $3D \to 1D$ linear mapping π is proposed. The method is based on a technique of two-dimensional scheduling. Restrictions for two-dimensional scheduling vector are obtained; a procedure to find two-dimensional scheduling vector $(\tau^{(1)}, \tau^{(2)})$ is proposed. The procedure uses the following assumptions: the total execution time of the schedule is directly proportional to $|\tau_1^{(i)}| + |\tau_2^{(i)}| + |\tau_3^{(i)}|$, $i = 1, 2$; $\tau^{(1)} \cdot \varphi \geq 1$ for one vector $\varphi \in \Phi$ at least; $\tau^{(1)}$ and $\bar{\pi}$ are linearly independent; components of vector $\tau^{(1)}$ are integer. Notice that following the procedure we can obtain almost optimal (or optimal) scheduling $t(v) = Pt_1(v) + t_2(v)$ even for the case of non-integral components of the vector $\tau^{(1)}$. It is easy to generalize the procedure for the case of $4D \to 2D$ and $5D \to 3D$ spatial mapping. Besides, the procedure can be generalized for the case of affine scheduling with the same linear part (such a scheduling is a more powerful scheduling).

References

1. Karp, R.M., Miller, R.E., Winograd, S.: The organization of computations for uniform recurrence equations. J. of the ACM. **14**(3) (1967) 563–590
2. Banerjee, U.: An introduction to a formal theory of dependence analysis. J. Supercomput. (2) (1988) 133–149
3. Kung, S.-Y.: VLSI array processors. (Prentice-Hall, Englewood Cliffs, NJ, 1988)
4. Lee, P., Kedem, Z.M.: Mapping nested loop algorithms into multidimensional systolic arrays. IEEE Trans. on Parallel and Distributed Syst. **1** (1990) 64–76
5. Kosianchouk, V.V., Likhoded, N.A., Sobolevskii, P.I.: Systolic architecture array synthesis. Prepr., n.6, Inst. of Math., Acad. of Sci. of Belarus, Minsk, 1992
6. Shang, W., Fortes, J.A.B.: On time mapping of uniform dependence algorithms into lower dimensional processor arrays. IEEE Trans. on Parallel and Distributed Syst. **3** (3) (1992) 350–362
7. Likhoded, N.A. Scheduling of algorithms with uniform dependencies: case of 3D → 1D mapping. Proc. 5th Australasian. Conf. on Parallel and Real-Time Systems. Adelaide, Australia, September 28–29, 1998. Springer-Verlag, 401–408
8. Feautrier, P.: Some efficient solutions to the affine scheduling problem, part II, multidimensional time. Int. J. of Parallel Programming **21**(6) (1992) 389–420
9. Darte, A., Vivien, F.: Revisiting the decomposition of Karp, Miller, Winograd. Parallel Processing Letters **5**(4) (1995) 551–562

Consistent Lamport Clocks
for Asynchronous Groups with Process Crashes

Achour Mostéfaoui [1], Michel Raynal [1], and Makoto Takizawa [2]

[1] IRISA - Campus de Beaulieu, 35042 Rennes Cedex, France,
{mostefaoui,raynal}@irisa.fr
[2] Dpt. of Comp. and Systems Eng., Tokyo Denki University, Japan,
taki@takilab.k.dendai.ac.jp

Abstract. Process duplication is a classical method to cope with process crashes: a set of replicated processes constitutes a group that implements some fault-tolerant service. Several distributed systems are structured as a set of interacting reliable groups.

This paper presents a clock management protocol where a logical clock is associated with each group (usually, logical clocks are associated with processes). The main problem that has to be solved is to ensure that all processes of a group behave in the same manner despite non-deterministic statements. It is shown that this problem can be reduced to the consensus problem. So, the proposed group clock protocol is based on an underlying building block providing a solution to the consensus problem.

Keywords: Asynchronous Distributed Systems, Consensus, Logical Clocks, Process Crash, Process Group, Reliable Multicast, Timestamp.

1 Introduction

Logical clocks are a powerful tool used as a basic mechanism in a lot of applications run on top of asynchronous distributed systems. A logical clock system is made of a set of logical clocks (one per process) plus a protocol that manages their progress. A logical clock allows a process to timestamp its events. The fundamental property of a logical clock system (called *consistency*) is the following: if two events are causally related [8] (one being the potential cause, the other being the effect) then the timestamp associated with a cause is smaller than the timestamp associated with its effect. Two main types of logical clocks have been investigated. Scalar clocks are particularly interesting when one is interested in obtaining a system-wide total ordering of events. Vector clocks [4, 9] have been introduced to decide whether two events are causally related or are independent.

A classical way to cope with process failures consists in using (active) replication. Every process is replicated, and the resulting set of replicated processes is called a *group*. From the point of view of an external observer the system must behave as a set of cooperating and interacting groups, each group being perceived as if it was composed of a single reliable process. Several systems have promoted such an use of the group concept; some of them are described in [10].

In this paper, we are interested in designing a logical scalar clock system for asynchronous group-based systems. Clocks are associated not with processes but with groups: each group g_x has a logical clock ($g_x.clock$) with which it can timestamp its events. Due to active replication, each process p_i of a group g_x has a clock $clock_i$ whose aim is to locally represent the "virtual" clock $g_x.clock$. So, the problem consists in defining a cooperation scheme among the processes of each group g_x that ensures each local clock $clock_i$ provides a correct implementation of $g_x.clock$. The fact that (i) the system is asynchronous (no bound on process speeds; no bound on message transfer delays) and that (ii) within each group, processes may crash, makes the problem non trivial. It is well-known that in such a context, it is not possible to distinguish a crashed process from a very slow process or from a process with which communications are very slow [3].

We show in this paper that within each group, the management of its process clocks can be actually reduced to an agreement problem, namely the consensus problem. This reduction is particularly interesting for two reasons. First, from a practical point of view, it provides modularity; more precisely, consensus executions never cross a group boundary. So, every group may have its own consensus protocol. This makes the group clock protocol efficient and is particularly interesting to cope with scalability-related issues. The second interest is from a theoretical point of view. The construction of a group clock by using an active replication technique amounts to order events. The consensus is used to produce this order. It has been shown that the problem of constructing a total order to deliver events to processes (e.g., the Atomic Broadcast problem) and the consensus problem are equivalent [3]. So, the design of group clocks by using active replication has the same limitations as the consensus problem.

The paper is composed of 4 sections. Section 2 points out the problem and introduces the model. Then, Section 3 presents the two underlying blocks on top of which the solution is constructed. Section 4 presents the group clock protocol based on active replication.

2 System Model and The Problem

2.1 The System at the Process Level

We consider a system composed of a finite set of sequential processes. Each process executes a program text; the execution of each operation produces an event. There are three types of events: internal, send and delivery events. Let op be an operation; $op.type \in \{\text{INT}, \text{SEND}, \text{DEL}\}$ will denote its type.

The behavior of a process, called its *history* is defined by the sequence of events it produces (Figure 1.a). We consider processes are *piece-wise deterministic*: the only non-deterministic operations a process can execute are message deliveries (if several messages have arrived, the execution of a delivery operation can deliver any of them). It is important to note that the history of a process depends on the order it has been delivered messages: two processes that execute the same program text can have distinct histories.

A process can fail by *crashing*, *i.e.*, by permanently halting. By definition, a *correct* process is a process that never crashes. A crashed process remains crashed forever.

Communication channels are assumed to be reliable. Every message that is sent is received by its destination processes, provided they are not crashed. There are neither message losses nor a bound on message transfer delays. Moreover, there is no bound on process relative speeds. So, the system is *asynchronous*.

A message is sent either by the environment (*e.g.*, an input or a message sent by an upper layer application) or by another process of the system. So, any message m has a type denoted $m.type$ whose value belongs to $\{ENVRT, SYSTEM\}$.

2.2 The System at the Group Level

The *group* paradigm is a powerful tool that has been introduced to structure distributed systems. At some abstraction level, a system can be seen as a set of interacting groups, each group being actually made of a finite set of processes.

We consider in this paper that each group g_x is made of processes that execute the same program text. The aim of such groups is, despite process crashes, to ensure the availability of the "service" they provide to upper layer application processes. So, from a logical point of view, each process of a group g_x considers (1) that it is the only process implementing the group, and (2) that any other group is composed of a single process (Figure 1).

2.3 The Problem

Group Consistency

The history of a group is the set of its process histories. As indicated previously, for an external observer, the system must behave as if it was composed of a single process per group. Consequently, the first problem (P1) that has to be solved is to ensure this property (see Figure 1.a).

Since processes are not fully deterministic but only piece-wise deterministic, the behavior of processes within each group must be controlled in order that correct processes produce the same history and that the history of a crashed process be a prefix of a correct process history. If this property is satisfied, the *group history* is said to be *consistent*. If follows that if the history of a group is consistent, then this group can be logically perceived as being composed of a single reliable process (see Figure 1.b).

Group Computation

Let e_1 and e_2 be two events of a consistent group history: so, they are produced in the same order by all correct processes of the group. If e_1 appears before e_2 in this history then (by definition) $e_1 \rightarrow_g e_2$.

Let e_1 and e_2 be two events belonging to two different consistent group histories. If it exists a message m such that $e_1 = send(m)$ and $e_2 = delivery(m)$, then (by definition) $e_1 \rightarrow_{msg} e_2$. Finally, let "$\rightarrow$" be the relation defined on events as $(\rightarrow_g \ \cup \ \rightarrow_{msg})^+$.

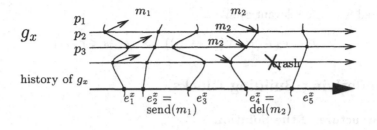

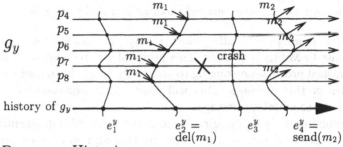

a. Processes Histories

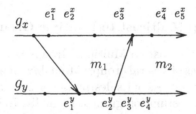

b. Corresponding Group Histories

Fig. 1. Processes and Group Computation

A *group computation* is a set of consistent group histories, one per group of the system, for which the relation "→" is acyclic (Figure 1.b). It is easy to see that if each group contains exactly one process, then "→" confuses with the usual *happened before* relation [8].

Consistent Group Clocks
Among all the events that appear in a group computation, only some of them are relevant for an observer (*i.e.*, at a given abstraction level). Let R be the set of relevant events.

The second problem (P2) that has to be solved consists in associating a group clock $g_x.clock$ with each group g_x, so that the relevant events be timestamped in a consistent way. We first consider scalar timestamps. More formally, this can be expressed in the following way where $e.ts$ denotes the integer timestamp associated with the relevant event e:

$$((e_1, \ e_2 \in \ R) \wedge (e_1 \rightarrow e_2)) \ \Rightarrow \ (e_1.ts < e_2.ts)$$

3 Underlying Building Blocks

3.1 Structure of the Solution

The protocol solving problems P1 and P2 is built on top of two underlying blocks. The next two subsections define these two underlying building blocks.

- The first underlying building block is any protocol implementing Reliable Multicast to Multiple Groups. This protocol will be used to ensure that all non-crashed processes belonging to groups that have been sent some message will deliver this message. This will ensure that processes of a group will deliver the same set of messages.
- The second underlying building block is any protocol implementing Consensus. This protocol will be used to ensure that all non-crashed processes of a given group that have to deliver the same set of messages will deliver them in the same order.

3.2 Reliable Group Multicast to Multiple Groups

The aim of Reliable Multicast to Multiple Groups is to allow a message to be reliably sent to processes of several groups. "Reliably" means here that if the message is delivered by one process of its destination groups then it is delivered by all correct processes of its destination groups. Formally, Reliable Multicast to Multiple Groups is defined by two primitives [6]: R_multicast(m) and R_deliver(m). The semantics of these primitives is defined by three properties, namely, Uniform Validity, Uniform Integrity and Termination. When a process p executes R_multicast(m) (resp. R_deliver(m)), we say it R-multicasts m (resp. R-delivers m). We assume all messages are different. Given any message m, $m.dest$ defines the set of groups that are destination of m.

- Uniform Validity. *If a process p R-delivers m, then some process has R-multicast m and p belongs to a group g such that $g \in m.dest$.*
  This property expresses there are no spurious messages: it defines the value domain of a delivered message.
- Uniform Integrity. *A process R-delivers a message m at most once.*
  This property expresses that there is no duplication.
- Termination. *If (1) a correct process R-multicasts m, or if (2) a process R-delivers m, then all correct processes that belong to a group of $m.dest$ R-deliver m.*
  This property defines the situations in which the multicast must terminate, *i.e.*, the message m must eventually be delivered to its correct destination processes. There are two such situations. The first one (case 1) is when the

sender is correct (in that case it executed R_multicast(m) without crashing). The second one (case 2) is when the message has been R-delivered by a process. Said another way, the only case in which a multicast can not terminate is when the sender process crashes (*e.g.*, during its invocation of R_multicast(m)).

Implementations of Uniform Reliable Multicast can easily be designed for asynchronous systems. A very simple (but inefficient) one is the following one: when a process receives a message m for the first time, it first forwards m to the processes belonging to groups in $m.dest$ and only then considers the delivery of m [6]. According to the underlying network topology, more efficient implementations can be designed.

3.3 The Consensus Problem

Definition
In the *Consensus* problem each process proposes a value and all correct processes have to decide on some value v that is related to the set of proposed values [5]. Formally, the *Uniform Consensus* problem is defined in terms of two primitives: propose and decide. As in previous works (*e.g.*, [3]), when a process p invokes propose(w), where w is its proposal to the consensus, we say that p "proposes" w. In the same way, when p invokes decide and gets v as a result, we say that p "decides" v (denoted decide(v)).

The semantics of propose and decide is defined by the following properties:

- Uniform Validity. *If a process decides v, then v was proposed by some process.*
  This property defines the value domain of the result.
- Uniform Integrity. *A process decides at most once.*
  This property states there is no "duplicates": from the point of view of each process, there is a *single* decision[1].
- Termination. *All correct processes eventually decide.*
  This property states that at least all correct processes decide.
- Uniform Agreement. *No two processes (correct or not) decide differently.*
  This property gives its global meaning to the consensus: from the point of view of all processes there is a *single* decision[2].

About Failures
It has been shown by Fischer, Lynch and Paterson [5] that the consensus problem has no deterministic solution in asynchronous distributed systems that are subject to even a single process crash failure. Intuitively, this negative result is due to the impossibility to safely distinguish (in an asynchronous setting) a crashed

---

[1] Here, the meaning of *single* is local: it locally forbids the occurrence of several decisions.
[2] Here, *single* has a global meaning: it forbids the occurrence of distinct decisions.

process from a slow process (or from a process with which communications are very slow).

This impossibility result has motivated researchers to find a set of minimal assumptions that, when satisfied by a distributed system, makes consensus solvable in this system. Chandra-Toueg's *Unreliable Failure Detector* concept constitutes an answer to this challenge [3]. From a practical point of view, an unreliable failure detector can be seen as a set of oracles: each oracle is attached to a process and provides it with a list of processes it suspects to have crashed. An oracle can make mistakes by not suspecting a crashed process or by suspecting a not crashed one. By restricting the domain of mistakes they can make, several classes of failure detectors can be defined. From a formal point of view, a failure detector class is defined by two properties: a property called *Completeness* which addresses detection of actual failures, and a property called *Accuracy* which restricts the mistakes a failure detector can make. Among the classes of failure detectors defined by Chandra and Toueg, the class $\Diamond S$ is characterized by Strong Completeness and Eventual Weak Accuracy. *Strong Completeness* states that *eventually, every crashed process is permanently suspected by every correct process. Eventual Weak Accuracy* states that *there is a time after which some correct process is never suspected.* It has been shown in [2] that, provided a majority of processes are correct, these conditions are the weakest ones to solve the consensus problem[3]. Consensus protocols based on unreliable failure detectors of the class $\Diamond S$ have been proposed in [3, 7].

These results are fundamental. Let Pb be any problem whose solution lies on a solution to the consensus problem. They show what are the minimal failure-related assumptions any system has to satisfy for Pb to be solved. This means that when these assumptions are not satisfied, Pb is impossible to solve.

4   A Group Clock Protocol

4.1   Data Structures

Each process is endowed with the following data structures:

$clock_i$: an integer variable initialized to 0. It locally represents $g_x.clock$, *i.e.*, the clock of the group to which p_i belongs.

$Received\_Q_i$: a fifo queue of messages. This queue stores the messages received by the process p_i.

$Ordered\_Q_i$: a fifo queue of messages. This queue stores the messages received by the process p_i after they have been ordered.

---

[3] This means that the consensus problem can not be solved in runs (of asynchronous distributed systems) in which these two properties are not satisfied. Furthermore, while the completeness property can always be realized by using timeouts, it is important to note that the accuracy property can only be approximated in purely asynchronous distributed systems (otherwise, this would contradict the Fisher-Lynch-Paterson's impossibility result!).

While all queues $Received\_Q_i(\forall p_i \in g_x)$ will eventually contain the same set of messages, the queues $Ordered\_Q_i(\forall p_i \in g_x)$ will eventually contain the same sequence of messages.

k_i : an integer variable initialized to 0. Its value is used to identify the successive consensus executed by processes of g_x.

4.2 The Three Tasks of the Protocol

Let us consider a process $p_i \in g_x$. The protocol is composed of three tasks T_RECEPTION$_i$, T_ORDER$_i$ and T_EXEC$_i$.

Task T_RECEPTION$_i$
The aim of this task is to handle message reception. As, due to reliable multicast, the same message can be received several times, this task filters these receptions. The first time a message is received, T_RECEPTION$_i$ puts it at the end of the queue $Received\_Q_i$. Due to the properties of reliable multicast primitive used to send messages (more precisely, part 2 of the termination property), it follows that if $m \in Received\_Q_i$, then eventually $m \in Received\_Q_j(\forall p_j \in g_x)$.

> **Task** T_RECEPTION$_i$:
>   **when** m is received **do**
>   **if** first reception of m **then**
>   **add** m to $Received\_Q_i$
>   **endif**

Task T_ORDER$_i$
The aim of this task is to order received messages in such a way that all processes of g_x order them in the same way. Non ordered messages are taken from $Received\_Q_i$ and ordered messages are put in $Ordered\_Q_i$.

> **Task** T_ORDER$_i$:
>   **while** true **do**
>   **wait** $(Received\_Q_i \neq \emptyset)$;
>   **let** m be the first element of $Received\_Q_i$;
> $k_i \leftarrow k_i + 1$; **let** k be the current value of k_i;
>   **propose**(k, m); **wait decide**(k, m');
>   **wait** $(m' \in Received\_Q_i)$; **suppress** m' from $Received\_Q_i$;
>   **add** m' to $Ordered\_Q_i$;
>   **enddo**

T_ORDER$_i$ proceeds in the following way. First, it waits until there is a message m in $Received\_Q_i$. Then it launches a new consensus by proposing m. As indicated before, the variable k_i (local to the task T_ORDER$_i$) is used to identify the successive consensus executed by p_i. Let k be the current value of k_i. So, T_ORDER$_i$ launches the consensus number k by invoking **propose**(k, m)

(note that k identifies the consensus while m is the value proposed by this p_i to this consensus). Then, it waits until a value (here, a message) has been decided by consensus number k (executed by the non crashed processes of g_x). Let m' be this message. Due to the property of consensus (agreement) all tasks T_ORDER of processes of g_x obtain the same message m' as the value decided by consensus number k. Due to asynchrony of channels, it is possible that m' has not yet arrived at p_i; if it is the case, T_ORDER$_i$ waits until m' has locally been received (as noted in the previous paragraph, due to the property of the reliable multicast primitive, m' will necessarily be received). Then, T_ORDER$_i$ suppresses m' from $Received\_Q_i$ and puts it at the end of $Ordered\_Q_i$.

$$p_i \qquad\qquad p_j \qquad\qquad \cdots$$

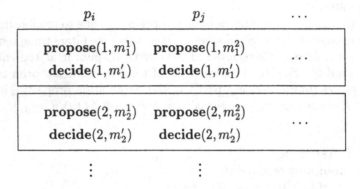

Fig. 2. Sequence of Consensus within a Group

As all processes of a group g_x execute consensus in the same order, they decide the same sequence of messages $m'_1, m'_2, \ldots$ As shown in Figure 2, and as announced in Section 4.1, the queues $Ordered\_Q_j (\forall p_j \in g_x)$ will contain the same sequence of messages. A similar task is found in [3] to implement Atomic Broadcast.

Task T_EXEC$_i$
This task acts as an interpreter for the program text p_i has to execute. Given a message m, $m.ts$ denotes the timestamp that has been associated with it by its sender ($m.dest$ denotes the set of groups to which the message is sent). A message m received from the environment has no timestamp ($m.type = ENVRT$ and $m.ts$ has no value). A message m sent by a group is timestamped before being sent ($m.type = SYSTEM$, and $m.ts$ has a value).

If the current operation is a delivery, T_EXEC$_i$ waits until a message m belongs to $Ordered\_Q_i$ and then takes the first one. If $m.type = SYSTEM$, T_EXEC$_i$ updates $clock_i$. The local clock $clock_i$ is incremented only if the current operation produces a relevant event. In that case, $op.ts$ denotes the timestamp associated with the corresponding event. Finally, T_EXEC$_i$ executes the operation op.

Task T_EXEC_i:
    while true **do**
        let $op.type$ be the type of the next operation;
        if $op.type$ = REC **then**
            wait $(Ordered\_Q_i \neq \emptyset)$;
            let m be the first element of $Ordered\_Q_i$;
            suppress m **from** $Ordered\_Q_i$;
            if $m.type = SYSTEM$ **then** $clock_i \leftarrow max(clock_i, m.ts)$ **endif**
        endif;
        if op is relevant (*i.e.*, it has to be timestamped) **then**
            $clock_i \leftarrow clock_i + 1$;
            $op.ts \leftarrow clock_i$
        endif;
        case $op.type$ **of**
            INT   execute the operation op
            SEND $m.type \leftarrow SYSTEM$;
                    $m.ts \leftarrow clock_i$;
                    R_multicast m **to** $m.dest$
            REC   **deliver** m **to** the upper layer
        endcase
    enddo

References

1. K. Birman and T. Joseph. Reliable Communication in the Presence of Failures, *ACM Trans. on Comp. Syst.*,5(1):47-76, 1987.
2. Chandra T., Hadzilacos V. and Toueg S. The Weakest Failure Detector for Solving Consensus. *Journal of the ACM*, 43(4):685-722, July 1996 (A preliminary version appeared in *Proc. of the 11th ACM Symp. PODC*, pp. 147-158, 1992).
3. Chandra T. and Toueg S. Unreliable Failure Detectors for Reliable Distributed Systems. *Journal of the ACM*, 43(1):225-267, March 1996 (A preliminary version appeared in *Proc. of the 10th ACM Symp. PODC*, pp. 325-340, 1991).
4. Fidge C.J. Logical Time in Distributed Computing Systems. *IEEE Computer*, 24(8):11-76, 1991.
5. Fischer M.J., Lynch N. and Paterson M.S. Impossibility of Distributed Consensus with One Faulty Process. *Journal of the ACM*, 32(2):374-382, April 1985.
6. Hadzilacos V. and Toueg S. Reliable Broadcast and Related Problems. In *Distributed Systems (Second Edition)*, ACM Press (S. Mullender Ed.), New-York, 1993, pp. 97-145.
7. Hurfin M. and Raynal M. A Simple and Fast Asynchronous Consensus Protocol Based on a Weak Failure Detector. *Distributed Computing*, to appear, 12(4), 1999.
8. Lamport, L. Time Clocks and the Ordering of Events in a Distributed System, *Communications of the ACM*, 21(7):558-565, 1978.
9. Mattern, F. Virtual Time and Global States of Distributed Systems. In Cosnard et al. Eds, *Proc. of the Int. Workshop on Parallel and Distributed Algorithms*, France, 1988, pp. 215-226, Elsevier Science Publishers B.V., North Holland, 1989.
10. Powell D. (Guest Editor). Special issue on Group Communication. *Communications of the ACM*, Vol. 39(4), April 1996.

Comparative Analysis of Learning Methods of Cellular-Neural Associative Memory

Sergey Pudov

Supercomputer Software Department
ICMMG of Siberian Branch
Russian Academy of Science
Pr. Lavrentieva, 6, Novosibirsk, 630090, Russia
E-mail: pudov@ssd.sscc.ru

Abstract. In this paper various methods of CNAM learning (synthesis) are compared in order to find their common features. This allows to transfer the important characteristics among the methods, and to do some assumptions about their capabilities. Also the influence of learning parameters in some methods on the CNAM stability is investigated, and recommendations on their choice are given.

1   Introduction

Cellular-Neural Associative Memory (CNAM) is a variant of Cellular Neural Networks (CNN) [1]. It has also a local connection structure and a neuron function of cells, but differs from general form of CNN in connection structure, each neuron having its own connection template. For each neuron the connection weights are determined depending on initial data either in a process of their iterative selecting *(learning)* or in a *synthesis* process, when the weights are calculated by some direct algorithm. So CNAM can be viewed as a hybrid of artificial neural network by Hopfield and CNN. The ideology of learning (synthesis) and all notions, connected with it, are inherited from Hopfield's networks. Also it concerns almost all learning (synthesis) methods. They were adapted for CNAM using one of two following approaches.

The first approach is as follows: firstly the fullconnected weight matrix is obtained, then the unnecessary connections are cut out. This approach has some obvious shortcomings. At first, there is no guarantee of individual stability of stored patterns. Next, a selfconnection weight has a dominant value as compared with fullconnected case, which leads to network degeneration and to a great number of spurious patterns.

The second approach is as follows: each neuron with its neighbourhood is considered as individual network containing of q neurons, which are learned by any appropriate method. Then a weight vector of this neuron is extracted from the obtained weight matrix. This allows to ensure individual stability of stored patterns, if it was present in fullconnected case, and to avoid the groundless increase of selfconnection weight values. This approach is more preferable than the first one, since only such information is used during the learning, which is acceptable in the process of CNAM functioning.

There exists also a number of methods (e.g. [15]), which were proposed specially for CNAM learning. They are based on the idea of perceptron learning rule, since it allows to use the needed information only. These methods are iterative and local, what is very important because they may be realized in the network to be learned.

All methods of CNAM learning (synthesis) have different characteristics because they are based on various points of view on the neural networks functioning. Some methods are investigated very well, there exist many theoretical and experimental results for them. For other methods, it is difficult to explain theoretically certain characteristics, and they are obtained by experimental way. Moreover, some methods have learning parameters, which in many cases are to be chosen randomly, though they may influence on the stability of taught CNAM.

The goal of this paper is to compare various methods of CNAM learning (synthesis) in order to find their common features. It allows to transfer the important characteristics among the methods, and to do some assumption about their capability. Also the influence of learning parameters on the CNAM stability is investigated and recommendations on their choice are given. This paper is organized as follows. In Section 2 formal representation of CNAM is given. Methods of synthesis and learning of CNAM are investigated in Section 3 and 4 respectively. In Section 5 main results of methods comparative analysis are given and the table of their common characteristics is presented.

2 Basic Definitions

Following [2] CNAM is defined by three notions: $\mathbf{N} = < \mathbf{C}, \mathbf{W}, \mathbf{\Phi} >$, where $\mathbf{C}$ is a rectangular array consisting of m rows and n columns of cells (or neurons) with states $c_{ij} \in \{-1, 1\}$. $\mathbf{W} = \{ W_{ij} \}$ is a set of *weight vectors* $W_{ij} = (w_1, \ldots, w_q)$, where w_k is a real number assigned to the connection between a neuron with coordinates (i, j) and its k-th neighbour. $\mathbf{\Phi}$ is a rule according to which CNAM acts.

Each neuron has exactly q different neighbours except itself, their states in array C form a vector $C_{ij} = (c_1, \ldots, c_q)$. Further a vector

$$D_{ij} = c_{ij} C_{ij} = (d_1, \ldots, d_q), \tag{1}$$

which is called a *normalized neighbourhood* of neuron (i, j) is also used. Both vectors C_{ij} and W_{ij} have q component each, their scalar product being defined as $\langle C_{ij}, W_{ij} \rangle = \sum_l c_l w_l$. If CNAM has non-zero self-connections, then c_0 and w_0 are states of a neuron and a self-connection weight respectively. In this case vectors (c_0, C_{ij}) and (w_0, W_{ij}) of length $q + 1$ are used instead of vectors C_{ij} and W_{ij} of length q.

The rule $\mathbf{\Phi}$ of CNAM without self-connections functioning is described by the following iterative procedure. Let $C(t)$ be the array after t-th iteration. Then

1. all cells in $C(t)$ compute the following function:

$$f_{ij} = \begin{cases} 1 & \text{if } \langle C_{ij}(t), W_{ij} \rangle \geq 0, \\ -1 & \text{otherwise,} \end{cases} \tag{2}$$

resulting in $C(t+1)$;

2. if $C(t+1) = C(t)$ then $C(t) = \Phi(C(0))$ is a result of the computation, which corresponds to a stable state of CNAM.

Operating in such a way CNAM performs storage and retrieval of a set of patterns $\{P^0, \ldots, P^{L-1}\}$, given as cellular arrays, and called *prototypes*. A pattern to be retrieved is input by setting the CNAM in the corresponding initial state $C(0)$. Application of the above iterative procedure to any $C(0)$ should terminate in a stable state, but for some initial state $C(0)$ the sequence of array states may terminate by a cycle of the form: $C_1, C_2, C_1, C_2, \ldots$

Network behavior is completely determined by weight vectors (w_0, W_{ij}), which should be calculated during a learning or synthesis process. Method of learning (or synthesis) should provide the following dynamic properties for prototypes $P^0, \ldots, P^{L-1}$, which are to be stored in CNAM:

(i) *individual stability*, i.e. each prototype should be a stable state, or $\Phi(P^K) = P^K$, $\forall K = 0, \ldots, L-1$;

(ii) *stability to distortions*, i.e. if P_{bad}^K lies near to P^K then $\Phi(P_{bad}^K) = P^K$;

(iii) there should be *no cycles*, or their number should be as small as possible.

It can be noticed that in the case of CNAM without self-connections only those set of patterns can be individually stable, which satisfy the condition of *local separability* [15]: patterns $P^0, \ldots, P^{L-1}$ are *locally separable* if there exists a set of weight vectors W_{ij} such that for all neurons (i, j) the following holds: $\langle P_{ij}^K, W_{ij} \rangle > 0, \forall K = 0, \ldots, L-1$.

3 Synthesis of CNAM

3.1 Hebb's Rule

Hebb's rule [3] was used for programming the Hopfield network. The main idea is that when patterns are weakly correlated, they can be stored independently one from another. In local case Hebb's rule [4] looks like this:

$$W_{ij} = \sum_{K=0}^{L-1} D_{ij}^K \tag{3}$$

in the case of neurons without self-connections,

$$(w_{ij}, W_{ij}) = \sum_{K=0}^{L-1} (1, D_{ij}^K) \tag{4}$$

otherwise. This rule is very simple, it has such a positive property as capability of additive learning-forgetting. For neurons with self-connections and symmetrical weight matrix W the absence of cycles is proved in [5].

A network learned by Hebb's rule is capable to store approximately $L \leq 0.15q$ patterns, which are desirable to be weakly correlated. But there is no guarantee that these patterns are individually stable. It follows from the above estimation that CNAM is capable to store 3 prototypes when neuron connection number is $q \geq 20$; 10 prototypes when $q \geq 66$. In [6] the capability of one dimensional CNAM to store information was experimentally investigated, only 10 patterns were stored using from 3 to 11 neighbours, which is very few. So the conclusion about impossibility of CNN to be used as associative memory was made. By contrast, in [4] for $L \leq q$ a CNAM is presented which has the same associative ability as its corresponding global interconnected network.

3.2 Projection Learning Rule

The main idea of Projection Learning Rule (PLR) [7] for fullconnected neural network is such that weight matrix W projects an input vector-image P on the linear subspace generated by vector-prototypes $P^0, \ldots, P^{L-1}$. It is obvious that each prototype is individually stable in such a network. Weight matrix **W** in this method can be obtained in the following way. Let's **P** be the matrix of prototypes as row-vectors, then

$$\mathbf{W} = \mathbf{P^T}(\mathbf{PP^T})^{-1}\mathbf{P}. \tag{5}$$

An additive modification of this method also exists. The method has not been applied to CNAM learning. To adapt it to the local case two above mentioned approaches may be used. The first one, which breaks off unnecessary connections has a number of obvious shortcomings. At first, as mentioned above, there is no guarantee of prototypes individual stability; at second, self-connection weights acquire more dominant values in comparison with fullconnected case [9], which leads to network degeneration and appearance of a great number of spurious patterns.

The second approach, in which neuron neighbourhood is learned as fullconnected network has the following advantages: guarantee of prototypes individual stability and capability of additive learning. It is supposed that $L \leq q/2$ prototypes are stable to distortions by analogy to fullconnected case. Probably, cycles can arise because the weight matrix W is nonsymmetric. Further, exactly this local PLR (LPLR) will be considered since it ensures best characteristics of both modifications.

LPLR provides for each neuron the following set of linear equalities:

$$\langle W_{ij}, D_{ij}^K \rangle = 1 - w_{ij} \geq 0.$$

If a selfconnection weight is equal to 1 ($w_{ij} = 1$), then a corresponding weight vector is zero ($W_{ij} = (0, \ldots, 0)$). So, this neuron keeps its state unchanged in time, i.e. the weight vector being referred to as a *degenerated* one. It is shown [8] that it takes place for prototypes which are not individually stable, and not only in this case.

Remark 1 *The case of degenerate weight vectors is encountered more often than not locally separable prototypes.*

In [9] acceptable characteristics of fullconnected associative memory were obtained up to $L = 0.75N$ prototypes by experimental selection of selfconnection weights. It provides a reason to suppose that by similar way a value $L \leq 0.75q$ can be achieved in LPLR.

Remark 2 *In the case when all vectors (p_{ij}^K, W_{ij}^K), $K = 0, \ldots, L-1$, are mutually orthogonal, the weight vectors (w_{ij}, W_{ij}) obtained by Hebb's rule are proportional to ones obtained by LPLR.*

3.3 Eigenstructure Method

Eigenstructure method [10] was proposed only for learning fullconnected neural network given by a system of first order differential equations of the form

$$\dot{x} = -Bx + TSat(x) + J, \tag{6}$$

where $x \in R^N$ is the state vector, $\dot{x}$ denotes the derivative of x with respect to time t, $B = diag[b_1, \ldots, b_N]$ with $b_i > 0$ for $i = 1, \ldots, N$, T is the real $N \times N$ connection matrix, $J = [J_1, \ldots, J_N]^T \in R^N$ is a bias vector, $Sat(x) = (Sat_1(x_1), \ldots, Sat_N(x_N))^T$ represents the activation function, where

$$Sat_i(x_i) = \begin{cases} 1, & x_i > 1 \\ x_i, & -1 \leq x_i \leq 1 \\ -1, & x_i < -1. \end{cases} \tag{7}$$

Later this method was adapted in [11] for learning of CNAM (*sparse method*). For representing a cellular neural network a index $N \times N$ matrix S was introduced, where $S_{ij} = 1$ or 0 depending on the existence of a connection between i-th and j-th neurons. Interconnection matrix T in this case looks like $T = T|S = [h_{ij}]$, where $h_{ij} = t_{ij}$ if $S_{ij} = 1$, and $h_{ij} = 0$ otherwise. It was shown in [8] that the sparse method is obtained by the second approach applied to eigenstructure method, its complexity increased as compared to fullconnected case.

Here, eigenstructure method is described for fullconnected neural network because it is easier to analyze than the sparse method, and nonetheless contains all its ideas. Suppose L vectors $P^0, \ldots, P^{L-1}$ are given which are to be stored in neural network. Then the following should be done.

1) Choose vectors $\beta^K = (\beta_1^K, \ldots, \beta_N^K)$ and a diagonal matrix B with positive diagonal elements such that $\beta_i^K P_i^K > 1$ and $B(\beta^K)^T = \mu(P^K)^T$ for all $i = 1 \ldots N$ and $K = 0 \ldots L-1$, where $\mu > \max_i\{B_{ii}\}$ such that $B_{jj}\beta_j^K = \mu P_j^K$.

2) Compute the $N \times (L-1)$ matrix:

$$Y = [Y^1, \ldots, Y^{L-1}] = [(P^0 - P^{L-1})^T, \ldots, (P^{L-2} - P^{L-1})^T]. \tag{8}$$

3) Perform a singular value decomposition of $Y = U\Sigma V^T$, where U and V are unitary matrices and Σ is a diagonal matrix with the singular values of Y on its diagonal. Let $U = [u^1, \ldots, u^N]$ and L_Y be equal to the dimension of span $\Omega_Y = \{Y^1, \ldots, Y^{L-1}\}$. From the properties of singular value decomposition it is known that $L_Y = rank(Y)$, $\{u^1, \ldots u^{L_Y}\}$ is an orthonormal basis of Ω_Y, and $\{u^1, \ldots, u^N\}$ is an orthonormal basis of R^N.

4) Compute

$$T^+ = [T_{ij}^+] = \sum_{K=1}^{L_Y} u^K (u^K)^T, \text{ and } T^- = [T_{ij}^-] = \sum_{K=L_Y+1}^{N} u^K (u^K)^T. \qquad (9)$$

5) Choose a positive value for the parameter τ an compute

$$T = \mu T^+ - \tau T^- \quad J = \mu (P^{L-1})^T - T(P^{L-1})^T. \qquad (10)$$

This method ensures individual and asymptotical (in the sense of differential equations theory) stability of stored patterns. Parameters μ and τ influence on the network stability to pattern distortions. Their values can be chosen randomly or by experimental way according to the following reason. Formula (9) is identical to that of Hebb's rule. Because all u^K are mutually orthonormal, and taking into account the remark 2, matrices T^+ and T^- are regarded as projectors of R^N on appropriate subspaces. From their properties the following equality

$$T^- = E - T^+ \qquad (11)$$

is obtained, where E is identity matrix. Taking (11) into account, (10) becomes $T = (\mu + \tau)T^+ - \tau E$, i.e. T is proportional to the matrix W from PLR with desaturating selfconnection weights. Consequently, the following suggestion may be done: the eigenstructure method with appropriate (experimental) choice of parameters μ and τ can store approximately $L \le 0.75q$ prototypes in the local case, since it is true for LPLR.

In the local case the obtained weight matrix T is a nonsymmetric one unlike that in fullconnected network, but in [12] the algorithm allowing to transform a matrix T into a symmetric form (if it is possible) is suggested. Also there exists [13] an additive modification of eigenstructure method. It can be noticed that calculation complexity of this method is high.

4 CNAM Learning

4.1 Perceptron Learning Rule

Perceptron learning rule [14] was adapted for a local case in the following way [15]. Let the prototypes $P^0, \ldots, P^{L-1}$ that must be stored in CNAM be given. From them an infinite sequence $P^0, \ldots, P^{L-1}, P^0, \ldots, P^{L-1}, P^0, \ldots$ obtained from the initial set of prototypes by its recycling is organized, and a through numbering of them is introduced, i.e. a chain of patterns

$$\{P^{(t)} \mid P^{(t)} = P^S \text{ at } t \equiv S \pmod{L}\}$$

is formed. Initial values of vector components W_{ij}^0 are chosen arbitrarily for all (i, j) (selfconnection weight $w_{ij} = 0$).

Then the weight vectors are updated according to the following iterative procedure for each (i, j):

$$W_{ij}^{t+1} = \begin{cases} W_{ij}^t & \text{if } \langle D_{ij}^{(t)}, W_{ij}^t \rangle > 0, \\ W_{ij}^t + D_{ij}^{(t)} & \text{otherwise.} \end{cases} \tag{12}$$

Calculation stops if the weight vectors don't change during one *macroiteration* (it is the learning period during which all L prototypes were input to the CNAM). It is shown [15] that this procedure converges in a finite number of iterations if initial prototypes are locally separable. In such a case, all prototypes are individually stable in the taught CNAM.

The described method is very easy, it guarantees the individual stability of prototypes, and, besides, their number L can be greater than neuron connection number q. But because there are no selfconnection weights in the taught CNAM it has a bad stability to pattern distortions and a great number of cycles.

Perceptron learning rule was also used for learning CNAM with selfconnections [19]. It was done by replacing the notations W_{ij} and D_{ij}^K by (w_0, W_{ij}) and $(1, D_{ij}^K)$, respectively. In this case there are no limitation on a set of stored prototypes; all of them being individually stable, due to the fact that selfconnection weights increase very fast during learning process. The disadvantage is that this leads to bad stability to distortions and to a great number of spurious memories.

4.2 Learning Method With Parameters

In [15] new learning method based on the idea of perceptron learning rule was elaborated. It provides the increase of the stability to distortions as compared with the above method and the reduction number of cycle states because of selfconnection weights calculation [17]. The main idea of proposed method is as follows. It is known that the greater the values

$$m_{ij}^K = \langle D_{ij}^K, W_{ij} \rangle,$$

in a CNAM, the better the network recognizes prototype distortions [16]. Perceptron learning rule guarantees in the case of learning process convergence $m_{ij}^K > 0$ $\forall (i, j)$, $\forall K = 0, \ldots, L - 1$, i.e. individual stability of prototypes only. If it is possible to obtain $m_{ij}^K > \alpha_{ij} > 0$, then some level of stability to distortions can be guaranteed, and, besides, the greater is the value of such α_{ij}, the better is CNAM stability. How can $m_{ij}^K > \alpha_{ij}$ be obtained? One of the obvious solutions is as follows: during the learning process in (12) the scalar product should be compared not with zero but with this α_{ij}. If such learning procedure converges then the needed inequality is achieved.

Remark 3 *In [15] it is shown that learning process with parameters α_{ij} converges in finite number of iterations, if stored prototypes are locally separable.*

Based on the above idea a method which iteratively increases the learning parameters α_{ij} is as follows. As in the perceptron learning rule the prototypes $P^0, \ldots, P^{L-1}$, which are to be stored in CNAM, are organized in an infinite sequence with a through numbering. Initial values of vector components W_{ij}^0 are chosen arbitrarily for all (i, j) (selfconnection weight $w_{ij} = 0$), the learning parameter $\alpha_{ij}^0 = 0$, $\tau = 0$ is the counter of macroiterations.

1. Macroiteration begins by setting $\mu_{ij}^\tau(t) = \infty$; the next step for the whole initial set of prototypes is executed.

2. The weight vectors are changed according to the following iterative procedure for each neuron (i, j):

$$
W_{ij}^{t+1} = \begin{cases} W_{ij}^t & \text{if } \langle D_{ij}^{(t)}, W_{ij}^t \rangle > \alpha_{ij}^\tau, \\ W_{ij}^t + D_{ij}^{(t)} & \text{otherwise.} \end{cases}
$$

$$
\mu_{ij}^\tau(t+1) = \min(\mu_{ij}^\tau(t), \langle D_{ij}^{(t)}, W_{ij}^t \rangle),
$$

3. If the stop condition is not met, then the new learning parameter is calculated by the following formula:

$$
\alpha_{ij}^{\tau+1} = \max(\alpha_{ij}^\tau, \mu_{ij}^\tau(t)),
$$

and go to item 1. If the stop condition is met and the weight vectors rest unchanged during the macroiteration, the calculation stops; if the weight vectors were changed, then go to item 1.

Let us note some properties of the above method. At some first macroiterations it coincide with perceptron learning rule as $\alpha_{ij}^0 = 0$, which provides individual stability of stored patterns. Further, learning stability to distortions is increased: $m_{ij}^K > \alpha_{ij}$, where $\alpha_{ij} > 0$ is the last learning parameter before algorithm stops.

Let's consider, now, the stop conditions of this algorithm. The greater is the number of macroiterations performed, the greater are m_{ij}^K values. The latter largely depend on the weight vector length, which increases during the learning. And, besides, the relative values $m_{ij}^K / \|W_{ij}\|$ may slightly change, so either experimental selection of learning time depending on the number of neuron neighbours q, or watching on the grows of the relative values $m_{ij}^K / \|W_{ij}\|$ is needed. It can be noticed, that there is no need to select the learning time for a new set of prototypes, if neuron neighbourhood is not changed. Tests of some models have shown that the above method provides a good level of m_{ij}^K optimization even when the number of macroiterations is 2-3 times greater than it is necessary for perceptron learning rule convergence.

This method produces CNAM without selfconnections, and though the number of cycles was reduced as compared with the basic method, still it is large enough. So it was decided to introduce the selfconnection after a successful end of learning [15,17]. This allows to get rid of cycles almost completely: during the simulations cycles occurred only when neighbourhood of two prototypes differs in state of one neighbour only.

Remark 4 *In such a case this two prototypes can't be stable to 1-distortions [18] (pattern P is a k-distortion of prototype P^K if they differ in states at most of k neighbours at each neuron neighbourhood).*

The proposed method inherits such properties of perceptron learning rule as its simplicity, and the guarantee of individual stability of prototypes (they are to be locally separable). Moreover it provides stability to distortions of stored patterns and small number of cycles.

This method provides

$$\min_K \langle D_{ij}^K, W_{ij} \rangle \to \max. \tag{13}$$

As compared with LPLR where all $\langle D_{ij}^K, W_{ij} \rangle = const$, it can be confirmed that this constant is equal to the maximum in (13) with an accuracy of a coefficient in the case when weight vector is not degenerate. So the weight vectors for both methods is said to be almost the same.

¿From above the following suggestion can be made about recommended number of stored patters. Since there exists an analogy between the proposed method and LPLR with desaturated selfconnection weights, so $L \leq 0.75q$ is good estimation for number L of stored patterns, though it is possible to store a greater number of prototypes. By this, there is no need to select the learning time for each set of stored patterns, it is enough to do it once for each pair L and q.

4.3 New Synthesis Approach

In [19] new approach to CNAM synthesis based also on the idea of perceptron learning rule was suggested. A model of the network to be learned coincides exactly with the one described in Sect.3.3. In this method selfconnection weights are determined during the learning process, which when the bias vector J is equal to zero looks as follows. Weight vectors (w_0, W_{ij}) have been obtained by perceptron learning rule using vectors $(1, D_{ij}^K)$. After that an arbitrary matrix $B = diag[b_1, \ldots, b_N]$ with $b_i > 0$ is chosen. The same is done for $l \neq r$ $T_{lr} = w_k$ for corresponding values k, l and r, and $T_{ll} = w_0 + b_l \mu_l$ with $\mu_l > 1$. By this, from the requirements of stable states being bipolar and of stability to 1-distortions, it was proved that optimal value of obtained selfconnection weight T_{ll} should be equal to b_l.

Consequently, the selfconnection weight w_0 obtained by perceptron learning rule, should be less than zero. This may be achieved as follows: if perceptron learning rule ends up with $w_0 \geq 0$ for some neuron (i, j), then this weight is replaced by a value which is less than zero, and the training is continued. It is proved in [19] that for prototypes which are locally separable such a training always ends up with $w_0 < 0$. Experimental tests showed that the suggested

Methods	Storage capability	Stability to distortions	Cycles	Method property
Hebb's rule	$L \leq 0.14q$	no guarantee	no cycles if $w_0 > 0$	additive
Eigenstruc. method	no limit	$L \leq 0.75q$	no cycles	matrix transform. additive
LPLR	no limit	$L \leq 0.5q$	cycles possible	additive
Perceptron	local separable	no guarantee	too many	iterative
Method [15]	local separable	$L \leq 0.75q$	cycles possible	iterative
Method [19]	local separable	$L \leq 0.75q$	no cycles	iterative

Table 1. Table of summaries characteristics of described CNAM learning methods.

method has a less number of spurious patterns, as compared with eigenstructure method, and, consequently, has the better stability to distortions.

The stability to distortions of this method can be explained as follows: weight vector (w_0, W_{ij}) being obtained by perceptron learning rule with selfconnection satisfies the inequality $\langle W_{ij}, D_{ij}^K \rangle > -w_0 > 0$. Hence, the selfconnection weight has the same significance, as the learning parameter from [15]. In [19] selfconnection weight value w_0 influence on the stability to distortions isn't investigated, it is considered that being less than zero is sufficient. Therefore, the stability to distortions in this method is not permanent, being different for each learning process even for the same set of prototypes, depending on a selfconnection weight value. Though it possible to obtain optimal value of selfconnection weight w_0 using the idea of learning method [15], therefore weight vectors W_{ij} can be the same as in the method mentioned above.

Unfortunately, it is very difficult to compare theoretically the choice of self-connection weight values obtained by this method and that of [17]. So the experimental inspection is needed. Connection weight matrix T obtained by this method is nonsymmetric, therefore the algorithm like that of for eigenstructure method [12] was suggested which allows to transform a matrix T to a symmetric form (if it is possible).

5 Analysis of Methods

It is useful after learning methods description to adduce the table of its generalized characteristics and properties as related to basic requirements (i) – (iii). The following suggestions based on the common features of different methods was made during the process of its analysis.

1) Though all matrix (LPLR, eigenstructure method) methods guarantee the individual stability of any set of patterns, weight vectors degenerate in the case when prototypes are not locally separable. Then such neurons have states unchangeable in time, consequently many spurious patterns can arise. Moreover it was noticed that degeneration of weight vectors can arise and in the case of locally separable patterns. Hence, it follows that matrix methods of CNAM synthesis ensuring the fulfillment of system of equalities possess less capability on information storing as compared with the iterative learning methods ensuring the fulfillment of inequality system.

2) The comparison of different methods allows to make some suggestions about the stability of CNAM to stored pattern distortions. If the statement for LPLR ($L \leq 0.5q$) about the number of stored patterns is true, then it is possible to predict the recommended number of stored patterns in the methods which are close to it from the point of view the stability to distortions (i.e. eigenstructure method, method [15]). Though the method [15] allows to store more individually stable patterns.

3) The stability to distortions for method [19] is explained by similarity with the learning parameter α^τ from [15], which enables to improve resulting characteristics of the method.

6 Conclusion

Currently known methods of CNAM synthesis and learning are compared. It is shown that the condition of local separability of stored patterns have a great significance for all methods. The common features for such methods as LPLR, eigenstructure method and method with parameters [15] were found. This allows to transfer certain important characteristics among the methods, and to do some assumptions about their capability to store patterns. Also the influence of learning parameters in eigenstructure method and selfconnection weights in the new synthesis approach [19] on the CNAM stability is investigated, and recommendations on their choice are given.

References

1. Leon O.Chua. CNN: a Paradigm for Complexity. World Scientific, Series on Nonlinear Science, Vol.31.
2. O.L.Bandman. Cellular-Neural Computations, Formal Model and Possible Applications. Lecture Notes in Computer Science, 964, 1995, p.21–35.
3. J.J. Hopfield, D.W.Tank. Computing with Neural Circuits: a Model. Science, Vol.233, 1986, p. 625.
4. J.Zhang, Li Zhang, D.Yan, A.He, L.Liu. Local Interconnection Neural Network and its Optical Implementation. Optics Communication, Vol.102, 1993, pp.13–20.
5. H.Harrer, J.A.Nossek. Discrete-time Cellular Neural Networks. Int. j. c. th. appl. 20, 453 (1992).

6. E.Pessa, C.Palma, M.Penna. Cellular Neural Networks for Realizing Associative Memories. Proceedings of the Second Conference on Cellular Automata for Research and Industry, Milan, Italy, 16-18 October 1996, pp. 127-134.
7. L.Perzonas, I.Guyon, G.Dreyfus. Collective Computational Properties of Neural Networks: New Learning Mechanism. Physical Review, A, vol 34, November, 1986,p. 4217 – 4228.
8. S.G.Pudov. Cellular-Neural Associative Memory Learning. Master's Thesis in Mathematics (Novosibirsk State University, 1997).
9. D.O.Gorodnichy. Desaturating Coefficient for Projection Learning Rule. Lecture Notes in Computer Science, 1112, 1996, p.469 – 476.
10. J.Li, A.N.Michel, W.Porod. Analysis and Synthesis of a Class of Neural Networks: Linear Systems Operating on a Closed Hypercube. IEEE Transactions on Circuits and Systems, v.36, N.11, 1989, p.1405–1422.
11. D.Liu, A.N.Michel. Sparsely Interconnected Neural Networks for Associative Memories With Applications to Cellular Neural Networks. IEEE Transactions on Circuits and Systems – II: Analog and Digital Signal Processing, v.41, N.4, 1994, p. 295–307.
12. A.Michel,K.Wang, D.Liu, H.Ye. Qualitative Limitations Incurred in Implementations of Recurrent Neural Networks. IEEE Control Systems, June 1995, pp.52–65.
13. G.Yen, A.N.Michel. A Learning and Forgetting Algorithm in Associative Memories: The Eigenstructure Method. IEEE Transactions on Circuit and Systems-II: Analog and Digital Signal Processing, vol.39, pp. 212–225, Apr.1992.
14. F.Rosenblatt. Principles of Neurodynamics. Washington, Spartan, 1959.
15. S.G.Pudov. Cellular-Neural Associative Memory Learning. Optoelectronics, Instrumentation and Data Processing, 2, 1997, pp.98–110.
16. M.Cottrell. Stability and Attractivity in Associative Memory Networks. Biological Cybernetics 58, 1988, p. 129–139.
17. S.G.Pudov. Influence of Self-Connection Weights on Cellular-Neural Network Stability. Lecture Notes in Computer Science, 1277, p.76-82.
18. O.L.Bandman, S.G.Pudov. Stability of stored patterns in cellular-neural associative memory. Bulletin of the Novosibirsk Computer Center. Series: Computer Science, issue 4, 1996, p. 1–16.
19. D.Liu, Z.Lu. A New Synthesis Approach for Feedback Neural Networks Based on the Perceptron Training Algorithm. IEEE Trans. Neural Networks, Vol.8, pp.1468–1482, Nov.1997.

Emergence and Propagation of Round Autowave in Cellular Neural Network

A.V.Selikhov

Supercomputer Software Department
ICMMG of Siberian Branch
Russian Academy of Sciences
Akad. Lavrentiev ave., 6, Novosibirsk, 630090, Russia
tel: +7 3832 343994, fax: +7 3832 324259
E-mail: selikhov@ssd.sscc.ru

Abstract. In this paper, some results of investigation of a round autowave emerging and propagating in two-layer Cellular Neural Network (CNN) are presented. The round autowave is initiated by one cell. Cell phase plane properties and their influence on the autowave emergence process are considered. On the base of theoretical investigation of two-cell communication, required conditions for the autowave emergence in two CNN types are suggested. Simulating results in form of characteristic dependencies for two types of the autowave process, namely for traveling front and traveling pulse, are presented.

1 Introduction

Autowaves are objects of investigation in various disciplines. They represent oscillations in active media, which have constant properties (amplitude, waveform and other) without external supply. Autowaves may be considered as basic processes for more complex ones because they are rather simple and inherent for many complex systems.

In spite of the maturity of the partial differential equations theory used as a background for mathematical models of autowaves, there are a number of problems concerning computer realization of such models. In this connection other approaches deserve much attention, particularly those ones, which allow to obtain processes *similar* to real autowaves. Among such approaches, application of Cellular Neural Networks (CNN) may be of considerable interest.

As a formal model, CNN was first introduced in [1] and was headed for development of image processing VLSI circuits. Further investigations showed, that many complex processes such as autowaves [2, 3], chaotic [4] and stable structure [5] emergence processes can be observed in CNNs.

Though much attention is paid to investigation of various complex processes in CNNs, up-to-day there are no methods for obtaining CNN parameters required for realization of a desirable distributed dynamic process. Deep study of CNN properties may become a first step to such methods construction. In this connection the purpose of this work is to investigate properties of two simplest autowave processes, namely, traveling front and traveling pulse, emerging and propagating in a two-layer CNN and initiated by one-cell state change (one-cell initial condition). Traveling pulse and traveling front may be considered as simplest basic processes being a background for more complex ones. Besides that, a choice of one-cell state change as initial condition for the autowaves emergence allows to study the emergence of autowave in CNN in more detail and to determine a possibility to control this process.

The paper contains five sections. In the next one, the formal representation of the CNN under investigation will be presented on the base of general CNN formalism. The third section is devoted to peculiarities of the CNN cell phase plane. In the forth section, an autowave emergence required conditions are proposed and discussed for two types of CNNs differing in properties of cell phase planes. The fifth section contains some results of computer simulation of the autowave processes.

2 CNN Formal Representation

Cellular Neural Network is a 1-, 2- or 3-dimensional lattice, which has cells placed in its nodes. Generally, each cell is described by an external *input* $u \in R^u$, a *bias* $z \in R^u$, a *state* $x \in R^x$, an *output* $y \in R^y$. In this paper, it is assumed that z is a constant and all other variables are functions of continuous time t. Each cell has weighted connections with cells in its *neighbourhood*. Configuration of the neighbourhood is defined by a neighbourhood template and used for each CNN cell. The size of neighbourhood is defined by the neighbourhood radius r and contains 3×3 cells when $r=1$, 5×5 cells when $r=2$ and so on. CNN can operate either in discrete or in continuous time.

CNN with identical cells has a general cell state equation

$$\frac{dx_W}{dt} = f(x_W, y_W, z_W, u_W) \tag{1}$$

where w is a spatial coordinate vector of each CNN cell. In the following, it will be omitted for simplicity.

Each component of the cell output vector $y = [y_1, y_2, \ldots, y_n]$ is usually defined as nonlinear function of the corresponding state variable x_k, i.e.

$$y_k = g(x_k) \tag{2}$$

where $k = 1, \ldots, n$.

Accordingly, each CNN cell described by a state variable vector $x = [x_1, x_2, \ldots, x_n]$ may be represented as a set of interconnected *neurons*, each of which is described by the state equation

$$\frac{dx_k}{dt} = f_k(x_k, z_k, u_k, y_k) \tag{3}$$

where $k = 1, \ldots, n$, and by the output equation (2). In the state equation (3), vectors u_k and y_k contain values of their own inputs u'_k and outputs y'_k and values of inputs $\mathbf{u}_m''$ and outputs $\mathbf{y}_m''$ of its neighbour neurons, i.e. $\mathbf{u}_k = u_k' \cup \mathbf{u}_m''$, $\mathbf{y}_k = y_k' \cup \mathbf{y}_m''$. Here $m = 1, \ldots, n$ and the neighbourhood configuration and size are defined by corresponding neighbourhood template.

The above general CNN representation allows to underline some CNN features, which define a possibility of more detailed approach to complex process realization in CNN. First, the CNN definition is based on two laws: the state evolution law of isolated cell and the intercell communication law. Second, each cell may be defined as a set of communicating neurons, each of which represents separate nonlinear component of the whole system. The last feature results in decomposition of the CNN into a set of *layers*, where the number of layers corresponds to the number of system components and to the number of cell state variables $x_1, \ldots, x_n$, respectively.

Let us denote neighbourhood template matrices as $\mathbf{A}_{km}$ and $\mathbf{B}_{km}$ which determine connection weights between the neuron in k-th layer and its neighbours' outputs and inputs in m-th layer respectively. When a distributed process is realized in CNN, elements of the matrix $\mathbf{A}$ obviously play the role of diffusion coefficients between k-th and m-th layers of the CNN (and also between neurons in the same layer when $m=k$). Similarly, elements of the matrix $\mathbf{B}_{km}$ can reflect the value of external influence on the neurons of each layer (i.e. on each component of the whole system separately). The form of matrix $\mathbf{A}_{km}$ in accordance with the role of elements corresponds to Laplacian operator ∇^2. Hence, defining diffusion coefficients between neurons of k-th and m-th layer as D_{km}, $k, m = 1, \ldots, n$, connections of each k-th layer neuron with those of m-th layer are represented by a neighbourhood template in the form of matrix

$$\mathbf{A}_{km} = D_{km}\nabla^2 = \begin{pmatrix} 0 & D_{km} & 0 \\ D_{km} & -4D_{km} & D_{km} \\ 0 & D_{km} & 0 \end{pmatrix}. \tag{4}$$

Thus, the general equation, which define the state evolution of a neuron in k-th layer may be written as follows

$$\frac{d\mathbf{x}_k}{dt} = f(x_k, z_k, u_k', y_k') + \sum_m \mathbf{A}_{km}' \mathbf{y}_m'' + \sum_m \mathbf{B}_{km}' \mathbf{u}_m'' \tag{5}$$

where $\mathbf{A}_{km}'$ and $\mathbf{B}_{km}'$ are vectors obtained from the matrices $\mathbf{A}_{km}$ and $\mathbf{B}_{km}$ in accordance with neighbourhood output and input vectors, the function $f(.)$ in right hand part of the equation defines communications between neurons within a cell and second and third items determine communications between neurons from different cells.

Equations (1), (2) and (5) represent complex CNN structure, which can be easily transformed into a simpler one when the number of variables of each cell is restricted on the base of prior information about the media properties required to realize desirable process. Particularly, it is known [6] that most of autowaves emerge and propagate in active media with strongly pronounced presence of two communicating components, e.g. presence of two communicating agents in chemical reactions.

For two-component systems modeling, the state vector $\mathbf{x} = [x_1, x_2]$ contains two components and, in the absence of external influence ($\mathbf{B}_{km} = 0$), equations (5) are as follows:

$$\begin{cases} \frac{\partial x_1}{\partial t} = F_1(x_1, y_1, y_2, z_1) + D_{11}\nabla^2 y_1 \\ \frac{\partial x_2}{\partial t} = F_2(x_2, y_1, y_2, z_2) + D_{22}\nabla^2 y_2 \end{cases} \tag{6}$$

where variables x_1 and x_2 correspond to the media active components.

The system of equations (6) represents the CNN with each cell consisting of two communicating neurons – a *neuron pair* and the lattice of cells forms a two-layer structure with interneuron communications both within a layer and between them.

The CNN under investigation is a two-dimensional lattice of cells ($\mathbf{w} = [i, j]$) and capable to realize autowaves in 2-dimension space. This CNN is a special case of (6) and yields in the following system of equations

$$\begin{cases} \frac{\partial x_{1,ij}}{\partial t} = -x_{1,ij} + (1 + \mu)y_{1,ij} - sy_{2,ij} + z_1 + D_{11}\nabla^2 y_{1,ij} \\ \frac{\partial x_{2,ij}}{\partial t} = -x_{2,ij} + sy_{1,ij} + (1 + \mu)y_{2,ij} + z_2 + D_{22}\nabla^2 y_{2,ij} \end{cases} \tag{7}$$

where the output value of each neuron is determined by piece-wise linear function

$$y = \frac{1}{2}(|x + 1| - |x - 1|). \tag{8}$$

This function is shown in Fig.1.

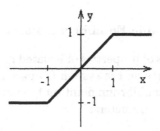

Fig. 1. Piece-wise linear output function

The type of functions $F_1(.)$ and $F_2(.)$ and values of parameters μ, z_1, z_2 required to obtain useful CNN properties were determined in [3], where they were applied to generate various autowave processes (such as vortex, concentric waves and spirals) involving initial change of more than one cell states. To study the process of emergence and propagation of a single round autowave initiated by one-cell state change, these values of parameters had been previously studied from the viewpoint of its ability for realization of the process in CNN and accepted as a background for the investigation.

3 Neuron Pair Phase Plane Properties

Analysis of the isolated neuron pair evolution law may be done on the base of properties investigation of the neuron pair phase plane formed by the state variables x_1 and x_2. The piece-wise linear function being used (8) divides the phase plane onto nine linear regions where methods of qualitative analysis of phase plane trajectories and equilibrium points may be applied. In this case, an additional characteristic appears for each equilibrium point on the phase plane, namely, the equilibrium point is called "real" if it belongs to its own region and that one called "virtual" if it belongs to any other region. The virtuality of equilibrium point in a certain region doesn't change qualitatively its influence on the neuron pair state trajectory in this region. In [3] it is shown that each region of the neuron pair (7) phase plane contains a single (real or virtual) equilibrium point.

Analysis of the system (7) presented in [4] for $z_1 = z_2 = 0$ showed the presence of isolated closed limit trajectory (limit cycle) on the isolated neuron pair phase plane. Non-zero values of these biases lead to the change of the position of trajectory and equilibrium points on the phase plane. Therefore it is possible to set up such values of z_1 and z_2 that two equilibrium points become superposed. In the CNN represented by (7) it is possible to make one or two such superpositions. In both cases, considered below, a real stable equilibrium point is superposed onto a virtual unstable one. Because the number of real stable equilibrium points on the phase plane in these cases corresponds to the number of superpositions, the two different CNNs under investigation are called "CNN with one stable equilibrium point" and "CNN with two stable equilibrium points" with respect to the number of superpositions.

3.1 CNN with One Stable Equilibrium Point

Being based on the analysis of properties of isolated neuron pair phase plane and on the properties dependence on the system (7) parameters, construction of the CNN with one real stable equilibrium point on the phase plane is determined by the following values of the parameters:

$$\mu = 0.7, \quad s = 1.0, \quad z_1 = -0.2, \quad z_2 = 0.3 \tag{9}$$

In this case the neuron pair phase plane contains also one real unstable equilibrium point with coordinates $(-0.11, -0.28)$ in the linear region $R^{l,l} = \{(x_1, x_2) : -1 < x_1 < 1, -1 < x_2 < 1\}$. All other equilibrium points are virtual ones, however their positions also define trajectory direction. The real equilibrium point has coordinates $(-2.9, 1.0)$ and is denoted as P in Fig.2.

The presence of one stable equilibrium point and the limit trajectory L, which converge to this point on the phase plane defines an existence of a traveling pulse as a single possible type of autowave. Here, as a traveling pulse we consider an oscillating process propagating from the wave source to CNN boundaries, when the state of each neuron pair begins its motion on the phase plane from

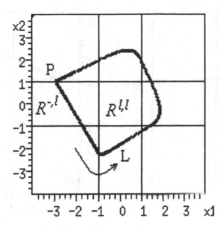

Fig. 2. The phase plane of neuron pair with one stable equilibrium point

the equilibrium point and then moves along the limit trajectory L to the same equilibrium point.

3.2 CNN with Two Stable Equilibrium Points

Similarly with the case of CNN having one equilibrium point, construction of the CNN with two stable equilibrium points on the phase plane of an isolated neuron pair is defined by the following parameters of (7):

$$\mu = 0.7, \quad s = 1.0, \quad z_1 = -0.3, \quad z_2 = 0.3 \tag{10}$$

As in the case of phase plane with one stable equilibrium point, the phase plane with two stable equilibrium points contains one real unstable equilibrium point with coordinates $(-0.06, -0.34)$ in the linear region $R^{l,l}$. All other equilibrium points are virtual ones, but their positions also define the trajectory direction. The two real stable equilibrium points P_1 and P_2 have coordinates $(-3.0, 1.0)$ and $(-1.0, -2.4)$, respectively.

The presence of two stable equilibrium points defines an existence of two limit trajectories L_1 and L_2 converging to these points. According to this, a transition of the neuron pair state from one stable equilibrium point to another one along the limit trajectory and propagation of this transition from the wave source to CNN boundaries defines the traveling front. Since the mutual influence of communicating neuron pairs leads to the changes of coordinates of all equilibrium points on the phase plane, it is possible for one or both real equilibrium points to become virtual (the changes of coordinates of equilibrium points don't influence on their stability). In the case when only one stable real equilibrium point becomes virtual, an emergence of traveling pulse becomes possible. Here the traveling pulse assumed to be a distributed process similar to that of the CNN with one stable equilibrium point. The phase plane of the CNN with two stable equilibrium points is depicted in Fig.3.

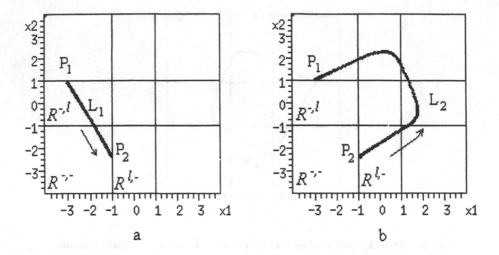

Fig. 3. The phase plane of neuron pair with two real stable equilibrium points

4 Autowave Emergence Conditions

4.1 CNN with One Stable Equilibrium Point

Emergence of any distributed process in CNNs requires to consider intercell communications determined by a communication law and dynamical properties of CNN cells.

Since the autowave under investigation is generated by the state change of one neuron pair, called "central" for simplicity, the emergence process may be assumed identical for all four directions determined by neuron pair connections. Hence, it is sufficient to consider only one direction and only for two neuron pairs, respectively.

Furthermore, since the initial state of all neuron pairs but the central one corresponds to equilibrium point P (see Fig.2), and beginning of the motion along the limit trajectory L on the phase plane corresponds to a neuron pair transition to instability region $R^{-,l} = \{(x_1, x_2) : x_1 < -1, -1 < x_2 < 1\}$ (i.e. the region where the state of neuron pair moves away from the stable equilibrium point), the emergence condition for a traveling pulse in this CNN may be defined as a necessity to shift the state of each neuron pair (placed on the way of traveling pulse propagation) to the instability region $R^{-,l}$.

Let us denote the central neuron pair as C_a and one of its neighbour neuron pairs as C_N. Then C_N state equations (7) which have the parameters values (9) looks as follows:

$$\begin{cases} \frac{\partial x_{1,N}}{\partial t} = -x_{1,N} + 1.7y_{1,N} - y_{2,N} + z_{1,N} + \\ \qquad + D_{11}(y_{1,a} + y_{1,\alpha} + y_{1,\beta} + y_{1,\gamma} - 4y_{1,N}) \\ \frac{\partial x_{2,N}}{\partial t} = -x_{2,N} + y_{1,N} + 1.7y_{2,N} + z_{2,N} + \\ \qquad + D_{22}(y_{2,a} + y_{2,\alpha} + y_{2,\beta} + y_{2,\gamma} - 4y_{2,N}) \end{cases} \qquad (11)$$

The neuron pair C_N being in equilibrium state has output values $y_{i,N}$ equal to $y_{i,\alpha}$, $y_{i,\beta}$, $y_{i,\gamma}$, $i = 1, 2$ of three neuron pairs from its neighbourhood, which are also in equilibrium state. Since the state of C_N is not equal only to the state of C_a, the equations (11) may take the following form:

$$\begin{cases} \frac{\partial x_{1,N}}{\partial t} = -x_{1,N} + 1.7y_{1,N} - y_{2,N} + z_{1,N} + D_{11}(y_{1,a} - y_{1,N}) \\ \frac{\partial x_{2,N}}{\partial t} = -x_{2,N} + y_{1,N} + 1.7y_{2,N} + z_{2,N} + D_{22}(y_{2,a} - y_{2,N}) \end{cases} \tag{12}$$

For the neuron pair C_N, an emergence of instability defined by shifting to the region $R^{-,l}$ may be determined by the following inequality:

$$\frac{\partial x_{2,N}}{\partial t} < 0 \tag{13}$$

So, it is necessary to find the required value of $y_{a,2}$.

Let us rewrite the second equation of the system (12) in accordance with the inequality (13):

$$-x_{2,N} + y_{1,N} + 1.7y_{2,N} + z_{2,N} + D_{22}(y_{2,a} - y_{2,N}) < 0$$

Relative to the desired value $y_{a,2}$ it looks as follows:

$$y_{2,a} < \frac{1}{D_{22}}(x_{2,N} - y_{1,N} - (1.7 - D_{22})y_{2,N} - z_{2,N})$$

Substitution of the values $x_{1,N} = -2.9$, $y_{1,N} = -1.0$, $x_{2,N} = 1.0$ and $y_{2,N} = 1.0$ results in

$$y_{2,a} < \frac{1}{D_{22}}(1 + 1 - (1.7 - D_{22}) - 0.3)$$

or

$$y_{2,a} < 1 \tag{14}$$

The inequality (14) represents the required condition for traveling pulse emergence in the CNN represented by the system (7) with parameters (9) and with one stable equilibrium point on the neuron pair phase plane.

4.2 CNN with Two Stable Equilibrium Points

As in the case discribed above, it is assumed, that all neuron pairs in the CNN, except the central one, have the state placed in stable equilibrium point P_1 (see Fig.3.). It is also assumed that the consideration of only two connected neuron pairs is sufficient, namely the central neuron pair and the one from its neighbourhood.

It is necessary for emergence of traveling front to make possible the transition of the state of each neuron pair from the point P_1 to point P_2 (all the following is similar for the transition from P_2 to P_1). This transition corresponds to the first limit trajectory L_1 (see Fig.3a.) and is possible as a result of a smallest shift of the neuron pair state to the instability region $R^{-,l}$. Generally speaking, for both the CNN with one stable equilibrium point and for the CNN with two ones, the emergence of propagating autowave requires shifting of a neuron pair state from a stable equilibrium point to an instability region. Therefore, (14) represents the required condition for emergence of both autowaves under consideration.

In CNN with two stable equilibrium points, emergence of traveling pulse is possible only in the case when the stable equilibrium point P_2 becomes virtual, i.e. it shifts to the region $R^{l,-} = \{(x_{1,N}, x_{2,N}) : -1 < x_{1,N} < 1\}$, while the neuron pair state passes by. This may be achieved by shifting the coordinate $x_{1,N}$ of the stable equilibrium point P_2 belonging to region $R^{-,-} = \{(x_{1,N}, x_{2,N}) : x_{1,N} \leq -1; x_{2,N} \leq -1\}$, to the region $R^{l,-}$. Since the equalities $y_{1,N} = -1$ and $y_{2,N} = -1$ are satisfied in the region $R^{-,-}$, according to (12) we have:

$$x_{1,N} = -1.7 + 1 - 0.3 + D_1(y_{1,a} - y_{1,N})$$

Transition of the equilibrium point P_2 to the region $R^{l,-}$ is defined by inequality

$$-1 + D_1(y_{1,a} - y_{1,N}) > -1.$$

Then

$$D_1(y_{1,a} - y_{1,N}) > 0$$

or

$$y_{1,a} > y_{1,N}$$

Since for all t in the interval $t_0 < t \leq t_{P_2}$ it follows that $y_{1,N} = -1$, where t_0 is the time of starting of the process and the t_{P_2} is the time when the state of neuron pair C_N reaches the equilibrium point P_2, the last inequality may be transformed to the following:

$$y_{1,a} > -1 \tag{15}$$

As a result, inequalities (14) and (15) represent the required conditions, which should be satisfied for the traveling pulse emergence, restrict the set of initial state values of central neuron pair. For both CNN types, obtaining of sufficient conditions for the initial state values on the base of analytical methods seems to be rather difficult because of the CNN peculiarities. In Fig.4, the experimentally obtained region of the central cell state initial values for a certain fixed $D_{11} = D_{22}$ is presented.

5 Simulation Results

Simulation results for both CNN types are obtained using a program model developed by the author. This program model is made for UNIX-compatible operating systems and allows to observe the change of CNN one layer outputs, the state evolution of the required neuron pair, the neuron pair phase plane

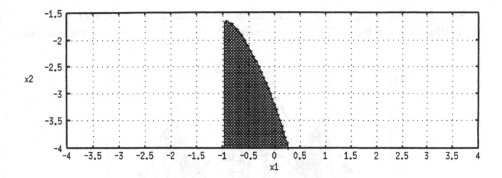

Fig. 4. The initial state values of central neuron pair required for emergence of traveling front in the CNN with two stable equilibrium points

trajectory, and the state changes of a row of neuron pairs. In the program, the Euler numerical algorithm is used. The requirement of rather small Δt for this algorithm determines a great number of iterations and leads to round off accumulation. To avoid this accumulation, the "sensitivity" parameter ϵ for the state variable x_i was used. If the new value of the state variable x_i differs from the previous one more than by ϵ, then x_i is changed, else it remains unchanged. In simulating process, the value $\epsilon = 10^{-7}$ was used. It is assumed that inaccuracy appearing due to this sensitivity restriction has no substantial influence on the simulated process.

The CNN with 149×149 neurons in each layer was simulated. Initially, all neuron pair states were set up in the equilibrium point $P = P_1 = (-2.4, 1.0)$ except the central neuron pair with coordinates $(75, 75)$ which was set up in the initial state corresponding to the emergence condition for desired autowave type in each of two CNNs under investigation. The CNN parameters were stated in accordance with (9) and (10). The value $\Delta t = 0.05$ was chosen corresponding to values $D_{11} = D_{22} = [0.005, \ldots, 5.0]$ and a well known correlation $\Delta t \leq \frac{1}{4D}$ was used. The fon-Newman boundary conditions were used.

The investigation of the process of autowave emergence and propagation in the CNN was aimed to determine the following process characteristics:

1. The autowave form dependence on the diffusion coefficient value;
2. The autowave speed dependence on the diffusion coefficient value;
3. The result of two autowaves interaction

These investigations were performed for each of two CNN types described above.

5.1 CNN with One Stable Equilibrium Point

As it was mentioned above, the CNN with one stable equilibrium point is capable to realize (for a chosen D range) only a traveling pulse.

The traveling pulse form dependence on the diffusion coefficient $D = D_{11} = D_{22}$ is illustrated in Fig.5 The curves presented are formed by the state x_1 values

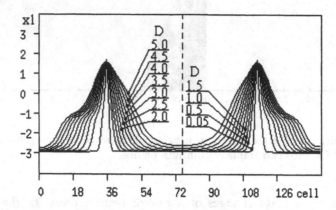

Fig. 5. The traveling pulse form dependence on diffusion coefficient in the CNN with one stable equilibrium point

of the central (75-th) CNN row. The central neuron pair position is marked by a vertical dashed line.

The autowave speed dependence on the diffusion coefficient value is illustrated by the graph in Fig.8a. For construction of this graph, the time (the number of CNN iterations) required for the instability propagation from the central neuron pair to some fixed one was detected. The instability was observed for the state variable x_1. The "line" presented in the same figure allows to estimate a nonlinearity of the curve obtained.

The interaction of two colliding pulses and interaction of these pulses with the CNN boundary are illustrated in Fig.9a. This figure represents the image of CNN first layer outputs. Here, two colliding pulses annihilate and travel through the CNN boundary without any dependence on the values of diffusion coefficients. These properties of autowave in CNN are also typical for real autowave processes.

5.2 CNN with Two Stable Equilibrium Points

CNN with two stable equilibrium points is capable to realize two different autowave types with identical initial conditions and different diffusion coefficient values $D = D_{11} = D_{22}$.

The traveling pulse form dependence on the diffusion coefficient value for this CNN type is shown in Fig.6. When $\Delta t = 0.05$, the emergence of traveling pulse may be observed for $D = [0.025 \ldots 0.225]$. The diffusion coefficient values outlined in the figure are given over equal intervals to emphasize the character of dependence. Besides, more than one traveling pulse may appear at certain value of $D = [0.6 \ldots 0.9]$.

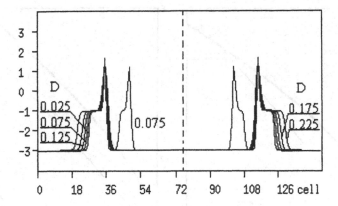

Fig. 6. The autowave form dependence on the diffusion coefficient in CNN with two stable equilibrium points

In Fig.7 the traveling front form dependence on the diffusion coefficient value is illustrated.

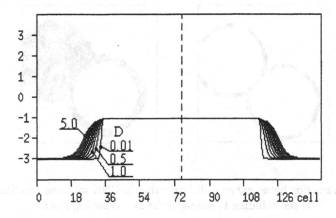

Fig. 7. The traveling front form dependence on diffusion coefficients in CNN with two stable equilibrium points

The autowave speed dependence on the diffusion coefficient is illustrated in Fig.8b. Construction of the graph was made similarly to the case of CNN with one stable equilibrium point.

Interaction of two colliding autowaves in CNN with two stable equilibrium points has properties characterized by the same quality as in CNN with one stable equilibrium point. In Fig.9b, interaction between traveling pulse and traveling front is illustrated.

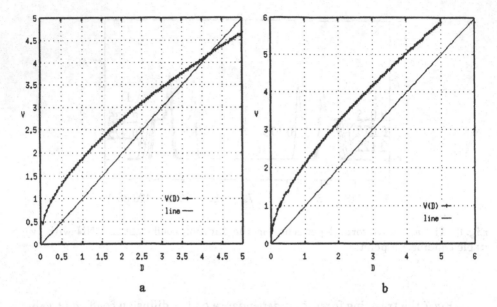

Fig. 8. The autowave speed dependence on the diffusion coefficient value: a – in CNN with one stable equilibrium point, b – in CNN with two equilibrium points

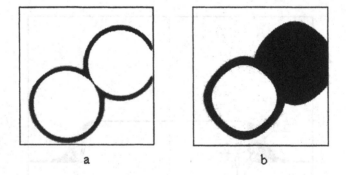

Fig. 9. a – interaction between two colliding pulses in CNN with one equilibrium point; b – interaction between colliding traveling pulse and traveling front

6 Conclusion

In this paper, the emergence and propagating of autowave generated by changing of a single CNN neuron pair state is presented. The neuron pair phase plane properties are studied and their influence on the autowave emergence is discussed. On the base of theoretical investigation of communications between two neuron pairs, the required conditions for emergence of autowaves are obtained for two types of CNN. The computer simulation results for two types of autowaves, namely for traveling front and traveling pulse, are presented and differences between their properties for two different CNN types under investigation are also illustrated.

Since the autowave in the CNNs has a *similarity* to autowaves in real media, application of the CNNs may be considered as an alternative approach to investigation of complex processes. Besides that, an inherent parallelism of the CNN and possibility to realize it as high-performance CNN Universal Machine [8] allows to increase an effectiveness of the computer simulation of complex processes. However, to have the CNN as a useful tool, it is necessary to explore the CNN possibility and construct effective methods of their application.

References

1. L.O.Chua, L.Yang, "Cellular Neural Networks: Theory and Applications", IEEE Transactions on Circuits and Systems, vol.35, pp.1257-1290, 1988.
2. A.P.Munuzuri, V.Perez-Munuzuri, M.Gomez-Gesteira, L.O.Chua and V.Perez-Villar, "Spatiotemporal structures in discretely-coupled arrays of nonlinear circuits: a review", Int. Journal of Bifurcation and Chaos, Vol.5, no.1, pp.17-50, 1995.
3. P.Aerna, S.Baglio, L.Fortuna, G.Manganaro, "Self-Organization in a Two-Layer CNN", IEEE Transactions on Circuits and Systems - Part I, vol.45, no.2, pp.157-163, Feb.1998.
4. F.Zou, J.A.Nossek, "Bifurcation and Chaos in Cellular Neural Networks", IEEE Transactions on Circuits and Systems - Part I, vol.40, pp.166-173, 1993.
5. P.Thiran, K.R.Crounse, G.Setti, "Analytical approach to pattern formation in arrays of coupled systems", International Symp. on Nonlinear Theory and its Applications (NOLTA95), 10-14 Dec. 1995, Las Vegas, USA, pp.465-470.
6. V.A.Vasil'ev, Yu.M.Romanovsky, V.G.Yakhno, Avtovolnovye Processy (Autowave processes), Moscow: Nauka, 1987.
7. L.O.Chua (editor), Special Issue on Nonlinear Waves, Patterns and Spatio-Temporal Chaos, IEEE Transactions on Circuits and Systems - Part I, vol.42, no.10, 1995.
8. T.Roska, L.O.Chua, "The CNN Universal Machine: An Analogic Array Computer", IEEE Transactions on Circuits and Systems, Part II, vol.40, no.3, pp.163-173, 1993.
9. L.O.Chua, CNN: A Paradigm for Complexity, Worl Scientific series on Nonlinear Science, Series A, Vol.31, World Scientific, 1998

Parametric Behaviour Analysis
for Time Petri Nets *

I.B. Virbitskaite and E.A. Pokozy

Institute of Informatics Systems
Siberian Division of the Russian Academy of Sciences
6, Acad. Lavrentiev av. 630090, Novosibirsk, Russia
{virb,pokozy}@iis.nsk.su

Abstract. The intention of the paper is to develop an algorithm for timing behaviour analysis of concurrent and real time systems. To this purpose we introduce a notion of the parametric time net that is a modification of the time Petri net [4, 7] by using parameter variables in specification of timing constraints on transition firings. A property of the system is given as a formula of Parametric TCTL (PTCTL), a real time branching time temporal logic with timing parameter variables in its operators [6]. Timing behaviour analysis consists in finding necessary and sufficient conditions on parameter values under which the checked PTCTL-formula is valid in the given system. Thus the approach allows 'mutual adjustment' of timing specifications of both the system and the property via a single execution of verification procedure. It is further shown the correctness and evaluated the complexity of the algorithm proposed.

1 Introduction

Within the last decade, model checking has turned out to be useful and successful technique for verification of temporal properties in finite state systems. More recently, serious attempts have been made to extend the success of model checking to the setting of real time systems represented by timed automata (see, for example, [1]). However, concurrency can not be modelled directly by such timed state-graphs. On the other hand, the paper [4] proposed time Petri nets which are an adequate model of timed concurrent systems, generalizing other models in a natural way. Some verification algorithms for time net models and real time temporal logics were put forward in the literature [3, 5, 7].

One of the major obstacles for real time model checking is that it usually requires overly detailed specification of timing characteristics of the system and its properties. In the case when the checked formula is not satisfied by the system the timing characteristics are changed, and verification algorithm is applied again. It leaves users in repetitive trial-and-error cycles to select a proper parameter valuation. As Alur, Henzinger, and Vardi [2] have observed: "Indeed, when

---

* This work is supported in part by the Russian State Committee of Higher Education for Basic Research in Mathematics.

studying the literature on real time protocols, one sees that the desired timing properties for protocols are almost invariably parametric". Further, Wang [6] proposed a specification language for timed automata, called Parametric TCTL (PTCTL), that is an extension of the real time temporal logic TCTL [1] by using parameter variables, representing unspecified timing constants, in logical operators.

The intention of the paper is to develop an algorithm for parametric timing behaviour analysis of concurrent and real time systems represented by net models with real (dense) time. To this purpose we introduce a notion of the parametric time net that is a modification of the time Petri net [4,7] by using parameter variables in specification of timing constraints on transition firings. A property of the system is given as a formula of PTCTL. Timing behaviour analysis consists in constructing general linear equations of timing parameter variables whose solution makes the system working w.r.t. the checked formula. Thus the approach allows 'mutual adjustment' of timing specifications of both the system and the property via a single execution of verification procedure.

The rest of the paper is organized as follows. The basic definitions concerning parametric time nets are given in the next section. Section 3 recalls the syntax and semantics of PTCTL. Section 4 describes our observations and algorithm for solving the problem. Due to the space limitations, the proofs are omitted, they are presented in a forthcoming paper.

2   Parametric Time Nets

In this section, we introduce a notion of the parametric time net whose transitions are associated with time predicates representing unspecified timing constraints on transition firings.

We let $\mathbf{N}$ be the set of natural numbers, and $\mathbf{R}^+$ the set of nonnegative real numbers. Assume a finite set Par of parameter variables and an arbitrary set A. The syntax of a *time predicate* η over Par and A is defined as follows: $\eta = false \mid x \sim \theta \mid \eta_1 \to \eta_2$, where $x \in A$, $\theta \in Par \cup \mathbf{N}$, η_1, η_2 are time predicates, and $\sim$ stands for one of the binary relations $<, \leq, =, \geq, >$. Let B^A_{Par} be the set of all time predicates over Par and A. A *parameter valuation* χ is a mapping from Par into $\mathbf{N}$. A parameter valuation χ is said to be *c-bounded* if there exists a constant $c \in \mathbf{N}$ such that $\chi(\theta) \leq c$ for all $\theta \in Par$. Given a time predicate η and a parameter valuation χ, we shall let η^χ be the time predicate obtained from η by replacing every occurrence of θ with $\chi(\theta)$ for all θ appearing in η. With different parameter valuations a time predicate may impose different timing requirements.

Definition 1. A *parametric time net* is a tuple $\mathcal{N} = (P, T, F, Par, \tau, m_0)$, where P is a finite set of places; T is a finite set of transitions $(P \cap T = \emptyset)$; $F \subseteq (P \times T) \cup (T \times P)$ is a flow relation; Par is a finite set of parameter variables, $(Par \cap (P \cup T) = \emptyset)$; $\tau : T \to B^T_{Par}$ is a function that associates each transition $t \in T$ with a time predicate $\tau(t) \in B^T_{Par}$; $m_0 \subseteq P$ is the initial marking.

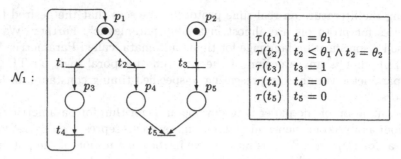

$$\mathcal{N}_1:$$

$\tau(t_1)$	$t_1 = \theta_1$
$\tau(t_2)$	$t_2 \leq \theta_1 \wedge t_2 = \theta_2$
$\tau(t_3)$	$t_3 = 1$
$\tau(t_4)$	$t_4 = 0$
$\tau(t_5)$	$t_5 = 0$

Fig. 1.

An example of a parametric time net is shown in Fig. 1. Let $c_\mathcal{N}$ be the biggest constant from $\mathbf{N}$ appearing in $\mathcal{N}$. For $t \in T$, ${}^\bullet t = \{p \in P \mid (p, t) \in F\}$ and $t^\bullet = \{p \in P \mid (t, p) \in F\}$ denote the *preset* and *postset* of t, respectively. Given a parameter valuation χ, we shall let $\mathcal{N}^\chi$ be the parametric time net obtained from $\mathcal{N}$ by replacing $\tau(t)$ with $\tau(t)^\chi$ for all $t \in T$.

A *marking* m of $\mathcal{N}^\chi$ is any subset of P. A transition t is *enabled* in a marking m if ${}^\bullet t \subseteq m$ (all its input places have tokens in m). We shall use $enable(m)$ to denote the set of transitions, enabled in m.

Let $\mathcal{V} = [T \to \mathbf{R}^+]$ be the set of *time assignments* for transitions from T. Assume $\nu \in \mathcal{V}$ and $\delta \in \mathbf{R}^+$. We let $\nu + \delta$ denote the time assignment of the value $\nu(t) + \delta$ to each t from T. Given $\tau(t) \in B_{Par}^T$, we use $\tau(t)_\nu$ to denote the result of replacing every occurrence of a transition t' with the value $\nu(t')$ for all t' appearing in $\tau(t)$.

A *state* q of $\mathcal{N}^\chi$ is a pair $\langle m, \nu \rangle$, where m is a marking in $\mathcal{N}^\chi$ and $\nu \in \mathcal{V}$. The *initial state* of $\mathcal{N}^\chi$ is the pair $q_0 = \langle m_0, \nu_0 \rangle$, where $\nu_0(t) = 0$ for all $t \in T$. The states of $\mathcal{N}^\chi$ change, if time passes or if a transition fires. Let $q = \langle m, \nu \rangle, q' = \langle m', \nu' \rangle$ be states of $\mathcal{N}^\chi$. In a state q, a transition $t \in T$ is *fireable*, if $t \in enable(m)$ and the predicate $\tau(t)_\nu^\chi$ is true. In this case, the state q' is *obtained by firing t from q* (written $q \xrightarrow{0} q'$), if $m' = (m \setminus {}^\bullet t) \cup t^\bullet$, and for all $t' \in T$, $\nu'(t') = 0$, if $t' \in enable(m') \setminus enable(m)$, else $\nu'(t') = \nu(t')$. In a state q, time $\delta \in \mathbf{R}^+$ *can pass*, if for all $t \in enable(m)$ there exists $\delta' \geq \delta$ such that the predicate $\tau(t)_{\nu+\delta'}^\chi$ is true. In this case, the state q' is *obtained by passing δ from q* (written $q \xrightarrow{\delta} q'$), if $m' = m$ and $\nu' = \nu + \delta$. A state q is *reachable* in $\mathcal{N}^\chi$ if $q = q_0$ or there exists a reachable state q' such that $q' \xrightarrow{\delta} q$ for some $\delta \in \mathbf{R}^+$. Let $RS(\mathcal{N}^\chi)$ denote the set of all reachable states of $\mathcal{N}^\chi$.

A *q-run* r in $\mathcal{N}^\chi$ is an infinite sequence of states $q_i \in RS(\mathcal{N}^\chi)$ and time values $\delta_i \in \mathbf{R}^+$ of the form: $q = q_1 \xrightarrow{\delta_1} q_2 \xrightarrow{\delta_2} \ldots q_n \xrightarrow{\delta_n} \ldots$ We define $time(r, n) = \sum_{1 \leq i < n} \delta_i$. Let us consider the parametric time net $\mathcal{N}_1$ (see Fig. 1) and the parameter valuation χ_1 with $\chi_1(\theta_1) = 1$ and $\chi_1(\theta_2) = 0$. We construct the following q_0-run r_1 of $\mathcal{N}_1^{\chi_1}$: $\langle \{p_1, p_2\}, \nu \equiv 0 \rangle \xrightarrow{\delta_1 = 0} \langle \{p_2, p_4\}, \nu \equiv 0 \rangle \xrightarrow{\delta_2 = 0.7} \langle \{p_2, p_4\}, \nu \equiv 0.7 \rangle \xrightarrow{\delta_3 = 0.3} \langle \{p_2, p_4\}, \nu \equiv 1 \rangle \xrightarrow{\delta_4 = 0} \langle \{p_4, p_5\}, \nu \equiv 1 \rangle \xrightarrow{\delta_5 = 0} \langle \emptyset, \nu \equiv 1 \rangle \xrightarrow{\delta_6 = 1} \ldots$. Then $time(r_1, 6) = 1$.

We shall call $\mathcal{N}$ *one-safe*, if for each parameter valuation χ, state $\langle m, \nu \rangle \in RS(\mathcal{N}^\chi)$ and transition $t \in enable(m)$ it holds $t^\bullet \cap m = \emptyset$. In the sequel, $\mathcal{N}$ will always denote the one-safe parametric time net.

3 PTCTL: Syntax and Semantics

In this section, we review the syntax and semantics of PTCTL (Parametric Timed Computation Tree Logic) proposed in [6] as a specification language for timed automata. We rephrase it in a form suitable for the specification of properties of parametric time nets. Let $\mathbf{AP}$ be a set of atomic propositions. For our purpose, it is convenient to take $\mathbf{AP} = P$.

Definition 2. The *PTCTL-formula* ϕ is inductively defined as follows: $\phi := false \mid p \mid \phi_1 \rightarrow \phi_2 \mid \forall \phi_1 \mathcal{U}_{\sim\theta} \phi_2 \mid \exists \phi_1 \mathcal{U}_{\sim\theta} \phi_2$, where $p \in \mathbf{AP}$, $\theta \in Par \cup \mathbf{N}$, ϕ_1 and ϕ_2 are PTCTL-formulas, $\sim$ stands for one of the binary relations $<, \leq, =, \geq, >$.

Informally, $\exists \phi_1 \mathcal{U}_{\sim\theta} \phi_2$ means that for some computation path there exists an initial prefix of time corresponding to $' \sim \theta'$ such that ϕ_2 holds in the last state of the prefix, and ϕ_1 holds in all its intermediate states.

In addition, some of commonly used abbreviations are: $\forall \Diamond_{\sim\theta} \phi \equiv \forall true \, \mathcal{U}_{\sim\theta} \phi$, $\exists \Diamond_{\sim\theta} \phi \equiv \exists true \, \mathcal{U}_{\sim\theta} \phi$, $\forall \Box_{\sim\theta} \phi \equiv \neg \exists \Diamond_{\sim\theta} \neg \phi$, $\exists \Box_{\sim\theta} \phi \equiv \neg \forall \Diamond_{\sim\theta} \neg \phi$.

Let c_ϕ be the biggest constant from $\mathbf{N}$ appearing in ϕ. Given a PTCTL-formula ϕ and a parameter valuation χ, we let ϕ^χ be the PTCTL-formula obtained from ϕ by replacing every occurrence of θ with $\chi(\theta)$ for all θ appearing in ϕ. With different parameter valuations a PTCTL-formula may impose different timing requirements. Given $q = \langle m, \nu \rangle \in RS(\mathcal{N}^\chi)$ and a PTCTL-formula ϕ^χ, we define the *satisfaction* relation (written $\mathcal{N}^\chi, q \models \phi^\chi$) inductively as follows:

$$\mathcal{N}^\chi, q \not\models false;$$
$$\mathcal{N}^\chi, q \models p^\chi \iff p \in m;$$
$$\mathcal{N}^\chi, q \models (\phi_1 \rightarrow \phi_2)^\chi \iff \mathcal{N}^\chi, q \not\models \phi_1^\chi \text{ or } \mathcal{N}^\chi, q \models \phi_2^\chi;$$
$$\mathcal{N}^\chi, q \models (\exists \phi_1 \mathcal{U}_{\sim\theta} \phi_2)^\chi \iff \text{for some } q\text{-run } r \text{ in } \mathcal{N}^\chi, \; r \models (\phi_1 \mathcal{U}_{\sim\theta} \phi_2)^\chi;$$
$$\mathcal{N}^\chi, q \models (\forall \phi_1 \mathcal{U}_{\sim\theta} \phi_2)^\chi \iff \text{for every } q\text{-run } r \text{ in } \mathcal{N}^\chi, \; r \models (\phi_1 \mathcal{U}_{\sim\theta} \phi_2)^\chi.$$

For a q-run $r : \langle m, \nu \rangle = \langle m_1, \nu_1 \rangle \overset{\delta_1}{\Rightarrow} \langle m_2, \nu_2 \rangle \overset{\delta_2}{\Rightarrow} \ldots$ in $\mathcal{N}^\chi$ the relation $r \models (\phi_1 \mathcal{U}_{\sim c} \phi_2)^\chi$ holds iff there exists k and $\delta \leq \delta_k$ such that: (1) $(\delta + time(r, k)) \sim \chi(\theta)$; (2) $\langle m_k, \nu_k + \delta \rangle \models \phi_2^\chi$; (3) $\forall 1 \leq i < k \, (\langle m_i, \nu_i \rangle \models \phi_1^\chi \land \forall 0 \leq \delta' < \delta_i . \langle m_i, \nu_i + \delta' \rangle \models \phi_1^\chi)$; (4) $\forall 0 \leq \delta' < \delta . \langle m_k, \nu_k + \delta' \rangle \models \phi_1^\chi$.

$\mathcal{N}^\chi$ *satisfies* a PTCTL-formula ϕ^χ (written $\mathcal{N}^\chi \models \phi^\chi$) iff $\mathcal{N}^\chi, q_0 \models \phi^\chi$. Let us consider the parametric time net $\mathcal{N}_1$ (see Fig. 1), the PTCTL-formula $\phi_1 = \exists \Diamond_{\geq \theta}(p_4 \land p_5)$, and the parameter valuation χ_1 with $\chi_1(\theta) = 1$, $\chi_1(\theta_1) = 1$ and $\chi_1(\theta_2) = 0$. $\mathcal{N}_1^{\chi_1}$ satisfies the PTCTL-formula $\phi_1^{\chi_1}$ because along the q_0-run r_1 (see above) the places p_4 and p_5 contain tokens at time moment equal to 1. Notice, the PTCTL satisfiability problem is undecidable [6]. Given $\mathcal{N}$ and ϕ, *the c-bounded timing behaviour analysis problem* instance of $\mathcal{N}$ w.r.t. ϕ (written $TBA(\mathcal{N}, \phi, c)$) is defined as the problem of finding c-bounded parameter valuation χ, if any, which makes $\mathcal{N}^\chi \models \phi^\chi$.

4 Parametric Timing Behaviour Analysis

Our analysis algorithm to decide $TBA(\mathcal{N}, \phi, c)$ is based on the concepts of regions (equivalence classes of states) and region graphs [1].

In order to simplify the checking of timing constraints, we introduce an additional transition $t^* \notin T$ which is disabled in any marking of the net, and its time assignment therefore keeps time elapsed since some initial moment. We shall use $\mathcal{V}^*$ to denote the set of time assignments for transitions from $T \cup \{t^*\}$.

Before introducing the notion of a region in the context $TBA(\mathcal{N}, \phi, c)$, we have to give the following auxiliary definitions. We let $c_{\mathcal{N}:\phi} = \max\{c, c_{\mathcal{N}}, c_\phi\}$. For any $\delta \in \mathbf{R}^+$, $\{\delta\}$ denotes the fractional part of δ, and $\lfloor \delta \rfloor$ denotes the integral part of δ. Given $\nu, \nu' \in \mathcal{V}^*$, $\nu \simeq_{c_{\mathcal{N}:\phi}} \nu'$ iff the following conditions are met: (1) for each $t \in T$ if $\nu(t) \leq c_{\mathcal{N}:\phi}$ or $\nu'(t) \leq c_{\mathcal{N}:\phi}$, then $\lfloor \nu(t) \rfloor = \lfloor \nu'(t) \rfloor$; (2) for each $t, t' \in T \cup \{t^*\}$: (a) $\{\nu(t)\} \leq \{\nu(t')\} \Leftrightarrow \{\nu'(t)\} \leq \{\nu'(t')\}$; (b) $\{\nu(t)\} = 0 \Leftrightarrow \{\nu'(t)\} = 0$. When the context of $TBA(\mathcal{N}, \phi, c)$ is obvious, we shall write $\nu \simeq \nu'$, for simplicity. Given $\nu \in \mathcal{V}^*$, we use $[\nu]$ to denote the equivalence class of ν w.r.t. $\simeq$. Let $[\nu]$ and $[\nu']$ be two distinct equivalence classes w.r.t. $\simeq$ for ν and ν' from $\mathcal{V}^*$, respectively. Then $[\nu']$ is said to be a *successor* for $[\nu]$ (written $[\nu'] = succ([\nu])$), if (1) $\nu' = \nu + \delta$ for some positive $\delta \in \mathbf{R}^+$; (2) there is no $[\bar{\nu}]$ and $\bar{\delta} \in \mathbf{R}^+ (0 < \bar{\delta} < \delta)$ such that $[\bar{\nu}] \neq [\nu]$, $[\bar{\nu}] \neq [\nu']$, $\nu + \bar{\delta} = \bar{\nu}$ and $\bar{\nu} + \delta - \bar{\delta} = \nu'$. We define $succ^k([\nu]) = \underbrace{succ(succ(\ldots succ([\nu])\ldots))}_{k}$.

Let $TBA(\mathcal{N}, \phi, c)$ and a c-bounded parameter valuation χ be given. A *region* of $\mathcal{N}^\chi$ is called to be a set $\langle m, [\nu] \rangle = \{\langle m', \nu' \rangle \in RS(\mathcal{N}^\chi) \mid m = m' \wedge \nu' \simeq \nu\}$. The *region graph* of $\mathcal{N}^\chi$ is defined to be the labelled directed graph $G^\chi = (V^\chi, E^\chi, l^\chi)$. The vertex set V^χ is the set of all regions of $\mathcal{N}^\chi$. The edge set E^χ consists of two types of edges: (1) the edge $(\langle m, [\nu] \rangle, \langle m', [\nu'] \rangle)$ may represent firing a transition if $\langle m', \nu' \rangle$ is obtained from $\langle m, \nu \rangle$ by firing some $t \in T$; (2) the edge $(\langle m, [\nu] \rangle, \langle m', [\nu'] \rangle)$ may represent the passage of time if $m = m'$ and $[\nu'] = succ([\nu])$. The function l^χ labels an edge either with the symbol $'t'$ (if the edge represents firing t) or with the symbol $'\delta'$ (if the edge represents the passage of time). The *c-bounded region graph* of $\mathcal{N}$ is defined to be the labelled directed graph $G = (V, E, l)$ with $V = \cup_{\chi \in \chi_c} V^\chi$, $E = \cup_{\chi \in \chi_c} E^\chi$, $l = \cup_{\chi \in \chi_c} l^\chi$, where χ_c is the set of all possible c-bounded valuations. Given a vertex $v = \langle m, [\nu] \rangle$ and a PTCTL-formula ϕ', we write $v \models \phi'^\chi$ iff $\mathcal{N}^\chi, \langle m, [\nu] \rangle \models \phi^\chi$ for some c-bounded parameter valuation χ. For some $\tau(t) \in B_{Par}^T$, we write $\tau(t)_{[\nu]}$ iff $\tau(t)_\nu$.

We need to introduce a number of auxiliary notions and notations. Let $G = (V, E, l)$ be the c-bounded region graph of $\mathcal{N}$. A (finite or infinite) *path* in G is a (finite or infinite) sequence $\Gamma = \langle v_1 v_2 \ldots \rangle$ of vertices from V such that for every $i \geq 1$, $(v_i, v_{i+1}) \in E$ if v_{i+1} exists. A *cycle* is a finite path $\langle v_1 \ldots v_m \rangle$ such that $m \geq 2$ and $v_1 = v_m$. For some $(\langle m, [\nu] \rangle, \langle m', [\nu'] \rangle) \in E$, we write $\varepsilon(\langle m, [\nu] \rangle, \langle m', [\nu'] \rangle) = \uparrow$ if going from $\langle m, \nu \rangle$ to $\langle m', \nu' \rangle$ the value of t^*'s time assignment increments from an integer to a noninteger. For a given path $\Gamma = \langle v_1 v_2 \ldots v_m \rangle$, we write $time(\Gamma)$ to denote the number of edges (v_i, v_{i+1}) such that $\varepsilon(v_i, v_{i+1}) = \uparrow$ for all $1 \leq i < m$. A path Γ in G is *correct* if Γ is a path in G^χ for some c-bounded parameter valuation χ; Γ is *slim* if each its cycle of zero time is traversed at most once along Γ. For a path Γ, we let $Tr(\Gamma) = \{v \in \Gamma \mid \exists v' \in \Gamma \,.\, l(v,v') =' t'\}$ and $\Delta(\Gamma) = \{v \in \Gamma \mid \exists v' \in \Gamma \,.\, l(v,v') =' \delta'\}$. Given $v \in Tr(\Gamma)$, we use $t(v)$ to denote the transition $t \in T$ such that $l(v,v') =' t'$ for some $v' \in \Gamma$.

We now give some intuition behind our decision algorithm. Any path in G from a vertex v to a vertex v' can always be decomposed into a simple path, say Γ, and a set, say H, of simple cycles. It is also obvious that by repeating any of the simple cycles in H a few more times, we still get a path from v to v'. Thus the time of a path constructed from Γ and H can be represented as the sum of the time of Γ and a positive linear combination of the times of cycles in H. Based on the paper [6], it can be observed that the repetition patterns of path time from v to v' are expressible in terms of the greatest common divisor and the least common multiple of the times of nonzero simple cycles traversable by paths from v to v'. And this relationship can then be expressed as conditions on parameter variables from Par.

Given a simple path $\Gamma = \langle v_1 v_2 \ldots v_k \rangle$ and a finite set H of simple cycles in G, we call (Γ, H) a *cactus structure* from v_1 to v_k iff for each $\Omega \in H$ there is a finite sequence $\Omega_1, \cdots \Omega_m$, $m \geq 1$, of simple cycles in H such that (1) $\Omega_1 = \Omega$; (2) given $\Omega_m = \langle u_1 \ldots u_n \rangle$ for some $1 \leq i \leq k$, $v_i = u_1$; (3) for each $1 \leq h < m$ with $\Omega_h = \langle u_1 u_2 \ldots u_n \rangle$ and $\Omega_{h+1} = \langle u'_1 u'_2 \ldots u'_{n'} \rangle$, there is $1 \leq i \leq n'$ such that $u'_i = u_1$. Given a cactus-structure $(\Gamma, \{\Omega_1, \ldots, \Omega_m\})$ from v to v' we call (Υ, Ψ) the *characteristic pair* from v to v' iff $\Upsilon = time(\Gamma) + \sum_{1 \leq i \leq m} r_i + m \cdot lcm(r_1, \ldots, r_m)$ and $\Psi = gcd(r_1, \ldots, r_m)$, where $r_i = time(\Omega_i)$ for each $1 \leq i \leq m$, $gcd(r_1, \ldots, r_m)$ and $lcm(r_1, \ldots, r_m)$ are respectively the *greatest common divisor* and the *least common multiple* of nonzero elements in $r_1, \ldots, r_m$.

We construct the function $ptime_{\sim\theta}^{\phi'}(v,v')$ which, given two vertices v, v' in G and a timing requirement $' \sim \theta'$ on paths, returns a condition for the existence of a correct path from v to v' satisfying ϕ' and $' \sim \theta'$.

$ptime_{\sim\theta}^{\phi'}(v,v')$ {

(1) let U be the set of simple paths from v to v';
(2) for each $\Gamma \in U$ {
    (1) compute the set SC_Γ of vertices from G strongly connected to vertices from Γ;
    (2) compute the set H_Γ of simple cycles from G made of vertices from SC_Γ;
    (3) compute the characteristic pair $(\Upsilon_\Gamma, \Psi_\Gamma)$ for (Γ, H_Γ) }
(3) let $\overline{\Upsilon} := \max\{\Upsilon_\Gamma \mid \Gamma \in U\}$ and $\gamma := false$;
(4) for each $0 \leq d < \overline{\Upsilon}$ and each slim path Γ of time d from v to v' let $\gamma := \gamma \vee (d \sim \theta \wedge \theta \leq c_{N:\phi} \wedge \tilde{\mathbf{L}}^{\phi'}(\Gamma))$;
(5) for each $\Gamma \in U$ let $\gamma := \gamma \vee [(\exists i \geq 0 (\Upsilon_\Gamma + i \cdot \Psi_\Gamma \sim \theta)) \wedge \theta \leq c_{N:\phi} \wedge \tilde{\mathbf{L}}^{\phi'}(\Gamma) \wedge \bigwedge_{\Omega \in H_\Gamma} \tilde{\mathbf{L}}^{\phi'}(\Omega)]$;
(6) return γ }

Here $\tilde{\mathbf{L}}^{\phi'}(\Gamma) = \bigwedge_{1 \leq j < n} \mathbf{L}^{\phi'}(v_j) \wedge \bigwedge_{\langle m, [\nu] \rangle \in \Delta(\Gamma)} \bigwedge_{t \in enable(m)} \bigvee_{k \geq 1} \tau(t)_{succ^k([\nu])}$
$\wedge \bigwedge_{\langle m, [\nu] \rangle \in Tr(\Gamma)} \tau(t(\langle m, [\nu] \rangle))_{[\nu]} \wedge$ for a given path $\Gamma = \langle v_1, \ldots, v_n \rangle$ in G.

To decide $TBA(\mathcal{N}, \phi, c)$ we label a pair of the initial vertex v_0 of G and a PTCTL-formula ϕ by a first-order-logic formula $\mathbf{L}^\phi(v_0)$, which we call *a condition*, with parameter variables as free variables. Like [6], we use a top-down recursive form of the labelling algorithm for convenience.
Label($\mathcal{N}, \phi, c$) {

1. construct the c-bounded region graph $G = (V, E, l)$ of $\mathcal{N}$;
2. for the initial vertex v_0 of G compute $\mathbf{L}^\phi(v_0)$; }

$\mathbf{L}^{\phi_i}(v = \langle m, [\nu] \rangle)$ {

1. if $\phi_i = false$, then $\mathbf{L}^{false}(v) := false$;
2. when $\phi_i \in P$, if $\phi_i \in m$ then $\mathbf{L}^{\phi_i}(v) := true$ else $\mathbf{L}^{\phi_i}(v) := false$;
3. if $\phi_i = \phi_j \to \phi_k$, $\mathbf{L}^{\phi_j \to \phi_k}(v) := \mathbf{L}^{\phi_j}(v) \to \mathbf{L}^{\phi_k}(v)$;
4. if $\phi_i = \exists \Box_{\geq 0} \phi_j$ then $\mathbf{L}^{\exists \Box_{\geq 0} \phi_j}(v) := \bigvee_{u \in V}(ptime_{\geq 0}^{\phi_j}(\langle * \rangle v, u) \wedge ptime_{\geq 0}^{\phi_j}(u, u))$;
5. if $\phi_i = \exists \phi_j U_{\geq \theta} \phi_k$ then $\mathbf{L}^{\exists \phi_j U_{\geq \theta} \phi_k}(v) := \bigvee_{u \in V}(ptime_{\geq \theta}^{\phi_j}(\langle * \rangle v, u) \wedge \mathbf{L}^{\phi_k}(u) \wedge \mathbf{L}^{\exists \Box_{\geq 0} true}(u))$;
6. if $\phi_i = \forall \phi_j U_{\geq \theta} \phi_k$ then $\mathbf{L}^{\forall \phi_j U_{\geq \theta} \phi_k}(v) := \neg[\mathbf{L}^{\exists \Diamond < \theta \neg \phi}(\langle * \rangle v) \vee ((\mathbf{L}^{\exists \Box_{\geq 0} \neg \phi}(\langle * \rangle v) \vee \mathbf{L}^{\exists (\neg \phi_k) U_{\geq 0} \neg (\phi_j \vee \phi_k)}(\langle * \rangle v)) \wedge \theta = 0) \vee (\theta > 0 \wedge \bigvee_{u_1, u_2 \in V}(ptime_{=\theta-1}^{\phi_j}(\langle * \rangle v, u_1) \wedge \mathbf{L}^{\phi_j}(u_1) \wedge \epsilon(u_1, u_2) = \uparrow \wedge (\mathbf{L}^{\exists \Box_{\geq 0} \neg \phi_k}(u_2) \vee \mathbf{L}^{\exists (\neg \phi_k) U_{\geq 0} \neg (\phi_j \vee \phi_k)}(u_2))))]$. }

Here $\langle * \rangle v$ denotes the vertex from G that agrees with v in every aspects except that the value of t^*'s time assignment is an integer.

We establish the correctness of the labelling algorithm.

Theorem 1. Given $TBA(\mathcal{N}, \phi, c)$, a PTCTL-formula ϕ' such that $c_{\phi'} \leq c_{\mathcal{N}:\phi}$, a c-bounded parameter valuation χ, and a vertex v in G^χ, after executing $\mathbf{L}^{\phi'}(v)$ in the labelling algorithm, χ satisfies $\mathbf{L}^{\phi'}(v)$ iff $v \models \phi'^\chi$.

Solutions for linear equations of parameter variables obtained after executing the labelling algorithm can be found by using the Solve algorithm from [6].

Theorem 2. There exists a procedure for deciding $TBA(\mathcal{N}, \phi, c)$ which is linear in the size of ϕ and double-exponential in the size of $\mathcal{N}$.

References

1. ALUR, R., DILL, D. *A theory of timed automata.* Theoretical Computer Science **126** (1994) 183–235.
2. ALUR, R., HENZINGER, T., VARDI, M. *Parametric real time reasoning.* Proc. 25th ACM STOC (1993) 592–601.
3. BENGTSSON, J., JONSSON, B., LILIUS, J., YI, W. *Partial order reductions for timed systems.* Proc. CONCUR'98 (1998) 485–496.
4. MERLIN, P., FABER, D.J. *Recoverability of communication protocols.* IEEE Trans. of Communication **COM-24(9)** (1976).
5. VIRBITSKAITE, I.B., POKOZY, E.A. *Towards efficient verification of time Petri nets.* Logical Journal of IGPL **5(6)** (1997) 921–924.
6. WANG F. *Timing behavior analysis for real-time systems.* Proc. 10th IEEE LICS (1995) 112–122.
7. YONEDA, T., SHIBAYAMA, A., SCHLINGLOFF, B.H., CLARKE, E.M. *Efficient verification of concurrent real-time systems.* Lecture Notes in Computer Science **697** (1993) 321–333.

A Blackboard Approach for the Automatic Optimization of Parallel I/O Operations

Helmut Wanek and Erich Schikuta

Institute for Applied Computer Science and Information Systems
Department of Data Engineering, University of Vienna,
Rathausstr. 19/4, A-1010 Vienna, Austria
schiki@ifs.univie.ac.at
wanek@vipios.pri.univie.ac.at

Abstract. The performance of parallel I/O operations is highly dependent on various parameters like disk transfer rates, speed of processor (network) interconnections, size of available memory for data buffers and so forth. Tuning of parallel I/O to achieve optimum performance is a very complex task for application programmers. This paper presents a method to perform I/O optimization automatically. The approach used is based on a combination of a blackboard system and an A^* algorithm, which allows to achieve (near) optimal performance in reasonable time. The architecture of the blackboard is described in detail and illustrated on an example based on a simple cost model.

1 Introduction

Parallel I/O has been an important topic in high performance computing research in the last few years. Many parallel file systems and I/O libraries have been developed. These are either proprietary systems, which are sold with specific hardware (e.g. IBM's Vesta [2]) or portable multipurpose systems that can be used on different hardware platforms (e.g. PASSION [12], Galley [8], PANDA [10] or ViPIOS [4]). In addition to those systems MPI-IO ([7]) has been proposed as a standard parallel file interface for MPI. With a reference implementation available (ROMIO [13]) this standard has been widely accepted by now.

Despite of all the efforts to provide application programmers with means to perform parallel I/O efficiently, very few work has yet been done to automatically optimize the performance of I/O systems. Considering how tedious and complex performance tuning generally turns out to be, it is desirable to build a system which can perform all the necessary optimizations without any human intervention. The user of such a system only has to specify what data has to be read or written, not how it should be performed (i.e. which disks to use, how to distribute data over the disks etc.). The system is expected to provide a (near) optimal throughput for the requested operations.

Only a limited number of research projects have addressed automatic optimization of parallel I/O operations so far. An extension to PASSION using compiler inserted library function calls for prefetching and caching has been proposed in [11]. PPFS uses a trained neural network and a Hidden-Markov model to identify I/O access patterns and to optimize operations accordingly. The PABLO performance analysis tool and a fuzzy logic based adaptive control enable PPFS to react dynamically to changing system characteristics at application's runtime ([6]). And finally PANDA uses an optimizer based on adaptive simulated annealing and generic algorithms ([1]).

Very similar problems have however been studied extensively in the research on parallel and distributed databases. Requests to a database are accomplished by applying a sequence of basic primitive database operations, which is called a query execution plan. In general a huge number of possible execution plans can be found for a single request. It is the responsibility of the database system to select the one which can be executed most efficiently. Different techniques have been developed for this automatic optimization of query execution plans and blackboard architectures have been found to be quite efficient ([5]).

In the following a novel blackboard method is presented, which automatically optimizes parallel I/O operations.

2   The Blackboard

The basic idea of a blackboard system is to solve hard problems like a group of human experts would do. In this metaphor the experts use a common blackboard where all of them could write down their ideas. Every expert then uses his or her knowledge to enhance the information already on the blackboard by reformulating or adding additional information. The whole process is iterated until (hopefully) a solution to the initial problem has been found. Note that none of the experts has to have a complete model of the problem or its solution. Everyone just adds his or her specific knowledge until the solution finally emerges.

To put it more formally a blackboard system basically consists of the following three components:

- A *global blackboard*, which is represented by a database and contains all input data and partial solutions.
- A *knowledge base*, which contains the specific expert knowledge in independent modules. Each module corresponds to one expert and the only way to communicate between modules is the global blackboard. The modules are often also referred to as regions (assuming that each expert has a reserved region on the blackboard where to put all his or her results).
- A *control component*, which decides about the course of the problem solving approach (i.e. when can which expert add to or change the contents of the blackboard). In order to enable the control component to make reasonable decisions, every knowledge module that wants to contribute to the blackboard has to supply estimations of the expected costs and profits of the operation (i.e. how long will the calculation of the new result take and how much will it be of interest for the final solution).

More information about blackboard systems in general can be found in [3].

2.1 Parallel I/O Optimization

The following will concentrate on a blackboard, which provides basic optimization capabilities only. Emphasis is put on the demonstration of the design principles, which are also illustrated by an example. It is assumed that the applications are executed on a parallel hardware with dedicated I/O nodes like depicted in figure 1. Each I/O node receives requests from the application processes and performs the necessary disk accesses on its local disks only. Requests and data are sent via message passing between the processors affected. The hardware may be inhomogeneous in the connections between processors and in the disks attached to the I/O processors (i.e. the time needed to transfer a message may vary depending on the sending and the receiving processors and speed and size of disks may also differ).

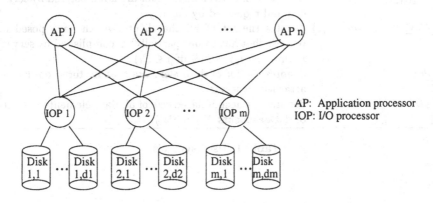

Fig. 1. Basic hardware model

I/O operations are considered to be collective, which means that all the application processes that are taking part in an I/O operation have to pose their requests simultaneously. This way the operation as a whole, which lasts from the issue of the requests until the last processor's data has been read/written completely, can be optimized. For non collective operations the optimization of overall performance is by far harder to achieve. The model could be extended to account for the probability of a request in certain time intervals. The proper probability values however are extremely difficult to calculate.

Additionally only blocking I/O operations are modeled in this paper. This simplifies the cost calculations by assuring that any application processor can send/receive data at the maximum speed possible at any time during the I/O operation. During non blocking operations an application processor could be busy with calculations and thus lower data transfer rates would apply. Since these rates depend on the utilization of the application processor, they are also hard to estimate.

The presented model already enables plenty of possibilities to optimize I/O performance and thus clearly demonstrates the usefulness and strengths of the blackboard approach. In the following a number of symbols and abbreviations will be used, which are summarized in table 1

symbol	meaning
$no_{clients}$	number of application processors (clients)
$no_{servers}$	number of I/O processors (servers)
$no_{disks,i}$	number of disks available on server processor i
$tr_{i,j}$	disk transfer rate of disk number j on server i (in MB/s)
$send_{i,j}$	transfer rate for messages from server i to client j (in MB/s)
$S = \{1, \ldots, no_{servers}\}$	the set of all possible server numbers
$D_i = \{1, \ldots, no_{disks,i}\}$	the set of all possible disk numbers on server i
$req(i, j)$	the set of all data elements that are administered by server i and requested by client j
$C_i \subseteq \{1, \ldots, no_{clients}\}$	denotes the set of all the clients, which have posed a request that has to be (partially) accomplished by server i (thus $req(i, j) <> \emptyset$ iff $j \in C_i$)
$data(i, j)$	denotes the set of data elements that is stored on disk j attached to server i
$size(X)$	denotes the accumulated size of all data elements in a set of data elements X (in MB)

Table 1. Used symbols

2.2 The Blackboard Regions

The search for an optimal strategy to accomplish specific I/O requests can basically be divided into three decision levels:

1. Find a suitable distribution of the data items among the available I/O processors.
2. Distribute the data items assigned to a specific I/O processor among the disks available at that processor.
3. Find a communication scheme that allows the data to be transferred to/from the application processors in minimum time. Assuming that every processor only can participate at one communication at a time, I/O processors serving more than one client have to serve all the clients successively. Vice versa a client accessing data, which is spread across a number of I/O processors only can send/receive data to/from one I/O processor after the other. An optimal communication scheme has to provide maximum overlap of all the communication necessary. This still applies even if simultaneous communication to more than one processor is possible because the maximum bandwidth available is always a limiting factor.

Accordingly the blackboard devised here contains three regions, which are called *server distribution region*, *disk distribution region* and *communication scheme region* respectively. Figure 2 shows how each region corresponds to a level in a decision tree which selects an execution plan for a given I/O request.

At the server distribution level it may appear natural to use the same distribution as the one used by the application program. So if data among the application processes is BLOCK distributed then it should be BLOCK distributed among I/O processors too. Normally that should yield optimal performance. But different layout strategies could be advantageous due to the following reasons.

1. The number of I/O processors generally is (far) less than the number of application processors. So different mappings have to be used.
2. An access may be to a persistent file which already is stored in a distribution different than the actual distribution used by the application (for example the file could have been written by an other application previously). The server distribution region then has to decide whether data should be redistributed or not. Clearly redistribution, which is a very costly operation, in general will only pay off if the number of accesses using the new distribution is large enough.
3. Server processes may run on processors with a wide variety of hardware and software characteristics (like number and quality of disks, network interconnection speed and so on). This is especially true in the case of distributed computing.

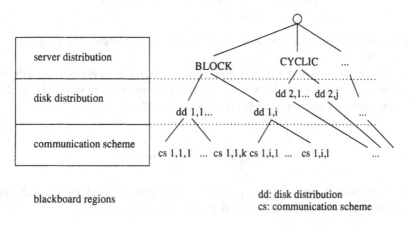

blackboard regions

dd: disk distribution
cs: communication scheme

Fig. 2. Blackboard regions and decision tree

2.3 The Cost Model

Every region estimates the minimum time needed to perform the I/O operation according to the following formulas:

Server Distribution Region. In this region the time needed by server i to read the data from disk is estimated by

$$t_{read}(i) = size(\bigcup_{j \in C_i} req(i,j))/\sum_{j \in D_i} tr_{i,j} \qquad (1)$$

This estimation is calculated for a hypothetical optimal data layout on disks, which ensures that all the disks can be accessed simultaneously and no disk is ever idle during the read operation. The overall data transfer rate from disk can therefore be calculated by the sum of all the individual disk's data rates. The amount of data to be processed can however not be calculated by simply summing up the requests from all the different clients. If requests overlap (i.e. different clients access the same data items on a server simultaneously) data has to be read from disk only once. Therefore the size is computed using the union of all the requests to server i. Formula (1) also does not account for the time needed for disk seek operations when data items are not stored contiguously on disk. So it actually gives a lower bound for the time the read operation will take to complete.

Ignoring message latency we can similarly calculate a lower bound for the time needed to transfer the data from the ith server process to the respective client processes.

$$t_{send}(i) = \sum_{j \in C_i} (size(req(i,j))/send_{i,j}) \qquad (2)$$

This just sums up the times needed to send all the requested data to each client process.

Using formulas (1) and (2) and considering that the operation is only completed when all the servers have fully accomplished their part of the task the overall time needed can be computed by formula (3).

$$t_{overall} = \max_{i \in S}(t_{read}(i) + t_{send}(i)) \qquad (3)$$

Disk Distribution Region. For a specific distribution of data on disk the costs for the disk accesses can be calculated more accurately.

$$\bar{t}_{read}(i) = \max_{j \in D_i}(size(data(i,j))/tr_{i,j}) \qquad (4)$$

It is the maximum time required by any disk attached to the specific server. Since each data element is only stored on exactly one of the disks available, formula (4) does not have to account for overlapping requests. (For specific optimizations the use of redundant copies of data elements could also be of interest. But this would need an additional region to be added to the blackboard.)

The actual distribution of data on disk does not influence the time needed to transfer the data from the server to the clients. So the overall cost can be estimated using formulas (2) and (4).

$$\bar{t}_{overall} = \max_{i \in S}(\bar{t}_{read}(i) + t_{send}(i)) \tag{5}$$

Communication Scheme Region. The overall cost estimation is basically the same as in the previous region. But since the costs are now calculated for a specific communication scheme (sequence of communications between processors) possible collisions have to be considered too. A collision is a situation where according to the scheme a specific communication should take place but cannot be performed because at least one of the two processors involved already has another communication operation active (see the example in chapter 3 for a communication scheme causing collisions). Extending formula (5) the overall costs are then computed by

$$\bar{\bar{t}}_{overall} = \max_{i \in S}(\bar{t}_{read}(i) + t_{send}(i) + stall(i)) \tag{6}$$

Here $stall(i)$ gives the total time that server processor i is idle due to communication collisions. It can be calculated using the following algorithm.

1. Provide a clock count and a stall time count for every server processor and initialize all counters with 0. Also provide a pointer for every server processor that points to the currently active communication on that server and initialize them with nil. Set $stall(i)$ to 0 for all server processors.
2. If all server processor's clock counts are set to infinity then terminate. Else select the server processor with minimum clock count value. (Precedence rules are applied to determine the process to select in case of a tie. These rules can either depend on the processor numbers or on priorities of the client requests. It must however be the same precedence rules that are used when the communication scheme is actually executed.)
3. For the selected server processor lookup the next communication to be performed according to the communication scheme. If no more communication is to be scheduled set the server processor's clock count to infinity and continue with step (2). Otherwise check if this communication does not provoke a collision (i.e. no other server processor is having an active communication with the same client processor).
4. If a collision is detected then set the clock count of the selected server processor to the value of the clock count of the server processor causing the collision, add the same amount that the clock count is being incremented to the selected server processor's stall time count ($stall(i)$) and continue with step (2). Otherwise calculate the time needed for the communication (by just dividing the amount of data to be sent by the transfer rate $send_{i,j}$ using appropriate values for i and j) and add it to the clock count value of the

selected server processor. Mark that communication as active by setting the server processor's pointer appropriately. Continue with step(2).

Based on these cost estimations the blackboard's control component directs the search so that only the most promising alternatives are processed by each region. This is done by interpreting the blackboard as a decision tree (like in figure 2), which has all the nodes associated with the appropriate cost estimation. The search for the minimum cost then can be done by using an A^* algorithm ([9]) to prune the search space and thus to avoid exhaustive work. The algorithm starts at the root of the decision tree and it only expands a node to the next level if the estimated costs associated with that node are lower than the costs of any solution that has been found so far. The example in chapter 3 shows this method in more detail. The A^* algorithm only can be guaranteed to find the optimal solutions if all the costs in the branch nodes underestimate the actual costs associated with the respective leaf nodes. This condition is satisfied by the cost model given above. In addition to the pruning by the control component each blackboard region can independently discard possible solutions which are heuristically known or otherwise proven to be inefficient. Some care has to be taken here however in order to prevent the unintentional removal of nodes which are deemed inefficient by a special region but actually could lead to an optimal solution.

2.4 Performance Considerations

The search for an optimal execution plan for a given sequence of I/O operations can take a considerable amount of time. Since it makes no sense to spend more time on the optimization than it would take to perform the operations in a suboptimal way, a 'good enough' execution plan often will suffice too. Each blackboard region does therefore not only estimate the minimum costs possible to achieve but also how long it will take that region to scan for the optimum solution. The blackboard's control component uses this information to decide whether an exhaustive search should be done in a specific region or an already evaluated possible solution can be considered good enough and passed on to the following regions. (This process is often called ballooning because possible suboptimal solutions can pass through the blackboard bypassing costly optimization operations.)

3 A Simple Example

Figure 3 shows the blackboards course of action for an example I/O operation. Three clients request 60 MB each of 2 server nodes. The nodes of the decision tree representing the blackboard are numbered in order to show the sequence in which they are generated. Each node is additionally marked with the decision made in the previous level and the estimated cost value. The cost for the root value is calculated by applying the models parameters, which are indicated in

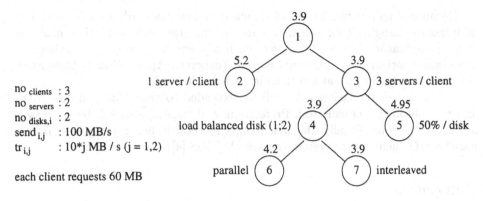

no clients : 3
no servers : 2
no disks,i : 2
send $_{i,j}$: 100 MB/s
tr $_{i,j}$: 10*j MB / s (j = 1,2)

each client requests 60 MB

Fig. 3. A simple example

the left of the figure without any further restrictions (i.e. assuming the maximum throughput possible for the given constellation).

First the server distribution region generates new nodes for BLOCK and CYCLIC distribution of data among the disks respectively. The associated cost estimation function yields a better result for the CYCLIC distribution, which is therefore passed to the next region. The disk distribution region tests for different block sizes that are cyclically distributed among the disks. Cost values are equal for both block sizes tested. This comes as no surprise because the specific cost estimation formula does not account for message latency and disk seek times. Considering these parameters too, the bigger block sizes should normally perform better.

Finally the communication scheme region tests two schemes:

Parallel: server one sends data to client one, two and three in that succession and server two does the same. This results in collisions which in turn worsen the estimated cost value. (This node only has been created to exemplify collision effects. The communication scheme region normally will use heuristics to avoid collisions and thus the interleaved scheme would be examined first.)

Interleaved: server one sends data to client one, two and three and server two first sends to two and three and to one at last. Since all send operations are expected to take the same time no collisions should occur here and the cost value is computed to be equal to the one at the root. At this point the algorithm can stop because no better solution can be found any more. (Remember that all the cost values are underestimated.)

4 Conclusions and Future Work

In this paper the application of a blackboard system for the automatic optimization of parallel I/O operations has been developed. An appropriate cost model has been given and the system was demonstrated by an example.

Because of its modularity the blackboard system can easily be extended and adopted to changing conditions. It also can integrate different other problem solving approaches like neural networks, fuzzy sets, and so on by adding appropriate algorithms as additional regions (experts). Application of ballooning allows to find near optimal solutions in reasonable time.

In the future the cost model will be extended to apply for non collective, and non-blocking I/O calls too. Prefetching and caching also will be addressed in specific regions. Finally the blackboard method is being integrated into a parallel I/O client-server system (namely ViPIOS [4]).

References

1. Y. Chen, M. Winslett, Y. Cho, and S.Kuo, *Automatic parallel i/o performance optimization in panda*, Proceedings of the 10th Annual ACM Symposium on Parallel Algorithms an Architectures, ACM Press, June 1998.
2. Peter F. Corbett and Dror G. Feitelson, *The Vesta parallel file system*, ACM Transactions on Computer Systems **14** (1996), no. 3, 225–264.
3. D. D. Corkill, *Blackboard systems*, AI Expert (1991), no. 6(9), 40–47.
4. E.Schikuta, T.Fuerle, and H.Wanek, *The vienna parallel input/output system*, L-NCS 1470: Euro-Par'98 Parallel Processing, Springer, September 1998, pp. 953–958.
5. A. Kemper and G. Moerkotte, *A blackboard architecture for query optimization in object bases*, Proc. 19th Int'l Conf. Very Large Data Bases, Dublin, Ireland, 1993, pp. 543–554.
6. Tara M. Madhyastha and Daniel A. Reed, *Input/output access pattern classification using hidden Markov models*, Proceedings of the Fifth Workshop on Input/Output in Parallel and Distributed Systems (San Jose, CA), ACM Press, November 1997, pp. 57–67.
7. *MPI-IO: a parallel file I/O interface for MPI*, The MPI-IO Committee, April 1996, Version 0.5. See WWW http://lovelace.nas.nasa.gov/MPI-IO/mpi-io-report.0.5.ps.
8. Nils Nieuwejaar and David Kotz, *The Galley parallel file system*, Proceedings of the 10th ACM International Conference on Supercomputing (Philadelphia, PA), ACM Press, May 1996, pp. 374–381.
9. J. Pearl, *Heuristics*, Addison-Wesly, Reading, Massachusetts, 1984.
10. Kent E. Seamons, *Panda: Fast access to persistent arrays using high level interfaces and server directed input/output*, Ph.D. thesis, University of Illinois at Urbana-Champaign, May 1996.
11. Tarvinder Pal Singh and Alok Choudhary, *ADOPT: A dynamic scheme for optimal prefetching in parallel file systems*, Tech. report, NPAC, June 1994.
12. Rajeev Thakur, Alok Choudhary, Rajesh Bordawekar, Sachin More, and Sivaramakrishna Kuditipudi, *Passion: Optimized I/O for parallel applications*, IEEE Computer **29** (1996), no. 6, 70–78.
13. Rajeev Thakur, Ewing Lusk, and William Gropp, *Users guide for ROMIO: A high-performance, portable MPI-IO implementation*, Tech. Report ANL/MCS-TM-234, Mathematics and Computer Science Division, Argonne National Laboratory, October 1997.

Routing and Embeddings in Super Cayley Graphs

Chi-Hsiang Yeh, Emmanouel A. Varvarigos, and Hua Lee

Department of Electrical and Computer Engineering
University of California, Santa Barbara, CA 93106-9560, USA
E-mail: yeh@engineering.ucsb.edu

Abstract. In this paper, we introduce *super Cayley graphs*, a class of communication-efficient networks for parallel processing. We show that super Cayley graphs can embed trees, meshes, hypercubes, as well as star, bubble-sort graphs, and transposition networks with constant dilation. We also show that algorithms developed for star graphs can be emulated on suitably constructed super Cayley graphs with asymptotically optimal slowdown, under several communication models. Basic communication tasks, such as the multinode broadcast (MNB) and the total exchange (TE), can be executed in suitably constructed super Cayley graphs in asymptotically optimal time. Moreover, no interconnection network with similar node degree can perform these communication tasks in time that is better by more than a constant factor than that required in suitably constructed super Cayley graphs.

1   Introduction

In [2], Akers and Krishnamurthy develop a group-theoretic model, called the *Cayley graph* model, for designing, analyzing, and improving symmetric interconnection networks. They showed that Cayley graphs are vertex-symmetric and that most vertex-symmetric graphs can be represented as Cayley graphs; it was also shown that every vertex-symmetric graph can be represented as a *Cayley coset graph*. Both the Cayley graph model and the Cayley coset graph model have been used to derived a wide variety of interesting networks for parallel processing and have since received considerable attention [2, 3, 6, 7, 9].

In this paper, we introduce a mathematical game called the *ball-arrangement game (BAG)* and apply it to the design of communication-efficient interconnection networks. Each Cayley graph corresponds to a ball-arrangement game where different balls have different numbers. In [20, 24], we derived an analogous result showing that every graph corresponds to a certain ball-arrangement game. We have also used the underlying idea of the ball-arrangement game to derive a variety of efficient networks [18–20, 23, 25], such as super Cayley graphs [22] and super-IP graphs [24], that have their respective advantages.

In [20, 22, 24] and this paper, we show that numerous networks can be formulated by simple ball-arrangement games and that algorithms for networks derived from a similar set of movements can usually be developed in a unified manner. In this paper, we derive efficient embeddings and communication algorithms for ten classes of super Cayley graphs, including macro-star (MS) networks, rotation-star (RS) networks, complete-rotation-star (Complete-RS) networks, macro-rotator (MR) networks, rotation-rotator (RR) networks, complete-rotation-rotator (Complete-RR) networks, insertion-selection (IS) networks, macro-insertion-selection (MIS) networks, rotation-insertion-selection (RIS) networks, and complete-rotation-insertion-selection (Complete-RIS) networks. These super Cayley graphs have various desirable properties, such as optimal diameters (given their node degree) and small node degrees. We show that algorithms for many of these super Cayley graphs can be developed in a unified manner. We derive constant-dilation embeddings of a variety of important topologies, such as trees, meshes, hypercubes, star graphs, bubble-sort graphs [2], and transition networks [12, 13], for some of these super Cayley graphs. We also show that a macro-star, macro-IS, complete-rotation-star, or complete-rotation-IS network can embed a star graph of the same size with constant dilation and asymptotically optimal congestion, and emulate the star graph with asymptotically optimal slowdown under several communication models. As a consequence, we obtain through embeddings and emulation many efficient algorithms for super Cayley graphs under several communication models, thus indicating its versatility. In particular, we derive asymptotically optimal algorithms to execute basic communication tasks, such as multinode broadcast (MNB) and total exchange (TE) [4, 10, 17]. We also show that the MNB and the TE tasks cannot be performed in an interconnection network of similar node degree in time that is asymptotically better by more than a constant factor than the time required in balanced macro-star, macro-IS, complete-rotation-star, and complete-rotation-IS networks. The traffic on all the links of suitably constructed super Cayley graphs is uniform within a constant factor for all algorithms considered in this paper.

The remainder of this paper is organized as follows. In Section 2 we present the ball-arrangement game and several classes of super Cayley graphs. In Section 3, we present efficient algorithms for emulating star graph algorithms under the single-dimension communication model. In Section 4, we present efficient algorithms for emulating star graph algorithms under the all-port communication model, and obtain optimal algorithms to execute certain prototype communication tasks in super Cayley graphs. In Section 5, we present $O(1)$-dilation embeddings of several important topologies in super Cayley graphs. Finally, in Section 6 we conclude the paper.

2   The Ball-Arrangement Game and Super Cayley Graphs

In this section, we introduce the *ball-arrangement game (BAG)* with boxes and distinct balls.

Ball-Arrangement Game with l Boxes and nl + 1 Balls:

*We are given l boxes and $k = nl + 1$ balls, one of which has color 0 and n of which has color i for all $i = 1, 2, ..., l$. These boxes do **not** have color (at the beginning). Initially, $k - 1$ of the balls are mixed together in the l boxes, so that each box contains n balls (of different colors, in general), and one ball is left outside the boxes. The goal of the game is to rearrange the balls and the boxes so that balls with the same color ends up in the same box, with proper order. Also, these boxes should be sorted so that the balls of color i, $i \in \{ 1, 2, ..., l \}$, appears in the ith box from the left. At each step the player can take one of the following two types of actions: (1) rearrange the order of the leftmost $n + 1$ balls (i.e., the outside ball and the balls in the leftmost box), or (2) rearrange the order of boxes.*

In what follows, we relate the ball-arrangement game to network topologies and (unicast) routing in them. For a ball-arrangement game with k balls, there are k! distinct configurations (i.e., states), each of which can be visualized as a node of a network. Given a set of actions for moving the boxes and balls, we can visualize a movement between two configurations as a link connecting those two corresponding nodes. That is, the network can be obtained by drawing the state transition graph for the ball-arrangement game.

In other words, if d possible actions are allowed in a ball-arrangement game, then each node in the derived network has d outgoing links connecting it to d other nodes in the network. Sending a packet from node $X^{(0)}$ to node $X^{(1)}$ through link i corresponds to moving the boxes or balls according to action i so that the configuration is changed from $X^{(0)}$ to $X^{(1)}$. Therefore, we can relate routing in the network to sorting boxes and balls in the corresponding game, where the source and destination nodes corresponds to the initial and final configurations, the routing path consists of the links corresponding to the actions taken to solve the game, and the diameter is the maximum number of steps required to solve the game for any initial and final configurations.

2.1 Super Cayley Graphs

In this subsection we present the definition of super Cayley graphs, which are derived from the ball-arrangement game.

Each node of a super Cayley graph is represented as a permutation of k distinct symbols, where k is the number of balls in the ball-arrangement game it is derived from. We define the ith *super-symbol* of node label U as the n-long sequence of symbols at positions $(i - 1)n + 2, (i - 1)n + 3, ..., in + 1$ in the permutation label of node U. On the set of all possible permutations of k symbols, we introduce two classes of operators:

- *nucleus generators:* permute the leftmost $n + 1$ symbols (i.e., the leftmost symbol and super-symbol, corresponding to the outside ball and the balls within the leftmost box) in the ball-arrangement game.
- *super generators:* permute super-symbols without changing the contents of each of these super-symbols (i.e., corresponding to moving boxes in the ball-arrangement game).

For example, transposition generators T_i [21] are nucleus generators and swap generators $S_{n,i}$ [21] are super generators. A *super Cayley graph* is a (directed) Cayley graph [2, 6, 7] defined by nucleus generators and super generators. For example, macro-star networks $MS(l, n)$ [21] are Cayley graphs defined by n transposition nucleus generators T_i, $i = 2, 3, ..., n + 1$, and $l - 1$ swap generators $S_{n,i}$, $i = 2, 3, ..., l$. A super Cayley graph that is defined with l super-symbols is called an l-level super Cayley graph.

According to the preceding definition, node U of a super Cayley graph is connected to node V by a directed link if and only if the permutation label of node V can be obtained from that of node U either by permuting the leftmost $n + 1$ symbols of U using one of the nucleus generators in its definition, or by permuting super-symbols of U using one of the super generators in its definition. Links corresponding to the former are called *nucleus links*; while links corresponding to the latter are called *inter-cluster links*. Clearly, a super Cayley graph is a directed Cayley graph [2], whose in-/out-degree is equal to the number of generators in its definition. Since any directed Cayley graph is vertex-symmetric and regular [2, 6, 7], super Cayley graphs are vertex-symmetric and regular. Note that in some Cayley graphs, such as macro-star networks, each directed link has a corresponding directed link that has the same ending nodes and opposite direction. These graphs can be viewed as undirected Cayley graphs [2], by merging each pair of such directed links.

2.2 Definitions of Several Generators and Super Cayley Graphs

In this subsection we present several other super Cayley graphs, which corresponds to the ball-arrangement game that uses different moves. Before doing so, we introduce some operators, which will be useful in defining these networks. These generators corresponds to the actions that insert the outside ball into the leftmost box in the ball-arrangement game.

Definition 1 (Insertion Generator I_i).: Given a permutation $U = u_{1:k}$, we define the *dimension-i insertion generator I_i*, $i = 2, 3, ..., k$, as the operator that cyclicly shift the leftmost i symbols $u_{1:i}$ to the left by one position.

In other words, for $i = 2, 3, ..., k$,

$$I_i(U) = u_{2:i} u_1 u_{i+1:k}.$$

It can be viewed as inserting the outside ball to the $(i - 1)^{th}$ position of the leftmost box (i.e., the ith position from the left).

The following generators are the *inverse* of the corresponding insertion generators.

Definition 2 (Selection Generator I_i^{-1}).: Given a permutation $U = u_{1:k}$, we define the *dimension-i selection generator I_i^{-1}*, $i = 2, 3, ..., k$, as the operator that cyclicly shift the leftmost i symbols $u_{1:i}$ to the right by one position.

In other words, for $i = 2, 3, ..., k$,

$$I_i^{-1}(U) = u_i u_{1:i-1} u_{i+1:k}.$$

It can be viewed as selecting the ith ball from the leftmost box. We can see that

$$I_i^{-1} I_i(U) = U$$

so I_i^{-1} is the *inverse generator* of I_i.

The last type of generators corresponds to the actions that cyclicly shift all the boxes.

Definition 3 (Rotation Generator R_n^i).: Given a permutation $U = u_{1:k}$, we define the *rotation generator* R_n^i as the operator that cyclicly shift the rightmost $k - 1$ symbols $u_{2:k}$ to the right by ni positions.

Therefore, for $i = 2, 3, ..., l$, we have

$$R_n^i(u_{1:k}) = u_1 u_{k-in+1:k} u_{1:k-in}$$

In what follows, we will use R^i instead of R_n^i, suppressing the dependence on n, unless explicitly stated otherwise. We may also use R instead of R^1. We can see that

$$R^i = R^{i \bmod l} = \underbrace{RR\cdots R}_{i \bmod l}, \ R^i R^{-i}(U) = U.$$

We are now ready to define various interesting super Cayley graphs as directed or undirected Cayley graphs. In particular, insertion, selection, and transposition T_i generators will be used as nucleus generators in the definition of these super Cayley graphs; swap $S_{n,i}$ and rotation generators will be used as super generators. In what follows we give nine classes of super Cayley graphs generated by different combinations of these nucleus and super generators. Each of the proposed networks has its respective advantages, while algorithms for them as well as the macro-star networks can be developed on a common platform. More details and formal definitions for these networks can be found in [20–22].

- Rotation-star (RS) networks and complete-rotation-star (complete-RS) networks are super Cayley graphs derived by the ball-arrangement game where boxes are moved by rotation and balls are moved by transposition.
- Macro-rotator (MR) networks are super Cayley graphs derived by the ball-arrangement game where boxes are moved by transposition and balls are moved by insertion.
- Rotation-rotator (RR) networks and complete-rotation-rotator (complete-RR) networks are super Cayley graphs derived by the ball-arrangement game where boxes are moved by rotation and balls are moved by insertion.
- The insertion-selection (IS) network is defined as an undirected Cayley graph derived by the ball-arrangement game with one box and an outside ball, where balls are moved by insertion and selection.
- Macro-IS (MIS) networks, rotation-IS (RIS) networks, and complete-rotation-IS (complete-RIS) networks are super Cayley graphs derived by the ball-arrangement game with l boxes, where balls in the leftmost box are moved by insertion and selection.

3 Parallel Algorithms under the Single-Dimension Communication Model

In this section, we show how to emulate algorithms developed for a k-dimensional star graph on super Cayley graphs. In our emulation algorithms, a node in the k-star is one-to-one mapped on the node that has the same permutation label in super Cayley graphs.

We assume the *single-dimension communication (SDC) model* [20, 21], where the nodes are allowed to use only links of the same dimension at any given time. This communication model is used in some SIMD architectures to reduce the cost of implementation, and is also suitable for parallel systems that use wormhole routing. Many algorithms developed for the star graph as well as many other networks naturally fall into this category [13, 15, 20, 21].

The following theorem shows that a macro-star or complete-rotation-star network can emulate a star graph with a slowdown factor not exceeding 3, under the SDC model.

Theorem 1. *Any algorithm in an $(ln + 1)$-star under the SDC model can be emulated on the $MS(l, n)$ or complete-$RS(l, n)$ network with a slowdown factor of 3.*

Proof: The k-dimensional star graph is derived by a game where the outside ball can be exchanged with any other ball in a single step. To emulate such an action in the macro-star and complete-rotation-star networks, we need to bring the box containing the ball to be exchanged to the leftmost position, exchange the two balls, and finally return the box to its original position. This requires at most 3 steps in the macro-star and complete-rotation-star networks.

More precisely, the dimension-j links T_j in an $(ln + 1)$-star can be emulated by the paths consisting of links

$$S_{j_1+1} T_{j_0+2} S_{j_1+1}$$

in an $MS(l, n)$ network, and

$$R^{-j_1} T_{j_0+2} R^{j_1}$$

in an complete-$RS(l, n)$ network, where $j_0 = j - 2 \bmod n$ and $j_1 = \lfloor (j - 2)/n \rfloor$, when $j_1 \neq 0$. That is, each node in an $MS(l, n)$ network (or complete-$RS(l, n)$ network) sends the packet for its dimension-j neighbor via its S_{j_1+1} (or R^{-j_1}, respectively) link in step 1, then each node forwards the packet received in step 1 via its T_{j_0+2} link in step 2, and finally each node forwards the packet received in step 2 via its S_{j_1+1} (or R^{j_1}, respectively) link in step 3. It can be seen that each node receives the packet from its dimension-j neighbor (in the emulated star graph) in step 3. When $j_1 = 0$, emulating the T_j links requires only one step. $\qquad\square$

Insertion-selection (IS) networks are closely related to star graphs in that they can emulate a star graph of the same size with a slowdown factor not exceeding 2 under the SDC model, the single-port communication model, or the all-port communication model.

Theorem 2. *Any algorithm in a k-star can be emulated on the k-dimensional insertion-selection (IS) networks with a slowdown factor of 2, under the SDC model, the single-port communication model, or the all-port communication model.*

Proof: Transposition of two balls x_1, x_2 (an action of the ball-arrangement game corresponding to the star graph) can be replaced by insertion of the outside ball x_1 to the original position of ball x_2, followed by selection of ball x_2 (actions of the ball-arrangement game corresponding to the insertion-selection (IS) network). Since emulation of all the $k - 1$ possible actions of a k-star can be performed on the insertion-selection (IS) network at the same time without conflict, the slowdown factor is at most equal to 2 under all the three communication models. □

Similarly, a macro-insertion-selection (MIS) or complete-RIS network can emulate a star graph with a slowdown factor not exceeding 4 under the SDC model.

Theorem 3. *Any algorithm in an $(ln + 1)$-star under the SDC model can be emulated on the $MIS(l, n)$ or complete-RIS(l, n) network with a slowdown factor of 4.*

Proof: To emulate such an action in the MIS or complete-RIS network, we need to bring the box containing the ball to be exchanged to the leftmost position, insert outside ball x_1, select ball x_2 as the outside ball, and finally return the box to its original position. This requires at most 4 steps in the macro-insertion-selection (MIS) or complete-RIS network. □

The *dilation* for embedding a k-star in a k-IS network is equal to 2; the *dilation* for embedding an $(ln + 1)$-star in an $MS(l, n)$ or complete-RS(l, n) network is equal to 3; the dilation for embedding an $(ln + 1)$-star in an $MIS(l, n)$ or complete-RIS(l, n) network is equal to 4. That is, if we map each node of the k-star onto a node in an these networks, and map each link of the k-star onto a path in these networks, the maximum length of such paths is equal to 2, 3, and 4, respectively. The maximum number of such paths that are mapped onto a link in these networks is called the *congestion* of the embedding. The congestion for embedding a k-star in a k-IS network is equal to 1; the congestion for embedding an $(ln + 1)$-star in an $MS(l, n)$, complete-RS(l, n), $MIS(l, n)$, or complete-RIS(l, n) network is equal to max$(2n, l)$. However, the congestion for embedding all the links of a certain dimension i in an $MS(l, n)$, complete-RS(l, n), $MIS(l, n)$, or complete-RIS(l, n) network is only 2 when $i > n + 1$ and is equal to 1 otherwise. Therefore, the slowdown factor for an insertion-selection network to emulate a star-graph algorithm under the single-dimension, single-port, or all-port communication model is approximately equal to 1, and the slowdown factor for an MS, complete-RS, MIS, or complete-RIS network to emulate a star-graph algorithm under the SDC model is approximately equal to 2 if the network uses wormhole or cut-through routing or if it uses packet switching and each node has many packets to be sent along a certain dimension.

Two basic communication tasks that arise often in applications are the multinode broadcast (MNB) and the total exchange (TE) [4, 10]. In the MNB each node has to broadcast a packet to all the other nodes of the network, while in the TE each node has to send a different (personalized) packet to every other node of the network. Mišić and Jovanović [15] have proposed strictly optimal algorithms to execute both tasks in time $k! - 1$ and $(k + 1)! + o((k + 1)!)$, respectively, in a k-star with single-dimension communication. Using Theorem 1, the algorithms proposed in [15] give rise to corresponding asymptotically optimal algorithms for the MS and complete-RS network.

4 Parallel Algorithms under the All-Port Communication Model

In this section, we consider the *all-port communication model*, where a node is allowed to use all its incident links for packet transmission and reception at the same time. The packets transmitted on different outgoing links of a node can be different. Given two graphs G_1 and G_2 of similar sizes, and node degrees d_1 and d_2, a lower bound on the time required for G_1 to emulate G_2 is $T(d_1, d_2) = \lceil d_2/d_1 \rceil$. When G_1 can emulate G_2 with a slowdown factor of $\Theta(T(d_1, d_2))$, we will say that graph G_1 can *(asymptotically) optimally emulate* graph G_2. The following theorem shows that an $MS(l, n)$ or a complete-$RS(l, n)$ network can emulate a star graph of the same size with asymptotically optimal slowdown. Its proof is similar to the one given in [20, 21] for emulation in macro-star networks under the all-port communication model.

Theorem 4. *Any algorithm in a k-star with all-port communication can be emulated on the $MS(l, n)$ or complete-$RS(l, n)$ network with a slowdown factor of* $\max(2n, l + 1)$.

Proof: In Theorem 1, we have shown that an $MS(l, n)$ or complete-$RS(l, n)$ network can emulate an $(nl + 1)$-star with a slowdown factor of 3 under the SDC model. The emulation algorithm with all-port communication simply performs single-dimension emulation for all dimensions at the same time with proper scheduling to minimize the congestion. In particular, a packet for a dimension-j neighbor, $j \geq n + 2$, in the emulated star graph will be sent through links $S_{j_1+1}, T_{j_0+2}, S_{j_1+1}$ on the macro-star network and through links $R^{-j_1}, T_{j_0+2}, R^{j_1}$ on the complete-rotation-star network, where $j_0 = j - 2 \bmod n$ and $j_1 = \lfloor (j - 2)/n \rfloor$. There exist several schedules that guarantee the desired slowdown factor. Let B_i be the super generator that brings the ith super-symbol (i.e., box) to the leftmost position, and B_i^{-1} be the inverse generator of B_i. That is, $B_i = B_i^{-1} = S_i$ for the MS network; $B_i = R^{-i-1}$ and $B_i^{-1} = R^{i+1}$ for the complete-RS network. Then, we present a possible schedule as follows:

We first consider the special case where $l = rn + 1$ for some positive integer r.

- At time 1, each node sends the packets for its dimension-j neighbors (in the emulated k-star), $j = 2, 3, 4, \ldots, n + 1$, through links T_j.

- At time t, $t = 1, 2, 3, \ldots, n$, each node sends the packets for its dimension-$u_i(t)$ neighbors, $i = 2, 3, 4, \ldots, l$, through links B_i, where $u_i(t) = (i - 1)n + 2 + (i + t - 3 \bmod n)$.
- At time t, $t = sn + 2, sn + 3, sn + 4, \ldots, (s+1)n + 1$ for $s = 0, 1, 2, \ldots, r - 1$, each node forwards the packets for dimension-$v_i(t)$ neighbors, $i = sn + 2, sn + 3, sn + 4, \ldots, (s + 1)n + 1$, through links $T_{v_i(t)-(i-1)n}$, where $v_i(t) = (i - 1)n + 2 + (i + t - 4 \bmod n)$.
- At time t, $t = n + 1, n + 2, \ldots, 2n$, each node forwards the packets for its dimension-$u_i(t)$ neighbors, $i = 2, 3, 4, \ldots, n + 1$, through links B_i^{-1}, where $u_i(t) = (i - 1)n + 2 + (i + t - 3 \bmod n)$.
- At time t, $t = sn + 3, sn + 4, sn + 5, \ldots, (s+1)n + 2$ for $s = 1, 2, 3, \ldots, r - 1$, each node forwards the packets for dimension-$u_i(t)$ neighbors, $i = sn + 2, sn + 3, sn + 4, \ldots, (s + 1)n + 1$, through links B_i^{-1}, where $u_i(t) = (i - 1)n + 2 + (i + t - 5 \bmod n)$.

Figure 1a shows such a schedule for emulating a 13-star on these super Cayley graphs.

In what follows we extend the previous schedule to the general case where l is not of the form $l = rn + 1$. The schedule for $l \leq n$ can be easily obtained by removing the unused part of the schedule for an $MS(n + 1, n)$ or complete-$RS(n + 1, n)$ network. Other possible cases can be formulated by assuming that $l = rn - w$ for some integers $r \geq 2$ and $0 \leq w \leq n - 2$, in which case we can modify the schedule as follows. We initially start with the schedule for an $MS(rn + 1, n)$ or complete-$RS(rn+1, n)$ network. Clearly, the transmissions in the schedule that correspond to the emulation of dimensions $j > ln + 1$ are not used by the $MS(l, n)$ or complete-$RS(rn + 1, n)$ network. Therefore, we can now perform each of the transmissions over links T_{j_0+2} originally scheduled for time $l + 1$ through $rn + 1$ at time earlier than $l + 1$ by rescheduling these transmissions to the unused part of the schedule. Note that the modified part of the schedule are for the emulation of some dimensions larger than $(r - 1)n^2 + n + 1$ (that is, some of the dimensions that correspond to the last $l - (r - 1)n - 1 = n - w - 1$ blocks). We then swap generators T_{j_0+2} in the modified part of the schedule with part of the schedule for the emulation of dimensions smaller than $(r-1)n^2 + n + 2$ (that is, for some of the dimensions that correspond to the first $(r - 1)n + 1$ blocks). Due to the previous modifications, we also have to move the schedule for some generators B_{j_1+1} and $B_{j_1+1}^{-1}$. In particular, we will move the final generator $B_{j_1+1}^{-1}$ in each of the 3-step single-dimension emulations one time step after the use of T_{j_0+2} generators when possible. When $l + 1 < 2n$, the schedule for some generators $B_{j_1+1}^{-1}$ can not be moved before time $2n$. As a result, the time required for emulation under the all-port communication model is equal to $l + 1$ if $l + 1 \geq 2n$, and is equal to $2n$ otherwise. Figure 1b shows such a schedule for emulating a 16-star on these super Cayley graphs. $\square$

Theorem 5. *Any algorithm in a k-star with all-port communication can be emulated on the $MIS(l, n)$ or complete-$RIS(l, n)$ network with a slowdown factor of $\max(2n, l + 2)$.*

(a) Emulating a 13-star on an MS(4,3) or complete-RS(l,n) network

generators of an RS(4,3) network	dimension j of the 13-star being emulated											
	1	2	3	4	5	6	7	8	9	10	11	12
Step 1	T_2	T_3	T_4	R^{-1}	—	—	—	R^2	—	—	—	R^3
Step 2	T_2	R^1	—	—	T_3	R^2	R^3	—	T_4			
Step 3	—	T_3	R^1	R^2	—	T_4	T_2	R^3	—			
Step 4	R^1	—	T_4	T_2	R^2	—	—	T_3	R^1			
Step 5	R^1	—	—	R^2	R^3	—						
Step 6	R^1	R^2					R^3					

(b) Emulating a 16-star on an MS(5,3) or complete-RS(l,n) network

generators of an RS(5,3) network	dimension j of the 16-star being emulated														
	1	2	3	4	5	6	7	8	9	10	11	12	13	14	15
Step 1	T_2	T_3	T_4	R^{-1}	—	—	—	R^2	—	—	—	R^3	—	R^4	—
Step 2	T_2	R^1	—	—	—	R^2	R^3	—	T_4	—	T_2	R^4			
Step 3	—	T_3	R^1	R^2	—	T_4	T_2	R^3	—	R^4	—	—			
Step 4	R^1	—	—	T_2	—	R^1	—	T_3	R^2	—	R^4	T_4			
Step 5	R^1	T_4	R^1	T_3		R^2	—		T_2		R^4				
Step 6	R^1	R^1			R^2	R^4									

Fig.1. Schedules for emulating star graphs on macro-star and complete-rotation-star networks, under the all-port communication model. Note that a generator appears at most once in a row, and each column $j > 4$ consists of generators $B_{j_1+1}, T_{j_0+2}, B_{j_1+1}^{-1}$, where $j_0 = j - 2 \bmod 3$ and $j_1 = \lfloor (j-2)/3 \rfloor$. (a) Emulating a 13-star on an MS(4,3) or complete-RS(l,n) network. (b) Emulating a 16-star on an MS(5,3) or complete-RS(l,n) network. The links in the MS or complete-RS network are fully used during steps 1 to 5, and are 93% used on the average.

Proof: A schedule for emulating an $(nl+1)$-star on an MS(l,n) or complete-RS(l,n) network can be modified to obtain a schedule for an MIS(l,n) or complete-RIS(l,n) network by replacing each transposition generator T_{j_0+2} with an insertion nucleus generator I_{j_0+2} and a selection nucleus generator $I_{j_0+1}^{-1}$. The result follows. □

By properly choosing the parameters l and n, we can emulate a star graph with all-port communication on the above four classes of super Cayley graphs with asymptotically optimal slowdown with respect to the node degrees.

Corollary 1. *Any algorithm in a k-star with all-port communication can be emulated on the MS(l,n), complete-RS(l,n), MIS(l,n), or complete-RIS(l,n) network with asymptotically optimal slowdown if $l = \Theta(n)$.*

Proof: It follows from Theorems 4, and 5, and the fact that a graph of degree $\Theta\left(\sqrt{\frac{\log N}{\log \log N}}\right)$ cannot emulate a graph of degree $\Theta\left(\frac{\log N}{\log \log N}\right)$ with a slowdown smaller than $\Theta\left(\sqrt{\frac{\log N}{\log \log N}}\right)$, under the all-port communication model. □

Note that the slowdown factor of $\Theta\left(\sqrt{\frac{\log N}{\log \log N}}\right)$ is also the congestion for embedding a k-star on the above super Cayley graphs with $l = \Theta(n)$. Therefore, no graph that has N nodes and degree $\Theta\left(\sqrt{\frac{\log N}{\log \log N}}\right)$ can embed an N-node star graph with asymptotically better congestion (by more than a constant factor) than that achieved by these super Cayley graphs with $l = \Theta(n)$.

Fragopoulou and Akl [8] have given optimal algorithms to execute the MNB and the TE communication tasks in a k-star with all-port communication in time $\Theta((k-1)!) = \Theta(N \log \log N / \log N)$ and $\Theta(k!) = \Theta(N)$, respectively. Emulating their algorithms leads to the following asymptotically optimal algorithms for several super Cayley graphs.

Corollary 2. *The multinode broadcast task can be performed in time $\Theta\left(N\sqrt{\frac{\log\log N}{\log N}}\right)$ in an $MS(l,n)$, complete-$RS(l,n)$, $MIS(l,n)$, or complete-RIS (l,n) network with $l = \Theta(n)$, and in time $\Theta\left(\frac{N\log\log N}{\log N}\right)$ in a k-dimensional insertion-selection (IS) network, under the all-port communication model. This completion time is asymptotically optimal for the multinode broadcast task over all interconnection networks that have N nodes and degree $\Theta\left(\sqrt{\frac{\log N}{\log\log N}}\right)$ (or degree $\Theta\left(\frac{\log N}{\log\log N}\right)$, respectively), under the all-port communication model.*

Corollary 3. *The total exchange task can be performed in time $\Theta\left(N\sqrt{\frac{\log N}{\log\log N}}\right)$ in an $MS(l,n)$, complete-$RS(l,n)$, $MIS(l,n)$, or complete-$RIS(l,n)$ network with $l = \Theta(n)$, and in time $\Theta(N)$ in a k-dimensional insertion-selection (IS) network, under the all-port communication model. This completion time is asymptotically optimal for the total exchange task over all interconnection networks that have N nodes and degree $\Theta\left(\sqrt{\frac{\log N}{\log\log N}}\right)$ (or degree $\Theta\left(\frac{\log N}{\log\log N}\right)$, respectively), under the all-port communication model.*

Proof: Since the TE can be performed in an N-node star graph in time $\Theta(N)$ [8], it can be completed in time $O\left(N\sqrt{\frac{\log N}{\log\log N}}\right)$ in the first four classes of super Cayley graphs with N nodes of degree $\Theta\left(\sqrt{\frac{\log N}{\log\log N}}\right)$ through emulation (Theorems 4 and 5), assuming all-port communication and $l = \Theta(n)$. By arguing as in the derivation of the universal diameter lower bound $D_L(d, N)$, we can show that the mean internodal distance of an N-node graph with degree $\Theta\left(\sqrt{\frac{\log N}{\log\log N}}\right)$ is at least $\Omega\left(\frac{\log N}{\log\log N}\right)$. The total number of packets that have to be exchanged to perform a TE is $N^2 - N$, for a total of $\Omega\left(\frac{N^2\log N}{\log\log N}\right)$ packet transmissions. Since at most $O\left(N\sqrt{\frac{\log N}{\log\log N}}\right)$ transmissions can take place simultaneously in an N-node interconnection network of degree $\Theta\left(\sqrt{\frac{\log N}{\log\log N}}\right)$ under the all-port communication model, the time required to complete the TE is at least

$$\Omega\left(\frac{\frac{N^2\log N}{\log\log N}}{N\sqrt{\frac{\log N}{\log\log N}}}\right) = \Omega\left(N\sqrt{\frac{\log N}{\log\log N}}\right).$$

Similarly, we can obtain a TE algorithm for the k-IS network through emulation of a k-star graph (Theorem 2) and show that executing time is asymptotically optimal. □

5 Embeddings of Trees, Meshes, Hypercubes, and Transposition Networks

Several embeddings of the star graph on super Cayley graphs have been presented in the previous subsections. In this section, we present constant-dilation embeddings of other important graphs in super Cayley graphs.

A k-dimensional transposition network k-TN [12, 13] is a Cayley graph defined with a generator set consisting of all the generators that interchange any two of the k symbols in the label of a node. A k-TN graph has $k!$ nodes, degree $k(k-1)/2$, and diameter $k-1$. It contains a k-star or a k-dimensional bubble-sort graph [2] as a subgraph and has been shown to be a rich topology that can efficiently embed many other popular topologies, including hypercubes, meshes, and trees. The following theorem provides $O(1)$-dilation embedding of transposition networks in macro-star and complete-RS networks.

Theorem 6. *A k-dimensional transposition network can be one-to-one embedded in an $MS(l,n)$ or complete-RS(l,n) network with load 1, expansion 1, and dilation 5 when $l = 2$, or dilation 7 when $l \geq 3$.*

Proof: Similar to Theorem 1, we map each node in the k-TN graph onto the node with the same label in the $MS(l,n)$ or complete-RS(l,n) network. Therefore, the load and expansion of the embedding are both equal to 1. We let $T_{i,j}$ be the generator that interchanges the ith and j^{th} symbols in the label of a node, where $1 \leq i < j$. Then the generator set for a k-TN graph consists of generators $T_{i,j}$ for any combination of integers i, j satisfying $1 \leq i < j \leq k$. Let B_i be the super generator that brings the ith super-symbol (i.e., box) to the leftmost position, and B_i^{-1} be the inverse generator of B_i. That is, $B_i = B_i^{-1} = S_i$ for the MS network; $B_i = R^{-i-1}$ and $B_i^{-1} = R^{i+1}$ for the complete-RS network. Also, let $i_0 = i - 2 \bmod n$, $i_1 = \lfloor (i-2)/n \rfloor$, $j_0 = j - 2 \bmod n$, and $j_1 = \lfloor (j-2)/n \rfloor$. It is easy to verify the following equivalence

$$
T_{i,j} = \begin{cases} T_j \\ B_{j_1+1} T_{j_0+2} B_{j_1+1}^{-1} \\ T_i T_j T_i \\ T_i B_{j_1+1} T_{j_0+2} B_{j_1+1}^{-1} T_i \\ B_{i_1+1} T_{i_0+2} T_{j_0+2} T_{i_0+2} B_{i_1+1}^{-1} \\ B_{i_1+1} T_{i_0+2} B_{j_1+1} T_{j_0+2} B_{j_1+1}^{-1} T_{i_0+2} B_{i_1+1}^{-1} \end{cases} \quad \text{when} \quad \begin{cases} i = 1, \ j_1 = 0; \\ i = 1, \ j_1 > 0; \\ i_1 = j_1 = 0; \\ i_1 = 0, \ j_1 > 0; \\ i_1 = j_1 > 0; \\ i_1 \neq j_1, \ i_1, j_1 > 0. \end{cases}
$$

As a result, the dilation for embedding a k-TN graph in an $MS(l,n)$ or complete-RS(l,n) network. is at most equal to 7. When $l = 2$, only the first five cases are possible, so that the dilation is equal to 5 for an $MS(2,n)$ or complete-RS$(2,n)$ network. □

Theorem 7. *A k-dimensional transposition network can be one-to-one embedded in a k-dimensional insertion-selection network with load 1, expansion 1, and dilation 6, and in an $MIS(l,n)$ or complete-RIS(l,n) network with load 1, expansion 1, and dilation $O(1)$.*

Proof: The embeddings on k-IS networks follows from the fact that a star graph can embed a k-TN with dilation 3 and a k-IS networks can embed a k-star graph with dilation 2. The rest of the proof is similar to to that of Theorem 6. $\square$

Since a k-dimensional bubble-sort graph is a subgraph of a k-TN graph, it can also be embedded in these super Cayley graph with constant dilation.

A variety of embedding results are available for star graphs, bubble-sort graphs, and transposition networks [5, 11, 12, 14]. These results, when combined with Theorems 1, 3, 2, 6, and 7, give rise to a variety of $O(1)$-dilation embeddings in super Cayley graphs. The following corollaries summarize some of the results.

Corollary 4. *The complete binary tree of height 5 can be embedded in*

- *a k-IS network with dilation 2,*
- *an $MS(2,2)$ or complete-$RS(2,2)$ network with dilation 3, and*
- *an $MIS(2,2)$ or complete-$RIS(2,2)$ network with dilation 4.*

For $k \geq 7$, the complete binary tree of height at least equal to $(1/2 + o(1))k \log_2 k$ can be embedded in

- *a k-IS network with dilation 2,*
- *an $MS(l,n)$ or complete-$RS(l,n)$ network with dilation 3, and*
- *an $MIS(l,n)$ or complete-$RIS(l,n)$ network with dilation 4.*

Proof: In [5], it has been shown that for $k = 5$ or 6 there exists a dilation-1 embedding of the complete binary tree of height $2k - 5$ into the k-star. For $k \geq 7$, there exists a dilation-1 embedding of the complete binary tree of height at least equal to $(1/2 + o(1))k \log_2 k$ into the k-star. The rest of the proof follows from Theorems 1, 2, and 3. $\square$

Corollary 5. *There exists a dilation-$O(1)$ embedding of the d-dimensional hypercube into an $MS(l,n)$, complete-$RS(l,n)$, $MIS(l,n)$, complete-$RIS(l,n)$, or k-IS network, provided $d \leq k \log_2 k - \frac{3k}{2} + o(k)$, where $k = nl + 1$.*

Proof: In [14], it has been shown that there exists a dilation-$O(1)$ embedding of the d-dimensional hypercube into a k-star, provided that $d \leq k \log_2 k - (3/2 + o(1))k$. This, combined with Theorems 1, 2, and 3, completes the proof. $\square$

Corollary 6. *The $m_1 \times m_2$ mesh can be embedded in an $MS(2,n)$ or complete-$RS(2,n)$ network with load 1, expansion 1, and dilation 5, and in an $MIS(2,n)$ or complete-$RIS(2,n)$ network with load 1, expansion 1, and dilation $O(1)$, where $m_1 \times m_2 = (2n+1)!$. The $m_1 \times m_2$ mesh can be embedded in a k-IS network with dilation 6, $m_1 \times m_2 = k!$. The $m_1 \times m_2$ mesh can be embedded in an $MS(l,n)$ or complete-$RS(l,n)$, $MIS(l,n)$, or complete-$RIS(l,n)$ network with dilation $O(1)$, where $m_1 \times m_2 = k!$ and $l \geq 3$.*

Proof: It follows from Theorems 6 and 7 and the fact that there exists a load-1, expansion-1, and dilation-1 embedding of $m_1 \times m_2$ mesh into a k-TN graph, where $m_1 \times m_2 = k!$ [12]. $\square$

Corollary 7. *There exists a load-1, expansion-1, and dilation-$O(1)$ embedding of the $2 \times 3 \times 4 \times \cdots \times (k-1) \times k$ mesh into an $MS(l, n)$, complete-$RS(l, n)$, $MIS(l, n)$, complete-$RIS(l, n)$, or k-IS network.*

Proof: In [11] it has been shown that there exists a load-1, expansion-1, and dilation-3 embedding of the $2 \times 3 \times 4 \times \cdots \times (k-1) \times k$ mesh into a k-star. This, combined with Theorems 1, 2, and 3 completes the proof. □

6 Conclusions

The super Cayley graphs presented in this paper form a new class of interconnection networks for the modular construction of parallel computers. Super Cayley graphs have several desirable algorithmic and topological properties, while using nodes of small degree. We derived constant-dilation embeddings of a variety of important topologies, such as trees, meshes, hypercubes, star graphs, bubble-sort graphs [2], and transition networks [12, 13], for some of these super Cayley graphs. We also developed efficient algorithms to emulate the star graph, and asymptotically optimal algorithms to execute the MNB and TE communication tasks. In all parallel algorithms presented, the expected traffic is balanced on all links of suitably constructed super Cayley graphs.

References

1. Akers, S.B., D. Harel, and B. Krishnamurthy, "The star graph: an attractive alternative to the n-cube," *Proc. Int'l Conf. Parallel Processing*, 1987, pp. 393-400.
2. Akers, S.B. and B. Krishnamurthy, "A group-theoretic model for symmetric interconnection networks," *IEEE Trans. Comput.*, Vol. 38, Apr. 1989, pp. 555-565.
3. Akl, S.G. and K.A. Lyons, *Parallel Computational Geometry*, Prentice Hall, Englewood Cliffs, NJ, 1993.
4. Bertsekas, D.P. and J. Tsitsiklis, *Parallel and Distributed Computation – Numerical Methods*, Athena Scientific, 1997.
5. Bouabdallah, A., M.C. Heydemann, J. Opatrny, and D. Sotteau, "Embedding complete binary trees into star networks," *Proc. Int'l Symp. Mathematical Foundations of Computer Science*, 1994, pp. 266-275.
6. Corbett, P.F., "Rotator graphs: an efficient topology for point-to-point multiprocessor networks," *IEEE Trans. Parallel Distrib. Sys.*, vol. 3, no. 5, pp. 622-626, Sep. 1992.
7. Faber, V., J.W. Moore, and W.Y.C. Chen, "Cycle prefix digraphs for symmetric interconnection networks," *Networks*, Oct. 1993, vol. 23, no. 7, pp. 641-649.
8. Fragopoulou, P. and S.G. Akl, "Optimal communication algorithms on star graphs using spanning tree constructions," *J. Parallel Distrib. Computing.*, Vol. 24, 1995, pp. 55-71.
9. Huang, J.-P., S. Lakshmivarahan, and S.K. Dhall, "Analysis of interconnection networks based on simple Cayley coset graphs," *Proc. IEEE Symp. Parallel and Distributed Processing*, 1993, pp. 150-157.
10. Johnsson, S.L. and C.-T. Ho, "Optimum broadcasting and personalized communication in hypercubes," *IEEE Trans. Comput.*, vol. 38, no. 9, Sep. 1989, pp. 1249-1268.

11. Jwo J.S., S. Lakshmivarahan, and S.K. Dhall, "Embedding of cycles and grids in star graphs," *Proc. IEEE Symp. Parallel and Distributed Processing*, 1990, pp. 540-547.

12. Latifi, S. and P.K. Srimani, "Transposition networks as a class of fault-tolerant robust networks," *IEEE Trans. Parallel Distrib. Sys.*, Vol. 45, no. 2, Feb. 1996, pp. 230-238.

13. Leighton, F.T., *Introduction to Parallel Algorithms and Architectures: Arrays, Trees, Hypercubes*, Morgan-Kaufman, San Mateo, CA, 1992.

14. Miller, Z., D. Pritikin, and I.H. Sudborough, "Bounded dilation maps of hypercubes into Cayley graphs on the symmetric group," *Math. Sys. Theory*, Vol. 29, no. 6, Springer-Verlag, Nov.-Dec., 1996, pp.551-572.

15. Mišić, J. and Z. Jovanović, "Communication aspects of the star graph interconnection network," *IEEE Trans. Parallel Distrib. Sys.*, Vol. 5, no. 7, Jul. 1994, pp. 678-687.

16. Varvarigos, E.A., "Static and dynamic communication in parallel computing," Ph.D. dissertation, Dept. Electrical Engineering and Computer Science, Massachusetts Institute of Technology, 1992.

17. Varvarigos, E.A. and D.P. Bertsekas, "Multinode broadcast in hypercubes and rings with randomly distributed length of packets," *IEEE Trans. Parallel Distrib. Sys.*, vol. 4, no. 2, Feb. 1993, pp. 144-154.

18. Yeh, C.-H. and B. Parhami, "Recursive hierarchical swapped networks: versatile interconnection architectures for highly parallel systems," *Proc. IEEE Symp. Parallel and Distributed Processing*, Oct. 1996, pp. 453-460.

19. Yeh, C.-H. and B. Parhami, "Cyclic networks – a family of versatile fixed-degree interconnection architectures," *Proc. Int'l Parallel Processing Symp.*, Apr. 1997, 739-743.

20. Yeh, C.-H., "Efficient low-degree interconnection networks for parallel processing: topologies, algorithms, VLSI layouts, and fault tolerance," Ph.D. dissertation, Dept. Electrical & Computer Engineering, Univ. of California, Santa Barbara, Mar. 1998.

21. Yeh, C.-H. and E.A. Varvarigos, "Macro-star networks: efficient low-degree alternatives to star graphs," *IEEE Trans. Parallel Distrib. Sys.*, vol. 9, no. 10, Oct. 1998, pp. 987-1003.

22. Yeh, C.-H. and B. Parhami, "A new representation of graphs and its applications to parallel processing," *Proc. Int'l Conf. Parallel and Distributed Systems*, Dec. 1998, pp. 702-709.

23. Yeh, C.-H. and E.A. Varvarigos, "Parallel algorithms on the rotation-exchange network – a trivalent variant of the star graph," *Proc. Symp. Frontiers of Massively Parallel Computation*, Feb. 1999, pp. 302-309.

24. Yeh, C.-H. and B. Parhami, "The index-permutation graph model for hierarchical interconnection networks," *Proc. Int'l Conf. Parallel Processing*, Sep. 1999, to appear.

25. Yeh, C.-H. and B. Parhami, "Routing and embeddings in cyclic Petersen networks: an efficient extension of the Petersen graph," *Proc. Int'l Conf. Parallel Processing*, Sep. 1999, to appear.

Implementing Cellular Automata Based Models on Parallel Architectures: The CAPP Project

Stefania Bandini(*), Giovanni Erbacci(°), Giancarlo Mauri(*)

(*)Dipartimento di Informatica Sistemistica e Comunicazione
Università di Milano-Bicocca
Via Bicocca degli Arcimboldi, 8 - 20126 Milano - ITALY
tel.: +39 0264487828 - fax: +39 0264487839
email: bandini,mauri@dsi.unimi.it
(°)CINECA – Inter University Computing Center - Supercomputing Group
Via Magnanelli 6/3 - 40033 Casalecchio di Reno (BO) - ITALY
tel: +39 0516171475 - fax: +39 0516132198
email: erbacci@cineca.it

1. Introduction

This paper will present the main ideas and results of the CAPP -- Cellular Automata for Percolation Processes – Project, funded by European Union in the frame of the activity of the Technology Transfer Node NOTSOMAD. The aim of the project was to implement on parallel machines codes for simulation of specific applicative models based on Cellular Automata for a variety of industrial applications like the design of new products in the coffee industry, the experimentation of elasticity properties of batches for tires and the monitoring of chemical contamination of soils, all sharing the need of dealing with percolation phenomena.

Parallel implementation is here a crucial issue, since sequential codes proved to be uneffective when dealing with the required simulations, for which many hours or even days of computation where necessary. Hence, the porting of the code to parallel platforms using High Performance Computing Networks (HPCN) technology was mandatory to reduce the global computational time to less than one hour in order to meet the industrial end-users requirements. Then, the parallel codes have been optimized, and an extensive analysis af their performance and scalability has been carried out. Finally, laboratory data, to be compared with simulations results, have been collected through specifically designed experimental campaigns, and Cellular Automata models fitting end-users data on different sized computational platforms have been tested for:

- water flow behavior into percolation channels in a grounded and toasted coffee portion;
- visco-elastic properties of solicited carbon black networks filled in rubber compounds and the dynamical behavior of percolation clusters between aggregates representing deformations and fractures;
- reaction-diffusion phenomena of soluble chemical substances (pesticides) in different geological structures in order to evaluate percolation indexes in the monitoring of chemical contamination of soils.

In the next section, we will shortly describe the needs of the three end users we worked with, stressing the presence of percolation phenomena, to which Section 3 will be devoted.

Section 4 will motivate the choice of Cellular Automata as basic model, and will present them in an informal way; for more detailed and formal definitions, the reader is referred to the extensive literature (e.g., [Toffoli *et al.*, 1987], [Goles *et al.,* 1990]).

Finally, in Section 5, after describing the main characteristics of the models we have developed for the three end users, we will focus on their parallel implementation and on the performance evaluation of the code we have developed for different parallel architectures, and will present the results of the simulations done with the experimental data collected by the end users.

2.   The Users Needs

The three end-users involved in the project share the same need of applying HPCN in the simulation of percolation processes, but in three different application fields (i.e. simulation of water flow behavior into percolation channels of coffee, experimentation of elasticity properties of filler networks for tires, soil chemical contamination control strategies), in order to achieve shorter time to market, reduce development costs and increase the quality of the final product and the efficiency in respect to 'time to market' requirements.

Percolation can be seen from an experimental point of view as the flow of a fluid through a porous medium, which consists of a structure of interconnected channels. Theoretical models of percolation which allow to deal with several physical phenomena have been developed during the time [Stauffer *et al.*,1992]. They play a central role in many cases of great interest; so the possibility of simulating them through efficient and cost effective computer programs would give substantial benefits. However, the simulation with conventional numerical computation techniques is completely unsatisfactory [Sahimi, 1994], hence there is the need for different approaches, such as Cellular Automata.

2.1.   The Case of Illycaffè

The first case concerned Illycaffè, a producer of roasted coffee. Illycaffè is interested in percolation because brewing a cup of espresso actually means percolating a certain quantity of hot water through a bed of ground coffee particles. The determination of the features connected to percolation of hot water through coffee with different granulometric distributions are of great importance, in order to understand the processes which take place within a coffee pod, where water is transformed into the well known espresso. Percolation is in fact highly connected to the quality obtained in the cup. The monitoring of the dynamical behavior of water flow through different granulometric patterns is hence a crucial step for obtaining a good espresso, and this requires expensive and time consuming experiments.

In order to optimize the product design (for example, to establish the optimal granulometric distribution), a design tool that allows experiments to be performed in a "soft" way, that means without requiring the physical handling of the real substances (coffee, water, machines) is needed.

A totally experimental approach, that means a design of experiment considering all the involved variables, would lead to excessively time-consuming or difficult to implement working plans. This would result in an increase of the time to market, whose reduction is on the contrary a key success factor for this industrial sector. Hence, Illycaffè needs cost effective computational tools to simulate in reasonable time the percolation phenomenon with realistic parameters.

2.2. The Case of Pirelli Tires

In the case of Pirelli tires, the main needs we take into account are related to the material development, which is a very significant part in the product development cycle for tires.

The typical development process of compounds for tires goes through a loop including the following stages: experiment design, laboratory sample production, testing in the laboratory, selection of two or three recipes for further testing, industrial prototype production (one prototype per recipe), tire building, tire testing. The total time required for the launch of a new product (responding to performance requirements coming from cars producers) is around 3 years and the time needed for the material development varies between 1 and 2 years. It is expected that this time could be at least six months shorter if the developers could reduce the number of passages through the loop by means of suitable simulation models. For example, the number of experimental compounds produced and tested in the laboratory is over 3,000 per year. Any method or mathematical model apt to reduce the number of compounds to be tested is highly desirable, in order to reduce the cost of testing and the product time to market. In particular, we considered three aspects:

- the testing of mechanical and percolation properties of rubber compounds (as suggested in [Kluppel et al., 1995]) in order to map the obtained properties into the set of required performances, by-passing standard steps in the production line of prototypes to be evaluated by cars producers;
- the optimization of the dispersion of carbon black in the polymer production step in the production line;
- the design of particular morphological percolation beds and the related mechanical properties test in order to cooperate with carbon black providers for the production of optimized reinforcing structures.

2.3. The Case of ICPS

The third case we considered was that of a public research institute in Italy, the International Center of Pesticide Safety (ICPS). One of the main tasks of ICPS is to verify percolation indexes of chemical substances, in particular of pesticides, in different types of soils.

Pesticides are essential elements in modern agriculture and they are also used in public health to control communicable diseases. More than two million tons of pesticide product, that are derived from 700 active ingredients, are used yearly world-wide.

Modeling of pollution transfer processes due to pesticide contamination and making effective decisions for environment protection are complex problems. The main difficulties we have to face with when trying to solve them are related to the fact that we have an incomplete mathematical formulation of the interaction mechanisms for involved physical, chemical and mechanical processes and an inadequate knowledge on interaction among polluting substances. Furthermore, often the initial parameters and data are incomplete or not completely valid.

For the evaluation of pesticide leaching into ground water, ICPS generally makes use of mono-dimensional deterministic-mathematical models. Since the modeling of leaching is strongly dependent on spatial information related to soil properties, climate and agricultural practice, a huge number of leaching tables would be necessary to reflect all combinations occurring at different spots in the «real world». To limit the number of tables to a manageable amount and since not all data related to soil properties and climate are available in the form of digitized maps, it is common practice to create so called soil-climate scenarios. For this purpose a number of representative soils (criteria: covered area, use as arable land) might be characterized by the parameters needed as input for the leaching models. Any method or mathematical model apt to reduce the number of elaborations to be linked to scenarios is highly desirable.

3. Simulation of Percolation Phenomena

Percolation is a complex physical phenomenon which has been studied from several theoretical [Stauffer et al., 1992], applicative and computational [Sahimi, 1994] standpoints. Within this framework, several formal tools have been developed as possible solution to the problem of modeling percolation and simulating its behavior in different experimental situations.

Percolation standard theory was developed in the mathematics field as the simplest model of disordered system whose theoretical problems are not exactly solved [Stauffer et al., 1992]. In particular, percolation transition is an example of phase transition phenomenon and many real problems, like materials conductivity and magnetic properties, involve similar processes.

According to a classical definition, given a square two-dimensional grid where each place can be filled, with probability p, or empty, with probability 1-p, a *percolation cluster* is a continuous path of filled places starting from one edge of the grid and reaching the opposite one: it is made up of adjacent places and is infinite. The existence of such an infinite cluster depends on the value of p: when p is small there are only finite clusters, when p is large enough there is an unique infinite cluster. The *percolation phenomenon* can be defined really as the transition of the system from the first situation to the second one and, thus, it is considered as a geometric phase transition [Bunde et al., 1991]. The lowest value p_c corresponding to an unique infinite cluster is called *percolation threshold*. By formulating the problem in this way we obtain the so called *site percolation* model; another, dual, possibility is the *bond percolation* model, where the links are filled with probability p, rather than the places.

In order to avoid a numerical approach, some researchers proposed to represent percolation by *cellular automata* [Succi *et al.*,1989], [Bandini *et al.*, 1992], [Sahimi, 1994]. One main advantage of using cellular automata is that any configuration of the pore space can be used. Thus even the exact digital image of a natural porous medium can be used in cellular automata simulation. Once the desired pore-space configuration has been generated, the simulation can be started. At the beginning of the simulation, one constructs a transition table that tells us how the present state (determined, for each place in the grid, by the velocity of the incoming particles) is transformed into the next state. The updating of the rules depends of the local state of each involved particle.

4. Why Cellular Automata

All the end-users found that conventional numerical computation techniques are completely unsatisfactory; hence they were looking for different approaches. The approach chosen was to model the different situations to be studied with the same abstract model, Cellular Automata [Toffoli *et al.*, 1987], [Goles *et al.*, 1990], differently customized for the three cases.

A CA is an aggregation of many identical components, named *cells,* that evolve in the time by modifying their state. The main properties of the CA and of its evolution are the following:
- the CA evolves through a sequence of discrete time steps;
- at each time step, every cell is characterized by a (local) state belonging to a finite set, that does not vary from one cell to another;
- the (global) state of the automaton is updated at every step according to a function simultaneously applied to every cell *(evolution rule)* ;
- the evolution rule for cell states is the same for every cell *(uniformity)*;
- the evolution rule determines the new state of every cell from the states of a given finite set of cells (called *neighborhood* of the cell) and the state of the cell itself *(locality)*;
- the evolution rule is simultaneously applied to all cells *(intrinsic parallelism).*

These properties make it particularly easy to implement CA on machines with parallel architectures.

CA are capable of a lot of complex behaviors we associate with natural dynamical systems, including all known types of attractors, phase transitions at critical values, self-organization through the formation of dissipative structures, etc. [Wolfram, 1983]. So, they are commonly used to simulate dynamical systems at a microscopic (or sub-macroscopic) level, introducing a grid of interconnected cells where each cell describes a small volume in the space. The evolving properties are associated with each cell as state variables.

Derivatives in differential equations are replaced by computational rules associated with each cell that update the state-variables at discrete time steps.

A classical and well studied example of this approach is the modeling of phenomena in fluid dynamics [d'Humieres *et al.*, 1987]. Within this topic, the phenomena that one expects in fluid flow, such as diffusion, wave propagation, emerging vortices, etc. can be convincingly simulated.

There is a growing amount of activity in many areas of physics to use such as computational approach: there appear to be substantial advantages compared to partial differential equations [Toffoli, 1984].

Starting from the analysis of the specific problems to be solved, we have first designed models for:

- the generation of percolation beds in accordance with experimental parameters such as particle size and morphology, density and granulometric distributions;
- the simulation of water flow behavior into percolation channels in a grounded and toasted coffee portion;
- the simulation of visco-elastic properties of solicited carbon black networks filled in rubber compounds and the dynamical behavior of percolation clusters between aggregate representing deformations and fractures;
- the simulation of reaction-diffusion phenomena of soluble chemical substances (pesticides) in different geological structures.

Then, programs for the above tasks have been written, ported on different parallel architectures and experimented with sets of real data.

5. The HPCN Issue: Implementation and Performance Results

We are not interested here in describing in detail the specific models we developed, that have been presented in other papers [Borsani *et al.*, 1998], [Bandini *et al.*, 1998a] [Bandini *et al.*, 1998b]. We will rather discuss some implementation issues and the performances of the produced code. The main problem in simulating CA dynamics for the cases we considered with significant data is computation time: on a (sequential) workstation, simulations for Illycaffè, for example, required from 15 to 18 hours, a time too high to allow an effective use of the code in real situations. Hence, the need to reduce this time using parallel computation.

5.1. The FHP-N Model for Coffee Percolation

The model used to simulate coffee percolation is the FHP-N model, an extension of the classical FHP model [Frish *et al.*, 1986], with an arbitrary number of rest particles per cell. It is a fluid-dynamic model based on LGA, which derives the Navier-Stokes equation on a hexagonal lattice of boolean cells by imposing conservation of mass and momentum. An averaging procedure over space and time leads to calculate the required physical quantities.

Without entering into details we can state that it is not a heuristic model. On the contrary, it is based on the physics occurring during the process and it reproduces differential equations which rule the processes occurring during percolation. The flow of particles that leave the lattice or just a region of the lattice is calculated, so as the distribution of the modulus of the momentum, which is a good indicator of the presence of high-velocity channels.

The analysis of the sequential code and the computational power necessary to the simulations suggested to use a message-passing programming paradigm, portable on high-end super-computers like Cray T3E, middle-end super-computers like Origin 2000, and low-end cluster of PCs. The MPI message-passing library has been selected and the code has been ported to the parallel platforms following this paradigm.

Finally, a series of simulations on Cray T3E and Origin 2000 was started. The following table give the speed up of the program, from a sequential machine to the Cray T3E, as a function of the number of processors (PE) used. It can be seen that the computational time has been drastically reduced, from more than 15 hours to half an hour.

Number of PE's	Number of iterations	Simulation time (sec)	Number of cells per second (10^6)	Speed up theor/exper
1 (Pentium 200)	5000	5466	1.92	
2	5000	1513	7	2/2
4	5000	719	14	4/4
8	5000	375	28	8/8
16	5000	187	56	16/16
32	5000	98	107	30/32
64	5000	54	109	56/64
128	5000	32	338	95/128

Table 1. Speed-up table on the system Cray T3E1200 for the Illycaffè model

The next tables show the speed up obtained, for the most time consuming routines, i.e. propagation (prop), collision (coll) and media routines, and for the complete code (tot) on the systems Cray T3E and Origin 2000, respectively, as a function of the number of processors.

N PEs	Prop	Coll	Media	Tot
2	2.00	2.00	2.00	2.00
4	4.42	3.86	5.04	4.79
8	8.05	6.73	9.99	9.16

16	17.09	12.67	19.74	17.84
32	32.61	20.46	38.08	32.48
64	58.34	28.76	70.35	54.05
128	114.22	35.32	127.87	79.40

Table 2. Speed-up reference table on the system Cray T3E1200 for the Illycaffè model

N PEs	Prop	Coll	Media	Tot
2	2.00	2.00	2.00	2.00
4	5.76	5.13	7.65	6.90
8	17.72	8.26	25.43	18.23

Table 3. Speed-up reference table on the system SGI Origin 2000 for the Illycaffè model

The end-users, with the speed-up tables, can easily decide the best number of PEs on which it is better to run the simulations, depending on the maximum time that they are able to wait for the answers and on the availability of the machines. For the Illycaffé model the machine that better fits the big computational load of the simulations is the Cray T3E, where the 128 processors can give a significant advantage in terms of time.

The speed-up report shows a super-linear speed-up (the gain running the code on a parallel architecture with p processors is greater than p) for the media and propagation routines and a sub-linear speed-up for the entire code and the collision routine.

This model can never be fitted in the small cache of the processor of the Cray also when the data allocated by the program is split on 128 processors. From our performance evaluations, the importance of an optimized access to the memory is evident: the stream buffer device can optimize the access in memory and gives a great increase of performance for the code. On SGI Origin 2000 the cache is very large and can contain the entire allocated simulation between 4 through 8 processors. The processor maintains all data in cache, giving an impressive speed-up from 4 to 8.

Finally, the program has been run on a set of porous beds, generated according to the hints given by Illycaffe'. The total surface exposed to water as a function of the granulometric distribution has been computed. The program generating the percolation bed builds the particles starting from a given centre and a radius, with a pseudo-fractal growth, which leads to a larger surface than the corresponding sphere. This is big step towards the real phenomenon.

Some parameters have been calculated, which characterise the behaviour of the fluid. Since they depend on the initial conditions, which have been set just once for every simulation so that the results can be compared, they are equal for every simulation..

The Reynolds number, which is a standard parameter in fluid-dynamic simulations to compare different models and physical situations, is not computable in this case, because the granulometric distribution leads to a lack of a significant one dimensional characteristic length. This index is not very useful for our purpose anyway. The mass density, i.e. the average particles number in each cell (under the hypothesis of constant mass particles) has been computed instead.

The flow rate is the actual physical quantity, which can be monitored and compared with real data. If the flow is measured on the border of the lattice the results have the opposite trend compared to the experimental data recorded outside the percolation bed. The flow rate increases when the void ratio decreases. The effect is due to the presence of many obstacles, which causes vortexes on the exit edge. A greater number of particles is then counted due to their presence in the vortexes inside the sensitive surface of counting. When an additional empty layer is considered the simulations agree at least qualitatively with the experimental recordings as far as the maximum value is regarded, showing a decrease of the flow rate when the tamping degree increases.

5.2. Simulation of Dynamic Properties of Filled Rubber Compounds

In the case of Pirelli Tires an original CA based model for the simulation of dynamic properties of filled rubber compounds has been developed [Bandini *et al.*, 1999a].

Figure 1 summarizes the speed-up results for the Pirelli Tires model on Cray T3E.

The Pirelli model performs very well on the parallel architectures tested. On the Cray T3E, the real problem takes a total time ranging from 720 seconds on 2 PEs to less than 11 seconds on 128 PEs. The same scalability can be observed also on SGI Origin 2000 where the code takes 780 and 195seconds on 2 and 8 CPUs respectively. This is a very important result because using these parallel systems, the output of a simulation run will be available in a few seconds.

It can be observed that for a given number of processors the total time is of the same order of magnitude on Cray T3E and Origin 2000, despite of the fact that the Cray T3E has a more powerful processor than Origin 2000 (600MHz versus 200 Mhz). For example, with 4 processors the code takes 361 seconds on Cray T3E and 437 seconds on Origin 2000. Possible reasons for this behavior can be the structure of the algorithm that requires a few arithmetic operations in comparison to the data moving and the dimension of the data cache available on the systems. The Cray T3E provides a very small data cache system compared to Origin 2000: 8 KByte primary plus 96 KByte secondary data cache for Cray T3E and 32 KByte primary plus 4 MByte secondary data cache for Origin 2000.

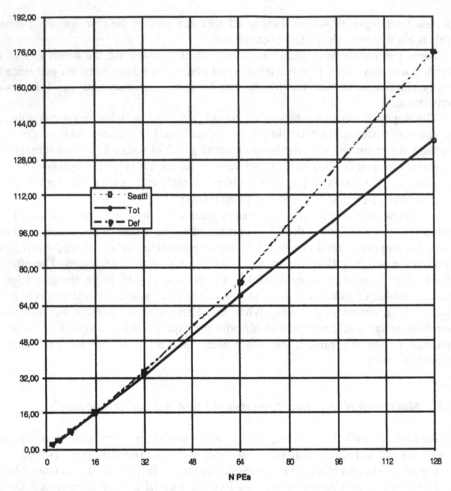

Figure 1. Speed-Up of the Pirelli model for the system Cray T3E

The speed-up report shows in some cases a super-linear speed-up; this phenomenon can be explained with the data cache missing occurring when the simulation runs on a small number of processors.

Even in this case, after the implementation and the performance evaluation, the model has been run on real physical and morphological data collected in order to improve the quality and reliability of the simulation of the material behaviour in an stress-strain experiment. The steps of this activity were planned according to the following scheme:

1. Preparation of the reference compounds composed by natural rubber, carbon blacks and chemicals for the vulcanization. Three different carbon blacks were selected with different particle size and each carbon black was introduced in the compound at 2 different concentrations. Since the reinforcing effect is related to the dimensions of particles and aggregates, this choice will provide a wide range of condition coming to finer C.B (carbon blacks) to coarser.

2. Determination for each compound above of the vulcanization kinetics in order to check the proper time of the vulcanization.
3. Vulcanization and moulding of the specimens in the suitable shape. The condition selected was 10 minutes at 170 °C.
4. Characterization of the vulcanized material and determination of the mophology of the filler network by AFM (Atomic Force Microscopy), and of the grain size distribution of the recovered carbon-black by DCP (Disc Centrifuge Photosedimentometry). The distribution of the aggregates size ranges from 0.25 to 0.50 microns.
5. Determination of the behaviour of the vulcanized reference compound in a dynamic stress-strain experiment at different levels of strain and at 3 different temperatures. This set of data represents the output that the simulation should provide and may be assumed as a representation of the mechanical properties of the material.

5.3. A Reaction-Diffusion Machine for Studying Pesticide Leaching

In the case of ICPS the specialization in terms of CA of a Reaction–Diffusion Machine for simulating the chemical extraction of soluble substances occurring during the washing process in porous media has been created [Bandini et al., 1999b].

Each cell can be of three different types: *water* (i.e. containing a given amount of water), *soil* (i.e. containing a given amount of soil) or *empty*. Moreover, each cell can contain a given amount of pesticide (provided that the cell is not empty), expressed as an integer number of *particles*. The number of particles in water and soil cells cannot be greater than a given *saturation constant* (respectively WSC and SSC). The number of particles in each cell is evenly split in four directions.

The simulation can be divided in three stages:
- **Reaction** : Neighbouring cells containing pesticide exchange some particles according to the equilibrium search law.
- **Balance** : The number of particles in each cell is evenly divided in the four directions.
- **Diffusion** : Water particles move inside the percolation bed.

The results of the performance evaluation of the parallel code implementing the above model are synthesized in Figure 2.

The ICPS model performs well on the parallel architectures tested. On the Cray T3E, the time decreases from 267.61 seconds (with 2 PEs) to 16.98 seconds when 128 PEs are used.

The scalability is very good up to 32 PEs, but after that number the model does not scale at all. The total time is quite the same with 32 PEs and with 128 PEs (20.42 seconds and 16.98seconds respectively). The same phenomenon can be observed also on the SGI Origin 2000 where the code takes 314.07 seconds and 128.80 seconds on 2 and 8 CPUs respectively, and the total time does not decrease moving from 4 to 8 CPUs.

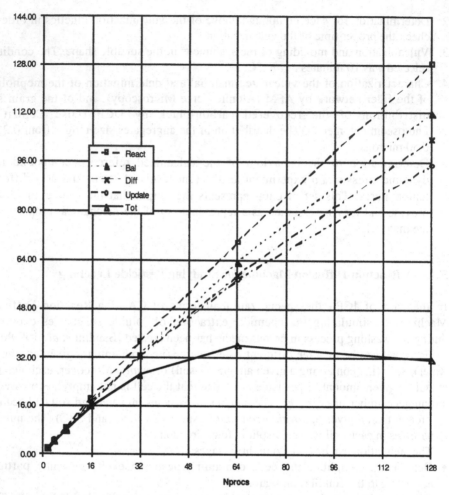

Figure 2. Speed-Up of the ICPS model for the system Cray T3E

The phenomenon needs to be investigated more in depth but at a first analysis, the communication seems the responsible for the bad scalability (after 32 PEs for Cray T3E and after 4 CPUs for SGI Origin 2000), considering also that a big amount of arithmetic operations is not involved for this problem, respect to the big activity concerning the data movement. Perhaps a more in depth analysis of the problem allows to introduce a new algorithm with less communication activity and a better scalability when a big number of PEs is utilized.

For the ICPS model the parallel architectures used represent a good choice also with a limited number of PEs (32 for Cray T3E and 4 for Origin 2000).In fact, the problem size can be fitted in the global memory of that systems (a minimum of 2 PE are required to host all the data structures involved) and the total time can be very acceptable (in the order of a few seconds) to do all the tests need for the simulations.

Acknowledgements

The CAPP (Cellular Automata for Percolation Processes) project has been supported by the ESPRIT HPCN programme from the European Commission and was one of the High Performance Computing and Networking Technology Transfer Nodes (HPCN-TTN) projects.

References

[Bandini et al., 1992] Bandini, S., G. Cattaneo, G. Tarantello, *Distributed AI Models for Percolation*, "Intelligent Scientific Computation", AAAI Fall Symposium Series, Cambridge (MA), 1992.

[Bandini et al., 1998a] Bandini, S., G. Giuliani, M. Magagnini, *A Cellular Automaton Based Computational Model for the Simulation of Dynamic Properties of Filled Rubber Compounds*, in S. Bandini, R. Serra, F. Suggi Liverani (eds.), «Cellular Automata: Research towards Industry», Springer Verlag, London, 1998.

[Bandini et al., 1998b] Bandini, S., E. Illy, C. Simone, F. Suggi Liverani, *A Computational Model Based on the Reaction-Diffusion Machine to Simulate Transportation Phenomena*, in S. Bandini, R. Serra, F. Suggi Liverani (eds.), « Cellular Automata: Research towards Industry», Springer Verlag, London, 1998.

[Bandini et al., 1999a] Bandini, S., M. Magagnini, *Parallel Processing Simulation of Dynamic Properties of Filled Rubber Compounds based on Cellular Automata*, Parallel Computing, to appear, 1999.

[Bandini et al., 1999b] Bandini, S., C. Simone, *Integrating Forms of Interaction in a Distributed Coordination Model*, Fundamentae Informaticae, to appear, 1999.

[Borsani et al., 1998] Borsani C., G. Cattaneo, V. de Mattei, U. Jocher, B. Zampini, *2D and 3D Lattice Gas Techniques for Fluid-Dynamics Simulations*, in S. Bandini, R. Serra, F. Suggi Liverani (eds.), «Cellular Automata: Research towards Industry», Springer Verlag, London, 1998.

[Bunde et al., 1991].Bunde A., S. Havlin (eds.), *Fractals and Disordered Systems*, Springer Verlag, Berlin, 1991.

[d'Humieres et al., 1987] d'Humieres, D., P. Lallemand, *Numerical Simulations of Hydrodynamics with Lattice Gas Automata in Two Dimensions*, Complex Systems, vol. 1, n. 4, 1987.

[Goles et al., 1990] Goles, E., S. Martìnez, *Neural and Automata Networks: Dynamical Behavior and Applications*, Kluwer Academic, Boston, 1990.

[Kluppel et al., 1995] Kluppel, M., G. Heinrrich, Rubber Chemistry and Technology, 68, 297, 1995.

[Toffoli, 1984] Toffoli, T., *Cellular Automata as an Alternative to (rather than an approximation of) Differential Equations in Modeling Physics*, Physica 10D, North-Holland, 1984.

[Sahimi, 1994] Sahimi, M., *Applications of Percolation Theory*, Taylor & Francis, London, 1994.

[Stauffer et al.,1992] Stauffer, D., A. Aharony, *Introduction to Percolation Theory*, 2nd ed., Taylor & Francis, London, 1992.

[Toffoli et al., 1987] Toffoli, T., N., *Margolus, Cellular Automata Machines: a New Environment for Modeling*, MIT Press, Cambridge, MA, 1987.

[Wolfram 1983] Wolfram, S., *Statistical Mechanics of Cellular Automata*, Rev. of Modern Physics, vol. 55, n. 3, 1983.

Methods for Achieving Peak Computational Rates for Linear Algebra Operations on Superscalar RISC Processors

Oleg Bessonov[1], Dominique Fougère[2], Ky Dang Quoc[2], Bernard Roux[2]

[1] Institute for Problems in Mechanics of Russian Academy of Sciences,
101, Vernadsky ave., 117526 Moscow, Russia
[2] Institut de Recherche sur les Phénomènes Hors Equilibre,
IRPHE–IMT, Technopôle de Château-Gombert, 13451 Marseille Cedex 20, France

Abstract. The paper presents methods for developing high performance computational cores and dense linear algebra routines. Different approaches for performing matrix multiplication algorithms are analysed for hierarchical memory computers, taking into account their architectural properties and limitations. Block versions of matrix multiplication and LU-decomposition algorithms are described. The performance results of these new algorithms for several processors are compared with the results obtained for optimized LAPACK and BLAS libraries.

1 Introduction

Modern superscalar RISC processors are characterized by the sharp disbalance between potentially high computational speed and relatively low memory performance. The latter is partially compensated by integrating the hierarchy of smaller cache memories. This however leads to the complicated problem of revealing memory locality properties of algorithms.

The most successful for a such sort of processors are implementations of high performance dense linear algebra algorithms. These algorithms are used in numerous time consuming applications to solve dense systems of linear equations [1] and to perform multigrid relaxation sweeps [3]. For more general sorts of problems, locality properties of algorithms are considered in [2, 3, 4].

Much experience has been obtained in the development of block algorithms in LAPACK project [1]. The idea of block approach is based on the use of BLAS 3 matrix multiplication software. The BLAS 3 performs $O(n^3)$ operations on $O(n^2)$ data elements, which helps to improve the balance between computations and memory references. However, the blocked LAPACK approach is effectively applicable only to large problems, when it benefits from the relation $O(n^3) \gg O(n^2)$.

In real practice the matrix size is often not so big to efficiently use LAPACK. On the other hand, it usually exceeds the size of biggest cache in the memory hierarchy. Therefore, new methods should be developed which can be used for implementing efficient solvers for linear systems of moderate size.

The present paper describes the approach based on multiplication of block vector by matrix, as opposed to vector–matrix (BLAS 2) and matrix–matrix

(BLAS 3) approaches. Employing the instruction level parallelism (ILP) in the optimized inner loops using the level 1 cache as a pool of vector registers results in achieving near-peak computational rates. The slower speed of outer levels of memory hierarchy (L2-cache and main memory) is taken into consideration for different sorts of RISC processor architecture. The new method therefore combines efficiency of BLAS 3 with flexibility and scalability of BLAS 2.

The developed computational cores are used as building blocks for implementation of out-of-cache matrix multiplication and LU-decomposition routines. Different variants of adaptive blocking algorithms are considered in conjunction with main microprocessor architectures. The performance results are compared with the results for standard LAPACK and BLAS 3 libraries, as well as with the peak results registered by J. Dongarra for the famous Linpack benchmark [5].

The performance gain of this new approach (tens of percents) is comparable to the effect of 2-processor parallelization, or to the result of costly CPU upgrade. Unlike them both, this gain is obtained for free, without additional hardware. The new algorithm can be subsequently used as a base of parallelized code.

All considerations are done for double precision (`real*8`) floating point arithmetic. The Fortran style of array organization (column by column) is assumed.

2 Analysis of Computational Cores

The programming style for achieving peak computational rates strongly depends on the architectural properties of target microprocessor. Consider SGI/MIPS R10000 processor as a typical example. Its main characteristics are:

- 4-way superscalar architecture with out-of-order execution;
- pipelined floating point (FP) unit with short latency and execution rate 2 operations per cycle (for multiplication and addition operations combined in `MADD` machine instruction) giving 390 MFLOPS peak for 195 MHz processor;
- load/store unit with issue rate 1 load/store instruction per cycle;
- 32 64-bit floating point registers;
- 32 KByte level 1 data cache with instant access and non-blocking cache miss;
- 2 MByte level 2 cache with short latency and limited throughput;
- relatively slow main memory with more limited throughput.

Other modern microprocessors are very similar to the R10000. They may differ in cache organization and have, for example, wider superscalarity, double FP unit (4 FP operations per cycle) and less restrictive load/store issue rate limitation.

The most important of these characteristics is the memory access rate. In our example, the optimal balance is 1 load/store instruction per 1 multiply/add pair (`MADD` instruction). Consider the matrix multiplication algorithm from the point of view of this balance. Figure 1 represents 3 main forms of the algorithm, depending on the choice of inner loop: scalar product (a), column update (b) and matrix update (c) approaches. For each approach, 3 memory accesses per loop iteration (i.e. one `MADD` instruction) are required. One of them is eliminated by placing the loop-invariant variable into a register, another one can be considered as addressing L1-cache, and the last refers to uncached memory. Therefore, we have 2 times more load/store instructions than necessary for the optimal balance.

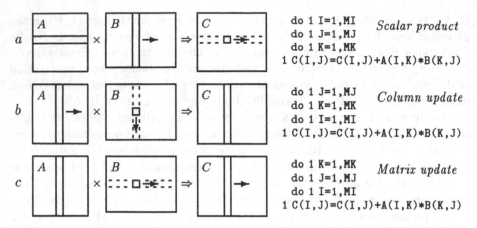

Fig. 1. Main forms of the matrix multiplication algorithm

The way to solve this problem is to block vectors for the inner loop. Imagine, that for the scalar product form of the algorithm (Fig. 1, a) a block row of width N_i in matrix A is multiplied by a block column of width N_j in matrix B producing the rectangular block of size $N_i \cdot N_j$ in matrix C. The inner loop iteration in this case contains $N_i + N_j$ memory accesses and $N_i \cdot N_j$ MADD instructions (Fig. 2). The balance relation is therefore $N_i + N_j \leq N_i \cdot N_j$. Similarly, a block column of width N_k in A, a block of size $N_k \cdot N_j$ in B and the resulting block column of width N_j in C can be considered for the forms (b) and (c) of the algorithm. The balance relation is in these cases $N_k + 2 \cdot N_j \leq N_k \cdot N_j$.

The next aim is to reduce the access rate to the matrix in uncached memory. For the form (a) of the algorithm above, 1 memory access is performed every N_i cycles (Fig. 2). Therefore N_i (the width of the cached block row in A) should be made as large as possible. The same rule applies to the widths of the cached block columns for another forms of the algorithms, N_j for (b) and N_k for (c).

The factor that limits the width of cached block vector is the number of FP registers available. For 32 registers total, 16 can be usually used to keep loop-invariant variables (e.g. a block of size $N_i \cdot N_j$ in matrix C, Fig. 2). Also, the complexity of instruction scheduling can restrict the choice of variants, especially when scheduling is performed by Fortran compiler, rather than manually. The SGI compiler, for example, can generate near-optimal loops with the following parameters: (a) $N_i = 8$, $N_j = 2$; (b) $N_k = 4$, $N_j = 4$; (c) $N_k = 8$, $N_j = 2$.

For all 3 forms (Fig. 1), the two innermost loops comprise the computational cores representing the following sorts of block vector by matrix multiplication:

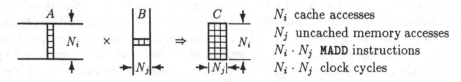

N_i cache accesses
N_j uncached memory accesses
$N_i \cdot N_j$ MADD instructions
$N_i \cdot N_j$ clock cycles

Fig. 2. The inner loop iteration of the blocked scalar product algorithm

(*a*) multiplying the block row in *A* by the matrix *B*;
(*b*) multiplying the matrix *A* by the block column in *B*;
(*c*) multiplying the block column in *A* by the block row in *B* (outer product).
This approach can be considered as a block extensions to the BLAS 2 approach.

In the presented algorithm, the part of L1-cache (usually 50 %) is used as a pool of vector registers. If the length of block vector is too big to fit into the cache, strip-mining should be applied. Unlike BLAS 3, the new computational cores achieve near–peak performance even for multiplication of narrow block vector by matrix, that is very convenient for performing triangular solves in LU-decomposition routines. Allocation of narrow long arrays in L1-cache (rather than small square submatrices, as in more traditional approach) ensures the reasonable performance level for small and moderate scale problems.

3 General Matrix Multiplication Algorithm

For implementing matrix multiplication (MxM) routines, the most efficient of 3 forms of computational cores is the scalar product approach (Fig. 1, *a*). The other forms are suitable for LU-decomposition and will be considered later.

The accurate implementation of MxM codes, with either automatic (SGI) or manual (Intel) instruction scheduling, allowed to achieve the following performance levels close to the peak values: SGI PowerChallenge R10000-195 – 366 MFLOPS (peak 390 MFLOPS), R8000-90 – 349 MFLOPS (peak 360), Intel Celeron-333 – 190 MFLOPS (peak 333), i860-40 – 42.7 MFLOPS (peak 45.7).

For the i860 processor, the special algorithm has been developed employing the idea of Strassen–Winograd for multiplication of 2×2 submatrices [6]. This algorithm is applicable to processors with different costs of multiplication and addition operations and can increase the peak performance by 14 %.

Consider now the blocking strategy for big matrices. As mentioned above, strip-mining can be applied if the block row in matrix *A* (Fig. 2) is bigger than L1-cache. For processors with 2 cache levels, horizontal strips of matrix *B* should be further split into smaller blocks (tiles) to fit into L2-cache (Fig. 3).

The adaptive blocking algorithm has been developed, which is parametrized for different cache architectures and sizes. Performance results for SGI Power-Challenge R8000 and R10000 computers are presented on Fig. 4 in comparison with the results for optimized BLAS libraries from SGI. The new MxM code written in Fortran outperforms the BLAS code for both machines. For R10000, the BLAS results reveal sharp drops and illustrate that the implementation is not cache–aware. Instead, the new algorithm demonstrates steady behaviour.

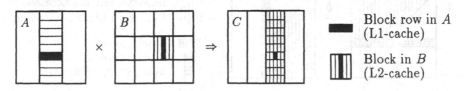

Fig. 3. Illustration of the blocking strategy for the matrix multiplication algorithm

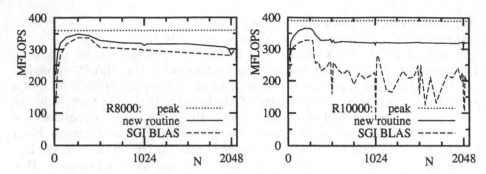

Fig. 4. Performance of MxM routines depending on matrix size (for square matrices)

4 Solving Dense Systems of Linear Equations

The algorithms based on the scalar product approach (Fig. 1, a) may be used for solving linear systems. The top-looking variant [7] of LU-decomposition (Fig. 5, a) has been implemented for i860 processor. It employs the idea of Strassen–Winograd mentioned above. The record performance result for J. Dongarra's Linpack-1000 benchmark (34.5 MFLOPS) has been obtained on Intel iPSC/860 and Delta computers and registered in [5].

However, the splitting into vertical strips cannot be applied to the top-looking strategy due to problems with pivoting and column interchange. Therefore, this approach is applicable only for processors with relatively fast main memory missing level 2 cache (for example, IBM P2SC, widely used in SP-2 supercomputers).

The left-looking variant (Fig. 5, b) can be used for processors with 2 levels of cache (SGI R10000/R12000, IBM P3, DEC 21264 etc.) as well as for processors with the only cache of very large size (HP PA8x00 and SGI R8000, where L2-cache is addressed directly by FP unit). For the last class of processors, splitting the matrix into vertical strips is sufficient to ensure the necessary locality.

For processors with 2 levels of cache, the 2-dimensional blocking should be applied. Then most operations will be expressed through multiplication of sub-matrices. For example, the update of submatrix C on Fig. 6 (a) is performed as $C = C + AB$. The matrix update variant of computational core (Fig. 1, c) is the most efficient for this operation, when a narrow block column in A (L1-cache) is used to update the whole submatrix C (L2-cache). It can also be used for triangular solves. Additionally, splitting the matrix into vertical strips permits partial interchange of rows reducing the cost of interchange twice as a result.

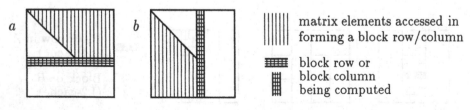

Fig. 5. The top-looking (a) and the left-looking (b) variants of LU-decomposition

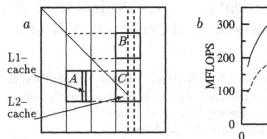 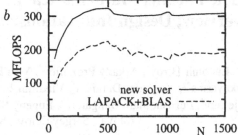

Fig. 6. (a) Blocked LU-decomposition; (b) Performance of linear solvers for R10000

The blocking algorithms have been implemented for SGI PowerChallenge R8000 and R10000 computers. For R8000, the obtained Linpack-1000 result is 312.3 MFLOPS, which is higher than the record value (308 MFLOPS) registered in [5]. The Linpack-1000 result for R10000 is 312.2 MFLOPS. Performance of the new linear solver for R10000 processor is presented on Fig. 6 (b) in comparison with the results of LAPACK solver with optimized BLAS library. The new algorithm is more than 50 % faster for all matrix sizes. Note that the new code is wholly written in Fortran. Implementing assembler code with manual instruction scheduling and prefetch would further improve the performance.

5 Conclusion

The methods described in the paper allow to implement high performance dense linear algebra codes for modern superscalar RISC processors with hierarchical memory organization. These methods combine the efficiency of large block approach with the flexibility and scalability of vector–matrix operations. The new routines have been implemented based on the developed methods, that demonstrate the record level of performance for several processor architectures.

The work was supported by the program "Réseau Formation-Recherche Franco-Russe" of the French Ministry MENRT and by Silicon Graphics France.

References

1. J. Dongarra, D. Walker. The design of linear algebra libraries for high performance computers. LAPACK working note 58, University of Tennessee, Knoxville, TN, 1993.
2. S. Carr. Combining optimization for cache and instruction-level parallelism. Proceedings of PACT 96, Boston, MA, 1996.
3. U. Rüde. Iterative algorithms on high performance architectures. Proceedings / Euro-Par '97, Lecture Notes in Computer Science, **1300**, 1997, 57-71.
4. O. Bessonov, B. Roux. Optimization techniques and performance analysis for different serial and parallel RISC-based computers. Proceedings / PaCT-97, Lecture Notes in Computer Science, **1277**, 1997, 168–174.
5. J. Dongarra. Performance of various computers using standard linear equations software. CS-89-85, Knoxville, Oak Ridge, TN, 1999.
6. A. Aho, J. Hopcroft, J. Ullman. The design and analysis of computer algorithms. Addison-Wesley, Reading, 1974.
7. J.M. Ortega. Introduction to parallel and vector solution of linear systems. Plenum Press, New York, 1988.

The Parallel Mathematical Libraries Project (PMLP): Overview, Design Innovations, and Preliminary Results [1]

Lubomir Birov[*], Arkady Prokofiev[†], Yuri Bartenev[†], Anatoly Vargin[†], Avijit Purkayastha[*2], Yoginder Dandass[*], Vladimir Erzunov[†], Elena Shanikova[†], Anthony Skjellum[*], Purushotham Bangalore[*], Eugeny Shuvalov[†], Vitaly Ovechkin[†], Nataly Frolova[†], Sergey Orlov[†], Sergey Egorov[†]

[*]Mississippi State University, High Performance Computing Laboratory
Department of Computer Science and NSF Engineering Research Center for Computational Field Simulation, PO Box 9627, Mississippi State, MS 39762, USA
lubo@cs.msstate.edu; {avijit, yogi, tony, puri}@erc.msstate.edu
[†]Russian Federal Nuclear Center, Mira 37, Sarov City, N.Novgorod region, Russia
{ark, bart, vargin, erzunov, shan, trump, assist, Lonn, seo, sne}@rstl.vniief.ru

Abstract. In this paper, we present a new, parallel, mathematical library suite for sparse matrices. The Parallel Mathematical Libraries Project (PMLP), a joint effort of Intel, Lawrence Livermore National Laboratory, the Russian Federal Nuclear Laboratory (VNIIEF), and Mississippi State University (MSU), constitutes a concerted effort to create a supportable, comprehensive "Sparse Object-oriented Mathematical Library Suite." With overall design and software validation work at MSU, most software development and testing at VNIIEF, and logistics and other miscellaneous support provided by LLNL and Intel, this international collaboration brings object-oriented programming techniques and C++ to the task of providing linear and non-linear algebraic-oriented algorithms for scientists and engineers. Language bindings for C, Fortran-77, and C++ are provided.

1 Introduction

The Parallel Mathematical Library Project builds on over a decade of flexible, portable, and performance-oriented scalable library efforts that commenced with research on the Multicomputer Toolbox [13, 15]. Unlike the fixed-distribution approach used in libraries such as Scalapack [5, 7], PMLP and Multicomputer

[1] Support from the United States Industry Coalition (USIC) through DOE under subcontracts #B319811, #B329138, and #B342021 from LLNL, is gratefully acknowledged. This work was also supported in part under contract from the LLNL funded by the Initiatives for Proliferation Prevention Program (IPP) which is in the U.S. DoE Office of Arms Control and Non-Proliferation. Additional support from the NSF Career Program, Grant #ASC-9501917 is acknowledged.

[2] Additional support is also acknowledged from the University of Puerto Rico, Mayaguez for sabbatical leave.

Toolbox emphasize flexible, application-relevant data layouts. Also, PMLP differs from other major library efforts in its systematic use of software engineering and design, including design documents that drive the implementation effort, coupled with efforts to provide high performance, portability, and usability. The advantage of the PMLP parallel library is that it supports current and future parallel application architectures, as shown in Figure 1. Parallel scientific applications have to cope with significant software complexity resulting from the problem being solved, the management of memory hierarchies, and the size of the software itself. In addition, mathematical applications need to use different languages, according to what is most appropriate or mandated, for a given part of the work, and need to leverage reusable and standard components. The application architecture to be supported by this project assumes that the best approach is to develop all portable, high-performance codes in C and/or C++, while supporting application-level software in these languages and FORTRAN-77. Interoperability interfaces for multi-language programming, library layer with parallel C++ functionality, library layer with sequential C++ functionality and concrete, standard sequential kernels are supported, as shown in Figure 1.

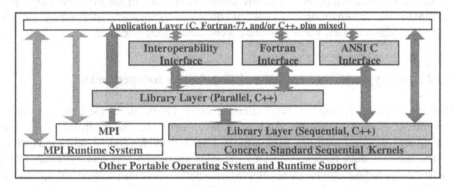

Fig. 1. Canonical parallel architecture supported by PMLP

The current scope of PMLP includes sequential sparse BLAS, parallel sparse matrix vector products, and sequential and parallel iterative solvers with Jacobi and ILU preconditioners. Direct solvers, Multi-grid solvers, and parallel precondioners are under consideration for further development. The only other library that is closest in functionality to PMLP is PetSc [1,2]. However, it differs in design and technological features.

The remainder of the paper is organized as follows. Section 2 briefs the main technical contributions of the PMLP effort. Section 3 presents the design of PMLP. Section 4 describes the current release and initial set of results. In Section 5 we conclude with a summary of the main design goals and achievements thus far.

2 Main Features of PMLP

The Parallel Mathematical Library Project is a third-generation scalable library effort. By combining features such as object-oriented (OO) design, sequential and parallel modes, and regular (dense) and irregular (sparse) kernels, PMLP achieves ease of use while also being amenable to runtime optimization, and thus offers an efficient tool for parallel scientific and engineering applications. Portability in PMLP is achieved through the use of MPI-1.1 for inter-process communication [16]. In addition, the C and Fortran bindings for the functionality in PMLP make it interoperable with most existing applications. The remainder of this section highlights the important characteristics of the library, generalizing the framework presented in [14].

2.1 Poly-algorithmic Approach

Single algorithm can not always provide the best performance given the diversity of architectures and physical constraints. Even if an algorithm is the best one in the general (average) case, it may not be optimal under a specific configuration such as a particular storage format or a particular distribution of data. Therefore, providing poly-algorithmic features becomes a requirement for the implementation of a powerful and efficient parallel software library [11]. One of the primary design goals of PMLP is in enabling the use of different algorithms depending on data representation schemes, while providing a consistent user interface.

2.2 Matrix Type, Storage Format and Distribution Independence

PMLP includes operations on various matrix types such as general, banded, symmetric, banded symmetric, skew symmetric, hermitian, skew hermitian, and lower and upper triangular matrices. Furthermore, PMLP provides functionality independent of the internal data representation of irregular sparse objects and different storage matrix formats (*e.g.* coordinate, compressed sparse column, compressed sparse row, sparse diagonal, dense, Ellpack/Itpack, and skyline) are included.

As a poly-algorithm library, an important part of PMLP is the implementation of additional data-distribution-independent (DDI) algorithms. The DDI algorithms used in PMLP are based on the Multicomputer Toolbox [13, 15] implementation of a concurrent BLAS library, which in turn arose from concepts due to Van de Velde [18]. Because of the data redistribution potentially required by fixed-data-distribution algorithms, the DDI approach used in PMLP is more efficient in many cases. The structure of the library allows combining fixed-data-distribution and DDI algorithms, offering further potential for runtime optimization.

2.3 Persistent Operation Interface

In order to maximize efficiency, PMLP library also provides a persistent operation interface. When a persistent operation is initiated, an opaque handle encapsulates the information associated with the operation and enables optimized repeated execution of the same operation. When one or a few kernels have dominant complexity, this type of optimization may be extremely beneficial to overall performance, because it removes error checking and dynamic memory allocation from inner loops, while supporting the deployment of poly-algorithms.

For every persistent operation, there are several corresponding global functions. The *function_name_init(initial_parameter_list, int flag, Handle &handle)* function initializes the internal persistent handle for the operation *function_name*. The persistent mode supports both synchronous (blocking) and asynchronous (non-blocking) modes, which are specified by the *flag* parameter. *BLASP_Start(Handle& handle)* starts the operation encapsulated by the handle. A generalization for this call is *BLASP_Startall(const Handle &*array_of_handles, ...)* which starts the operations contained in *array_of_handles*. There are similar functions that wait for completion of, return the status of, and halt the execution of a single operation or an array of operations.

3 PMLP Design and Implementation

In the design of the library, OO methodology, generic programming, parameterized types, run-time polymorphism, compile-time polymorphism, iterators, and reference counting are utilized in order to implement a flexible, robust, and maintainable library that also provides maximum efficiency. An OO approach is used for high-level and user-level management of objects. OO provides both data encapsulation and polymorphism [6]. Generic programming, supported by iterators, is used to avoid virtual functions and reduce the size and complexity of the code. The poly-algorithmic approach maximizes the efficiency of important kernels; function overloading for the different matrix types and storage formats makes such specialization transparent to the user. Handles and reference counting are used for efficient memory management.

The motivation behind the use of C++ in the project has been to exploit the software engineering advantages that the OO paradigm offers along with the efficiency of compile-time polymorphism provided by C++ templates. Parameterized types, or templates, supported in C++, is the engine of the PMLP library. Templates provide code reuse for different precision of the objects and enables building of static, compile-time polymorphism, while preserving the efficiency of the code. In addition, C++ is compatible with C and Fortran.

The generic class hierarchy used in the presentation of domain entities in PMLP's design is discussed in detail in [4]. In this section, we describe of the major techniques and technologies used in the design and realization of PMLP, with an overview of the compile-time and run-time polymorphism used in the library. In addition, the implementation of iterators, which allows generic programming, is discussed.

3.1 Polymorphism

Both compile-time and run-time polymorphism are strongly supported in the design and the implementation of the library. They are deployed according to their specific benefits and drawbacks. Static, compile-time, polymorphism provides efficiency. It enables compiler optimizations such as inlining of the code and flow analysis.

However, overuse of compile-time polymorphism, which is based on heavy use of templates, can easily lead to code bloat, a complex user interface, and misleading error messages. In addition, it is difficult to debug and maintain. By contrast, run-time polymorphism provides user-friendly interface but also has hidden, run-time overheads, and prevents compiler optimizations. In the design and implementation of the library, both benefits and drawbacks of each type of polymorphism have been considered according to the specific situation. For example, in the heavily used lightweight functions (i.e. matrix element access, basic kernel of the library) run-time polymorphism has been completely avoided. The matrix class hierarchy is based on compile-time information and both storage format and matrix type are known at compile-time. Run-time polymorphism is enabled for high-level, heavyweight functionality such as for solvers.

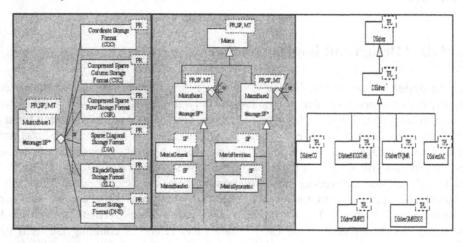

Fig. 2. Polymorphism in PMLP. Static, compile-time polymorphism in matrix hierarchy (*left and middle*) and run-time polymorphism in parallel solvers hierarchy (*right*)

Two types of static polymorphism provided by templates are used in PMLP. The first one is used in the implementation of the handle class for different storage formats, which efficiently and automatically manage the allocation, copying, and deallocation of memory [4]. Handles have a value semantic rather than pointer semantic, and internal reference counting of handles, transparent to users, provides a safe and easy means for sharing objects [17, p.294]. Figure 2 uses Unified Modeling Language [9] to illustrate the parameterized matrix handle classes. Class *MatrixBase1* encapsulates different storage formats and forwards its functionality to the underlying storage format classes (*e.g.* COO, CSC, CSR, DIA, etc.). This delegation is performed at compile-time so there is no performance penalty. Each storage format class has a template parameter specifying the precision of data elements and provides an interface for accessing the data.

The second use of compile-time polymorphism is in the implementation of classes that optimize their functionality based on different matrix types. The recursive template pattern [10] is used in this case, as shown in Figure 2. The base class, *Matrix*, encapsulates the functionality of the various matrix classes at the leaves (*e.g.* *MatrixSymmetric* and *MatrixGeneral*). The type of the leaf matrix class, storage format and precision, *MT*, *SF*, and *PR* respectively, are forwarded as template parameters to the base class. This information enables the base class to delegate its interface to the corresponding implementation in the leaf class. Since this delegation is performed at compile-time, efficiency is preserved.

Run-time polymorphism is used in the implementation of high-level functionality, such as in solvers, where the cost of one virtual call is a small fraction of the total cost of the function. Figure 2 presents the class hierarchy of distributed solvers. *DSolver* is a base class for all solvers and defines the solver interface. *DISolver* is a base class for all iterative solvers. *DSolver* contains a pure virtual function *Solve()* that is implemented in each of the leaf classes. Each of the leaf classes implements a different iterative solver which is invoked by calling the virtual *Solve()* function.

3.2 Iterators

Iterators in PMLP provide a convenient means for users to iterate over elements in vectors and matrices, regardless of their internal data storage format. They also provide a storage format independent means for writing functions that access the elements in objects using disparate storage formats. This reduces the size and complexity of the code. However, since iterators are not the most efficient mechanism for accessing elements in sparse matrices, some of the core functionality in PMLP, such as matrix-vector operations, is written using data access mechanisms specific to particular storage formats. The resulting combinatorial explosion in the number of efficient internal functions is hidden from the users via function overloading.

There are four kinds of iterators in the sequential PMLP storage classes: row, column, put, and general iterators. Row and column iterators iterate through all matrix elements along rows or columns respectively. Put iterators are used to efficiently set elements in an empty storage object. In order to achieve optimal performance, general iterators iterate over elements according to the storage *substructure* of the matrix. The substructure of a matrix depends on the storage format of the matrix. In column-oriented (*e.g.*, compressed sparse column) and row-oriented (*e.g.* compressed sparse row) storage formats, a substructure is defined by columns or rows, respectively, of the matrix. For the sparse diagonal, Ellpack/Itpack, and skyline formats, substructures are defined by the non-zero diagonal of the matrix, or non-zero row, or non-zero row of the lower/upper triangular part of the matrix, respectively.

4 State of the Implementation and Initial Results

The project is in a pre-release integration-testing phase. Currently, the iterative solvers implemented include Conjugate Gradient, Generalized Minimal Residual, Transpose Free Quasi-Minimal Residual, Bi-conjugate Gradient Stabilized, and Jacobi iterative methods as well as Jacobi and ILU(0) preconditioners [3].

Although that the first release emphasizes wider functionality, rather than performance, which will be targeted in the second release, the most important kernels have been optimized and initial results shows performance of up to 80% efficiency of some of the matrix-vector functionality [4].

Figure 3 shows preliminary results for GMRES and TFQMR parallel iterative solvers for different precision type of the elements. The tests are run on a banded matrix, stored in compressed sparse row storage format. The matrix size is 100,000 with 1,098,517 nonzero elements and bandwidth of 272. In the parallel test, the matrix is distributed linearly on 4x1 grid. The 4 processes are mapped onto 4 Pentium Pro 200 MHz hosts connected using Myrinet. The results show that the float and complex float GMRES solvers achieve the best performance at 76% and 83% efficiency respectivly, closely followed by TFQMR.

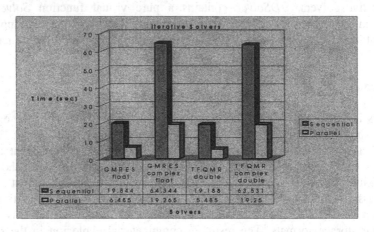

Fig. 3. Performance result for iterative solvers in PMLP

We gratefully acknowledge the implementation efforts and design feedback from Andrew Lomtev, Vladimir Basalov, Nadezhda Mustaeva, Nadezhda Vyskubenko, Nataly Davydova, Nina Poburinnaya (VNIIEF), as well as feedback from Bruce Greer and Ken Pocek (Intel) and Dale Nielsen (LLNL).

5 Conclusions

The Parallel Mathematical Libraries Project (PMLP) is developing parallel mathematical libraries of numerical methods that are required by a wide range of scientific and engineering simulation codes. The advantage of PMLP is that it anticipates current and near-term future parallel application architectures. The PMLP philosophy is to develop a portable, high-performance library using OO design and C++ while supporting an API binding for C and Fortran-77 which are widely used in the scientific parallel environment.

The incorporation of significant front-end software engineering process, together with key design principles (poly-algorithms, data-distribution independence, storage-format independence, mathematical entity type independence, and persistent operation techniques) provide this library with unparalleled ability to exploit high performance, while providing portable interfaces. The opportunity to utilize underlying optimized kernels is enhanced through the support of persistent operations, which support poly-algorithmic selection, and eliminate repetitive error checking and reduce dynamic memory management. These techniques couple effectively with storage format independence to provide greater control over resources and operational policies, while providing seamless results to the user.

References

1. Balay, S., W. D. Gropp, L. C. McInnes, and B. F. Smith, Efficient management of parallelism in object oriented numerical software libraries, in *Modern Software Tools in Scientific Computing*, E. Arge, A. M. Bruaset, and H. P. Langtangen, eds., Birkhauser Press, 1997, pp. 163--202.
2. PETSc home page. http://www.mcs.anl.gov/petsc, 1998.
3. Barrett, R. et al.: *Templates for the solution of Linear Systems*. Published by Society for Industrial & Applied Mathematics, November 1993.
4. Lubomir Birov, Yuri Bartenev, Anatoly Vargin, Avijit Purkayastha, Anthony Skjellum, Yoginder Dandass and Purushotham Bangalore. The Parallel Mathematical Libraries Project (PMLP) -- A Next Generation Scalable, Sparse, Object-Oriented, Mathematical Library Suite. In *Proceedings of the Ninth SIAM Conference on Parallel Processing for Scientific Computing*, March 1999.
5. Blackford et al.: *Scalapack Users' Guide* Society for Industrial & Applied Mathematics, July 1997. Also available at http://www.netlib.org/scalapack/slug/scalapack_slug.html.
6. Booch, G. *Object Oriented Design With Applications*. The Benjamin/Cummings Publishing Company, Inc. Redwood City, California, 1991.
7. Choi, J., J. J. Dongarra, R. Pozo, and D. W. Walker, ScaLAPACK: A scalable linear algebra library for distributed memory concurrent computers, in *Proceedings of the fourth symposium on the frontiers of massively parallel computation*, IEEE Computer Society Press, 1992, pp. 120--127.
8. Coplien, J.: Advanced C++: Programming Styles and Idioms. Addison-Wesley, 1992.
9. Fowler, M., Scott, K. UML Distilled. Addison-Wesley, 1997
10. Furnish, G.: Disambiguated Glommable Expression Templates. Computer in Physics 11(3), May/June 1997, pp. 263-269.
11. Li, J., Skjellum, A., Falgout, R.D.: A Poly-Algorithm for Parallel Dense Matrix Multiplication on Two-Dimensional Process Grid Topologies. Concurrency: Practice and Experience 9(5), 1997, pp.345-89.
12. Musser, D.R., Saini, A.: STL tutorial and reference guide: C++ programming with the standard template library. Mass.: Addison-Wesley, 1996.
13. Skjellum, A., Baldwin, C.H.: The multicomputer toolbox: Scalable parallel libraries for large-scale concurrent applications. Lawrence Livermore National Laboratory. Technical Report UCRL-JC-109251, 1991.
14. Skjellum, A., Bangalore, P.: Driving Issues in Scalable Libraries: Poly-Algorithms, Data Distribution Independence, Redistribution, Local Storage Schemes. Proceedings of the Seventh (SIAM) Conference on Parallel Processing for Scientific Computing, San Francisco, California, February 1995, pp. 734-37.
15. Skjellum, A., A. P. Leung, S. G. Smith, R. D. Falgout, C. H. Still, and C. H. Baldwin, The Multicomputer Toolbox -- First-Generation Scalable Libraries, in Proceedings of HICSS--27, IEEE Computer Society Press, 1994, pp. 644--654. HICSS--27 Minitrack on Tools and Languages for Transportable Parallel Applications.
16. Grop, William, E. Lusk, and A. Skjellum. Using MPI: Portable Parallel Programming with the Message-Passing Interface. MIT Press, Cambridge, Mass. 1996.
17. Stroustrup, B.: The C++ Programming Language. Third Edition. Addison-Wesley, 1997
18. van de Velde, E. F. Data redistribution and concurrency. Parallel Computing, 16, 1990.

Implementing
Model Checking and Equivalence Checking
for Time Petri Nets
by the RT-MEC Tool *

A.V. Bystrov and I.B. Virbitskaite

Institute of Informatics Systems
Siberian Division of the Russian Academy of Sciences
6, Acad. Lavrentiev av., 630090, Novosibirsk, Russia
{avb,virb}@iis.nsk.su

Abstract. RT-MEC is a tool box for validation (via graphical simulation) and verification (via model checking and equivalence checking) of real time systems based on partial order reduction [11] and on–the–fly technique [10]. It is appropriate for systems that can be modelled as Petri nets with real (dense) time. The tool is available within the system PEP (Programming Environment based on Petri nets) [4]. In this note, we present the RT-MEC tool, including general unique features, and summarize our development and usage experience.

1 Introduction

Recently, a growing interest can be observed in modelling and analyzing complex distributed and real time systems such as communication protocols, process control systems, production and management systems, etc. The development of such systems requires sophisticated verification methods to guarantee correctness, and the increase in details rapidly becomes unmanageable without computer assistance.

Model-checking and equivalence checking are widely accepted techniques for automatic verification of distributed systems. Unfortunately, verification of complex systems suffers from the so-called state-space explosion problem. Several heuristics to confine this problem have been proposed: partial order reduction [11], on-the-fly technique [10], symmetry [7], symbolic states [3], compositional model checking [6]. More recently, these and other techniques have been extended to the framework of real time systems and implemented into the tools UPPAL [14], COSPAN [2], HYTECH [12], and CMC [13], which are based on timed automata models.

In this note, we present the RT-MEC tool that supports validation (via graphical simulation) and verification (via model checking and equivalence checking)

---

* This work is partially supported by the Russian State Committee of High Education for Basic Research in Mathematics.

of real time systems modelled as Petri nets with real (dense) time. A goal in the design of the RT-MEC tool is to incorporate several verification methods for different classes of time Petri nets. The versatility of the tool implies many advantages: it should support mixed verification strategies which use more than one method, it should facilitate a comparison between many techniques for reasoning about the timing behaviour of nets. This versatility contrasts with the existing automated tools, which typically embody a particular time extension of Petri nets and a particular form of verification (see [9] and [18] for a comparison). The RT-Mec tool is available within the system PEP (Programming Environment based on Petri nets) [4] and can be viewed as its real time extension. This extension appears in two PEP modules: editor/simulator and verificator. Thus RT-MEC is not a stand-alone tool.

The plan of the paper: the next section describes the design principles and features of RT-MEC; section 3 presents experimental results; some remarks on the future work are finally given in section 4.

2 Overview of RT-MEC

The efficient representation and manipulation of time information is key to any successful implementation of a verification and analysis tool. The RT-MEC tool uses both time Petri nets [15] and parametric time nets [20], as a fundamental framework, which are based on a dense time domain (i.e., an unbounded (although finite) number of transitions can fire between two successive time moments). Time Petri nets are Petri nets whose transitions are labelled by two timing constraints that indicate their earliest and latest firing times. A state of the time Petri net is a set of its places containing tokens, equipped with a finite set of clocks corresponding to the transitions and recording the time elapsed since the transitions were enabled. A time Petri net progresses through a sequence of states in one of two ways: by firing transitions and letting a certain amount of time pass. In parametric time nets, timing constraints are described by using parameter variables with unknown, fixed values. We shall denote a representative of the classes of time Petri nets and parametric time nets by P&TN.

The main features of the RT-MEC tool are the following:

– *Editor/Simulator*, that provides GUI to design and simulate real time systems by means of P&TN's. Editor is a graphical tool supporting design of P&TN using intuitive constructs such as places, transitions, arcs, timing constraints. The graphical simulator enables visualization and recording of executions of P&TN. During a simulation the following information is presented to the user:
  • the current state of P&TN visualized by highlighting marking (a set of places containing tokens) directly in the graphical description and timing constraints of transitions displayed in a separate window;
  • the transitions or time amounts which may be selected and displayed to move to a next state;

- the executions that lead to the current state of P&TN. They are displayed and may be saved, reexamined, and reset from any intermediate point.

The simulator may run in both interactive and automatic modes of operation. In addition, such features as break points and reverse execution are provided.

- *Analyzer*, that supports some standard algorithms for checking structural and behavioural properties (e.g. free-choice property, liveness, deadlock-freeness, reachability, etc.).
- *Model checker*, that currently includes modules supporting a real time model checking algorithm for TCTL [1] and its partial order improvements [19]. They can determine whether P&TN satisfies a property given in terms of a TCTL-formula.

Since P&TN constitutes a dense time model, the size of its state-space is infinite. In order to get a finite representation of the behaviour of P&TN, we use the concepts of regions and regions graphs defined in [1]. States of P&TN are in the same region, i.e. they are in some sense equivalent, iff their marking coincide and the corresponding clock values agree on the integral parts and on the ordering of the fractional parts. The region graph (RG) of P&TN is defined to be the graph with vertices corresponding to regions, and edges representing firings of transitions and the passage of time. Notice that the size of the RG is in general exponential in the size of P&TN. The idea of partial order reduction is that from each vertex of a reduced region graph (RRG), the set of enabled transitions is examined, and (neglecting concurrent transitions) only a subset of it is used to generate successors. This contrasts with the construction of the RG, where all of enabled transitions are explored. Notice that the complexity of construction of a reduced set from each vertex of an RRG is linear in the size of P&TN. The correctness of the reduction method is based on the notion of timed stuttering equivalence [19] between the RG and an RRG. This guarantees that the truth value of any checked TCTL-formula under the RG is the same as under an RRG. Hence the model checking problem of the RG is reduced to model checking problem of an RRG. Therefore, our verification method is based on the idea of: (1) constructing an RRG of P&TN by exploiting the concurrency of the net, and (2) labelling all the regions with subformulas of the checked formula by using standard labelling procedure. P&TN satisfies a TCTL-formula iff the initial region of an RRG is labelled with the formula.

The transparency, and thus a full functionality of the model checker is obtained by a formula translator which transforms an abstract formula (such as 'is P&TN terminated in 5 time units', 'will a transition fire within 2 time units', etc.) into a formula referring to the corresponding places of P&TN. This offers a comfortable interface to the model checker.

- *Equivalence checker*, that currently includes usual and timed bisimulation checking modules. An important key to the efficiency of the engines is the application of the region [1] and on-the-fly [11] techniques. In addition, it offers both breadth-first and depth-first search of the state-spaces of P&TN's.

The RT-MEC tool is written in C/C++ and executes under X-Windows. Its graphical interface is built on the top of the Tcl/Tk graphics library. It currently running under PC Linux.

3 Experimental Results

We have tested RT-MEC on three example systems represented by time Petri nets. Using first two examples, we compare the basic TCTL model checking algorithm and its partial order improvement. The third example is used to evaluate the on-the-fly implementation of timed bisimulation checking. All tests were performed on a Pentium 166 MHz with 128 MBytes of memory.

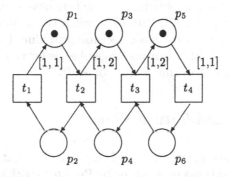

Fig. 1.

The first example extends a concurrent n-buffer taken from [8] with timing constraints. The corresponding time Petri net has $2n$ places, $n + 1$ transitions, and the first and $(n + 1)$th transitions have the time interval [1,1], whilst the others are associated with the time interval [1,2]. A time Petri net of 3-buffer system is shown in Figure 1. As an example property, we verified, if the nth slot of n-buffer is not empty at least once during the time interval $(n, 2n - 1)$ along any computation run. The table below shows the impact of reduction on the effectiveness of the model checking. The 'n' column refers to the capacity of buffer. In the 'RG' and 'RRG' columns, we list the numbers of vertices ('$|V|$'), edges ('$|E|$') and times ('T') in seconds measured for checking the fixed TCTL-formula in the RG and an RRG of the net, respectively.

	RG			RRG		
n	$\|V\|$	$\|E\|$	T	$\|V\|$	$\|E\|$	T
2	36	43	0.02	33	39	0.01
3	130	168	0.10	117	153	0.08
4	1368	1813	0.39	923	1187	0.30
5	10928	14632	29.3	7341	10015	21.1
6	117745	151250	5020	85136	99814	3127
7	−	−	−	506138	679254	18812

The second example is a system from [16] which is a local area network linking stations by a shared hardware bus. As an example property, we checked, if after sending a message, a station will starts its next activity within a fixed time. The size of the corresponding time Petri net is linear in the number n of stations, thus the basic model checking algorithm is exponential in n. Since all stations operate more or less independently, concurrency also increases with n, therefore, the partial order algorithm has turned out to be linear in n.

The third example is a decision of 'readers/writer' problem ensuring starvation to be avoided. A time Petri net corresponding to a decision in which two reader processes and one writer process are involved is given in [5]. By varying the number of readers and the frequencies of their access to resources, time Petri nets of different sizes can be obtained. These nets have been compared, with respect to timed bisimulation [21]. However, when the number of readers exceeds 30, the memory required by the basic decision procedure becomes too large, and consequently the verification can no longer be performed with this procedure, whereas the on-the-fly algorithm works correctly.

4 Conclusion and Future Work

In this paper, we have presented RT-MEC, a toolset that supports the formal analysis of real time systems represented by Petri nets with real (dense) time. The core idea was to use partial order and on-the-fly techniques in order to reduce the cost of the analysis. The usage of RT-MEC was demonstrated on three examples. Partially based on the experimental results, our conclusion is that: (1) the real time temporal logics constitute convenient specification languages for P&TN's, and (2) reduction heuristics can be used for the models in effective and efficient manner.

Our experiences have prompted us to consider the following future aims:

- an algebraic language for specification of P&TN's are considered suitable for extending the interfaces of the tool,
- new model checking algorithms based on such reduction methods as unfolding [8], symmetry [7], symbolic states [3], etc. are expected to be added,
- an interface with the INA system [17] is desirable to provide the possibilities of the system (in particular, its state graph checker and its theorem data base) to the user.

References

1. R. Alur, C. Courcoubetis, D. Dill. Model-Checking for Real-Time Systems. In *Proceedings of 5th Symposium on Logic in Computer Science (LICS'90)*, pages 414–425, 1990.
2. R. Alur, R.P. Kurshan. Timing Analysis in Cospan. Volume 1066 of *Lecture Notes in Computer Science*, pages 220–231, 1996.

3. J.R. Burch, E.M. Clarke, L. McMillan, D. Dill, J. Hwang. Symbolic Model Checking: 10^{20} and Beyond. In *Proceedings of the 5th Symposium on Logic in Computer Science (LICS'90)*, pages 428–439, 1990.

4. E. Best, B. Grahlmann. PEP — More Than a Petri Net Tool. Volume 1055 of *Lecture Notes in Computer Science*, pages 397–401, 1996.

5. B. Berthomieu, M. Menasche. A State Enumeration Approach for Analyzing Time Petri Nets. *Proceedings of the 3th European Workshop on Application and Theory of Petri Nets*, pages 27–65, 1982.

6. E.M. Clarke, D.E. Long, K.L. Mc Millan. Compositional Model Checking *Proceedings of the 4th Symposium on Logic in Computer Science (LICS'89)*, pages 353–362, 1990.

7. E. Emersen, A. Sistla. Symmetry and Model Checking. Volume 697 of *Lecture Notes in Computer Science*, pages 463–478, 1993.

8. J. Esparza. Model Checking Using Net Unfoldings. *Science of Computer Programming*, 23:151–195, 1994.

9. F. Feldbrugge. Petri Net Tools Overview 1992. Volume 674 of *Lecture Notes in Computer Science*, pages 169–209, 1993.

10. J.-C. Fernandez, L. Mounier. 'On the fly' Verification of Behavioral Equivalences and Preorders. Volume 577 of *Lecture Notes in Computer Science*, pages 181–191, 1991.

11. P. Godefroid. Partial-Order Methods for the Verification of Concurrent Systems. An Approach for State-Explosion Problem. Volume 1032 of *Lecture Notes in Computer Science*, pages 1–143, 1996.

12. T.A. Henzinger, P.H. Ho, H. Wong-Toi. A Model Checking for Hybrid Systems. Volume 1254 of *Lecture Notes in Computer Science*, pages 220–231, 1997.

13. F. Laroussenie, K.G. Larsen. CMC: a Tool for Compositional Model Checking of Real-time Systems. In *Proceedings of FORTE XI/PSTV XVIII'98* , November 1998, Paris, France, pages 439–456, 1998.

14. K.G. Larsen, P. Pettersson, W. Yi. UPPAAL: Status and Developments. Volume 1254 of *Lecture Notes in Computer Science*, pages 456–459, 1997.

15. P. Merlin, D.J. Faber. Recoverability of Communication Protocols: Implications of a Theoretical Study. *IEEE Trans. of Commun.*, COM-24(9):1036–1043, 1976.

16. J.-L. Roux, B. Berthomieu. Verification of Local Area Network Protocol with Tine, a Software Package for Time Petri Nets. In *Proceedings of the 7th European Workshop on Application and Theory of Petri Nets*, pages 183–205, 1986.

17. P. Starke. INA: Integrated Net Analyzer. Handbuch, 1992.

18. H. Störrle. Tool Comparison, to be published, 1998.

19. I.B. Virbitskaite, E.A. Pokozy. A Partial Order Algorithm for Verifying Time Petri Nets. In *Proceedings of International Workshop on Discrete Event Systems (WoDES'98)*, August 1998, Cagliari, Italy, IEE Publisher, London, pages 514–517, 1998.

20. I.B. Virbitskaite, E.A. Pokozy. Parametric Behaviour Analysis for Time Petri Nets (see this volume).

21. I.B. Virbitskaite, I.V. Tarasyuk. Equivalence Notions and Refinement for Time Petri Nets. Volume 8 of *Joint Bulletin of NCC and IIS, Series Computer Science*, Novosibirsk, 1998.

Learning Concurrent Programming:
A Constructionist Approach

Giuseppina Capretti, Maria Rita Laganà and Laura Ricci

Università degli Studi di Pisa, Dipartimento di Informatica, Corso Italia 40,
56125 Pisa ITALIA
{capretti, lagana, ricci}@di.unipi.it

Abstract. We present a software environment in which students learn concurrency by programming the behaviour of a set of interacting agents. The language defined puts together the turtle primitives of the Logo language, the classic sequential imperative language constructs and the concurrent ones. It is possible to program a dynamic world in which independent agents interact with one another through the exchange of messages.

1 Introduction

Today computer science is very important in society. The new working environments require an interaction with computers that, today, are the new medium through which ideas are expressed and programming is the means by which this can be accomplished. For this reason, learning to program has become more and more important for young people.

The concurrent programming paradigm is particularly interesting because of the diffusion of intrinsic parallel systems such as the massively parallel ones and networks. Our teaching experience shows that the learning of concurrent programming is often hard for students. We believe that this is due to the fact that the concurrency paradigm is often considered only as an evolution of the sequential one and, furthermore, students learn it after having acquired the latter.

This situation can be overcome if the first experience in programming is acquired through the concurrent paradigm at an early age. The concept of concurrency is intrinsic in the real world because it is *naturally* concurrent. If we give a student a concurrent programming environment, she/he may create and simulate all the fantastic and real situations s/he wants.

The theory underlying this approach is the constructionism [7]. Papert, the father of this theory, believes that students will be more deeply involved in their learning if they are constructing something that others will see, judge, and perhaps use. Through that construction, students will face complex issues, and they will make the effort to solve the problem and learn because they are motivated by the construction. A student should not be considered like a bottle to fill with notions but as a self-constructor of his/her knowledge: students need instruments to make the assimilation of new schemes and personal re-elaboration easier.

Our idea is to create a new system allowing the definition of the behaviour of automata able to interact with one another and react to the outside stimuli. In this case the term "animate system" is perfect to describe this sort of dynamic world that involves active and inter-active objects.

Animate systems are simulated dynamic worlds that contain
multiple independent but interacting graphic actors [10]

The environment we are describing in this paper allows the definition of animated concurrent worlds programmable by an agent-based programming language.

An agent is any component of a program or system that is designed to be animated. The term agent - asserts Travers in [10] - suggests a variety of attributes that have not generally been built into the underlying metaphors of existing programming languages, attributes such as autonomy, purposefulness and the ability to react to the surrounding environment. In our case the creatures are autonomous and have the ability to react to the outside stimuli.

We have analysed several educational systems: KidSim [9], Starlogo [8] and ToonTalk [6]. We think that even if these systems are concurrent, they are not suitable for teaching concurrency.

The **Orespics** system, developed at the Computer Science Department of the University of Pisa [1, 2, 3] is programmable with Logo-PL language.

Logo-PL has control flow, movement and communication commands and expressions. The Logo-PL language defines a set of communication primitives. In particular, the prototype version implements basic primitives to send and receive messages. The receive primitive is synchronous and asymmetric while the send primitive is synchronous and symmetric [5]. As you can see, in this prototype, the set of the communication primitives is extremely poor.

In this paper, we introduce our new system, Advanced Orespics, its Orespics-PL language that includes a richer set of communication primitives and we propose an example of didactic training to learn the semantics of different types of communications.

2   The Advanced Orespics System

The Advanced Orespics system is born from the Orespics system described above. Its programming language is called Orespics-PL and is based on the local environment model and on the explicit use of the communication primitives. The Advanced Orespics system has substituted the previous one because a richer set of communication primitives is defined, activation and termination constructs are introduced and no limit to the number of interacting actors in the world is imposed. Each actor is an agent of an animate system and has the attributes of autonomy, purposefulness and the ability to react to the surrounding environment by the exchange messages paradigm. An agent is characterised by a set of properties: the initial position on the screen, its appearance and the code of its program

The system gives the users an interface to define all these properties. The system has a set of pre-defined fantastic and real characters like aliens and animals. The students may choose the most suitable character according to the situation to solve.

The sequential part of Orespics-PL includes traditional imperative sequential constructs (*repeat, while, if* ...) and all turtle primitives of the Logo language [4]. Orespics-PL language offers all the elementary data types (integer, boolean..): the only data structure is the list. Some of the operations defined on list type are *getFirst(list)*, *first(list)* and *second(list)*: *getFirst* returns the first item of *list* and pops it up; *first* and *second* return respectively the first and the second ones and do not pop them up.

The set of primitives, functions and procedures used in the following examples are:
- *versus(x, y)*, which returns the direction to assume to reach the point of co-ordinates *x* and *y*,
- *distance(x, y)*, which returns the distance between the position of agent and the point *(x, y)*,
- *set_heading(angle)*, which turns the agent in the direction given by the *angle*,
- *set_color(color)*, which sets the colour of the agent trace to that of *colour*. A set of pre-defined colour is available,
- *jump(x, y)*, the agent jumps to the point of co-ordinates *(x, y)*,
- *random(val)*, which returns a random value included in +/- *val*. If parameter is zero, it returns a random value according to the common definition.

As regards the concurrent part, the new language defines the following types of primitives:
- synchronous send and receive,
- asynchronous send and receive
- termination and activation commands,
- broadcast send primitive,
- asymmetric receive primitive.

The didactic training we present in this paper uses only synchronous and asynchronous communication primitives: hence, we only show the syntax and the semantics of these primitives. The syntax of the synchronous primitives is changed in:

send&wait *msg* **to** *agent*

wait&receive *var* **from** *agent*

The semantics of synchronous and asynchronous primitives is well known in literature [5]. With regard to the synchronous primitives, when an agent sends a message to another one and its partner is not ready for communication, it waits until the message has been received. The semantics of synchronous receive primitive is analogous.

The syntax of the asynchronous primitives is:

receive&no_wait *var* **from** *agent*

send&no_wait *msg* **to** *agent*

As for the asynchronous primitives, an agent sends/receives a message to/from another one but it does not wait for the successful issue of the communication. When an agent executes a *send&no_wait*, it does not wait for the receiver to get the message and it goes on with its execution. Hence a queue of messages is created, where messages are inserted and taken according to the order of arrival. When an agent executes a *receive&no_wait* it checks the existence of some incoming messages and goes on. If the queue is empty the message has no meaning and no value is assigned to the *var*. The meaning of *var* may be checked through the function *in_message()* which returns the **true** value if the last executed *receive&no_wait* has picked up a valid message, and the **false** value otherwise.

A process executing the *receive&no_wait* performs a non-deterministic choice: we suppose that a suitable introduction of non-determinism in concurrent programs has been given when this primitive is introduced to the students.

3 Teaching Synchronous and Asynchronous Communication

We now wish to introduce an example of didactic training to learn the semantics of the communication paradigm we described above. In particular the goal of the training is to allow the students to learn the difference among different kinds of communication.

According to the constructionist approach, this is obtained by proposing a set of proper problems to the students and letting them solve them in the way they prefer. The whole process is obviously guided by the teacher; nevertheless, the student may try different solutions and verify the effects of his program directly on the screen, eventually changing the program. We present only the code of the agents used to solve the problems proposed: we suppose they are just created and that every one of them has properly been defined.

The task of the first problem is the comprehension of the concept of synchronisation among agents. Let us consider the following problem:

"The Quasar 40 and the Star 23 space shuttles move about the solar system. They have to meet to transfer the crews of Star-23 to Quasar-40 for the party for the captain of the latter. They use the radio communication to exchange the position. Try to describe their behaviour."

To define a correct synchronisation between these two agents, it is necessary that each of them knows the behaviour of the other one; in particular, if and when the other one is disposed to accept synchronisation. In the following solution, the two agents[1] employ synchronous send and receive to exchange their positions: this is probably the first solution given by the students, but it is not correct.

```
Agent Quasar_40                        Agent Star_23
   repeat                                 repeat
      x ← random(25);                        x ← random(25);
      y ← random(15);                        y ← random(15);
      right x;                               right x;
      forward y;                             forward y;
      send&wait [myX, myY] to                send&wait [myX, myY] to
      Star_23;                               Quasar_40;
      wait&receive [x, y] from               wait&receive [x,y] from
      Star_23;                               Quasar_40;
      d ← distance(x, y);                    d ← distance(x, y);
   until d < 10;                          until d < 10;
   show "It's time to stop";              show "It's time to stop";
end                                    end
```

The variables *myX* and *myY* are predefined variables that represent the position of the agent on the screen.

This kind of solution determines a deadlock situation between agents. In fact, the agents move and execute a *send&wait*, waiting for the reception of the corresponding message: the agents are now blocked. It is possible to use this example to deal with the deadlock subject and discuss the semantics of prevention, avoidance, recognition or elimination of the deadlock with students. Our system may help teachers to create situations in which the deadlock is not a difficult concept, but only one of the innate characteristics of a concurrent environment. To solve the problem of the deadlock it is sufficient to invert the order of send and receive in the code of one of the agent

---

[1] Each agent represents a space shuttle

```
Agent Quasar_40                          Agent Star_23
......                                    ......
    forward y;                               forward y;
    send&wait [myX, myY] to Star_23;         wait&receive [x, y] from Quasar_40;
    wait&receive [x, y] from Star_23;        send&wait [myX, myY] to Quasar_40;
    d ← distance(x, y);                      d ← distance(x, y); ......
......                                    end
end
```

In the above examples we use synchronous primitives. We could also propose to solve the deadlock problem through asynchronous primitives: the following is a possible solution.

```
Agent Quasar_40                          Agent Star_23
......                                    ......
    forward y;                               forward y;
    send&no_wait [myX, myY] to Star_23;      send&no_wait [myX, myY] to
    wait&receive [x, y] from Star_23;        Quasar_40;
    d ← distance(x, y);                      wait&receive [x, y] from Quasar_40;
......                                        d ← distance(x, y); ......
end                                      end
```

It is important to notice that the *receive* command must be synchronous in this case because each shuttle needs the message from the other one before computing the distance. This version is similar to the one described previously, but it presents no deadlock. The comparison between the two versions can be used to study and probe the semantics of the two kinds of primitives.

The concept underlying the following problem is the understanding of the asynchronous communication. We propose a problem requiring only that the messages exchanged be picked up from the receiver according to the arrival order.

The problem proposed is:

"A leader pen orders the red pen to draw the roof of a house and the black pen to draw the walls. It gives them the co-ordinates of the points. The coloured pens draw the segments creating the roof and the walls of the house. How do they do it?".

```
Agent leader_pen                          Agent black_pen
    walls ← [[5,9], [5,4], [10,2],            wait&receive [x, y] from leader_pen;
    [10,7], [14,7], [14,2], [10,2]];          jump(x, y); set_color(black);
    roof ← [[14,7], [12,10], [10,7],          pen_down:
    [5,9], [8,11], [12,10]];                  repeat
    repeat                                        wait&receive msg from leader_pen;
        send&no_wait getFist(walls) to            if msg <> nil
        black_pen;                                then
    until (walls = nil);                              x ← first(msg);
    send&no_wait nil to black_pen;                    y ← second(msg);
    repeat                                            set_heading (versus(x, y));
        send&no_wait getFirst(roof) to                forward (distance (x, y));
        red_pen;                                  endif
    until (roof = nil);                       until (msg = nil)
    send&no_wait nil to red_pen;          end
end
```

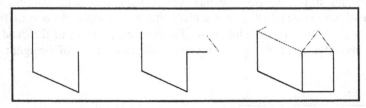

Fig. 1 Evolution of drawing: first case

The code of *red_pen* is identical to that of the *black_pen*. In this version the *leader_pen* agent first sends all the walls' points to *black_pen* and then the list of the roof points to *red_pen*. In fig. 1, we show a possible evolution of the drawing: the black line is thicker than the red one to grant the visual identification of the lines.

In the following version, *leader_pen* alternatively sends a point to *red_pen* and one to *black_pen*. The code of coloured pens is identical to the precedent while the one of *leader_pen* is modified as follow:

```
Agent leader_pen
    walls ←[[5,9], [5,4], [10,2],
    [10,7], [14,7], [14,2], [10,2]];
    roof ← [[14,7], [12,10], [10,7],
    [5,9], [8,11], [12,10]];
    repeat
        if (walls <> nil)
            send&no_wait getFirst(walls)
            to pen_black;
        endif

        if (roof <> nil)
            send&no_wait getFirst(roof)
            to pen_red;
        endif
    until ((roof=nil) AND (walls=nil))
    send&no_wait nil to pen_red;
    send&no_wait nil to pen_black;
end
```

Fig. 2 Evolution of drawing: second case

The purpose of the last example is to show that a realistic situation, like the modelling of animal behaviour, may be programmed in our system. In this example both *send&no_wait* and *receive&no_wait* primitives are used. Since the latter primitive requires a clear knowledge of the concept of non-deterministic behaviour of an agent, we suppose it has been given in another didactic training.

"In a field there were two ants called Z ant and T ant. They are searching for food and have a term: the first who finds it tells the other the position of food. "Good luck T". "Good luck Z. Let us begin"

We present one of the possible implementation of the Z ant and T ant agents.

```
Agent Z_ant
    I_found ←false; You_found ←false;
    repeat
        x ← random(25);
        y ← random(15);
        right x; forward y;
        if here_food(myX, myY)
        then
            send&no_wait [myX, myY] to
            T_ant;
            I_found← true;
        else
            receive&no_wait [x, y] from
            T_ant;
            if in_message()
            then You_found← true; endif
        endif
    until (I_found OR You_found);
    if You_found
    then
        set_heading (versus(x, y));
        forward distance(x, y);
    endif
end
```

```
Agent T_ant
    I_found ←false; You_found ←false;
    repeat
        x ← random(25);
        y ← random(15);
        right x; forward y;
        if here_food(myX, myY)
        then
            send&no_wait [myX, myY] to
            Z_ant;
            I_found ←true;
        else
            receive&no_wait [x, y] from
            Z_ant;
            if in_message()
            then You_found ← true; endif
        endif
    until (I_found OR You_found);
    if You_found
    then
        set_heading (versus(x, y));
        forward (distance(x, y));
    endif;
end
```

Each ant moves randomly checking for presence of food. If an ant finds it, it sends the food co-ordinates to the other one and stops moving. If it does not find it, it checks the presence of an incoming message from the other ant. If no message is present it goes on searching. If a message is present it gets the co-ordinates to reach the food.

It is important to stress that in this case the agents are completely autonomous. Each one may be programmed without knowing the behaviour of the other agent: this is the main difference between this example and the previous ones. The autonomy increase is obtained through the use of the *receive&no_wait* primitive, which allows each agent to perform a non-deterministic choice whose result depends on its interaction with the surrounding world.

4 Conclusions

We may create lots of new examples in which the agents co-ordinate and synchronise themselves. Classic problems like the game of life, the simulation of a biological system, and so on may be naturally realised in our system.

We have studied the possibility of creating several typologies of agents characterised by a richer set of personal properties, for example, in the case of the ants we give them the ability to move the antennae or in the case of the dog the ability to bark. We are implementing a version in which the character may be created or imported by the student.

We are just planning experimentation of the Advanced Orespics system with teenagers to test the suitability of the Orespics-PL language.

5 References

1. Capretti G.: *Strumenti per l'apprendimento della concorrenza nella didattica dell'informatica*, Master of Computer Science Thesis, Computer Science Department, University of Pisa, December 1997.
2. Capretti G., Cisternino A., Laganà M. R. and Ricci L.: A concurrent microworld, *ED-MEDIA 99 World Conference on Educational Multimedia, Hypermedia & Telecommunications*, Seattle, Washington, June 19-24th.
3. Capretti G., Laganà M. R. and Ricci L.: Micro-world to learn concurrency, *SSCC'98*, 22-24 September 1998, Durban, South Africa, 255-259.
4. Harvey B.: *Computer Science Logo style*, The Mit Press, Cambridge, 1997
5. Hoare C. A. R.: Communicating Sequential Process, *Comm. of the ACM*, Vol. 21, No. 8, Aug. 1978, pp. 666-677.
6. Kahn K.: ToonTalk - An Animated Programming Environment for Children, *Journal of Visual Languages and Computing*, (7), 197-217, 1996.
7. Papert S.: *Mindstorm: children, computer and powerful ideas*, Basic Books, New York, 1980.
8. Resnick M.: *Turtles, termites and traffic jam: exploration in massively parallel micro-world*, The MIT Press, Cambridge, 1990.
9. Smith D. C. and Cypher A.: KidSim: end users programming of simulation, Apple Computer Inc., 1997. **http://www.acm.org/sigchi/chi95/Electronic/documnts/papers/ac1bdy.htm**.
10. Travers M. D.: *Programming with agents: new metaphors for thinking about computation*, Bachelor of Science Thesis at Massachusetts Institute of Technology, 1996.

The Speedup Performance of an Associative Memory Based Logic Simulator

Damian Dalton

Dept of Computer Science, University College Dublin, Belfield, Dublin 4, Ireland.
E-mail:damian.dalton@ucd.ie

Abstract. As circuits increase in size and complexity, there is an ever demanding requirement to accelerate the processing speed of logic simulation. Parallel processing has been perceived as an obvious candidate to assist in this goal and numerous parallel processing systems have been investigated. Unfortunately, large speedup figures have eluded these approaches. A large communication overhead due to basic passing of values between processors, elaborate measures to avoid or recover from deadlock and load balancing techniques, is the principal barrier to achieving high speedup. This paper presents an Associative memory architecture which is the basis of a machine APPLES(Associative Parallel Processor for Logic Event Simulation), specifically designed for parallel discrete event logic simulation. A scan mechanism replaces inter-process communication. This mechanism is well disposed to parallelisation. The machine has been evaluated theoretically and empirically.

1 Parallel Processing and Logic Simulation: The Problem

The ever-expanding size of VLSI circuits has further emphasized the need for a fast and accurate means of simulating digital circuits. A compromise between model accuracy and computational feasibility is found in *Logic Simulation*. In this simulation paradigm, signal values are discrete and may acquire in the simplest case logic values 0 and 1. More complex transient state signal values are modeled using up to 9-state logic. Logic gates can be modeled as ideal components with zero switching time or more realistically as electronic components with finite delay and switching characteristics such as inertial, pure or ambiguous delays.

Due to the enormity of the computational effort for large circuits, the application of parallel processing to this problem has been explored. Unfortunately, large speedup performance for most systems and approaches has been elusive.

Sequential (uni-processor) logic simulation can be divided into two broad categories *Compiled code* and *Event-driven* simulation [1]. These techniques can be employed in a parallel environment by partitioning the circuit amongst processors. In compiled code simulation, all gates are evaluated at all time steps, even if they are not active. The circuit has to be levelised and only unit or zero delay models can be employed. Sequential circuits also pose difficulties for this type of simulation. A compiled code mechanism has been applied to several generations of specialized parallel hardware accelerators designed by IBM, the Logic Simulation Machine LSM [2], the Yorktown Simulation Engine [3] and the Engineering Verification Engine EVE [4] and performance figures as high as 2.2 billion gate evaluations/sec reported. Agrawal et al [5], have analyzed the activity of several circuits and their results have indicated that at any time instant circuit activity (i.e. gates whose outputs are in transition) is typically in the range 1% to 0.1%. Therefore , the *Effective* number of gate evaluations of these engines is likely to be smaller by a factor of a hundred or more. Speedup values ranging from 6 to 13 for various compiled coded benchmark circuits have been observed on the Shared memory MIMD Encore Multimax multiprocessor by Soule and Blank [6]. A SIMD (array) version was investigated by Kravitz[13] with similar results.

The intrinsic unit delay model of compiled code simulators is overly simplistic for many applications.

Some delay model limitations of compiled code simulation have been eliminated in parallel *Event-driven* techniques. These parallel algorithms are largely composed of two phases; a *Gate evaluation phase* and an *Event-scheduling phase*. The gate evaluation phase identifies gates that are changing and the scheduling phase puts the gates affected by these changes (the fan-out gates) into a time-ordered linked schedule list, determined by the current time and the delays of the active gates, see Figure (1). Soule and Blank [6] and Mueller-Thuns et al [7] have investigated both Shared and Distributed memory *Synchronous* event MIMD architectures. Again, overall performance has been disappointing the results of several benchmarks executed on an 8-processor Encore Multimax and an 8-processor iPSC-Hypercube only gave speedup values ranging from 3 to 5.

Asynchronous event simulation permits limited processor autonomy. Causality constraints require occasional synchronization between processors and rolling back of events. Deadlock between processors must be resolved. Chandy, Misra [8] and Bryant [9] have developed deadlock avoidance algorithms, while Briner [10] and Jefferson [11] have explored algorithms based on deadlock recovery. The best speedup performance figures for Shared and Distributed memory asynchronous MIMD systems were 8.5 for a 14-processor system and 20 for a 32-processor BBN system.

Optimising strategies such as load balancing, circuit partioning and distributed queues are necessary to realise the best speedup figures. Unfortunately, these mechanisms themselves contribute large *Overhead communication costs* for even modest sized parallel systems. Furthermore, the gate evaluation process despite its small granularity, incurs between 10 to 250 machine cycles per gate evaluation.

2   Design Objectives

The design framework for a specific parallel logic simulation architecture originated by identifying the essential elemental simulation operations that could be performed in parallel and minimising the tasks that support these operations and which are totally intrinsic to the parallel system.

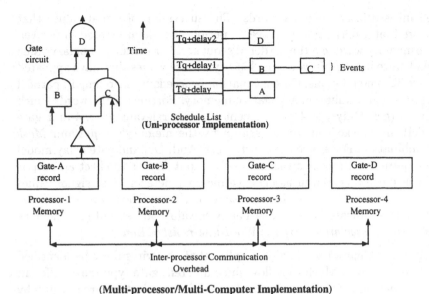

Fig. 1. Event-driven simulation on a multiprocessor/multicomputer system.

The essential elemental tasks identified were:

1. *Gate evaluation.*
2. *Delay model implementation.*
3. *Updating fan-out gates.*

Notice that activities such as event scheduling and load balancing are perceived as implementation issues which need not be incorporated necessarily into a new design. An important additional critique was that the design must execute directly in hardware as many parallel tasks as possible, as fast as possible, but without limiting the type of delay model.

The machine which evolved subject to these objectives incorporated several special Associative memory blocks and was accordingly named *APPLES* (Associative Parallel Processor for Logic Event-driven Simulation).

3 Basic Parallel Processing Mechanisms in APPLES

The Gate evaluation/Delay model implementation and Update/Fanout process will be explained with reference to the APPLES architecture, see Figure(2).

3.1 Gate Evaluation/Delay Model Implementation

A gate can be evaluated once its input wire values are known. In conventional uni-processor and parallel systems these values are stored in memory and accessed by the processor(s) when the gate is activated. In APPLES, gate signal values are stored in associative memory words. The succession of signal values that have appeared on a particular wire over a period of time are stored in a given associative memory word in a time ordered sequence. For instance, a binary value model could store in a 32-bit word, the history of wire values that have appeared over the last 32 time intervals. Gate evaluation proceeds by searching in parallel for appropriate signal values in associative memory. Portions of the words which are irrelevant (e.g. Only the 4 most recent bits are relevant for a 4-unit gate delay model) are masked out of the search by the memory's *Input* and *Mask* register combination. For a given gate type (e.g. And, Or) and gate delay model there are requirements on the structure of the input signals to effect an output change. Each pattern search in associative memory detects those signal values that have a certain attribute of the necessary structure. Those wires that have *all* the attributes indicate *active* gates.The wire values are stored in a memory block designated *Associative Array1b(Word-line-register Bank)*.

This simple evaluation mechanism implies that the wires must be identified by the type of gate into which they flow since different gate types have different input wire sequences that activate them. Gates of a certain type are selected by a parallel search on gate type identifiers in *Associative Array1a*.

Each signal attribute corresponds to a bit pattern search in memory. Since several attributes are normally required for an activated gate, the result of several pattern searches must be *recorded*. These searches can be considered as *Tests* on words.

The result of a test is either successful or not. This can be recorded as single bit in a corresponding word in another register held in a register bank termed the *Test-result register Bank*. Since each gate is assumed to have two inputs (inverters and multiple input gates are translated into their 2-input gate circuit equivalents) tests are *combined* on pairs of words in this bank. This combination mechanism is specific to a delay model and defined by the the *Result-activator register* and consists of simple And or Or operations between bits in the word pairs.

The results of each combining each word pair, the final stage of the gate evaluation process, are stored as a single word in another associative array, the *Group-result register Bank*. Active gates will have a unique bit pattern in this bank and can be identified by a parallel search for this bit pattern. Successful candidates of this search set their bit in the 1-bit column register *Group-test Hit list*.

In essence the APPLES gate evaluation mechanism selects gates of a certain type, applies a sequence of bit patterns searches (Tests) to them and ascertains the active gates by recording the result of each pattern search and determining those that have fulfilled all the necessary tests. *This mechanism executes gate evaluation in constant time—the parallel search is independent of the number of words. This is an effective linear speedup for the evaluation activity. It also facilitates different delay models—delay model is defined by a set of search patterns.*

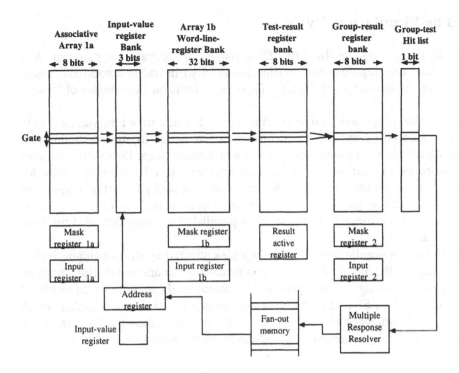

Fig. 2. The APPLES Architecture.

3.2 Fan-out/Update

Active gates set their bits in the column hit list. A *Multiple Response Resolver* scans through this list. The resolver can be a single counter which inspects the entire list from top to bottom which stops when it encounters a set bit and then uses its current value as a vector for the fan-out list of the identified active gate. This list has the addresses of the fan-out gate inputs in the *Input-value register Bank*. The new logic value of the active gates are written into the appropriate word of this bank.

It then clears the bit before decrementing through the remainder of the list and repeating this process. All hit bits are Ored together so that when all bits are clear this can be detected immediately and no further scanning need be done.

This scanning process can be accelerated by introducing *several scan registers* in the resolver, each scanning independently and in parallel a sub-section of the hit list.

When all gate types have been evaluated for the current time interval all signals are updated by *shifting in parallel the words of the Input-value register into the corresponding words of the Word-line register bank*. For 8 valued logic (i.e 3 bits for each word in the Input-value register) this phase requires 3 machine cycles.

4   The Simulation Cycle

A circuit to be simulated by APPLES is parsed to generate the gate type and delay model and topology information required to initialise associative arrays 1a, 1b and the fan-out vector tables. There is no limit on the number of fan-out gates.

Simulation progresses in discrete time units. For any time interval, each gate type is evaluated by applying tests on associative array 1b and combining and recording results in the neighbouring register banks. Regardless of the number of gates to be evaluated this process occupies between 10 machine cycles for the simplest, to 20 machine cycles for the more complex gate delay models, see Figure(3). Once the fan-out gate inputs have been amended, as previously stated all wires are time incremented through a parallel shift operation of 3 machine cycle duration.

Of the entire simulation cycle, the only task affected by the circuit size is that of scanning the Hit list. As a circuit grows in size the list and sequential scan time expand proportionately. Analogous to the conventional communication overhead problem, the APPLES architecture needs to incorporate a scan mechanism which can effectively increase the scan rate as the hit list expands. This has been investigated and inplemented as a multiple scan register structure.

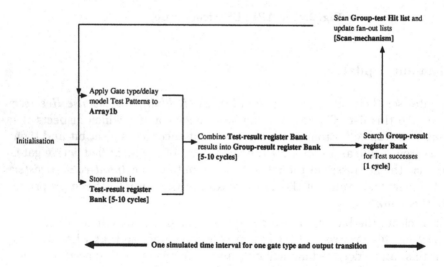

Fig. 3. The Apples simulation cycle.

5   Architecture Performance Evaluation

For each gate type, the evaluation time $T_{\text{gate-eval}}$ remains constant, typically ranging from 10 to 20 machine cycles. The time to scan the Hit list depends on its length and the number of registers employed in the scan. N scan registers can divide a Hit list of H locations into N equal partitions of size H/N. Assuming a location can be scanned in 1 machine cycle, the scan time, T_{scan} is H/N cycles. Likewise it will be assumed that 1 cycle will be sufficient to make 1 fan-out update.

For one scan register partition, the number of updates is $(Prob_{hit})H/N$. If all N partitions update without interference from other partitions this also represents the total update time for the entire system. However, while one fan-out is being updated other registers continue to scan and hits in these partitions may have to wait and queue. The probabilty of this happening increases with the number of partitions and is given by $^N C_1 (Prob_{hit})H/N$.

A *Clash* occurs when two or more registers simultaneously detect a hit and attempt to access the single ported fan-out memory. In these circumstances, a semaphore arbitrarily authorises waiting registers accesses to memory. The number of clashes during a scan is,

$$\text{No. Clashes} = (\text{Prob of 2 hits per inspection})H/N$$
$$+\text{Higher order probabilities.} \tag{1}$$

The low activity rate of circuits implies that higher order probabilities can be ignored. Assume a uniform random distribution of hits and let Prob_{hit} be the probability that the register will encounter a hit on an inspection. Then (1) becomes,

$$\text{No. Clashes} = {}^N C_2 (\text{Prob}_{hit})^2 H/N \tag{2}$$

Thus, T_N, the average total time required to scan and update the fan-out lists of a partition for a particular gate type is,

$$T_N = T_{\text{gate-eval}} + T_{\text{scan}} + T_{\text{update}} + T_{\text{clash}}$$
$$= T_{\text{gate-eval}} + H/N + {}^N C_1 (\text{Prob}_{hit})H/N + {}^N C_2 (\text{Prob}_{hit})^2 H/N \tag{3}$$

Since all partitions are scanned in parallel, T_N also corresponds to the processing time for a N scan register system. Thus the speedup $Sp = T_1/T_N$, of such as system is,

$$T_1/T_N = \frac{T_{\text{gate-eval}} + T_{\text{scan}} + T_{\text{update}}}{T_{\text{gate-eval}} + H/N + {}^N C_1 (\text{Prob}_{hit})H/N + {}^N C_2 (\text{Prob}_{hit})^2 H/N} \tag{4}$$

Eqt (4) has been validated empirically. Predicted results are within 20% of observed for circuits C7552 and C2670 and 30% for C1908. Non-uniformity of hit distribution appears to be the cause for this deviation.

Differentiating T_N w.r.t N and ignoring 2nd order and higher powers of Prob_{hit} the optimum number of scan registers N_{optimum} and corresponding optimum speedup S_{optimum} is given by,

$$N_{optimum} = \sqrt{2}/\text{Prob}_{hit} \qquad (5)$$
$$S_{optimum} = 1/(2.4\text{Prob}_{hit}) \qquad (6)$$

Thus, the optimum number of scan registers is determined inversely by the probability of a hit being encountered in the Hit list. In APPLES, the important processing metric is the rate at which gates can be evaluated and their fan-out lists updated . As the probability of a hit increases there will be a reciprocal increase in the rate at which gates are updated. Circuits under simulation which happen to exhibit higher hit rates will have a higher update rate.

When the average fan-out time is not one cycle, $Prob_{hit}$ is multiplied by Fout, where Fout is the effective average fan-out time.

A higher hit rate can also be accomplished through the introduction of extra registers. An increase in registers increases the hit rate and the number of clashes. The increase halts when the hit rate equals the fan-out update rate, this occurs at $N_{optimum}$. This situation is analogous to a saturated pipeline. Further increases in the number of registers serves to only increase the number of clashes and waiting lists of those registers attempting to update fan-out lists.

5.1 Experimental Results

The APPLES processor was implemented, validated and evaluated using a Verilog model. **ISCAS-85** benchmarks **C1908**(786 gates) and **C2670**(1736 gates) and
C7552(4392 gates) were simulated to generate statistics and performance figures. The gate counts refer to expanded circuits. Averages were compiled from the execution of 10 trials per circuit, each trial being a distinct input vector exercised over 1000 to 10000 machine cycles for the smallest to the largest circuit respectively.

The average number of cycles, taking into account the scan and fan-out cycle times, executed per gate processed for the 3 benchmark circuits are shown in figure 4. The fixed size overheads such as gate evaluation and time incrementation have been excluded from this analysis, since in a smaller circuit they form a proportionately larger overhead. Excluding these overheads is representative of large circuits where the fixed overheads are insignificant to the scan and update times.

Naturally as more registers are employed the average cycle time per gate processed reduces. In the first column of figure 4, depicting cycle times for one scan register, the variation in performance is attributable to the distribution of hits in the Hit-list. As more registers are introduced, the number of cycles per gate is progressively dominated by the number of cycles required to update the fan-out lists; the scan time becomes less significant.

Figure 5 illustrates the speedup performance for the circuits. Again, the adjusted figures give a more balanced analysis. As the fan-out updates converge to the fan-out memory bandwidth, maximum speedup is attained.

No. Scan Registers	1	15	30	50
Circuit				
C7552	154.6	11.3	6.4	5.2
C2670	101.9	8.0	5.1	3.9
C1908	86.9	6.8	5.1	3.9

Average No. Cycles/Gate Processed

Fig. 4. Cycles per Gate processed

No. Scan Registers	1	15	30	50		1	15	30	50
Circuit									
C7552	1	12.5	19.9	24.3		1	13.6	24.3	29.6
C2670	1	9.7	13.8	15.9		1	12.5	20.0	25.1
C1908	1	8.4	10.8	11.8		1	11.8	17.3	20.9
		Speedup				**Speedup (excl Fixed size Overheads)**			

Fig. 5. Speedup as a function of Scan-registers.

For comparison purposes figure 6 uses data from Banerjee [12] which illustrates the speedup performance on various parallel architectures for circuits of similar size to those used in this paper. This indicates that APPLES consistantly offers higher speedup.

6 Conclusion

The APPLES architecture was designed to provide a fast and flexible mechanism for logic simulation. The technique of applying test patterns to an associative memory culminates in a fixed time gate processing and a flexible delay model. Multiple scan registers provide an effective way of parallelising the fan-out updating procedure. This mechanism eliminates the need for conventional parallel techniques such as load balancing and deadlock avoidance or recovery. Consequently, parallel overheads are reduced. As more scan registers are introduced the gate evaluation rate increases, ultimately being limited by the average fan-out list size per gate and consequently the memory bandwidth of fan-out list memory. APPLES is still a prototype model and further research investigating technology implementation issues need to be addressed.

Architecture	Synchronous		Asynchronous	
	Shared Memory	Distributed Memory	Shared Memory	Distributed Memory
Circuit				
Multiplier (4990 gates)	5.0/8	/	5.0/8, 5.8,14	/
H-FRISC (5060 gates)	3.7/8	/	7.0/8, 8.2/14	/
S15850 (9772 gates)	/	3.2/8	/	/
S13207 (7951 gates)	/	3.2/8	/	/
Adder (400 gates)	/	/	4.5/16, 6.5/32	/
QRS(1000 gates)	/	/	5.0/16, 7.0/32	/

Speedup Performance for Various Parallel Systems.
Notation a/b, where a=Speedup value, b=No. Processors.
Double entries denote two different systems of the same architecture

Fig. 6. A Speedup comparison of other parallel architectures.

References

1. Breur et al: Diagnosis and Reliable Design of Digital Systems. Computer-Science Press, New York (1976).
2. Howard et al: Introduction to the IBM Los Gatos Simulation Machine. Proc IEEE Int. Conf. Computer Design: VLSI in Computers. (Oct 1983) 580–583.
3. Pfister: The Yorktown Simulation Engine. Introduction 19th ACM/IEEE Design Automation Conf, (June 1982), 51–54.
4. Dunn: IBM's Engineering Design System Support for VLSI Design and Verification. IEEE Design and Test Computers, (February 1984) 30–40.
5. Agrawal et al: Logic Simulation and Parallel Processing Intl Conf on Computer Aided Design (1990).
6. Soule et al: Parallel Logic Simulation on General purpose machines. Proc Design Automation Conf, (June 1988), 166–171.
7. Mueller-Thuns et al: Benchmarking Parallel Processing Platforms: An Application Perspective. IEEE Trans on Parallel and Distributed systems, 4 No 8 (Aug 1993).
8. Chandy et al: Asynchronous Distributed Simulation via Sequence of Parallel Computations. Comm ACM 24(ii) (April 1981), 198–206.
9. Bryant: Simulation of Packet Communications Architecture Computer Systems. Tech report MIT-LCS-TR-188. MIT Cambridge (1977).
10. Briner: Parallel Mixed Level Simulation of Digital Circuits Virtual Time. Ph.D thesis. Dept of El.Eng, Duke University, (1990).
11. Jefferson: Virtual time. ACM Trans Programming languages systems, (July 1985) 404–425.
12. Banerjee: Parallel Algorithms for VLSI Computer-Aided Design. Prentice-Hall, 1994
13. Kravitz et al: Massively Parallel Switch Level Simulation: A Feasibility Study. IEEE Trans. Computer-aided-Design Integrated Circuits Systems, 10(7), (July 1991).

A High-Level Programming Environment for Distributed Memory Architectures*

W.K. Giloi, H.W. Pohl, A. Schramm

GMD FIRST, Rudower Chaussee 5, 12489 Berlin, Germany, E-mail: giloi@first.gmd.de

Abstract. The programming of distributed memory architectures can be significantly facilitated by abstract, application-oriented models. The Promoter model reconciles generality and easiness of use by a new concept of high-level data parallelism that leads to distributed types with parallel operations. The model enables the user to describe the spatial structures for a wide spectrum of numerical and non-numerical application in a uniform algebraic formalism, so that the compiler can readily generate the optimized message-passing program.

I. Introduction

Scaleable distributed memory architectures can deliver any desired performance at maximum cost-effectiveness. From a hardware point of view, this makes them the ultimate architecture. What keeps them from becoming the standard form of computer, however, is the related message-passing programming paradigm that forces the application programmer to take care of inter-thread communication and coordination and to provide a favorable initial data distribution. Tools like PVM or MPI that make programming machine-independent and provide library routines for communication mitigate these difficulties but work only for standard applications. Another cure has been seen in the provision of a global address space that allows the use of shared variables. Specific hardware or software provisions such as *distributed shared memory* [1] or *virtual shared memory* [2] have been developed to make a distributed memory architecture look like a shared memory machine. However, these approaches incur higher hardware cost and/or additional software overhead, while programming is not really so much easier. There is an additional argument against the global address space: Pointers as means to construct spatial structures fail to preserve any high-level structural information.

A better solution is to have programming models that are based on an application-oriented *abstract machine*, rather than reflecting the manner in which the physical machine works. In this case, the compiler has to bridge the semantic gap between the abstract machine and the actual architecture. If the application is described at a sufficiently high level of abstraction, the compiler is enabled to generate a corresponding optimized message-passing program, thus unburdening the user from the low level tasks of communication, coordination, and (optimized) data distribution. A step in this direction are data parallel languages and compilers such as *High Performance Fortran* (HPF) and others. The downside of these Fortran versions is their confinement

---

* This work was funded by the Real World Computing (RWC) Partnership, Tsukuba, Japan

to rigid array structures. Irregular structures can be expressed only through indirect indexing. This degrades the array to a mere memory heap.

This paper shows a more flexible and general approach to data parallel computing [3,4]. The high-level model and the *Promoter* language based on it provides expressive means for explicitly defining all kinds of application-specific data structures, array-like or hierarchical, static or dynamic, regular or irregular. Lifting the operations to these structures makes the parallelism in an application explicit to the compiler. Such an approach contrasts to the attempt to automatically extract parallel code from a sequential program, e.g., by loop parallelization. Hence, like data parallel languages Promoter exploits data parallelism; however, unlike those languages it offers a concept for creating data structures of almost any kind such as arrays, trees, graphs, or whatever the application may demand. In numeric applications, data structures are usually viewed as geometric patterns, whereas in non-numeric applications they are typically hierarchic, and there may be structures that combine both aspects (e.g., in multi-level methods).

The Promoter model is based on an abstract formalism in which programs are written independent of a particular architecture. The semantic gap between the abstract description and the executing platform is closed by the compiler. The issues of data distribution, communication, and coordination are hidden from the user.

2. The Promoter Model

2.1 High-Level Data Parallelism

In contrast to the common understanding of data parallelism, Promoter exploits a more flexible, polymorphic form, in which homogeneity of data domains and temporal coordination may exist only at a sufficiently high level of abstraction. In this *high-level data parallelism*, parallel algorithms are described by their temporal and spatial structures under two assumptions: (i) there is always some temporal coherence and coordination, however loose, and (ii) within each unit of temporal coherence there exists spatial homogeneity of the individual parallel operations.

Programs are written at a level where the data types look homogeneous, so that the nominally same method can be called in all points of a domain or subdomain. Yet there may be local differences in the method body to be dealt with at run time. Thus, we have global uniformity "in the large", while spatial heterogeneity and temporal incoherence may exist at lower levels of abstraction and are taken care of by local control flow autonomy and object-oriented polymorphism.

2.2 Structured Universe and Topology

The Promoter approach to describing application-specific data structures, data hierarchies, partitions, or coverings is to define them as collections of subsets of an appropriately defined *structured universe* [5]. A universe is an index space with group property. The two ends of the spectrum are Abelian groups for arrays and free groups for trees. Other structures may be somewhere in between, combining geometric and hierarchical aspects (e.g., multi-level grids). Universes may be infinite but are regular and static. A universe provides the basis for constructing the actual domains of computation, i.e., the application-specific data structures which we call *topologies*. Topologies are defined as finite substructures that inherit the geometric properties of their generating universe. By forming unions of substructures, the user has complete control over the topologies and their granularity. This concept covers the entire spectrum between fully regular and totally irregular structures. One extreme is the regular array; the other is the union of single points. Between these, any degree of regularity or irregularity is possible, determined by the shape and size of the regular constituents. Hence, unlike their universe, topologies may be irregular or sparse; moreover, they may be dynamic. For example, a family of triangulations may be derived by uniform or adaptive refinement of an initial triangulation, given by a single three-dimensional universe [5]. Thus, it is possible to provide an appropriate index space for multilevel algorithms.

In general, topologies are sets of spatially distributed discrete points, defined as subsets of Z^n (Z denoting the set of integer numbers). They are explicitly described by index expressions. Irregular topologies may be obtained by adding constraints that "cull off" the irrelevant points. Fig. 1 presents the simple example of an irregular topology, *Tridiag*, created by applying a constraint to a regular structure, a matrix. The result is a band matrix.

```
topology Tridiag (int N): 0:N, 0:N {
    $i, $j |: abs(i-j) <= 1;
};
```

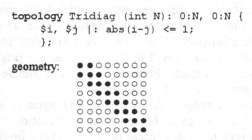

Fig. 1. Simple topology declaration with constraints for a NxN diagonal matrix (N=8)

Rather than evaluating constraints, index spaces may be constructed as Abelian groups restricted by linear boundaries. It is here not the space to go into the topic of group based index spaces; please refer to [6]. New topologies may be derived from existing ones by composition and/or specialization. Composition means that the index space of a new topology either inherits the index space of an existing topology or is defined as the Cartesian product of several other topologies. Specialization means to add constraints. A simple example of a topology specialization is the topology *Twotridiag* which takes every second row of the topology *Tridiag* defined above:

```
topology Twotridiag(int N) : Tridiag(N) > {
    $i, $j |: i%2 = 0;
};
```

The problem-specific algebraic topology descriptions have a geometric interpretation which makes it easy for the user to compose irregular structures out of regular substructures. Topologies may be dynamic and combine regular and irregular aspects (e.g., multi-level linear solver for a dynamically adaptive discretization of an irregular domain). The declaration of a dynamic topology usually requires the use of parameterized index expressions that are evaluated at run time. The topology specifications of a program enable the compiler to optimally map them onto a given target platform.

2.3 Distributed Types

Computation in high-level data parallelism is the parallel execution of methods replicated over the elements of a *distributed type*, that is, a class of topologies (data structure objects) and the methods applicable to them. All values of a distributed object are of the same element type (any type of the host language). As usual in data parallel programming, parallelism is obtained by *function lifting*, i.e., by constructing new functions as multiple applications of a function of one of the element types. The properties of distributed types may be summarized as follows:

- they reconcile the different notions of indexable point sets and recursive types; thus unifying geometric and algebraic models;
- they are polymorphic, thus providing a powerful scheme for formalizing sparseness, irregularity, and dynamic spatial structures.

3. Communication and Coordination

3.1 The View of Communication

In contrast to the low-level message-passing model, communication is separated from synchronization. Communication is viewed simply as the act of data points observing the states of some other points. Thus, "observation of state" means a call (by value) of elements of distributed variables. This approach frees the programmer from having to call communication constructs. Furthermore, it is as simple as the shared memory model but safer, because it is side-effect-free.

The observation of states is determined by the argument expression of the replicated operations. The so given set of pairs of communication partners may be described by a relation between the index spaces of the topologies involved. By specifying that relation, the programmer enables the compiler find an optimized data distribution. The advantage of this model is that data domains and communication patterns both are expressed by the same concept, viz. the specification of topologies.

Communication topologies are created by a specific language construct, called *communication product*, which has the form of a generalized vector-matrix multiplication. Let i,j,r be index tuples of the index spaces I,J,R, respectively, and let A,B,Y denote product spaces $A \subseteq I \times R$, $B \subseteq R \times J$, and $Y \subseteq I \times J$. Then we have

$$y_{ij} = \sum_{(i,r) \in A, (r,j) \in B} a_{ir} * b_{rj} \tag{1}$$

Of the two operations of the communication product, "+" stands for a *reduction* and "*" for a *transfer* (replication). The result is a distributed value that may serve as input argument in a parallel operation. For any point of the target operand, the operation is performed only if both source operands are defined; thus, we have some kind of *data flow* mechanism. This approach allows for the modeling of sparseness, irregularity, and dynamic communication structures. In the communication product, the vector-operand may be a distributed variable and the matrix a Boolean *connectivity matrix* that selects the values to be read. In most applications, however, communication matrices are numeric. Communication may be many-to-one, in which case the result is obtained by a reduction operation.

3.2 Thread Coordination

In each point of a topology, a method, represented by a program thread, is to be executed. Parallel computation means to process all the elements of a potentially large data structure in one step. All threads are embedded in a global control flow such that the individual threads proceed collectively yet with meaningful variations of synchronization requirements. The global control flow is determined by a programmer-selected *coordination scheme* and may consist of any combination of parallel atomic steps. The choice of coordination schemes of Promoter is:

- lock-step synchronization
- wave fronts
- asynchronous iteration
- chaotic iteration

Thus, in contrast to the common message-passing model, thread coordination is separated from communication. All the programmer need do is to select the appropriate coordination scheme, which is then automatically carried out by the system. The coordination schemes listed above proved sufficient for a large variety of applications. They even allow for applications that are usually not associated with data parallelism, e.g., discrete-event simulation.

4. Promoter Language and Compiler

To avoid acceptance problems, the Promoter language is an extension of C++. The extensions are mainly the constructs for defining structured universes and topologies, for declaring distributed variables and functional replications, and for the communication product. Specific constructs such as *reduction, multicast, outer product,* and *scan* allow for the convenient programming of such forms of communication. Distributed types with a dynamic topology are denoted by the keyword **dynamic**.

Based on the specification of data and communication topologies in conjunction with the selected coordination scheme, the Promoter compiler automatically inserts the appropriate message passing constructs into the code. A less trivial task for the compiler is to optimally partition the set of data points of a program into entities that are to be mapped onto the nodes of the target platform so that (i) the computational load is approximately the same on all nodes and (ii) the data movement caused by communication is minimized. Mapping is an NP-complete optimization problem; consequently, one must resort to appropriate heuristics. Dynamic data structures may have to be re-mapped during program execution; thus, the speed of the mapping algorithm is very important. The suitability of some popular mapping heuristics, e.g., the *Kernighan-Lin algorithm* [7] and *Recursive Spectral Bisection* [8], was tested. In addition, a new mapping algorithm, called *balanced hypersphere tessellation* (BHT), has been developed [6]. BHT proved to work well for the partitioning of irregular domains of arbitrary dimensions.

5. Promoter Implementations

The Promoter runtime system provides portability between different platforms. The system has been implemented on the experimental MANNA supercomputer developed by GMD FIRST, on the experimental RWC-1 platform, and on the IBM SP-2. There exist also an implementation for the standard message-passing library MPI, which allows Promoter to be run on workstation clusters. There exists even an implementation for SUN workstations. Though there is no parallel computing on the single-processor workstation, there still is the benefit of the highly abstract, application-oriented programming style of Promoter.

A variety of applications programmed in Promoter for workstations, clusters of workstations, and parallel computers reflects the fact that Promoter enables its user to formulate potentially parallel application algorithms in a highly abstract form, leaving it to the system to execute them in parallel to the degree allowed by the executing platform. The performance proved to be at least as good as that of message passing programs programmed in Fortran under PVM. For more details please look up <http://www.first.gmd.de/org/promot.html>.

References

[1] Li K.: Shared Virtual Memory on Loosely Coupled Multiprocessors, Ph.D.thesis, Yale University 1986

[2] Lenoski D. et al.: The Stanford DASH Multiprocessor, COMPUTER (March 1992)

[3] Giloi W.K., Schramm A.: PROMOTER, An Application-Oriented Programming Model for Massive Parallelism, in Giloi W.K., Jaehnichen S., Shriver B.D.(eds.): *Programming Models for Massively Parallel Computers*, IEEE-CS Press order no. 4900-02 (Sept. 1993)

[4] Giloi, W.K., Kessler, M., Schramm, A.: "PROMOTER: A High Level, Object-Parallel Programming Language, Proc. Internat. Conf. on High Performance Computing, McGraw-Hill Publishing Co., New Delhi, India 1995

[5] Schramm A.: PROMOTER: A Programming Model for Massive Parallelism, PhD. thesis, Tech. University of Berlin 1997

[6] Besch M.: Extracting Application-Specific Knowledge for Mapping Scientific Computations to Parallel and Distributed Systems, Ph.D. thesis, Tech. University of Berlin 1997

[7] Kernighan B.W., Lin S.: An Efficient Heuristic Procedure for Partitioning Graphs, The Bell System Technical Journal, Feb. 1970, 291-307

[8] Pothen A., Simon H.D., Liou K.P.: Partitioning Sparse Matrices With Eigenvectors of Graphs, SIAM J. Matrix Anal. 11 (1990), 430-452

Virtual Shared Files: Towards User-Friendly Inter-Process Communications

Alexandr Konovalov, Victor Samofalov, Sergei Scharf

Inst. Mathematics and Mechanics UrB RAS,
ul. S.Kovalevskoi 16, 620219, Ekaterinburg, Russia,
{avkon, svv, scharf}@imm.uran.ru,
WWW home page: http://www.imm.uran.ru/

Abstract. This paper presents conception of virtual shared files (VSF) as paradigm of parallel components interaction. Metaphor of virtual shared files space ensures a compromise between flexibility of explicit message passing and transparency of shared memory model. VSF are based on ordinary I/O notion and look like matrixes and ordinary files for application programmers. The most essential design issues are: all operations are applied to a file as a whole; operations remotely changing the content of file are prohibited; memory is explicitly allocated by user what is essential for massively-parallel computers.

1 Introduction

Mechanism of parallel components interaction is a critical issue of creating programs for massively-parallel computers. Traditionally there are 3 kinds of parallel interaction paradigms [8]: shared memory, message passing, RPC. Usually to compare them such criteria as effectiveness, overhead of implementation and portability are used. As can be seen from the experience of using supercomputer MBC-100 [4], for application programmers it's also very important that interaction paradigm should be customary and convenient.

From the above mentioned interaction paradigms RPC is the closest to the practice of application programmers. However such feature of RPC as synchronous interaction presents great difficulty for parallel programming in real world and requires either construction of asynchronous procedures above it [7] or introduction of asynchronism in RPC itself, thus destroying the metaphor.

From the point of view of asynchronous communication and error recovery it seems that message passing (which has become techniques of choice for massively parallel systems) looks more natural. But in this case a regular user also has to deal with a number of complicated problems, far from his own tasks. For example, what is the best way to distribute MPI_Isend, MPI_Irecv, MPI_Wait (or their analogues) along parallel branches for superposition of computation and exchange? It requires understanding of considerable number of new entities.

We believe many difficulties can be avoided by choosing file space metaphor based on ordinary I/O notion as the foundation of interaction paradigm. It's the essence of this metaphor and the problem whether it can satisfy the demands of an application programmer as well as some questions of implementation that the present article is devoted to.

2 Files: Metaphor Reusing

"All is a File" paradigm has a history of long and successful application in programming, the most well-known example of following it being canonical Unix shell programming.

Matrixes which are widely used in the field of scientific computing can also be regarded as files. Differently from Unix shell where files-as-stream are used these files are direct access files (files-as-arrays). In case of such approach the procedure of coping a file as a whole known to a user may be applied instead of sequential reading by records.

Of course application of files as communication media requires careful consideration of the choice of both file space structure and operations set. Let's dwell upon the most essential design issues, worked out while designing VSF.

- It's quite natural to demand that not all arrays, but only declared ones will function as shared resources (i.e., files). The same thing happens in the case of one-sided communications [5]. Evident results of this limitation are growing program's expressiveness, possibility of more efficient implementation as well as the necessity to introduce a separate "file creation" operation.
- In order to get scalability the file space should be structured. Creation of adequate universal structure is hardly possible as the needs of application are usually specific. We believe that main efforts should be concentrated on creating easily applied basic namespace which would form the foundation for construction of different systems taking into account peculiarities of diverse application. As such we suggest the system in which addressing a file by name it's also necessary to give the number of the process-owner. File name is represented by tuple of numbers, which makes it possible to operate the names in loops. Thus file space is divided into subspaces consisting of files owned by one process.
- All operations are applied to a file as a whole. The only operations which are allowed to be performed with files from remote nodes are moving to itself and copying to itself. Operations remotely changing the content of file are prohibited (for example, it's impossible to create neighbor's file). The fact that remote modification is prohibited:
  - makes radically lower the amount of programmer's mistakes (such as races) typical for systems with shared memory,
  - rises the effectiveness of implementation on computers that don't ensure cache coherence of main and communication processors (for example, MBC-100 [10]),
  - spares the necessity of having remote locks,
  - creates a lot of possibilities for caching data between different processes.

- Operating of file data and memory allocation can only be performed by the owner, using regular programming languages constructions. Atomicity of data change is ensured by local locks. Explicit memory allocation is caused by optimization demands, as the memory size available for application at each node of massively parallel computers is usually strictly limited by RAM.
- Application programmer should be oriented towards superposition of computation and data exchange because without it effective application of massively parallel computers is possible only for a limited class of tasks. This superposition is made easy in two ways. It can be done by supplying resources (files) with the possibility of their asynchronous requests from other processes. The second way is the implementation of data copying by the system in parallel with carrying out user's procedures.
- It's necessary to aim at reducing the number of introduced entities. Users are, as s rule, familiar with files operations, which makes it possible to take into account a well-known rule for designing API for application programmers "No one will read a manual which is longer than on page".

The above given criteria determine file operations, rules of processing its contents, a set of file attributes. Direct singling out, besides the contents, of system-controlled file attributes gives a possibility to carry out adaptation for tasks of a definite kind, as the set and interpretation of attributes can change depending on user's needs.

3 Operations and Attributes

In current implementation a file is a named data set with the following attributes: state, name of file, a number of process-creator, maximal and current length, a number of readings from the file after the latest writing.

As has been stated the contents of file can be changed only by the owner performing operation of copying f_r_copy (or moving by f_r_move) or ordinary assignment. Operation f_r_copy (f_r_move) only initializes asynchronous copying (moving) of file from remote process towards request sender and immediately returns. Data copying is performed asynchronously by the communication system. The request is sent to a remote process from which the content of the file is transferred with its attributes to local file. If the required file is missing issuing of request is delayed till the appearance of the file. The user either checks (f_test) whether data copying has been completed or waits for it (f_wait).

Copying (moving) operations also sets such attributes as names of source file and its owner, the length of source file. Metadata sent together with data enables the user to organize cooperative data processing without evident description of system arrays. For example, in case of dynamic distribution of matrix blocks file name may correspond to block number. Then by the name of source file the working process can determine the number of neighboring blocks and download them. In this case the user must be spared the necessity to definitely include block number into his data or organize additional message sending.

An operation of copying into a local file can't be initiated before the previous operation with this file is completed. The user may determine the reason by analyzing the returned value, that's different for reading, writing and lock. Operations f_lock, f_unlock are devised to ensure atomicity of changes of the file contents by common assignments. The f_lock execution is suspended till the previous reading is completed. If writing in required file is not completed, this operation will return a condition code immediately. Changes, made in the file content by the process-owner, are guaranteed to be visible by other processes after return from f_unlock.

Operation of moving f_r_move besides copying the contents removes the source file. The possibility to perform moving makes implementation of farm-like schemes of parallelization simpler.

Local file can be removed by calling f_unlink. Removing is delayed till the end of reading out the given file. If a file is removed the copying which has been performed into it is cancelled by sending special message. If the attempt to stop the starting of copying has failed removing doesn't take place, the user is given a certain condition code. Such design makes the implementation of complex protocols simpler, as the part of the work is performed on the level of interaction mechanisms, practically speaking without any overhead for simple cases.

Thus using metaphor of virtual shared files space ensures a compromise between flexibility of explicit message passing and transparency of shared memory model.

4   Comparison with Other Paradigms

Let's consider the problem of tasks distribution in the farm of dynamic working pool. Below this rather typical problem is expressed in terms of VSF.

```
producer() {
  while(...) {
     current_job = Mat[...];
     ... /* prepare next current_job */
 /* put the next task for the workers into file i */
     f_create(i++, current_job, curr_size);
  }
 /* wait for the finish of all the tasks, checking
       the existence of files */
  for(...; ...; i++)
    while(FREE_INODE_STATE != f_state(i))               ;
  ...
}
worker() {
 /* create file for received tasks */
 MyFile=f_create(0, Buf, SIZE);
 while(1) {
 /* begin moving arbitrary task from master to itself */
```

```
   f_r_move(MyFile, 0, ANY_FILE);
/* wait for a task */
   f_wait(MyFile);
   ... /* perform received task */
  }
}
```

Let's compare the suggested implementation with the similar procedure of dynamic tasks distribution, expressed in the terms of traditional message passing. It's not difficult to see that in cases of the simplest implementation the master has to store the workers states and add the poll "Aren't there any workers without a job?" to the loop of generation of works. When we complicate the implementation the polls can be replaced by threads creation, which encapsulates the state of workers. Creation of the threads by the user is possible not in all systems, and, what's still more important, explicit control of threads shouldn't be included into everyday facilities of an application programmer.

Using one-sided communications MPI-2 [5] it's possible to avoid problems of explicit and asynchronous tracing of worker's states by master. However joint creation of window (communication unit of one-sided communications MPI-2) will lead either to every worker taking part in the distribution of every task or to remote locks of working pool on master.

In [6] collective communications was used for Galley parallel file system design. The extension of VSF file attributes will allow to directly support not only collective communications, but such notions as interleaved files and sparse data structures as well.

5 Related Work

Among the systems ensuring intermediate model between explicit message passing and shared memory full emulation it's possible to distinguish the system [9]. The system ensures remote access to segments of memory, operations WRITE, READ, COMPARE-N-SWAP with them and asynchronous reaction to remote messages. The system outperforms TCP due to the absence of copying out of data and was used as the transport layer for advanced distributed file system. In our opinion it's just similar construction of transport layer, supplied with files metaphor that gives to application programmers a chance to use advantages of low overhead of such systems.

Extension of MPI — MPI-2 [5] seems to be the most often mentioned system with one-sided communications. Remote memory in MPI-2 is represented as Windows, over which operations of remote memory reading, writing into remote memory and remote operations with remote memory are defined. To provide atomicity of changes, including remote ones lock procedure can be used. It seems that the main aim of standards of MPI family is not to be used directly by applied programmers, but to serve as transferable substratum for designing end-user systems.

6 Conclusion

The described system prototype has been implemented under Digital Unix 4.0 in MPICH 1.1.1, with use of POSIX threads. Transfer time for short messages (40-byte) in our prototype is 0.5 ms on Alpha-based workstations connected by 100 Mb/s Ethernet. The same characteristic for MPICH is 0.04 ms.

Preliminary considerations show that concepts VSF, presented in the article are easy to understand for real application programmers for massively parallel computers, as they seem usual and familiar. We are planning to develop namespace systems for supporting high-level schemes of addressing files, to reach integration of VSF with traditional file systems by means of introducing persistent files, to support heterogeneous systems on the basis of typed files. Transport level of implementation for network of workstations is planned to be transformed for using active message interface designed in the frames of GAMMA [1] project, which makes it possible to improve performance considerably.

References

1. Chiola, G., Ciaccio, G.: Implementing a Low Cost, Low Latency Parallel Platform. Parallel Computing. **22** (1997) 1703–1717
2. The Common Object Request Broker: Architecture and Specification. Revision 2.0, July 1995
3. Dagum, L., Menon, R.: OpenMP: An Industry-Standard API for Shared-Memory Programming. IEEE Computational Science & Engineering. Vol. 5, No. 1 (January/March 1998)
4. Igumnov, A., Konovalov, A., Samofalov, V., Scharf, S.: Development and Adaptation of System Programming Tools for MBC-100. Algorithms and Programing Tools of Parallel Computing, Ekaterinburg: UrO RAN, Vip. 2, 123—133, in russian
5. MPI-2: Extension to the Message-Passing Interface. Message Passing Interface Forum, 1997. http://www.mpi-forum.org/
6. Nieuwejaar, N., Kotz, D.: The galley parallel file system. ICS'96. Proc. of the 1996 international conference on Supercomputing. 374-381
7. Seshadri, G.: How Do I Implement Callbacks with Java's RMI? Dr.Dobb's Journal. **283** (March 1998) 123–124
8. Tanenbaum, A. S.: Distributed Operating System. Prentice-Hall, Inc. (1995)
9. Thekkath, Ch. A., Levy, H. M., Lazowska, E. D.: Separating Data and Control Transfer in Distributed Operating Systems. ASPLOS-VI Proceedings — Sixth International Conference on Architectural Support for Programming Languages and Operating Systems, San Jose, California, October 4-7, 1994. SIGPLAN Notices, **29(11)** (1994) 2–11
10. Zabrodin, A. V., Levin, V. K., Korneev, V. V.: The Massively Parallel Computer System MBC-100. Parallel Computing Technologies, Proceeding, 1995. LNCS 964. (1995) 341–355

An Object Oriented Environment to Manage the Parallelism of the FIIT Applications

Michaël Krajecki

Loria, projet RESEDAS
Campus Scientifique, B.P. 239
F54506 Vandœuvre-Lès-Nancy Cedex
Michael.Krajecki@loria.fr

Abstract The main goal of this paper is to propose an environment helping the user to parallelize a FIIT application. This object oriented environment is not only independent of the particular application considered, but also of the target parallel machine. It offers a facility of programming: in fact, parallelism is managed by the environment, it is thus completely transparent for the user. We experiment this environment in the framework of parallel ray tracing and show the main advantages.

1 Introduction

One of the main purposes of distributed and parallel systems is to optimise the use of the available resources. In a distributed system, it is highly probable that at least one idle processor exists. In practice, a large number of load balancing schemes has been studied [1, 2]. When the behaviour of an application is unpredictable, only dynamic load balancing algorithms can yield significant time enhancement.

In this paper, we define the notion of *FIIT application* (application with a Finite number of Independent and Irregular tasks). We explain why we choose to use dynamic load balancing schemes to parallelize these applications. To help the user, we offer an object oriented environment responsible for the parallelisation of the application. To highlight the advantages of this solution, we apply this method to the ray tracing. Finally, we sum up the main results obtained and give some perspectives for this work.

2 The FIIT Applications

A FIIT application is made up of a Finite number of Independent and Irregular tasks. We assume that each task satisfies these three features. Firstly, a task cannot make any hypothesis about the execution of any other task. Hence, there is no communication between tasks. Secondly, the execution time of each task is unpredictable. In other words, we cannot have a good estimate of the execution time before the task is completed. Thirdly, The same algorithm is applied to compute all the tasks of the application. Hence, two tasks are distinguished by the data they process.

Due to the task irregularity, we have to propose some suitable load balancing strategies in order to effectively parallelize the FIIT applications. Due to the lack of information on the task behaviour, we exhibit dynamic load balancing strategies. The communication overhead induced by the load balancing strategy should be reasonable if we want to observe a good acceleration of a FIIT application. We focus on dynamic load balancing strategies in section 3.2.

To help the FIIT environment to bring an effective parallelization, the user must answer two questions: he has to cut out its problem in a finite number of tasks and to provide a function that solves a task identified by its number. The choices carried out by the user are significant. He must choose a granularity (a number of tasks) adapted to the parallel machine which he wants to exploit. Indeed, the granularity influences the quality of the load balance but also the level of use of the interconnected network.

We proposed a general matrix iterative model to represent a range of dynamic load balancing strategies in the framework of FIIT applications [3]. Different measure parameters are expressed only on theoretical data. Our model is an interesting tool to select the best algorithm before implementing it.

3 A Parallel Environment for the FIIT Applications

We developed a FIIT environment which proposes the user with various tools such as five MIMD load balancing strategies (presented in section 3.2) and a virtual parallel machine. The goal of this environment is to produce a first parallel solution which solves the load balancing problem on a dynamical scale. As this solution should be easily portable on different machines, we choose the object oriented approach.

3.1 Definition of a Parallel Virtual Machine

In order to make FIIT applications independent of the target machine, our MIMD computational model assumes the following hypothesis. We assume the machine uses a distributed memory, so the data are shared through explicit message passing. Moreover, the topology of the network is fully connected, so there is a path between any two processors of the parallel machine. And finally, we consider that each processor is accessible using an unique identifier. Our parallel virtual machine was made useful, thanks to a set of C++ classes we have developed. The class ParallelMachines provides a set of member functions possibly called by the user in his FIIT application. For example, the user can call the functions SendMsg(void *, int) and ReceiveMsg(void *, int) to communicate. There are some other member functions provided by the class in order to have the kind of message sent or receive, to test if an expected message is arrived...

The target parallel computer we use to experiment FIIT applications corresponds to a particular class of `ParallelMachines` which obviously inherits from all of its services. In our work, we experimented two specific parallel computers: a CM-5 and a cluster of workstations. The class `CM5Machines` is implemented using the library *CMMD* provided by the Thinking Machine Corporation. Like the class `CM5Machines`, `PvmMachines` inherits from the virtual class `ParallelMachines`. Each of the member functions defined is implemented using the PVM library.

3.2 Dynamic Load Balancing Strategies

In literature, many dynamic load balancing schemes have been proposed. Each algorithm tries to reduce the overall communications and to optimize the use of each processor. Nevertheless, it is very difficult to compare the different methods proposed. Thus, some algorithms have been proposed for a particular execution model like SIMD, SPMD, MIMD and hypotheses made by authors are very different in each case. A first approach is to propose a hierarchical classification which answers the following question: who has to distribute the load among the processors?

Thanks to the FIIT environment, the user is not in charge of the dynamic management of the load since he only has to choose one of the available strategies. We have proposed five different dynamic strategies summarised in the next sections. Each task is represented on the load balancing strategy level, by a single number. It is the FIIT application which carries out the link between this number and the work associated to it. Thanks to this representation, the dynamic load balancing strategies are independent of the FIIT application considered.

The class `Loads` is that of higher level. It defines the various services offered by the dynamic load balancing strategies. Moreover, it carries out an elementary static placement of the tasks on the whole of the processors. All the strategies carried out by the environment inherit from the class `Loads`.

Client-Server Strategies Client-server strategies are simple to implement and are, in a large number of cases, efficient. Therefore, centralized strategies are widely used by the scientific community [4].

In the case of FIIT application, we can easily group together all the tasks on a processor, so a very simple algorithm can be used. The server has the set of tasks in its spool. It sends a task to a processor when it makes a request. The other processors are all clients and request the tasks to perform, as soon as they are idle. Finally, the program ends when there is no more task in the server spool.

This kind of algorithms is very efficient. The key advantage of client-server scheme is that it makes a good load distribution without any hypothesis on tasks (execution time, memory resource, ...). Nevertheless, if the granularity is too fine or the number of processors is too high, the server can become a bottleneck.

Distributed Strategies When a distributed strategy is applied, any processor can trigger a new load balancing step. Y. T. Wang et R. J. T Morris introduced the distinction between source and server initiated algorithms in 1985 [1]. A load balancing strategy is source initiated if the load balancing management is initiated by the overloaded processors. In the same way, a dynamic load balancing algorithm is server initiated, if the idle processors are responsible for load balancing [2]. Some dynamic load balancing algorithms behave both as source and server initiated, they are hybrid algorithms.

In [5], we presented three dynamic load balancing algorithms: the first one is source initiated, the second server initiated and the last one is an hybrid algorithm. The reader who wishes more information concerning these three strategies, will refer to this paper. The aim of the new hybrid algorithm is to taking into account the advantages of both source and server initiated algorithms. This hybrid algorithm is based on a temporal variation: at the beginning of the execution, it behaves like a server initiated algorithm whereas it turns into source initiated algorithm during the execution.

A Semi-Distributed Strategy Client-server strategies are very efficient since the load is distributed at a global level. But when the number of processors is large, the server can become a bottleneck. At the opposite, distributed strategies are bottleneck free, but a large number of communications are induced by the distributed methods. This is the reason for, we proposed a semi-distributed algorithm. This one will avoid the bottleneck while keeping the number of communications at a reasonable level. I. Ahmad and A. Ghafoor have proposed a semi-distributed load balancing algorithm [6]. The strategy uses a partitioning of the interconnection structure. The central processor (*scheduler*) of each sphere applies a client-server strategy in order to balance the load in its sphere. If the load has to be balanced at a global level, a source initiated strategy is applied by each scheduler.

In our study, the load balancing is only concerned with the tasks of a FIIT application. The system is composed of r regions named R_0 to R_{r-1}. All the regions have the same size. The semi-distributed strategy will balance the load at two levels: a local and a global one.

At a local level, the load is evenly distributed among the processors which are in the same region. Since we have shown that server initiated strategies are more efficient than source initiated ones and as efficient as client-server strategies [5], we proposed to apply the server initiated strategy presented in [5].

When a processor cannot find any task to perform in its region, a global load balancing step is required. The processor in charge of the region will apply a server initiated strategy. Suppose $P^{(i)} = P_{i \times m}$, responsible for the region R_i, wants to find some tasks for its region. $P^{(i)}$ will send a request to $P^{(i+1)}$, responsible for the region R_{i+1}. If $P^{(i+1)}$ is overloaded, the global load balancing step succeeds. In fact, the other processors of the region R_{i+1} are also overloaded, since they all apply the local load balancing scheme. If this try is unsuccessful, $P^{(i)}$ will try to find some tasks on the region R_{i+2}. This principle is applied until the global load balancing step succeeds or all the regions are idle. If the global load balancing is unsuccessful, the end of the program is detected.

4 Parallel Ray Tracing Algorithm

Ray tracing is a well known algorithm in the visualization area for its image quality and its simplicity. Unfortunately, it is computationally expensive. This algorithm considers multiple reflections and transparencies to visualize a scene. Several techniques have been proposed in order to reduce the cost of this algorithm. Despite these numerous improvements, the ray tracing algorithm is still too slow on sequential computers. In addition, it is intrinsically a parallel algorithm because each pixel can be evaluated independently. Several parallel ray tracing algorithms have been developed in literature.

The ray tracing is a FIIT application. Indeed, it is possible to break up work to be achieved in a set of elementary and independent tasks. For this reason, we divide the screen into a set of rectangles. Each rectangle (identified by an integer) is composed of several *pixels* .

In our parallel ray tracing algorithm, the whole scene is duplicated on each processor. This hypothesis does not limit our study because we focus on load balancing strategies. However, each processor computes only some regions of the scene. In order to solve dynamically the load balancing problem, the best known strategy is the centralized client-server one which distributes the regions to processors as soon as they are idle [7]. In the following section, we will show that our semi-distributed load balancing strategy gives better results.

We experimented all the load balancing strategies studied in this paper, on a Connection Machine (CM-5). All the tests were made with different scenes made up of 50 to 450 primitives. We show here the result obtained for three particular scenes. We used two scenes proposed by E. Haines which are *mount* and *sphere-flake*. We present this particular experimental setting, in order to be concrete about the experiments; however the qualitative results of our experiments were observed in a variety of other scenes.

Table 1 recapitulates time executions for the server and source initiated strategies, the semi-distributed scheme and the centralized client-server algorithm. In our study, the semi-distributed and server strategies seem to be more efficient than the fully centralized client-server algorithm. In addition, we observe in the case of the semi-distributed strategy, we observe an improvement from 30 to 50 % of the execution time. Moreover, we observe that the semi-distributed solution realizes less load balancing steps than both source and server initiated strategies. This result fits with our initial objectives.

5 Conclusion

In this paper, we formally defined the FIIT applications we wish to parallelize. A FIIT application is characterized by a finite set of independent and irregular tasks. We expressed why a parallel implementation of these applications was

Table1: Comparison of the algorithms execution times (in seconds)

Strategy	Sphereflake		Mount		CubeSphere	
	$p=32$	$p=64$	$p=32$	$p=64$	$p=32$	$p=64$
No load balancing	187.45	94.92	264.07	139.46	92.23	56.08
Source initiated alg.	148.28	91.15	155.27	87.96	60.88	39.34
Server initiated alg.	135.17	67.96	133.74	70.86	54.97	31.19
Semi-distributed alg.	134.07	67.03	128.64	70.04	58.15	30.01
Client-server alg.	136.70	68.26	134.33	70.08	58.99	31.77

desirable. So that parallelization is effective, it is necessary to develop adapted dynamic load balancing strategies.

We proposed an environment which helps the user to parallelize FIIT applications. This object oriented environment is not only independent of the particular application considered, but also of the target parallel machine. In fact, parallelism is managed by the environment, it is thus completely transparent for the user. We used this tool to parallelize the ray tracing application on a CM-5. In this particular study, the performances obtained are very satisfactory.

The prospects for this work are numerous. In particular, we plan the extension of the FIIT concept in order to consider other irregular problems where the tasks can be subdivided. For example, the CSP problems (Constraint Problem Satisfaction problem) are solved by algorithms for which it is possible to define a set of independent and irregular tasks. However, a task is divisible. This is why, we should extend the definition of FIIT to allow the subdivision of a task in order to resolve such problems.

References

[1] Wang Y. T., Morris R. J.: Load sharing in distributed systems. IEEE transactions on Computers. **C(34)** (1985) 202–217

[2] Willebeek-LeMair M., Reeves A. P.: Strategies for dynamic load balancing on highly parallel computers. IEEE Trans. on Parallel and Distributed Systems. **4(9)** (1993) 979–993

[3] Krajecki M., Habbas Z., Herrmann F., Gardan, Y.: A performance prediction tool for parallel ray tracing. 6th Int. Conf. in Central Europe on Computer Graphics and Visualisation (WSCG'98), Plzen-Bory (1998)

[4] Hamdi M., Lee C. K.: Dynamic load-balancing of image processing applications on clusters of workstations. Parallel computing, **22(11)** (1997) 1477–1492

[5] Krajecki M., Habbas Z., Herrmann F., Gardan, Y.: Distributed load balancing strategies for parallel ray-tracing. 9th Int. Conf. on Parallel and Distributed Computing Systems, Dijon (France) (1996) 50–55

[6] Ahmad I., Ghafoor A.: Semi-distributed load balancing for massively parallel multi-computer systems. IEEE Trans. on Software Engineering, **17(10)** (1991) 987–1004

[7] Badouel D., Bouatouch K., Priol T., Arnaldi B.: Distributing data and control for ray tracing in parallel. IEEE Comp. Graphics and Applications (1994) 69–77

Performance Studies of Shared-Nothing Parallel Transaction Processing Systems

Jie Li[†], Jiahong Wang[‡], and Hisao Kameda[†]

[†]Institute of Information Sciences and Electronics, University of Tsukuba
Tsukuba Science City, Ibaraki 305-8573, Japan
{lijie, kameda}@is.tsukuba.ac.jp
[‡]Faculty of Software and Information Sciences
Iwate Prefectural University, Iwate, 020-0173, Japan
wjh@iwate-pu.ac.jp

Abstract. We study the system performance affected by Degree of Declustering (DD) and the additional overheads in shared-nothing parallel transaction processing systems with the widely used two-phased locking (2PL) concurrency control method by simulation. We show that for the environment of high resource contention, a large DD is beneficial. For a system in the environment of low resource contention, if we have infinite frontend resource, a large DD is beneficial; otherwise a large DD would degrade system performance. It is shown that as the level of the resource contention in disks decreases, the additional overhead of parallelism increases. Furthermore, it is shown that the functions attached to frontend nodes affect system performance to a significant degree for shared-nothing parallel TP systems. These results provide insights for improving performance of shared-nothing parallel transaction processing systems.

Keywords: Additional overheads, degree of declustering, performance studies, resource contention, shared-nothing parallel transaction processing systems, simulation, two-phased locking.

1 Introduction

Of late, the *shared-nothing* parallel Transaction Processing (TP) systems [1][13][22] have become increasingly popular for their cost effectiveness, scalability, and availability. Commercially available systems and research prototypes include DBC/1012 from Teradata [18], Non-Stop SQL from Tandem [15], Gamma at the University of Wisconsin [4], and Bubba at MCC [2]. In such systems, there are many processing elements (PEs) connected by an interconnection network where each PE has its processor and memory. Records of each relation in the database are declustered across disk drives attached directly to each PE's and the execution of a transaction is distributed over the network. A transaction is divided into several sub-transactions, all of which can be executed in parallel.

For parallel transaction processing to be conducted in a shared-nothing system, it is important to decide the Degree of Declustering (DD) that declusters a relation of database, i.e., to decide the number of network nodes over which this relation should be declustered. DD is an essential performance factor that reflects the degree of parallelism of the system. Two other performance factors for shared-nothing systems are the additional overheads caused by the parallel processing, and the method of the Concurrency Control (CC). These factors interfere with one another, and thus shared-nothing systems behave in an intricate way.

Like the centralized TP systems, most of the shared-nothing parallel TP systems use the Two-Phase Locking (2PL) [7] Concurrency Control (CC) method to resolve the data contention to maintain data consistency and integrity. By 2PL, a transaction has to be blocked, if it requests data that have been locked by another transaction. It is well accepted that for TP systems with 2PL, blocking the transactions has a big negative effect on system performance [17][19][23]. Especially, as the level of the data contention increases (for example, by increasing the MultiProgramming Level (MPL), i.e., the total number of transactions running concurrently in a TP system), the interaction between data contention and 2PL causes such a snowball effect that the blocked transactions hold locks that they have acquired, and result in further blocking [17][19]. As an extreme of this negative effect, *data contention thrashing* (a sudden performance degradation caused by a MPL breaking through some threshold) may occur [17][20].

In this paper, we study the system performance affected by DD and the additional overheads in shared-nothing parallel transaction processing systems with 2PL by careful simulation. We show that for the environment of high resource contention, a large DD is beneficial. For a system in the environment of low resource contention, if we have infinite frontend resource, a large DD is beneficial; otherwise a large DD would degrade system performance. It is shown that as the level of the resource contention in disks decreases, the negative effect (i.e., the additional overhead) of parallelism increases. Furthermore, it is shown that the functions attached to frontend nodes affect system performance to a significant degree for shared-nothing parallel TP systems. Based on the simulation results, we suggest that for shared-nothing parallel TP systems, frontend nodes are necessary in order to improve the system performance, although many existing systems are not configured with them. And the number of frontend nodes should be computed by considering both the maximal possible arrival rate of transactions and the DD of data. The frontend nodes should be configured with two layers. The nodes of the first layer distribute transactions over that of the second layer uniformly, which in turn, start transactions and coordinate transaction execution.

Many related studies have conducted on the performance study for shared-nothing parallel TP systems[12]. In [5], a *single-user* workload was used, and thus the effect of the multiprogramming was ignored. In [15][16], the Debit-Credit transaction was used. This transaction accesses exactly four data granules, and thus increasing DD beyond four do little to alter the parallelism within an individual transaction. In [2], read-only transactions were used, and thus the effect of CC was ignored. Many other simulation studies (e.g., [11] and [9]) have the same limitations as above. Here we study the system performance of shared-nothing parallel TP systems in more real environments with the consideration of the combination of DD, CC (Concurrency Control) and the additional overheads. These results provide comprehensive insights for improving the performance of shared-nothing parallel transaction processing systems.

This paper is organized as follows. In the next section, we present the system description considered in this paper. The simulator for the study of shared-nothing systems is described in section 3. In section 4, we describe the simulation experiments. Sections 5 and 6 show the system performance in the environment with low level of resource contention and with high level of resource contention, respectively. Section 7 studies the data contention thrashing behavior. Section 8 concludes the paper.

2 System Description

A shared-nothing parallel TP system is shown in figure 1. Here a non-replicated relation database is used. A relation consists of a number of records. One or more records constitute a granule, which is a lockable unit. Each relation in the database is horizontally declustered across all the network nodes called data Processing Elements (PEs) [4]. Transactions arriving at the system are accepted and started by *transaction managers* that reside at the *frontend nodes*. The results are also routed by these frontend nodes to their users. Each frontend node has an identical copy of a global directory of a relation in the database telling which PEs hold which data of this relation. We consider the *fork* and *join* type of transactions [3], e.g., a transaction that scans a relation in the database in parallel for the required data. A transaction of this type consists of several sub-transactions, each of which works on the PE where the data to be used reside, and all of which are executed in parallel. Generally, we assume that sub-transactions do not need data from each other. A sub-transaction is modeled as a sequence of *data-processing steps*. The number of steps is called the *size* of this sub-transaction. Each step involves a lock request for the granule to be accessed, followed by the granule access to a disk, and a period of CPU usage for processing this granule. The two-phase locking (2PL) concurrency control (CC) method is used to resolve data contention, and to maintain data consistency and integrity. To ensure transaction atomicity, the two-phase commit (2PC) protocol is applied.

3 Developing a Simulator

In order to study the performance of CC methods, we developed a comprehensive simulator [21] for shared-nothing parallel TP systems which follows the real-life systems such as Bubba [2] and Gamma [4]. Simulation study allows us to deal with the system performance by considering the system factors in detail. The structure of the simulator is given in figure 2. There are four parts of this

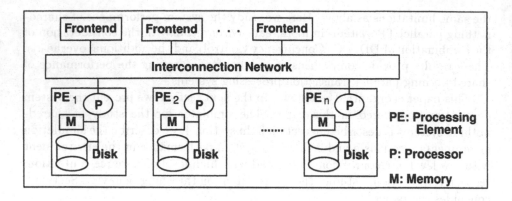

Fig. 1. A shared-nothing parallel TP system

simulator described as follows. Note that although the operations such as sending and receiving messages consume CPU time, they are not depicted in figure 2 for the sake of simplicity.

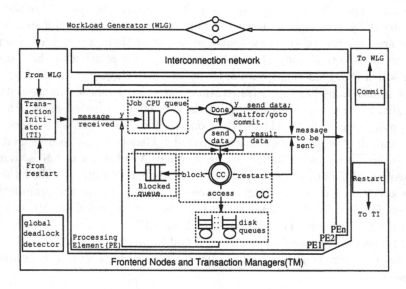

Fig. 2. The parallel TP system model

1. Computer System The computer system consists of n network nodes called data Processing Element (PE) connected by an interconnection network. Each PE has its own processor, memory, disks, and communication processor. Each PE also has a copy of the operating system that supports a multi-threaded process environment. A database cache is provided for each PE for caching local data. Frontend nodes are configured for interfacing with users and handling all the centralized functions, such as commit, abort, global deadlock detection, and transaction initiation.

2. Database   The database is a collection of relations, and a relation is a collection of records. One or more records constitute a granule, which is a lockable unit. We suppose that all granules have the same size. The size of database is measured by the number of granules in the database. In this study, a non-replicated database is assumed. A relation is horizontally declustered across all the PEs in the system, one partition per PE [4].

3. Transaction   Since we are interested in the relative performance of the scheduling algorithms to be evaluated, granules are assumed to be accessed in an exclusive mode (i.e., one granule cannot be locked by more than one transaction) [8]. A transaction is viewed as a collection of update operations on the database, each of which involves a lock request for the granule to be accessed, followed by the granule access to disk, and followed by a period of CPU usage for processing this granule. The granules accessed by a sub-transaction are distributed uniformly over all the disks at the PE where this sub-transaction is executed.

According to its size, a sub-transaction cycles through the CPU and disk queues several times. Before a granule is accessed, a lock is requested for it. If the lock request is granted, the sub-transaction enters a disk queue to perform I/O operation; otherwise it enters the blocked queue to wait until it can proceed again. Results are produced in each cycle. These results are sent to their user each time they can contribute to a network packet. When a transaction completes all its data processing work, a two-phase commit protocol is started. The modified data are forced into the stable storage as a part of the commit processing. The committed transaction is immediately replaced by a new one.

For 2PL, deadlock is possible. In this model, local deadlock is detected immediately based on a local wait-for-graph whenever a lock conflict occurs. A global deadlock is resolved by a specified transaction manager by periodically collecting local wait-for information from all PEs. In resolving a deadlock, the youngest transaction among those involved in the deadlock is aborted and to be restarted. A restarted transaction is made to wait until all its blockers are committed or aborted.

4   Simulation Experiments

By using the developed simulator, we study the performance of shared-nothing parallel TP systems.

The parameter settings for the simulation experiments are shown in Tables 1 to 4, most of which are typical parameters from previous studies [8][10] [?].

The global deadlock detection interval is varied from 100 to 500ms adaptively by the step of $\pm 5ms$ according to whether a deadlock is found for a detection process. The time taken for commit in Table 4 integrate those for pre-committing and completing transactions.

Tab. 1: Workload related parameters

Tab. 2: Database related parameters

Num. of granules required by a transaction: 192	Num. of relations in the database: 8
Num. of relations accessed by a transaction: 1	Num. of records per relation: 320,000
Num. of partitions accessed per relation: DD	Num. of partitions per relation: DD
Num. of granules accessed per partition: 192/DD	Num. of records per partition: 320,000/DD
Num. of trans. executed concurrently: MPL	Record size in bytes: 200
	Lock granularity (record num. per lock): 1

Tab. 3: Computer system related parameters

Tab. 4: Transaction processing related parameters

Num. of processing elements in the system: 32	Deadlock detection interval: 100-500ms
Num. of disks per processing element: 10	CPU time requirement per granule: 0.05ms
Network speed: 17.76 MBits/sec	CPU time (re-)starting a trans. at FEs: 1.0 (0.5) ms
CPU time for sending/receiving a message: 0.05ms	CPU time (re-)initiating a thread at PE: 0.1 (0.05) ms
Control/Data message size: 512/4,096 bytes	CPU time for commit at FE/PE: 0.35/0.26ms
I/O time for accessing a granule from disk: 13.0ms	CPU time for abort at FE/PE: 0.12/0.10ms
Hit ratio of database cache: 0%, 60%, 100%	

Note: E: Exponential, G: Geometric, FE: FrontEnd node, PE: Processing Element.

According to many previous studies (e.g., [14]), for shared-nothing systems, it is the CPU that restricts message transmission rate between two processors, rather than the interconnection network. Therefore, in this paper we focus on the effect of CPU and rule out the interconnection network by setting a bandwidth large enough for it. In addition to interconnection network, we note that the frontend nodes are also shared resources. Therefore, the effect of the frontend nodes is examined by assuming that there are finite and infinite frontend resource, respectively. The former is achieved by configuring a single frontend node, which reflects the extreme of the finite case. The latter is achieved by assuming that the functions attached to frontend nodes can be served without delay, which corresponds to such a TP system with which numerous frontend nodes are configured.

By our parameter settings, before data contention thrashing occurs, only disks can become system bottleneck. By changing the hit ratio of database cache, the effect of resource contention in disks can be taken into account. The level of data contention is varied by changing MPL.

The primary performance metric with which we are concerned is the system *throughput* that is defined to be the transaction completion rate. The *mean response time* of a transaction can be obtained easily by the Little's law. Two other metrics are also employed. The one is the *sub-transaction execution time per PE* that is defined to be the average execution time of all the sub-transactions at a PE, excluding the time for initiating and committing sub-transactions. Sub-transaction execution time reflects the work of sub-transactions. The other is the *additional overhead* that is defined to be the time for (sub-) transaction initiation, two-phase commit protocol, abort processing, and network communication.

The simulation results will be given in the next section. For each simulation result, the 90% confidence intervals of measured indices are within ±5% of the mean of the indices.

To study the system performance of shared-nothing parallel TP systems, we have conducted extensive simulation studies. Specifically, we study the system performance in environment of low resource contention in which the hit ratio of database cache is high, and the environment of high resource contention in which the hit ratio of database cache is low. Based on these studies, we provide a clear explanation on two contradictory viewpoints in previous studies about DD in shared-nothing parallel TP systems.

5   System Performance in Environment with Low Level of Resource Contention

In the environment with low level of resource contention, the hit ratio of database cache of a system is relatively high. For the purpose of demonstration, we set the hit ratio of database cache to 60%.

We study two cases in this environment: the case that infinite number of frontend nodes and the case that there are finite number of frontend nodes. The former is achieved by assuming that the functions attached to frontend nodes can be served without delay, which corresponds to such a TP system with which numerous frontend nodes are configured. The latter is achieved by configuring a single frontend node, which reflects the extreme of the finite case.

The system performance for the case with infinite number of frontend nodes is illustrated in figure 3.

There are four curves in figure 3. The first curve shows that the additional overhead (in ms) increases slightly as DD increases. The second curve plots that the maximal system throughput (in transactions per second) increases as DD increases. Furthermore, we look into the sub-transaction execution time (in ms) and the amount of work of a sub-transaction (in granules). Curves 3 and 4 show that the sub-transaction execution time divided by 3 and the amount of work of a sub-transaction decrease as DD increases.

Figure 4 shows the system performance for the case with finite number of frontend nodes. Comparing with the results in figure 3, we find that the additional overhead increases greatly as DD increases beyond 24 (curve 1 in figure 4) which results in the decrease in of the maximal system throughput (curve 2 in figure 4).

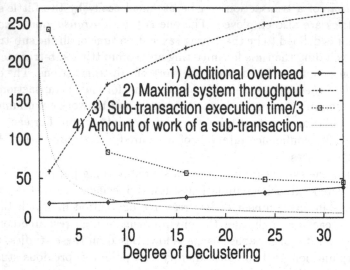

Fig. 3. Results for 1) Additional overhead (in ms) vs. DD; 2) Maximal system throughput (in transactions per sec.) vs. DD; and 3,4) Load balancing effect of DD. Curve 4) illustrates the function of 192/DD. All the results are obtained by fixing DD and increasing MPL as large as possible without thrashing.

For the environment with low level of resource contention, we also find that the number of frondend nodes has a big effect on the system performance of shared-nothing parallel transaction systems.

In order to improve the system performance in the environment with low level of resource contention, we have the following consideration based on the results in figures 3 and 4.

Firstly, for shared-nothing parallel transaction systems, frontend nodes are necessary although many existing systems are not configured with them. Naturally, PEs can function as the frontend nodes. It, however, is not beneficial since the management operations at frontend nodes affect system performance greatly, and these operations would be interfered by the data-processing operations at PEs.

Secondly, the arrival requests at a frontend node should be served with little delay. This means that a large DD should correspond to a large number of frontend nodes, and there should be no access skew for these frontend nodes. Therefore, the number of frontend nodes should be computed by considering both DD and the maximal possible MPL. In addition, two layers of frontend nodes should be provided. The first layer is used to distribute the arriving transactions uniformly over the nodes of the second layer, which in turn start transactions and coordinate their execution.

Thirdly, transactions should be started, committed, and aborted by using multicase messages. Otherwise, for example, for starting a transaction at a fron-

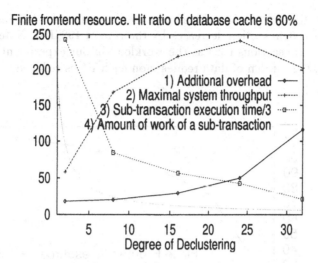

Fig. 4. Results for 1) Additional overhead (in ms) vs. DD; 2) Maximal system throughput (in transactions per sec.) vs. DD; and 3) Load balancing effect of DD. The results are obtained by fixing DD and increasing MPL as large as possible without thrashing.

tend node, a DD of 32 leads to queuing at least 32 messages into the CPU queue at this node to initiate all the 32 sub-transactions. Committing transactions doubles this message number. If the multicast message is used, the message number becomes only 1/32 of the above. Naturally, multicast messages may waste network bandwidth since all the necessary data for all the PEs involved should be included. By many previous studies (e.g., [14]), however, for shared-nothing architecture, message transmission rate between two processors is limited by CPU speed rather than network bandwidth. Considering that all the additional overheads stated in section 2 are caused by splitting a single data stream into several independent streams, it is suggested that the destinations of a splitting operation should be grouped as a single destination virtually by a multicast message, and thus the additional overheads caused by parallel processing is reduced at the cost of sacrificing network bandwidth to some extent.

6 System Performance in Environment with High Level of Resource Contention

In the environment with high level of resource contention, the hit ratio of database cache of a system is relatively low. For the purpose of demonstration, we set the hit ratio of database cache to 0%. Figure 5 shows the system performance in the environment with high level of resource contention. From this figure we see that in this case, the amount of frontend resource has little effect on system performance, and a large DD is always acceptable. The results may be explained as follows. In the environment with high level of resource contention, the resource contention in disks dominates the system performance. As DD increases, the work of each sub-transaction decreases by the rate of 192/DD. Note that 192 is the size of the transactions used as the workload in our experiments (see Table 1). Therefore, the burden of data requests on each PE is reduced.

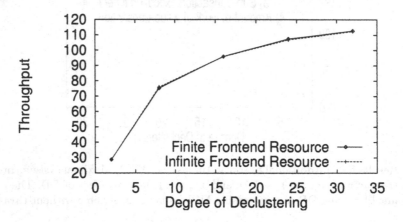

Fig. 5. DD vs. maximal system throughput (in transactions per sec.). The results are obtained by fixing DD and increasing MPL as large as possible without thrashing. Hit ratio of database cache is 0%.

7   Data Contention Thrashing Behavior

Furthermore, we study the system performance from the viewpoint of data contention thrashing. For this purpose, the simulation experiments are performed with infinite frontend resource and with the hit ratio of database cache being set to 100%, so that the resource contention in frontend nodes and in disks can be eliminated. The maximal MPL is limited to such a value that an arrival request can be served by a CPU with little delay. Under such an environment, the effect of the data contention on system performance can be studied without the interference of the resource contention. The simulation results are shown in figure 6. Note that we do not turn off the disk accesses for committing a transaction at individual PE. However, this does not affect our conclusion, as interpreted below.

As shown in figure 6, as DD increases, the data contention thrashing point tends to shift toward the right. We also have conducted extensively simulation experiments for the cases with larger DD. For the sake of brevity, we do not give the results in figures. In the simulation experiments, we find that a large DD always leads to a high throughput after MPL becomes 110. We note that the data contention becomes strong enough to dominate the system performance, after MPL becomes 110, and a large DD can relieve data contention by reducing sub-transaction sizes. Therefore, it can be concluded that a large DD is preferable

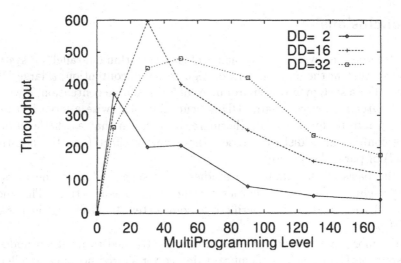

Fig. 6. Throughput vs. MPL with hit ratio of database cache = 100%

for a TP system with high level of data contention (i.e., high value of MPL). Note that the overhead for committing sub-transactions at PEs increases as DD increases, which slows down the speed by which thrashing point shifts towards the right. Nevertheless, we have observed the tendency of this shifting, as shown in figure 6.

For the experiments here, such a DD is beneficial that leads to a good tradeoff between the effect of the data contention and the overhead for committing sub-transactions at PEs. In the case of low data contention environment, a relatively small DD is acceptable. For example, for MPL=10, the optimal DD is 8 in our simulation study. The result is expected since a large DD increases the overhead for committing sub-transactions at PEs. As the level of the data contention increases, the optimal DD shifts towards the right, since a large DD helps to reduce the level of the data contention. When MPL becomes 30, the optimal DD becomes 16.

Furthermore, we can conclude that as the level of resource contention in disks decreases, the effect of the additional overhead caused by parallel processing increases, since the cost for maintaining parallelism becomes a significant fraction of the actual execution gradually. $C_{init}^{TM} + C_{init}^{PE} + C_{comm}^{TM-PE} + C_{dp}^{PE} + C_{2PC}$, where C_{init}^{TM} is the average time for starting transactions at frontend nodes; C_{init}^{PE} is the average time for initiating sub-transactions at PEs; C_{comm}^{TM-PE} is the average time of communication between frontend nodes and PEs; C_{dp}^{PE} is the average execution time of sub-transactions, including that for lock requests, data accesses from disks, and data processing; C_{2PC} is the time for committing transactions. It is obvious that as C_{dp}^{PE} decreases, the other kinds of time dominate response times of transactions gradually. For example, in the case of finite frontend resource for our experiments with DD of 24, at the thrashing point, the ratio of the additional overhead to the response time are 2.73%, 9.64%, and 19.90% for the hit ratio of database cache of 0%, 60% and 100%, respectively.

8 Conclusions

We have studied the system performance of shared-nothing parallel TP systems. It is shown that in the environment of high resource contention, a large DD is beneficial. For a system in the environment of low resource contention, if we have infinite frontend resource, a large DD is beneficial; otherwise a large DD would degrade system performance. Furthermore, it is shown that as the level of the resource contention in disks decreases, the negative effect (i.e., the additional overhead) of parallelism increases.

On the basis of the simulation studies, it is suggested that the messages should be sent by the way of multicast rather than one-at-a-time. This means that the network bandwidth is sacrificed to some extent to offsetting the negative effects of parallelism.

Furthermore, it is shown that the functions attached to frontend nodes affect system performance to a significant degree for shared-nothing parallel TP systems. Based on the simulation results, we suggest that for shared-nothing parallel TP systems, frontend nodes are necessary in order to improve the system performance, although many existing systems are not configured with them. And the number of frontend nodes should be computed by considering both the maximal possible arrival rate of transactions and the DD of data. The frontend nodes should be configured with two layers. The nodes of the first layer distribute transactions over that of the second layer uniformly, which in turn, start transactions and coordinate transaction execution.

References

1. P. Bernstein and E. Newcomer, *Principles of Transaction Processing.* Morgan Kaufmann, Inc., San Francisco, California, 1997.
2. H. Boral, et al., Prototyping Bubba, A Highly Parallel Database System, *IEEE Trans. Knowledge Data Eng.*, Vol.1, pp.4-24, 1990.
3. S.P. Dandamudi, and C.Y. Chow, Performance of Transaction Scheduling Policies for Parallel Database Systems, *Proc. 11th IEEE Conf. Distributed Computing Sys.*, pp.116-124, 1991.
4. D.J. DeWitt, et al., GAMMA - A High Performance Dataflow Database Machine, in: *Proc. 12th VLDB Conf., (Kyoto, Japan, 1986)* 25-28.
5. D.J. DeWitt, S. Ghandeharizadeh, D. Schneider, A Performance Analysis of the Gamma Database Machine, in *Proc. ACM SIGMOD Conf. on Management of Data*, pp.350-360, Chicago, 1988.
6. S. Englert, R. Glasstone and W. Hashan, Parallelism and Its Price: A Case Study of NopStop SQL/MP, *ACM SIGMOD Rec.*, Vol.24, No.4, pp.61-71, Dec. 1995.
7. K.P. Eswaran, J.N. Gray, R.A. Lorie and I.L. Traiger, The Notions of Consistency and Predicate Locks in a Database System, *Commun. ACM*, Vol.11, pp.624-633, 1976.

8. P.A. Franaszek, J.R. Haritsa, J.T. Robinson and A. Thomasian, Distributed Concurrency Control Based on Limited Wait-Depth, *IEEE Trans. Parallel Distributed Sys.*, Vol.11, pp.1246-1264, 1993.

9. S. Ghandeharizadeh and D.J. DeWitt, "Hybrid-Range Partitioning Strategy: A New Declustering Strategy for Multiprocessor Database Machines," *Proc. 16th VLDB Conf.*, pp.481-492, Melbourne, Australia, 1990.

10. B.C. Jenq, B.C. Twitchell, and T.W. Keller, "Locking Performance in a Shared-Nothing Parallel Database Machine," *IEEE Trans. Knowledge Data Eng.*, Vol.1, No.4, pp.530-543, Dec. 1989.

11. R. Maret and E. Rahm, "Performance Evaluation of Parallel Transaction Processing in Shared Nothing Database Systems," *Proc. PARLE'92, Lecture Notes in Computer Science*, Vol. 605 (Springer) pp.295-310, 1992.

12. K. Salem, H. Garca-Molina and J. Shands, "Altruistic Locking" *ACM Trans. on Database Systems*, Vol.19, pp.117-165, 1994.

13. M. Stonebraker, "The Case for Shared Nothing," *Database Eng. Bull.*, Vol.9, No.1, pp.4-9, Mar. 1986.

14. Tandem, "Cyclone/R Message System Performance," *Technical Report, Tandem Computers*

15. Tandem Database Group, "NonStop SQL, A Distributed, High-Performance, High-Reliability Implementation of SQL," *Proc. 2nd Workshop on High Performance Transaction Systems*, pp.60-104. CA, 1987.

16. Tandem Performance Group, "A Benchmark of NonStop SQL on the Debit Credit Transaction," *Proc. ACM SIGMOD Conf. on Management of Data*, pp.337-341, Chicago, 1988.

17. Y.C. Tay, N. Goodman, and R. Suri, "Locking Performance in Centralized Databases," *ACM Trans. Database Sys.*, Vol.10, No.4, pp.415-462, 1985.

18. Teradata, "DBC/1012 Data Base Computer Concepts & Facilities," Document No. C02-001-00, Teradata Corp., 1983.

19. A. Thomasian, "Centralized Concurrency Control Methods for High-End TP," *ACM SIGMOD Rec.*, Vol.20, No.3, pp.106-115, Sep. 1991.

20. A. Thomasian, "Two-Phase Locking Performance and Its Thrashing Behavior," *ACM Trans. Database Sys.*, Vol.18, No.4, pp.579-625, 1993.

21. J. Wang, J. Li, and H. Kameda, "Simulation Studies on Concurrency Control in Parallel Transaction Processing Systems," *Parallel Computing* Vol.23,, Issue 6, pp.755-775, June, 1997.

22. J. Wang, J. Li, and H. Kameda, "Distributed Concurrency Control with Local Wait-Depth Control Policy," *IEICE Trans. on Information and Systems*, Vol.E81-D, No.6, pp.513-520, June, 1998.

23. P. S. Yu, "Modeling and Analysis of Transaction Processing Systems" *Lecture Notes in Computer Science*, **729**, pp.651-675, 1993.

Synergetic Tool Environments*

Thomas Ludwig, Jörg Trinitis, Roland Wismüller

Technische Universität München (TUM), Informatik
Lehrstuhl für Rechnertechnik und Rechnerorganisation (LRR-TUM)
Arcisstr. 21, D-80333 München
email: {ludwig|trinitis|wismuell}@in.tum.de

Abstract. In the field of parallel programming we notice a considerable lack of efficient on-line tools for debugging, performance analysis etc. This is due to the fact that the construction of those tools must be based on a complicated software infrastructure. In the case of such software being available tools from different vendors are almost always incompatible as they use proprietary implementations for it. We will demonstrate in this paper that only a common infrastructure will ease the construction of on-line tools and that it is a necessary precondition for eventually having interoperable tools. Interoperable tools form the basis for synergetic tool environments and yield an added value over just integrated environments.

1 Introduction

In the area of programming parallel and distributed applications we find tools of various types to help us to develop, optimize, and maintain parallel code [10]. Tools can be categorized as on-line and off-line and as interactive and automatic. Off-line tools are trace based and allow a post-mortem program analysis for e.g. performance bottleneck detection or debugging. By their technology they are not able to manipulate the program under investigation. This can only be performed by on-line tools. They provide instant access to the program, thus supporting a wider variety of tools. Interactive tools can be used for e.g. debugging [2], performance analysis [6], program flow visualization, or computational steering, whereas automatic tools offer services for e.g. dynamic load balancing and resource management.

Although we nowadays find many tools from various developers from industry and academia there is a decisive problem when applying them: on-line tools can almost never be used in combination. Due to their complex software infrastructure needed for program observation and manipulation (usually called monitoring system) they require the parallel program to be linked with special libraries and run under strictly specified execution conditions such as especially adapted runtime environments. Unless different tools are implemented by the same producer they are based on incompatible infrastructure concepts which do not allow a concurrent tool usage (see Figure 1).

* This work is partly funded by *Deutsche Forschungsgemeinschaft*, Special Research Grant SFB 342, Subproject A1.

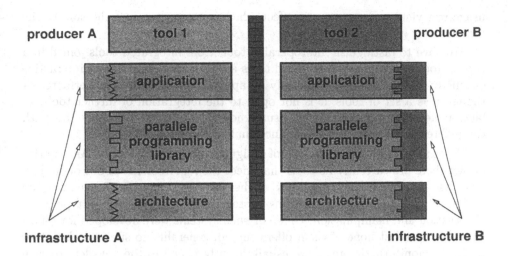

Fig. 1. Incompatible on-line tools

Thus, synergetic effects of applying more than one tool during the same program run are impossible. It is the goal of our project to change this situation and to develop concepts and means for the implementation of environments of interoperable tools.

2 The Concepts of Interoperable Tools

Interoperable tools is a concept that is hardly covered in the literature on development and maintenance tools for parallel programs. Let us first have a closer look on the basic ideas behind this concept.

The concept of interoperable tools is to provide a synergetic effect to the developer by allowing to apply more than one tool at a time to a program run. The synergy results from complementary functions in the individual tools which add new features to each other.

Consider the usage of a debugger. You will monitor programs to find errors in the code. With parallel programs that exhibit difficult timing behavior and are used for long running applications like e.g. fluid dynamics simulations this might result in long debugging sessions where the programmer waits for errors to occur. If we add a second tool that can can perform regular and on-demand checkpoints of a set of processes we will end up with a more powerful development environment: If an error occurs we will set the program back to one of its recent checkpoints and start with exploring the causes of the error. By this the debugger will be much more efficient. We will even be able to checkpoint the debugger itself and thus can restart not only the parallel program but a complete debugging session.

Interoperable tools are thus a combination of two or more on-line tools. They may belong to the class of interactive and automatic tools. Their concurrent usage will yield some synergetic effect which is more than just the sum of the functionality of the individual tools.

We have to distinguish interoperable tools from integrated tools joined in a certain tool environment. Integrated tools are usually a collection of interactive on-line tools that can not necessarily be applied concurrently. Furthermore, although it is a set of tools, it is not open to the integration of further tools. In fact, its development concepts are usually identical to those of a single tool with the difference that a larger set of functionality is supported.

What are the inherent problems of designing interoperable tools? As a matter of fact there are currently no tools that meet the requirements of our definition. The first problem is the complexity of the software infrastructure required by on-line tools. A powerful monitoring system is necessary to support program observation and manipulation. Different such systems were developed for different tool types but none of them offers enough generality to support also other tools. As monitoring systems are usually tightly joined to the parallel program and its runtime environment, only one such system can be active at a time. Second, there are hardly any powerful standards available, especially for interfaces between tools and monitoring systems. Having such standards could greatly simplify the construction of interoperable tools and would allow to serve several tools with a single monitoring system (see Figure 2).

Finally, as there are no concepts for a general purpose tool infrastructure there are consequently also no concepts for tool interoperability. It has not yet been worked out how tools should be designed in order to be interoperable with other, possibly yet unknown tools.

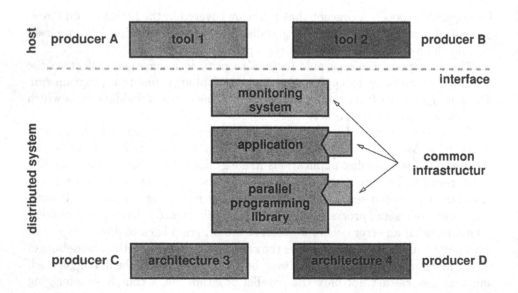

Fig. 2. Interoperable on-line tools

3 Levels of Interoperability

With the concept of interoperability being applied to tools we first have to consider the levels of interoperability that are to be distinguished.

- The first level is characterized as co-existence. Several tools can be applied concurrently to the same program run. However, they have no knowledge of the existence of the other tools. The benefit of having more than one tool is reduced by the danger of a potentially conflicting behavior of the tools. If they manipulate the same objects of the program they might generate an inconsistent program state. Consider a debugger that initiates a single step mode on a process in combination with a load balancer that migrates exactly this process to another node. A program abortion might be the consequence of these tool activities.
- At the second level we have a concept called consistent co-existence. Tools are obliged to preserve consistency of the program system under investigation. In detail this implies that manipulations of objects are treated as critical regions. It has to be guaranteed that only one tool is in the critical region with respect to specific objects at a time. As with consistency mechanisms in other application fields we can determine several concepts to meet this requirement. One possibility would be that the monitoring system itself coordinates the access to objects by the various tools. Another way can be provided with means for observing tool activities and controlling access to individual objects. In any way there is no direct tool cooperation but a coordinated co-existence.
- The third level is thus characterized by direct cooperation. By means of a communication mechanism tools exchange control information and data. A debugger could inform others of its single-step activity, a load balancer could send its current load evaluation heuristics to some interactive tool to be presented to the user. Direct cooperation is the most advanced concept of interoperability. However, it might already limit the synergetic effects by pre-defining them with the messages to be sent.

The three levels of interoperability require different concepts for their realization. Concepts get more complex with each level. For the first level to be reached it is sufficient to be able to run the tools concurrently. This can easily be achieved by basing them on an identical software infrastructure which is powerful enough to support the sum of the functionality required by the tools. Note that there are hardly any realizations available that provide such a functionality. With the second level we must require concepts for coordination in addition to all concepts for the first level. Coordination could be performed automatically by the infrastructure itself. However, as the monitoring system knows nothing of the tools' semantics it might follow a worst case approach where everything is coordinated by locks etc. even when this would not be necessary. A more flexible approach is to provide the tools with mechanisms to coordinate their activities. This comprises detection of object manipulation by other tools and locking of objects against manipulation from other tools. It is essential to distinguish between object observation and object manipulation. In most cases only the latter has to be coordinated as it bears the chance for inconsistencies in the tools and the programs. Finally, with the third level we also require concepts for tool cooperation. This can be achieved by a message passing mechanism by which tools can control cooperation. Two issues are to be considered. Message passing must follow a protocol that does not depend on the actual receivers to be present. Usually we do not know in advance how many tools will be used concurrently in a session. Messages must correspond to a fixed though expandable format. Different types of message formats must be offered for vice versa tool control and information messages. Problems of this kind are already handled in the ToolTalk approach from Sun. However, there is no methodology how to integrate this into the individual tools.

We conclude that tool interoperability is a goal that is characterized by many different aspects. Various degrees can be achieved with different effort providing the tool user with more or less powerful tool environments and more or less possibilities for synergetic effects.

4   The Infrastructure Concept: OMIS

The last section showed that for interoperable tools to be designed and implemented we can identify one crucial prerequisite: We need a common software infrastructure for all tools that is powerful enough to support their individual functionalities and that allows for the various levels of interoperability. Such an infrastructure concept was conceived in the OMIS project in our research group [5].

The on-line monitoring interface specification (OMIS) was developed in 1995 and first published in January 1996. Its goal is to define an interface between tools and on-line monitoring systems that allows to base various types of tools on top of it. It covers on-line and off-line tools as well as interactive and automatic tools. The interface is currently oriented towards tools for parallel and distributed programming based on the message passing paradigm. It offers a single function by which tools can send requests to the monitoring system to invoke certain activities. Requests are structured as event/action-relations where each such relation tells the monitoring system to watch for the occurrence of the specified event and to invoke the specified actions when it occurs. By sending sets of requests, a tool is able to program the monitoring system to perform a certain functional behavior. Events and actions are composed by the name of a service and a list of parameters. The latter usually identify objects of interest of our parallel program. Event services are e.g. "a process terminates", "a node is added", "a message arrives". Action services fall into two categories, one for observation, one for manipulation. We offer e.g. "get node status information", "show message contents", "perform single step on process", and "modify message contents". Consequently, the set of object types that can be dealt with comprises nodes, processes, threads, message queues and messages. Additional object types stem from the monitoring system itself: service requests, timers, and counters.

The interface specification offers a set of basic services that covers all typical types and the most common activities performed by current tools. For future adaptations to new tools and new programming paradigms with new objects it employs a mechanism for extensions to be brought in.

Based on this specification we implemented an OMIS compliant monitoring system (OCM) for the PVM programming library on workstations clusters as target architecture [13]. In a first step we put our already existing tools on top of this software infrastructure [12]. This is already level one of interoperability as the tools can execute concurrently, but do not perform coordination or cooperation.

How does the interface specification support the higher levels of interoperability? For a coordinated co-existence the interface offers a comprehensive set of event services. Using them, it is possible for a tool to observe object manipulations invoked by other tools. It may then react appropriately. In order to execute actions without being interrupted, a service for locking is offered. By that a tool is guaranteed to have an exclusive object access.

Cooperation in form of direct tool-to-tool communication is not yet supported by OMIS. Although it would be a minor effort to integrate the messaging mechanism, it is a very complex task to specify the cooperation protocol and the message format. In addition, no profound knowledge is available what features are really useful when having cooperating tools. An investigation of this issue will be preceded by implementing interoperable tools at level two.

Our current research activity concentrates on the definition of co-existence for various tools. Starting with a comprehensive list of on-line tools we investigated, which tool combinations do provide synergetic effects. Among them we identified two combinations that seem to be most promising: the synergy of debugging and checkpointing and the one of performance analysis and load balancing. The results of the first will be presented here. Before going into details we will have a look at other infrastructure concepts supporting tool development and possibly interoperability.

5 Infrastructure Concepts for Tool Development

There are a few other approaches that aim at providing concepts for monitoring systems. Some of them also deal with interoperability. Let us first consider those which concentrate on monitoring.

One such approach is the DAMS environment (Distributed Applications Monitoring System) [1]. DAMS is already a distributed monitoring system where a server runs on each node to be controlled and clients (tools) connect to a central service manager. The individual components of DAMS exhibit well defined interfaces for communication. Thus, a multi-vendor environment could be supported. DAMS is configurable with respect to monitoring services offered. Although it allows multiple clients to attach to the service manager and also partly supports indirect tool interactions, it does not integrate interoperability concepts that satisfy our additional requirements.

The DPCL approach (Dynamic Probe Class Library) [8] is an effort to provide an API for simplifying tool construction. DPCL daemons act as node local monitoring systems. They are controlled by the DPCL library which gets linked to the user's tools. DPCL is by itself not yet a full distributed monitoring system. The merge of the node local views has to be provided by the tools themselves. Consequently, as it does not cover the higher levels of abstraction of our infrastructure layer it does also not support tool interoperability. DPCL concentrates on performance analysis but its functionality allows also any type of manipulation services.

We also find concepts and approaches to support interoperability. Unfortunately, they are not dedicated to parallel run time tool environments.

The most interesting approach for interoperability is ToolTalk [3]. It was conceived by SunSoft and aims at providing a messaging mechanism for multiple clients in a distributed environment. ToolTalk is applied in the Common Desktop Environment to take care of inter-window cooperation. This role would also be appropriate for a multi-tool environment. ToolTalk's working paradigm is to send requests via messages to others that might provide services to handle the requests. In case of no appropriate client listening the message yields no effect. The ToolTalk semantics is well adapted to environments with a varying number of partners potentially being unknown to each other at startup.

Another approach exists in the realm of software engineering. PCTE (Portable Common Tool Environment) [4] aims at integrating tools of multiple vendors. The concepts in PCTE are based on an object management system, where the individual objects are specifications, software modules etc. Thus, it does not fit with our field of application which is event oriented. Nevertheless, PCTE exhibits clever concepts for interoperability in general which could be transferred to other areas of interest.

There are also other approaches for multi-client interoperability, e.g. SNMP and Corba. Their level of abstraction is very high and a link with low-level monitoring concepts will necessarily lead to a loss of efficiency in the implementation. Furthermore, it is not clear how the stated requirements can be met.

With respect to these requirements OMIS/OCM seems currently to be the most appropriate candidate to support tool interoperability.

6 Interoperability of Debugging and Checkpointing

We will now have a closer look at an example environment.

The first set of interoperable tools implemented at our chair were a parallel debugger (DETOP) [7] and a checkpointing tool that is based on CoCheck [9]. The initial goal was to achieve consistent co-existence of the two tools.

Our OMIS compliant monitoring system (OCM) is powerful enough to support both kinds of tools. The debugger utilizes services to read and write memory, stack, etc. and to control the program's execution (stop, continue, single-step).

The checkpointing tool makes use of OMIS' checkpoint/restore services. These are implemented as a tool extension to the monitor and ensure atomicity of the operations with respect to other services by locking. Thus, OMIS/OCM offers the possibility to achieve *co-existence* of the two tools.

This co-existence, however, is up to this point only a *non-aware* co-existence, where the two tools don't know anything about each other. As both kinds of tools manipulate common objects (e. g. the processes of the parallel application), this can lead to trouble whenever assumptions are made about the state of such objects.

To achieve *consistent co-existence*, additional measures have to be taken. Either the monitoring system has to hide manipulations from the other tools, or the tools have to react appropriately in the event of such manipulations. Because the first approach is far too complicated and expensive in the general case (e. g. saving "before images" in case a process is killed by one tool), we decided to follow the second approach.

As a first step, the tools have to be *aware* of each others critical actions. When such actions take place, the tools have to react on them to achieve consistent co-existence. This of course requires some form of communication.

Our approach was to have the monitoring system support this through a special form of indirect communication, which fits perfectly well into the event/action scheme applied by OMIS. Whenever a checkpoint is to be written, a *will_be_checkpointed* and a *has_been_checkpointed* event are triggered at the appropriate points of time and for each process in question. The debugger configures the monitoring system to have special actions executed before and after checkpoints are written[1]. Through this, modifications done to the processes can be saved and hidden from the checkpointing system. On the other hand, whenever a restore takes place, the debugger is noticed and will update its state (variable views, etc.). Finally, of course, the debugger can initiate checkpoint and restore actions for the processes being debugged, thus potentially dramatically shortening the testing and debugging cycle and reducing software development costs.

More details on the current status of this environment can be found in [11].

7 Project Status and Future Work

The status of the interface specification is currently fixed. Version 2 was published in June 1997. Based on this document we developed an OMIS compliant monitoring system (OCM) for PVM. First results are available with two debugging tools being based on OMIS.

The next step is to combine already available tools to interoperable tools. Within the framework of two research grants we will not only finish the combination of the debugger and the checkpointing facility, but also look into combining a performance analysis tool and a dynamic load balancer. The design phases of these projects are finished (see Figure 3). All tools refer to the same monitoring system OCM as well as to traces produced by it during runtime.

---

[1] Of course the same applies to restores

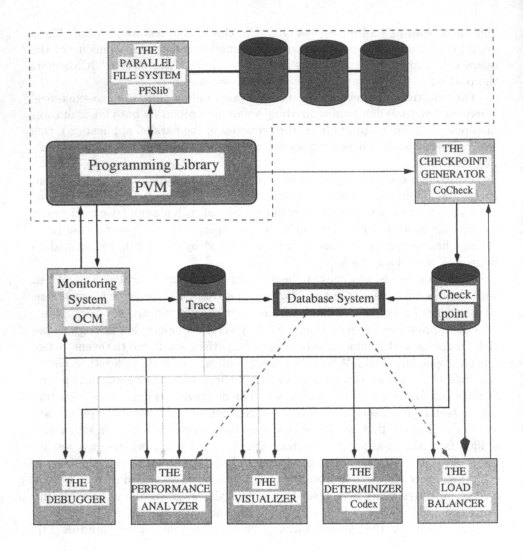

Fig. 3. The Tool-set environment

OMIS itself will be adapted to the shared memory programming model. This research is also embedded in a national research program.

References

1. J. Cunha and V. Duarte. Monitoring PVM Programs Using the DAMS Approach. In V. Alexandrov and J. Dongarra, editors, *Recent Advances in Parallel Virtual Machine and Messag Passing Interface, Proc. 5th European PVM/MPI Users' Group Meeting*, volume 1497 of *Lecture Notes in Computer Science*, pages 273–280, Liverpool, UK, Sept. 1998. Springer Verlag.

2. R. Hood. The *p2d2* project: Building a portable distributed debugger. In *Proc. SPDT'96: SIGMETRICS Symposium on Parallel and Distributed Tools*, pages 127–136, Philadelphia, Pennsylvania, USA, May 1996. ACM Press.

3. A. Julienne and B. Holtz. *ToolTalk & Open Protocols — Inter-Application Communication*. A Prentice Hall Title. SunSoft Press, Englewood Cliffs, NJ, 1994.

4. F. Long and E. Morris. An Overview of PCTE: A Basis for a Portable Common Tool Environment. Technical Report CMU/SEI-93-TR-1, Software Engineering Institute, Carnegie Mellon University, Pittsburgh, Pennsylvania, Mar. 1993.

5. T. Ludwig, R. Wismüller, V. Sunderam, and A. Bode. *OMIS — On-line Monitoring Interface Specification (Version 2.0)*, volume 9 of *LRR-TUM Research Report Series*. Shaker Verlag, Aachen, Germany, 1997. ISBN 3-8265-3035-7.

6. B. P. Miller, J. M. Cargille, R. B. Irvin, K. Kunchithap, M. D. Callaghan, J. K. Hollingsworth, K. L. Karavanic, and T. Newhall. The Paradyn parallel performance measurement tools. *IEEE Computer*, 11(28), Nov. 1995.

7. M. Oberhuber and R. Wismüller. DETOP - An Interactive Debugger for PowerPC Based Multicomputers. In P. Fritzson and L. Finmo, editors, *Parallel Programming and Applications*, pages 170–183. IOS Press, Amsterdam, May 1995.

8. D. Pase. Dynamic Probe Class Library (DPCL): Tutorial and Reference Guide, Version 0.1. Technical report, IBM Corporation, Poughkeepsie, NY, 1998.

9. G. Stellner and J. Pruyne. *CoCheck Users' Guide V1.0 - PVM Version*. Technische Universität München, Institut für Informatik, Lehrstuhl für Rechnertechnik und Rechnerorganisation, Nov. 1995.

10. T. Sterling, P. Messina, and J. Pool. Findings of the second pasadena workshop on system software and tools for high performance computing environments. Technical Report 95-162, Center of Excellence in Space Data and Information Sciences, NASA Goddard Space Flight Center, Greenbelt, Maryland, 1995.

11. R. Wismüller and T. Ludwig. Interoperable run time tools for distributed systems – a case study. In *PDPTA'99*, Juli 1999. Accepted for publication.

12. R. Wismüller, T. Ludwig, A. Bode, R. Borgeest, S. Lamberts, M. Oberhuber, C. Röder, and G. Stellner. THE TOOL-SET Project: Towards an Integrated Tool Environment for Parallel Programming. In *Proc. 2nd Sino-German Workshop on Advanced Parallel Processing Technologies, APPT'97*, Koblenz, Germany, Sept. 1997.

13. R. Wismüller, J. Trinitis, and T. Ludwig. OCM — a monitoring system for interoperable tools. In *Proceedings of the SIGMETRICS Symposium on Parallel and Distributed Tools*, pages 1–9. ACM Press, August 1998.

Logically Instantaneous Communication on Top of Distributed Memory Parallel Machines

Achour Mostéfaoui[1], Michel Raynal[1], and P. Veríssimo[2]

[1] IRISA - Campus de Beaulieu, 35042 Rennes Cedex, France,
E-mail: {mostefaoui,raynal}@irisa.fr
[2] Univ. Lisboa, C5 Campo Grande, 1700 Lisboa, Portugal
E-mail: pjv@di.fc.ul.pt

Abstract. Communication is *Logically Instantaneous* (LI) if it is possible to timestamp communication events with integers in such a way that (1) timestamps increase within each process and (2) the sending and the delivery events associated with each message have the same timestamp. So, there is a logical time frame in which for each message, the send event and the corresponding delivery events occur simultaneously. LI is stronger than Causally Ordered (CO) communication, but weaker than Rendezvous (RDV) communication. This paper explores *Logically Instantaneous* communication and provides a simple and efficient protocol that implements LI on top of asynchronous distributed systems. LI is attractive as it includes co and provides more concurrency than RDV. Moreover it allows to adopt the following approach: first design a distributed application assuming Rendezvous communication, and then run it on top of an asynchronous distributed system providing only LI communication.

Keywords: Asynchronous Distributed System, Communication Protocol, Logical Time, Logically Instantaneous Communication, Rendezvous.

1 Introduction

Among the services offered by a distributed system to upper layer application processes, Communication Services are of crucial importance. A communication service is defined by a pair of matching primitives, namely a primitive that allows to send a message to one or several destination processes and a primitive that allows a destination process to receive a message sent to it. Several communication services can coexist within a system. A communication service is defined by a set of properties. From a user point of view, those properties actually define the *quality of service (QoS)* offered by the communication service to its users. These properties usually concern reliability and message ordering.

A reliability property states the conditions under which a message has to be delivered to its destination processes despite possible failures. An *ordering* property states the order in which messages have to be delivered; usually this order depends on the message sending order. FIFO, causal order (CO) [4, 18] and total order (TO) [4,7,11] are the most encountered ordering properties [12]. Reliability and ordering properties can be combined to give rise to powerful communication primitives such as Atomic Broadcast [4] or Atomic Multicast to asynchronous groups [9]. The ISIS system [4] pioneered research in this domain. Other systems that have proposed powerful communication services are described in [17].

Another type of communication service is offered by CSP-like languages (*e.g.*, the *Occam* distributed programming language). This communication type assumes reliable processes and provides the so-called *rendezvous* (RDV) communication paradigm [2, 3, 13] (also called *synchronous* communication.) "A system has synchronous communications if no message can be sent along a channel before the receiver is ready to receive it. For an external observer, the transmission then looks like instantaneous and atomic. Sending and receiving a message correspond in fact to the same event" [5]. Basically, RDV combines synchronization and communication. From an operational point of view, this type of communication is called *blocking* because the sender process is blocked until the receiver process accepts and delivers the message. "While asynchronous communication is less prone to deadlocks and often allows a higher degree of parallelism (...) its implementation requires complex buffer management and control flow mechanisms. Furthermore, algorithms making use of asynchronous communication are often more difficult to develop and verify than algorithms working in a synchronous environment" [8]. This quotation expresses the relative advantages of synchronous communication with respect to asynchronous communication.

This paper focuses on a particular message ordering property, namely, *Logical Instantaneity* (LI [21]). This property is weaker than RDV in the sense that it does not provide synchronization; more precisely, the sender of a message is not blocked until the destination processes are ready to deliver the message. But LI is stronger than CO (*Causally Ordered* communication). CO means that, if two sends are causally related [14] and concern the same destination process, then the corresponding messages are delivered in their sending order [4]. CO has received a great attention as it simplifies the design of protocols solving consistency-related problems [18]. It has been shown that these communication modes form a strict hierarchy [8, 21]. More precisely, RDV $\Rightarrow$ LI $\Rightarrow$ CO $\Rightarrow$ FIFO, where X $\Rightarrow$ Y means that if the communications satisfy the X property, they also satisfy the Y property. (More sophisticated communication modes can found in [1].) Of course, the less constrained the communications are, the more efficient the corresponding executions can be. But, as indicated previously, a price has to be paid when using less constrained communications: application programs can be more difficult to design and prove, they can also require sophisticated buffer management protocols. Informally, LI provides the illusion that communications are done according to RDV, while actually they are done asynchronously. More precisely, LI ensures that there is a *logical* time frame with respect to which communications are synchronous. As a very simple example let us consider a system made of only two processes p and q plus a single directed channel from p to q. If the channel is FIFO, then it ensures the LI property: it is possible to build a logical time such that matching send and receive events occur at the same date, *i.e.*, at the same logical instant. When considering (non realtime) distributed programs, LI can not be distinguished from RDV. So, any program designed with the assumption that communications satisfy RDV can actually be run with LI communications. This is particularly interesting and suggests the following approach[1]: first design (and prove) programs[2] assuming RDV communications; and then run the obtained programs on top of a system offering LI communications. So, the LI communication paradigm can benefit to high performance computing when applications are run top on distributed memory parallel machines. In that sense this paper contributes to the definition of a communication service that can be used to provide efficient executions of Rendezvous-based parallel algorithms.

This paper explores the LI communication paradigm. It is composed of four sections. Section 2 introduces the underlying asynchronous distributed system model and defines logically instantaneous communication. Then, Section 3 presents a protocol implementing LI communication on top of an asynchronous distributed system. Finally, Section 4 considers the case of unreliable systems and provides a few concluding remarks.

2 Asynchronous Distributed Systems and LI Communication

2.1 Underlying Asynchronous Distributed System

The underlying asynchronous distributed system consists of a finite set P of n processes $\{P_1, \ldots, P_n\}$ that communicate and synchronize only by exchanging messages. We assume that each ordered pair of processes is connected by an asynchronous, reliable, directed logical channel whose transmission delays are unpredictable but finite[3]. The capacity of a channel is supposed to be infinite. Each process runs on a different processor, processors do not share a common memory, and there is no bound on their relative speeds.

A process can execute internal, send and receive operations. An internal operation does not involve communication. When P_i executes the operation $send(m, P_j)$ it puts the message m into the channel connecting P_i to P_j and continues its execution. When P_i executes the operation $receive(m)$, it remains blocked until at least one message directed to P_i has arrived, then a message is withdrawn from one of its input channels and delivered to P_i. Executions of internal, send and receive operations are modeled by internal, sending and receive events. Processes of a distributed computation are *sequential*; in other words, each process P_i produces a *sequence* of events $e_{i,1} \ldots e_{i,s} \ldots$ This sequence can be finite or infinite. Moreover, processes are assumed to be reliable, *i.e.*, they do not suffer failures (Section 4 will consider process crash failures).

---

[1] This is similar to the *Distributed Shared Memory* (DSM) paradigm. DSM allows to execute parallel programs, made of processes communicating through shared variables, on top of distributed memory systems.

[2] We only consider here non realtime programs.

[3] Note that channels are not required to be FIFO.

Let H be the set of all the events produced by a distributed computation. This computation is modeled by the partially ordered set $\hat{H} = (H, \overset{hb}{\rightarrow})$, where $\overset{hb}{\rightarrow}$ denotes the well-known Lamport's *happened-before* relation [14]. Let $e_{i,x}$ and $e_{j,y}$ be two different events:

$$e_{i,x} \overset{hb}{\rightarrow} e_{j,y} \Leftrightarrow \begin{cases} i = j \wedge x < y \\ \vee \; \exists m : e_{i,x} = send(m, P_j) \wedge e_{j,y} = receive(m) \\ \vee \; \exists e : e_{i,x} \overset{hb}{\rightarrow} e \wedge e \overset{hb}{\rightarrow} e_{j,y} \end{cases}$$

So, the underlying system model is the well known reliable asynchronous distributed system model. Our aim is to build on top of it a distributed system whose communications satisfy the LI property.

2.2 Communication Primitives at the Application Level

The communication interface offered to application processes is composed of two primitives denoted SEND and DELIVER.

- The SEND$(m, dest_m)$ primitive allows a process to send a message m to a set of processes, namely $dest_m$. This set is defined by the sender process P_i (without loss of generality, we assume $P_i \notin dest_m$). Moreover, every message m carries the identity of its sender: $m.sender = i$. The corresponding application level event is denoted SEND$_{m.sender}(m)$.
- The DELIVER(m) primitive allows a process (say P_j) to receive a message that has been sent to it by an other process (so, $P_j \in dest_m$). The corresponding application level event is denoted DELIVER$_j(m)$.

Previous proposals [16, 21] consider a message is sent to a single destination process. Here, the SEND primitive allows to multicast a message to an arbitrary set of destination processes (this set is defined online by the sending process).

2.3 LI Communication

When a process executes SEND$(m, dest_m)$ we say that it "LI-sends" m. When a process executes DELIVER(m) we say that it "LI-delivers" m. Communications of a computation satisfy the LI property if the four following properties are satisfied.

- *Termination.* If a process LI-sends m, then m is made available for LI-delivery at each process $P_j \in dest_m$. P_j effectively LI-delivers m when it executes the corresponding DELIVER primitive[4].

---

[4] Of course, for a message (that has been LI-sent) to be LI-delivered by a process $P_j \in dest_m$, it is necessary that P_j issues "enough" invocations of the DELIVER primitive. If m is the $(x + 1)$th message that has to be LI-delivered to P_j, its LI-delivery at P_j can only occur if P_j has first LI-delivered the x previous messages and then invokes the DELIVER primitive.

- *Integrity*. A process LI-delivers a message m at most once. Moreover, if P_j LI-delivers m, then $P_j \in dest_m$.
- *Validity*. If a process LI-delivers a message m, then m has been LI-sent by $m.sender$.
- *Logical Instantaneity*. Let $I\!N$ be the set of natural integers. This set constitutes the (logical) time domain. Let H_a be the set of all application level communication events of the computation. There exists a timestamping function $\mathcal{T}$ from H_a into $I\!N$ such that $\forall (e, f) \in H_a \times H_a$ [16]:

(LI$_1$) e and f have been produced by the same process with e first
  $\Rightarrow \mathcal{T}(e) < \mathcal{T}(f)$
(LI$_2$) $\forall m : \forall j \in dest_m : e = \text{SEND}_{m.sender}(m) \wedge f = \text{DELIVER}_j(m)$
  $\Rightarrow \mathcal{T}(e) = \mathcal{T}(f)$

From the point of view of the communication of a message m, the event $\text{SEND}_{m.sender}(m)$ is the **cause** and the events $\text{DELIVER}_j(m)$ ($j \in dest_m$) are the **effects**. The termination property associates effects with a cause. The validity property associates a cause with each effect (in other words, there are no spurious messages). Given a cause, the integrity property specifies how many effects it can have and where they are produced (there are no duplicates and only destination processes may deliver a message). Finally, the logical instantaneity property specifies that there is a logical time domain in which the send and the deliveries events of every message occur at the same instant.

Figure 1.a describes communications of a computation in the usual space-time diagram. We have: $m_1.sender = 2$ and $dest_{m_1} = \{1, 3, 4\}$; $m_2.sender = m_3.sender = 4$, $dest_{m_2} = \{2, 3\}$ and $dest_{m_3} = \{1, 3\}$. These communications satisfy the LI property as shown by Figure 1.b. While RDV allows only the execution of Figure 1.b, LI allows more concurrent executions such as the one described by Figure 1.a.

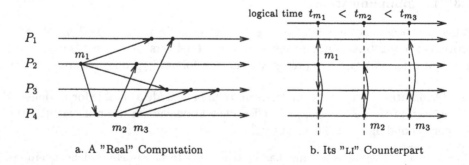

a. A "Real" Computation   b. Its "LI" Counterpart

Fig. 1. Logical Instantaneity

2.4   Communication Statements

We consider two types of statements in which communication primitives can be used by application processes.

- *Deterministic Statement.* An application process may invoke the DELIVER primitive and wait until a message is delivered. In that case the invocation appears in a deterministic context [20] (no alternative is offered to the process in case the corresponding SEND is not executed). In the same way, an application process may invoke the SEND primitive in a deterministic context.
- *Non-Deterministic Statement.* The invocation of a communication primitive in a deterministic context can favor deadlock occurrences (as it is the case, for example, when each process starts by invoking DELIVER.) In order to help applications prevent such deadlocks, we allow processes to invoke communication primitives in a non-deterministic statement (ADA and similar languages provide such non-deterministic statements). This statement has the following syntactical form:

$$\textbf{select\_com } \text{SEND}(m, dest_m) \textbf{ or } \text{DELIVER}(m') \textbf{ end\_select\_com}$$

This statement defines a non-deterministic context. The process waits until one of the primitives is executed. The statement is terminated as soon as a primitive is executed, a flag indicates which primitive has been executed. Actually, the choice is determined at runtime, according to the current state of communications.

3   A Protocol Implementing LI Communication

3.1   Underlying Principle

The protocol is based on a few simple ideas. First, a message sending is processed as a message delivery. Second, a Lamport timestamp (local clock value, sender identity) is associated with each message and messages are delivered according to their timestamp order [14]. Finally, after having initiated a message sending, its sender has to commit or to abort it.

The computation of the timestamp associated with a message m requires the cooperation of its sender and of its destination processes. This cooperation is done in a classical way: each process proposes a timestamp for m and the greatest proposal becomes the final timestamp of m. (This cooperation scheme is known as "Skeen's protocol", as described in [4].)

At the protocol level, a message m is made of several fields. Those are:
- $m.id$: the identity of m. All message identities are assumed to be distinct.
- $m.sender$: the identity of the sender (as seen before).
- $m.content$: the content of m (defined by the sender process).
- $m.ts$: the current timestamp associated with m.
- $m.final\_ts$: whose value is *true* or *false*. $m.final\_ts = true$ means that m

has got its final timestamp; $m.final\_ts = false$ means that the current timestamp of m is not necessarily its final timestamp, it is only a timestamp proposal.

Each process P_i manages a queue ($queue_i$) where it stores the messages that are currently candidates to be delivered at P_i. The primitive *append* allows to add a message into $queue_i$. The primitive *remove* allows to suppress a message from $queue_i$. This queue is assumed to be sorted according to the current timestamps of the messages it contains[5]. The primitive *head* returns the message that is currently the first of $queue_i$ (*i.e.*, the one with the smallest timestamp). To simplify the protocol description, we assume that $queue_i$ is never empty: it always contains a "sentinel" message m characterized by: $m.ts = +\infty$ and $m.final\_ts = false$. (As we will see in the protocol description, this message will never obtains a final timestamp, and consequently will never be delivered.)

Three procedures (Section 3.2) and a task T_i (Section 3.3) implements the protocol at each process P_i. A procedure implements a communication primitive in a given context: SEND called in a deterministic context, DELIVER called in a deterministic context, and the SEND/DELIVER non-deterministic statement. The task T_i manages the local data structure $queue_i$. It constitutes the core of the protocol by executing operations required by the three procedures and handling messages received from other processes.

3.2 Implementing the Primitives

SEND *in a deterministic context*
The primitive SEND is implemented by the procedure given below, where $sent\_msg$ and msg_dest denote the data value of the message and the set of its destination processes, respectively.

> **Procedure** SEND($sent\_msg, msg\_dest$)
>   **create** a new message identity msg_id;
>   **add_to_queue**($msg\_id, msg\_content, msg\_dest$);
>   **wait until** $head(queue_i).id = msg\_id \wedge head(queue_i).final\_ts$;
>   **commit**(msg_id); /* Event SEND$_i(m)$ */
>   **remove** $head(queue_i)$ **from** $queue_i$

After having defined a new message identity, P_i asks the task T_i to add this new message into $queue_i$. Then, it waits until this message becomes the head of the queue and has got its final timestamp. When this occurs, P_i commits the sending of the message: this means the event SEND$_{m.sender}(m)$ occurs. Then, P_i suppresses m from $queue_i$.

DELIVER *in a deterministic context*
DELIVER in a deterministic context is implemented by the procedure given below. P_i waits until the head of the queue contains a message that has got its final

---

[5] Let $m1$ and $m2$ be two messages in $queue_i$. The message $m1$ precedes the message $m2$ if $(m1.ts, m1.sender) < (m2.ts, m2.sender)$ (lexicographic order defined in [14]).

timestamp. When this occurs, the content of the message is delivered to P_i and the message is removed from the queue.

> **Procedure** DELIVER(del_msg)
>   **wait until** $head(queue_i).final\_ts$;
>   **let** m **be** $head(queue_i)$;
> $del\_msg \leftarrow m.content$; /* Event DELIVER$_i(m)$ */
>   remove m **from** $queue_i$

SEND/DELIVER *in a non-deterministic context*
This non-deterministic context communication statement is implemented by the function given below. First P_i initiates the sending of the message (so, the first two lines are the same as in the primitive SEND. Then, P_i waits until there is a message m with a final timestamp at the head of its queue. If m is the message it has just tried to send, then the SEND is successful: it is committed and "sending" is provided as a result of the call to the non-deterministic statement. If m is another message, then the DELIVER is successful: P_i aborts the sending of the message it has initiated, delivers the content of m and provides "delivery" as a result of the call to the non-deterministic statement.

> **function** SEND($sent\_msg, msg\_dest$)_or_DELIVER(del_msg)
>   **create** a message identity msg_id;
>   **add_to_queue**($msg\_id, sent\_msg, msg\_dest$);
>   **wait until** $head(queue_i).final\_ts$;
>   **let** m **be** $head(queue_i)$;
>   **case** $m.id = msg\_id$ $\rightarrow$ **commit**(msg_id);
>   **return** "sending" /* Event SEND$_i(m)$ */
> $m.id \neq msg\_id$ $\rightarrow$ **abort**(msg_id);
> $del\_msg \leftarrow m.content$;
>   **return** "delivery" /* Event DELIVER$_i(m)$ */
>   **endcase**;
>   remove m **from** $queue_i$

3.3 Queue Management

As indicated previously, the management of the local data structure $queue_i$ constitutes the core of the protocol. It is realized by a task T_i that runs in the background of P_i. Each set of statements of T_i is executed atomically. The work of T_i is [6]:

- The implementation of the local calls to **add_to_queue**, **commit** and **abort** issued by P_i. This entails the sending of control messages to peer tasks of other processes.
- The processing of the control messages received from the other tasks. These control messages are TS_REQUEST, TS_PROPOSAL, COMMITTED and ABORTED. The two first are related to the final timestamp determination of messages.

The third one is used to convey the final timestamp associated with a message. Finally, the last one is related to the the implementation of the non-deterministic communication statement.

In addition to $queue_i$, the task T_i manages three variables. The first one is h_i, a local Lamport clock handled in the usual way [14]. The other two, namely, $dest_i$ and $wait\_ts\_from_i$, are relevant only when P_i is engaged in a SEND(m) primitive (deterministic or not). They have the following meaning. The variable $dest_i$ is used to memorize the identities of the processes that are the destinations of m (namely, $dest_m$). The variable $wait\_ts\_from_i$ (which is initialized to $dest_i$) is updated ($wait\_ts\_from_i \leftarrow wait\_ts\_from_i - \{j\}$) when a timestamp proposal (TS_PROPOSAL) for m is received from P_j; so $wait\_ts\_from_i = \emptyset$ indicates that T_i has received all the timestamp proposals for the message m it wants to send: this means that m has got its final timestamp.

The behavior of T_i is the following:

- When **add_to_queue** is called (deterministic or non deterministic send primitive), T_i builds a message with the appropriate fields, and adds it to $queue_i$. Then, it sends to each destination process a TS_REQUEST control message asking it to send back a timestamp proposal for m. It also appropriately updates the local control variables $dest_i$ and $wait\_ts\_from_i$.

  When a task receives a TS_REQUEST control message concerning a message m, it first builds a corresponding entry in its queue, and then answers by proposing a timestamp for m.

  When, T_i receives a timestamp proposal for a message m, it updates the timestamp of m (namely, $m.ts$) to the max of its current value and the proposed value. If all the timestamp proposals have been received, then m has its final timestamp (the maximum of all proposed timestamps), consequently, $m.final\_ts$ is set to $true$. From now on, the message is "ready" to be sent (if P_i is its sender) or delivered (if P_i is a destination process). The message is "delayed" until either it is at the head of the queue and is required by P_i, or its sending is aborted by its sender (non-deterministic primitive) (^{6}).

- If the sending process commits the sending of m, then a COMMITTED control message is sent to all the processes of $dest_m$. When a destination receives this message, it provides its copy of the message with the final timestamp and makes the message ready to be locally delivered. The message will be locally delivered when it will be at the head of the local queue and will be required by the destination process.

  If the sender process aborts the sending of m (non-deterministic primitive), then an ABORTED control message is sent to all the processes of $dest_m$. When a destination process receives this message it destroys its copy of m.

---

^{6} Actually, this part of the protocol is close to Ricart-Agrawala's mutual exclusion protocol [19]. Both use the same message exchange pattern: one for ordering the critical section requests, the other for ordering the messages whose sending have been committed.

Task T_i
  $h_i \leftarrow 0$;
  cobegin
    $\|$ **upon a local call to add_to_queue**($msg\_id, msg\_content, msg\_dest$)
      $h_i \leftarrow h_i + 1$; $dest_i \leftarrow msg\_dest$;
      build a message structure m such that
          $m.sender \leftarrow i$, $m.ts \leftarrow h_i$, $m.id \leftarrow msg\_id$,
          $m.final\_ts \leftarrow false$, $m.content \leftarrow msg\_content$;
      append m to $queue_i$;
      $\forall k \in dest_i$ **send** TS_REQUEST($m.id, m.content$) to P_k;
      $wait\_ts\_from_i \leftarrow msg\_dest$

    $\|$ **upon reception of** TS_REQUEST($msg\_id, msg\_content$) **from** P_j
      /* first time P_i hears about this message */
      build a message structure m such that
          $m.sender \leftarrow j$, $m.ts \leftarrow h_i$, $m.id \leftarrow msg\_id$,
          $m.final\_ts \leftarrow false$, $m.content \leftarrow msg\_content$;
      append m to $queue_i$;
      send TS_PROPOSAL($m.id, h_i$) to $m.sender$

    $\|$ **upon reception of** TS_PROPOSAL(msg_id, msg_ts) **from** P_j
      if $\exists\, m \in queue_i$ such that $m.id = msg\_id$ **then**
          $m.ts \leftarrow max(m.ts, msg\_ts)$;
          $wait\_ts\_from_i \leftarrow wait\_ts\_from_i - \{j\}$;
          $m.final\_ts \leftarrow (wait\_ts\_from_i = \emptyset)$;
          $h_i \leftarrow max(h_i, msg\_ts)$
      endif /* $(m \notin queue_i) \Rightarrow$ (the sending of m has been aborted by P_i) */

    $\|$ **upon a local call to commit**(msg_id)
      let $m \in queue_i$ such that $m.id = msg\_id$;
      $\forall k \in dest_i$ **send** COMMITTED($m.id, m.ts$) to P_k

    $\|$ **upon reception of** COMMITTED(msg_id, msg_ts)
      let $m \in queue_i$ such that $m.id = msg\_id$;
      $m.ts \leftarrow msg\_ts$; /* the send has been committed */
      $m.final\_ts \leftarrow true$;
      $h_i \leftarrow max(h_i, msg\_ts)$

    $\|$ **upon a local call to abort**(msg_id)
      let $m \in queue_i$ such that $m.id = msg\_id$;
      $\forall k \in dest_i$ **send** ABORTED($m.id$) to P_k;
      remove m from $queue_i$ /* the send has been aborted */

    $\|$ **upon reception of** ABORTED(msg_id)
      wait until $\exists m \in queue_i$ such that $m.id = msg\_id$;
      /* The wait is required because channels are not necessarily FIFO: */
      /* ABORTED(msg_id) can arrive before */
      /* the corresponding TS_REQUEST($msg\_id, -$) */
      remove m from $queue_i$ /* the send has been aborted */
  coend

3.4 Sketch of Proof

Due to space limitation, only a proof sketch is given.

Integrity and Validity

The integrity property (a message is LI-delivered at most once) follows from the fact that a message that has been LI-delivered is immediately removed from the queue.

The validity property (if a message is LI-delivered, it has been LI-sent) follows from the fact that no application message is coined by the protocol. The only message that is coined by the protocol is a control message: the "sentinel" m such that: $m.ts = +\infty$ and $m.ts\_final = false$. This message is used to simplify the protocol description by ensuring the local queues are never empty. As its ts_final field is never set to *true* this message can not be delivered.

Logical Instantaneity

This property is made of two parts LI_1 and LI_2 (Section 2.3). Note that all non-aborted messages are totally ordered by their timestamps [14]. LI_2 follows from the fact that the send event and the corresponding delivery events of each non-aborted message receive the same timestamp. LI_1 comes (1) from the management of the local clocks (h_i) that are non-decreasing, and (2) from the fact that non-aborted messages are removed from the queues according to their timestamp order.

Termination

The termination property states that if the event $\text{SEND}_{m.sender}(m)$ is produced, then m is made available for LI-delivery at each destination process.

Let us first remark that each message that has been aborted is eventually withdrawn from the queues in which it has been added. So, it is not necessary to consider aborted messages: they cannot prevent committed messages from arriving at the head of the queue. So, in the following we consider only committed messages.

The proof follows from the fact that the two-way handshake sub-protocol that computes the final timestamp of m (implemented by the sequence of control messages TS_REQUEST, TS_PROPOSAL) is not blocking. The processing of a TS_REQUEST or TS_PROPOSAL message is done unconditionally by its receiver and any TS_REQUEST entails the sending of the corresponding TS_PROPOSAL.

So, there is eventually a message m at the head of all $queue_j$ ($\forall j \in dest_m \cup \{m.sender\}$) such that $m.final\_ts = true$. This message can be delivered by all destination processes. The sender withdraws it from its queue when it commits the sending; a destination process withdraws it from its queue when it LI-delivers it. Then a simple induction shows all committed messages can be LI-delivered (provided that their destination processes issue "enough" DELIVER).

3.5 Cost of the Protocol

For each application message, the proposed protocol is actually a three-way handshake protocol (defined by the sequence of control messages: TS_REQUEST,

TS_PROPOSAL, COMMITTED/ABORTED). The protocol is *minimal* in the sense that, for each message, it involves only its sender and its destination processes, no other process has to participate in the protocol.

Let d_m be the number of destination processes of m and assume all control messages take one time unit. For each application message, the protocol costs $3d_m$ messages and 3 time units. If the message is aborted, these costs actually are upper bounds. In the broadcast case (all application messages are sent to all processes), the protocol come very close to Lamport's mutual exclusion protocol [14] and has the same message cost, namely $3(n-1)$.

4 Conclusion

Communication is *Logically Instantaneous* (LI) if there is a time frame in which matching send and delivery events occur at the same date. LI is stronger than Causally Ordered communication, but weaker than Rendezvous communication. This paper has explored *Logically Instantaneous* communication and has provided an efficient protocol that implements it on top of asynchronous distributed systems.

LI communication is very close to what is needed to implement a parallel discrete event simulation system. In a discrete event simulation model, actions issued by agents consume time but their interactions do not [10, 15]. The main problem of a simulation model is to implement the so called *virtual time* (simulation time). Among other uses, the proposed LI protocol can be used to implement agent interactions in such a system.

Last but not least, let us note that the proposed protocol can be extended to cope with process crashes by using the techniques introduced and used in [9].

References

1. Ahuja M. and Raynal M., An implementation of Global Flush Primitives Using Counters. *Parallel Processing Letters*, Vol. 5(2):171-178, (1995).
2. Bagrodia R., Process Synchronization: Design and Performance Evaluation for Distributed Algorithms. *IEEE TSE*, SE15(9):1053-1065, (1989).
3. Bagrodia R., Synchronization of Asynchronous Processes in CSP. *ACM TOPLAS*, 11(4):585-597, (1989).
4. Birman K.P. and Joseph T.A., Reliable Communication in the Presence of Failures. *ACM TOCS*, 5(1):47-76, (1987).
5. Bougé L., Repeated Snapshots in Distributed Systems with Synchronous Communications and their Implementation in CSP. *Theoretical Computer Science*, 49:145-169, (1987).
6. Brinch Hansen P., Distributed Processes: A Concurrent Programming Concept. *Communications of the ACM*, 21(11):934-941, (1978).
7. Chandra T. and Toueg S., Unreliable Failure Detectors for Reliable Distributed Systems. *Journal of the ACM*, 43(1):225-267, (1996).
8. Charron-Bost B., Mattern F. and Tel G., Synchronous, Asynchronous and Causally Ordered Communications. *Distributed Computing*, 9:173-191, (1996).

9. Fritkze U., Ingels Ph., Mostefaoui, A. and Raynal M., Fault-Tolerant Total Order Multicast to Asynchronous Groups. *Proc. 16th IEEE Int. Symposium on Reliable Distributed Systems*, Purdue University, pp. 228-234, (1998).

10. Fujimoto R., Parallel Discrete Event Simulation. *Communications of the ACM*, 33(10):31-53, (1990).

11. Garcia-Molina H. and Spauster A., Ordered and Reliable Multicast Communication. *ACM TOCS*, 9(3):242-272, (1991).

12. Hadzilacos V. and Toueg S., Reliable Broadcast and Related Problems. In *Distributed Systems*, ACM Press (S. Mullender Ed.), New-York, pp. 97-145, (1993).

13. Hoare C.A.R., Communicating Sequentail Processes. *Communications of the ACM*, 21(8):666-677, (1978).

14. Lamport, L., Time, Clocks and the Ordering of Events in a Distributed System, *Communications of the ACM*, 21(7):558-565, (1978).

15. Misra J., Distributed Discrete Event Simulation. *ACM Computing Surveys*, 18(1):39-65, (1986).

16. Murty V.V. and Garg V.K., Synchronous Message Passing. *Tech. Report* TR ECE-PDS-93-01, University of Texas at Austin, (1993).

17. Powell D. (Guest Editor), Special Issue on Group Communication. *CACM*, 39(4), (1996).

18. Raynal M., Schiper A. and Toueg S., The Causal ordering Abstraction and a Simple Way to Implement it. *Information Processing Letters*, 39:343-351, (1991).

19. Ricart G. and Agrawala A.K., An Optimal Algorithm for Mutual Exclusion in Computer Networks. *Communications of the ACM*, 24(1):115-123, (1981).

20. Silberschatz A., Synchronization and Communication in Distributed Systems. *IEEE TSE*, SE5(6):542-546, (1979).

21. Soneoka T. and Ibaraki T., Logically Instantaneous Message Passing in Asynchronous Distributed Systems. *IEEE TC*, 43(5):513-527, (1994).

Three Complementary Approaches to Parallelization of Local BLAST Service on Workstation Clusters

K.T. Pedretti, T.L. Casavant, R.C. Braun, T.E. Scheetz,
C.L. Birkett, C.A. Roberts

Coordinated Laboratory for Computational Genomics
Department of Electrical and Computer Engineering
University of Iowa
Iowa City, IA 52242, USA
genome@eng.uiowa.edu
http://genome.uiowa.edu

Abstract. This paper describes approaches to improving the performance of one of the most common and increasingly important aspects of the Human Genome Project (HGP) – large-volume, batch comparison of DNA sequence data. This basic comparison operation, usually carried out by the well-known BLAST program on one subject sequence against the internationally-available databases of over 3 million target sequences, is already used hundreds of thousands of times each day by researchers around the world. At present, it is still used primarily in single query, or small batch query mode. As the entire sequence of the human genome nears completion, the area of functional genomics, and the use of microarrays of sets of genes, is coming to the fore. These developments will demand ever more efficient means of BLASTing sets of data that will make single processor implementation on powerful workstations infeasible. We describe the three primary parallel components to BLAST. The first is at the sequence-to-sequence comparison level. The second parallelizes a single query across a partitioned and distributed database. And finally, the set of queries themselves are partitioned across a set of servers with replicated or partitioned databases. The three methods may be employed alone or in concert. Our current implementation is described which parallelizes batch requests, and our plans for implementation of the other levels is also described. The results will ultimately be applied to hardware assistance for this soon-to-be primitive computer operation.

1 Introduction

Modern genome sequencing, discovery and mapping research efforts *are* parallel/distributed processing systems. The processing involved is computationally demanding, but the basic nature of the entire process of gene discovery and understanding is highly parallel, heterogeneous, and distributed. To date, the dominant component of the *human genome project* (HGP) has been the discovery of the entire 3 billion base pairs of sequence of the human genome. This has been a worldwide parallel/cooperative effort in which the dimensions of parallelism have been drawn at the boundaries of organisms (e.g., human, mouse, rat, C.elegans, etc.) [DOE95, BlR97, Ber95], and chromosomes of these organisms. However, close examination of this phase of the effort reveals that the parallelism being exploited is mostly at the job-level [HoJ88]. Partitioning of the sequencing effort along organism and chromosomal lines requires only very rudimentary parallel task structure, inter-process communication (IPC) and synchronization (e.g., often via human examination of WWW sites displaying similar regions of differing organisms).

As the entire sequence of the Human Genome nears completion (draft expected in 2000, and finished sequence expected in 2003), the frequency and intensity of inquiries against this data will expand exponentially. The area of *functional genomics* will require batch processing of large numbers of requests to identify homologous groups of sequences. The current mode used by 90% of researchers is to submit single queries for comparison of a segment of sequence data (a subject string of 300-600 characters) against one or more databases being served at a national or international repository. The most common such repository is GenBank which is housed in the National Center for Biotechnology Information (NCBI) at the National Institutes of Health (NIH) in Bethesda, Maryland in the United States. (Two other large repositories also exist – one in Europe and one in Japan). The most common sequence comparison tool is the well-known BLAST [AlM97] (Basic Local Alignment Search Tool) program, which is also available for download for local execution. While it is possible for anyone to download the contents of GenBank (as of 4/15/1999 containing 2,569,578,208 bases, from 3,525,418 reported sequences) for processing of queries on a dedicated server, this is rarely done. Rather, many thousands of single queries "hit" a large bank of database server systems at NCBI on a daily basis. Not only does this cluster of servers continue to diminish in its ability to serve the ever mounting numbers of requests, but the network traffic generated by this load is also becoming intolerable. The databases themselves are growing at an increasing rate, and single queries on a dedicated high-performance system can also be time consuming. While some efforts have been made in the past to parallelize BLAST searches, none of the methods exploit all levels of available parallelism, and none of these tools has been implemented for easy public access. Lastly, a comprehensive understanding, and a robust, near-optimal solution to this problem is a necessary first step toward development of parallel architectures, and hardware assists for this soon-to-be ubiquitous and primitive computer operation.

In this paper, we describe a comprehensive approach to exploitation of three distinct types of parallelism in BLAST searches. The three types derive from various granularities of searches, and different inherent parallel aspects of BLAST searching. Figure 1 summarizes the three complementary approaches.

Conceptually, the lowest level involves speeding up the comparison of a single pair of DNA sequences – a subject and target – by performing all the alignments of the comparison in parallel. These operations may be performed in an "embar-

	Fine Grained	Medium Grained	Coarse Grained
Subject(s)	1 sequence	1 sequence	N sequences (batch request)
Target(s)	1 sequence	M sequences (in database)	M sequences (in database)
Parallelism	Multiple alignments on single sequence pairs.	Partition Database Multiple targets examined at once	Replicate Database Partition Input Sets

Fig. 1. Three Levels of Parallelism Exploitable in Large Batch BLAST Processing.

rassingly parallel" manner with no data dependencies between them. It should be noted that this lowest level may be best performed on a node with special parallel capabilities as well – beyond those of the typical symmetric multi-processor (SMP) system. In the second case, a large target database can be partitioned into subsets, and distributed to the static (disk) storage devices of a cluster of workstations – possibly replicating each subset some number of times on several nodes of the cluster. Single queries would then be replicated to the multiple nodes and the comparisons against each partition of the database would proceed in parallel. While non-trivial, the merging of the results is feasible, and can be done efficiently at an appropriate level of granularity. Finally, if a large set of queries is to be processed in a "batch" mode, partitioning of the multiple query requests can also be done to allow even more parallelization.

Our current implementation exploits only the last of these three approaches. Implementation of the second method is proceeding and is expected to be deployed by Fall 1999, and the final level is a subject of further research. The eventual goal is to implement all three of these granularities in a hybrid cluster-server architecture for use in the local BLASTing of expressed sequence tag (EST) and functional genomics study at the University of Iowa. All developed software would be made available to the research community. Architecture enhancements to greatly improve exploitation of fine-grained parallelism will be a natural extension of this work.

2 Background

BLAST is a heuristic search algorithm employed by a number of genetic search tools. These tools are used by researchers to identify similarity between genetic sequences. Typically, there is an input sequence that is *BLASTed* against a database of known sequences – the target set. The result of a BLAST search is a list of sequences from the target set that were found to have significant regions matching regions of the input sequence. In large-scale sequencing projects, this data can be useful to determine if a particular sequence has already been discovered or if contamination has occured. BLAST can also be useful in a broader sense by providing insight into a sequence's function by matching it with some sequence of known function.

The specific implementation of BLAST used at the University of Iowa is NCBI BLAST (freely available from *ftp://ncbi.nlm.nih.gov/blast*). NCBI BLAST recognizes two types of sequences: *nucleotide* and *peptide*. Both sequence types are represented as a string of ASCII characters. Nucleotide sequences are made up of four letters (A, T, C, and G). These represent the 4 bases in DNA – Adenine, Thymine, Guanine, and Cytosine. Thus, a short nucleotide sequence input into BLAST might be ACCTGACTACCT. This string also codes for the complementary DNA strand TGGACTGATGGA (A bonds with T, C bonds with G). One can imagine these two sequences of nucleotides being placed in parallel and then twisted to create the familiar DNA double helix. For nucleotide to nucleotide queries, NCBI BLAST takes the complementary strand of the query into account when searching. A peptide sequence (a protein sequence) is also made up of a string of letters but, in this case, each represents one of twenty amino acids. Peptides are encoded by triplets of nulceotides, as specified by the genetic code. There are three possible reading frames (+0, +1, +2) in both directions, and therefore there are six ways to translate a nucleotide sequence into a peptide sequence.

The NCBI BLAST distribution contains five variations of BLAST – blastn, blastx, tblastx, blastp, and tblastn. blastn compares a nucleotide sequence against a nucleotide database and is relatively quick. blastx compares a nucleotide sequence against a protein database. To do this, the nucleotide subject needs to be translated into a peptide sequence. Since there are six different translations, the basic BLAST algorithm must be applied six times to complete the query. Like blastn, tblastx compares a nucleotide sequence to a nucleotide database only in this case each is translated (in all 6 reading frames) into a peptide sequence before BLASTing. This is the most computationally intensive of the blast programs since the BLAST algorithm must be invoked 36 times for each sequence to sequence comparison. blastp compares a peptide sequence to a peptide database and is relatively quick. tblastn compares a peptide sequence against a nucleotide database. As with blastx, each sequence to sequence comparison requires six calls to BLAST.

A sample output from a blastn BLAST run is shown in figure 2. The query sequence was 296 bases long and 15 sequences were found to have significant alignments. The two figures of merit for an alignment are its *score* and *E* value. Long matches get high scores. In the sample output, the hit that matched 296 bases received a score of 587 while the hit that matched 13 bases only received a score of 26. The E value (or "expect" value) represents the number of significant alignments one would expect to see by chance. It is dependent on the size of the target database and it decreases exponentially with score. An E value of zero is ideal.

3 Approach and Options

3.1 Local BLAST

Although NCBI, along with several other research centers, maintain public BLAST servers, these have their limitations. Foremost, depending on the application, is the speed at which the searches are performed. During peak times, the servers become extremely saturated. Many projects rely on data being processed in a timely manner. In such cases, this possible delay and reliance on an outside provider is unacceptable. Additionally, the databases which can be selected for use, although current, are limited to those available on the remote server. The ability to create custom, real-time databases to BLAST against, is increasingly becoming a necessity for many projects. For these reasons, local installation of a BLAST server and the basic set of public databases is essential for any large-scale sequencing or functional genomics effort.

3.2 Local Parallel BLAST

Given the need for local BLAST services, the need to complete these searches in a timely manner becomes evident. Parallelizing the BLAST algorithm pays dividends by effectively reducing the processing time in relation to the number of compute nodes utilized. In addition to reducing the processing time, parallelizing can in some cases reduce costs by utilizing commodity workstations and even PCs. Finally, a locally-scheduled parallel algorithm allows for prioritization and a level of control over individual searches not afforded by any other option.

3.3 Types of Parallelization

Three basic approaches to parallelizing BLAST can be readily identified, and are currently in various stages of implementation at Iowa. They are summarized in Figure 1, and are described below.

Pairwise Multiple Alignment Parallelization The notion of multiple alignments of a single pair of DNA subsequences was described in section 2. It is clear that if 2 subsequences are to be compared – of lengths n and m respectively – then there are $O(nxm)$ possible alignments to be examined for possible similarity for the pair. Since these comparisons are mutually independent, the parallelization of the comparisons is potentially very efficient. The granularity of this operation is such that effective implementation would greatly benefit from specialized hardware, or a large scale MPP system with a custom interconnect. Implementation on a modest-sized SMP would be feasible using threads. However, single nodes of a cluster utilizing this level of parallelism could possibly be an IBM

```
BLASTN 2.0.6 [Sept-16-1998]

Reference:
Altschul, Stephen F., Thomas L. Madden, Alejandro A. Sch ffer,
Jinghui Zhang, Zheng Zhang, Webb Miller, and David J. Lipman (1997),
"Gapped BLAST and PSI-BLAST: a new generation of protein database search
programs", Nucleic Acids Res. 25:3389-3402.

Query=
        (296 letters)

Database: CustomBlastDB
          104 sequences; 43,616 total letters

Searching..................................................done

If you have any problems or questions with the results of this search
please refer to the BLAST FAQs

                                                          Score    E
Sequences producing significant alignments:              (bits)  Value

UI-R-A0-ah-b-10-0-UI        800     0    800  ABI          587   e-170
UI-R-A0-av-f-10-0-UI.s1     798     0    798  ABI           26   0.15
UI-R-A0-ar-g-06-0-UI        790     0    790  ABI           26   0.15
UI-R-A0-ar-h-09-0-UI        790     0    790  ABI           24   0.59
UI-R-A0-ax-e-06-0-UI        718     0    718  ABI           24   0.59
UI-R-A0-bi-d-06-0-UI.s1     719     0    719  ABI           22   2.3
UI-R-A0-bk-f-10-0-UI.s1     789     0    789  ABI           22   2.3
UI-R-A0-ae-d-01-0-UI        697     0    697  ABI           22   2.3
UI-R-A0-ak-h-08-0-UI.s1     461     0    461  ABI           22   2.3
UI-R-A0-aj-f-02-0-UI.s3     753     0    753  ABI           22   2.3
UI-R-A0-aj-d-08-0-UI.s3     632     0    632  ABI           22   2.3
UI-R-A0-ao-a-12-0-UI.s1     802     0    802  ABI           22   2.3
UI-R-A0-aw-d-02-0-UI.s1     779     0    779  ABI           22   2.3
UI-R-A0-bd-a-10-0-UI.s1     766     0    766  ABI           22   2.3
UI-R-A0-bl-a-03-0-UI.s1     729     0    729  ABI           22   2.3

   UI-R-A0-ah-b-10-0-UI     800     0    800  ABI
       Length = 391

   Score =  587 bits (296), Expect = e-170
   Identities = 296/296 (100%), Positives = 296/296 (100%)

Query: 1    ctaaaaacatggtgttcgttaaagcgggacctgggatggaggaactgcagacaaggcatt 60
            ||||||||||||||||||||||||||||||||||||||||||||||||||||||||||||
Sbjct: 55   ctaaaaacatggtgttcgttaaagcgggacctgggatggaggaactgcagacaaggcatt 114

Query: 61   gcaagcagaaagtgcattcgaaaccaataagcgtgcactcctggctctctggccacccag 120
            ||||||||||||||||||||||||||||||||||||||||||||||||||||||||||||
Sbjct: 115  gcaagcagaaagtgcattcgaaaccaataagcgtgcactcctggctctctggccacccag 174

Query: 121  gggcagcaaggcaagtggaggcccaaaggctcactccttagaatgcccactagggagggg 180
            ||||||||||||||||||||||||||||||||||||||||||||||||||||||||||||
Sbjct: 175  gggcagcaaggcaagtggaggcccaaaggctcactccttagaatgcccactagggagggg 234

Query: 181  aggccagaactccaccatcgtggaggggagggaaatgagagaacaggaacgtgagaaggg 240
            ||||||||||||||||||||||||||||||||||||||||||||||||||||||||||||
Sbjct: 235  aggccagaactccaccatcgtggaggggagggaaatgagagaacaggaacgtgagaaggg 294

Query: 241  gtgccagaccaaggggtcatgggacaaagaacagaccccaagcatctggcacctag 296
            ||||||||||||||||||||||||||||||||||||||||||||||||||||||||
Sbjct: 295  gtgccagaccaaggggtcatgggacaaagaacagaccccaagcatctggcacctag 350

   UI-R-A0-av-f-10-0-UI.s1   798     0    798  ABI
       Length = 372

   Score = 26.3 bits (13), Expect = 0.15
   Identities = 13/13 (100%), Positives = 13/13 (100%)

Query: 124  cagcaaggcaagt 136
            |||||||||||||
Sbjct: 243  cagcaaggcaagt 231

CPU time:     0.06 user secs.      0.06 sys. secs       0.12 total secs.

   Database: CustomBlastDB
     Posted date:  May 19, 1999  8:13 AM
   Number of letters in database: 43,616
   Number of sequences in database:  104

Lambda     K       H
   1.37    0.711   1.31

Gapped
Lambda     K       H
   1.37    0.711   1.31
```

Fig. 2. Sample BLAST Output

SP-2 class system. Of greatest importance would be a high-speed, low-latency interconnection network to allow rapid selection and scoring of the best possible alignment.

Database (Target Set) Partitioning The next larger grain of parallelization involves distributing "chunks" of the database(s) across a collection of compute nodes. This allows for less demanding memory requirements as smaller pieces of the database are held in persistent storage, and loaded into memory of each node. Additionally, when not at peak load across compute nodes, individual jobs can be completed much more quickly as the power of multiple nodes is leveraged. In this scheme, a master node coordinates the scheduling of jobs and collates the results from each submission. A typical scenario might involve 8-10 workstations with several different chunks of the database, which may have been broken into 4-6 pieces. This will allow for a useful level of redundancy for robustness and reliability, and to incrementally add compute power as databases grow, and more queries are being submitted.

Batch Query (Subject Set) Partitioning The largest grain method of parallelization involves batch processing and scheduling of sets of queries, while keeping full copies of the database stored on each compute node. While this does not reduce the time for an individual search to complete, it is quite effective when used in situations where multiple searches need to be performed in a sustained way on a daily basis, or at the same time. Several methods of optimization can be used when scheduling, including prioritization of interactive jobs if necessary. One disadvantage of this method is the large amount of memory still necessary to allow the entire database to be stored and loaded on each node.

4 Current Implementation

To date, only the coarse-grained batch approach has been implemented and used in a production setting. This allows for efficient processing of daily workloads generated by the many ongoing large-scale sequencing projects at the University of Iowa [ScB98, SoB98]. Without this system in place, it would be impossible to complete BLASTing each day's sequence data within a 24-hour period.

4.1 The Batch Scheduler

The foundation of the local batch BLAST system is the Portable Batch System (PBS) developed for NASA for their diverse set of high-performance computing resources [FeR95]. At the University of Iowa, this system is used to manage an on-site heterogeneous cluster of SUN, HP, and SGI workstations. In addition, PBS can be used with commodity architectures such as Intel PCs. Such systems, when combined with powerful operating systems such as Linux, allow for the low-cost, high-performance addition of computer resources to a local batch BLAST system. A PBS system consists of three distinct parts: the *job server*, the *scheduler*, and *compute nodes* (see figure 3).

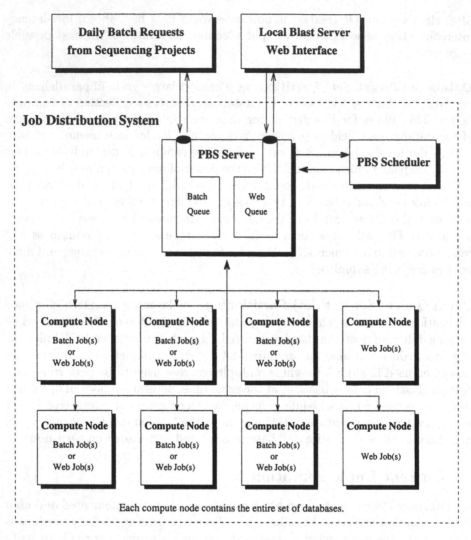

Fig. 3. Software Architecture of Current Implementation

Server The PBS job server is responsible for managing a queue of incoming jobs. In the current system, all jobs are BLAST jobs but this need not be the case. Other computationally-intensive jobs such as sequence clustering and the creation of radiation hybrid maps can just as easily share computing resources with BLAST. There are currently two job queues in the system, one for batch BLAST jobs and a second for jobs interactively submitted to the Local BLAST Server through a web interface.

Scheduler The PBS scheduler applies a scheduling algorithm to allocate compute nodes to jobs in the two incoming job queues. Some compute nodes in the current cluster of workstations have several CPUs and therefore can handle more than one simultaneous BLAST job. The PBS scheduler knows about this and will assign multiple jobs to such nodes.

Compute Nodes Each compute node has a PBS node monitor running on it that communicates with the PBS job server. This allows the server to query the node for job status information and also ensure that the node is still on-line. Should a node go off-line, the PBS job server marks it as down and the scheduler ceases to schedule jobs to it. Each compute node has its own set of the sequence databases. This requires that nodes each have enough disk storage for the databases in use (currently over 2.5 gigabytes).

4.2 Job Types

There are two types of jobs that are submitted to the Local BLAST Server: batch and web. Batch jobs can be executed at any time and can be restarted if necessary. Web jobs are created when users submit BLAST jobs via the UI Local Blast Web Interface. These are time-critical and should therefore have priority over batch jobs. Ideally, if a web job arrives and all of the compute nodes are busy executing batch jobs, one of the batch jobs should be rescheduled and the web job should take its place on the compute node. If possible, the batch job should be check pointed before being interrupted so that no work is lost.

In the current implementation, we have opted for an approach in which only 75% of the compute nodes are allowed to execute batch jobs. The remaining 25% of the compute nodes are always available for time critical web jobs. If there are no batch jobs executing, then 100% of the computing resources are available for web jobs. Although this approach limits the overall throughput for both web and batch jobs under heavy loads, it means that neither will ever be starved of resources. Although this was meant to be a short-term implementation, our experience to date has led us to maintain this as our continuing production configuration.

One of the benefits of using PBS is that it is relatively easy to write a custom scheduling algorithm. We are currently developing a scheduling policy that interrupts executing batch BLAST jobs when web jobs arrive. In addition, once a more fine-grained parallel BLAST has been implemented, it will be possible to speedup individual web jobs by allocating them to a group of compute nodes. PBS allows for this flexibility. There are a number of different scheduling policies and database "chunk" distribution strategies that we are evaluating.

4.3 Database Updates and Performance Tuning

It is critical that all of the replicated databases on the compute nodes in the Local BLAST Server are updated periodically to reflect the most recent contents of the globally-shared databases. In addition, it is also necessary to assure that all nodes' copies of the database(s) are consistent with each other. Otherwise, the results obtained from a BLAST query would depend upon the compute node on which it was executed. In the current implementation, we have chosen to replicate databases in their entirety on each of the compute nodes. This is a trade-off between performance and the ease of maintaining database consistency. At the time of implementation, it was decided that using some sort of networked filesystem would be too large a bandwidth bottleneck given the large database sizes. However, the databases themselves are now reaching sizes that are making full replication less attractive. These databases not only consume (and require) large amounts of local disk space on each node, but they also require large amounts of internet, and intranet bandwidth at the time of updating. The intranet load is particularly problematic. If the local bandwidth consumed to update replicated databases becomes substantial, it will eventually interfere with the ability of the system to serve actual requests for BLAST service from the PBS scheduler.

As an alternative, with faster commodity networks such as Gigabit Ethernet, and with large file system caches on each node, the performance penalty of a networked file system solution may not be as large now as it was when that initial decision was taken. A hybrid solution which we are pursuing, is to have several *I/O servers* in the system, each with a complete copy of the database set in a switched partition of the intranet. Compute nodes would rely on these I/O servers for access to the databases. As long as the ratio of compute nodes to I/O nodes is below a computed threshold, the performance loss should be negligible. As compute nodes are added to the Local BLAST Server, such a system will be necessary since the network traffic caused by database updates will become excessive. These issues, as well as others, will need to be addressed continuously as networked architectures for local intranet BLAST service continue to evolve.

5 Status and Discussion

The Coordinated Laboratory for Computational Genomics at the University of Iowa currently operates ten sequencing systems, three shifts per day, with 96 sequencing lanes each. At full capacity, 2880 sequences are generated each day. Of these, approximately 80% would be expected to pass through an initial verification step and move on to be BLASTed. The length of a typical sequence is about 450 bases.

The daily sequence dataset has BLAST run on it three times. First, blastn is run against the NCBI non-redundant nucleotide database nt (404,657 sequences). Second, blastx is run against the NCBI non-redundant peptide database nr (356,412 sequences). Finally, tblastx is run against the NCBI non-redundant nucleotide database $dbest$ (2,119,879 sequences). The blastn and blastx queries are relatively quick and take a minute at most. The tblastx queries take substantially longer – averaging about 15 minutes each.

For a daily load of 2310 sequences, running tblastx alone would take approximately 576 hours (over 3 weeks) on a single CPU. Clearly, there is a need for some level of parallelism. In the current implementation, there are 25 CPUs in the Local BLAST Server. This can handle the maximum daily load, requiring about 20 hours to run the `tblastx` program. As the number of sequences generated each day increases, it will be a simple matter to add compute nodes to the Local BLAST Server.

Thus far, the compute load generated by the web interface to the Local BLAST Server has been negligible compared to the batch service load. This trend is likely to continue in the future because users generally run quick programs such as `blastn` and `blastp` when using this interface. If the load were to increase significantly, it would again be straight-forward to modify the scheduling policy to favor web jobs more. Alternatively, more compute nodes could be purchased.

6 Conclusion

As projects such as the Human Genome Project near completion, the size of sequence databases and the frequency of BLAST queries against them will grow exponentially. In this paper, we have discussed three ways to exploit parallelism in BLAST searches. A coarse grained approach has been described that is currently in production use at the University of Iowa. Without such a system, it would be impossible to meet the daily computational demands of BLAST searches. Work on a medium grained solution is in progress and is scheduled to be completed by Fall 1999. A fine grained solution has been outlined for future research.

References

[AlM97] S. Altschul, T. Madden, A. Schäffer, J. Zhang, Z. Zhang, W. Miller, D. Lipman, "Gapped BLAST and PSI-BLAST: a new generation of protein database search programs," Nucleic Acids Res. 25:3389-3402, 1997.

[Ber95] M. Berks, "The C. elegans genome sequencing project," Genome Research, Volume 5, 1995, pp. 99-104.

[BlR97] J. A. Blake, J. E. Richardson, M. T. Davisson, J. T. Eppig and the Mouse Genome Informatics Group. "The Mouse Genome Database (MGD). A comprehensive public resource of genetic, phenotypic and genomic data," Nucleic Acids Res, Volume 25, Number 1, 1997, pp. 85-91.

[DOE95] Deparment of Energy, "Five Years of Progress in the Human Genome Project," Human Genome News, Volume 7, Numbers 3-4, September-December 1995. Available via the WWW from www.ornl.gov in TechResources/Human_Genome/publicat/hgn/v7n3/04progre.html (September, 1997).

[FeR95] D. G. Feitelson and L. Rudolph (eds.), Springer-Verlag. "Job Scheduling Under the Portable Batch System," Lecture Nodes in Computer Science Vol. 949, 1995.

[HoJ88] R. W. Hockney and C. R. Jesshope, Parallel Computers 2: Architecture, Programming, and Algorithms, IOP Publishing, 1988.

[ScB98] T. E. Scheetz, C. L. Birkett, T. A. Braun, D. Nishimura, V. C. Sheffield, M. B. Soares, T. L. Casavant, Depts. of Electrical and Computer Engineering, Pediatrics, and Physiology and Biophysics, University of Iowa, Iowa City. "Informatics for preparation of EST reads in a mixed-tissue cDNA library setting," *Proceedings of the 1998 meeting on Genome Mapping, Sequencing, and Biology*, Cold Spring Harbor, New York, pp. 205.

[SoB98] M. B. Soares, G. Beck, B. Berger, C. L. Birkett, E. A. Black, M. F. Bonaldo, R. C. Braun, T. A. Braun, M. Donahue, S. Kaliannan, R. Kincaid, V. Miljokovic, K. J. Munn, D. Nishimura, K. T. Pedretti, T. E. Scheetz, L. H. Stier, T. L. Casavant, V. C. Sheffield, Depts. of Electrical and Computer Engineering, Pediatrics, and Physiology and Biophysics, University of Iowa, Iowa City. "A program for rat gene discovery and mapping, " *Proceedings of the 1998 meeting on Genome Mapping, Sequencing, and Biology*, Cold Springs Harbor, New York, pp. 212.

An Implementation of the Lifecycle Service Object Mobility on CORBA

Yvan Peter and Hervé Guyennet

Laboratoire d'Informatique de Besançon
16, route de Gray – 25030 Besançon cedex – France
Yvan.Peter@pu-pm.univ-fcomte.fr
guyennet@lib.univ-fcomte.fr

Abstract. Standards such as CORBA are spreading in the development of large scale projects. However, CORBA lacks a mobility mechanism which is an interesting feature to deal with the system's dynamics. In this paper, we propose a generic solution for object mobility in CORBA in the framework of the *lifecycle service*. Implementation at the object level handles the migration process using intermediary objects. A group mechanism is used to manage the object creation infrastructure so as to allow scalability. We have chosen a multi-agent auto-organizational group mechanism so as to reduce the administration task for a large system. The performance tests show that reasonable performance can be achieved using a high level generic and portable implementation.
keywords : CORBA, Lifecycle Service, object mobility, group mechanism, multi-agent group.

1 Introduction

Object-oriented distributed environments such as *CORBA (Common Object Request Broker Architecture)* alleviate the development complexity by providing a programming model which hides distribution and takes care of heterogeneity. However, these environments do not handle the dynamics of large scale systems properly. These systems are characterized by a large number of interacting components and the constant evolution of the global system where resource availability (either software or hardware) may change. To deal with the system dynamics we feel that object mobility is important. It can support either manual adaptation through a graphical administration tool or automatic adaptation for example in a load-balancing service. For this reason we propose an implementation of the CORBA *Lifecycle Service* which enables the manipulation of components. This implementation can be divided into two parts : (i) the mechanisms used at the object level to make them mobile and (ii) the infrastructure used to find destination sites and create objects on these sites. Because we are interested in large scale systems, we have chosen to use a group mechanism for this infrastructure. It must be stressed that our aim is to provide a generic and portable mechanism. For this reason, we have only used standard parts of existing products and we have avoided proprietary extensions. The first part of this article includes a brief introduction to CORBA, an overview of the lifecycle service and reviews existing work before discussing implementation choices. In the second part we present the actual implementation at the object level. The third part deals with the object creation infrastructure. It covers groups mechanisms and presents their characteristics. Then the chosen solution is presented which is based on a multi-agent group mechanism that combine group organization and a search mechanism. The fourth part is dedicated to performance tests. Finally we analyze the work still to be done.

2   Object Mobility in CORBA

In this section we recall some elements about CORBA before presenting the lifecycle service which defines how to manipulate objects, then we will consider existing work before discussing implementation choices.

2.1   The CORBA Standard

The CORBA standard has been defined by the OMG *(Object Management Group)* to enable interaction of distributed components [2]. The OMG has defined a framework for their specifications, the OMA (*Object Management Architecture*) which describes the object model used by the OMG and sets of services (e.g., naming service) and facilities (e.g., printing). The ORB is the central part of the architecture and serves as a communication medium between objects.

The ORB is a "software bus" which enables a client to access a service in a transparent manner according to localization and heterogeneity. This transparency is achieved by using *interfaces* which describe the service supplied by a server regardless of its implementation. An interface is written in *IDL (Interface Definition Language)*. The IDL interface is then used to generate stubs for the client and the server sides which handle communication and heterogeneity. To invoke a server, a client needs an object reference either found in a naming service or given by another server.

2.2   The Lifecycle Service

CORBA's mobility model is based on the *LifeCycle Service* [1] which defines a set of interfaces and a general architecture for object management. Manageable objects must support the *LifeCycleObject* interface (cf. figure 1) and implement its methods. We will particularly focus on the *move()* method.

Object creation is done using *factories*. A factory is a plain object which knows how to create some kinds of objects. To find a suitable factory, one can use a *factory finder*. Such an object is associated to a search area and returns a list of appropriate factories for a given object. The only search mechanism considered in the specification is based on the naming service. However we feel this is a serious shortcoming to the usefulness and efficiency of the search. For this reason, we propose a slight modification of the factory finder's interface to

```
interface LifeCycleObject {
  LifeCycleObject copy(in FactoryFinder there,
    in Criteria the_criteria)
    raises(NoFactory, NotCopyable, InvalidCriteria,
      CannotMeetCriteria);
  void move(in FactoryFinder there,
    in Criteria the_criteria)
    raises(NoFactory, NotMovable, InvalidCriteria,
      CannotMeetCriteria);
  void remove()
    raises(NotRemovable);
};
```

Fig. 1. LifeCycle Service's interface

allow the use of criteria in the search. Criteria are defined in the specification as a $< name, value >$ pair and have no semantics attached. We will see in the next sections how these criteria can be used.

During a move operation (cf. figure 2), the client provides a reference to a factory finder to the object it wants to move (1). This object invokes the factory finder to get a list of factories (2). The object then chooses a factory using the criteria provided by the client. This factory is then invoked to create a new instance of the object (3). Handling of mobility between the two instances (e.g., state transfer) is outside the scope of the specification.

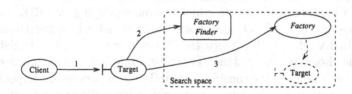

Fig. 2. Object mobility model in CORBA

2.3 Existing Work

Object mobility has already been thoroughly studied in the past, *Emerald* being one of the most known projects [12]. However, much work rely on an homogeneous environment and propose a system level (as in *COOLv2* [3]) or a language level (as in *Emerald*) management of mobility. This is no longer possible with highly heterogeneous environments such as CORBA.

Some proprietary extensions to the standard proposed by some ORB vendors provide useful functionalities to build a mobility mechanism. *VisiBroker*

[20] from Visigenic is an ORB with support for fault tolerance that handles re-binding of object references transparently. *Orbix* [13] from IONA proposes *Smart Proxies* that allow a programmer to inherit from generated stubs so as to change the default behavior. This can be very convenient to implement transparent reference lookup in the naming service when a reference is stale. However this is not enough to implement all the functions of our model. *OmniORB2* from ORL proposes a proprietary mobility mechanism [10] based on special stubs to handle migration transparency and incoming invocations. An object is kept on the primary creation site that knows the valid object reference. The client stubs refer to the "home" object when they cannot invoke the actual object instance. The problem with this scheme is that fault tolerance cannot be achieved. If the "home" object fails, clients have no means to find the server anymore.

In [14], the author studies object mobility on CORBA for graphics applications. His work is targeted at fine grain objects and the solution does not consider active objects. It provides an implementation of the LifeCycle Service but management of object references relies on the ability of ORBeline (now VisiBroker) to rebind object references transparently.

Finally, research done at the university of Munich to build a load balancing mechanism on CORBA is very similar to our work regarding invocation management (only passive migration is handled). However factories create incoming objects in their process. For this reason, they must include the objects' code. We feel this is less flexible since all objects must be known beforehand and they must be developed in the same language as the factory.

For the sake of transparency and efficiency, migration should be handled at the lowest (i.e., system) level. However one must bear in mind that implementing at a low level hinders portability. Regarding CORBA, one has to choose between an integration approach which means modifying an ORB and implies changing its interface (cf. [11]) and a service approach which means building on top of CORBA (cf. [15, 16]). Since the lifecycle service is already defined as a service, the choice is almost done. The actual migration mechanism could still be handled at any level. We consider portability is of paramount importance. So, we have concentrated on high level implementation while trying to provide good performance. This means we have restricted ourselves to the use of standard elements and interfaces. Because of this we cannot benefit from low level ORB functionalities such as LOCATION_FORWARD messages that are used by the object adapter to update a client's knowledge of a server location. However, to use such messages, there must be an object adapter (i.e., a server) on the site to handle invocations from client having a stale object reference. This is not the case in our solution where nothing is left on a site after migration.

3 Implementation at the Object Level

Our implementation at the object level deals with the *state* and *activities* elements and also with referential integrity (i.e., keeping object references up to date). We will first describe the two migration mechanisms we propose. Then, we present the objects defined to implement these two mechanisms.

3.1 Migration Process

Our aim is to keep object's availability to its maximum. For this reason, we propose two mechanisms : a simple *passive migration* where migration is delayed until the end of the last activity and a *state sharing migration* where the original and the destination instances run concurrently to reduce the unavailability.

Passive migration. This is the simplest solution. As soon as migration is requested, new invocations are blocked. We do not handle internal activities because this is very difficult at a high level. Solutions have been proposed to do this [5] but they are a burden for the programmer. For this reason we prefer invocation handling than activity handling (although we propose a minimal set of methods to do this). Because of this, migration is delayed until this end of the last activity. However, the creation of the destination instance can be done right away using factory finders and factories. At the end of the last activity, the state is transfered to the new instance whose object reference is published in naming services. The blocked invocations are released and redirected to the new instance. The former instance can then be terminated.

The drawback of this solution is that migration can be delayed for quite a long time and thus the service is not available. We propose a second solution to reduce unavailability.

State sharing migration. We have seen in the first solution that the new instance of the server can be created right away, but it cannot be used since is has no access to the state. To be able to use this new instance, we propose to share the state between the two instances. This way, the service availability is improved. After the new instance is created it gets a reference to the state hold by the former instance. The access to the state is serialized so as to avoid state inconsistencies. The server can then be published in naming services and the invocations blocked at the former instance can be redirected to the new one. At the end of the last activity in the former instance, the state is transfered and the instance is terminated. This way, the service is still available during the whole migration but the time to get the state reference at the beginning and the state transfer at the end of the migration. Of course remote access is far more costly than a local access but one has to keep in mind that it is a transient situation.

The state is managed in a separate object which has got an IDL interface with methods to manipulate it. The object reference is private to the migrating instances thus preserving encapsulation. We have defined rules to write state access methods similar to a language mapping. These methods are necessary since using IDL *attributes* is not convenient. An attribute can be used for a simple type but for a constructed or scalar type (e.g., structure, sequence or array), there is no way to access a single element. One can only get or set a whole structure for example. The table 1 illustrates the rules we have defined for structures and arrays.

IDL type	Access methods
structure	*type* get_structurename_variablename() *void* set_structurename_variablename(*type* val) *fieldtype* get_structurename_fieldname_variablename() *void* set_structurename_fieldname_variablename(*fieldtype* val)
array[a]	*type* get_1d_variablename(*long* row) *void* set_1d_variablename(*long* row, *type* val) *type* get_2d_variablename(*long* row1, *long* row2) ...

[a] Name and number of arguments depend on the array dimension.

Table 1. State access methods

3.2 The Objects

To handle migration at the object level, we have defined three objects (cf. figure 3) : a *proxy* on the client side to handle relocation transparency, a *representative* on the server side to gain control on incoming invocations and a *controller* object also on the server side which performs the migration and manages activities and the server's characteristics.

Fig. 3. Objects layout and invocation path

The proxy object. This object is on the client side and, as the stub, is generated from the IDL interface of the server. Its role is to encapsulate the stub to handle stale object references and broken invocations. This object is used in the same way as the stub in the client code and, consequently, there are few changes in the programming model. The proxy provides methods to set the name of the corresponding server and the name service in which to get a new object reference transparently after a migration.

The representative object. The *representative* object is on the server side and is also generated from its interface. It encapsulates the server object and is used as a mean to intercept invocations and to perform some extra invocation management tasks before calling the server's actual methods or the controller if a *LifecycleObject*'s method is called.

Handling of invocations that occur during the migration process is done the following way : they are trapped by the *representative* until migration is done. These invocations are then released with a MOVED exception raised by the *representative*. This exception comprises the object reference of the new instance of the server to be used by the client's *proxy*.

The controller object. A server which must be mobile must have an interface that inherits from *LifeCycleObject*. The controller actually implements these methods. Regarding migration, the controller has three roles :

Activities management. The controller provides a set of methods to manage activities. Some of these methods are used by the representative and they are also provided to enable a programmer to manage internal activities.

Criteria management. An object's characteristics are described by a set of criteria. The controller provides methods to get and set criteria and uses these criteria during migration to select an appropriate factory (i.e., site).

Migration management. The controller uses the given factory finder to get appropriate factories and chooses one to create the new instance of the server. The controller also handles the management of the state and keeps the naming services up to date. For this it provides methods to register/unregister the naming services in which the object reference is exported and to define the export name.

4 Object Creation Infrastructure

In this part, we focus on the object creation infrastructure which is composed of factories and factory finders. This infrastructure should be carefully designed to have desirable properties such as scalability and fault tolerance and it should adapt to the client's needs. Indeed, some clients have little or no knowledge of the system and the infrastructure should find the appropriate destination sites while some other clients can choose one on their own. To do this we have to concentrate on the architecture of the infrastructure and the management of the information used to find sites.

4.1 Information Management

We have already mentioned that the criteria defined in the lifecycle service are used to describe objects and sites characteristics. To find the appropriate sites, a factory finder must know the sites composing the system and their characteristics. Building such a view of the system is very costly. The problem is similar to load balancing where many researches have been done about gathering and scattering information throughout a system. The information exchanged should be kept to a minimum and the periodicity of updating should be enough to take good decisions. For this reason, we consider two types of information :

Structural information which pertain to static properties of the system (e.g., processor type of a computer). These information are scarcely subject to change.

Conjonctural information which pertain to dynamic properties. The trustworthiness of such information decreases rapidly and it should be frequently updated.

This distinction can be used in a two phase search mechanism. The structural characteristics are used to describe sites and objects. They are considered during the selection of the destination site. The selected sites can then be probed for their conjonctural characteristics. This way we can reduce the number of communications.

Having taken care of the nature of information, we still have to handle a great number of sites. One way to deal with this is to use group mechanisms described in the next section.

4.2 Group Mechanisms

The notion of group in distributed systems can be applied to all types of resources: processes, processors, communications, memory, peripherals, files, etc. The group concept allows us to define a group of entities as one virtual entity, thus making it possible to give only one and the same name to each member of a particular group, and to communicate with them using only one address. In wide area distributed systems, acquiring information, moving objects or processes, and decision-making are difficult problems which cannot be solved for all the nodes. Therefore, in order to deal with these problems, subsets can be formed called groups [4] , domains [18], clusters [21], partitions [8], and territories [17]. These groups are made up of members. In each group, one member plays a particular role. It is referred to as a leader [4], manager [6] or Interlevel Contact Point [19], and is responsible for managing the communication between groups or levels, receiving information and sending it to other members, and supervising internal group organization. The notion of hierarchy is very important in this concept since it allows us to order the various elements of a group. Scalability problems are replaced by a different problem related to the choice of elements making up the group. With group self-organization protocols, the arborescence can adapt to the dynamics of the system. When a group is too large, these protocols allow it to be divided into several smaller groups. Moreover, when group members have the same location, they can be better distributed in order to strengthen the group.

For our problem, a group mechanism provides a mean to manage a great number of sites. Group formation can be done using either geographical or administrative criteria or using common characteristics of the members. The first approach has the advantage of being close to the organization of the system while the other can be the basis of an efficient search mechanism based on sites' characteristics.

To build our infrastructure, we have chosen to use the mechanisms proposed in [16]. It is an auto-organizational multi-agent group mechanism. Each member of a group is described by its competencies (i.e., characteristics). The group protocols take care of the evolution of the group hierarchy when members join or leave the group or when their competencies change (which should not be too often). This auto-organization structures the search space so as to pose a limit on communication costs during a search. The structuration is also controlled by parameters such as the maximum number of members in a group thus keeping the groups sizes reasonable.

Using this group mechanism, a factory is considered as a server which has a number of competencies (i.e., its characteristics). This factory registers in the group hierarchy using a *server object* which represents the factory in the arborescence in the appropriate groups. A factory finder is considered as a client and uses the group protocols to find sites corresponding to a set of characteristics.

One of the main advantages of the mechanisms used is that the administration tasks are significantly reduced since adding a new factory requires only to describe the site's characteristics. Everything else is taken care by the group protocols.

5 Performance

In this section, we would like to provide some performance results showing how our mechanism performs. We will first pay attention to the overhead imposed by our mechanisms which should not affect normal execution too badly. Then we will compare the efficiency of the two migration mechanisms presented and study the parameters that influence the migration duration. For these tests we have used the traditional *grid* example provided with Orbix which is a simple array with methods to get and set its values. The performance presented have been collected using *Visibroker* on Sun Workstations.

5.1 Overhead

The proposed mechanisms impose an overhead on the invocation time because of the intermediary objects and on execution because of the particular management of the state. The figure 4 shows the invocation durations over 100 series of invocations. The lowest curve corresponds to a normal invocation. We can see that the next two curves corresponding to the two proposed mechanisms expose quite the same overhead. This is not surprising because the intermediary objects are the same and so the overhead. The small gap is due to the difference in the management of the state but it is not very remarkable in this case because the state is not intensively accessed during an invocation. Finally, the upper curve corresponds to the case where the object is migrating with the state sharing mechanism. In this case the state is still in the original instance and the invocation is done on the destination instance. An additional invocation is necessary to access the state, thus, the invocation duration is roughly twice the time of a normal invocation.

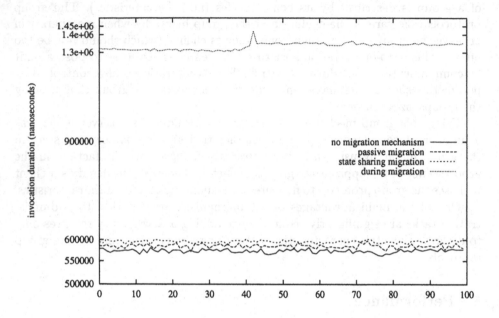

Fig. 4. Invocation duration

Similar results have been found with *omniORB*. The overhead is roughly 3% of the normal invocation time. The overhead of the state access has been found to be 43% to 231% of a simple access in an array depending on the mechanism, ORB and compiler used. This is not as much as one can think since a normal access in an array is really short (around 585-870 nanoseconds).

5.2 Migration Duration

We have considered two important parameters : migration duration and unavailability. Migration duration is the time during which the client waits for the object to move while unavailability is the time during which the service is not accessible. We have aimed at reducing the second parameter. Migration implies the same operations for the two mechanisms and thus they have the same migration duration (the figure 5 represents measures for the state sharing migration over 10 migrations series). With the first mechanism, the object is not available for the whole migration, while with the second one we can see on figure 5 that unavailability is only a part of the total migration time.

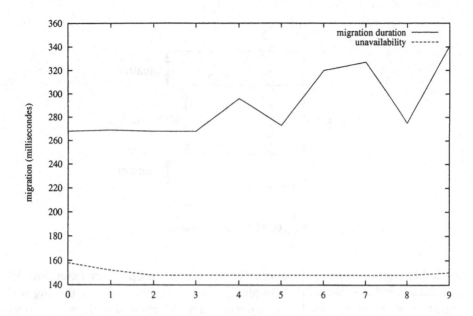

Fig. 5. Migration and unavailability

For the tests we have done, unavailability represents 84.97% of the total migration duration. This is the worst result expected because the tests have been done with quiescent objects. If there were activities in the objects, then migration duration would have been greater while unavailability is not affected.

The figure 6 summarize the different steps of the migration and shows the potential improvement of the second solution we propose. Destination object creation and state transfer represent initial and final unavailability. The transfer can be done only after the end of the last activity. By sharing the state, the destination object can be available while there are activities in the original instance.

Destination object creation depends on how the group search mechanism behave. The state transfer time depends mostly on the state size. It depends also on the data types since marshaling performance vary from one type to another [7].

6 Conclusion and Future Work

Object mobility is an interesting feature to handle the system's dynamics. New standards such as CORBA lack this functionality. In this article we have proposed an implementation of the CORBA *lifecycle service* using a high level implementation. This approach is necessary because of the variety of systems on which CORBA can be found and also because CORBA is only a standard and some variations exist between different implementations. For this reason we have

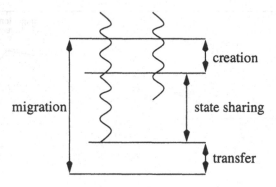

Fig. 6. Migration duration

decided to stick to the standard and did not use any proprietary extension. We have considered two parts in the implementation. An internal part dealing with migration at the object level using intermediary objects and a global part dealing with the object creation infrastructure. We have extensively used the criteria defined in the specification to describe sites and objects characteristics and to find appropriate destination sites. These criteria are used in a multi-agent group mechanism that takes care of the infrastructure organisation. The performance tests have shown that it is possible to improve the availability of the object during migration by sharing the state between the original and the destination instances. The proposed mechanisms have been successfully integrated in an administration tool enabling a system administrator to manipulate objects graphically and in a load balancing mechanism.

Object mobility raises serious issues regarding security. We are starting to investigate these problems. A first step will be to use an ORB with SSL (Secure Socket Layer) to provide a first level of security. We will then look at the CORBA security specification to provide a better level of security. Research regarding mobile agents will also be of great interest (e.g., Agent TCL [9]).

References

1. Common Object Services Specification, Volume I. Technical Report 94-1-1 Revision 1.0, Object Management Group, March 1994.
2. Common Object Request Broker Architecture and Specification. Technical Report 96-03-04 Revision 2.0, Object Management Group, July 1995.
3. Paulo Amaral, Christian Jacquemot, Peter Jensen, Rodger Lea, and Adam Mirowski. Transparent object migration in COOL2. In Yolande Berbers and Peter Dickman, editors, *Position Papers of the ECOOP '92 Workshop W2*, pages 72–77, Utrecht, The Netherlands, June 1992.
4. C. Balayer, C. Daval-Frerot, and H. Guyennet. The Processor Group Approach to Dynamic Load Balancing. In *ISMM Parallel and Distributed Computing and Systems*, Washington, October 1995.

5. Adam Beguelin, Erik Seligman, and Peter Stephan. Application level fault tolerance in heterogenous networks of workstations. Technical Report CMU-CS-96-157, School of Computer Science, Carnegie Mellon University, Pittsburg, PA15213, USA, August 1996.

6. D.J.Evans & W.U.N. Butt. Load Balancing with Network Partitionning Using Host Groups. *Parallel Computing*, (20):325–345, 1994.

7. DSRG. CORBA comparison project. Technical report, Distributed Systems Research Group – Department of Software Engineering, Faculty of Mathematics and Physics, Charles University, Malostranske namesti 25 – Praha, Czech Republic, June 1998.

8. E. Rosti et al. Robust partitioning policies of multiprocessor systems. *Performance Evaluation North Holland*, 19(2-3):141–165, 1994.

9. Robert Gray, David Kotz, Saurab Nog, Daniela Rus, and Georges Cybenko. Mobile agents for mobile computing. Technical Report PCS-TR96-285, Dept. of Computer Science, Dartmouth College, May 1996.

10. Duncan Grisby. *How to use the omniORB2 LifeCycle Support*. ORL, December 1997.

11. IONA. An introduction to Orbix+ISIS. Technical report, IONA technologies Ltd. et ISIS Distributed Systems Inc., July 1994.

12. Eric Jul, Henry Levy, Norman Hutchinson, and Andrew Black. Fine-Grained Mobility in the Emerald System. *ACM Transactions on Computer Systems*, 6(1):109–133, February 1988.

13. IONA Technologies Ltd. *Orbix 2 - Programming Guide*, 1996.

14. Vijay Machiraju. A Framework for Migrating Objects in Distributed Graphics Applications. Master's thesis, University of Utah, June 1997.

15. Silvano Maffeis. Adding group communication and fault-tolerance to CORBA. In *Proceedings of the USENIX Conference on Object Oriented Technologies*, Monterey, Canada, June 1995.

16. Eric Malville and François Bourdon. Task allocation: A group self-design approach. In *Proceedings International Conference on Multi-Agent Systems (ICMAS'98)*, 1998.

17. P.G. Raverdy. *Gestion de Resources et répartition de Charge dans les Systèmes Hétérogènes à Grande Échelle*. PhD thesis, Paris VI, 1996.

18. K. Raymond. Reference Model of ODP. Technical report, CRC for Distributed Systems Technology, University of Queensland, Australia, 1996.

19. J.G. Vaughan. A Hierarchical Protocol for Decentralizing Information Dissemination in Distributed Systems. *The Computer Journal*, 38(1):57–70, 1995.

20. Visigenic. *Visibroker for C++ - Programmers Guide*, 1996.

21. Zhou. Utopia - A Load Sharing Facility for Large, Heterogeneous Distributed Computer Systems. Technical Report TR CSRI-257, Toronto, 1992.

SKiPPER: A Skeleton-Based Parallel Programming Environment for Real-Time Image Processing Applications

Jocelyn Sérot, Dominique Ginhac, Jean-Pierre Dérutin

LASMEA UMR 6602-CNRS
Campus des Cézeaux, F-63177 Aubière Cedex, France
E-mail: Jocelyn.Serot@lasmea.univ-bpclermont.fr
Tel : +33 (0)4 73 40 73 30 Fax : +33 (0)4 73 40 72 62

Abstract. This paper presents SKiPPER, a programming environment
dedicated to the fast prototyping of parallel vision algorithms on MIMD-
DM platforms. SKiPPER is based upon the concept of algorithmic skeletons, i.e. higher order program constructs encapsulating recurring forms
of parallel computations and hiding their low-level implementation details. Each skeleton is given an architecture-independent functional (but
executable) specification and a portable implementation as a generic process template. The source program is a purely functional specification of
the algorithm in which all parallelism is made explicit by means of composing instances of selected skeletons, each instance taking as parameters the application specific sequential functions written in C. SKiPPER
compiles this specification down to a process graph in which nodes correspond to sequential functions and/or skeleton control processes and
edges to communications. This graph is then mapped onto the target
topology using a third-party CAD software (SynDEx). The result is a
dead-lock free, optimized (but still portable) distributed executive, which
SKiPPER finally turns into executable code for the target platform. The
initial specification, written in ML language, can also be executed on
any sequential platform to check the correctness of the parallel algorithm.
The applicability of SKiPPER concepts and tools has been demonstrated
by parallelising several realistic real-time vision applications both on a
multi-DSP platform and a network of workstations. It is here illustrated
with a real-time vehicle detection and tracking application.
Keywords: *Parallelism, skeleton, Caml, image processing, fast prototyping, vehicle tracking*

1 Introduction

In recent years, there has been a growing interest in so-called *skeleton-based* parallel programming models [1][11] in which the programmer's task is to select and
compose instances of pre-defined templates, chosen from a fixed repertoire, rather
than to deal with low-level parallel constructs such as message-passing calls or
shared-memory access. The idea is that recurring patterns of parallel computations can be encapsulated into higher-order program constructs which can

be parameterized to suit a given parallel application, thus hiding all low-level, error-prone implementation details to the application programmer. Skeleton-based programming models are simple, abstract and make it possible to conciliate *portability* and *efficiency*: skeletons can be defined in a target-independent manner but their implementation on a given platform — being done once — can be carefully handcrafted [12]. However, their applicability to *general-purpose* parallel programming remains an open question, because it seems very difficult (impossible ?) to exhibit a fully generic repertoire of skeletons, *i.e* one sufficient to express *every* parallel algorithm. This limitation does not hold if the class of encompassed algorithms is deliberately restricted to a given application domain. In this case, the definition of the skeleton repertoire can be made in a bottom-up manner, starting from an identifiable corpus of applications and/or expert knowledge. This paper assesses this approach by taking our primary application domain as target, namely real-time image processing. In this context, we have found skeletons to be a very effective programming paradigm for *encapsulating* the expertise gradually gained by parallel programmers and making it readily available for the rapid prototyping of subsequent applications.

The paper is organized as follows: section 2 briefly recalls the most salient features of the parallel skeleton concept and presents a repertoire of such skeletons specifically dedicated to real-time image processing applications. Section 3 presents SKiPPER, a complete parallel programming environment built on this skeleton basis. Section 4 demonstrates the effectiveness of the presented concepts and tools, both in terms of code performance and programmability, through a realistic case study. Section 5 is a brief survey of related work. Section 6 concludes this paper by summarizing the main results of this work and giving hints for further investigations.

2 Skeletons for parallel image processing

Within our application domain — low and intermediate level image processing — a retrospective analysis of legacy implementations on MIMD-DM platforms (especially the TRANSVISION [8] platforms, for which we had a large corpus of working, hand-coded parallel applications) showed that most of parallel applications were actually built upon a limited number of recurring *patterns*. Three broad classes of patterns could readily be identified:

- Patterns devoted to "geometric" processing of iconic data. These are all instances of an elementary form of *data parallelism* in which the input image is decomposed into sub-domains, each sub-domain is processed independently with the same function, and the final result is obtained by merging those computed on each sub-domain.
- Patterns encapsulating generic parallel control structures such as *data farms* or *task farms*. These typically involve processing lists of features when the size of the list and/or its elements depends on the input data and thus requires some form of dynamic load-balancing to achieve good efficiency.

- Patterns reflecting the iterative nature of the vision algorithms, *i.e.* the fact that an embedded vision system does not process single images but continuous *streams* of images.

From the implementation point of view, each pattern can be be viewed as a fixed, generic communication harness embedding a set of application-specific sequential functions. Following the skeleton approach, it will therefore be abstracted into a reusable parallel construct, *i.e.* a higher-order function encapsulating all its parallel behaviour and accepting as parameters the sequential functions. This led to the following four "elementary" skeletons making the basis of our programming environment:

- The SCM skeleton (Split, Compute and Merge) encompasses the first class of patterns, *i.e.* those dedicated to regular, data-parallel processing. The SCM skeleton has been illustrated for example in [7].
- The DF (Data Farming) skeleton is an abstraction of the processor farm model, devoted to irregular data-parallelism. Its implementation relies on a *master* process dynamically dispatching data packets to a pool of *worker* processes and accumulating partial results until each input data is processed.
- The TF (Task Farming) skeleton is a generalisation of the DF one, in which each worker can recursively generates new packets to be processed. Its main use is for implementing the so-called *divide-and-conquer* algorithms. It will not be discussed here.
- The ITERMEM skeletons is used whenever the stream-based model of computation has to be made explicit, in particular when computations on the nth image depends on results computed on the $n+1^{th}$. Such "looping" patterns are very common in tracking algorithms, based upon system-state prediction, such as the one presented in section 4.

Practically, each skeleton is given *two* definitions: a *declarative* one and an *operational* one.

The goal of the *declarative* definition, which is written once, is to give the skeleton an architecture-independent, purely *applicative* interpretation. Because of its higher-orderness, this definition is classically and elegantly written using a functional language. For example, here's a declarative definition of the DF skeleton in CAML, a well-known dialect of the ML functional language[2]:

```
let df n comp acc z xs = fold_left acc z (map comp xs)
```

This definition states the skeleton semantics as a simple combination of calls to its functional arguments[1]. Here, it says that the result of applying (`df n comp acc z`) (*i.e* the parameterized skeleton) to a list `xs` is obtained by first applying the `comp` function to each element of the list[2] and then accumulating all the resulting values[3]. Note that the first argument (`n`), actually related to the oper-

---

[1] In (CA)ML function application associates to the right and is denoted without parenthesis, so that `f a b` reads `(f a)(b)` or, more simply, `f(a,b)`

[2] `map` is the CAML builtin higher-order function defined by `map f [x1;x2;...xn] = [f x1;f x2; ... f xn]` where `[a;b;...]` is the CAML notation for lists

[3] `fold_left` is the CAML builtin higher-order function defined by `fold_left f z [x1;x2;...;xn] = f ( ... (f (f z x1) x2) ... xn)`

ational definition, is not used here. The CAML definition classically comes with a *type signature*, the goal of which is to express all the generic type constraints that the arguments of the **df** skeleton will have to meet in order to build *consistent* programs. Here's the signature for the DF skeleton:

```
val df : int              (* Number of workers *)
      -> ('a -> 'b )       (* Compute function *)
      -> ('c -> 'b -> 'c)  (* Accumulating (folding) function *)
      -> 'c                (* Initial accumulator value *)
      -> 'a list           (* Input list *)
      -> 'c                (* Result *)
```

Type *variables* (denoted by letters 'a, ..., 'c) introduce *polymorphism, i.e* the ability for the skeleton to accommodate arguments with various (but related) types. For example, if the second argument (**comp**) of DF has type 'a->'b (*i.e.* function from any type 'a to any type 'b) then its fifth argument (**xs**) must have type 'a list (*i.e* list of 'a), its fourth argument (**z**) type 'c and its third argument (**acc**) type 'c->'b->'c (*i.e.* function from types 'c and 'b to type 'c).

Being real CAML code, the applicative definition can be viewed as an *executable* specification, which can be used to assign a target independent semantics to skeleton-based programs. Practically, this gives the programmer the opportunity to *sequentially emulate* a parallel program on "traditional" stock hardware before trying it out on a dedicated parallel target (by supplying relevant input data, observing results and, if a problem arises, using *sequential* debugging tools to overcome it, for example).

The goal of the *operational* definition is to make explicit the parallel behaviour of the skeleton by specifying its actual implementation on a given platform. For this a classical representation of skeletons as *process network templates* (PNTs) is used. PNTs are incomplete graph descriptions, which are parametric in the degree of parallelism (for example, in the number of **comp** nodes for the DF skeleton), in the sequential function computed by some of their nodes and in the data types attached to their edges. Figure 1 is a representation of a PNT for the DF skeleton on a ring-connected architecture.

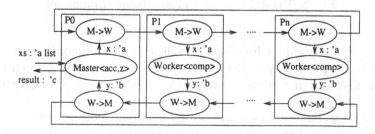

Fig. 1. A process network template for the DF skeleton

Rectangular boxes represent processors (numbered 0 to n), ellipsis sequential processes and arrows communications. Four types of processes are involved: **Master** for dispatching data items and accumulating results, **Worker** for applying the **comp** function and two auxiliary processes (**W->M** and **M->W**) for routing data

The operational definition must be written for each target architecture. It is of course the *implementor*'s responsibility to prove its equivalence with the declarative one (*i.e.* the compatibility of the sequential and parallel semantics). For the DF skeleton, for example, this requires that the **acc** function is commutative and associative, since the accumulation order in the parallel case is intrinsically unpredictable.

3   The software environment

The components of SKiPPER programming environment are depicted in figure 2.

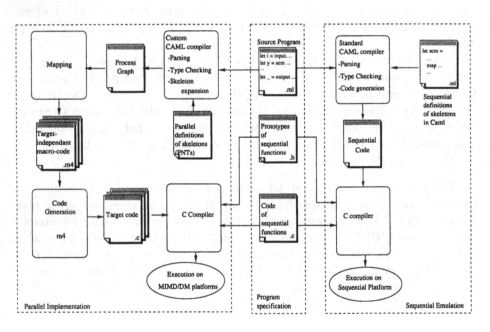

Fig. 2. The skeleton-based programming environment

The source program is a functional specification of the algorithm, in which all parallelism is explicited by means of composing instances of the aforementioned skeletons. Each instance takes as parameters application-specific sequential functions written in C.

SKiPPER starts from this specification for deriving both a parallel implementation on target hardware and an sequential emulated version on a workstation. Only the first possibility will be described further in this paper.

First a custom CAML compiler performs parsing and polymorphic type-checking. The resulting annotated abstract syntax tree is then expanded into a (target-independent) parallel process network by instantiating each skeleton PNT.

This process graph — whose nodes are associated to user computing functions and/or skeleton control processes and edges indicates communication — is then mapped onto the target architecture, which is also described as a graph, with nodes associated to processors and edges representing communication channels. This task is handled by a third-party CAD software called SynDEx[13] which performs a static distribution of processes onto processors and a mixed static/dynamic scheduling of communications onto channels. This tool generates a dead-lock free distributed executive with optional real-time performance measurement. This executive takes the form of processor-independent programs ($m4$ macro-code, one per processor) which are finally transformed into compilable code by simply inlining a set of kernel primitives. The code of these primitives — which basically support thread creation, communication and synchronisation and sequentialisation of user supplied computation functions and of inter-processor communications — is the only platform-dependant part of the programming environment, making it highly portable.

4 A realistic case study

SKiPPER has used to parallelize several algorithms for real-time vision applications including connected-component labelling [7], road-following by white line detection [6] and vehicle tracking [9]. The latter is illustrated in this section.

A video camera, installed in a car, provides a gray level image of several lead vehicle (one to three, in practice). Each lead vehicle is equipped with three visual marks, placed on the top and at the back of it (see figure 3).

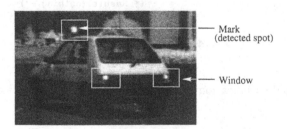

Fig. 3. Tracking algorithm

Algorithmically, the application can be divided into two main parts:

- First, detection of the marks in the image. Marks are detected as connected groups of pixels with values above a given threshold. Each mark is then characterized by computing its center of gravity and an englobing frame.

– Second, tracking each lead vehicles by a classical *predict-then-verify* method. The englobing frames of marks detected at iteration i are used to predict the position and size of the *windows of interest* in which the detection process will search for marks at iteration i+1. This is done using a 3D-modelling of each vehicle trajectory, coupled to a set of rigidity criteria to resolve ambiguous cases (occultations, *etc*). If less than three marks were detected at iteration i, it is assumed that the prediction failed, and windows of interests are obtained by dividing up the whole image into n equally-sized sub-windows, where n is typically taken equal to the total number of processors.

Two skeletons can be put into operation in this application:

– The input of the detection process is a list of windows. This list may vary in length (from 3,6 or 9 in normal tracking to n for the reinitialization phase) and each window may itself vary widely in size (its size depends on the apparent size of the marks, which in turn depends in the distance to the lead vehicle). Such dynamic behaviour, involving a very uneven work load, calls for a DF skeleton.

– The top-level prediction exhibits iterative behaviour, in which results computed at iteration i are used at iteration i+1. This is exactly what the ITERMEM, whose definition is given on figure 4, is designed for.

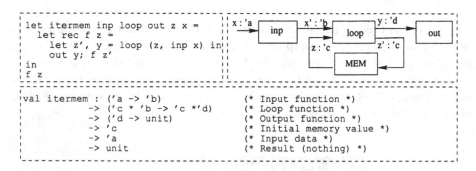

Fig. 4. The ITERMEM skeleton

The functional specification of the application can then be expressed as follows in Caml:

```
let nproc = 8;;
let s0 = init_state ();;
let loop (state, im) =
  let ws = get_windows nproc state im in
  let marks = df nproc detect_mark accum_marks empty_list ws in
  predict marks;;
let main = itermem read_img loop display_marks s0 (512,512);;

    where
```

- init_state returns the initial state value for initiating the prediction algorithm (this state contains all the information required for positioning the windows),
- get_windows extracts the windows of the current image,
- detect_mark and accum_marks respectively detects and accumulates the position and size of marks in the selected windows
- predict returns both the position of the detected marks at the current iteration for display and the updated state value for the next iteration.

The associated C prototypes are:

```
void read_img(/*in*/ int nrows, /*in*/ int ncols, /*out*/ img *im);
void init_state(/*out*/ state *s);
void get_windows(/*in*/ int np, /*in*/ state *s, /*in*/ image *im,
  /*out*/ windowList *ws);
void detect_mark(/*in*/ window *w, /*out*/ mark *m);
void accum_marks(/*in*/ markList *old, /*in*/ mark *m,
  /*out*/ markList *new);
void predict(/*in*/ markList *marks, /*out*/ markList *ms,
  /*out*/ state *st);
void display_marks(/*in*/ markList *ms);
```

Starting from the above CAML specification and C code, SKiPPER has been used both to check the correctness of the parallelisation process (by using the sequential emulation facilities mentioned in section 3) and to derive a parallel implementations on a parallel vision machine with real-time video i/o facilities, the TRANSVISION platform [8]. This architecture is built upon Transputer processors and can be configured according to various physical topologies. The experiment here has been conducted using a ring-topology.

With a ring of 8 Transputers (T9000, 20MHz) operating on a 25 Hz 512×512 video stream, the minimal latencies obtained is 30ms for the tracking phase and 110 ms for the reinitialization phase, with the application processing each image of the video stream in first case, and one image out of 3 in the second. These performances are similar to the ones obtained by an existing hand-crafted parallel version of the algorithm and satisfy the timing constraints of the target application.

The main lesson drawn from this testbench, however was not on raw performances but on the effectiveness of the skeleton approach for writing complex portable parallel applications:

First, the programmer's work here reduced to writing 6 sequential C functions and the CAML specification given above. All underlying parallel implementation details (including process placement, communication scheduling, buffer allocation, provision for deadlock avoidance, etc.) were transparently handled by the environment. The result is that it took less than one day to get a first working implementation on the target platform and that it was then almost instantaneous to get variant versions with different numbers of processors. The previously hand-crafted parallel version had required at least ten times longer to implement. Moreover, it could not be scaled in a straightforward way (modifying the number of processors, for instance required significant changes in the C code).

Second, thanks to the SynDEx retargetable back-end, it would be straightforward to port the application to another parallel platform, provided an executive kernel is available for this platform.

Third, the possibility to emulate the parallel code on a sequential workstation, though not described here has proven to be a very useful approach for debugging the application *functionality* without having to deal with a complex parallel environment. Several bugs in the *sequential* C functions have been uncovered this way. Tracking them down in the *parallel* version would have been much more difficult (if not impossible, given the very limited debugging support offered by our machine).

5 Related work

The concept of algorithmic skeletons is not new and many researchers have worked (and are still working) to demonstrate their usefulness for portable parallel programming. Darlington's group at Imperial College [5] shares our view of skeletons as *coordinating* constructs for sequential functions written in C or Fortran, but mainly targets numerical applications with no real-time constraints. Michaelson's group at Heriot-Watt University [10] use skeleton in ML programs to denote sites of *potential* parallelism, leaving the responsibility of expanding them into parallel constructs to the compiler, on the basis of profiling information collected by an *instrumentation* phase. The P3L project at Pisa University [3] has developed a complete skeleton-based parallel programming language, in which sequential functions are written in C and skeletons are introduced as special constructs. Recently, Danelutto *et al.* [4] have proposed an integration of the P3L skeletons within the CAML language. Their work is very similar to ours. It is more general both in terms of the target application domain and expressibility (their skeletons can be freely nested ours not, in particular) but the provided implementation requires either a good OS-level support (Unix sockets) or a generic message passing library (MPI), thus precluding their use on embedded an/or dedicated vision platforms.

6 Conclusion

This paper has presented a methodology dedicated to the rapid prototyping of image processing applications on dedicated MIMD-DM architectures, based upon the concept of algorithmic skeletons. This methodology provides a tractable solution to the parallelisation problem, by restricting the expression of parallelism to a few forms admitting both a well-defined abstract semantics and one or more efficient implementations. A prototype system level software has been developed to support this methodology. It uses both a custom ML to process network compiler and an existing distributing/scheduling tool to turn a high-level skeletal specification into executable code. Preliminary results of this system — illustrated here with a realistic vision application — are encouraging, showing a dramatic reduction in development time while keeping satisfactory performances. Further developments are needed, however, first to see whether the approach can be extended to higher levels of image processing — for which the higher irregularity of algorithms may require more complex skeletons, and second to study inter-skeleton transformational rules, which are needed when applications are built by composing and/or nesting a large number of skeletons.

References

1. M. Cole. *Algorithmic skeletons: structured management of parallel computations.* Pitman/MIT Press, 1989.
2. G. Cousineau and M. Mauny. *The functional approach to programming.* Cambridge University Press, 1998 - see also: http://pauillac.inria.fr/caml.
3. M. Danelutto, F. Pasqualetti, and S. Pelagatti. Skeletons for data parallelism in p3l. In C. Lengauer, M. Griebl, and S. Gorlatch, editors, *Proc. of EURO-PAR '97, Passau, Germany,* volume 1300 of *LNCS,* pages 619–628. Springer, August 1997.
4. Marco Danelutto, Roberto DiCosmo, Xavier Leroy, and Susanna Pelagatti. Parallel functional programming with skeletons: the OCamlP3L experiment. In *Proceedings ACM workshop on ML and its applications.* Cornell University, 1998.
5. J. Darlington, Y. K Guo, H. W. To, and Y. Jing. Skeletons for structured parallel composition. In *Proceedings of the 15th ACM SIGPLAN Symposium on Principles and Practice of Parallel Programming,* 1995.
6. D. Ginhac. *Prototypage rapide d'applications de vision artificielle par squelettes fonctionnels.* PhD thesis, Univ. B. Pascal, 1999.
7. D. Ginhac, J. Sérot, and J.P. Dérutin. Fast prototyping of image processing applications using functional skeletons on a MIMD-DM architecture. In *IAPR Workshop on Machine Vision and Applications,* pages 468–471, Chiba, Japan, Nov 1998.
8. P. Legrand, R. Canals, and J.P. Dérutin. Edge and region segmentation processes on the parallel vision machine Transvision. In *Computer Architecture for Machine Perception,* pages 410–420, New-Orleans, USA, Dec 1993.
9. F. Marmoiton, F. Collange, P. Martinet, and J.P. Dérutin. A real time car tracker. In *International Conference on Advances in Vehicle Control and Safety,* Amiens, France, July 1998.
10. G. J. Michaelson and N. R. Scaife. Prototyping a parallel vision system in standard ML. *Journal of Functional Programming,* 1995.
11. D. B. Skillicorn. Architecture-independent parallel computation. *IEEE Computer,* 23(12):38–50, December 1990.
12. D. B. Skillicorn and D. Talia. Models and languages for parallel computation. *Computing Surveys,* June 1998.
13. Y. Sorel. Massively parallel systems with real time constraints. The "Algorithm Architecture Adequation" Methodology. In *Proc. Massively Parallel Computing Systems,* Ischia Italy, May 1994.

A Queuing Model of a Multi-threaded Architecture: A Case Study

Vladimir Vlassov[1] and Alexander Kraynikov[2]

[1] Department of Teleinformatics, Royal Institute of Technology,
Electrum 204, S-164 40 Kista, Sweden
vlad@it.kth.se
[2] Department of Computer Science, State Electrotechnical University,
Popov str. 5, St.Petersburg, 197376, Russia
kray@eltech.ru

Abstract. We present an evaluation of a coarsely multithreaded architecture (MTA). The architecture is represented as a queuing network with finite population of jobs (statistically identical threads). The Markovian model is solved by the Matlab environment and the network is simulated in GPSS. A modelling technique reported in the paper allows rough performance prediction in the first stage of top-down system design.

1 Introduction

Most of the recent scalable shared-memory architectures typically provide different combinations of latency reducing and tolerating mechanisms, such as caching, weak ordering, data prefetching, and multithreading [2, 4, 6]. Multithreading [3, 6, 8, 12] is used for hiding long memory latency in multiprocessor systems, and aims to increase system efficiency.

A few attempts of mathematical evaluation of block-multi-threaded Multi-Threaded Architectures, MTAs, have resulted in deterministic analytical models [1, 14] and stochastic models [1, 5, 13–15]. For example, a first-order approximation for MTA efficiency is reported by Saavedra-Barrera et al. in [14]. Agarwal in [1] proposes to model an MTA by a simple queuing system with a fixed number of threads. Queuing models of MTAs are reported in [5, 15].

In this article we present a Markovian model for a coarsely multithreaded architecture executing a set of statistically identical threads. The presented model is a case study for a particular state diagram for a thread execution cycle with context switch on local memory misses. While other researchers simplify a thread state diagram [1, 5, 14], we consider the execution of a thread in more detail. Because the modelling technique reported in this paper, is based on a finite state machine, a new model of MTA with specific design features can be developed easily by adding new states or expanding existing states.

The remainder of this article is organized as follows: Section 2 describes a basic state diagram of a thread. Section 3 introduces a queuing model of the studied multithreaded architecture. Section 4 presents a typical usage of the model and deals with validation of the model by comparison with simulation results. Conclusions are given in Section 5.

2 A Thread State Diagram

Consider a coarsely multithreaded shared-memory MTA with context switching on local memory misses, which cause an executing thread to suspend until a remote access completes. We ignore the possibility of thread suspension caused by synchronization faults, because the probability of such events and duration of the synchronization latency are totally unpredictable. We assume that the MTA has a typical structure including the processing element (PE), a cache, a main memory, part of which is shared. The behaviour of a thread while accessing shared memory is similar to an algorithm for the processing of a shared-address space reference as reported in [10] for the MIT Alewife architecture.

Assume that during its life time the thread cyclically passes through the following states (we annotate a state by the mean time of being in the state):

- C: context switch, where the thread is being scheduled for execution. It takes C_R cycles to activate a thread whose context resides in the processing element of the MTA (resident thread), and C_M cycles to activate a thread from the main memory of the MTA (memory thread).
- r: run state, where the thread is executing during a time between two consecutive cache accesses.
- L_C: cache memory access (cache latency).
- T: locality test, which is performed when the cache misses, to check if data resides in local or remote memory.
- L_M: local memory access (local memory latency) which is performed if the cache misses and the requested data is in the local memory.
- L: remote memory access, caused by a local memory miss (remote memory latency). The interval may include the time required to send a remote fetch request, communication round-trip time, and the time needed to maintain cache coherency and to load the requested data to a register.
- t_r: ready state, where the thread is ready for execution. The duration of this state depends on the behaviour of other threads allocated to the node and does not need to be specified as an input parameter.

Assume also that a local memory miss may occur with probability P_{L_M} (local memory miss ratio), and the probability of a cache miss is P_M (cache miss ratio).

Figure 1 illustrates thread state transitions. Execution of the newly reactivated thread (C) resumes from the state r, where the PE executes thread instructions passing through L_C (cache access) and returning back to r if requested data is currently cached (probability $1 - P_M$). This loop continues until the cache misses with probability P_M, and the thread passes to the locality-test state (T) where it checks the locality of the requested address. On a local memory miss (probability P_{L_M}), the thread initiates a remote memory access and becomes suspended in the state L. If the local memory hits (probability $1 - P_{L_M}$), the thread performs a local memory access (L_M) and returns to r.

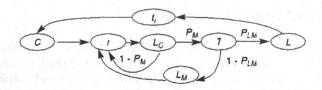

Fig. 1. State Diagram of a Thread

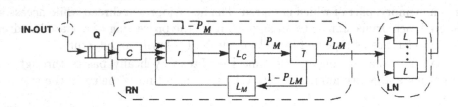

Fig. 2. The Closed Queuing Network of the MTA with Fixed Number of Threads

3 The Queuing Model of an MTA

Assume that an MTA executes a fixed number (n) of identical threads forever. In this case the MTA can be represented as a closed queuing network (Fig. 2) with a finite number n of circulating jobs (threads). The network consists of a queue Q and two sub-networks called RN and LN. Each server of the network corresponds to a thread state and is labelled by its mean service time. For example, the server L_C (Fig. 2) matches the L_C state (Fig. 1) and is marked by the L_C service time. Assume that all timing parameters, r, L, L_M, L_C, C_R, C_M and T have exponential distributions with corresponding means, and that the mean context switch time C is defined as:

$$C = \begin{cases} C_R & \text{if } n \leq n_R \\ \left(C_R \cdot n_R + C_M \cdot (n - n_R)\right)/n & \text{if } n > n_R \end{cases} \tag{1}$$

where n_R is the number of contexts which may reside in the processing element.

The sub-network RN can not serve more than one job at a time, i.e. not more than one thread can be active at any time. The behaviour of the network with the above restriction can be described by the CT Markov chain depicted in Fig. 3. Each state of the chain is marked by a triple index (q, S, l), where:

- q - number of jobs in the queue Q, $q_s \in \{0, 1, 2, \ldots, (n-1)\}$.
- S - the name of the server where the job is located, $S \in \{C, r, L_C, T, L_M, L\}$.
- l - the number of jobs in sub-network LN, $l \in \{0, 1, 2, \ldots, n\}$.

The chain (Fig. 3) contains $(5n + 1)$ states and can be analytically explored using well-known methods [9]. To define the limiting probabilities of states, the following system of equilibrium equations must be solved:

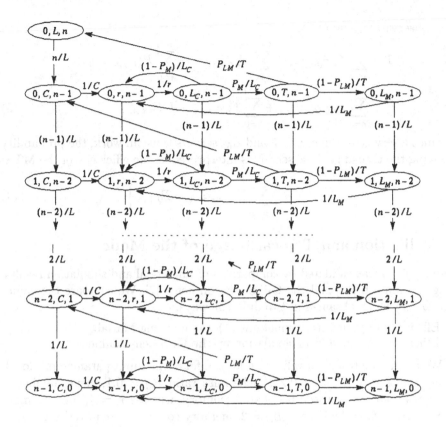

Fig. 3. The Markov Chain of the MTA Queuing Network

$$
\begin{cases}
0 = -n\lambda_L P_{0,L,n} + \lambda_T P_{L_M} P_{0,T,n-1} \\
0 = -(\lambda_C + \Phi)P_{i,C,n-i-1} + \Psi P_{i-1,C,n-i} + \phi\lambda_T P_{L_M} P_{i+1,T,n-i-2} + \\
\quad (1-\psi)n\lambda_L P_{0,L,n} \\
0 = -(\lambda_r + \Phi)P_{i,r,n-i-1} + \Psi P_{i-1,r,n-i} + \lambda_C P_{i,C,n-i-1} + \\
\quad \lambda_{L_C}(1 - P_M)P_{i,L_C,n-i-1} + \lambda_{L_M} P_{i,L_M,n-i-1} \\
0 = -(\lambda_{L_C} + \Phi)P_{i,L_C,n-i-1} + \Psi P_{i-1,L_C,n-i} + \lambda_r P_{i,r,n-i-1} \\
0 = -(\lambda_T + \Phi)P_{i,T,n-i-1} + \Psi P_{i-1,T,n-i} + \lambda_{L_C} P_M P_{i,L_C,n-i-1} \\
0 = -(\lambda_{L_M} + \Phi)P_{i,L_M,n-i-1} + \Psi P_{i-1,L_M,n-i} + \lambda_T(1 - P_{L_M})P_{i,T,n-i-1}
\end{cases}
\tag{2}
$$

where:

$$\Phi = \phi(n - i - 1)\lambda_L, \quad \Psi = \psi(n - i)\lambda_L$$

$$\phi = \begin{cases} 1 & \text{if } i < n - 1 \\ 0 & \text{if } i = n - 1 \end{cases}, \quad \psi = \begin{cases} 1 & \text{if } i > 0 \\ 0 & \text{if } i = 0 \end{cases}$$

$$\lambda_L = 1/L, \quad \lambda_{L_M} = 1/L_M, \quad \lambda_{L_C} = 1/L_C, \quad \lambda_C = 1/C, \quad \lambda_r = 1/r, \quad \lambda_T = 1/T$$

$$i = 0, 1, \ldots, n - 1$$

The conservation relation is:

$$1 = \sum_{i=0}^{n-1} P_{i,C,n-i-1} + \sum_{i=0}^{n-1} P_{i,r,n-i-1} + \sum_{i=0}^{n-1} P_{i,L_C,n-i-1} +$$

$$\sum_{i=0}^{n-1} P_{i,L_M,n-i-1} + \sum_{i=0}^{n-1} P_{i,T,n-i-1} + P_{o,L,n} \qquad (3)$$

Since a service in the r, L_C, T and L_M servers is useful work, the probability of having the thread in these servers is interpreted as the efficiency of the MTA:

$$E_n = 1 - \left(\sum_{i=0}^{n-1} P_{i,C,n-i-1} + P_{0,L,n} \right) \qquad (4)$$

4   Validation and Typical Usage of the Model

Model (1)–(4) was validated by comparison of analytical and simulation results, using the Matlab [11] and the GPSS environments [7]. We compare the values of MTA efficiency obtained in two different ways:

- Efficiency obtained from equations (1)–(4) by using Matlab.
- Efficiency obtained from simulation by the GPSS environment.

We report the results of validation for the following input parameters[1]: local-memory miss ratio $P_L M = 0.25$, cache miss ratio $P_M = 0.1$, mean number of cycles between two consecutive shared-memory accesses $r = 4$, local-memory latency $L_M = 8$, cache latency $L_C = 2$, memory context switch overhead $C_M = 16$, resident context switch overhead $C_R = 2$, locality test $T = 1$, the number of L servers $k = 16$. Table 1, Fig. 4 and Fig. 5 compare the performance estimates obtained from the model with the experimental results from the GPSS simulator.

The modelling technique illustrated by the case study can be used to investigate the impact of various architectural and work-load parameters on the performance of MTAs. A typical usage of the model is illustrated by two series of estimates. One that investigates the impact of remote memory latency on the efficiency (Fig. 4); and another that estimates the effect of increasing the number of resident contexts (Fig. 5). The results were obtained, on the one hand, from equations (1)–(4) using the Matlab environment and, on the other hand, from the GPSS simulator. In both cases, we used the input parameters listed above.

In the first series, the number of threads was changed from 1 to 8 for remote memory latency 32, 64, 128, and 256. Fig. 4 depicts efficiency as a function of n and L for a fixed number of hardware contexts $n_R = 4$. Figure 4 indicates that more threads are required to hide increased communication latency.

In the second series, we estimate efficiency as a function of the number of threads ($n = 1, \ldots, 16$) and the number of hardware contexts ($n_R = 0, 4, 8, 16$) for latency $L = 128$. The remaining input parameters are similar to those in the first series. Figure 5 indicates that the efficiency of the MTA degrades when the number of threads becomes greater than the number of hardware contexts.

---

[1] All timing parameters have exponential distribution with means given in cycles.

Table 1. Efficiency predicted by the model and measured from GPSS ($L = 128$, $n_R = 4$)

n	1	2	3	4	5	6	7	8	9	10
E_n Model	0.6734	0.9234	0.9822	0.9914	0.9823	0.9757	0.9710	0.9675	0.9648	0.9626
GPSS	0.69	0.923	0.983	0.99	0.98	0.973	0.968	0.963	0.962	0.96

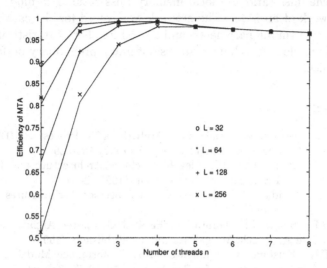

Fig. 4. Efficiency vs. number of threads and latency, $n_R = 4$ (solid curves correspond to the model, symbols correspond to simulation)

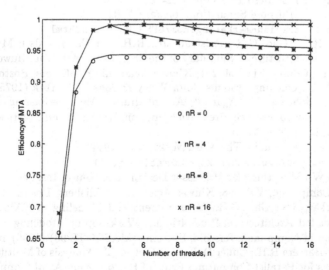

Fig. 5. Efficiency vs. number of threads and number of hardware threads, $L = 128$ (solid curves correspond to the model, symbols correspond to simulation)

5 Conclusions

We presented a modelling of a multithreaded architecture with context switching on local memory misses. The architecture and its workload are specified in terms of communication, cache and local memory latencies, context switching overhead, number of threads, number of cycles between two consecutive cache accesses, cache miss ratio and local memory miss ratio. The model is a closed queuing network of an MTA. The network was solved for the case of exponentially distributed timing parameters and a fixed number of statistically identical threads. This modelling technique allows obtaining preliminary performance estimations quickly.

References

1. Agarwal, A: Performance Tradeoffs in Multithreaded Processors. IEEE Transactions on Parallel and Distributed Systems **3** (1992) 525-539
2. Agarwal, A., et al.: The MIT Alewife Machine: Architecture and Performance, Proc. 22nd Ann. Int. Symp. on Comp. Arch. (1995) 2-13
3. Byrd, G.T., Holliday, M.A.: Multithreaded Processor Architectures. IEEE Spectrum **32** (1995) 38-46
4. Culler, D.E., Singh, J.P., Gupta, A.: Parallel Computer Architecture: A Hardware/Software Approach. Morgan Kaufmann Publishers (1999)
5. Dubey, P.K., Krishna, A., Squillante, M.S.: Performance Modeling of a Multithreaded Processor Spectrum. In: Bagchi, K., Walrad, J., Zobrist, G. (eds.): State-of-the-Art in Performance Modeling and Simulation of Advanced Computer Systems. Gordon and Breach Publishers, Newark, New Jersey (1996)
6. Eggers, S.J., et al.: Simultaneous Multithreading: A Platform for Next-generation Processors, IEEE Micro **15**:5 (1997) 12-18
7. GPSS General Purpose Simulation Software. URL: http://www.meridian-marketing.com/GPSS_PC/index.html
8. Iannucci, R.A., Gao, G.R., Halstead, Jr., R.H., Smith, B. (eds.): Multithreaded Computer Architecture. A Summary of the State of the Art. The Kluwer Int. Series in Eng. and Comp. Sci., Vol. 281, Kluwer Academic Publishers, Boston (1994)
9. Kleinrock, L.: Queuing Systems. John Wiley & Sons, New York (1975)
10. Kranz, D., Johnson, K., Agarwal, A.: Integrating Message-Passing and Shared-Memory: Early Experience, Proc. 4th Symp. on Principles and Practices of Parallel Programming (1993) 54-63
11. MATLAB User's Guide. The MathWorks, Inc. (1994) (See also http://www.mathworks.com/matlab.html)
12. Moore, S.W.: Multithreaded Processor Design. The Kluwer Int. Series in Engineering and Comp. Sci., Vol. 358, Kluwer Academic Publishers, Boston (1996)
13. Nemawarkar, S.S., Gao, G.R.: Measurement and Modeling of EARTH-MANNA Multithreaded Architecture, Proc. 4th Int. Workshop on Modeling, Analysis and Simulation of Comp. and Telecom. Systems (MASCOTS'96) (1996) 109-114
14. Saavedra-Barrera R.H., Culler D. E., von Eicken, T.: Analysis of Multithreaded Architectures for Parallel Computing. Proc. of the 2nd Ann. ACM Symp. on Parallel Algorithms and Architectures (1990) 169-178
15. Vlassov, V., Ayani, R., Thorelli, L.-E.: Modeling and Simulation of Multi-Threaded Architectures, SIMULATION, **68** (1997) 219-230

BSP Performance Analysis and Prediction: Tools and Application

Weiqun Zheng, Shamim Khan and Hong Xie

School of Information Technology, Murdoch University
Perth, Western Australia 6150, Australia
E-mail: {zheng, sk, xie}@it.murdoch.edu.au

Abstract. Load balance is one of the critical factors affecting the overall performance of the BSP (Bulk Synchronous Parallel) programs. Without sufficient performance profiling information generated by effective profiling tools, it is often difficult to find out what extent and where load imbalance has occurred in a BSP program. In this paper, we introduce a new parallel performance profiling system for the BSP model. The system traces and generates comprehensive information on timing and communication by each process in each superstep. Its aim is to assist in the improvement of BSP program performance by identifying load imbalance among processors. The profiling data is visualised via a series of performance profiling graphs, making it easier to identify overloaded processes in a superstep. The visualising component of the system is written in Java, thus runs on almost any type of computer systems.

1   Introduction

This paper is concerned with improving parallel performance analysis, prediction and visualisation for parallel programs under the BSP (Bulk Synchronous Parallel) model [5, 4]. We concentrate on load balancing of BSP supersteps among different processors, which is important to good BSP performance. The effect of load imbalance could be magnified by the need to synchronise all processes at the end of each superstep under the BSP model. It is also quite difficult for most users to identify performance bottlenecks and load imbalance and make any performance improvement, without the support of effective performance evaluation techniques and tools to provide sufficient performance profiling information.

The Oxford *BSP toolset* [3] provides a BSP library, *BSPlib* and a collection of profiling tools. *BSPlib* is smaller and simpler than PVM [2] and MPI [1] and it offers a useful vehicle for parallel programming with popular languages such as C and Fortran. The Oxford profiling tools use command lines with options in producing profiling data and analysing BSP performance. The profiling results, however, do not include a complete breakdown in terms of different types of time costs for a superstep for each process. Without such information, it is difficult to make a comprehensive performance analysis to detect load imbalance among different processes and then to improve performance efficiency in BSP programs. Also, command lines with options lack the ease-of-use characteristic typical of graphical user interfaces. A good performance tool is fundamental to achieving performance tuning and improvement.

In this paper, we present a new BSP performance profiling system called *BSP Pro*, which aims at evaluating and improving BSP program performance assisted by exposing process load imbalance. *BSP Pro* is composed of a performance profiling tool, *BSP Profiler*, and a performance visualisation tool, *BSP Visualiser*. *BSP Pro* uses *BSP Profiler* to trace and generate comprehensive profiling information including various time costs for both computation and interprocess communication for each process. The profiling information is then visualised and shown as performance profiling graphs using *BSP Visualiser*. This visualising component of *BSP Pro* is fully developed in the Java language and utilises Java graphics to expose and highlight process load imbalance. Given its profiling and visualising features as well as Java-based graphical user interface, *BSP Pro* is different from other existing systems, such as the profiling tools within the Oxford *BSP toolset*.

Section 2 discusses the BSP model. Section 3 outlines important characteristics of parallel performance and then details BSP performance and profiling analysis with *BSP Profiler*. In section 4, we introduce our BSP performance profiling visualisation tool. Finally, the effectiveness and ease-of-use of *BSP Pro* are demonstrated in section 5 by analysing and profiling a BSP volume rendering application [6].

2 The BSP Programming

The BSP model was proposed by Valiant [5] as a model for architecture independent parallel computing. Over the last several years, active research has been conducted in Oxford and elsewhere to design FORTRAN and C interfaces for BSP programming. The first BSP library provides 6 programming primitives. It supports the SPMD (single program multiple data) style of program executions, and allows the direct access to the memory of remote processes. Recently there is an initiative to standardize the BSP programming interface for Fortran and C [3]. This proposal combines the direct remote memory access with the bulk synchronous message passing. It also allows the access to remote memory allocated in the stack and the heap.

A BSP computation consists of a collection of processes, proceeding in phases. Each phase is called a *superstep*. All processes are synchronised by a barrier synchronisation at the end of each superstep. Within each superstep, a process performs computation on data held locally. It also initiates remote data accesses, i.e., writing to a variable in a different process or reading from a variable from a different process. These remote data accesses, however, are asynchronous (i.e. non-blocking), and none is guaranteed to complete until the end of the superstep, where the barrier synchronisation of all processes takes place. Therefore these remote data are not guaranteed to be available until the start of the next superstep.

An important characteristic of the BSP synchronisation is that, at the end of each superstep, *all* processes must perform a *barrier synchronisation* before any process is allowed to proceed the next superstep. Therefore the time cost of each superstep is the time taken by the *slowest* process in that superstep. The total time cost of a BSP program for a given execution is the sum of the time costs by all supersteps. When there is a load imbalance in one superstep, all processes will have to wait for the slowest process to complete, unable to do anything useful. The accumulation of such time wastes in successive supersteps may then lead to low performance BSP programs. Therefore, it is important to identify load imbalances among the processors in all supersteps in order to obtain good performance improvement.

3 Superstep Performance Profiles

Unlike programs written in a general message passing style, performance analysis of programs based on the BSP model is made easier. The BSP model provides a simple and composite cost model with the BSP parameters that capture the computation, communication and synchronisation aspects of a parallel computer system. The cost analysis is straightforward under the BSP model. The essence of the BSP performance analysis is that the cost of a BSP program is merely the sum of the costs of each separate superstep. In turn, the cost within an individual superstep can be decomposed into the local computation cost, the global communication cost and the barrier synchronisation cost. The superstep methodology facilitates profiling BSP programs and enhances profiling effects. We can profile time information within individual processes or supersteps. We can also profile communication information within individual processes or supersteps.

```
. . . . . .

From                    kelp
Number_of_Processes     4
Number_of_Supersteps    5

. . . . . .

Process 1:
IP_domain_name          gull
IP_number               134.7.110.22
Operating_System        SunOS release 4.1.2, version 2
Machine                 sun4c
Tic_Per_Second          60
Starting_Time           Thu Mar 13 20:20:15 1997
Finishing_time          Thu Mar 13 20:21:42 1997
(in seconds)            User_Time    Sys_Time    CPU_Time    Wall_Time
Computation                45.03        8.72       53.75        54.02
Communication               0.08        0.28        0.37        32.69
Total_times                45.12        9.00       54.12        86.71

. . . . . .

sstep 1    utime          stime          wtime          send      receive
P 0   25.05 25.05    2.20  2.22    27.44  27.45    2292   48     0    0
P 1    0.02  0.02    0.03  0.03    27.44  27.44       0    0   764   16
P 2    0.02  0.02    0.00  0.00    27.44  27.44       0    0   764   16
P 3    0.00  0.00    0.03  0.03    27.42  27.42       0    0   764   16

. . . . . .
```

Under the BSP model, all interprocess communication within a superstep is completed by the barrier synchronisation at the end of a superstep. The total cost of all communication is therefore attributed to the barrier synchronisation and it is unnecessary to consider the costs of individual communication operations separately, as required in conventional message passing systems. This makes the evaluation and demonstration of profiling results easier compared with message passing systems.

One effective way to generate BSP performance profiling information is to use an appropriate profiling tool to trace profiling data, and produce data files when a BSP program is executed. With *BSPlib*, the performance profile of a BSP program can be obtained by setting a profiling flag during the compilation and then running the executable program. Performance analysis usually requires different time cost data to detect load imbalance among processes. These include user time, system time and the total elapsed time in computation and communication sessions for each process in each superstep. However, the profiling data generated by the *BSPlib* profiling tools only provide one overall elapsed time for all processes in a superstep. Such information is not sufficient to identify the load imbalance among different processes in the same superstep.

Our BSP performance profiling tool, *BSP Profiler*, was to produce more extensive and readable BSP profiling information including the following items: (1) General Information: hostname (eg, kelp), number of processes, number of supersteps. (2) Process Information: process number; starting time and finishing time of each process; total user time, system time, CPU time (= user time + system time) and total elapsed time (wall-clock time) of computation and communication within each process. (3) Timing Information for each superstep: user time, system time and wall-clock time of both computation and communication for each process within each superstep; (4) Data Communication Information for each superstep: number of send (*put*) operations and receive (*get*) operations, and number of bytes sent and received by each process within each superstep. The above table shows part of a trace file containing BSP profiling information after profiling a BSP volume rendering program [6] using *BSP Profiler*.

4   The Profile Visualiser

The *BSP Profiler* described above generates comprehensive timing and communication data profiles for each process in each superstep. However it is very difficult to identify the hot spots with this set of raw profile data without effective visualisation. To help visualising the load imbalance, we have developed a BSP performance profiling visualisation tool, *BSP Visualiser*. This visualisation program was written in Java, hence it runs on any platform with a Java virtual machine.

BSP Visualiser analyses the performance profiling information generated by *BSP Profiler,* and shows the profiling results with performance graphs. For each superstep, it displays: (1) different computation times: user time, system time, CPU time, wall-clock time of every processes; (2) different communication times: user time, system time, CPU time, wall-clock time of all processes; (3) number of send (*put*) and receive (*get*) operations for communication by each process; (4) number of bytes sent or received by each process.

Load balancing is fundamental to good BSP program design, which requires balanced computation and communication among processes for each superstep. One of the main purposes of *BSP Visualiser* is to identify and display workload imbalance in both computation and communication among processes for each superstep. This is achieved by using profiling visualisation, which aims to help programmers improve BSP programs for better performance. The imbalance between light load processes and heavy load processes may cause extra idle (waiting) time costs when these processes reach the common barrier synchronisation within a superstep. Balancing workload among processes within supersteps can minimise idle (waiting) time costs.

The profiling graphs are displayed by *BSP Visualiser* in a style different from the *BSPlib* profiling tools. For instance, in the *time* profiling graphs, the X-axis represents time, and the Y-axis represents processes executing in parallel. For each process within a superstep, computation time is displayed first in the order of user time, system time, CPU time (= user time + system time) and wall-clock time (elapsed time), each shown in a different colour. The communication time is then displayed in a similar manner. This display strategy clearly highlights profiling results for different time costs in computation and communication (see Figure 1).

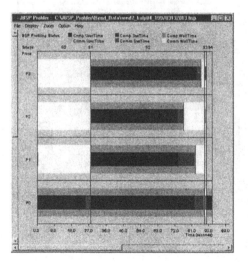

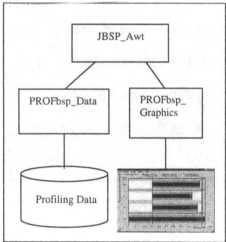

Figure 1   Figure 2

BSP Visualiser combines useful profiling functions with a more friendly graphical user interface than the command based profiling systems. Users can select menu items, click on them, and then do profiling to display visualising graphs. Visualising graphs can be zoomed in or out to a proper scale. Users can select any BSP profiling data file and view its corresponding profiling graphs in a window. The contents of the selected data file can be viewed optionally in a pop-up window for comparison.

The system structure of *BSP Visualiser* is shown in Figure 2. It principally consists of the following Java classes: (a) PROFbsp_Data.java: to read, analyse and convert the BSP profiling data into suitable data format before profiling visualisation; (b)

PROFbsp_Graphics.java: to visualise and display various profiling graphs; (c) JBSP_Awt.java: to design the user interface, and integrate profiling functions (classes) into a unified environment.

5 An Example – Performance Analysis of a Volume Renderer

A BSP volume rendering program [6] was developed by using the Oxford *BSP toolset* in C. To test the *BSP Pro* profiling system, the volume rendering program has been rewritten with *BSP Pro,* and tested on a network of SUN workstations. Execution of the volume rendering program results in the generation of a trace information file by *BSP Profiler.* Information in this file is used by *BSP Visualiser,* which displays the profiling graph (shown in Figure 1) for six different time costs. From the graph, it is clear that, for all four processes, user time and system time of computation suffer from load imbalance in supersteps 0 and 2, especially in superstep 0. The total elapsed time of this BSP program is more than ninety seconds.

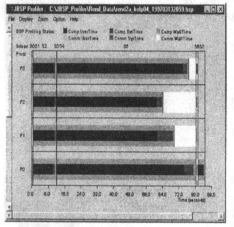

Figure 3

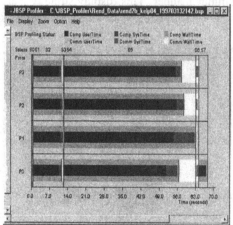

Figure 4

Since *BSP Pro* exposes computation load imbalance among supersteps that are usually represented by code segments enclosed between two successive *bsp_sync()* operations, the program can be modified to address imbalances among the supersteps. Improvements in the volume rendering program were carried out to minimise the load imbalance demonstrated in Figure 1. Figure 3 displays the profiling graph for the new profiling data file generated after these improvements. It is evident from the graph that, for all processes, user time and system time of computation have been balanced in most supersteps, and the total elapsed time is less than 90 seconds. This is smaller than the total elapsed time in Figure 1 (greater than 90 seconds), even though the number of supersteps has increased. However, the user time and system time of computation still exhibits imbalance in superstep 5.

Further improvement to reduce imbalance resulted in the profiling graph shown in Figure 4. As the graph displayed, a significant improvement in load balancing in all supersteps has been achieved by program modification based on the earlier visualisation graphs. The use of *BSP Pro* has enabled a reduction in the total elapsed time from greater than 90 seconds (Figure 1) to less than 70 seconds (Figure 4).

6 Conclusion

The BSP profiling tool described in this paper generates comprehensive timing and communication information for each process in each superstep. Such information makes it possible to identify the load imbalance among different processors. The visualiser makes the comprehensive profiling data understandable by the program developers, thus helping them identify the source of imbalance and suggest possible modification to improve the load balance strategy. As the superstep load balance plays a particularly role in determining the overall parallel performance under the BSP model, the BSP profiling tools such as the one presented will become very valuable tools for the BSP program developers. This work can further in the following areas:

- a high level integrated BSP performance environment including various performance analysis and visualisation tools;
- superstep management and transformation tools that can combine closely related supersteps or expand some supersteps;
- program optimisation tools that, based on profiling results, can provide suitable load migration facilities to reschedule or redistribute tasks evenly among processes within supersteps.

References

1. Dongarra, J.J., Otto, S.W., Snir, M. and Walker, D.: A Message Passsing Standard for MPP and Workstations. Communications of the ACM, Vol. 39, No. 7, (1996), pp. 84-90.
2. Geist, A., Beguelin, A., Dongarra, J., Jiang, W., Manchek, R. and Sunderan, V.: PVM: Parallel Virtual Machine - A Users' Guide and Tutorial for Networked Parallel Computing. The MIT Press, Cambridge, Massachusetts, USA. (1994).
3. Hill, J.M.D., McColl, W.F., Stefanescu, D.C., Gougreau, M.W., Lang, K., Rao, S.B., Suel, T., Tsantilas, T. and Bisseling, R.: BSPlib - The BSP Programming Library. Technical report PRG-TR-29-97, Oxford University Computing Laboratory, U. K. (1997).
4. McColl, W. F.: Scalable Computing. In J. van Leeuwen (Ed.), Computer Science Today: Recent Trends and Developments, LNCS Vol. 1000, (1995) pp. 46-61, Springer-Verlag.
5. Valiant, L.G.: A Bridging Model for Parallel Computation. Communications of the ACM, Vol. 33, No. 8, (1990) pp. 103-111.
6. Xie, H.: Slit-light Ray Tracing of Medical Slices on Multiple Processors: the BSP Approach. Proc. of the 21st Australiasian Computer. Science Conference (ACSC'98), Perth, 4-6 February (1998). In Australian Computer Science Communications, Vol.20, No.1, pp. 145-155, Springer-Verlag.

Message Passing vs Tuple Space Coordination in an Aerodynamics Application *

S. Sancese and P. Ciancarini and A. Messina

Department of Computer Science, University of Bologna
Mura Anteo Zamboni 7, 40127 Bologna, Italy
E-mail: {ciancarini,messina}@cs.unibo.it

Abstract. We study how two well known platform for parallel programming, namely PVM and Linda, compare for designing a computation-intensive simulation program running on a cluster of networked workstations. The program has been developed as a component of the DREAM system, a distributed problem solving environment oriented to the domain of aerodynamics. We compare the available programming environments for PVM and Linda in our domain from a software engineering point of view, namely we discuss how effective they are in the design phase of a parallel application with special requirements of load balancing and distributed data allocation.

1 Introduction

A *Problem Solving Environment* (PSE) [4] should provide all the computing facilities to solve a well defined target class of problems, for instance in the field of aerospace design [13]. Numerical simulation is a major part of a PSE which requires much computing power and large memory space.

In our research project we have developed for an aeronautical industry a prototype PSE useful for designing and simulating (parts of) an aircraft. These problems require high-performance architectures to be solved in a reasonable time [13, 2]. We present here a mathematical model as well as the basic structure of the related numerical algorithm for the simulation of potential transonic flows using a boundary integral equation method. In such an algorithm there are two time consuming steps: the evaluation of all the influence coefficients matrix and the construction of the known vector terms at each time step of the simulation. Matrices involved in the computation of non–linear terms can reach a dimension of $10^5 \times 10^5$ floating point elements. These matrices in general are not sparse, so an important issue is how to allocate in memory their representation when using a cluster of workstations to run the programs that manipulate them. Luckily, both computing steps described above can be easily distributed to take advantage of parallel computing techniques since each subset of coefficients is completely independent from each other.

---

* This paper has been partially supported by the Italian MURST.

In order to build a prototype PSE we have used two different software platforms: PVM and Linda. In this paper we describe our experience, and compare the usage of PVM and Linda in our application.

This paper has the following structure: Sect.2 describes the application and its context and discusses the basic algorithms and why they are expensive in terms of space and time. Sect.3 presents a PVM implementation; Sect.4 presents a Network Linda implementation. Sect.5 compares the PVM and Linda implementations; Sect.6 includes some performance results.

2 An Aerodynamical Application

Aerodynamical analysis applications are used to simulate the behaviour of fluid flows around moving bodies without resorting to actually build and test mechanical prototypes. For the aeronautical industry, simulation tools are particularly convenient, being cheaper, faster, and safer than the real thing. The interest in this area mainly concerns the ability to face the problems related to a highly reliable prediction of the aircraft physical behaviour, so that all the production activities can benefit: design, production, flight testing, etc.

In this way, it is possible to reduce the number of expensive and time-wasting re-design loops usually imposed by the lack of integration among the different design phases, and at the same time to satisfy the requirements of flexibility and compliance with future trends. There are at least two difficult issues:

- algorithms for scientific simulations are almost always very computational-intensive: hours or even days of computing may be needed for a single run;
- visualization of the results of the simulation algorithm can be not straightforward, particularly when tracking and steering are to be implemented (usually the user interface has to be especially designed to the application domain, in order to allow the desired information to be conveyed to the user).

In this paper we report how we designed a simulation tool which can compute forces and moments over a helicopter's rotor blade or airplane wing in hover fly with transonic speeds. This module is part of the DREAM (Dynamic Rotorcraft Evaluation by Advanced Modeling) PSE (Problem Solving Environment) [11]. The DREAM project aims at defining the hardware and software technologies necessary to aeronautics modeling by means of integrated efforts of different expertise.

Figure 1 is a screen snapshot showing the visualization of an actual simulation of a rotor blade. The picture shows the surface of the wingtip and the representation of two physical quantities of interests for the case study: the velocity of the air on the surface of the body and the related pressure values resulting from the flow. The former is represented by means of small green cones, which give a quite immediate 3D representation of the velocity vectors by means of height and orientation: higher cones mean higher speeds in the direction of the cone height. The pressure related quantity is represented using different color values inside the body panels with higher values shown with purple shade and lower

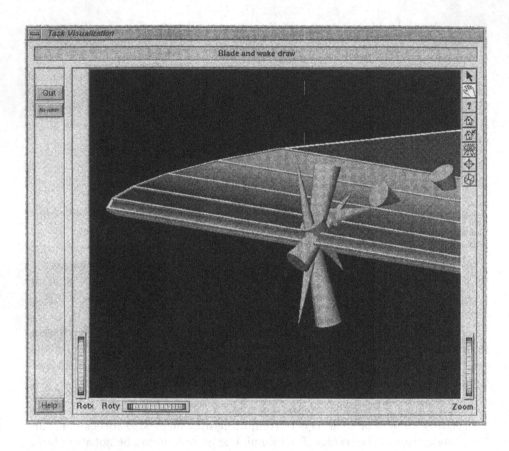

Fig. 1. Visualization of air speed and pressure–related values on the surface of a rotating helicopter blade. Values of velocity shown with cones, values of pressure–related values are shown using panels of different colors.

values shown with orange shade. Each pressure related vector is orthogonal to its panel.

The algorithm used in this work has been described in [12, 7, 8], where extensive mathematical details can be found. In short, the discretized representation of the integral aerodynamical problem is

$$[b]_B = B_B [\chi]_B + C_B [\phi]_B + F_B [\Delta\phi]_B + H_B [\sigma]_B ,$$ (1)
$$[\phi]_B = A^{-1} [b]_B ,$$
$$[\phi]_V = B_V [\chi]_B + C_V [\phi]_B + F_V [\Delta\phi]_B + H_V [\sigma]_V .$$

These equations describe the distribution of the potential function in a region of fluid volume around a solid body moving with transonic speed. The method has been widely validated in the past through comparisons with existing numerical results obtained with well assessed CFD methods (e.g. Iemma and Morino [7], [8]) and is being applied to two– and three–dimensional analysis of airplane wings and helicopter rotors in steady motion.

The matrices $B_B, C_B, F_B, H_B, B_V, C_V, F_V, H_V$ are called Influence Coefficients (IC) and depend only on the geometrical characteristics of the aerodynamical problem. The potential is calculated both on the surface of the discretized body ($[\phi]_B$) and in the discretized volume ($[\phi]_V$), in the form of arrays.

The temporal evolution of the system can be studied by iterating the solution procedure for different time steps.

Two phases are clearly defined as composing the whole algorithm: the construction of the IC matrices and the computation of the terms $[b]_B$ and $[\phi]_V$, needed for the time domain solution of the system (TDSL).

The suitability of a parallel implementation comes mostly from the IC matrices, in which each element can be independently calculated. These matrices are very large: for instance H_V can reach a dimension of $10^5 \times 10^5$ floating point elements. Hence, the design of a distributed implementation has to deal with both the computational load and memory requirements for data allocation.

3 A PVM Approach

We will now illustrate an existing application based upon the above formulation and designed using PVM [5] as the message-passing communication package.

Message passing offers a straightforward way to implement parallel programs in distributed environments. However, simple as it is, message passing offers little comfort to the programmer: each coordination operation has to be implemented directly in terms of low level send/receive operations.

In our application the most difficult issues to deal with are the *size* of the data structures and the *minimization* of the communication overhead.

Data structures are accommodated in the multicomputer RAMs by partitioning them in pieces and assigning each section to a different host. This implies that each host has to perform all the computation relative to the section of data it holds. The partition of data is *static* because it is determined at the start of execution depending on problem size and on the number of worker processes. Once these parameters are fixed, it is not possible to change the amount of work processes are assigned to.

A collection of worker nodes is in charge of the computations on different sections of the data structures, given that no relation holds between different computed elements. This approach has the advantage of requiring null IPC in the influence coefficients phase because computation is done on local data only. Of course, in the TDSL phase communication is required to keep the potential vector updated in order to perform matrix-vector products.

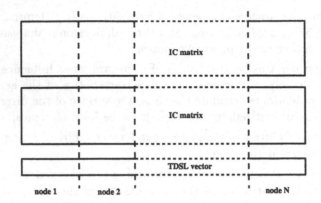

Fig. 2. Data distribution. Different sections of the data structures are allocated on different nodes.

4   The Linda Implementation

The adoption of the Linda coordination model [16] in designing the software architecture of the program provides a direct support for distributed data structures and agenda parallelism. Agenda Parallelism is a way to coordinate parallel activities focusing the attention on simple sub-activities which compose the global work to be performed.

The activities involved with Influence coefficient computation phase are:

- computation of the matrices of linear systems of equations B_B, C_B and F_B;
- computation of the matrix A^{-1} (AINV);
- computation of the matrices of non-linear systems H_B, B_V, C_V, F_V and H_V;

The parallel computation of the IC matrices is performed on a per-row basis, that is each task in the agenda indicates the computation of a single row of one of the matrices. A *bag of tasks* is created in the Tuple Space (TS) by means of tuples tagged **"Task of IC"**. This process is split in two, generating all the tasks for the linear matrices first, then waiting for computed data to appear in the TS by means of appropriate **rd()** operations.

The computation of the non-linear matrices is done similarly, except that the master process collects from TS a number of token tuples tagged **"Task done"**, one for each task created. When all the tokens are collected, a *poison pill* tuple is output in order to terminate the phase. The master process also computes and outputs in TS the A^{-1} matrix while the workers are computing non-linear coefficients.

The process iterates until a **POISON** condition is found. First, a **"Task of IC"** is picked up from the bag of tasks in the TS and identification parameters for the task are assigned to local variables **taskType** and **row**. The **taskType** parameter tells the worker the kind of computation to perform and the **row** parameter indicates which row to compute. If a **POISON** task is not encountered, the worker performs actual computation depending on **taskType** and outputs results in TS, otherwise the termination condition is recognized, the poisonous tuple is reinstated in TS and the phase ends.

The algorithm used is highly parallel because no relation holds between any two tasks and this advantage is exploited with the "bag-of-tasks" approach: no relation between activities means that no restriction is imposed on the ordering of the activities, thus the highest possible degree of parallelism is achieved.

Once the matrices in the IC computation phase are computed, it is possible to solve the non-linear system of Eq. 1 in the TDSL phase.

Here, unlike in the IC computation phase, some small dependencies hold between the activities. In fact, each vectorial equation in the system has to be completely solved before the next equation can be solved and this creates three distinct sub-phases inside each time-step. Coordination is used in this phase to keep these computational constraints satisfied. However, inside each sub-phase it is still possible to coordinate the activities using the master-worker architecture and the bag of tasks data structure.

Computational loads have been found to be smaller with respect to the IC phase (each vector element requires fewer flop to compute), so that we assigned a larger granularity of parallelism. The choice here has been to compute the potential vectors as distributed data structures made up of distributed *chunks* of elements. Each chunk of data is actually a section of a distributed vector and lives in TS as a tuple.

For each vector element to be calculated it is needed one row of the corresponding IC matrices in order to perform the inner product. Under the dynamical agenda paradigm, this implies that one **rd()** operation is needed in order to compute a single potential vector element because it is not possible for a worker to predict which task it is going to get next. Also, in the case where the TDSL phase iterates for multiple time steps, the IC rows are not "reused" for successive time steps computations and this may cause excessive IPC overhead. For this reason it has been added the option to buffer part of the IC data in the workers' local memory in order to eliminate multiple **rd()** operations for the same IC data over multiple time steps. This option significantly increases the memory requirements for the application, but allows better runtime performance. The bufferization option takes places at the very start of the TDSL phase, when the whole H_V matrix can be retrieved from TS. Actual computation starts with a synchronization with the master process, then the different subphases are worked out one at the time, creating the relative distributed data structures when completed.

The implementation of the agenda paradigm in the TDSL subphases relies on the use of the **inp()** predicate. Workers reach in the bag of tasks while tasks are available and the termination condition is detected by means of the **inp()** operator itself. This implementation has been chosen because of its simplicity, not requiring any additional termination protocol like those used in the IC phase. The **first** and **numItems** variables are the identifiers of the chunk of vector to compute for the current task, representing the index of the first element to compute and the size of the chunk, respectively. The starting in() operation removes from TS the previous time step instance of the vector chunk, so that TS is not flooded with old tuples as time advances. Actual computation for each vector element is achieved in the for() loop, where the inner products are carried out. Here, any IC row is retrieved from TS via appropriate rd() operations, as long as the IC buffering option is disabled. When all the vector elements in the chunk are computed, a chunk tuple is output in TS, tagged with the name of the vector and the index of the first element contained. Concurrent computation of vector chunks builds the distributed vector.

5 Comparing Software Tools in PVM and Linda

The message passing and the Linda models are very different approaches: as a result their programming environments offer different helping tools to the developer of parallel applications. We have used version 3.3.10 of PVM from ORNL [5] and version 3.1 of Network-Linda from SCA [9].

5.1 PVM

PVM gives the user the abstraction of a *virtual machine* - a set of hosts connected by a network that appears logically as a single large parallel computer. Either the hosts and the interconnections can be heterogeneous, so that various hybrids of different machines and various connections can be made available as a single parallel computer. Consoles are available for controlling the virtual machine and can be used to add hosts, spawn tasks, delete hosts and perform all the configuration work. Another useful PVM tool is XPVM, which is a graphical console and monitor that performs the functions of the PVM console, and that of a real-time performance monitor displaying network and space-time utilization, a call level debugger, and a post-mortem analysis tool.

XPVM [6] is a graphical user interface which helps programmers in developing applications. Fig. 3 shows a snapshot of the XPVM interface during use.

The interface window can be divided into four logical parts. The buttons on the top row perform the basic functions of the standard PVM console and is possible to manage the virtual machine by adding or deleting hosts and by spawning user processes on different nodes.

Below, there is the *network view* part of the interface, with a graphic representation of the virtual machine showing its nodes and the underlying network. While running an application the icons' colors change to reflect the current state of the host (idle, computing, communicating), so that a quick view can give an idea of the status of the virtual machine.

The third part of the XPVM window contains the view controls. Here the user can specify a trace file, enable additional views and control the flow of execution by means of VCR-like controls.

The bottom part of the window contains the *space-time view* of the application. All the PVM tasks running are listed and for each one an horizontal

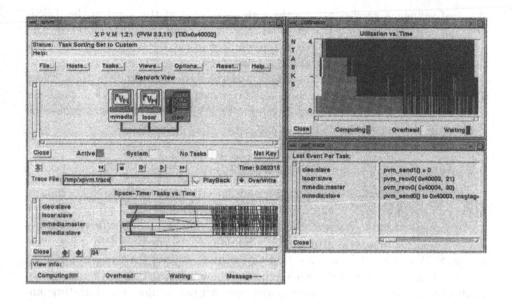

Fig. 3. Debugging the static-PVM aerodynamical application with XPVM.

bar is drawn (the horizontal axis represents time), extending to the right as the application progresses. Bars assume different colors depending on their actual activities: green means computing, yellow is for communication operations, white stands for idle time. Messages between tasks are shown by means of red lines connecting task bars. In addition, if any feature on the window is clicked on, a description of that feature is displayed at the bottom of the window. For a message, this would include the sender, receiver, message size and message tag.

Figure 3 shows an actual run of the static-PVM application using XPVM. In the network view appears the composition of the virtual machine with three SGI machines, one running Irix 5.3 and two running Irix 6.1. The network branches are colored with respect to the data communicated through them and the host icons are colored showing their status (computing, system activity, idle).

In the space–time view are shown the tasks running on the virtual machine. The application has been configured with one master process and three slaves. One machine (named **mmedia**) hosts both the master process and one slave process (it has to be remarked that all the tests we are reporting in Sect.6 were done in different working conditions). On the left there are the name of the executables and the name of the host they are running on. On the right, there is the "history" of each task.

The picture clearly shows the two-phase structure of the application, with the tasks computing influence coefficients up to about the half of the window. The main issue against the static work partition scheme is well shown here. The three hosts have very different computational powers, so that the fastest slave spends lots of time time waiting for the slowest one to finish computing its share of influence coefficients. In the rightmost part of the window the TDSL phase of the application is depicted, where communication is more intense. The utilization window of XPVM (right top window in the illustration) summarizes the space-time view discussed above, compacting the events into an x-y graph.

The right bottom window in Figure 3 is the *call_trace* window. Here, there are reported the last PVM function called for each task. the actual parameters used for each call and the returned values. This view offers a tool to probe the PVM side of the application for debug.

5.2 Linda

Linda, being a coordination model, does not specify how the Tuple Space and its operators are to be implemented, but leaves the solution to specific implementors.

In general, Linda systems have their foundations in compiler level tools because Linda forms a new programming language when matched to a host language. SCA's product is no exception and is built around the `clc` compiler (for C-Linda) and `flc` (for FORTRAN-Linda). The compiler itself is then made up of three main pieces [16]: a language-dependent precompiler, a prelink-time analyzer/optimizer and an architecture-dependent runtime library.

Besides, the Linda environment is completed by a distributed runtime system, based on tuple space server processes, which implement tuple space services on each node of the multicomputer. This approach allows to share the load of TS handling between processors and permits a high degree of parallelism for the TS operations. Together, the Linda compiler and the runtime system achieve a high degree of optimization with respect to application performance. Such optimization techniques for implementing tuple spaces in distributed environments have been studied extensively (e.g. [14], [15] and [18]).

SCA's Linda v3.1 is composed of two different operating environments: *Network Linda* and the *Code Development System* (CDS). The former is the "real" implementation of Linda, which allows the user to run parallel applications on an actual multicomputer, while the latter is a development and debugging environment which simulates a multiprocessor architecture on a single workstation. This allows fast application prototyping without wasting multicomputer resources.

For both environments it is possible to debug applications using TupleScope [17], which is an X-based visualization and debugging tool for Linda parallel programs. In addition to the debugger features such as single-step mode and breakpoints, TupleScope can display tuple classes, data in specific tuples and visual indications of process interactions with the tuple space. This gives complete control of all the tuple space activities carried out by parallel processes.

It is also possible to attach native debuggers like `dbx` to Linda processes in order to perform usual sequential code debugging.

Figure 4 is a screen snapshot of the TupleScope display when running the agenda-Linda application in the IC computation phase, where a number of different features of TupleScope are illustrated.

The TupleScope display consists of two parts: the control panel window (the top window in Figure 4) and separate windows for each tuple class (tuple classes

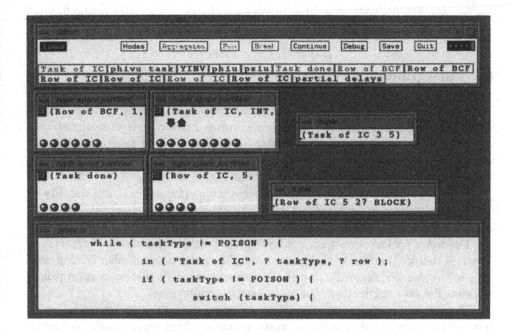

Fig. 4. Debugging the Linda aerodynamical application with TupleScope. A screen snapshot while computing Influence Coefficients.

are compiler-generated distinct partitionings of tuple space, based upon tuple field types and any unique constant strings).

The control panel provides the user the ability to set run modes and aggregate data display mode, to start and stop execution and to perform various debugging activities by means of menu buttons at its top. The control slider at the upper right corner of the window sets the execution speed of the user application.

Tuple class windows contain two kinds of items: spherical icons for each tuple that exists in TS and icons for processes which have accessed tuples in the class. It is possible to obtain further information about items in a tuple class window by clicking on the item.

Tuples show their actual data contents (like the tuple windows at the right side of Figure 4). For instance, it is shown a **"Task of IC"** tuple with integer fields **3** and **5** and a **"Row of IC"** tuple with integer fields **5** and **27** and the actual array of ICs shown collapsed as a **BLOCK**. It is also possible to display all the values in the block field via a menu option.

Processes are represented with different icons depending on the last Linda operation performed and their actual status (e.g. out()/in()/rd() and whether the operation has succeeded or the process is blocked). For example, in the **"Task of IC"** tuple class window, process number 3 has performed a out() operation, while process number 2 has performed a in() operation. Specifically, the exact Linda operation can be seen by opening a process code window by clicking on a process icon. In the bottom window in Figure 4 the in() operation is highlighted by means of a caret mark.

6 Performance Evaluation

We have tried to evaluate how well our agenda application performs when run in a time-sharing multi-user multicomputer composed of a cluster of workstations. For this purpose we have used a cluster of 15 SUN SPARClassics running on a standard Ethernet network. While always running in non-dedicated mode, all the tests were performed during weekends or night periods.

Two issues have been investigated in our work: performance and scalability of our Linda application and its load balancing capabilities. The comparison term for both measurements has been the PVM application.

The main performance metric adopted has been the *Hardware Performance* R_H [19] defined as $R_H = F_H/M_{et}$, where F_H is the total number of flop and M_{et} is the *Master Elapsed Time* of the application. This metric is appropriate because the two applications ran on the same architecture.

The raw performance has been measured using the same aerodynamical problem with increasing dimension of state vectors, which corresponds to higher spatial resolution. Corresponding Mflop give a measure of the increase in computational workload. The multicomputer was composed of a maximum number of 15 nodes (master + 14 workers) and exactly one process (master or worker) has been placed on each node. The reported values are an average of at least three independent measures.

The results for increasing number of nodes in the IC computation phase are reported in Figure 5 for 9 and 15 nodes, respectively.

It is clear that the Linda application scales properly with the number of nodes, i.e.

$$[Mflop/s]_{9nodes}/[Mflop/s]_{15nodes} \simeq 9/15,$$

and is roughly twice as fast as the PVM application for every computational workload measured, when the number of nodes increases to the maximum number available.

The previous two tests demonstrate that virtual shared memory systems can be at least as efficient as message passing systems, which are reputed to be the best suited for distributed architectures.

In fact, our application has been found to run considerably faster when the number of nodes exceeds 10.

Figure 6 show the performance of the Linda and PVM applications when run over an aerodynamical problem in the time domain phase, with dimension about 2.5 Mflop. Data refer to clusters of 4 nodes (master + 3 workers, at left) and 9 workstations (master + 8 workers, at right), respectively. The increasing parameter on the abscissa is now the number of iterations used in each time steps. Performance increases for both applications, but the Linda application clearly scales better.

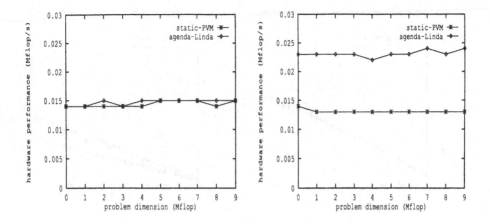

Fig. 5. Hardware performances of the Linda and PVM applications for increasing problem dimension. Left: 9 nodes multicomputer. Right: 15 nodes multicomputer.

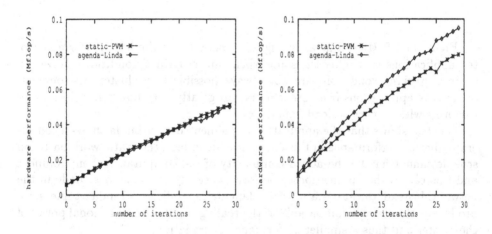

Fig. 6. Hardware performances of the Linda and PVM applications for increasing number of time steps in the TDSL phase. Left: 4 nodes multicomputer. Right: 9 nodes multicomputer.

In order to evaluate load balancing we set up a test using a 4-nodes multicomputer (master + 3 worker). We ran a time-consuming external application on one of the workers' nodes in order to simulate a time-sharing multi-user environment. On the busy processor the CPU time has been measured to be equally shared between the worker process and the "interfering" application, so that the computational power of the node could be considered reduced by roughly 50%.

Fig. 7 shows the performance results in these conditions.

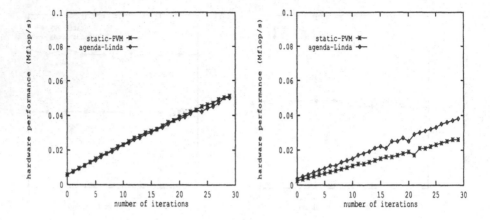

Fig. 7. Load balancing. Hardware performances of the Linda and PVM applications for increasing number of time steps in the TDSL phase. At left, "dedicated" environment. At right, environment is loaded with an external application which reduces the computing capabilities of one of the nodes by about 50%. 4 nodes multicomputer.

Figure at left (the same as in Figure 6) shows that the base performance of the applications is roughly the same when run in optimal conditions. However, optimal working conditions are not always possible in a cluster environment: interactive applications from other users can greatly vary how a multicomputer performs with respect to load balancing.

Our test shows that the application implemented with Linda shows a considerably better performance in this environment. In fact, the static work partition scheme cannot handle the added complexity of the computational environment and this causes the application to perform as slowly as the slowest node in the network. Instead, the automatic load balancing capabilities of Linda's tuple space produce performances comparable to the real aggregate computational power of the cluster and thus a smaller performance degradation.

The curves in Figure 7 reflect the expected values for the performance. The PVM application measured at right performed at about half speed with respect to that shown at left, because the whole computation proceeds with the speed of the slowest node in the network. Instead, the Linda application at right runs at about 70% the speed measured at left, thanks to the automatic load balancing capabilities of agenda parallelism when implemented by Tuple Space.

7 Conclusions

We have compared PVM and Linda in the design of a computation-intensive simulation program. Both platforms are well known, however lesser studied is their usage from a software engineering viewpoint.

The software engineering tools available for PVM and Linda influence the development costs. We have measured much shorter development times in the case of Linda. However, Linda was especially useful as rapid application development platform. We were able to perform several experiments rearranging the coordination of the main components of the program.

Our plans now include the full development of DREAM, a problem solving environment devoted to aerodynamics applications. We are building DREAM around the main tools offered by the Linda programming environment.

References

1. N. Carriero and D. Gelernter. *How to Write Parallel Programs*. MIT Press, 1990.
2. C. Everaars and B. Koren. Using Coordination to Parallelize Sparse-Grid Methods for 3D CFD Problems. (to appear), 1998.
3. MPI Forum. "MPI: a Message-Passing Interface Standard". *International Journal of Supercomputer Applications*, 8(3/4), 1994.
4. E. Gallopoulos, E. Houstis, and J. Rice. Computer as Thinker/Doer: Problem Solving Environments for Computational Science. *IEEE Computational Science and Engineering*, 1(2):11–23, 1994.
5. A. Geist, A. Beguelin, J. Dongarra, W. Jiang, R. Manchek, and V. Sunderam. *PVM: Parallel Virtual Machine. A User's Guide and Tutorial for Networked Parallel Computing*. The MIT Press, 1994.
6. A. Geist, J. Kohl, and P. Papadopoulos. "Visualization, Debugging, and Performance in PVM". In *Visualization and Debugging Workshop*, October 1994.
7. U. Iemma and L. Morino. "Transonic Analysis Using a Boundary Element Method". In 19th *ICAS Conference Proceedings*, Anaheim, California, 1994.
8. U. Iemma and L. Morino. Steady two-dimensional transonic analysis using a boundary integral equation method. *Journal of Fluids and Structures*, 11:633–655, 1997.
9. Scientific Computing Associates Inc. *Linda User's Guide & Reference Manual*. New Haven, CT, 1993.
10. O. Loques, J. Leite, and E. Carrera. P-RIO: A Modular Parallel Programming Environment. *IEEE Concurrency*, 6(1):47–57, 1998.
11. A. Messina, M. Borghesi, M Fustini, L Mazzoni, M Torrisi, and A. Russo. DREAM: A Problem Solving Environment for Aeronautical Industry. In *Client/Server Computing, 30–31 October, IBM La Hulpe, Belgium*, pages 6/1–6/4. IEE Computing and Control Division, Savoy Place, London WC2R 0BL, UK, 1995.
12. L. Morino and K. Tseng. "A General Theory for Unsteady Compressible Potential Flows with Applications to Aeroplanes and Rotors". In P.K. Banerjee and L. Morino, editors, *Boundary Elements Method In Nonlinear Fluid Dynamics, Developments in Boundary Elements Methods*, pages 183–245. Elsevier Applied Science, London, 1990.
13. J. Murphy. A perspective of HPCN requirements in the European Aerospace Industry. *Future Generation Computer Systems*, 11(4-5):409–418, 1995.
14. Carriero N. and Gelernter D. "The S/NET's Linda Kernel". *ACM Transactions on Computer Systems*, 4(2):110–129, May 1986.
15. Carriero N. and Gelernter D. "A Foundation for Advanced Compile Time Analysis of Linda Programs". In U. Banerjee, D. Gelernter, A. Nicolau, and D. Padua,

editors, *Languages and Compilers for Parallel Computing*, number 757 in Lecture Notes in Computer Science, pages 389–404. Springer-Verlag, Heidelberg, Germany, 1992.

16. Carriero N., Gelernter D., Mattson T.G., and Sherman A.H. "The Linda Alternative to Message Passing Systems". *Parallel Computing*, 20:633–655, 1994.

17. Bercovitz P. and Carriero N. "TupleScope: a Graphical Monitor and Debugger for Linda-Based Parallel Programs". Tehcnical Report 782, Yale University, Department of Computer Science, New Haven, CT, April 1990.

18. Bjornson R. *Linda on Distributed Memory Multiprocessors*. Phd thesis, Yale University, New Haven, CT, 1993.

19. Hockney R.W. *The Science of Computer Benchmarking*. SIAM, 1996.

Two Examples of Distributed Architecture for Solving Combinatorial Optimization Problems

S.M.Achasova

Supercomputer Software Department, ICMMG of SB RAS,
Lavrentieva 6, Novosibirsk, 630090, Russia, e-mail: achasova@ssd.sscc.ru

Abstract. Using the Parallel Substitution Algorithm, as a formal model of parallel computations, two examples of distributed architecture are given for implementation of fast parallel algorithms: for the maximal independent set problem and the minimum weighted vertex cover one.

1 Introduction

It is known that sequential algorithms for combinatorial optimization problems can not always be converted in fast parallel ones. This circumstance stimulates a search for completely different approaches to designing parallel algorithms than sequential ones. We refer to two such approaches. The first makes use of the Monte Carlo method [1], and it is illustrated by an algorithm for the maximal independent set (MIS) problem. The second makes use of the primal–dual technique based on the fact that the optimum value of a problem is equal to the optimum value of its dual [2], and it is applied to the minimum weighted vertex cover (MWVC) problem. For the fast parallel algorithms based on the above approaches, the question arises of mapping these into a distributed architecture with massive parallelism and local connections between processors. The cited algorithms are ideally suited to these features. The algorithms assume massive parallel computations (a parallel processing of all vertices or all edges), and these are satisfied with local connections in an architecture having the topology similar of the graph in hand (a processing of a vertex requires the information only from the adjacent vertices or from the incident edges; a processing of an edge requires the information only from the incident vertices). In this paper, design of distributed architectures is based on an original model of parallel computations named Parallel substitution algorithm (PSA) [3].

The PSA is a formal model which is intended for organizing the joint work of a massive number of simple processors with the aim to solve a given problem. Each processor is represented as a pair (a, m), where $a \in A$ (A is a set of states) and $m \in M$ (M is a set of names), which is said to be a cell. In our case, M is a set of symbols, corresponding to the vertices and the edges of the graph in hand. A finite set of cells is said to be a cellular array. A parallel substitution algorithm comprises parallel substitutions of the form: $\theta : S_1(m) * S_2(m) \Rightarrow S_3(m)$, where $S_1(m) = \{(a_1, \phi_1(m)) \ldots (a_p, \phi_p(m))\}$, $S_2(m) = \{(b_1, \psi_1(m)) \ldots (b_q, \psi_q(m))\}$, $S_3(m) = \{(c_1, \phi_1(m)) \ldots (c_p, \phi_p(m))\}$ and $\phi_i(m)$ ($i = 1, \ldots, p$) and $\psi_j(m)$ ($j =$

$1, \ldots, q)$ are functions over a set of names M with both the domain and the range equaled M. The functions define the neighbourhood of the processors. Each parallel substitution represents a set of copies of the same operation which can be executed in parallel in a cellular array. The left-hand side of a substitution is divided into the base and the context by the asterisk. PSAs of MIS and MWVC are performed in cellular arrays of size proportional to n for MIS and $n + m$ for MWVC taking $O(\log n)$ iteration steps for MIS and $O(\log m)$ for MWVC for an n-vertex, m-edge graph.

2 A PSA for the MIS Problem

The MIS problem is: given an n-vertex, m-edge undirected graph $G = (V, E)$, find $I \subseteq V$ (a MIS) such that no two vertices from I are connected by an edge from E, and on addition a new vertex to I, this property does not hold . The Monte Carlo algorithm (MC) finds a MIS taking $O(\log n)$ iteration steps [1]. Let $G' = (V', E')$ be a subgraph of $G = (V, E)$, $N(W) = \{i \in V' : \exists j \in W, (i, j) \in E'\}$ be the neighbourhood of $W \subseteq V'$, $d'(i)$ be the current degree of a vertex i. In each iteration, the MC for the MIS problem generates n pairwise independent random variables $r(i) = (x + y \times i) \bmod q$, $i = 1, \ldots, n$, where x, y are random numbers from the interval $[0, q-1]$, q is a prime number from the interval $[n, 2n]$, it defines the cardinality q^2 of a probability space each point $\{(x, y)\}$ of which corresponds to one of variants of X.

Algorithm MC
begin
    $G'(V', E') := G(V, E)$; $I := \emptyset$;
    while $G' \neq \emptyset$, *do*
        begin
            in parallel for all $i \in V'$
                compute $d'(i)$; *if* $d'(i) = 0$, *then* add i to I and remove from V';
            randomly select x and y from the interval $[0, q - 1]$; $X := \emptyset$;
            in parallel for all $i \in V'$ *do*
                $p(i) := q/2d'(i)$; $r(i) := (x + y \times i) \bmod q$;
                if $r(i) \leq p(i)$, *then* add i to X;
            in parallel for all $(i, j) \in E'$
                if $i \in X$ and $j \in X$, *then*
                      if $d'(i) \leq d'(j)$, *then* remove i from X, *else* remove j from X;
            $I := I \cup X$; $Y := X \cup N(X)$; $V' := V' \setminus Y$;
        end
end

MC can be implemented in a distributed architecture of the following kind. Let there be n nodes. The topology of connections of the nodes is similar to the graph in hand. A node has a name i as its respective vertex. Each node i is connected with nodes $j_1^{(i)}, \ldots, j_k^{(i)}$, where $k = d(i)$. Each node i contains six elementary processors $\langle i, 1 \rangle, \ldots, \langle i, 6 \rangle$. In addition to the above n nodes there is one more node with the name r which is connected with each of the n nodes.

The node r contains three cells $\langle r, 1 \rangle$, $\langle r, 2 \rangle$ and $\langle r, 3 \rangle$, two of which generate random numbers x and y, and the third cell works as a counter. The cell $\langle i, 2 \rangle$ computes $d'(i)$. The cell $\langle i, 1 \rangle$ calculates a random number for its node. The cell $\langle i, 3 \rangle$ has the state 1 if the vertex i still remains in G', and the state 0 if i has been removed from G'. The cell $\langle i, 4 \rangle$ has the state 1 if i is put into X, the state 2 if i has been put into I, and the state 0 if i is not put into both X and I. A PSA realizing MC comprises six parallel substitutions, " $-$ " is the "don't care" symbol.

$$\theta_1 : \{(-, \langle r, 1 \rangle)\,(-, \langle r, 2 \rangle)\,(0, \langle r, 3 \rangle)\} \Rightarrow \{(f_1', \langle r, 1 \rangle)\,(f_1'', \langle r, 2 \rangle)\,(1, \langle r, 3 \rangle)\},$$
$$f_1' = \langle \text{a random } 0 \le x \le q - 1 \rangle, \; f_1'' = \langle \text{a random } 0 \le y \le q - 1 \rangle,$$

$$\theta_2 : \{(-, \langle i, 2 \rangle)\} * \{(1, \langle i, 3 \rangle)\,(z_{j_1}, \langle j_1^{(i)}, 3 \rangle)) \ldots (z_{j_k}, \langle j_k^{(i)}, 3 \rangle)\,(0, \langle r, 3 \rangle)\}$$
$$\Rightarrow \{(f_2, \langle i, 2 \rangle)\}, \; f_2 = z_{j_1} + \ldots + z_{j_k},$$

$$\theta_3 : \{(-, \langle i, 1 \rangle)\,(1, \langle r, 3 \rangle)\}*$$
$$\{(z_2, \langle i, 2 \rangle)\,(1, \langle i, 3 \rangle)\,(x, \langle r, 1 \rangle)\,(y, \langle r, 2 \rangle)\,(i, \langle i, 5 \rangle)\,(q, \langle i, 6 \rangle)\}$$
$$\Rightarrow \{(f_3, \langle i, 1 \rangle)\,(2, \langle r, 3 \rangle)\}, \; f_3 = 2z_2((x + iy) \bmod q),$$

$$\theta_4 : \{(0, \langle i, 4 \rangle)\,(2, \langle r, 3 \rangle)\} * \{(z_1, \langle i, 1 \rangle)\,(1, \langle i, 3 \rangle)\,(q, \langle i, 6 \rangle)\}$$
$$\Rightarrow \{(f_4, \langle i, 4 \rangle)\,(3, \langle r, 3 \rangle)\}, \; f_4 = 1, \text{if } z_1 \le q,$$

$$\theta_5 : \{(1, \langle i, 4 \rangle)\,(3, \langle r, 3 \rangle)\} * \{(z_2, \langle i, 2 \rangle)\,(z_2^l, \langle j_l^{(i)}, 2 \rangle)\,(1, \langle j_l^{(i)}, 4 \rangle)\}$$
$$\Rightarrow \{(f_5, \langle i, 4 \rangle)\,(4, \langle r, 3 \rangle)\}, \; l = 1, \ldots, k, \; f_5 = 0, \text{if } z_2 \le z_2^l,$$

$$\theta_6 : \{(1, \langle i, 4 \rangle)\,(1, \langle i, 3 \rangle)\,(-, \langle j_1^{(i)}, 3 \rangle)) \ldots (-, \langle j_k^{(i)}, 3 \rangle)\,(4, \langle r, 3 \rangle)\}$$
$$\Rightarrow \{(2, \langle i, 4 \rangle)\,(0, \langle i, 3 \rangle)\,(0, \langle j_1^{(i)}, 3 \rangle)) \ldots (0, \langle j_k^{(i)}, 3 \rangle)\,(0, \langle r, 3 \rangle)\}.$$

The algorithm finishes when all cells $\langle i, 3 \rangle$, $i = 1, \ldots, n$, turn into the state 0, and returns a MIS specified with those cells $\langle i, 4 \rangle$, $i = 1, \ldots, n$, which have the state 2.

3   A PSA for the MWVC Problem

The MWVC problem is: given a graph $G = (V, E)$ with vertex weights $w(i)$ find $C \subseteq V$ such that for each edge (i, j) at least one of i and j belongs to C, and $\sum_{i \in C} w(i)$ is minimum. For the MWVC the dual problem is the maximum edge packing, which consists of finding the edge weights $w(i, j)$ such that the total weight assigned to the edges incident to any vertex i is at most $w(i)$ and the total weight assigned to all edges is maximum. A parallel approximation algorithm PD based on the primal–dual technique finds a vertex cover of weight at most $2/(1 - \epsilon)$ times the minimum taking $O(\log m)$ iteration steps, where $\epsilon \in (0, 1)$ [2]. In PD $\delta(i, j) = \min\left\{ \frac{w'(i)}{d'(i)}, \frac{w'(j)}{d'(j)} \right\}$, where $d'(i)$ is the current degree and $w'(i)$ is the current weight of $i \in G'$ and $Inc(i)$ is a set of edges incident to i.

Algorithm PD

begin

   $G'(V', E') := G(V, E)$; $C := \emptyset$;

   in parallel for all $i \in V'$ $w'(i) := w(i)$;

   while $G' \ne \emptyset$, *do*

```
      begin
          in parallel for all i ∈ V' compute d'(i);
          in parallel for all (i, j) ∈ E' compute δ(i, j);
          in parallel for all i ∈ V'
              w'(i) := w'(i) - Σ_{(i,j)∈Inc(i)} δ(i, j);  w'(i) ≤ εw(i),
              C := C ∪ i;  V' := V' \ i;  E' := E' \ {(i, j) ∈ Inc(i)};
      end
  end
```

The algorithm PD can be implemented in a distributed architecture of the following kind. Let there be $m + n$ nodes, n of which correspond to the vertices, m — to the edges of the graph in hand. A node corresponding to a vertex i has a name i, a node corresponding to a edge (i, j) has a name $[i, j]$. Each node i is connected with the nodes $[i, j_1^{(i)}], \ldots, [i, j_k^{(i)}]$, $k = d(i)$. A node i contains seven cells $\langle i, 1 \rangle, \ldots, \langle i, 7 \rangle$. A node $[i, j]$ contains two cells $\langle [i, j], 1 \rangle, \langle [i, j], 2 \rangle$. The cells $\langle i, 1 \rangle$ and $\langle i, 2 \rangle$ calculate $w'(i)$ and $d'(i)$, respectively. The state 1 of the cell $\langle i, 3 \rangle$ means that a vertex i belongs to G', the state 0 — it does not. The state 1 of the cell $\langle i, 4 \rangle$ means that a vertex i has been put in the cover C, the state 0 — it has not been. A cell $\langle [i, j], 1 \rangle$ calculates $\delta(i, j)$. A cell $\langle [i, j], 2 \rangle$ being in the state 1 indicates that an edge (i, j) belongs to G', in the state 0 — the converse. A PSA realizing PD comprises five parallel substitutions.

$$\theta_1 : \{(-, \langle i, 2 \rangle)(0, \langle i, 7 \rangle)\} * \{(1, \langle i, 3 \rangle)(z_{j_1}, \langle [i, j_1^{(i)}], 2 \rangle) \ldots (z_{j_k}, \langle [i, j_k^{(i)}], 2 \rangle)\},$$
$$\Rightarrow \{(f_1, \langle i, 2 \rangle)(1, \langle i, 7 \rangle)\}, \quad f_1 = z_{j_1} + \ldots + z_{j_k},$$

$$\theta_2 : \{(-, \langle [i, j], 1 \rangle)(1, \langle i, 7 \rangle)(1, \langle j, 7 \rangle)\} *$$
$$\{(z_{i1}, \langle i, 1 \rangle)(z_{i2}, \langle i, 2 \rangle)(z_{j1}, \langle j, 1 \rangle)(z_{j2}, \langle j, 2 \rangle)(1, \langle i, 3 \rangle)(1, \langle j, 3 \rangle)\}$$
$$\Rightarrow \{(f_2, \langle [i, j], 1 \rangle)(2, \langle i, 7 \rangle)(2, \langle j, 7 \rangle)\}, \quad f_2 = \min\{z_{i1}/z_{i2}; z_{j1}/z_{j2}\},$$

$$\theta_3 : \{(z_1, \langle i, 1 \rangle)(2, \langle i, 7 \rangle)\} * \{(1, \langle i, 3 \rangle)(z_{j_1}, \langle [i, j_1^{(i)}], 1 \rangle) \ldots (z_{j_k}, \langle [i, j_k^{(i)}], 1 \rangle)\}$$
$$\Rightarrow \{(f_3, \langle i, 1 \rangle)(3, \langle i, 7 \rangle)\}, \quad f_3 = z_1 - [z_{j_1} + \ldots + z_{j_k}],$$

$$\theta_4 : \{(0, \langle i, 4 \rangle)(3, \langle i, 7 \rangle)\} * \{(z_1, \langle i, 1 \rangle)(1, \langle i, 3 \rangle)(z_5, \langle i, 5 \rangle)(z_6, \langle i, 6 \rangle)\}$$
$$\Rightarrow \{(f_4, \langle i, 4 \rangle)(4, \langle i, 7 \rangle)\}, \quad f_4 = 1, \text{if } z_1 \le z_5 z_6,$$

$$\theta_5 : \{(1, \langle i, 3 \rangle)(4, \langle i, 7 \rangle)(-, \langle [i, j_1^{(i)}], 2 \rangle) \ldots (-, \langle [i, j_k^{(i)}], 2 \rangle)\} * \{(1, \langle i, 4 \rangle)\}$$
$$\Rightarrow \{(0, \langle i, 3 \rangle)(0, \langle i, 7 \rangle)(0, \langle [i, j_1^{(i)}], 2 \rangle) \ldots (0, \langle [i, j_k^{(i)}], 2 \rangle).$$

The algorithm finishes when all cells $\langle i, 3 \rangle$, $i = 1, \ldots, n$, obtain the state 0, and returns a vertex cover specified with those cells $\langle i, 4 \rangle$, $i = 1, \ldots, n$, which have the state 1.

References

1. M.Luby. A simple parallel algorithm for the maximal independent set problem // SIAM J. Comput. 1986. Vol. 15, No. 4, 1036-1053.
2. S.Khuller, U.Vishkin, and N.Young. Primal–Dual Parallel Approximation Technique Applied to Weighted Set and Vertex Cover // J. of Algorithms. 1994, 280-289.
3. S.Achasova, O.Bandman, V.Markova and S.Piskunov. Parallel Substitution Algorithm. Theory and Application. World Scientific, 1994.

Performance of the NAS Benchmarks on a Cluster of SMP PCs Using a Parallelization of the MPI Programs with OpenMP

Franck Cappello, Olivier Richard and Daniel Etiemble

LRI, Université Paris-Sud, 91405
Orsay, France
Email: fci@lri.fr.

Abstract. The availability of multiprocessors and high performance networks offer the opportunity to build CLUMPs (Cluster of Multiprocessors) and use them as parallel computing platforms. The main distinctive feature of the CLUMP architecture over the usual parallel computers is its hybrid memory model (message passing between the nodes and shared memory inside the nodes). To be largely used, the CLUMPs must be able to execute the existing programs with few modifications. We investigate the performance of a programming approach based on the MPI for inter-multiprocessor communications and OpenMP standards for intra-multiprocessor exchanges. The approach consists in the intra-node parallelization of the MPI programs with an OpenMP directive based parallel compiler. The paper details the approach in the context of the biprocessor PC CLUMPs and presents a performance evaluation for the NAS parallel benchmarks.

1 Introduction

Many computing centers are now equipped with parallel platforms using PCs as computing nodes and a high performance network like Myrinet as the interconnection network. Today, most of the microprocessors (and especially the Pentium II family) and their chip-sets are designed to easily build multiprocessors. Two-way multiprocessor PCs are now available as workstation PCs. They are about 1.5 times more expensive than uniprocessor PCs with the same microprocessor and memory size. Four-way PCs are also available for servers, but they are far more expensive. In this paper, we only consider 2-way multiprocessor PCs.

The main potential interest of multiprocessor nodes lies in the reduced number of the network connections for a given number of processors in a parallel platform. The speed-up of biprocessor nodes over single processor nodes promise identical performance for the parallel platforms composed of n single processor nodes or of n/2 biprocessor nodes. Since the cost of the network connection is a large portion of the cost of a PC node in a parallel platform, it becomes appealing to use multiprocessor PCs as the nodes for a parallel platform. Instead of reducing the global cost of a parallel platform, the multiprocessor nodes could be used to increase the global platform performance for a constant number of nodes. This approach increases the parallel platform cost. In both cases (constant number of processors or constant number of nodes) an intra-node speed-up study must be done to evaluate the actual speed-up of multiprocessor under uniprocessor nodes.

1.1 Programming and Testing the CLUMPs

Several ways exist to program the CLUMPs and measure their intra-node speed-up. Networks of multiprocessor PCs present an hybrid hardware memory model: message passing between nodes and shared memory inside each node and conform to the term of CLUMP (CLUster of MultiProcessors). In [1] and [2] the authors present respectively a taxonomy and a classification of the programming models for the CLUMPs. We may classify two main approaches by distinguishing the programmer view of the memory in a CLUMP:

- a single memory model (SMM) or
- an hydride memory model (HMM)

Message Passing SMM In [3], [4] and [2] the authors have developed a version of their message passing libraries to work in SMP platforms. A model to program the CLUMP through a small kernel of collective communication and computation primitives is described in [5]. The communication primitives are implemented on top of a message passing library and a SMP Library. Algorithms implemented with this model are programmed as a succession of collective computations and collective communications.

Shared Memory SMM Shared Virtual Memory environments provide the opportunity to program the CLUMPs with the shared memory model. Several projects have already published some design and performance results about the CLUMPs: [6], Shasta [7], Cashmere-2L [8] and SoftFLASH [9]. As for the uniprocessor platforms, the performance of DVSM mainly relies on the protocol efficiency. Recently, OpenMP [10] has been implemented on a network of workstations on top of the Treadmark DSM system. It provides a very convenient way to program the distributed memory architectures. Its performance relies on the shared virtual memory software.

HMM HMM has been the first approach used to program the CLUMPs. Original works include programming the PVPs (Parallel Vector Processor) where Vector Supercomputers are interconnected with a high speed network to form a parallel architecture. Recently the NAS parallel benchmarks repository has published the performance of a Power Challenge Array on a selection of the NPB2 benchmark programs [11]. A hybrid shared memory/distributed memory programming model for the CLUMPs is presented in [12]. Intra-node computation utilizes a multi-threaded programming style. Inter-node programming is based on message passing and remote memory operations.

Portability Requirement Both for SMM and HMM, the portability of code is a main issue. Moving from traditional supercomputers (vector machine) to shared memory or message passing parallel computers has already forced the users to reconsider their application programs. Moving from single processor nodes to multiprocessor nodes in the parallel architectures may also need some effort. Thus, a methodology to program the CLUMPs should seriously consider the portability and provides an approach compliant with a wide variety of CLUMP configurations.

1.2 A Method Based on MPI and OpenMP

In this paper, we investigate the performance of an approach which primary aims to provide portable codes with a reduced effort in the context of the HMM approach. The approach uses OpenMP for shared memory parallelism inside the nodes and MPI for message passing between nodes.

MPI is one of the post popular library for message passing for multi-PC parallel platforms. A lot of applications have been written or ported for the message passing paradigm. A methodology proposed to program the CLUMPs from MPI should provide a way to execute the MPI existing programs written for uniprocessor nodes.

OpenMP derives from the ANSI X3H5 standard efforts. It is a set of compiler directives and runtime library routines that extend a sequential programming language to express shared memory parallelism. The language is extended by a collection of compiler directives, library routines, and environment variables. OpenMP conforms to the SPMD programming paradigm. The OpenMP API uses the fork-join model of parallel execution.

2 OpenMP Parallelization of the NAS NPB 2.3 MPI Programs

2.1 The Basic Methodology

Parallelizing an application for the message passing following the SPMD paradigm often produces a program with the typical layout presented in figure 1. The program starts by initializing the communication system. Then it performs some local computations and calls some communication subroutines to split the data sets among the nodes participating to the application. The program continues executing a main block typically containing a loop nest. The main block is designed for parallel execution. The body of the loop nest can be described as a succession of three sections: local computations, communications, synchronization. The final part of the program gathers individual partial results and computes the final result.

The applications written from MPI programs come as one executable file running on each node of the parallel platform. Within each node, the program is executed inside a process. Parallelizing the program executed on each node

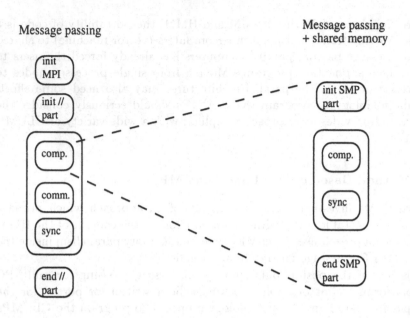

```
Message passing                          Message passing
                                         + shared memory

    init
    MPI
                                              init SMP
    init //                                   part
    part

    comp.                                     comp.

    comm.                                     sync

    sync

    end //                                    end SMP
    part                                      part
```

```
program cg                               subroutine conj_grad ( colidx, )
                                             do i = 1, l2npcols
call initialize_mpi                             call mpi_irecv( rho, )
                                                call mpi_send( sum, )
call setup_proc_info( num_procs, )              call mpi_wait( request, )
call setup_submatrix_info( l2npcols, )       enddo

do it = 1, niter                         !$OMP PARALLEL PRIVATE(k,sum)
                                         !$OMP DO
        call conj_grad ( colidx, )           do j=1,lastrow-firstrow+1
                                                sum = 0.d0
        do i = 1, l2npcols                      do k=rowstr(j),rowstr(j+1)-1
           call mpi_irecv( norm_temp2, )           sum = sum +
           call mpi_send( norm_temp1, )   a(k)*p(colidx(k))
                                                enddo
           call mpi_wait( request, )            w(j) = sum
                                             enddo
        enddo                            !$OMP END DO
                                         !$OMP END PARALLEL
endo
                                             do i = l2npcols, 1, -1
call mpi_finalize(ierr)                          call mpi_irecv( )
                                                 call mpi_send( )
end                                              call mpi_wait( request, )
                                             enddo

                                             return
                                             end
```

Fig. 1. *Parallelizing the MPI Code. The main loop nest of the CG code calls the conj-grad subroutine and contains some communication calls. The computation loop nest of conj-grad is parallelized for intra-node execution using the shared memory paradigm.*

leads to parallelize the main block. This block often encompasses an iterative calculus with inter-iteration dependencies. So intra-process parallelization could not be generally attempted at this level. For most of the NAS programs, we have parallelized the computational section of the main block. Figure 1 presents this hierarchy of parallelism: message passing between MPI processes and intra-node parallelism within each MPI process. The intra-node parallel execution is performed by a group of threads within the same process. The parallelization directives are simply applied to parallelizable loop nests of the original MPI code. From other nodes point of view, a biprocessor node with an intra node multi-threaded execution of a fraction of the MPI code behaves like a uniprocessor node.

The application may exhibit a large number of loop nests and subroutine calls. It can be difficult to discover manually (reading the text source) which loop nests worth to be parallelized. Table 1 gives the cost of the main parallel operations for several nodes of our platform.

	Pentium Pro 200	Pentium II 300	Pentium II 400
Fork-Join (Parallel DO)	5 us	3.5 us	3 us
Lock (Critical)	1.66 us	1.45 us	1.4 us
Barrier	1.36 us	1.33 us	1 us

Table 1. The Cost of the Parallel Operations of OpenMP on our Platform

Figure 2 presents a framework for selecting loop nests to parallelize.

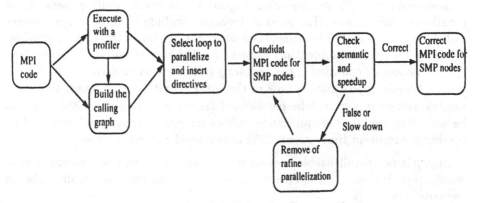

Fig. 2. *The Parallelization Framework*

The framework begins with the MPI source file. The profiled execution allows to discover the most expensive loop nests. The next step inserts OpenMP directives in the code in order to obtain a candidate MPI code for SMP nodes. Then the program is compiled and run on the platform. At the end of the execution, the result correctness and the speed-up must be checked. If the result is wrong or if the speed-up is less than one, the parallelization must be refined or removed. This process may require several iterations in order to provide an efficient and correct code.

A conceptual limit of the approach comes from the way the shared memory parallelization is applied to the message passing programs. With this method, we should not expect a local speed-up close to the speedup that can be obtained by directly parallelizing a sequential program. In contrast with a shared memory program directly derived from a sequential program, there is a lot of substantial work that cannot be parallelized. More precisely, the speed-up is not only bounded by the local sequential part contribution to the local execution time (Amdahl's law) but also by the communication and synchronization contributions to the local execution time.

Another limit of the approach comes from the way the OpenMP compiler distributes loop iterations among threads (e.g. processors). Our PGI compiler splits loop iterations in n sections where n is the number of threads. Each thread computes one section. We cannot control the loop splitting into sections (sections are always made of contiguous iterations) or the distribution of section among threads (processors). Uncontrolled distribution of sections may lead to higher execution time due to inappropriate cache fill at the interfaces between parallel and sequential parts.

2.2 Example: Intra Node Parallelization of MG Benchmark

MG uses a multi-grid algorithm to obtain an approximate solution of a three-dimensional scalar Poisson equation. Figure 3 presents the calling hierarchy of parallelized subroutines. The local cost doesn't include the cost of subroutines called by the current subroutine. The total cost includes the cost of routines called by the current subroutine. Values (% of the total execution time) must be understood by considering the very long initialization procedure. The initialization time is approximately 66% of the total execution time. Some time consuming subroutines cannot be parallelized (zran3, comm1p, norm2u3, comm3) because they contain communication calls or inter-iteration dependencies. Their combined execution time exceeds 30% of the total execution time.

mg3p is not parallelizable because it calls some communication subroutines. zero3, rprj3, interp, resid and psinv contain loop nests that are parallelizable at the outermost loop.

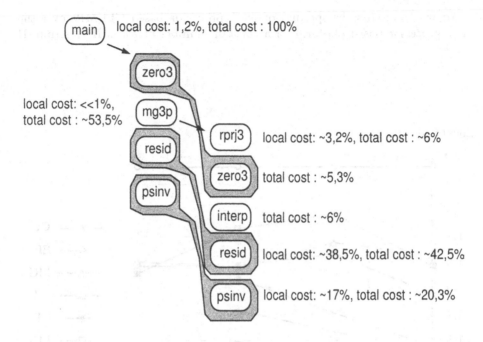

Fig. 3. *The Calling Graph of MG*

3 Performance

3.1 Platform Hardware and Software

Our platform contains a Myrinet network with four ports. We use two types of biprocessor nodes: Pentium II 300 MHz and Pentium II 400 MHz. Each Myrinet PCI interface has a 1MB local memory.

The software environment includes Linux 2.0.33, BIP 0.94c version of MPI library, F77 PGI 1.7 programming environment and Linux Pthread library. With BIP on Myrinet connected PCs, we have a latency of 5us and a bandwidth of 1 Gbit/s. MPI-BIP reaches 20 us (latency) and 1 Gb/s (bandwidth). All benchmarks have been compiled with the o2, unroll and P6 options.

3.2 Uniprocessor PC Versus Biprocessor PC

In this section, we compare a parallel platform based on uniprocessor nodes with a parallel platform based on biprocessor nodes. We compare these platforms for four different configurations: 1 node, 2 nodes, 4 nodes and 8 nodes. All the measurements are made with 400 MHz Pentium II nodes, except for figure 5 that compare performance between 300 MHz Pentium II nodes and 400 MHz Pentium II nodes .

Figure 4 presents the speedup of the biprocessor based CLUMPs over the single processor based platform for a constant number of 400 MHz Pentium II nodes.

Local Speed-up

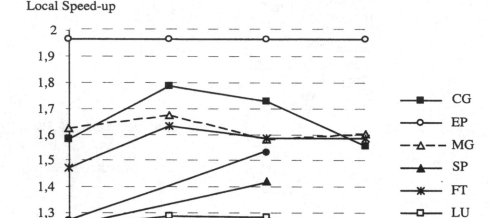

Fig. 4. *Intra-Node Speed-up of the Biprocessors over Uniprocessors for the NPB 2.3 Benchmarks and for the Same Number of Nodes*

The speed-up evolves with the number of nodes in the CLUMPs following one of two trends: it remains constant or it decreases. We have examined the breakdowns of the execution time of some key NAS programs. The analysis shows that the communications, the unparallelized computation loops and the cost of the local parallel execution (mainly bus conflicts) are the most significant bottlenecks.

Figure 5 compare the speed-up between 400 MHz nodes and 300 MHz nodes for the same number of nodes. It shows that Pentium II 400 biprocessors provide a more constant speed-up across the different benchmarks. They are also more sensitive to the communication cost.

Figure 6 presents the performance of the biprocessor based CLUMP against the single processor based platform for a constant number of 400 MHz processors.

We must consider the cost/performance ratio of the biprocessor nodes against the uniprocessor nodes. A biprocessor based platform requires half the connections of a uniprocessor based platform. In a typical uniprocessor PC based par-

Local Speed-up

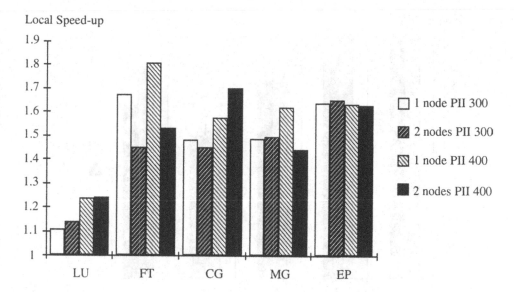

Fig. 5. *Local Speed-up of the Biprocessors Pentium II 400 MHz Nodes and of the Biprocessors Pentium II 300 MHz Nodes for the NPB 2.3 Benchmarks*

allel platform, the network cost is half the cost of the overall platform. As previously mentioned, a 2-way multiprocessor are about 1.5 times more expensive than the corresponding uniprocessor for a given microprocessor and memory size. Assuming these ratio, for a given number of nodes, a biprocessor based platform is 1.25 times more expensive than a uniprocessor based platform. According to the speed-up of figure 4, biprocessor nodes justify their extra cost (at least up to 4 nodes for all benchmarks and up to 8 nodes for all the measured benchmarks except LU). For a constant number of processors, a biprocessor based platform costs about 0.6 times a uniprocessor based platform. Figure 6 shows that the global speed-up of the biprocessor based platform is higher than 0.6 for all benchmarks up to 8 nodes, except for LU with 8 nodes. So biprocessor based platforms provide a cost-effective alternative to uniprocessor based platforms.

4 CLUMPs Versus Proprietary Supercomputers

The previous sections compared the relative performance of 2-way multiprocessor PC based CLUMPs with uniprocessor PC based CLUMPs. Users are mainly interested by the absolute performance. In this section, we compare the performance of uniprocessor and biprocessor CLUMPs with the performance of proprietary parallel supercomputers for the same number of nodes.

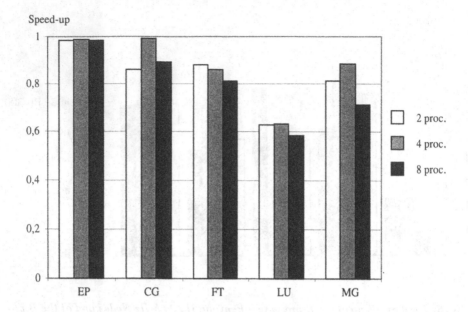

Fig. 6. *Global Speed-up of the Biprocessors over Uniprocessors for the NPB 2.3 Benchmarks and for the Same Number of Processors*

Figure 7 presents the performance 8 nodes platforms including the uniprocessor based CLUMP (called NOW), the biprocessor based CLUMP (called CLUMP) and the following parallel supercomputers for 8 nodes platforms:

- the SGI/CRAY T3E 900
- the SGI/CRAY T3E 1200
- the IBM SP2 with 66 MHz Power 2 processors
- the SGI Origin 2000 with 195 MHz processors
- the HP/Convex Exemplar SPP 2000
- the SUN Ultra Enterprise 4000

8 nodes CLUMPs use 400 MHz Pentium II processors. The figures for proprietary parallel computers come from the NAS NPB2.3 repository [11].

Figure 7 shows that performance of 8 nodes CLUMPS and performance of 8 nodes supercomputers have the same order of magnitude. In any case, no platform outperforms the other ones.

According to our measures, it is obvious that clusters of biprocessor PCs are a very cost effective solution for parallel computers, at least for small configurations. The results must be confirmed on actual applications.

Mflops

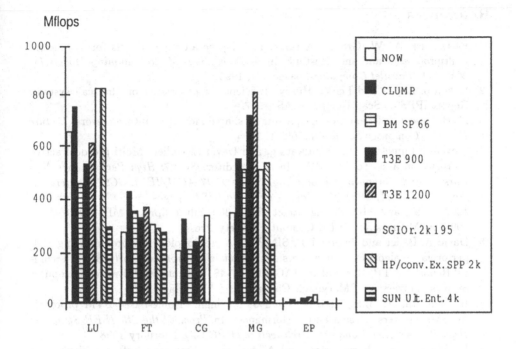

Fig. 7. *Performance of the CLUMPs and Some Parallel Supercomputer for the NAS NPB 2.3 Benchmark Suite with 8 Nodes*

5 Conclusion

In this paper, we have investigated the performance of a method based on HMM (hybrid memory model) for programming clusters of multiprocessors. This method requires the programmer to deal both with the message passing and the shared memory paradigms. It consists in the intra-node parallelization of the MPI programs by using an OpenMP directives based parallel compiler. We have presented a framework to select the loop to parallelize.

The intra-node speed-up for the NAS parallel benchmark is significantly lower than 2 (between 1.2 and 1.8 depending of the program for 400 MHz Pentium II nodes) except for EP. Moreover the speed-up can decrease with the number of nodes depending of the benchmark program features.

Although the method provides variable local speed-ups, it is much more practical than the manual parallelization approach to program the CLUMPs.

Finally, from the cost/performance point of view, biprocessors are a competitive alternative to uniprocessors as nodes of a PC based platform. This PC based platform is also a very cost effective alternative to proprietary parallel supercomputers, at least for small configurations.

References

1. E. L. Lusk W. W. Gropp. A taxonomy of programming models for symmetric multiprocessors and smp clusters. In *in Proceedings of Programming Models for Massively Parallel Computers*, pages 2–7, 1995.
2. Hakon o. Bugge and Per O. Husoy. Efficient sar processing on the scali system. Report IPPS97, Scali Computer AS, 1997.
3. M. Bernaschi. Efficient message passing on shared memory multiprocessors. *Lecture Notes in Computer Science*, 1156:221, 1996.
4. Steven S. Lumetta, Alan Mainwaring, and David E. Culler. Multi-protocol active messages on a cluster of SMPs. In ACM, editor, *SC'97: High Performance Networking and Computing: Proceedings of the 1997 ACM/IEEE SC97 Conference: November 15–21, 1997, San Jose, California, USA.*, pages ??–??, New York, NY 10036, USA and 1109 Spring Street, Suite 300, Silver Spring, MD 20910, USA, 1997. ACM Press and IEEE Computer Society Press.
5. David A. Bader and Joseph J J . SIMPLE: A methodology for programming high performance algorithms on clusters of symmetric multiprocessors (SMPs). Technical Report CS-TR-3798 and UMIACS-TR-97-48, Institute for Advanced Computer Studies, University of Maryland, College Park, MD, May 1997.
6. R. Samanta, A. Bilas, L. Iftode, and J. P. Singh. Home-based SVM protocols for SMP clusters: Design and performance. In *Proc. of the 4th IEEE Symp. on High-Performance Computer Architecture (HPCA-4)*, February 1998.
7. D. J. Scales, K. Gharachorloo, and A. Aggarwal. Fine-grain software distributed shared memory on SMP clusters. In *Proc. of the 4th IEEE Symp. on High-Performance Computer Architecture (HPCA-4)*, February 1998.
8. R. Stets, S. Dwarkadas, N. Hardavellas, G. Hunt, L. Kontothanassis, S. Parthasarathy, and Michael Scott. Cashmere-2L: Software coherent shared memory on a clustered remote-write network. In *Proc. of the 16th ACM Symp. on Operating Systems Principles (SOSP-16)*, October 1997.
9. Andrew Erlichson, Neal Nuckolls, Greg Chesson, and John Hennessy. SoftFLASH: Analyzing the performance of clustered distributed virtual shared memory. In *Proceedings of the Seventh International Conference on Architectural Support for Programming Languages and Operating Systems*, pages 210–220, Cambridge, Massachusetts, October 1–5, 1996. ACM SIGARCH, SIGOPS, SIGPLAN, and the IEEE Computer Society.
10. Charlie Hu Honghui Lu and Willy Zwaenepoel. Openmp on networks of workstations. In *Proc. of Super Computing 98*, Orlando, 1998.
11. NAS Parallel Benchmark Home page. http://science.nas.nasa.gov/software/npb/. Technical report.
12. M. Ando K. Kazuto Y. Tanaka, M. Matsuda and M. Sato. Compas: A pentium pro pc-based smp cluster and its experience. In *IPPS Workshop on Personal Computer Based Networks of Workstations*, pages 486–497. LNCS, 1998.

COOL Approach to Petaflops Computing

Mikhail Dorojevets

Dept. of Electrical and Computer Engineering

midor@ece.sunysb.edu

Abstract.

framework of the Hybrid Technology MultiThreaded architecture (HTMT) project. The objective of the current phase of the project is the proof-of-concept study of a computer that could be built with novel technologies such as RSFQ, optical networks, processors-in-memory, and holographic memory in order to achieve petaflops-level performance within a reasonable hardware and power budget by 2007. The COOL system design is based on a new multithreaded COOL-I architecture which supports two-level multithreading to hide latencies associated with memory and arithmetic operations in superconductor SPELL processors. Preliminary simulation results show that a COOL system with 4096 66-GHz processors can achieve petaflops-level performance on computationally-intensive parallel program kernels.

1 Introduction

Designing a system capable of achieving 10^{15} floating-point operations per second represents a real and daunting challenge to any computer designer. While an evolutionary approach to building such a petaflops computer by scaling current MPP teraflops systems implemented with CMOS technology seems to be a straightforward way to proceed, the resulting system would carry extremely high cost, power consumption, and system size tags. In the meantime, even if such a system of several hundred thousand processors were to be developed with traditional architectural approaches, with what kind of applications could it achieve an acceptable ratio of sustained to peak performance in order to justify the huge development costs? So, the question is whether there is any real need to worry about designing a petaflops system now when the current as well as the coming-soon CMOS technology will not be able to provide this almost 1000-fold leap in performance of current teraflops systems.

The answer to this question depends on the perspective. While a market-driven analysis says that there are no evident price-performance reasons to pursue this goal

initiating such a design process right now. This strategic approach to petaflops computing was clearly formulated in the 1998 President's Information Technology and Advisory Committee's (PITAC's) report [1] which concluded that:

- "…current scalable parallel high-end computing systems are not well suited to many applications of strategic importance to the nation;…"
- "…research should be focused on innovative architectures and devices that overcome the limitations of today's systems;…"
- "…research…can be effectively driven by an initiative to reach a petaflops by the year 2010."

2 HTMT Design Concept

Two years before PITAC's report was published, an ambitious research study called the Hybrid-Technology MultiThreaded architecture (HTMT)[1] project was initiated to develop and evaluate a new approach that would allow the first petaflops system to be built by 2005-2007 [2]. The HTMT design approach tries to solve both technological and architectural problems simultaneously. First, emerging electronic and

power consumption low. Second, a new architectural paradigm that changes the traditional role functions of processors and memory is being developed in order to tolerate huge disparities in processor and memory speeds in a petaflops system.

The target HTMT system has a hierarchical organization where each system level represents a distributed shared memory (DSM) subsystem with its own types of processors, memory, and interfaces to adjacent levels. The shared memory space visible to a processor of any subsystem includes the subsystem's memory as well as the memory of the adjacent system layer(s). This general definition leaves the question of the number of levels and the specific technologies used to implement each level open, thus allowing for flexibility in possible system implementations. What is crucial, however, is the availability of the HTMT execution model that is not bound to any technology, and meanwhile, highly effective in hiding communication and synchronization latencies within a multi-technology HTMT system where the relative speeds of processor and memory components can differ by 5-6 orders of magnitude.

The current HTMT system (Figure 1) has several levels of processing and main memory: a COOL[2] (sub)system consisting of superconductor RSFQ SPELL processors with cryo-memory (CRAM) interconnected by a cryo-network (CNET) [3]; semiconductor processors embedded in static and dynamic memories (S-PIMs and D-PIMs, respectively) [4]. Among all the processors, S-PIMs are the only processors which have direct access to all levels of the main memory hierarchy. This makes the SRAM subsystem a natural place where operating/runtime system functions can be performed.

An optical Data Vortex (DV) network [5] provides communication between the S-PIM and the D-PIM system layers as well as external I/O devices. Data storage is augmented with holographic photo-refractive memory (HRAM) connected directly to D-PIMs [6].

---

[1] The HTMT project and the work described in the paper are supported by DARPA, NSA, NASA via Jet Propulsion Lab., and in part by NSF under grant No. ECS-9700313.
[2] COOL acronym stands for Concurrency Out Of Limits.

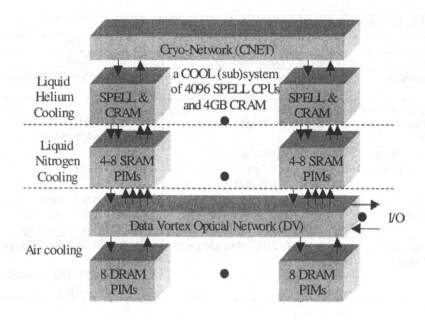

Fig. 1. The HTMT system block diagram

3 RSFQ Superconductor Technology

The superconductor RSFQ technology has two features, ultra-high speed and very low power dissipation, that make it a very attractive choice for implementing number-crunching SPELL processors. It is well known that previous attempts to exploit these properties of superconductor Josephson junction (JJ) devices to build a superconductor computer in the USA and Japan in the 1980s failed. However, since then, new superconductor materials such as niobium-trilayer have emerged, and a new RSFQ approach to signal coding and processing based on quantization of magnetic field in superconductor loops [7] has been developed. These developments raised a hope that a new attempt to build the first superconductor RSFQ processor will be more successful than the previous ones. Table 1 shows the state-of-the art of RSFQ technology at the end of the 1990s.

The current RSFQ logic family consists of the following elements:

- microstrip transmission lines (MSL) with ballistic propagation of 2mV picosecond pulses with velocity of the ~0.4 speed of light in vacuum over passive Nb wires;
- clocked gates (state elements): RS, D, T flip-flops, inverter, exclusive OR (XOR), Muller's C-element;

Table 1. The state-of-the-art of the RSFQ technolgy in 1999

Time	~10-15 years ago	1999
Logic	Latching logic	RSFQ
Materials	Soft: lead alloys	rigid: niobium with aluminum oxide
Logic features: a) binary signal coding b) switching between '0' and '1' c) clock and data signals	a) voltage levels b) non-symmetric: $T_{'0' \to '1'} = 1.5$ ps $T_{'1' \to '0'} = 100\text{-}300\ T_{'0' \to '1'}$ c) clock signal power >> data signal power; periodic reset with RF supply	a) pulses: 2 mV pulse /no pulse in clock window b) symmetric: 1 ps (0.25 µ m) c) no difference in power of data and clock signals, no need for RF power supply
Max. speed achieved	Up to 6 GHz for single gates	a) up to 770 GHz for T-trigger (0.25 µ m) b) 30 GHz (AC/DC converters of ~2K JJs (3.5 µ m)

- non-clocked (stateless) elements: 1-to-2 splitter (forks one pulse into two), 2-to-1 merger (merges pulses from 2 inputs into 1 output), Josephson transmission line (JTL) built with JJ loops providing current/power gain, MSL transceivers and receivers.

Our projections of the expected characteristics of 0.8-µm RSFQ circuits are based on our experimental designs manufactured in 3.5 µm technology as well as the RSFQ scaling rules confirmed in experiments with 1.5 µm and 0.25 µm devices. They show that 0.8-µm RSFQ circuits may have the following characteristics:

Logic:
- 1M Josephson Junctions/cm^2;
- impedance matching with microstrip transmission lines;
- 10 ps per individual 'clocked' gate with ~200-250 nW power dissipation;
- 15 ps per functional unit pipeline stage (~66 GHz pipeline clock rate);
- 160 GHz transfer rate with a bus-like switch built with non-clocked elements;

Memory:
- RSFQ address decoders, SFQ data matrices with latching/dc drivers;
- 33 GHz pipelined CRAM chips with ~ 120-150 ps read access time;
- 3M Josephson Junctions/cm^2;
- 0.002 µW power dissipation per memory bit when operating at a 33-GHz rate;

Microstrip transmission lines:
- ~200-300 GHz transmission rate of a FIFO- "pulse train" via a on-chip MSL;
- 33 GHz off-chip transmission rate on a cryo multi-chip module.

4 Key Challenges in Ultra-Gigahertz RSFQ Design

Based on the above projections, we can conclude that a COOL system of 4096 66-GHz SPELL processors[3] each with 4 floating-point pipelined functional units implemented with 0.8 μm RSFQ technology can achieve a peak performance of one petaflops. Sustained performance depends on many factors including: applications characteristics; data storage capacity, latency and bandwidth; an instruction set architecture and processor organization; parallel (micro)task management overhead and resource contention. Among these factors the problem of memory latency tolerance is the most challenging.

The roots of this problem lie in the difficulties of building a large and dense pipelined memory in RSFQ technology. The first reason is the RSFQ way of representing non-zero signals with short pulses rather than voltage levels. This makes it impossible to build memory arrays in a traditional way when inputs or outputs of multiple memory cells along a column are connected to the same wire. Although this interconnect problem can be solved by using additional split and merge elements, the resulting memory array is not as dense as it would be if a voltage-driven logic had been used[4].

The second reason can be considered typical for any multi-gigahertz technology, not just RSFQ. The problem is that a signal (pulse) propagation time within a memory array effectively determines the minimum clock period of the RSFQ memory pipeline. During 1 ps an RSFQ pulse can travel approximately 12.5 μm across a mictrostrip transmission line in 0.8-μm technology. This forces us to restrict the maximum size of any memory (sub)array to 128x128 bits if we need to support a 33 GHz memory access rate. This solution makes each memory chip have many relatively small subarrays and lots of wires providing separate data and clock

the area of a whole CRAM chip to the area that would be consumed by the array of cells of the same total density) will be definitely higher compared to that we would see in slower silicon SRAM/DRAM memory chips of the same capacity.

This analysis leads us to the conclusion that any superconductor system such as COOL will have to use its relatively small CRAM only as temporary storage (e.g., a software-or hardware-controlled cache), while its main memory will have to be silicon SRAM. An SRAM access time (3 ns in 2007 according to SIA roadmap [9]) is at least one order of magnitude larger than that of CRAM. Ribbon cables between a cryostat (where a COOL system will be immersed in liquid helium) and the SRAM subsystem can give additional 10-12 ns contribution to the total round-trip SRAM access delay. The existence of the 15-ns SRAM delay visible to any SPELL means that we need a technique allowing memory latencies of up to 1,000 66-GHz SPELL processor cycles to be tolerated.

---

[3] options, and the approach allowing for a combination of locally-synchronized blocks and asynchronous communication among them seems to be the most viable.

[4] use RSFQ logic only for address decoding at peripheral parts of memory chips and switch to a voltage-level signal representation when accessing a (non-RSFQ) memory array.

Besides the SRAM latency, the SPELL processor latencies related to arithmetic and CRAM load/store operations can be up to 100 cycles. The pipeline is so deep because it has to be built with clocked RSFQ elements which are used to implement almost any Boolean operation in RSFQ. In order to explore the enormous speed of these elements, however, a clock must be distributed to each clocked gate in the pipeline[5]. Thus, we can conclude that while RSFQ logic saves a lot of latches that would be necessary in the CMOS pipeline design, it requires additional clock distribution wires. How much these savings in latches (hardware budget) outweigh losses in "useful" layout area due to this additional clock wiring depends on many factors, and first of all on the number of metallization levels available on chips.

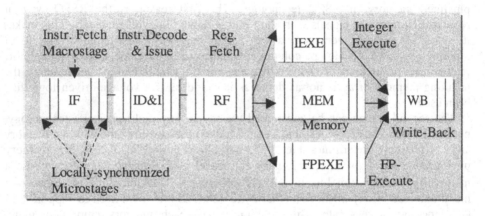

Fig. 2. Logical structure of the SPELL ultrapipelined datapath

A SPELL RSFQ pipeline (Fig. 2) consists of macrostages similar in function to traditional RISC processor stages. Any macrostage consists of several microstages, each of the latter typically including one clocked gate, non-clocked components, and transmission lines. The timing and other characteristics of a RSFQ macrostage are given in Equations 1, 2, 3, and Table 2.

$$Cycle\ time\ (CT)_{macrostage} \approx t_{cgsetup} + t_{cghold} + t_{Signal\ skew/microstage} \qquad (1)$$

$$Latency_{macrostage} \approx n_{clg} \times CT_{macrostage} + n_{non\_clg} \times t_{ncg\_delay} + L_{ms}/v \qquad (2)$$

$$Microstages/Macrostage = n_{clg} + (n_{non\_clg} \times t_{ncg\_delay} + L_{mtl}/v)/CT_{macrostage}, \qquad (3)$$

---

[5] Although an asynchronous design approach with dual-rail logic is also an option, we have found that it would require almost twice as much hardware as well as longer latency compared to a single-rail approach with locally-synchronized pipeline stages.

Table 2. RSFQ macrostage parameters

Parameter	Description	Projected value for 0.8 µm technology
$t_{cgsetup}$	the setup time for clocked gates	3 ps
t_{cghold}	the hold time for clocked gates	3 ps
t_{ncg_delay}	the delay of non-clocked gates	3 ps
$t_{Signal\ skew/microstage}$	the clock/data signal skew in a microstage	9 ps for an adder
n_{clg}	a number of clocked gates in a microstage critical path	4-50
n_{non_clg}	a number of non-clocked gates in a microstage critical path	4-8
V	the pulse propagation speed across MSL	~ 12.5 µm/1 ps
L_{msl}	a physical length of MSLs in a macrostage critical path	

The total number of microstages in the SPELL pipeline (Eq.3) represents the number of independent instructions to be in the pipeline in order to achieve its peak performance. It is well known, however, that the required level of parallelism (an order of 100 independent instructions) could be found almost exclusively in scientific programs with loops working on regularly-structured data objects. Thus, the capability of issuing multiple instructions during loop processing is a critical requirement for RSFQ processors.

The solutions for 66-GHz RSFQ processors, however, cannot be the same as those for superscalar or VLIW processors. The lack of a global clock makes the lock-step synchronization of execution of multiple instructions in very deep SPELL pipelines extremely difficult and, as a result, the implementation of compiler-controlled, synchronous VLIW computation unrealistic. The complexity of even moderate multi-way superscalar implementation is also prohibitive in 0.8 µm RSFQ technology.

5 COOL Multithreaded Architecture and Related Work

The COOL system design is based on a new parallel 64-bit COOL-I instruction set architecture with support for two-level multithreading [10]. Two-levels of multithreading are used to hide two different types of latencies in the COOL system.

The SRAM-SPELL communication latency of up to 1,000 SPELL cycles can be hidden with the assistance of latency-tolerance mechanisms in the HTMT percolation model of execution [11]. The percolation model relies on programming languages with explicit thread control, smart compilers, and effective runtime system running on SRAM and DRAM PIMs. According to the model, the runtime system starts the execution of a threaded program at the SRAM/DRAM levels. The execution of a threaded function is represented by a system object called a parcel that encapsulates the function code and all data needed to start and complete execution of the function without further references to other data or functions (Fig.3).

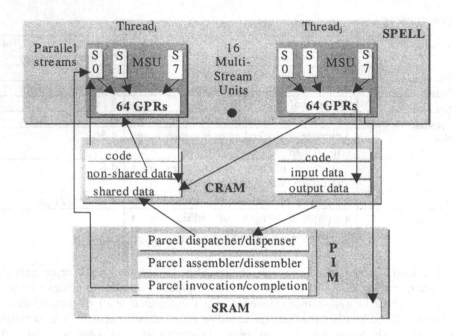

Fig. 3. Two-level multithreading in COOL-I architecture

The runtime system controls program execution by creating and moving parcels through processing levels of the HTMT hierarchical system. The percolation of a thread into a CRAM region of an associated SPELL processor involves the creation of the thread's CRAM memory context and the assignment of a free processor multistream unit (MSU) to execute the thread. Sixteen independent multistream units allow each SPELL processor to run up to 16 threads simultaneously.

The benefits of the percolation for the COOL system are due to two reasons. First, execution of any COOL thread (i.e., processing its COOL parcel by MSU) in general requires no references to data/code outside its local and remote CRAM modules.[6] Second, the percolation process allows for overlapping the computation in SPELLs with creating and loading new parcels into CRAM by PIMs.

To be successful, however, any SRAM/DRAM PIM implementation of the percolation model must keep the overhead of the runtime parcel management low enough. As usual, the best practical approach could be a combination of percolation with some traditional program control mechanisms with fewer overheads. The predecessors of the percolation model can be clearly seen in the active messages [12] concepts.

While the thread creation and percolation mechanisms are outside the scope of the COOL architecture, the second level of the COOL multithreading called multistreaming is the primary technique of hiding latencies inside SPELL processors

---

[6] The beginning/completion of thread execution can require synchronization operations to be performed on objects in local SRAM memory.

and CRAM. Compared to threads, streams are "lighter", and their creation does not involve the runtime system[7]. Any stream can create another stream by executing a single "create stream" operation. Stream communication and synchronization occurs via shared registers as well as CRAM.

The technique of two-level simultaneous multithreading was first implemented in the VLIW processors of the Russian MARS-M multithreaded computer built in the 1980s [13]. Several commercial high-performance computers using interleaved multithreading, such as HEP [14], and Tera [15], were built in the 1980s and the 1990s, and multithreading was the focus of several research projects [16], [17], [18].

The distinguishing features of our design approach are as follows:

1. Two-level multithreading has to be implemented in multi-gigahertz ultrapipelined SPELL processors where each (coarse-grain) thread has its own register file shared by all (medium-grain) parallel instruction streams (e.g., representing parallel loop iterations) created inside the thread. A total of up to 128 parallel instruction streams can simultaneously issue instructions and run in each SPELL processor.
2. The hardware supports flexible partitioning of each register file into variable-size register frames assigned to instruction streams and provides relative and absolute register addressing at run time. As a result, different instruction streams running simultaneously within the same processor can use a single copy of the program code.
3. Streams executing within the same thread can use general-purpose and special registers for very fast communication and synchronization. Data and control hazards are resolved with the assistance of scoreboard logic.
4. The architecture is scalable in the sense that it does not limit the number of streams/general-purpose registers per MSU.

The 64-bit COOL-I ISA (currently consisting of 85 instructions) has the following instructions groups:

- a traditional RISC core of load/store, logic, integer and floating-point arithmetic operations including fused FP multiply-add;
- bit-field and bit-matrix operations such pack/unpack, bit matrix multiply, and etc;
- stream control and synchronization operations such as create/quit stream, merge streams, (register) barrier, and etc.
- memory atomic read-modify operations such as swap, compare & set, and etc.

There are neither traps nor privileged instructions because any supervisor-type actions are to be performed by PIMs. The primary focus of COOL ISA is fast computing coupled with latency tolerance. This is in accordance with the HTMT execution model in which the computation process is driven by smart memory rather than fast RSFQ processors, thus forcing SPELLs to be humble servants of S-PIMs.

---

[7] More exactly, to start execution of a thread on an assigned MSU, an S-PIM sends the MSU an "awake" message containing the thread's initial instruction address in CRAM. Upon reception of the awake message, the MSU hardware creates a master stream 0 which begins the thread execution and if necessary creates other streams. This is the only time when a stream is to be created by an S-PIM operation.

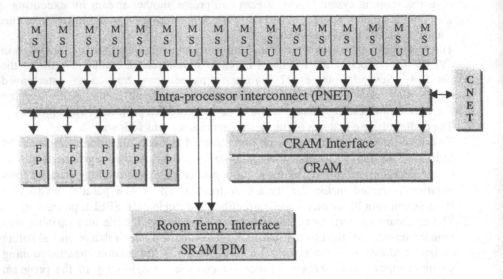

Fig. 4. The SPELL processor diagram

6 SPELL Multistream Organization

Figure 4 shows a block diagram of the proposed SPELL processor. SPELL has 16 multistream units (MSUs), 5 pipelined floating-point units (FPUs) operating with an average cycle time of 15 ps, and an 8-ported pipelined CRAM with a 30 ps cycle time. MSUs can communicate with the shared floating-point functional units and a processor-memory interface via an intra-processor interconnect (PNET).

Each MSU executes control, integer, and floating-point compare operations of up to eight parallel instruction streams. All parallel streams inside one MSU share:

- a 2KB multi-port instruction cache,
- a 64-bit integer arithmetic unit,
- a 32-bit instruction address adder,
- a PNET interface unit,
- 64 general-purpose registers (each of which is able to hold either 64-bit long integer or double-precision floating-point data).

Logically, the 64 general-purpose registers are partitioned into one set of global registers and multiple sets (one per stream) of local stream registers. Each such set is called a register frame. There can be one global frame starting from register 0 and up to eight local register frames. Partitioning of an MSU register file is done using eight (one per stream) frame base (FB) registers each specifying a starting frame address.

When creating a stream, the MSU hardware loads the stream's program counter (PC) and FB registers with specified values.

Any stream instruction can access global and local registers using two modes of register addressing: absolute and relative to the stream's FB register. Each stream can work with registers from the global frame, the stream's local frame, and remote registers from other local frames if the difference between the remote register numbers and the stream's FB value is less than 32. In the case of loops with recurrences, the capability of accessing registers from other local frames enables direct access to registers holding values calculated/loaded from memory during prior loop iterations.

All types of register dependencies (flow, anti- and output) among instructions belonging to one or different streams are enforced by scoreboard logic that sets/clears a Wait bit associated with each register. Also, execution of parallel streams can be synchronized using register-level barrier operations and/or atomic "compare & set" memory operations.

Non-shared hardware reserved for each stream includes an instruction fetch unit, an instruction decode/issue unit, 4 condition registers, and reservation stations where operations wait for their operands to become ready before issuing them to integer/floating-point units and memory.

All the units within MSU are pipelined and have a 15-ps cycle time (for 0.8-μm technology). Although the performance of any individual stream is limited by this 15-ps cycle (equivalent to a 66-GHz "clock" rate), other logic providing access to shared resources (registers and units) inside MSU can work at a much higher rate of up to 160 GHz.

Each SPELL has an eight-ported, 1 MB pipelined CRAM module to be implemented with 4 dual-port 256 KB chips. CRAM is based on Josephson junction technology, using both RSFQ and dc-biased latching circuits. Our estimates show that the memory chip pipeline can be built with four 30-ps stages. The peak CRAM bandwidth is eight 64-bit words per 30-ps cycle, i.e., more than 2 TB/s.

Communication between each SPELL/CRAM module and local SRAM is provided through a room-temperature interface with two ports (in and out) consisting of almost 1K signal and 1K ground wires and 8-10 Gb/s bandwidth per each signal wire. This gives a bandwidth of one 64-bit data (with additional bits for address and control) packet every 30 ps, i.e., ~512 GB/s in each direction.

SPELL communicates with remote CRAM/SRAM modules through RSFQ CNET to be implemented either as a Banyan network or a multi-dimensional pruned mesh with the peak data bandwidth of each input and output CNET port of ~ 256 GB/s. The average CNET latency visible to any SPELL is close to 18 ns for the analyzed COOL system implementation with a physical size of almost 1m in each direction [19]. The dominant contribution to the latency is the signal propagation time (~1cm/80ps for 0.8 μm RSFQ technology) across CNET. The minimum CNET latency (between SPELLs mounted on the same multichip module) is close to 1 ns.

Physically, each processing module (SPELL with 1MB CRAM) could be implemented as a set of seven 2x2 cm^2 chips. The chips are expected to be flip-chip mounted on a 20×20-cm^2 multi-chip module (CMCM), physically a silicon wafer with 2 layers of 3-μm wide superconducting microstrip lines. Each CMCM houses more than 60 chips, including 8 processing modules plus 5 CNET chips. A COOL system having 512 CMCMs would occupy a volume of less than 1 m^3.

Even with the current conservative estimates, the overall power load of the RSFQ COOL system at 4 Kelvin is about 1 kW. With the present-day efficiency of helium cooling, this leads to a total room-temperature power of approximately 300 kW. This number is almost two orders of magnitude smaller than that for a hypothetical petaflops system implemented with any prospective semiconductor transistor technology.

7   Performance Analysis: Preliminary Results

The peak performance of a SPELL processor with five floating-point units operating with 15-ps cycle time is more than 300 Gflops. Theoretically, up to eight instructions can be issued by 8 stream instruction decode/issue units and three instructions (control, integer arithmetic, and load/floating-point) can be completed in one cycle in each of 16 MSUs inside SPELL. The real performance depends on pipeline implementation, instruction mix, and data/control hazards.

We analyzed performance on a simple parallel program calculating an inner product of two vectors in CRAM. Our objective was to estimate the best integer and sustained performance we can achieve on a kernel of this program when all 8 streams are working in parallel. The following 16-threaded implementations of a 66-GHz SPELL processor have been analyzed:

- simultaneous (asynchronous) multistreaming with 8 parallel streams, 64 registers per MSU, 66-GHz Banyan intra processor networks with credit-based flow control, and 5 FP units per SPELL (SMS/64),
- interleaved (synchronous) multistreaming with 8 streams with 64 registers per MSU, 160-GHz synchronous bus-like switches without buffering, and 8 FP units per SPELL (IMS/64),
- interleaved (synchronous) multistreaming with 8 parallel streams, 160-GHz switches, and 88 registers allowing us to unroll the kernel twice in order to increase the frequency of floating-point operations to 33%, and 8 FP units per SPELL (IMS/88).

Figure 5 shows the maximum sustained performance we could achieve on this inner product kernel. The performance of the interleaved schemes based on 160-GHz instructions/data dispatch switches is better than that of the SMT one due to an almost two-fold increase in the instruction issue rate inside each stream. But these benefits do not go without price. When analyzing the IMS schemes, we placed two MSUs and a floating-point unit on same chip, i.e., in fact made each such chip a fully-fledged RSFQ microprocessor capable of running two threads, each with 8 parallel streams. A 2x2 cm^2 chip in 0.8 µm technology can have up to 4M Josephson junctions, an amount equivalent to more than 1M CMOS transistors. We think, however, that a 0.4 µm RSFQ technology would be a better choice for such IMS designs.

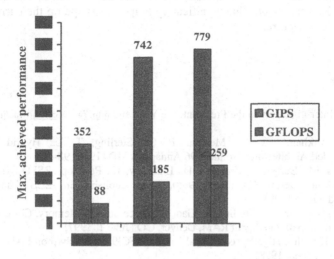

Fig. 5. The SPELL processor performance on the inner-product kernel

8 Conclusions

Our preliminary study shows that the design of superconductor processors for a petaflops computer will not be a joy ride, and will require significant effort and investment. However, the first results make us cautiously optimistic because at this stage we have not discovered any stumbling blocks on the way toward a compact petaflops superconductor subsystem with very low power consumption. We are carrying out simulations of the processor and system components on several levels. In particular, we are prototyping and measuring critical parameters of RSFQ circuits built with the commercially available 3.5-μm fabrication technology, as well as evaluating processor performance with simulation models. During HTMT Phase 3 that starts in the summer of 1999, we plan to design and evaluate a prototype of an integer multistream unit with 1.5 μm RSFQ technology.

Acknowledgements

This work is done jointly with a research team from the Physics Dept. of SUNY at Stony Brook, which has been working successfully on the development of RSFQ technology for many years. Without their team efforts and especially contributions from Konstantin Likharev, Dmitry Zinoviev, and Paul Bunyk the design and analysis of the RSFQ subsystem for petaflops computer would be impossible. I would also gratefully acknowledge very useful discussions with Burton Smith, Thomas Sterling, and other HTMT colleagues that significantly helped to shape up the current version of the COOL architecture.

References

1. PITAC - Interim Report to the President, see Web site http://www.ccic.gov/ac/interim/ (Aug. 6, 1998)
2. Gao, G., Likharev, K. K., Messina, P. C., Sterling, T. L.: Hybrid Technology Multithreaded Architecture. Frontiers'96 Annapolis MD (1996) 98–105
3. Dorojevets, M., Bunyk, P., Zinoviev, D., Likharev, K.: Petaflops RSFQ System Design. ASC'98, Palm Desert, CA (Sept. 1998), to be published in IEEE Trans. on Appl. Supercond. (June 1999)
4. Kogge, P., Brockman, J., Sterling, T., Gao, G.: Processing-In-Memory: Chips to Petaflops. ISCA Workshop on Intelligent RAM, Denver, CO (June 1, 1997)
5. Bergman, K.: Ultra-High Speed Optical LANs. OFC'98 Workshop on LANs and WANs, San Jose, CA (Feb. 1998)
6. Psaltis, D., Mok, F.: Holographic Memories. Scientific American, Vol. 273 (1995) 70-76
7. Likharev, K., Semenov, V.: RSFQ Logic/Memory Family: A New Josephson Junction Technology for Sub-Terahertz Clock Frequency Digital Systems. IEEE Trans. Appl. Supercond. Vol. 1 (March 1991) 3-28
8. Nagasawa, S., Hashimoto, Y., Numata, H., Tahara, S.: A 380-ps, 9.5 mW Josephson 4-Kbit RAM Operated at High Bit Yield. IEEE Trans. Appl. Supercond., Vol. 5, (March 1995) 2447-2250
9. National Technology Roadmap for Semiconductors. Semiconductor Industry Association, see Web site http://notes.sematech.org/mcpgs/roadmap4.pdf, San Jose, CA (1997)
10. Dorojevets, M.: The COOL-I ISA Handbook: Version 1.00. TR-11, RSFQ System Group, SUNY at Stony Brook (Jan. 1999)
11. Gao, G.R., Amaral, J.N., Marquez, A., Theobald, K.: A Refinement of the HTMT Program Execution Model. TR-TM22, CAPSL, University of Delaware, Newark, DE (July 1998)
12. von Eicken, T.D., Culler, D.E., Goldstein, S.C., Schauser, K.E.: Active Messages: A Mechanism for Integrated Communication and Computation. ISCA-19, Gold Coast, Australia (May 1992) 256-266
13. Dorojevets, M., Wolcott, P.: The El'brus-3 and MARS-M: Recent Advances in Russian High Performance Computing. J. Supercomputing, Vol. 6. (1992) 5-48
14. Smith, B.: Architecture and Applications of the HEP Multiprocessor Computer System. SPIE Real Time Signal Processing IV, SPIE, New York (1981) 241-248
15. Tera: Principles of Operation. Tera Computer Company (1997)
16. Hirata, H., Kimura, K., Nagamine, S., Mochizuki, Y., Nishimura, A., Nakase, Y., Nishizava, T.: An Elementary Processor Architecture with Simultaneous Instruction Issuing from Multiple Threads. ISCA-15, Los Alamitos, CA: IEEE Comput. Soc Press, (1988) 443-451
17. Dally, W.J., Keckler, S.W., Carter, N., Chang, A., Fillo, M., Lee, W.S.: M-Machine Architecture v 1.0. Concurrent VLSI Architecture TM-58, MIT, Cambridge, MA, (1994)
18. Eggers, S.J., Emer, J.S., Levy, H.M., Lo, J.L., Stamm, R.L., Tullsen D.M.: Simultaneous Multithreading: A Platform for Next-Generation Processors. IEEE Micro. J., Vol. 17 (Sept/Oct. 1997) 12-19
19. Wittie, W., Zinoviev, D., Sazaklis, G., Likharev, K.:CNET: RSFQ Switching Network for Petaflops Computing. ASC'98, Palm Desert, CA (Sept. 1998), to be published in IEEE Trans. on Appl. Supercond. (June 1999)

Hardware and Software Optimizations for Multimedia Databases

Bernard Goossens[1], Hassane Essafi[2], and Marc Pic[2]

[1] LIAFA, Université Paris 7, 2 place Jussieu, Paris Cedex 05, France
bg@liafa.jussieu.fr,
[2] LETI (CEA – Technologies Avancées)
DEIN – CE/Saclay
91191 Gif-sur-Yvette Cedex, France
Marc.Pic@cea.fr

Abstract. In this paper[1], we show that both software and hardware must be organized around a hierarchy of communications to perform well on todays multiprocessor machines. We classify data into three categories: the sedentary ones, the nomadic ones and the migrating ones. We show that the applications and the chips they are run on should concentrate on communications involving mainly sedentary and nomadic data, avoiding as much as possible to use migrations. Eventually, we present TiPi2, an on-chip multiprocessor particularly designed to this purpose.

1 Introduction

Two decades ago, a memory access was as fast as an ALU operation, i.e. roughly one CPU cycle. The consequence was that computation, storage in main memory and communication on a bus had an equal speed cost making the simple UMA multiprocessor model attractive. In the late 80's, the storage speed had to be divided into two categories: cache speed and main memory speed. Caches helped to keep communication speed close to computation speed in the COMA multiprocessor model. Today, we are entering the third generation due to the fact that on-chip caches make the off-chip communication speed far slower than the on-chip cache speed. This seems to limit the interest of the COMA approach in the current context. By splitting the communications in two sets, with on one side the local communications and on the other side the distant ones, we apply to communications the pattern that was applied the previous decade to memory access. Frequent local communications have to remain on-chip to keep fast. Distant communications must cross chip boundaries, hence must remain rare. To achieve this, the parallel programs must be organized to favour local communications as sequential programs are today being organized to favour data locality. Also, the processor chip architecture must evolve to allow local communications.

---

[1] Works partly done with the support of STRETCH, european project ESPRIT HPCN number 24977.

In this paper, we present the implications of such a goal on a sample application dealing with automatic document recognition, storage and retrieval ; we describe an on-chip multiprocessor (in short, a CMP [10] [6]) architecture that provides single cycle computation operators (thanks to pipelining), single cycle memory access (thanks to on-chip caches) and single cycle inter-processor communication (thanks to multiple on-chip processors). This section presents the parallel aspects of the sample application. The second section describes a parallel programming extension to C++ based on threads and named C_T++ and exhibits its task and data parallelism. The third section presents the main features of TiPi2, the proposed CMP architecture designed to give a good on-chip performance.

In the context of an european ESPRIT project, called STRETCH, we are involved in developing a system capable of storing and retrieving imaged documents by their pictural content. The system will allow users to search document databases with a series of techniques oriented on three main categories : texts, images and structures and some minor categories. It includes various Archival and Retrieval Engines (ARE). Each original document is analysed to produce information blocks which are themselves processed and archived in separate databases with appropriate links between the information blocks. Each query provided by end-users is decomposed in relations between basic queries corresponding to the previous categories. Each basic query is processed by the specific database to match the corresponding primitives. Specific answers are composed to produce a multi-ordered list of documents matching the query.

High-performance Algorithms involved in STRETCH Multimedia Databases.

- **Automatic Analysis**: low-level image processing for unskewing the original document, filtering to improve the quality, automatic segmentation [2], OCR[9]. The Document Enhancement process involves data-parallel programming based on images as primitive data structures (arrays of pixels). Each filtering can be considered as a very SIMD data-parallel program based on the pixels of the image, but the various filters can be applied concurrently, adding a SPMD task-parallelism over the data-parallelism.
- **Image Archiving**: content based retrieval requests specific indexing techniques allowing to deal with efficient data representations (reduced amount of data adapted to content based retrieval) in order to avoid prohibitive low level processing time on queries. Parallelism involved in this phase requires to be able to manage an irregular grid[7].
- **Text Archiving**: the text indexing engine retained for STRETCH is called SPIRIT [4], it is based on a Natural Language Processing (NLP) facility and allows the indexing of multilingual documents in free language. Parallelism is based on a tree decomposition of the relations between words in analysed statements and on multiple queries handling.
- **Structure Archiving**: text components of structured documents are divided into formal sections (titles, footnotes, ...) and content-bearing sections. Irregular processing is necessary.

- **Multimedia Queries**: the system splits the question in basic queries for the various primitive components of the database (texts, images, structures,...). Primitive component queries are matched separetely, introducing a client-server parallelism, and the results are merged to provide the final answers.

To summarize this section, the STRETCH application contains both task and data parallelism. A pure SIMD machine would perform poorly on task parallelism. A Network of Workstations (NOW) machine would perform poorly on data parallelism. A multiprocessor allowing both task and data parallelism is required if a high performance is needed.

2 Software Support for High-Performance Computing

Time critical aspects of the STRETCH projects implementation are developped using a specific compilation/library tool dedicated to exploit the various forms of parallelism required by the algorithms. This development tool is called C_T++ and has been originally conceived in collaboration between CEA and IRISA [1].

```
/* computation of an histogram */
TENSOR<INT8> ImageBW(512,512); /*input image*/
TENSOR<INT16> Histo(256)=0; /*histogram*/
/*parallel histogram computation in CT++ */
        Histo(ImageBW)++;
```

The concept of C_T++ is based on [3],[8] and [11] and is composed of 2 levels, one dedicated to data-parallelism and one dedicated to task-parallelism. Those 2 levels are hierarchically embedded in a common syntactic form in which data-parallel levels can be nested in task-parallel levels, like in Wavelet Transform example. Since C++ does not include Fortran90-like array operations, they are provided through a library based on 4 object classes and 2 special functions:
— **object classes:**
SECTION: defines a set of integer values characterized by an affine function (begin, end, stride). They represent iterations on parallelized dimensions:
SECTION J(1,10,2); corresponds to the set {1,3,5,7,9})
SHAPE: tensorial product of **SECTION**s and details the geometrical shape of parallel variables : number of dimensions, sizes of dimensions: **SHAPE** S(I,J);
TENSOR: distributed containers of data. Variants of regular arrays (like mesh, trees,...) extend the containers to more irregular data-structures able to be managed in a data-parallel mode.
FUNCTOR : **FUNCTOR**s represent independent scalar or parallel functions or methods able to be task-parallelized.
— **special functions:**
elemental: serves to promote a scalar function with scalar arguments to a data-parallel one with conformal parallel arrays as arguments.
nodal: serves to concurrently launch several **FUNCTOR**s.
Data accesses in **TENSOR** can be of three different types: a point of scalar coordinates, an affine sub-part or an indirect access.

We classify the data handled by $C_T{++}$ into three types:

sedentary data: data used by a single thread. For example, a local computation in data-parallel mode: A = B + C; where A, B and C are conform tensors handled by the same thread.

nomadic data: data used by neighbour threads. Two threads are defined as neighbours as a tractation between the limited number of threads on-chip and the volume of data they share, like in such standard filtering code:
A[I] = a*B[I+1]+b*B[I]+c*B[I-1];

migrating data: data used either by a large number of threads or by non-neighbour ones. An example of migrating data can be found in a reduction operation: a += B * C; the scalar a receives the sum of all the points in the tensor product of B by C. If B and C are large enough, it is more efficient to parallelize the computation of the reduction with a binary tree of threads. If the threads on the same height of the tree can be linearly ordered fixing the neighbourhood pattern, it is not possible to prolongate this pattern across height levels. Hence, data used by two threads having different heights can be migrating ones.

3 The TiPi2 Architecture

3.1 A High Performance CMP Architecture

To process n threads in a single processing chip machine we can either use time sharing (an on-Chip Single Processor or CSP) or multiprocessing (an on-Chip Multiple Processor or CMP). The CSP solution is not efficient because sequential execution is used instead of parallel execution. Task-parallelism is not exploited. Moreover, data sharing may lead to unceasing off-chip accesses due to cache pollution induced by time-sharing. The CMP solution can be implemented in at least three different ways:

- Maximal duplication: a single processor is fully duplicated n times on-chip. Threads have to communicate through a shared second level data cache (to avoid off-chip communications).
- Minimal duplication: only the register file and the PC-register are duplicated (this is very close to the SMT [12] architecture). Threads communicate through the single data cache.
- Intermediate duplication: only the set of functional units and the data cache are shared. Two threads may communicate through the shared data cache.

The maximal duplication has two major drawbacks: some rarely used operators are uselessly duplicated and the L1 (level 1) data caches have to be kept coherent which is not good for scalability. The minimal duplication is very close to the CSP architecture. The only difference is that thread interleaving is coarse-grain for the CSP and fine-grain for the SMT. But the set of resources is sized for a single thread, the multiple threads sharing it. The SMT architecture is more devoted to maximize resources utilization than to maximize multiple threads execution performance. The intermediate duplication offers the advantage to provide both parallel resources and shared ones. The shared resources serve two goals: fast inter-thread communications and chip area saving which helps to maximize the number of on-chip duplications.

The TiPi2 architecture is an intermediate duplication CMP.

3.2 The Tipi2 General Structure

The performance of a CMP chip is a function of the number of processors it contains, their respective IPC and the shared cycle. Of these three parameters, the cycle should be favoured to highly pipeline the operators. This helps to reduce the set of functional units, the pipelining acting as an operator duplication. Then we should maximize the number of processors on chip. In this respect, scalable structures are essential. The IPC is the least important of the three parameters in contrast with the usage in traditional CSP design. Nevertheless, it should remain reasonably high, essentially by using speculative and out-of-order execution.

The only part of the pipeline that has to be shared by all the on-chip processors is the set of functional units. If it is not shared, rarely used operators like the integer multiplier and divider must be uselessly duplicated. The fetch, issue and terminate parts of the pipeline must be duplicated to provide enough instruction bandwidth without a cycle width increase. In order to keep the L1 instruction cache access time reasonably short, the L1 instruction cache must be duplicated. Each copy must be small, thus an L2 (level 2) shared instruction cache is required.

In the data path, the data cache should be shared (this is the main difference with the TiPi processor we have presented in a previous work [5]). This has many advantages. First, it leads to treat load/store operations with shared functional units, as it is for the other operations. Second, dynamic load/store units partitionning per processor gives a higher throughput than a fix partition of duplicated units. In other words, for the same throughput, a dynamic partition will require less units than a fixed one. Third, shared data will not be duplicated. This is good for hit rate (more different data in the same cache size and prefetching effects). Fourth, it simplifies coherency control. Fifth, all the on-chip threads can be neighbours (in the sense given in the preceding section). Migrations only concern off-chip threads using on-chip data.

The main problem in a shared data-cache is its access time. If each processor in the CMP chip is designed with a superscalar degree d, it is reasonable to provide $d/3$ data cache accesses per processor per cycle (for an average of 33% of load/store instructions to be run), hence a total of $p*d/3$ ports. If we consider that for the p processors together, load/store accesses are uniformly distributed in the interleaved instruction flows and so are the memory addresses, a bank partitionning performs well. If $4p$ banks are provided, only $d/12$ ports per bank are required. If d equals the instruction L1 cache line size (say $d = 8$), a single port per bank is enough. Single port memory cells are better both for access time and bank size. Altogether, the banks form a big single level shared data cache. Because the data cache is big, it is likely to be physically addressed to avoid synonym problems. In such a case, each processor has its private TLB and translation logic, including TLB coherency control.

4 Conclusion

From the STRETCH application example, we have exhibited the two forms of parallelism a multiprocessor architecture must deal with, i.e. task parallelism and data parallelism. We have presented a corresponding model of hierarchical programming (C_T++). We have also divided the data sharing into three types: sedentary, nomadic and migrating data. We have stated that sedentary and nomadic types should be favoured both by the application structure and by the chip architecture; migrations should be kept rare to avoid inter-chip communications. We have shown that the expressivity of C_T++ allows an efficient compile-time/run-time identification of the nature of handled data in order to apply the correct software redistribution and prefetching mechanisms.

The TiPi2 architecture we have briefly described provides task parallelism by including multiple threads on-chip. It also provides data parallelism through single thread ILP and out-of-order execution and through multiple memory banks shared by multiple threads. In a multichip design, thanks to the shared banks in each chip, most of the nomadic data can be found on-chip. The banks set accessible from one chip can be extended off-chip by a private link to each neighbour chip (two such links in a ring topology). Migrations require a shared bus (full interconnection of the chips). But instead of avoiding contention through chips number limitation, it is avoided by reserving the bus usage to migrations only which should be kept rare.

References

1. F. Bodin, H. Essafi, and M. Pic. A specific compilation scheme for image processing architecture. In *CAMP'97*, Boston, USA, 1997.
2. R. G. Casey and K. Y. Wong. *Document Analysis Systems and Techniques*, pages 1–36. Marcel Dekker, New York, 1990.
3. DPCE Subcommittee. Data Parallel C Extensions. Technical Report X3J11/94-068, ANSI/ISO, 1994.
4. Ch. Fluhr. Multilingual information. In *Pacific Rim International Conference on Artificial Intelligence (PRICAI)*, Nagoya, 1990.
5. B. Goossens: TiPi, the threads processor. 1st MTEAC conference, Las Vegas, february 1998.
6. L. Hammond, B.A. Nayfeh, K. Olukotun: A single-chip multiprocessor. Computer, september 1997, pp79-85.
7. J.-M. Marie-Julie. PhD thesis, to appear in 1999.
8. Michael Metcalf and John Reid. *Fortran 90 Explained*. Oxford Science Publications, 1994.
9. S. Mori, C. Y. Suen, and K Yamamoto. Historical review of ocr research and development. 8(7):1029–1058, 1992.
10. K. Olukotun, B.A. Nayfeh, L.Hammond, K. Wilson, K. Chang: The case for a single- chip multiprocessor. ASPLOS 7, 1996, pp2-11.
11. R. Parsons and D. Quinlan. A++/P++ array classes for architecture independent finite difference computations. Technical report, 1994.
12. D.M. Tullsen, S.J. Eggers and H.M. Levy: Simultaneous multithreading: maximizing on-chip parallelism. 22nd ISCA, 1995, pp392-403.

Cellular Recursive Algorithm Architecture for Long Integers Multiplication in Arrays of Restricted Size

V.Markova

Supercomputer Software Department, ICMMG SB RAS
Pr. lavrentieva, 6, Novosibirsk, 630090, Russia
E-mail markova@ssd.sscc.ru
Tel.: (3832) 343994, Fax.: (3832) 324259

Abstract. A new cellular recursive algorithm architecture for multiplication of two long binary integers in arrays of restricted size is presented. The new algorithm is based on "divide and conquer" technique and performed in terms of a model of fine-grained parallelism – Parallel Substitution Algorithm. Time complexity of the new cellular recursive algorithm for multiplication of two long binary integers is obtained.

1 Introduction

In the design of high-speed algorithms it occurs rather frequently that the size of a task (the operand length) is larger than the size of a computing array (the number of processor elements). In this case, designing algorithms becomes more complicated because of an additional problem of the coordination of the task size and the array size.

To solve a task of "big" size, we use the well-known "divide and conquer" technique [1]. It consists in the following. The task of "big" size is broken into tasks of "smaller" size, formulated in a similar way. At first, tasks of "smaller" size are solved and then the solution of the "big" task is found as a composition of the obtained solutions. Moreover, for solving tasks of "smaller" size this technique can be applied recursively. It is known, that "divide and conquer" technique allows one to reduce the time complexity of the algorithm [1].

In this paper, we present a new recursive cellular algorithm architecture for multiplication of two long binary integers in arrays of restricted size and give the time complexity of the new algorithm.

The base of the new algorithm is a cellular algorithm for multiplying two long binary integers [2] (further referred to as *the basic* algorithm). This algorithm is based on "divide and conquer" technique and designed within the framework of a model of fine-grained parallelism – Parallel Substitution Algorithm [3]. The basic algorithm computes the shifted product in time $(1, 25n + 13 + \log_2 n)$. For comparison, the parallel version of the Karatzuba algorithm requires $(1, 75n + 2\log_2 n + 15)$ steps. The reduction of the time complexity of the basic algorithm is achieved due to the following. Firstly, the algorithm forms the shifted product, this reducing the number of shifts by half. Secondly, the algorithm generates four products instead of three. This allows us to conserve the multiplicand loading rate (4 steps) achieved due to the deep pipelining of multiplying.

In the proposed algorithm the calculation of the product of two long n-bit integers in the array of restricted size $(n' \times (2n'-1))$, where $n' = n/4$) is reduced to the recursive application of the basic algorithm for the calculation of the products of $n/2$-bit multipliers forming the product XY followed by their composition. The recursive algorithm forms the product in time $1\frac{5}{16}n + \log_2 n + 28$. Analogous to the basic algorithm, this time is less than the complexity of the recursive algorithm using the parallel version of the Karatzuba algorithm.

However, it is worth notice that the time complexity of both the basic and recursive algorithms is more than the time required for multiplying two n-bit integers in the array without size restriction $((n + \log_2 n + 5)$ steps) using the cellular algorithm. So, "divide and conquer" technique does not decrease the time complexity of the parallel algorithm as compared to the sequential one. It is explained by the fact that the multiplying speed of the cellular algorithm is so high that decrease in the time complexity due to the reduction of the operand length is less than the time needed to realize a composition of four products of integers of smaller size.

The article is organized as follows. In the second section is devoted to the cellular basic algorithm architecture for multiplication of two long n-bit binary integers in arrays of restricted size. An estimate of the time complexity is given. The new recursive cellular algorithm architecture for multiplication of two long binary integers and its time complexity are discussed in the third section.

2 Cellular Basic Algorithm Architecture for Long Integers Multiplication

In this section, we present the cellular algorithm architecture for long integer multiplication. The time complexity of the basic algorithm is given. First to be considered is the idea of the basic algorithm.

2.1 Idea of the Basic Algorithm

Let X and Y be two n-bit binary integers (for simplicity, n is a degree of integer 2) and let X and Y be split into two equal parts a and b, c and d, respectively. The basic algorithm calculates the product of n-bit integers X and Y as

$$P' = X'Y',$$

where X' and Y' – the new multipliers equal to $X2^{-n/4}$ and $Y2^{-n/4}$, respectively. The substitution of the shifted multipliers for the initial multipliers is associated with the wish to reduce the number of the products to be shifted and the number of shifts in the calculation of the product $P = XY$ according to the Karatzuba algorithm (Fig.1a). Recall that its computation scheme includes three multiplications, six additions, and two shifts: one by n and the other by $n/2$ bits; moreover, the 3-rd multiplier pair is two sums of $n/2$-bit integers.

In order for such reduction to be done, the integers a and b, c and d in the binary representation of the new multipliers should have the degrees of integer 2 with equal absolute values and opposite signs as distinct from the initial multipliers $X = a2^{n/2} + b$ and $Y = c2^{n/2} + d$. That is why the new multipliers are the initial multipliers shifted $n/4$ bits to the right along the axis j, and hence equal to $X' = a2^{n/4} + b2^{-n/4}$ and $Y' = c2^{n/4} + d2^{-n/4}$. Thus, the basic algorithm forms the product of n-bit integers X and Y as the following sum

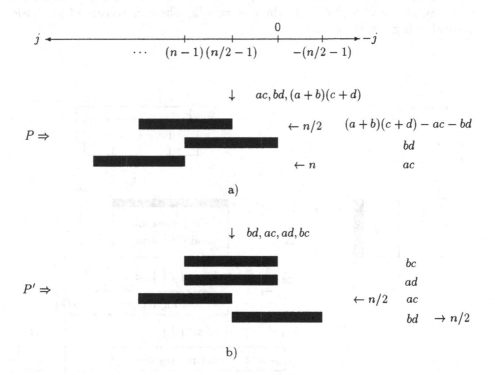

Fig. 1. Computation schemes of the algorithms. (a) Karatzuba, (b) Basic

$$P' = X2^{-n/4}Y2^{-n/4} = bd2^{-n/2} + ac2^{n/2} + ad + bc = P2^{-n/2}. \qquad (1)$$

From (1) we see that the obtained product is the initial product shifted $n/2$ bits to the right. The algorithm scheme (1) is given in Fig.1b. Below we list the distinguishing features of the basic algorithm.

– The algorithm computes four products. This allows us to conserve the multiplicand loading rate (4 steps) achieved due to the deep pipelining of computing the products from (1). In the Karatzuba scheme the loading rate must be changed beginning from $n > 64$ since the 3-rd multiplier pair cannot be calculated in time even if a fast carry-look-ahead adder (CLA) is used.

- To minimize the time complexity of the basic algorithm the order is introduced for calculating the products that form the product P' (Fig.1b).
- In the algorithm only two products ac and bd are shifted, moreover, they are shifted $n/2$ bits to the opposite sides.

2.2 Architecture of the Basic Algorithm

Thus, it is required to calculate the product of n-bit multipliers X and Y in an array of size $n' \times (2n' - 1)$, where $n' = n/2$. The architecture of the basic algorithm is given in Fig.2.

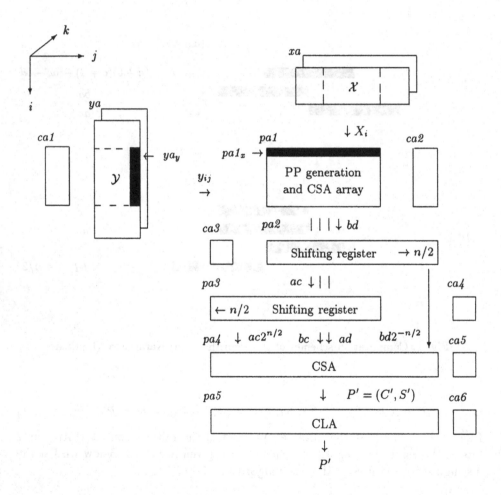

Fig. 2. Architecture of the basic algorithm

The sizes of the arrays ya and xa are $(n \times 4 \times 2)$ and $(3 \times n \times 2)$, respectively. The 0-th layer of each array is the processing one, and the 1-st layer is the controlling one. In the initial state the arrays ya and xa store two copies of the multipliers Y and X, respectively, which are then shaped into the initial data $\mathcal{Y}$ and $\mathcal{X}$ for computing the product P' according to (1). The first pair (d, b) to be multiplied is placed in the arrays ya_y and $pa1_x$ (in Fig.2 these arrays are marked). The former is the rightmost (the 0-th) column of ya; $n/4$ low-order and high-order bits of this column are equal to zero, the others are significant bits. The latter is the 0-th row of $pa1$; $n/2$ low-order bits of the row are significant bits, the others are equal to zero.

The arrays $pa1$, $pa2$, $pa3$, $pa4$, and $pa5$ are intended for computing the product P'. $pa1$ calculates four products in the form of the two-row code. The arrays $pa2$ and $pa3$ shift the products bd and ac $n/2$ bits to the right and to the left, respectively. $pa4$ (carry-save adder (CSA)) accumulates the two-row code of $P' = (C', S')$, which is then transferred into $pa5$ (CLA) to sum two last integers. Data loading is performed under the control of the arrays $ca1$, and $ca2$, data processing is performed under the control of the arrays $ca1$, $ca2$, $ca3$, $ca4$ and $ca5$.

The basic algorithm consists of two procedures carried out successively. The first one shapes the multipliers Y and X into the initial data arrays $\mathcal{Y}$ and $\mathcal{X}$. The second one computes the product P' itself.

Shaping procedure. According to the assumed order of calculation of the products forming the product P' (Fig.1.b), the arrays $\mathcal{Y}$ and $\mathcal{X}$ should take the forms $\mathcal{Y} = (c, d, c, d)$ and $\mathcal{X} = (b, a, a, b)$, respectively. The shaping scheme for 8-bit multipliers is given in Fig.3 (the controlling layers are not shown). Here the symbols ♠ and ♡ stand for bits in the integers c and d. Step 0 in Fig.3 shows the array ya in the initial state.

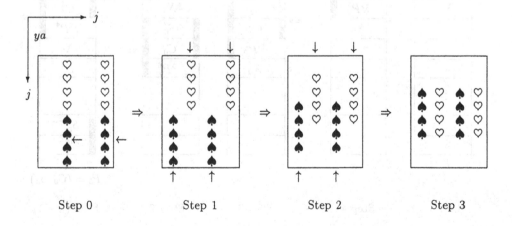

Fig. 3. Shaping scheme for 8-bit multipliers

The shaping procedure $Y, Y \Rightarrow \mathcal{Y}$ and $X, X \Rightarrow \mathcal{X}$ is carried out under the control of the first layers of ya and xa and consists of the following two steps.

1. Splitting the multipliers into two parts. It is carried out simply by shifting the integers a relative to b and c relative to d (step 1).
2. "Alignment" of the integers a, b, c and d. The alignment is realized by shifting the integers during $n/4$ steps as follows: the integers a and c are shifted in the direction of the low-order bits; the integers b and d are shifted in the direction of the high-order bits.

It is obvious that the shaping procedure together with the loading of the integer b in the 0-th row of the array $p1$ requires $(n/4 + 2)$ steps.

Multiplication procedure. To make the multiplication time shorter, the multiplication process is organized as follows.

– Loading of a new multiplier digit into ya is done at each step beginning from the least significant bit, placed in the 0-th row of ya. Loading of a new multiplicand is performed into the 0-th row of $p1$ at 3 step intervals. Such multiplier loading rate provides deep pipelining of the process of computing the products as the two-row codes in the array $pa1$ (Fig.4).

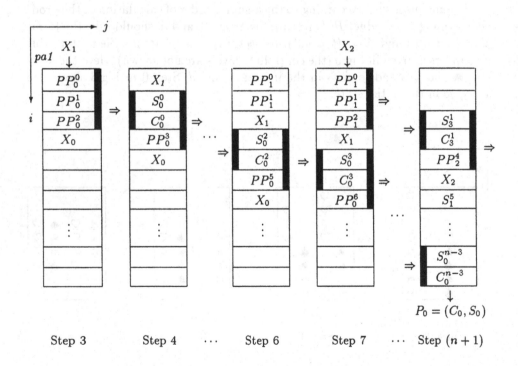

Fig. 4. Computation front propagation in the array $pa1$

– Loading of the initial data, transformation of the intermediate results (generation of partial products, their summation), shifting of the two-row code

of the products bd and ac $n/2$ bits and computing the two-row code of the product P' are done in parallel.
- Using a fast carry-save technique.

The two-row code (C_i, S_i) is formed as a result of the following three operations in the array $pa1$: one-row shift of the multiplicand to the bottom, generation of a partial product (PP), reduction of integer triple (the partial products or (and) the result of their addition). As we can see from Fig.4, the result of the 3-rd step situates in the first four rows and includes three partial products PP_0^0, PP_0^1, PP_0^2, and the multiplicand X_0. At the 4-th step, this quadruple is processed into a new quadruple by three operations (multiplicand shift, PP generation, and reduction) carried out in parallel. The new quadruple is shifted one row to the bottom and contains the following data: the two-row code (C_0^0, S_0^0), the partial product PP_0^3 and the multiplicand X_0. As a result, the 0-th row leaves the process of calculation of the first product and is ready to take the new multiplicand.

So, the computation front propagates one row per step to the bottom of the array $pa1$. At $(n-1)$-th step X_0 reaches the last row and after two steps the first product $P_0 = (C_0^{n-3}, S_0^{n-3}) = (C_0, S_0)$ is calculated in two last rows. At the 4-th step the multiplicand X_1 is loaded into the 0-th row and, starting from the 5-th step, two products are formed in parallel. The second product is obtained in 4 steps, and so on.

2.3 Time Complexity

The time complexity of the basic algorithm is defined from the its computation scheme (Fig.1b) and equal to

$$t_b = t_{shapy,x} + t_{ac2^{n/2}} + t_{CSA} + t_{CLA}.$$

Here $t_{shapy,x}$ – the time needed to generate the arrays X and Y and load the first multiplicand into $pa1$ ($(n/4+2)$ steps). $t_{ac2^{n/2}}$ – the time required to compute the two-row code of the product ac and shift $n/2$ steps to the right in $pa2$($(n+7)$ steps). t_{CSA} – the time needed to calculate the sum of four products in the form of the two-row code in $pa2$ (3 steps). t_{CLA} – the time required to sum two last integers in CLA ($\log_2 n$ steps).

As a result, the basic algorithm calculates the product of two n-bit integers in the array of restricted size in time $(1, 25n+13+\log_2 n)$. It is less than the time needed for the parallel version of the Karatzuba algorithm $((1, 75n+2\log_2 n+15)$ steps), but more than the time required for multiplying two n-bit integers in the array without size restriction $((n+\log_2 n+3)$ steps) using the cellular algorithm.

3   Cellular Recursive Algorithm Architecture for Long Integers Multiplication

In this section, we present the recursive cellular algorithm architecture for long integer multiplication. The time complexity of the basic algorithm is given.

3.1 Recursive Algorithm

Let X and Y be two n-bit binary integers and let the size of the array intended for the calculation of their product be $n' \times (2n' - 1)$, where $n' = n/4$. In this case the calculation of the product of n-bit multipliers is reduced to the recursive application of the basic algorithm for the calculation of the products of $n/2$-bit multipliers forming the product XY (1) followed by composition.

For this purpose, at first, $n/2$-bit multipliers a, b, c and d are split into two equal parts a_1, a_2, b_1, b_2 c_1, c_2, d_1 and d_2, respectively. Then the products of $n/2$-bit multipliers are formed similarly to the product of n-bit multipliers X and Y. For example, the product ac is calculated as

$$a'c' = a2^{-n/8}c2^{-n/8} = a_2c_22^{-n/4} + a_1c_12^{n/4} + a_2c_1 + a_1c_2 = ac2^{-n/4}. \quad (2)$$

Here the product $a'c'$ is equal to the product ac shifted $n/4$ bits (the multiplier length) to the right along the axis j (Fig.5). Further, substituting the obtained

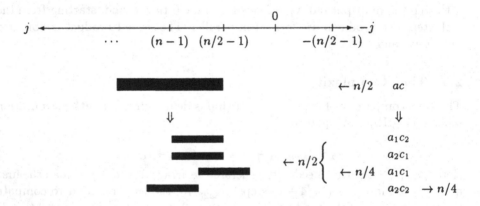

Fig. 5. Scheme for computing the product ac using the basic algorithm

products in (1) we obtain the product XY as

$$P'' = bd2^{-n/4}2^{-n/2} + ac2^{-n/4}2^{n/2} + +ad2^{-n/4} + bc2^{-n/4} = P'2^{-n/4}. \quad (3)$$

So, the basic algorithm computes n-bit products from (1) with the period equal to 4 steps. Therefore, the recursive algorithm can compute n-bit products from (3) with the period equal to 16 steps.

The computation of the product according to the formula (3) can be easily extended to the general case where the initial multipliers are split into m equal parts.

3.2 Recursive Algorithm Architecture

So, it is required to calculate the product XY in the array $p1$ of size $n' \times (2n' - 1)$, where $n' = n/4$. Fig.6 depicts the fragment of the recursive algorithm architecture. Here only the calculation of the product $a'c'$ is shown in detail (in Fig.6 it is placed in the large frame). The recursive algorithm architecture differs from the basic one by the following.

from $pa1$

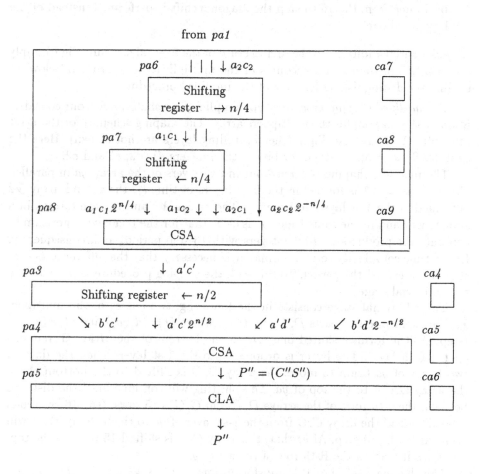

Fig. 6. Recursive algorithm architecture

- 3D arrays ya and xa used for storing the initial data for computing the product P'' have three information layers (0,1,2) and three controlling ones (3,4,5) (in Fig.6 these arrays are omitted). In the initial state the 0-th layer of each array stores two copies of the multipliers Y and X, respectively, which are then shaped into four initial data arrays $\mathcal{Y}1$, $\mathcal{Y}2$, $\mathcal{X}1$ and $\mathcal{X}2$, where $\mathcal{Y}1 = (d_1, d_2, d_1, d_2)$, $\mathcal{Y}2 = (c_1, c_2, c_1, c_2)$, $\mathcal{X}1 = (a_2, a_1, a_1, a_2)$ and $\mathcal{X}2 = (b_2, b_1, b_1, b_2)$.

– Six arrays $pa6$, $pa7$, $pa8$ and $ca7$, $ca8$, $ca9$ are introduced. The first three arrays are intended for computing n-bit products in the form of the two-row code under the control of the next three arrays. Beginning with $n > 64$, the shifting registers $pa6$ and $pa7$ have $n/4 - 13$ rows. Increasing the number of rows is explained by the fact that $n/2$-bit products arrive into the shifting registers at 16-step intervals. This makes it impossible to shift the two-row code of the product $n/4$ bits to the right (left) in the first two rows. Therefore, beginning from the 16-th step the diagonal shift is performed instead of the horizontal one.

Substantial additions to the architecture of the basic algorithm (Fig.6) imply modification of the main procedures of the multiplication algorithm. Below we outline the distinguishing features of the modified procedures.

The modified shaping procedure. For simplicity, we shall restrict our consideration to the shaping for the multipliers array. The shaping schemes for the n-bit multiplier Y is given in Fig.7 (the controlling layers are not shown). Here the symbols $\heartsuit$, $\spadesuit$, $\circ$ and $\bullet$ stand for bits in the integers $d1$, $d2$, $c1$ and $c2$.

The modified shaping is carried out in two layers of the array ya in parallel. The first array $\mathcal{Y}1$ is formed in the 0-th layers in time t_1, the second array $\mathcal{Y}2$ is formed in the 1-st layers in time t_2. (The arrays $\mathcal{X}1$ and $\mathcal{X}2$ are formed in a similar way and in the same time.) It is clear that for the recursive algorithm to compute the products of n-bit integers with 16-step period, and, consequently, for its time complexity to be minimal, it is necessary that the difference $t_2 - t_1$ should not exceed the period. To this end, the shaping procedure is preceded by an additional stage.

The additional stage consists in the following: two copies of the multiplier Y, Y are split into two parts D, D and C, C, where $D = (d_1, d_2)$ and $C = (c_1, c_2)$ (step 1). The former, shifted one row to the bottom of the array ya, remains on the 0-th layer. The latter is dropped into the 1-st layer. Then the data in two layers of ya begin to move: the array D, D is shifted to the bottom of ya, the array C, C – to the top of ya. This shifting will continue until the distance between the 0-th rows of the arrays D, D and C, C is 15 rows. (the 16-th step is needed to load the array C, C from the 1-st layer of ya to the 0-th layer). It will occur at $(n/4 - 6)$ step. After that, the array C, C is shifted 15 rows to the top, i.e., until it reaches the R-th row of the array ya.

The shaping itself, i.e., the transformations $C, C \Rightarrow \mathcal{Y}1$ and $D, D \Rightarrow \mathcal{Y}2$ are done similar to the transformation $Y, Y \Rightarrow \mathcal{Y}$ in the basic algorithm.

Only the 0-th layers of the arrays ya and xa take part in multiplying. The 1-st and the 2-nd layers are intended for storing the initial data $\mathcal{Y}2$ and $\mathcal{Y}1$, $\mathcal{X}2$ and $\mathcal{X}1$, respectively. The arrays $\mathcal{Y}1$ and $\mathcal{X}1$ are copied from the 0-th layers to the 2-nd layers when the generation of the product $b'c'$ begins. In the arrays ya and yx the 0-th layers contain the data of those pairs $(\mathcal{Y}1, \mathcal{X}1)$ and (or) $(\mathcal{Y}2, \mathcal{X}2)$ which are involved in the multiplication process.

The modified shaping procedure forms the first pair $\mathcal{Y}1$, $\mathcal{X}1$ in time $t_1 = (5n/16 + 11)$, consequently, one step later the generation of the first product begins.

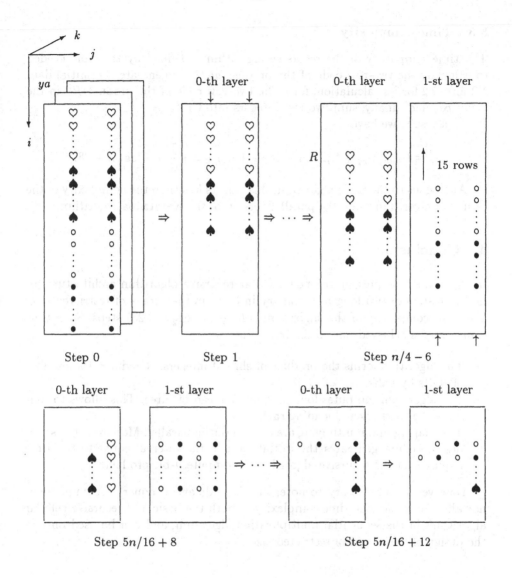

Fig. 7. Data moving in the array ya

The modified multiplication procedure has the following distinctions.

- The generation of the 1-st $n/2$-bit product and the arrays $\mathcal{Y}2$ and $\mathcal{X}2$ is performed in parallel.
- Additional shifts and compositions are used to form the product P'' from $n/2$-bit products according to (2).
- The generation of $n/2$-bit products and the copying of the initial data from the 1-st and the 2-nd layers of the arrays ya and xa into the 0-th layers are carried out in parallel. Moreover, the copying is performed row by row beginning from the moment when the 0-th row leaves the process of $n/2$-bit product generation, i.e., in 16 step intervals.

3.3 Time complexity

The time complexity of the recursive algorithm is defined by the time needed to calculate the two-row code of the product $alcl2^{n/2}$, generate the initial data $\mathcal{Y}2$ and $\mathcal{X}2$ for its calculation, form the two-row code of the product Pll in the array $pa4$ and, finally, sum two last integers into CLA.

As a result, we have

$$t_r = t_{shapy2,x2} + t_{alcl2^{n/2}} + t_{CSA} + t_{CLA} = 1\frac{5}{16}n + \log_2 n + 28.$$

Analogous to the basic algorithm, this time is less than the complexity of the recursive algorithm using the parallel version of the Karatzuba algorithm.

4 Conclusion

In this paper, we present the new cellular recursive algorithm architecture for multiplication of two long n-bit binary integers in the arrays of restricted size. The time complexity of this algorithm is $(1\frac{5}{16}n + \log_2 n + 28)$ steps. Such time complexity is achieved due to the following.

- The algorithm forms the product of shifted integers. It reduces the number of shifts by half.
- The algorithm computes four products instead of three. This allows to conserve the multiplicand loading rate.
- The shaping and multiplying are carried out in parallel. Moreover, the shaping procedure generates the initial data in the interval equal to the time required for the recursive algorithm to compute n-bit products.

However, it is necessary to note, that "divide and conquer" technique does not allow to reduce the time complexity of both the basic and recursive cellular algorithms in the sequential multiplication algorithm, and can be used only in the design of the arrays of restricted size.

References

1. Al.Aho, J.Hopcroft, J.Ullman. The Desing and Analysis of Computer Algorithms, Addison-Wesley Publishing Company, 1996.
2. V. Markova. Cellular Algorithm Architecture for Long Integers Multiplication in Array of Restricted Size. // Bulletin of Novosibirsk Computing Center, Series: Computer Science, issue 4, 1998, p.29-44.
3. S.M. Achasova, O.L. Bandman, V.P. Markova, S.V. Piskunov, *Parallel Substitution Algorithm. Theory and Application*, World Scientific, 1994.

A Parallel Model Based on Cellular Automata for the Simulation of Pesticide Percolation in the Soil *

Stefania Bandini[1], Giancarlo Mauri[1], Giulio Pavesi[2], and Carla Simone[3]

[1] Dept. of Informatics, Systemics and Communication
University of Milan–Bicocca
bandini,mauri@disco.unimi.it
[2] Dept. of Computer Science
University of Milan
pavesi@dotto.usr.dsi.unimi.it
[3] Dept. of Computer Science
University of Turin
simone@di.unito.it

Abstract. We present a parallel model based on Cellular Automata for the simulation of reaction–diffusion processes, that has been applied to the percolation of pesticides in the soil. The main contribution of our approach consists of a model where chemical reactions and the movement of fluid particles in a porous medium can be explicitly described and simulated. The model has been used to reproduce the process that causes pesticides, contained in the soil after their application to crops, to be released into water flowing through the soil and to be carried to the groundwater layer, polluting it. The model has been successfully implemented on Cray T3E and SGI Origin 2000 parallel computers.

1 Introduction

The main aim of this work regards the parallel simulation, based on cellular automata, of reaction–diffusion processes. Several works concerning the modeling of reaction–diffusion phenomena with cellular automata have been developed so far [1]. However, the main contribution of our approach consists of a model where chemical reactions and the movement of fluid particles in a porous medium can be explicitly described and simulated. In this paper we describe the application of the model to the simulation of the percolation of pesticides in the soil, developed in cooperation with the International Center for Pesticide Safety.

2 The Problem

Pesticides have become essential elements for modern agriculture, in order to obtain production yields sufficient to satisfy the growing needs of the increasing

* This work was part of the TTN/CAPP project, supported by European Commission DG3.

world population. The extensive use of pesticides can entail risks for the environment and human health. It is therefore very important to assess thoroughly the impact on the environment of a given pesticide, in order to minimize possible damages.

When applied to crops, pesticides are absorbed by soil. Then, when water flows (*percolates*) through the soil because of rain or floods, pesticides can be released into it. The amount of pesticide released changes according to the chemical properties of the pesticide itself and the physical and morphological properties of the soil. Water containing pesticide reaches the groundwater layer because of gravity. Since groundwater is usually the source of common tap water, it is straightforward to understand the polluting danger deriving from the excessive use of pesticides [2].

Simulation models are a very useful tool for assessing the leaching potential of a pesticide into groundwater. In the absence of experimental data, models are the only quantitative option. Several models based on differential equations have been proposed for predicting pesticide concentration in surface water and groundwater. Major differences are in modeling approach, complexity of the equations used, and amount of data required. In general, data required by these models are only in part available, difficult to obtain, and have a variable degree of quality. High quality data are needed to obtain a reliable prediction. Moreover, data available refer to specific locations (type of soil) and to specific characteristics of pesticides.

The use of cellular automata to simulate pesticide percolation into groundwater can be a chance to reduce the effort and the expenses in the evaluation of the environmental impact of pesticides.

3 The Model

The extraction process of soluble substances (i.e. pesticides) from the *percolation bed* (i.e. the soil) can be divided into two main phases: *washing* and *diffusion*. Washing corresponds to the reaction taking place between water flowing into the percolation bed and the surface of the soil particles. This phenomenon causes the release of pesticide from the soil to the water. Diffusion is due to the movement of water through the channels of the percolation bed, determined by gravity.

The process has been modeled in terms of *two–dimensional Cellular Automata* (CA), whose cells are arranged on a two–dimensional grid. CA evolve through a sequence of discrete time steps. At a given time, every cell is characterized by a *state*, belonging to a finite set. The state of the cells is updated simultaneously at each step according to the *update rule*. The rule determines the new state of each cell according to the current state of the cell itself and the state of the neighbouring cells, located on adjacent nodes of the grid. In our model we adopted the Von Neumann neighbourhood [3], where every cell has four neighbours.

The states of the cells represent the different entities (water, soil and empty spaces) involved in the process, and the update rule has been defined in order to simulate the interactions occurring during the percolation. Thus, a cell can be seen as a container, that can be *empty* or contain *water* or *soil*. Water or soil cells can also contain pesticide, expressed as an integer number of *particles*. Furthermore, each cell is divided in four parts (as shown in Fig. 1), and the overall number of particles contained in the cell has to be evenly distributed among the four portions.

The basic idea of this model (called *Reaction–Diffusion Machine*) has been applied to other similar problems and can also be used to study phenomena not strictly related to percolation [4]. It has been proved in [5] that CA are a special case of a Reaction–Diffusion Machine. In the following sections we describe in detail the cellular automaton and how simulations can be performed.

4 The Cellular Automaton

The automaton is contained in the infinite two–dimensional square grid $\mathbb{Z}^2$. We suppose that the cells are located on the nodes (i, j), with $0 \leq i < M$ and $0 \leq j < N$, where M is the number of rows of the automaton and N is the number of columns. With $C(i, j)$ we will refer to the cell located on the node (i, j). The neighbours of $C(i, j)$ will be thus denoted by $C(i - 1, j)$, $C(i + 1, j)$, $C(i, j - 1)$ and $C(i, j + 1)$. The state of each cell $C(i, j)$ of the automaton is defined by:

$$C(i, j) = <I, N, S, W, E, \mathbf{F}>$$

where:

1. I is the *identity*, that can assume one of the following values: *empty, water, soil*. The identity indicates whether a cell is empty, or contains water or soil.
2. N, S, W, E are four integer variables representing the number of pesticide particles contained in each portion of the cell.
3. $\mathbf{F} = <u, d, l, r>$ is a 4-tuple of one-bit variables, used in the diffusion phase in order to simulate the movement of water in the percolation bed.

From now on, we will refer with $N_{i,j}, W_{i,j}, E_{i,j}$, and $S_{i,j}$ to the number of particles contained in the four portions, with $u_{i,j}, d_{i,j}, l_{i,j}$ and $r_{i,j}$ to the four diffusion flags, and with $I_{i,j}$ to the identity of the cell $C(i, j)$.

Fig. 1. The structure of a cell of the automaton.

The initial configuration of the automaton contains some cells with $I = soil$, grouped together to form grains that resemble the morphology of actual percolation beds as shown in Fig. 2. It is worth mentioning that this step, the generation of the percolation bed, has been performed with another cellular automaton. This automaton allows to generate percolation beds reproducing in two dimensions the morphological properties (for example, shape and size of the grains) of different types of soil. Moreover, a given number of pesticide particles is assigned to the cells located on the surface of grains (that is, cells with $I = soil$ with at least one neighbour with $I = empty$). To start the simulation, water is added to the percolation bed by setting to *water* the identity of some empty cells according to a given rule.

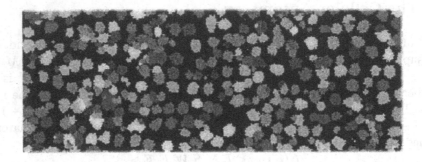

Fig. 2. The initial configuration of the automaton. Colored cells represent the grains forming the percolation bed.

5   The Update Rule

The update rule of the automaton can be divided into three separate steps: *reaction*, *balance*, and *diffusion*. In the first step water cells exchange pesticide particles with other water cells or with soil cells. In the second, the overall number of particles contained in each cell after the reaction step is evenly balanced in the four portions. In the last step, water is allowed to move inside the percolation bed, transferred from cell to cell.

5.1   Reaction

Reaction takes place as follows: for each cell, the amount of pesticide contained in each portion is balanced with the amount of pesticide contained in the adjacent portions of the neighbouring cells. For example, if the cell $C(i,j)$ contains $p = N_{i,j}$ particles in its northern portion, and the northern neighbour $C(i-1,j)$ contains $q = S_{i-1,j}$ particles in its southern portion, at the end of the reaction each portion will contain $\lfloor (p+q)/2 \rfloor$ particles. Since the number of particles must be integer, the possible particle corresponding to the remainder of the division is assigned randomly to one of the portions. The same rule is applied to the other three portions (eastern, southern and western) of the cell and the corresponding neighbours. Figure 3 shows two neighbouring portions before and after the reaction step.

The reaction rule can applied when two portions contain water, or when one of the portions contains water and the other soil. No reaction takes place between two soil portions, in order to keep pesticide particles only in cells located on the surface of grains. Likewise, no reaction is allowed when one of the portions is empty, since particles cannot be contained by an empty cell.

It is straightforward to see that, by applying the reaction rule to the four portions of a given cell, we also update the state of the adjacent portions of the neighbouring cells. For this reason, there is no need to apply the rule to every cell, since each portion would be updated twice. Thus, the rule can be applied only to one half of the cells, for example to all the cells with the same parity. If we figure that the cells of the automaton are arranged on a chess–board, the rule can be applied only to the cells located on white squares (or, vice versa, black squares). That is, we can update only the cells $C(i, j)$ such that $i + j$ is even, updating every portion exactly once.

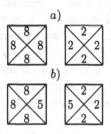

Fig. 3. Two cells before (a) and after (b) the reaction step. Numbers represent the particles contained in each portion of the cells.

5.2 Balance

During the *balance* step the total number of particles contained in a cell resulting from the reaction step is balanced in the four portions. That is, given $N_{i,j}, S_{i,j}, E_{i,j}$, and $W_{i,j}$ (the number of particles in the four portions of the cell $C(i, j)$ after the reaction), at the end of the balance step the number of particles in each portion will be $\lfloor (N_{i,j} + W_{i,j} + S_{i,j} + E_{i,j})/4 \rfloor$. Once again, the particles corresponding to the remainder of the division are assigned randomly to the four portions. Figure 4 shows two cells before and after the this step.

5.3 Diffusion

In the *diffusion* step, water moves from cell to cell inside the percolation bed. Basically, water always tries to move downwards (that is, to the southern neighbour of the cell). Otherwise, (if the southern neighbour is not empty) water tries to move laterally, choosing randomly between left and right if both the lateral neighbours are empty; if only one is empty, water tries to move in that direction.

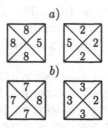

Fig. 4. Two cells before (a) and after (b) the balance step. Numbers represent the particles contained in each portion of the cells.

If also the lateral neighbours are not empty, water cannot move. In our model, water is transferred from one cell to another (provided that the latter is empty), by switching the parameters defining the state of the two cells.

Had the water moved only downwards, the rule would have been quite simple: exchange the parameters of a cell $C(i,j)$ containing water with the parameters of the empty neighbour $C(i+1,j)$ (all set to zero, since an empty cell cannot contain particles). The trouble comes from the lateral movement: that is, the same empty cell could be the destination chosen by water coming from more than one cell (at most three, the northern neighbour and the two lateral neighbours). Therefore, another rule must be added, deciding which one of the different water cells is allowed to transfer the water to the empty cell, while the others keep their state unchanged. For this reason, the diffusion step has been split into three sub-steps, employing the *diffusion flags*.

Given a cell $C(i,j)$, with $I_{i,j} = water$, the first sub–step is defined as follows:

1. If $I_{i+1,j} = empty$, $d_{i,j} = 1$. That is, if the southern neighbour is empty, water tries to move downwards, and the corresponding flag is set.
2. Else, if exactly one of the lateral neighbours is empty, set the corresponding flag ($l_{i,j}$ or $r_{i,j}$).
3. Else, if *both* the lateral neighbours are empty, choose one of the two directions at random, and set the corresponding flag.
4. Else, water cannot leave the cell: no flag is set.

At the end of the first sub–step, each cell containing water has therefore signaled the intention to transfer its content to an empty cell by setting the flag corresponding to the chosen neighbour.

In the second sub–step, empty cells examine the flags of their neighbours, and decide which one can transfer the water. This step is performed by setting to one the diffusion flag of the empty cell in the direction of the succeeding neighbour. Given a cell $C(i,j)$, with $I_{i,j} = empty$, the choice is based on the following criterion:

1. If $d_{i-1,j} = 1$, then $u_{i,j} = 1$. That is, water trying to move downwards always succeeds, and the empty cell sets its upper flag.

2. Else, if exactly one of the lateral neighbours has the diffusion flag set ($r_{i,j-1}$ or $l_{i,j+1}$), it wins, and the corresponding flag (respectively, $l_{i,j}$ or $r_{i,j}$) is set.

3. Else, if *both* the lateral neighbours have the diffusion flag set ($r_{i,j-1}$ and $l_{i,j+1}$), the cell chooses randomly the winner and sets its own corresponding flag ($l_{i,j}$ or $r_{i,j}$).

4. Else, none of the neighbours is trying to transfer its water; no flag is set.

Thus, at the end of the second sub–step, water can move to the empty cell indicated by its flag if the empty cell has the flag on its direction set. The rule has been defined in order to give the precedence to water moving downwards, while water trying to move laterally may have tough luck. The actual movement of water takes place in the third sub–step. Given a cell $C(i,j)$ containing water trying to move to a neighbouring empty cell:

1. If $d_{i,j} = 1$ and $u_{i+1,j} = 1$ then $C(i+1,j) = C(i,j)$ (all the parameters are copied to the empty cell) and $C(i,j) = EMPTY$ (the cell becomes empty and all its parameters are set to zero).

2. Else, if $l_{i,j} = 1$ and $r_{i,j-1} = 1$ then $C(i,j-1) = C(i,j)$ and $C(i,j) = EMPTY$.

3. Else, if $r_{i,j} = 1$ and $l_{i,j+1} = 1$ then $C(i,j+1) = C(i,j)$ and $C(i,j) = EMPTY$.

4. Else, the cell cannot transfer its water, and its state remains unchanged.

Figure 5 shows an example of the three diffusion sub–steps. The overall update of the automaton can be split in five different steps:

1. Reaction;
2. Balance;
3. Diffusion:
   (a) *Diffusion 1*
   (b) *Diffusion 2*
   (c) *Diffusion 3*

6 The Simulation

To start a simulation, we need to add two further parameters to the automaton: the *water saturation constant* and the *soil saturation constant*, representing, respectively, the maximum number of pesticide particles that can be contained by a water portion and by a soil portion. These parameters change according to the chemical properties of the pesticide and the soil employed in the simulation. Adding the saturation constants changes slightly the reaction rule, while the other rules remain the same. For instance, we show how the rule changes given two reacting portions $E_{i,j}$ and $W_{i,j+1}$. Let p and q be the number of particles contained respectively in the two portions; let $SC_{i,j}$ and $SC_{i,j+1}$ be the saturation constants of the two portions (corresponding to their content). Let us

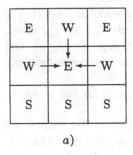 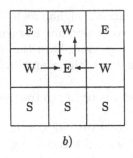

Fig. 5. The three diffusion sub–steps. Arrows leaving a cell represent a diffusion flag set and its direction. After step one (*a*) water cells (W) have signaled their intention to transfer their content and the direction chosen; after step two (*b*), the empty cell (E) has decided the winner; after step three (*c*) the winner has moved the water to the empty cell. Soil cells (S) remain inactive.

suppose that $\lfloor (p+q)/2 \rfloor > SC_{i,j}$, that is, the number of particles resulting from the reaction rule is greater than the saturation constant of one of the portions (notice that it cannot be greater than both the saturation constants). Then, the amount of particles resulting from the reaction step defined before changes in this way:

$$E_{i,j} = SC_{i,j}$$
$$W_{i,j+1} = (p+q) - SC_{i,j}$$

This ensures that after the reaction step neither portion contains more particles than its saturation constant. The possible exceeding particles are simply assigned to the other portion.

As mentioned before, the simulation starts with some cells of the automaton set to *soil* and containing pesticide particles, while the remaining cells are empty. Then, to start the simulation and during the simulation itself water is added to the automaton by setting to *water* the identity of some empty cells. For example, in order to simulate heavy rain, at each update step the empty cells located in the topmost row of the automaton are filled with water, or, if rain is not that heavy, the above operation can be performed every k steps, or at random (water is added at each step with probability p). Moreover, to reproduce a flood, all the empty cells can have their identity set to *water* at the beginning of the simulation, and water can added to the automaton before each update step according to one of the rules described above.

Water is also allowed to leave the percolation bed. After each update step, the cells in the bottom row of the automaton are emptied, that is, if their identity is *water*, it is set to *empty*, and their parameters are set to 0. During this operation, we also compute the overall number of pesticide particles contained in the cells that have been emptied. This allows to obtain the amount of pesticide that leaves the percolation bed at each update step, that is, the amount of pesticide leached from the bed that reached the groundwater.

The simulation can be stopped after a given number of steps, or when the percolation bed is empty. That is, we stop adding water to the bed and wait until all the water has left the percolation bed. However, water can form puddles when some cells cannot transfer the water contained (either downwards or laterally).

The steps performed during a simulation can be summed up as follows:

1. Set up of the percolation bed;
2. Set up of the saturation constants according to the chemical properties of the pesticide considered and the morphological and physical characteristics of the soil;
3. Add water (optional);
4. Update:
   (a) Reaction, modified to take into account the saturation constants;
   (b) Balance;
   (c) Diffusion $(1, 2, 3)$;
5. Remove water from the bottom row;
6. Update of the simulation statistics;
7. Go to 3.

To perform simulations consistent with real conditions, we have to employ a very large automaton, and the update rule has to be applied a large number of times. This makes the algorithm time consuming for sequential machines. Hence the need of a parallel implementation.

7   The Parallel Implementation

The parallel version of the CA has been implemented using the MPI (Message Passing Interface) library. This library has been chosen for its high level of efficiency and the great portability. The two-dimensional grid forming the automaton has been divided vertically into n layers, where n is the number of processors available. Basically, each processor updates a slice of the automaton. That is, at each update step (divided in the three phases), the processors update simultaneously the cells belonging to their part, divided in rows numbered from 1 to R/n, where R is the overall number of rows in the grid.

A problem arises with rows 1 and R/n of each layer, that have to be updated according (also) to the state of cells belonging to other processors. For this reason, we added rows 0 and $(R/n) + 1$ to each part. These two rows are composed of the so called *ghost cells*. Before each update step, processor number p communicates the status of its cells of row 1 to processor number $p - 1$, and the status of the cells of row R/n to processor number $p + 1$. It also receives the status of the cells of row R/n from processor $p - 1$, that form its own row 0, and the status of the cells of row 1 from processor $p + 1$, that form its own row $(R/n) + 1$ (see Fig. 6). In this way, each processor can update its border rows copying in its ghost cells the state of the neighbouring cells belonging to different processors.

The parallel implementation of the update routine of the automaton can be summed up as follows, where p is the processor number:

1. if $(p = 0)$ add water (optional);
2. if $(p > 1)$:
   - (a) send row 1 to processor $p - 1$;
   - (b) receive row 0 from processor $p - 1$;
3. if $(p < n)$:
   - (a) send row R/n to processor $p + 1$;
   - (b) receive row $(R/n) + 1$ from processor $p + 1$;
4. Reaction;
5. Balance;
6. Diffusion (1,2,3);
7. if $(p = n)$ remove water;

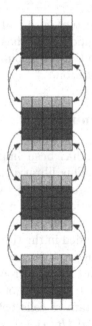

Fig. 6. The different layers composing the automaton. Each layer is assigned to a different processor. The top and bottom row of each layer are composed by *ghost cells*, used to store the state of neighbouring cells belonging to different layers.

8 Performance Analysis

Simulations with the parallel version of the model have been carried out on a Cray T3E (where we used a maximum of 32 processors) and a SGI Origin 2000 (where we used a maximum of 4 processors), in cooperation with the CINECA of Bologna, the most important italian center of supercomputing. The code has been tested on a grid formed by 512×512 cells, and 1000 iterations (update steps) on both machines. These parameters have been set only as a benchmark in order to assess the benefits deriving from the parallel implementation. The grid size and the number of iterations needed for real simulations are in fact much larger.

The results of the trials are shown in Tab. 1 and 2. The model showed a good performance on both platforms.

Table 1. Performance analysis on *Cray T3E*. From left to right columns represent: number of processors, number of rows and columns in the grid, number of iterations and overall time of the simulation. Time is measured in seconds. I/O was disabled during this benchmark.

PE	X	Y	T	Time
2	512	512	1000	267.61
4	512	512	1000	129.08
8	512	512	1000	66.26
16	512	512	1000	33.77
32	512	512	1000	20.42

Table 2. Performance analysis on *SGI Origin 2000*. From left to right columns represent: number of processors, number of rows and columns in the grid, number of iterations and overall time of the simulation. Time is measured in seconds. I/O was disabled during this benchmark.

PE	X	Y	T	Time
2	512	512	1000	314.07
4	512	512	1000	128.33

Acknowledgements

We wish to thank the staff of the International Center for Pesticide Safety for the advice and the interesting discussions on the subject of this paper. We also thank Giovanni Erbacci and Gianni de Fabritiis of CINECA for the help in the developement of the parallel version.

References

1. Dab D., Boon J.P., Cellular Automata to Reaction–Diffusion Systems. In Cellular Automata and Modeling of Complex Physical Systems, Springer Proceedings in Physics, Vol. 46, 1990.
2. Rao P.S.C, Hornsby A.G., Jessup R.E. Indices for Ranking the Potential for Pesticide Contamination of Groundwater, 1985.
3. Gutowitz H. Cellular Automata: Theory and Experiment. MIT Press, 1991.
4. Bandini S., Simone C., Reaction Diffusion Computational Models. In Proceedings of the 3rd Systems Science European Congress, Rome 1996.
5. Bandini S., Simone C., Integrating Forms of Interaction in a Distributed Model, to appear in Foundamenta Informaticae, 1999.

Comparative Study of Cellular-Automata Diffusion Models

Olga L. Bandman

Supercomputer Software Department
ICMMG of Siberian Branch
Russian Academy of Science
Pr. Lavrentieva, 6, Novosibirsk, 630090, Russia
E-mail: bandman@ssd.sscc.ru

Abstract. Cellular-automata diffusion models are studied by simulation and their characteristics are compared. The simulation results are obtained by process observation and by computing concentration distribution along one of the axis of the array. To prove the validity of the models and assess their macroscopic parameters the results are compared to those obtained by corresponding PDE solution. Stochastic and deterministic models are investigated. Stochastic models are shown to be more precise in reflecting pure diffusion dynamics and heat distribution, while the deterministic ones model more complex phenomena diplaying both diffusive and wavelike properties, inherent in gas and fluids.

1 Introduction

Investigation of spatial dynamics in physical media is a fundamental task of computational mathematics. Nowadays there are two alternative approaches to the problem: 1) a traditional one based on PDE solution and continuous data representation, and 2) a cellular-automaton approach, based on the presentation of micro-phenomena in terms of Boolean equations in discrete space. The first approach is perfectly developed, having a long history, the second one dates back about a quarter of a century [1] only, being stimulated at one hand by severe computational difficulties of nonlinear PDE solution, and at the other hand - by the increasing hardware capability of fine-grained parallel special-purpose processor implementation.

The kernel of cellular-automata approach is the fact that both time and space are initially given in discrete form, physical values (mass, speed vector component) being represented as Boolean states of the automaton cells. State transition rules are based upon mass and momentum conservation laws. The computation process is iterative, at each step state changes being performed simultaneously in all cells of the array. Real physical values are recovered by summing up the "ones" in an area around each cell. Rightfulness of cellular automata model was proved in [2] for diffusion and in [3] for gas dynamics ("gas-lattice") on the base of statistical physics.

Authors and apologists of cellular automata models consider them to mimic physical phenomena in more detail than PDEs, because the latter are artificially oriented to continuous representation. Moreover, Boolean operations are executed with absolute accuracy, the computation process is easily parallelized and implemented in special purpose computers [4].

All above stimulate intensive research in the field. Up till now a good deal of models are proposed for different aims, some of them being applied in industry [5].

The main problem in cellular automata approach development is to prove its adequacy to modeled phenomena, as well as to determine certain quantitative characteristics of the model and conditions of applicability. It is not always possible to use statistical physics to obtain analytical proof (as it is done in [2,3]), moreover in those proofs there are several assumptions, which require additional experimental verification. So, the only exact method of cellular automata models investigation is computer simulation with comparison of the results to those, obtained by the method, assumed to be correct. In this research the finite-difference method of PDE solution is taken as a standard. The reason for such a choice is in iterative character of computation process, which allows to compare the intermediate computation data. Diffusion is chosen here for experimental study of CA approach. The aim of such a choice is twofold. Firstly, there are several models to be compared. Secondly, diffusion is a basic physical phenomenon, being included as a part in more complex processes (heating, acoustics, hydrodynamics).

Besides the introduction (section 1), the paper includes three sections. The second section contains definitions of used concepts and cellular-automata models classification. In the third section the simulation results of two stochastic models are given and analyzed. Formulas to determine diffusion coefficient are derived. In the third part some deterministic models are presented and simulation results are discussed. And in the last section a general estimation of methods is given.

1.1 Continuous and Discrete Diffusion Representation

Diffusion is a process which aims at a stable distribution of concentration in a system, which is the result of a disordered wandering of system elements. In the simple two-dimensional case diffusion is represented by the following equation

$$\frac{\partial u}{\partial t} = d\triangle u, \tag{1}$$

where

$$\triangle u = \frac{\partial^2 u}{\partial^2 x} + \frac{\partial^2 u}{\partial^2 y}$$

is a Laplassian, $u(t, x, y)$ is a concentration, d is a diffusion coefficient (assumed to be constant), x, y are Cartesian coordinates of the plane space. When solving this equation by finite-difference method, time and space are discretised, so that $x = ih_x, y = jh_y$, and $t = n\tau$, i, j, n being integers. If $h = h_x = h_y = 1$, the equation (1) takes the following discrete form.

$$u_{i,j}(t+1) = u_{i,j}(t) + \tau d(u_{i-1,j}(t) + u_{i+1,j}(t) + u_{i,j+1}(t) + u_{i,j-1}(t) - 4u_{i,j}(t)). \tag{2}$$

Introducing a *cloning template*

$$\mathbf{A} = \begin{bmatrix} 0 & 1 & 0 \\ 1 & -4 + 1/d\tau & 1 \\ 0 & 1 & 0 \end{bmatrix} \tag{3}$$

and a cell *neighborhood*

$$\mathbf{U}_{ij}(t) = \begin{bmatrix} 0 & u_{i-1,j}(t) & 0 \\ u_{i,j-1}(t) & u_{i,j}(t) & u_{i,j+1}(t) \\ 0 & u_{i+1,j}(t) & 0 \end{bmatrix} \tag{4}$$

equation (1) may be brought to a cellular form

$$u_{i,j}(t+1) = D(\mathbf{A} \otimes \mathbf{U}_{i,j}(t)), \tag{5}$$

where $D = d\tau$ and " $\otimes$ " is a scalar product of two-dimensional vectors.

The solution of (5) is an iterative procedure, each step including the computation of $u_{i,j}(t+1)$ for all i, j and then changing cell states all over the array at once. Doing so we may observe the diffusion process at times $t = n\tau$. The choice of τ depends on convergence conditions, which are known to be met with $(d\tau)/(h^2) < 1/4$. Hence, further it is reasonable to take $D = 1/4$ with $h = 1$.

The above cellular form (5) is an approximation of (1). By contrast, Cellular Automata (CA) diffusion models are alternatives, rather than approximations of (1) [1]. Studying them, we shall compare simulation results with those computed by (5) and assess the models under investigation by the level of comparison agreement.

Cellular automaton (CA) is an array of finite automata (cells) with local interactions, all cells being characterized by one and the same *transition rule*. Boolean "ones" in the global state of the CA are thought of as abstract particles. Transition rules make them move and collide stimulating to distribute uniformly over the array. To obtain true physical concentration value at a certain point of the array one should sum up the "ones" over an area around this point. Such a procedure is referred to as *averaging*.

Following [6] a transition rule is represented by a set of substitutions $\Phi = \{\theta_1, \ldots, \theta_n\}$ of the form

$$\theta_k : C_{(t)} * S_{i,j}(t) \to S'_{i,j}(t+1), \tag{6}$$

where $C_{i,j}$ is a predicate referred to as a *context*, whose truth allows the substitution to be applied, $S_{i,j}$ and $S'_{i,j}$ are a cell neighborhoods, represented as cell sets with equal cardinalities $|S_{i,j}| = |S'_{i,j}| = q$, which differ only in state values.

$$S_{ij} = \{(u_0[i,j], u_1[i-1,j], \ldots, u_q[i+1,j+1]\}, \\ S'_{ij} = \{(u'_0[i,j], u'_1[i-1,j], \ldots, u'_q[i+1,j+1]\}. \tag{7}$$

To put it clear, each substitution rule is considered to be applicable at a cell (i, j), at time t when $C(t)$ is true and cell neighborhood U_{ij} coincide with $S_{ij}(t)$. If so, the states of the latter are replaced by the corresponding ones in $S'_{i,j}$.

In (7) cell states $u_0, \ldots, u_q$ in S_{ij} may be represented as Boolean vectors, real numbers, or variables. In the latter case states $u'_0, \ldots, u'_q$ in S'_{ij} are functions of these variables.

CA algorithm is a transition rule $\Phi = \{\theta_1, \ldots, \theta_n\}$ together with the indication which execution mode should be used. In CA diffusion models the following modes of execution are used.

1) *Synchronous mode*, when all applicable substitutions are executed simultaneously at each time step.

2) *Two-step synchronous mode*, when the set of cells is partitioned into two subsets forming a chessboard: *even* subset, such that for each its cell the sum of indices is even, and *odd* subset whose cells have odd sum of indices. At even time steps substitutions are applied to the cells of the even subset and are executed synchronously, at odd time steps the same is done at odd subset.

3) *Asynchronous mode*, when the transition rule is applied to only one cell at each step, the choice of the cell being undetermined.

Cellular automaton is referred to as a *probabilistic* one, if transition rule substitutions are provided with a probability to be executed.

To ensure that transition rules are adequate to simulate diffusion they should meet the following conditions:

1. conservation of mass and momentum, i.e. the number of "ones" in the array should be constant during the computation process,

2. symmetry in space, i.e. the rule should be invariant relative to a rotation at a certain angle .

All currently known CA diffusion models may be partitioned into two groups: *stochastic* models and *deterministic* ones. The first group is represented further by the following two models: *naive CA diffusion* , the name being taken from [8], but the model is essentially modified, and *block-rotation CA diffusion*, firstly mentioned in [8] and then studied in [2].

Deterministic models are based on microscopic gas theory, and were firstly intended to mimic gas and fluid behavior, but inherent spurious invariants constrained them to diffusive phenomena with wavelike features in gas and fluids. The following deterministic diffusion models are considered: HPP-gas [7], TM-gas [8], and 1D gas-lattice diffusion [9].

2 Stochastic CA Diffusion Models

2.1 Naive CA Diffusion

Naive model is the most primitive one. Unformally, the transition rule is as follows: each cell interchanges states with one of its neighbor with the probability $p_D = 1/q$, where q is amount of its neighbors. Such a rule being applied to an array in synchronous mode is "contradictory", i.e two different state values may occur in a single cell, resulting in disappearing or emerging "particles", which is in contradiction of the conservation laws. So, only asynchronous mode of conputation is admissible. Let p be a random value ranging from 0 to 1. Then according to [6] the formal repesentation of the transition rule is as follows:

$$\begin{cases} \theta_1 : (0 \le p < 1/4) \quad * \; (u[i-1,j], v[i,j]) \to (v[i-1,j], u[i,j]), \\ \theta_2 : (1/4 \le p < 1/2) * \; (u[i+1,j], v[i,j]) \to (v[i+1,j], u[i,j]), \\ \theta_3 : (1/2 \le p < 3/4) * \; (u[i,j+1], v[i,j]) \to (v[i,j+1], u[i,j]), \\ \theta_4 : (3/4 \ge p < 1) \quad * \; (u[i,j-1], v[i,j]) \to (v[i,j-1], u[i,j]), \end{cases} \quad (8)$$

where the conditions in the first pair of round brackets of each substitution provide the probability of its execution to be 1/4. At each time only one substituion is executed at a single cell of the array (a microoperation), the cells being chosen at random. An iteration consists of $M \times N$ microoperations, each microoperation being applied once to each cell. Diffusion coefficient is determined by comparing the function of concentration distribution $U_{naive}(j)$ with the similar one $U_{PDE}(j)$, calculated according to (5). Both function are taken along the j-axis going via the center of the array ($i = 0, j = 0$). A pair of time numbers (T_{naive}, T_{PDE}), such that two functions: $U_{naive}(j)$ at T_{naive} and $U_{PDE}(j)$ at T_{PDE} coincide, are referred to as *compatible times*. The diffusion coefficient D_{naive} is computed according to the following formula with $D_{PDE} = 0, 25$.

$$D_{naive} = D_{PDE} \frac{T_{naive}}{T_{PDE}} = 1/4 \frac{T_{naive}}{T_{PDE}}, \quad (9)$$

where T_{naive} and T_{PDE} form a pair of compatible times.

The simulation experiments were performed for an array with the size 200×200 cells, Fon-Neumann boundary conditions being used. The initial array had a square 40×40 cells in the center with states equal to 1, all other cells being in zero states (Fig.1, the left box). After 50 iterations the region of high concentration looses its square form and becomes round, as it is in real physical diffusion process (Fig.1, the right box).

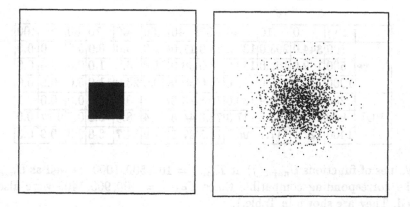

Fig. 1. Cellular-automaton naive diffusion simulation. Discrete representation: initial state of the array (the left box) and a snapshot of $T_{naive} = 300$ (the right box)

Averaging was done over a square 20×20 (averaging radius $r = 10$). The averaged picture of the process shows smooth transitions between areas of high and low density and looks like that obtained by using "continious" approach (Fig.2, the left box). The function $U_{naive}(j)$, which shows averaged values of concentration along the horizontal j-axis at $i = 0$ (i=0,j=0 are taken in the center of the array) ensures the similarity with continuous diffusion process (Fig.2, the right box).

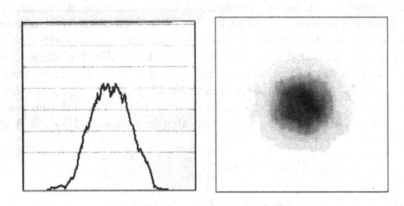

Fig. 2. Cellular-automaton naive diffusion simulation. Averaged representation: a snapshot at $T_{naive} = 300$ (the left box), and a function $U_{naive}(j)$ at $T_{naive} = 300$ (the right box)

Table 1 Simulation results for naive diffusion model

	$T\backslash j$	0	10	20	30	40	50	60	70	80	90	100
	100	344.0	293.0	187.0	75.0	11.0	1.0	0.0	0.0	0.0	0.0	0.0
Naive	500	162.0	169.0	138.0	78.0	38.0	21.0	6.0	1.0	0.0	0.0	0.0
	1000	127.0	115.0	95.0	76.0	50.0	30.0	23.0	11.0	5.0	0.0	0.0
	200	343.9	290.9	180.0	70.3	15.0	1.5	0.1	0.0	0.0	0.0	0.0
PDE	900	161.4	148.8	117.3	78.8	44.8	21.4	8.6	2.8	0.7	0.17	0.0
	1400	127.2	117.1	96.7	71.5	47.3	27.9	14.7	6.8	2.8	0.9	0.3

Values of functions $U_{naive}(j)$ at $T_{naive} = 100, 500, 1000$, as well as $U_{naive}(j)$ at the corresponding compatible times $T_{PDE} = 500, 900, 1400$ were also obtained. They are shown in Table.1.

Simulations showed, that diffusion coefficient is not constant, it decreases with the decrease of concentration gradient ($D = 0,5$ at $T_{naive} = 100$, $D = 0,45$ at $T_{naive} = 500$, and $D = 0,35$ at $T_{naive} = 1000$). The average deviation between two compatible functions does not exceed 3%.

2.2 Block-Rotation Model

Block-rotation model is meant to be executed in two-step synchronous mode. Accordingly, a partition of the array into two parts is to be constructed, both parts consisting of blocks 2×2 cells. The first part is called *even part*, its blocks having their diagonal cells with even sum of their indices. The second is referred to as *odd part*, its blocks having the same sum equal to an odd number. Such type of CA partitioning is called a *Margolus neighborhood* [8]. Each iteration is divided into two steps. At the even steps the transition rule is applied to all even blocks, at the odd steps - to all odd blocks. Alternating even and odd parts in execution process allows to avoid contradictoriness [6]. The transition rule is one and the same at odd and even steps: at each even (odd) step all even (odd) blocks are rotated $\pi/2$ clockwise or counterclockwise with equal probability p. Following the formalisms of [6] the rule is expressed as follows.

$$
\begin{cases}
\theta_1 : (rand < p) * \ (u[i,j], u[i,j+1], u[i+1.j+1], u[i+1,j]) \\
\qquad \rightarrow (u[i+1,j], u[i,j], u[i,j+1], u[i+1.j+1],); \\
\theta_2 : (rand \geq p) * \ (u[i,j], u[i,j+1], u[i+1.j+1], u[i+1,j]) \\
\qquad \rightarrow (u[i,j+1], u[i+1.j+1], u[i+1,j], u[i,j]);
\end{cases}
\tag{10}
$$

where $rand$ is a random number in the range equal to 1.

In [2] the coefficient $D = \tau d$ of this model is proved theoretically to be equal to $D_R = 3/2$ for the probability $p = 1/2$. This value characterizes the abstract diffusion model, but is too large to be used for simulating any physical process. So, it is necessary to know how to modify the transition rules to obtain a model of a real required process. Moreover, for the comparison of simulation results with PDE solutions be correct, the diffusion coefficients should be equal, and, hence, they have to meet the condition (9).

There are three possibilities to regulate diffusion coefficient $D = d\tau/h^2$ of the model.

1) Variation of time step τ. For example, if a coeffitient D is wanted, then the time step

$$
\tau' = D_R\tau/D = 3/2D
$$

. So, if $D = 0,25$, τ' is to be 6 times less than τ, i.e. each step should be considered as $\tau/6$.

2) Variation of the probability p. Taking

$$
p' = pD_R/D
$$

it is possible to model process with D as a diffusion coefficient.

3) Variation of spatial step h, which should be taken as

$$
h' = h\sqrt{D_r/D}
$$

. Simulation experiments of this model pursued two goals. The first is to determine whether the process coincide with that of corresponding PDE. The second is to check whether the above methods of determining diffusion coefficients yield the wanted results.

Functions $U_R(j)$ were calculated at times $T_R = 100$ and $T_R = 750$ with the probability value $p_1 = 1/2$ as well as at times $T_R = 600$ and $T_R = 3000$ with $p_2 = 1/12$. The size of the array was 400×400, its initial global state had a square 100×100 of "ones" at the center surrounded by a square 200×200 of randomly placed "ones" with the density equal to $1/2$, all remaining cells being empty. The obtained function values were compared with those of U_{PDE} at compatible times $T_{PDE} = 600$ and $T_{PDE} = 3000$, respectively (Table 2). Average deviation between curves $U_R(j)$ and $U_{PDE}(j)$ for the case $p_1 = 1/2$ does not exceed 2.5%, while that of the case $p_2 = 1/12$ is slightly larger. (Probably. it is due to computation inaccuracy provoked by random numbers generator imperfection).

Table 2

Simulation Results for Stochastic Diffusion Models

	Initial	Bl.rot.p=1/2		Bl.rot.p=1/12		Bl.rot.as		PDE	
$j\backslash T$	0	100	750	600	3000	240	1200	600	3000
0	400.0	400.0	290.0	400.0	322.0	396	284.0	396.3	289.9
10	400.0	399.0	285.0	394.0	311.0	391.0	277.0	393.6	285.0
20	400.0	389.0	270.0	385.0	286.0	365.0	277.0	382.8	274.0
30	400.0	371.0	257.0	368.0	291.0	330.0	248.0	356.7	256.4
40	395.0	314.0	224.0	325.0	270.0	280.0	223.0	310.3	233.5
50	250.4	230.0	210.0	238.0	231.0	245.0	189.0	248.2	206.8
60	100.0	178.0	179.0	166.0	213.0	193.0	170.0	185.3	180.1
70	100.0	134.0	144.0	115.0	173.0	144.0	137.0	135.3	149.0
80	100.0	93.0	120.0	100.0	128.0	106.0	122.0	100.3	121.0
90	95.0	74.0	93.0	72.0	91.0	74.0	98.0	86.4	95.3
100	50.0	53.0	77.0	56.0	70.0	53.0	56.0	61.2	72.8
110	0	24.0	58.0	27.0	43.0	35.0	44.0	38.1	53.8
120	0.0	13.0	52.0	7.0	28.0	21.0	35.0	19.6	38.3
130	0	5.0	33.0	2.0	21.0	8.0	25.0	.0	26.3
140	0.0	0.0	22.0	0.0	13.0	5.0	17.0	2.5	17.3
150	0.0	0.0	14.0	0.0	8.0	1.0	5.0	0.6	11.0
160	0.0	0.0	10.0	0.0	2.0	5.0	5.0	0.1	6.6
170	0.0	0.0	5.0	0.0	1.0	1.0	4.0	0.0	3.7
180	0.0	0.0	2.0	0.0	0.0	0.0	0.0	0.0	1.9

It makes sense also to know whether block rotating method may be used in asynchronous mode. The reason of such an interest is in that Cellular Nonlinear Networks (CNN) analogous (asynchronous) VLSI chips and based on them a special-purpose processor (CNN-machine) with extremely high performance are under construction [4]. So, the substitution set under asynchronous execution mode was also tested. The simulation was done with the same initial conditions as in the synchronous case. Functions $U_{R-as}(j)$ at times $(T_{R-as} = 240$ and $T_{R-as} = 1200$, compatible with those given for synchronous case, were obtained (Table 2). It is seen, that the diffusion coefficient $D = 0.512$, it differs from that of the synchronous case, calculated according to (9). The deviation from the corresponding PDE solutions at compatible times is not more 5%.

Block-rotating method was also tested for a diffusion through a porous wall. The holes are chosen to be not less than 20 cells wide as it is recommended in [9] for the mean density (the mean number of particles in a block) $\rho = 2$ (Fig3. the left box). In order to campare the averaged concentration function the rotation probability is taken equal to $p = 1/12$. Two curves for U_R and U_{PDE} are shown together in Fig3, the right box)

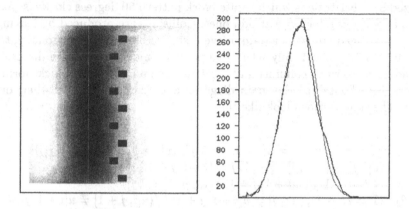

Fig. 3. Block-rotating diffusion ($p = 1/12$) through a porous wall: a shnapshot at $T = 2000$ (the left box), and the curves U_R (with imperfections) and U_{PDE} (smooth), (the right box)

From the right part of Fig.3 it is seen that the dynamics of the block-rotating method is very close to finite-difference solutioons.

3   Deterministic CA Diffusion Models

As distinct from stochastic CA-models, where diffusion process is thought of as a chaotic motion of abstract particles, deterministic models represent diffusion as a combination of particles propagation and collisions, propagation being responsible for convective and wavelike phenomena, while collisions correspond to diffusion. Such models reflect microscopic gas dynamics, which is described by Boltzmann or Navier-Stokes equations, rather than by PDE (1). Models to be studied in this section are invertible, obeying all conservation laws mentioned in section 1. But the determinism and rough rotation invariant of 90° lead to spurious conservation laws (conservation of momentum along each axis) and, hence, result to significant departure from physical behavior of gas or fluid flow. Nevertheless, it displays correctly the dynamics of concentration distribution and is considered in [7,8,10] as a gas diffusion phenomenon.

3.1 TM-Gas

TM-gas takes its name from the authors of [8]. The array is partitioned in the same manner than it is done in block-rotation model. The execution mode is two-step synchronous. Like all gas-lattice models this one provides two phases of abstract particles actions. The first is a *propagation phase*, in which particles advance one cell at each step. The second is a *collision phase*, which occurs if two particles moving in opposite directions meet in one and the same block of cells, and results in changing by 90 degrees the direction of propagation. Propagation is realized by substitutions which rotate block pattern 90 degrees clockwise at even steps, and counterclockwise at odd ones. Collisions are produced by leaving cell states unchanged during one (odd or even) step in blocks with diagonal patterns. Such blocks may occur only when two particles move in opposite directions in two adjacent rows or columns and meet in one and the same block, forming a pattern with "ones" at the main diagonal and "zeros" - at the other, or vice versa. The substitutions look like this.

$$\begin{cases} \theta_1 : (T = 2k), (u[i,j] \neq u[i+1, j+1]) \bigvee (u[i, j+1] \neq u[i+1, j])) * \\ \quad (u[i,j], u[i+1,j], u[i+1,j+1], u[i,j+1]) \\ \quad \rightarrow (u[i+1,j], u[i+1,j+1], u[i,j+1], u[i,j]) \\ \theta_2 : (T = 2k+1), (u[i,j] \neq u[i+1,j+1]) \bigvee (u[i,j+1] \neq u[i+1,j])) * \\ \quad (u[i,j], u[i+1,j], u[i+1,j+1], u[i,j+1]) \\ \quad \rightarrow (u[i,j+1], u[i+1,j+1], u[i+1,j], u[i,j]) \end{cases} \quad (11)$$

It is easily seen, that both conditions (conservation law and spatial symmetry) are met in the model. Moreover, the model exhibits a spurious conservation law, leaving invariant mass and momentum along each propagation direction. This property is a significant disadvantage to be used to model Navier-Stokes PDE, but is assumed to fit for diffusion in gas and fluids.

Due to the fact that a change of propagation direction may occur only as a result of a collision, the initial array in simulation experiments should have no "vacuum space" (array space filled with zeroes). The reason is that in the vacuum "particles" will propagate without collisions, which corresponds to the case of rarefied gas where diffusion phenomenon show no evidence.

The share of wavelike component depends on the density ρ of the concentration, which is measured as the mean amount of "ones" in a block on a given area A of the array.

$$\rho = 1/4 \sum_{ij \in A} u_{ij},$$

To test the influence of the density on the diffusion dynamics two experiments have been performed. Both have the initial array state as follows: a square 20×20 cells in the center of the array is randomly filled with "ones" in such a way, that the density is $\rho = \rho_1$, the remaining area of array having $\rho = \rho_2$. The boundary conditions are taken to be Neumann ones. In the first experiment $\rho_1 = 2, \rho_2 = 1$. The beginning of the process is characterized by fast propagation of particles from the dense area to the borders of the array, leaving the center almost empty (Fig.4, the left box), which is conditioned by the wavelike component of its behavior. The wave is reflected from the borders forming a moving structure which gradually blurs due to the influence of diffusion component (Fig.4, the right box). At last (in our experiment at $T \approx 500$) concentration distribution becomes completely homogeneous.

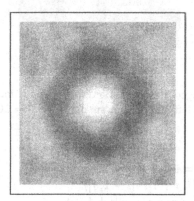 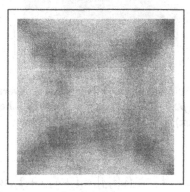

Fig. 4. TM-gas diffusion simulation. Averaged representation, initial conditions with $\rho_1 = 2, \rho2 = 1$ a snapshot at $T = 25$ (the left box) and a snapshot of $T = 100$ (the right box)

The second experiment was performed with $\rho_1 = 3, \rho_2 = 2$. It is seen (Fig.5, the left box) that the wave is less distinguished, compared with the above case at the same time, and the steady state comes earlier.

3.2 HPP-Gas

There are two different algorithms of HPP-gas model: the compact one, where elementary automata states are represented as Boolean vectors 4 bits long [3], and a one-bit model based on Margolus neighborhood with two-step mode of operation. Here, the latter variant is studied, since it is similar to the algorithms considered above.

HPP-gas model differs from TM-gas only in particles propagation direction: particles move along the diagonals, rather than along array axes. Collisions occur when particles meet in a block, resulting in rotating 90 degrees the way they came up. Partitioning of the array is done in the same way than in block-rotation model. The mode of execution is two-step synchronous. Each iteration consists of two steps: the even part operates at even steps, the odd part - at odd ones, transition rule being identical in both cases. The set of substitutions is as follows.

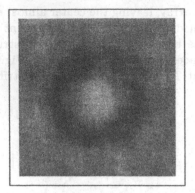

Fig. 5. TM-gas diffusion simulation. Averaged representation, initial conditions with $\rho_1 = 3, \rho_2 = 2$ a snapshot at $T = 25$ (the left box, and a snapshot of $T = 100$ (the right box)

$$
\begin{cases}
\theta_1 : (u[i,j] = u[i+1,j+1] = \bar{u}[i,j+1] = \bar{u}[i+1,j])* \\
\quad (u[i,j], u[i+1,j+1], u[i,j+1], u[i+1,j]) \\
\quad \rightarrow (\bar{u}[i,j], \bar{u}[i+1,j+1], \bar{u}[i,j+1], \bar{u}[i+1,j]), \\
\theta_2 : ((u[i,j] \neq u[i+1,j+1]) \bigvee (u[i,j+1] \neq u[i+1,j]))* \\
\quad (u[i,j], u[i+1,j+1], u[i,j+1], u[i+1,j]) \\
\quad \rightarrow (u[i+1,j+1], u[i,j], u[i+1,j], u[i,j+1]).
\end{cases} \tag{12}
$$

The first substitution of (12) represents the collision phase: if there are two "ones" in diagonal cells of a block, the other diagonal having "zeros", then all states of the block are inverted. New positions of "ones" make them propagate in the other diagonal direction. The propagation is represented by θ_2. Diffusion dynamics is similar to that of TM-gas, except the direction of initial propagation (Fig.6).

It is clear that the larger is the number of propagation directions, the better is the correspondence between the model and the real diffusion. So, the composition of HPP and TM models yields in a new model with eight propagation directions. Mode of execution is 4-step synchronous. Each iteration consists of four steps: at the first two steps HPP transition rule (11) is applied, the third and the fourth are left for TM substitutions (10). Diffusion process differs from the two previously considered only at the first 20 iterations, until the round wave is formed. As expected the time of reaching steady state is less than that of each model-component more than twice.

3.3   1D Gas-Lattice Diffusion

1D Gas-Lattice diffusion model (GL-model) [10] has the peculiarity consisting in that two particle velocity values and two particle mass values are allowed to

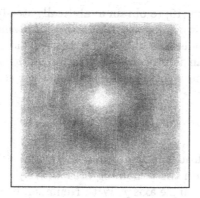

Fig. 6. HPP-gas diffusion simulation. Averaged representation, initial conditions with $\rho_1 = 2, \rho_2 = 1$ a snapshot at $T = 15$

characterize cell state. It has been proposed and studied, because of its simplicity as distinct from its counterparts in higher dimensions, which makes more accessible the theoretical analysis, and, thus it allowed to obtain analytically some macroscopic properties.

Cell states are four bit vectors of the form (n_3, n_2, n_1, n_0), each bit representing the presence ($n_i = 1$) or the absence ($n_i = 0$) of a particle characterized by a mass and a speed vector according to the following table.

n_i	n_3	n_2	n_1	n_0
M	m	$2m$	$2m$	$2m$
C	$2c$	$-2c$	c	$-c$

Like all gas-lattice models this one also provides propagation and collision phases. During the propagation phase all particles advance one or two cells according to the values and directions of their speeds. For example, if a $(j+1)$th cell state has $n_0 = 1$, then the corresponding particle with a mass equal to $2m$ (a heavy particle) propagates to the jth cell, if a $(j-2)$th cell state has $n_3 = 1$, then a light particle (with the mass equal to m) moves from the $(j-2)$th cell to the jth one. Collision occurs when two particles with different masses meet in an one and the same cell. Colliding they exchange their velocities. It means that if a cell state is "0110", then is changes to "1001" and vice versa, which asserts that all conservation conditions are met. The substitution set, describing the process is as follows.

$$\theta_1 : (T = 2k) * (u[i]) \rightarrow$$
$$(u[j+1]\&0001) \bigvee (u[j+2]\&0100) \bigvee (u[j-1]\&0010) \bigvee (u[j-2]\&1000);$$
$$\theta_2 : (T = 2k+1) * (n_0 = n_3 \& n_1 = n_2) \rightarrow$$
$$(\bar{n}_0, \bar{n}_1, \bar{n}_2, \bar{n}_3);$$

$$(13)$$

The model is used in [10] to obtain analytically steady state solution in non-convective case, which is in good accordance with Boltzmann equations solution, As in all gas-lattice models the wave-like component is present, its influence diminishing with the mean density of concentration. In this model the mean density ρ is measured as the mean total mass of particles per cell over a given area.

$$\rho = \sum_{j \in A} \sum_{1}^{4} n_i M_i$$

Having initial conditions in the form of a vertical strip with $\rho_1 = 4.5$ in the middle of the array with the remaining area with $\rho_2 = 3$ we obtained a plane wave moving along the single axis j. With Neumann boundary conditions twice being reflected from the borders the wave disappeared completely (Fig.7).

Fig. 7. 1D-gas-lattice diffusion simulation. Averaged representation, initial conditions with $\rho_1 = 4.5, \rho_2 = 3$ a snapshot at T=30

4 Conclusion

The scope of known up till now cellular automata diffusion models form two groups: stochastic and deterministic models. Stochastic models exhibited are in a good accordance with the dynamics represented by finite difference PDE solution. Block-rotating model in synchronous mode of operation corresponds to dynamics with constant diffusion coefficient, and, hence, is the most practical one. It is shown how to modify the model for obtaining dynamics with a given diffusion coefficient. Simulations of asynchronous version of this model showed, that its diffusion coefficient depends on the concentration gradient. Deterministic models are based on gas-lattice ideas and may be used to mimic dynamics in rarefied gas. Their dynamics exhibits both a wavelike and a diffusive component, the influence of the first being stronger with decreasing concentration density. Quantitative characteristics of deterministic models are not yet studied.

References

1. T.Toffolli. Cellular automata as an alternative to (rather than an approximation of) differential equations in modelling physics. //Physica D, vol. 10 (1984),pp.117-127.
2. G.G.Malinetski, M.E.Stepantsov. Modelling diffusive processes by cellular automata with Margolus neighborhood. // Zhurnal Vychislitelnoj Matematiki i Matematicheskoj Physiki, vol.38, N 6 (1998), pp.1017-1021. (in Russian)
3. U.Frish, D.d"Humiere, B.Hasslacher, P.Lallemand, Y.Pomeau, J.-P.Rivet. Lattice gas hydrodinamics in two or three dimensions.// Complex Systems, Vol.1 (1987),pp.649-707.
4. T.Roska, L.Chua. The CNN Universal Machine: An Analogic Array Computer // IEEE Trans.on Circuits and Systems - part II, vol.40 (1993), pp. 163-173.
5. S.Bandini, G.Mauri (Eds).Proceedings of the Second (and Third) Conference on Cellular Automata for Research and Industry.- Milan (Trieste), 1996 (1998), Springer, 1996 (1998).
6. S.Achasova, O.Bandman, V.Markova, S.Piskunov. Parallel Substitution Algorithm. Theory and Application. - World Scientific, Singapore, 1994, 180 pp.180.
7. J.Hardy, O..de Pazzis, Y.Pomeau. Molecular dynamics of a classical lattice gas. Transport properties and time correlation functions.// Physical Review, A13(1976), pp.1949-1960.
8. T.Toffolli, N.Margolus. Cellular Automata Machine.- MIT Press, 1987, 280pp.
9. D.H.Rothman. Cellular-automaton fluids: a model for flow in porous media. // Geophysics. Vol. 53, N 4, 1988. p.509-518.
10. Y.H.Qian, D. d"Humieres, P.Lallemand. Diffusion Simulation with a Deterministic One-Dimensional Lattice-Gas Model. // Journal of Statistical Physics, Vol.68, N 3/4,1992. p.563-572.

Creating and Running Mobile Agents with XJ DOME

Kirill Bolshakov, Andrei Borshchev, Alex Filippoff,
Yuri Karpov, and Victor Roudakov

Distributed Computing & Networking Dept.
St.Petersburg Technical University
195251 St.Petersburg Russia
Experimental Object Technologies (XJ)
dome@xjtek.com
http://www.xjtek.com

Abstract. XJ DOME is a set of tools and techniques for those who wish to speed up development of Distributed COM applications and improve their quality. DOME supports graphical modeling, code generation, simulation, deployment, monitoring and management. The simulation mode enables the developer to simulate the entire distributed application in virtual time on a single machine. After simulation step the application can be deployed onto the target network and managed via DOME Application Viewer. During run-time DOME platform enables the developer to collect and watch statistics, inspect threads and synchronization objects, view logs. DOME platform supports building of mobile agent systems on top of DCOM services. It provides for agent migration and employs DCOM security.

1 Introduction

Mobile agents are attracting interest from fields of distributed systems, information retrieval, electronic commerce and artificial intelligence as a rapidly evolving technology. This area suffers a lack of industrial-strength development tools support.

In this paper we present XJ DOME – run-time and development environment for building mobile agent system on top of Microsoft DCOM services [2,3]. It also provides graphical specification of object behavior, as well as simulation and visualization services. XJ DOME may tightly integrate with MS Visual C++ Developer Studio. Thus, DOME provides the developer with friendly environment from specification through debugging to real execution stage.

2 The Current State of Mobile Agent Systems Market

The vast majority of the agent systems available are research prototypes and only a few of them have users outside their own university or research institute [1]. The most known are Aglets (IBM, Japan), Mole (University of Stuttgart, Germany), Telescript

(General Magic, USA) and AgentTcl (Dartmouth College, USA). Aglets and Mole sup-port Java, AgentTcl supports Tcl, Telescript has its own language.

However, there are no high-level rapid application development (RAD) environ-ments for agents development. Also, at the moment there is no mobile agent system based on DCOM platform. The implementation of mobile agent system for DCOM enables to utilize its performance advantages (execution of native code and full access to OS services) and integration with MS Windows NT security.

3 XJ DOME Run-Time Environment

XJ DOME run-time environment supports the following models of mobile agents:

- Lifecycle
- Computational
- Communication
- Navigation
- Security

The lifecycle model provides services to create, destroy, save and restore mobile agents. The computational model heavily relies on Win32 services at the moment. The navigation model handles all issues referring to transporting an agent between two places. The communication model defines communication between agents. The secu-rity model defines rules of mutual access for agents and network.

We build our communication, navigation and security models on top of Microsoft DCOM. This allows the developer to fully exploit the advantages of Microsoft indus-try standard for Windows environments. This also greatly simplifies dealing with numerous security issues intrinsic to mobile agent systems.

4 DOME Application Editor

The basic services provided by XJ DOME Developer Studio are:

- Creation of COM components in visual environment with complete code gen-eration (for both static and dynamic components)
- Debugging of timings and synchronization and performance estimation of a distributed application by simulating it in virtual time on the developer's ma-chine
- Deployment of the application components over the target network
- Monitoring of the distributed application: collect and display statistics, inspect threads and synchronization objects, view logs, etc.
- Management of the distributed application via COM interfaces using standard controls

For rapid prototyping of distributed COM applications XJ DOME offers Applica-tion Editor, see Figure 1. It includes graphical COM Object Diagram and Statecharts editors. DOME Application Editor generates the complete application code including IDL, C++, resources, and MS Visual C++ project. It builds the application components using MS Visual C++ command-line compiler. DOME Application Editor drastically saves developer's time on the early design stages. Later on, when "COM skeleton" of the application becomes more stable, the developer can continue with MS Visual C++ environment using built-in DOME Wizards.

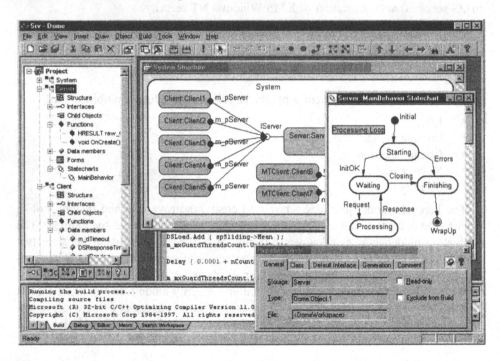

Fig. 1. XJ DOME Application Editor

5 Wizards for MS Visual C++

DOME can be used with new projects as well as with the legacy software. In the latter case DOME functionality can be added to the application gradually. By following a set of simple rules one can easily instrument COM objects under development to use DOME simulation, deployment, visualization and management facilities. To automate this work DOME adds to MS Visual C++ development environment a set of wizards covering all related tasks:

- *DOME App Wizard* — creates a skeleton application project.
- *Add DOME Object* — adds an object with support of standard DOME interfaces and skeleton implementation to the application project.

- *Add Child Object* — adds aggregated or contained child object to DOME object.
- *Add COM pointer* — adds a COM pointer to DOME object. DOME Objects communicate by calling methods of each other via COM pointers that are in turn set up by DOME run-time environment.
- *Add DOME Thread* — adds a control thread to DOME object. DOME objects can have several control threads and spawn them dynamically.
- *Add DOME Statistics* — adds an ability to collect statistics to DOME object. On execution stage the statistics is available for monitoring in DOME Viewer.
- *Add DOME Log* — adds a log access point to DOME object. DOME a feature that allows the user to watch logs of several objects deployed to different hosts.

6 Simulation

Simulation is used for preliminary analysis of the application correctness and estimation of its performance. In the simulation mode the most detailed information on threads and synchronization objects is available online in DOME Application Viewer, see Figure 2. The user can run the application step-by-step, stop upon a certain condition, e.g. when enough statistics is collected, etc. Using automation the developer can program DOME to run multiple simulation sessions to find optimal parameter values or to test the application scalability. All the simulation is performed on a single developer's machine.

DOME simulates the application in virtual time, thus making arbitrary complex experiments possible on a single workstation.

Simulation is supported by DOME Engine that implements IDomeEngineSite interface. The application objects developed according to DOME technology invoke the functions creating new objects, threads, synchronization objects, delaying thread execution, waiting for events, etc. through IDomeEngineSite. In the normal execution mode such call is transparently passed to the local operating system (in fact, the call does not even leave the local machine, as the engine is represented there by a lightweight DOME Engine Proxy object). In the simulation mode, the engine takes care of thread scheduling, synchronization and time.

7 Visualization

The user can monitor the running application with DOME Application Viewer. The viewer retrieves the information via IDomeObject interfaces implemented by DOME-compatible application components and displays the global picture of the application, including:

- Application objects and their hierarchy
- Threads
- Synchronization objects

- Statistics
- Logs
- Inspection views
- IDispatch interfaces of objects

The details of the displayed information depend on the execution mode. Namely, in the simulation mode the user can watch the current states of the synchronization objects and threads, and wait queues, whereas in the normal mode these details are not available.

The user can request information about running agents on the specific nodes and view their statistics, as well as access their properties and status information.

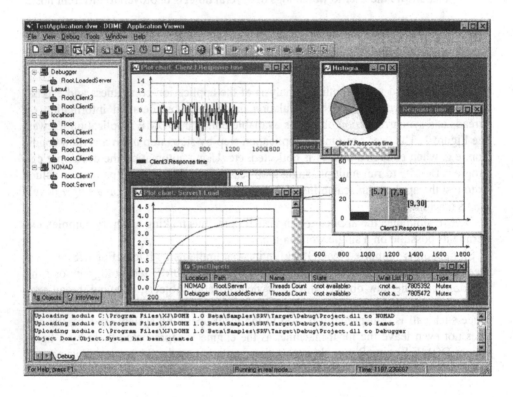

Fig. 2. XJ DOME Application Viewer

8 Management

The user can manage DCOM application with DOME Application Viewer. Before the application starts the user chooses the execution mode (simulation or normal), root objects and gives deployment instructions for static objects.

When the application is running, commands available in the viewer depend on the execution mode. In simulation mode the user has full control over the application execution. Since DOME Engine manages time and synchronization, the user can run the application step-by-step, stop, watch the activity of the selected object, etc. In the normal execution mode time and synchronization are managed by the operating system. In any mode the user can change the COM properties of any application object with DOME IDispatch Browser.

9 Example

As an example (see Figure 3), consider a file searching system. Its purpose is to find a file with a name corresponding to the given pattern and containing given text in it. The search system consists of two parts. The first one is an application that interacts with the user, requests corresponding patterns and reports the result on search completion. Another part of the search system is a mobile agent that travels through the domain and performs search procedure on every host in the domain. Due to the use of DCOM security model the agent has the same privileges as the user who launched it. As the agent finishes visiting hosts in the domain, it returns to the launching system and transfers the results to the front-end application, which reports them to the user.

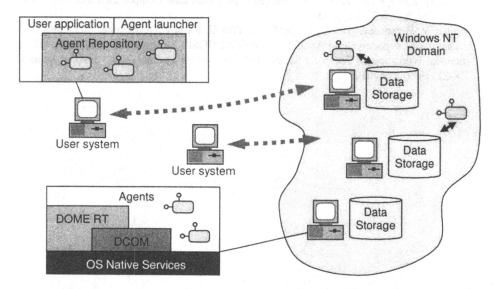

Fig. 3. An example of information retrieval system for distributed data storage

10 Future Work

As DOME is considered as a framework technology that can be used as a basis for building distributed applications with predictable quality of service, we are working in three directions:

- Implementing general-purpose distributed algorithms in DOME objects, such as distributed termination, distributed snapshot and distributed deadlock detection.
- Developing DOME object-compatible simulation models of communication and navigation models for mobile agent systems and communication media (networks and protocols) for better prediction of application performance.
- Incorporating UML Statecharts engine into DOME objects for enhancing clarity and expressive power of object behavior specification.

References

1. J. Baumann, F. Hohl, K. Rothermel and M. Strasser. Mole - Concepts of a mobile agent system. World Wide Web, 1 (1998), pp.123-127.
2. D. Krieger and R.M. Adler. The Emergence of Distributed Component Platforms. IEEE Computer, March 1998, pp. 43-53.
3. Andrei V. Borshchev, Alex E. Filippoff and Yuri G. Karpov. Developing, Simulating and Managing Distributed COM Applications with XJ DOME. In Proceedings of the 1st International Workshop on Computer Science and Information Technologies, Moscow, January 18-22, 1999, Volume 2.

Parallelization and Integration of the LU and ILU Algorithm in the LINSOL Program Package

Hartmut Häfner, Willi Schönauer, and Rüdiger Weiss

Numerical Research group for Supercomputers, Computing Center, Universität
Karlsruhe, 76128 Karlsruhe, Germany,
haefner@rz.uni-karlsruhe.de, schoenauer@rz.uni-karlsruhe.de,
weiss@rz.uni-karlsruhe.de,
WWW home page: http://www.rz.uni-karlsruhe.de/Uni/RZ/Forschung/Numerik/

Abstract. In order to provide generally applicable iterative linear
solvers for the community of scientific computing the LINSOL program
package has been designed. The focus of this package is on portability,
robustness and on an efficient implementation on massively parallel systems. LINSOL uses iterative solvers as basic methods that are state of
the art. Different normalization methods can be used to improve the
convergence rates of the iterative solvers. Now preconditioners like the
(in)complete Gaussian algorithm are being implemented. The paper is
focussed on this type of algorithm. LINSOL is tuned to massively parallel
systems with distributed memory. Therefore, the message passing programming style is used. LINSOL supports many matrix formats for the
convenience of the users. Moreover, adaptive method selection schemes
called polyalgorithms are implemented.

1 Background

LINSOL [1997] [1998] is a parallel iterative linear solver package solving

$$Ax = b.$$

The program package is adapted to the application of sparse matrices, but can
also be efficiently applied to full matrices. It presently contains fourteen iterative
methods and ten polyalgorithms of generalized Conjugate Gradient (CG) methods. The polyalgorithms use the fourteen iterative methods as basic algorithms
and differ by switching automatically between different methods.

Ten different data structures are supported by LINSOL to ease the embedding of LINSOL into an application as well as the mapping of arbitrary sparse
matrices to appropriate storage patterns.

The basic concepts of LINSOL are:

- **Flexibility or ease of use** - the design of LINSOL allows to use three types
  of interfaces and supports ten different data structures and storage patterns,
  respectively.

- **Portability** - by using the standardized Fortran77 and Fortran90 programming languages on single processor systems and additionally the *message passing* paradigm on parallel computers.
- **Robustness** - is obtained by fourteen different iterative solvers; they are suitable for different classes of matrices; additionally, adaptive polyalgorithms are provided that choose an appropriate solver from the fourteen methods. To enhance the robustness of LINSOL an (incomplete) LU algorithm embedded as a preconditioner into the iterative methods is being integrated into the program package.
- **Optimized code** for workstations (PCs), vectorcomputers and parallel computers - by reusing data in the highest memory hierarchy as far as possible and by using vector pipelining and parallel algorithms with a high *volume-to-surface* ratio. Two absolutely essential features for parallel software and thus for LINSOL are: scalability regarding the computation time and scalability regarding the memory. The second feature is achieved by the rowwise distribution of the matrix A onto matrix blocks and by the distribution of all vectors of LINSOL in vector parts adapted to the distribution of the matrix.

There are three essential features of LINSOL. First LINSOL is designed as "Black Box" solver which means that as few parameters as possible should be user-defined. Second the convergence behaviour and the results of LINSOL do to not depend on the number of processors (at least if we neglect the roundoff errors). Third many storage patterns are supported by LINSOL. These basic data structures are: main diagonal (assumed full), full (non-main) diagonal, packed diagonal (elements and their indices, from the first to the last nonzero element), indexed column (one element per row and the corresponding column index, from the first to the last nonzero element), indexed row (similarly one element per column and its row index), starry sky (nonzero elements with row and column indices), full row, full column, packed row (nonzero elements in a row and their column indices from the first to the last nonzero element) and packed column (similarly nonzero elements in a column and their row indices). They can be assembled without cutback to the matrix A, if A is nonsymmetric. If A is symmetric the only cutback is that the storage pattern "main diagonal" must exist and all main diagonal elements must be stored there.

If all iterative methods fail or converge very slowly, the incomplete or full Gaussian algorithm is being provided as a preconditioner for the iterative methods. The full Gaussian algorithm can be used as "emergency exit", if all iterative solvers fail to converge. Incomplete stands for the dropping of small matrix elements before and during the elimination process. To enable the preconditioning of large matrices the algorithm from Gibbs, Poole, Stockmeyer is being inserted as a bandwidth optimizer and the elimination process is executed in a dynamically used buffer whose size is determined by the bandwidth of the matrix. The parallelization of the bandwidth optimizer will be presented in a separate subsequent paper from W. Schönauer, D. Zundel and H. Häfner. For the parallelization of the Gaussian elimination process the matrix and the dynamically used buffer are wrapped row by row onto the processors. The goal is to embed

Basic data structures of the matrix A supported by LINSOL and the corresponding basic
vector operation types of the matrix-vector multiplication (c=A*r):

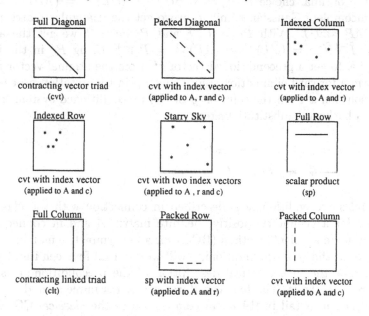

Fig. 1. Basic Data Structures of LINSOL

the LU/ILU algorithm into LINSOL so that the direct solver can be used as a
preconditioner transparently to the user for all classes of matrices and for all
processor numbers. C. Vuik, R.R.P. van Nooyen and P. Wesseling developed a
parallel ILU-preconditioned GMRES method for matrices with nine non-zero
diagonals [1998]; thus the algorithm only works for a special class of matrices.
Within the PARASOL project (http://192.129.37.12/parasol) parallel sparse direct methods are being developed, too. But these methods can only be used as
direct solvers; another difference in comparison to LINSOL is that the approach
will be based on the multifrontal method as developed by Ian Duff and John
Reid. The principal feature of the approach is that the matrix factorization can
be represented by a tree where each edge represents the communication of data
and each node some elimination operation on dense submatrices.

2 Mathematical Outline

The embedding of the Gaussian algorithm into the iterative methods reads
as follows. Instead of the linear system $Ax = b$ the preconditioned system
$P_L A P P_R y = P_L b$ with $x = P_R y$ must be solved. P_L $(P_R) \in R^{n \times n}$ is a nonsingular left-hand (right-hand) preconditioning matrix acting on the equations
(solutions); P is a permutation matrix emerging from the partial pivoting in
the Gaussian elimination. By the full Gaussian elimination we get the trian-

gular matrices U and L with $AP = UL$. With $P_L = U^{-1}$ and $P_R = L^{-1}$ we get the optimal choice $P_R P_L = L^{-1} U^{-1} = (UL)^{-1} = (AP)^{-1} = PA^{-1}$. By the incomplete Gaussian elimination we get the triangular matrices $\tilde{U}$ and $\tilde{L}$ with $AP \approx \tilde{U}\tilde{L}$. With $P_L = \tilde{U}^{-1}$ and $P_R = \tilde{L}^{-1}$ we get the approach $P_R P_L = \tilde{L}^{-1}\tilde{U}^{-1} = (\tilde{U}\tilde{L})^{-1} \approx (AP)^{-1} = PA^{-1}$. Using P_L in the iteration process, i.e. to get a preconditioned vector r^P from the original vector r, means to perform a forward elimination step; using P_R in the iteration process, i.e. to get the solution x from the solution y of the preconditioned system, means to perform a backward substitution step:

$$Ur^P = r \Leftrightarrow r^P = U^{-1}r$$
$$Lx = y \Leftrightarrow x = L^{-1}y$$

As examples preconditioning is described in connection with the *classical* CG algorithm for a symmetric positive definite matrix A and in connection with the biconjugate gradients method (BCG) for a nonsymmetric matrix A. It must be mentioned that the preconditioning will work for all fourteen iterative methods and that the mathematical description of the preconditioning is varying for different methods. The fourteen iterative solvers implemented in LINSOL are described in detail in [1996]. In comparison to the *classical* CG algorithm the residual $r_k = Ax_k - b(k = 0, 1, 2, ...)$ has to be substituted by $r_k^P = P_L r_k$ and the matrix A by $P_L A P P_R$. Thus the term Ar_k must be substituted by $\hat{r}_k = P_L A P P_R r_k^P$.

For an arbitrary *initial guess* x_0 holds:

$$Ax = A(\tilde{x} + x_0) = b \Leftrightarrow A\tilde{x} = b - Ax_0 \Leftrightarrow A\tilde{x} = \tilde{b}.$$

Now we solve $P_L A P P_R \tilde{y} = P_L \tilde{b}$ with $\tilde{x} = PP_R\tilde{y}, \tilde{x}_0 = 0$ and calculate

$$r_0 = -\tilde{b}, \ r_0^P = P_L r_0, \ \hat{r}_0 = P_L A P P_R r_0^P \text{ and for } k \geq 0:$$

$$\alpha_{1,k}^P = -\frac{\left(r_k^P\right)^T \hat{r}_k}{\left(r_k^P\right)^T r_k^P}$$

$$\alpha_{2,k}^P = -\frac{\left(r_{k-1}^P\right)^T \hat{r}_k}{\left(r_{k-1}^P\right)^T r_{k-1}^P}$$

$$\phi_k^P = \frac{1}{\alpha_{1,k}^P + \alpha_{2,k}^P}$$

$$r_{k+1}^P = \phi_k^P (P_L A P P_R r_k^P + \alpha_{1,k}^P r_k^P + \alpha_{2,k}^P r_{k-1}^P)$$

with $r_k^P = P_L r_k$, $\tilde{r}_k = PP_R r_k^P$ and $\hat{r}_k = P_L A P P_R r_k^P$

$$\tilde{x}_{k+1} = PP_R\tilde{y}_{k+1} = \phi_k^P (PP_R r_k^P + \alpha_{1,k}^P PP_R\tilde{y}_k + \alpha_{2,k}^P PP_R\tilde{y}_{k-1})$$
$$= \phi_k^P (\tilde{r}_k + \alpha_{1,k}^P \tilde{x}_k + \alpha_{2,k}^P \tilde{x}_{k-1}).$$

In BCG we solve $P_L A P P_R \tilde{y} = P_L \tilde{b}$ with $\tilde{x} = P P_R \tilde{y}, \tilde{x}_0 = 0$ and calculate

$$r_0 = -\tilde{b}, \quad r_0^P = p_0^P = P_L r_0, \quad (r_0^P)^* = (p_0^P)^* = P_R^T r_0^* \text{ and for } k \geq 0 :$$

$$\delta_k^P = -\frac{\left(r_k^P\right)^T \left(r_k^P\right)^*}{\left(p_k^P\right)^T P_R^T P A^T P_L^T \left(p_k^P\right)^*} = -\frac{\left(r_k^P\right)^T \left(r_k^P\right)^*}{\left(p_k^P\right)^T \left(\hat{p}_k^P\right)^*}$$

$$r_{k+1}^P = r_k^P + \delta_k^P P_L A P P_R p_k^P = r_k^P + \delta_k^P P_L A \tilde{p}_k^P$$

$$\left(r_{k+1}^P\right)^* = \left(r_k^P\right)^* + \delta_k^P \left(\hat{p}_k^P\right)^*$$

$$\beta_k^P = \frac{\left(r_{k+1}^P\right)^T \left(r_{k+1}^P\right)^*}{\left(r_k^P\right)^T \left(r_k^P\right)^*}$$

$$p_{k+1}^P = r_{k+1}^P + \beta_k^P p_k^P$$

$$\left(p_{k+1}^P\right)^* = \left(r_{k+1}^P\right)^* + \beta_k^P \left(p_k^P\right)^*$$

$$\tilde{x}_{k+1} = P P_R \tilde{y}_{k+1} = P P_R (\tilde{y}_k + \delta_k^P p_k^P)$$

$$= \tilde{x}_k + \delta_k^P \tilde{p}_k^P.$$

Thus the CG algorithm needs one forward elimination step and one backward substitution step per iteration and the BCG algorithm two forward elimination steps and two backward substitution steps per iteration. To apply a vector to the permutation matrix P means to perform a permutation of the vector elements by an index list.

If the matrix A is symmetric we can use a Cholesky decomposition and get the triangular matrices L^T and L with $AP = L^T L$. Thus the elimination can be performed completely on L reducing the storage requirements to the halfth. It holds $P_L = P_R$ and the forward elimination takes place on P_L and the backward substitution on P_L^T.

To minimize the storage requirements of the preconditioning matrices P_L and P_R for sparse matrices they are stored in a packed storage pattern. During the elimination process the rows of the matrix to be eliminated are wrapped around onto the processors on parallel computers to obtain scalability and a good load balancing.

3 Brief Description of the LU/ILU-Preconditioner

The preconditioning process within the program package LINSOL consists of four parts:

- preparation of the LINSOL-matrix,
- application of the bandwidth optimizer,
- the elimination process and
- the repeated application of the forward elimination and of the backward substitution within the iterative solution process.

Between these four steps several permutation algorithms resorting the matrix and the right hand side respectively must be applied.

3.1 Preparation of the LINSOL-Matrix

The LINSOL-matrix (A) can be made up of the ten different data structures supported by LINSOL. However the preconditioning matrix (A^P) only works on the storage pattern "packed row". Thus the matrix A is completely reassembled "in place" in the storage pattern "packed row", and zero entries are eliminated to reduce the storage requirements. On parallel computers this algorithm can be performed locally on all processors. In a second preparation step rows with only one non-zero entry ("explicit" variables) are used to eliminate entries of all other rows in the column, corresponding to the single non-zero entry, by shifting the entries multiplied by the solution component of the row with the single non-zero entry to the right hand side. Thus new rows with only one non-zero entry can arise and again entries in the matrix A can be eliminated. If the matrix would be a permuted triangular matrix, this algorithm is equivalent to a backward substitution step on the original triangular matrix. In the next step a graph of the matrix A is created. As the LINSOL-matrix A is distributed in blocks of rows onto the processors and the graph has to be "symmetrized" for the application of the bandwidth optimizer, the generation process of the graph requires communication over all processors.

3.2 Application of the Bandwidth Optimizer

In the graph the row numbers of the matrix A are interpreted as nodes and the row indices (not equal to their row number) are interpreted as undirected edges. Thus we get a finite undirected graph without loops or multiple edges, on which the bandwidth optimization process is performed. In paper [1976] the used algorithm of Gibbs, Poole, Stockmeyer (GPS) is described in detail. The GPS-algorithm returns a permutation vector that is used to resort both rows and columns of the matrix A and the right hand side. Running LINSOL on more than one processor resorting of the rows of matrix A requires communication over all processors (see also Fig. 3).

3.3 The Elimination Process

Before the elimination process can be started, the matrix A must be copied into the preconditioning matrix A^P. To determine the size of the buffer in which the Gaussian elimination is processed on unpacked rows we need two definitions. The bandwidths β_U and β_L of the matrix A^P are defined by

$$\beta_U = \max_{a_{ij} \neq 0, j > i} (j - i) \text{ and } \beta_L = \max_{a_{ij} \neq 0, i > j} (i - j).$$

β_U is the maximal distance of elements above the main diagonal to the main diagonal; β_L is the maximal distance of elements below the main diagonal to the main diagonal. In the elimination process pivoting by columns is performed. Then the size of the buffer must be set to $(\beta_L + 2\beta_U)(\beta_L + \beta_U)$. $(\beta_L + 2\beta_U)$ is the buffer size of each row and the maximal number of rows in the buffer is $(\beta_L + \beta_U)$. The buffer consists of the pivot row and all further rows that have non-zero entries in the pivot column (in Fig. 2 the elimination process for the pivot rows 1 to 4 is depicted). The buffer is a one-dimensional array that is managed by an information array containing a pointer to the row elements, the global row number and the length of the row for each row stored in the buffer. In Fig. 2 the global row number can be seen below the entry "Row" for the elimination process of the pivot rows 1 to 4. Row by row is stored contiguously in the buffer till the end of the buffer is reached. Then a "garbage collection" is performed; this means that "active" rows (rows with row indices greater than the pivot row index) are shifted to a contiguous array at the beginning of the buffer.

The pivot column is the column with the maximal element in the pivot row. The permutation of column indices - caused by column pivoting - is stored in two permutation vectors assigned to the global matrix A^P (in Fig. 2 P_{global}) and the local buffer (in Fig. 2 P_{local}). The global permutation vector is used in the iteration process instead of the matrix P. The local permutation vector is used to assign matrix elements to the buffer.

For each pivot row the preconditioning matrix A^P must be searched for rows with non-zero entries in the pivot column. In parallel mode the processor with the pivot row has to broadcast the index of the pivot column to all processors and then each processor searches for rows in the locally stored matrix A^P. These rows must be unpacked and put into the buffer. E.g. in Fig. 2 the rows with the global row number 1,2 and 4 must be put into the buffer for pivot row 1 and pivot column 4. The buffering is done by the permutation vector P_{local} assigned to the local buffer. Thus the buffered part of the matrix A^P corresponds to the permuted matrix $(A^P P)$. The elimination process then runs on the unpacked rows in the buffer with the vectorlength of the pivot row reduced by 1. In Fig. 2 the computation area is surrounded by bold lines in the tables. After one computation step in the buffer the pivot row and the actual leftmost column of the buffer are restored to the preconditioning matrix A^P as packed row and packed column respectively. Restored values are depicted by a grey background in Fig. 2.

The parallelization of the elimination process is done by wrapping around the rows of the preconditioning matrix onto the processors. Unpacked rows in the buffer are stored on the same processor as the corresponding packed rows of the preconditioning matrix A^P. This kind of parallelization leads to a simple communication pattern. Only two "broadcasts" of the pivot indices and of the elimination coefficients, that are processed by the pivot processor, are necessary per one elimination step in the buffer for the update of the unpacked matrix rows in the buffers of all processors.

Actually the elimination is processed on unpacked rows in the buffer. If the matrix is very sparse within the bandwidth of the matrix A^P, the buffer contains

Elimination process: A = U * L * P

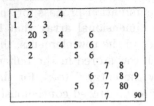

Matrix A with an upper bandwidth of 3
and a lower bandwidth of 3 stored in the
storage scheme of „packed rows"

For row 1

P_{global}	4	2	3	1	5	6
Row/P_{local}	4	2	3	1	5	6
1	4	2	0	1		
3	4	20	3	0	0	6
4	4	2	0	0	5	6

P_{global}	4	2	3	1	5	6
Row/P_{local}	4	2	3	1	5	6
1	4	0.5	0	0.25		
3	4	18	3	-1	0	6
4	4	0	0	-1	5	6

3 elements stored as 1th column of U in storage
scheme „packed columns"
2 elements stored as 1th row of L in storage
scheme „packed rows"

For row 2

P_{global}	3	2	1	5	6
Row/P_{local}	3	2	1	4	5
2	3	2	1		
3	3	18	-1	0	6
4	0	0	-1	5	6

P_{global}	3	2	1	5	6
Row/P_{local}	3	2	1	4	5
2	3	0.66	0.33		
3	3	16	-2	0	6
4	0	0	-1	5	6

2 elements stored as 2th column of U
2 elements stored as 2th row of L

For row 3

P_{global}	2	1	5	6
Row/P_{local}	2	1	3	4
3	16	-2	0	6
4	0	-1	5	6
5	2	0	5	60

P_{global}	2	1	5	6
Row/P_{local}	2	1	3	4
3	16	-0.125	0	0.375
4	0	-1	5	6
5	2	0.25	5	59.25

2 elements stored as 3th column of U
2 elements stored as 3th row of L

For row 4

P_{global}	6	5	1	7	8	9
Row/P_{local}	3	2	1	4	5	6
4	6	5	-1			
5	59.25	5	0.25			
7	6	0	0	7	8	9
8	6	5	0	7	80	

P_{global}	6	5	1	7	8	9
Row/P_{local}	3	2	1	4	5	6
4	6	0.83	-0.16			
5	59.25	-44.37	10.125			
7	6	-5	1	7	8	9
8	6	0	1	7	80	

4 elements stored as 4th column of U
2 elements stored as 4th row of L

And so on for rows 5 to 9

Fig. 2. The elimination process for a nonsymmetric sparse 9x9-matrix

Distribution of matrix

A in the iteration process A^P in the elimination process

onto the processors

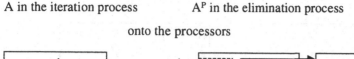

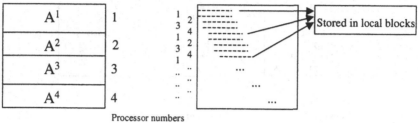

Processor numbers

Fig. 3. Distribution of matrices A and A^P onto the processors

many zero elements and many unnecessary computations on zero elements are performed. Therefore we are just now implementing the elimination process in a second version so that it can take place on packed rows in the buffer. Nevertheless we will not use index lists for the access to the buffered elements, but will resort the rows stored in the buffer according to the entries of the index list of the pivot row (e.g. in Fig. 2 for pivot row 1 we will drop the zero entry with column index 3 in row 1; this means that the entries of row 3 with the column indices 3 and 1 must be exchanged and the column width of the computation window is reduced by 1). By this strategy the buffer size can be reduced and unnecessary computations on zero elements can be avoided.

3.4 Forward Elimination and Backward Substitution

After the elimination process there are the two eliminated matrices U and L ($A^P = ULP$) for nonsymmetric matrices and one eliminated matrix L ($A^P = L^T LP$) for symmetric matrices. The matrix U is a lower triangular matrix and the matrix L is a columnwise permuted upper triangular matrix.

The matrix U is stored in packed columns. As the matrix L is stored in packed rows it must be converted into the storage pattern "packed column". The benefit of the columnwise storing of U and L is that the update of the right hand sides can be done by vector operations. The forward elimination process on U is a "usual" forward elimination and the backward substitution process differs from the "usual" backward substitution by the access to the columns of L via the permutation vector corresponding to P. After calling the backward substitution the result vector (e.g. $\tilde{r}$) must be permuted by the above mentioned permutation vector (e.g. $L\tilde{r} = b, r = P\tilde{r}$) (see also Fig. 4).

As result we get a lower triangular matrix   and a permuted upper triangular matrix

U

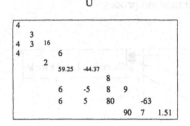

L

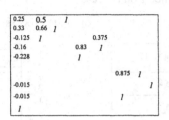

and a permutation matrix P

stored as index list

(4,3,2,6,5,8,9,7,1)

Fig. 4. The resulting matrices U, L and P

The parallelization of these two algorithms is similar to the parallelization of the elimination process. The computed solution component is broadcasted to all other processors and each processor updates the components of the right hand side according to the list of the row indices stored in the matrix for the column corresponding to the index of the solution component.

4 Results

This is a report on work in progress. We have designed and implemented all algorithms. Now we are stabilizing the system and doing tests for the complete and incomplete Gaussian elimination. Thus up to the conference we will have many test examples for quite different matrices. We want to mention that the parallel iterative solver package is running stable and that measurements have been published in the papers [1997] and [1998].

At least we want to show that it can be reasonable to use the complete Gaussian algorithm for a bandmatrix even if the implemented iterative solvers could solve the problem. To simplify the model we assume that $\beta_U = \beta_L$ holds ($\beta = \beta_U = \beta_L$); l be the dimension of the matrix. Then one matrix-vector multiplication needs $ops_{iter}(l, \beta) = 2(l(1+\beta) - \beta(\beta+1))$ operations; the Gaussian elimination needs in the best case, if the pivot elements are always the main diagonal elements, $ops_{Gauss}(l, \beta) = (l - \beta)(2\beta^2 - 3\beta + 1) + ((\beta - 1)(\beta - 2)/2)(1 + (\beta - 2)(\beta - 1))$ operations. In the worst case the buffer is six times as large as the buffer in the best case; thus the Gaussian elimination needs six times more opertations than in the best case. Now we want to compute the number of matrix-vector multiplications (mvm) with $mvm * ops_{iter}(l, \beta) > ops_{Gauss}(l, \beta)$. E.g. for $l = 10000$ and $\beta = l/10 = 1000$ we get $mvm \approx 13000$ and for $l = 10000$ and $\beta = l/100 = 100$ we get $mvm \approx 3$, if we assume the best case for the Gaussian elimination. Thus one can say that for a bandmatrix with a broad band the complete Gaussian elimination never pays. For bandmatrices with smaller bands one has to consider that usually bandmatrices within the band are also sparse; this means that the number of operations for a matrix-vector multiplication must be reduced by the sparsity factor within the band of the bandmatrix and thus mvm must be divided by the sparsity factor. Nevertheless the complete Gaussian algorithm can pay; if we set for example the sparsity factor to 0.1 and take the worst case for the Gaussian algorithm, mvm will be approximately $(3 * 6)/0.1 = 180$; this number says that the complete Gaussian algorithm pays, if the iterative solver needs more than 180 matrix-vector multiplications. Note that the number of matrix-vector multiplications required to achieve a certain accuracy depends on inner properties of the matrix.

References

[1998] C. Vuik, R.R.P. van Nooyen, P. Wesseling: Parallelism in ILU- preconditioned GMRES, Parallel Computing 24, 1998, pp. 1927-1946, Elsevier Science B.V.

[1997] W. Schönauer, H. Häfner, R. Weiss: LINSOL, a parallel iterative linear solver package of generalized CG-type for sparse matrices, in M. Heath et al. (Eds.), Proceedings of the Eigth SIAM Conf. on Paralel Processing for Scientific Computing, SIAM, Philadelphia 1997, CD-ROM (ISBN 0-89871-395-1), 8 pages.

[1998] H. Häfner, W. Schönauer, R. Weiss: The parallel and portable linear solver package LINSOL, in H. Lederer, F. Hertweck (Eds.), Proceedings of the Fourth European SGI/Cray MPP Workshop, IPP R/46, October 1998, Max-Planck-Institut für Plasmaphysik, Garching bei München, Germany, pp. 242-251.

[1996] R. Weiss: Parameter-Free Iterative Linear Solvers, Akademie Verlag, Berlin 1996, Book (ISBN 3-05-501763-3).

[1976] N.E. Gibbs, W.G. Poole, P.K. Stockmeyer: An algorithm for reducing the bandwidth and profile of a sparse matrix, SIAM J. of Numerical Analysis, Vol. 13, No. 2, 1976, pp. 236-250.

CDL++ for the Description of Moving Objects in Cellular Automata

Christian Hochberger[1], Rolf Hoffmann[2], and Stefan Waldschmidt[2]

[1] University of Rostock, 18059 Rostock, Germany,
hochberg@informatik.uni-rostock.de
[2] Darmstadt University of Technology, 64283 Darmstadt, Germany,
{hoffmann,waldsch}@informatik.tu-darmstadt.de

Abstract. We introduce a new model for objects which can move around on a cellular grid. The model consists of two phases, the movement phase and the conflict resolution phase. In the movement part of the description objects specify their desired direction. The conflict, which occurs when alternative objects want to move to the same free cell, is resolved in the conflict resolution part. The cellular description language CDL was extended to CDL++ in order to describe moving objects. This extension is automatically converted into a two–phased CDL program.

1 Introduction

In the *cellular automaton* (CA) model cells are located on a regular grid. The next state of a cell is computed by the local rule depending on the cell state and the cell states of the neighbour cells. All cells may execute their local rule in parallel, because they can act independently from each other.

The locality principle of the CA means that a cell has only read access to its neighbours and only write access within itself. Thinking in the object oriented programming paradigm, this means that a cell (an object) may only call methods of their neighbour objects, which do not change the state of the neighbours. The locality principle also implies the massively parallel principle, because write conflicts cannot occur.

The language CDL [1] was developed for an easy and concise description and the simulation of CA applications on software [2] and hardware platforms [3].

There is a certain class of applications, where cells also interact locally with their neighbours, but the way of interaction is different. Such applications typically contain objects, which are moving around.

- Physical, chemical or biological systems: Moving particles.
- Artificial life: Creatures are exploring the environment and interact with other creatures.
- Traffic simulation: Cars want to move to the next site.

Moving an object to a neighbours site means that the neighbours state has to be modified. In other words: A cell wants to modify directly its neighbour states.

Can these applications also be mapped to the classical CA model? The answer is yes, but the mapping is somewhat artificial, and difficult to understand. E.g. in a traffic simulation an empty site "is pulling" a car from a neighbour site. This means that instead of the car the empty neighbour plays the active role in the movement.

As can be seen by this example, there is a demand for describing such applications in a non artificial, easy to understand and concise way in which the user is not forced to express his ideas in the restricted classical CA programming model.

In contrast to the concept of agents in CELLANG [4] it is presumed that only one object of the same kind is hosted by one cell at the same time. The objects do not vanish or appear unless explicitly specified. Thus their number will usually be constant over the time. In analogy with the cellular principle of locality objects cannot "jump". They can only move to one of their adjacent cells. Objects carry attributes like the velocity of a car or the mass of a particle. Thus moving an object means that these attributes are moved.

2   The Two-Phase Conflict Resolution Model

Collisions. While the objects are moving around, they occasionally meet each other. In both cases shown in Fig. 1 the two objects A and B can not "see" each other – the other object is not within the (Moore–)neighbourhood of distance one. The dark shaded areas are not within the neighbourhood of any of the two cells, the gray shaded cells are within the neighbourhood and the white cells are in the neighbourhood of both cells.

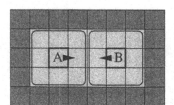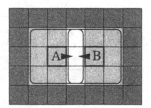

Fig. 1. Moving may cause collisions

In the case shown in the left part of Fig. 1 the two objects can move to the desired places without any problem. In the following generation both objects will be able to see each other, to realise their conflict and be able to resolve it without any additional help. They will not be able to interchange their places, because objects can only move to free cells. The situation shown in the right part is more interesting. The objects cannot see each other. Therefore they may intend to move to the same cell which causes an undesired collision if it is not resolved.

Conflict Resolution. The white cells in Fig. 1 in between A and B can see both objects moving towards each other. Thus they can foresee the collision.

Therefore the middle cell must take over the task of an acceptor, selecting only one of the two objects. In the CDL++ programming model conflict resolution is specified from the view of this middle cell. The programmer has to describe a decision which one of the cells A or B is allowed to move on and which one has to wait. This decision may take into account all the data of all accessible cells around the middle cell, especially the states of cells A and B or even the individual data of the competing objects.

This selection needs some additional time. The movement and selection is assigned to two alternating phases. In the *movement phase* objects specify where they want to move. In the *conflict resolution phase* each cell decides which object it will accept. The result of the decision is indicated to all surrounding cells. In the following movement phase the object evaluates the acceptance indicator of the target cell. If it was accepted it deletes itself, if not it remains in its old position (Fig. 2).

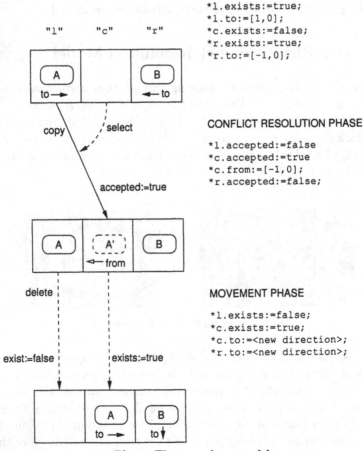

```
*l.exists:=true;
*l.to:=[1,0];
*c.exists:=false;
*r.exists:=true;
*r.to:=[-1,0];
```

CONFLICT RESOLUTION PHASE

```
*l.accepted:=false
*c.accepted:=true
*c.from:=[-1,0];
*r.accepted:=false;
```

MOVEMENT PHASE

```
*l.exists:=false;
*c.exists:=true;
*c.to:=<new direction>;
*r.to:=<new direction>;
```

Fig. 2. The two-phase model

Each moving object contains four hidden control variables: The boolean values **exists** and **accepted** and the relative celladdresses **to** and **from**. Semantically, **to** (desired direction) is related to **exists** and **from** (accepted direction) is related to **accepted**, in each case the cell address is only valid if the boolean flag is true. The actions of the two phases can be described as follows:

- *Conflict Resolution Phase.* If there is no object on the cell and objects on neighbouring cells want to move to it, one of them is selected. The address of the selected object is stored in **from** and **accepted** is set to true and the object is copied. If the cell is already occupied or it is not a destination of other objects, no object is accepted.
- *Movement Phase.* The variable **to** stores the address of the neighbour to which the object wanted to move in the previous movement phase, if there is an object on the regarded cell. It is tested whether the destination cell has accepted this object (**to=inv(from)**)[1]. In this case the copied object starts to exist (**exist** is set to true) and its movement direction can be specified. The **exist** of the original object is set to false. If the object was not copied in the previous conflict resolution phase the programmer may alter its destination using the **move** statement.

3 Moving Objects in CDL++

The language CDL has been extended [5] in order to support the description of moving objects. Here is a short example.

3.1 Example

This example shows the general structure of a CDL++ program and the usage of the most common elements. It implements creatures that move randomly over the cellular field. Creatures move either vertically or horizontally. Each creature has a lifetime which is decremented in every generation. Once the lifetime counter reaches zero the creature dies and is deleted from the field. If two creatures intend to move to the same cell, the creature with the smaller remaining lifetime is selected.

```
(1) cellular automaton moving;
(2) const
(3)    dimension = 2;        distance  = 1;
(4)    max_life  = 100;      c         = [0,0];
(5) type
(6)    celltype  = record
(7)       kind      : (normal,generator);
(8)       creature : mob
(9)          lifetime: 0..max_life;
```

---

[1] The function inv, which is not a standard CDL function, takes a relative celladdress and returns it with every component inverted in order to construct the opposite direction.

```
(10)     end;
(11)    end;
(12) colour
(13)    [0,255,255] ~ *c.kind=generator;
(14)    [*c.creature.lifetime*2+50,0,0] ~ exists(*c.creature);
(15)    [0,0,0] ~ true;
(16)
(17) var mlife    :0..max_life+1;
(18)     n,sel     :celladdress;
(19) rule *c.kind:=*c.kind;
(20)
(21) movement begin
(22)   if exists(*c.creature) then
(23)     if *c.creature.lifetime>0 then begin
(24)       if random(1)=0 then move(*c.creature,[2*random(1)-1,0]);
(25)                      else move(*c.creature,[0,2*random(1)-1]);
(26)       *c.creature.lifetime:=*c.creature.lifetime-1;
(27)     end else
(28)       delete(*c.creature)
(29)   else
(30)     if *c.kind=generator and random(9)<3 then begin
(31)       create(*c.creature);
(32)       *c.creature.lifetime:=max_life;
(33)     end;
(34) end;
(35)
(36) conflict resolution begin
(37)   mlife:=max_life+1;
(38)   for n in intended(*c.creature) do
(39)     if *n.creature.lifetime<mlife then begin
(40)       mlife:=*n.creature.lifetime;
(41)       sel:=n;
(42)     end;
(43)   if mlife <= max_life then select(*c.creature,sel);
(44) end;
```

3.2 Language Elements of CDL++

The most evident difference between a CDL program and a CDL++ program is
the new structure of the rule. In CDL++ programs it is divided into three parts:
(1) a static rule (19), which has no influence to the movement of objects, (2)
a movement specification part ((21)-(34)), in which the destination direction
for each object can be specified and (3) a conflict resolution part ((36)-(44)),
where the destination cell decides, which object will be accepted in the case of
a conflict.

The type declaration of CDL also had to be extended to introduce the notion of a **mob**. This can be seen as a new compound data type to describe moveable objects. The components of a **mob** can be used like the components of a record and they represent the attributes of the **mob**. Whenever a **mob** is moved, its attributes are automatically moved to the new cell. In this example a mob with a single attribute (**lifetime**) is declared as part of the cellstate in lines **(8)**– **(10)**. Note, that the declaration of local variables may not contain a **mob**.

CDL++ contains new statements which are used in the movement specification part to specify the destination of objects (**move**, **(24)** and **(25)**) and to create and delete objects (**create**, **(31)** and **delete**, **(28)**). In the conflict resolution part the new statement **select** is used to choose the accepted object.

Furthermore there are new expressions in CDL++. **exists()** (lines **(14)** and **(22)**) can be used in any part of the rule to check whether an object of certain kind exists in a cell. The addressed cell need not necessarily be the centre cell. In the specification part the expressions **was_moved()** and **from_dir()** can be used. **was_moved()** evaluates whether an object has been moved in the previous phase. This can be used to change attributes of an object in case it was rejected by the accepting cell. Such an attribute can be a priority, which in turn can be used by the conflict resolution to decide which object to accept and thereby granting a minimum of fairness. The expression **from_dir()** gives the direction from where an object came and can be used to track the motion of an object. The results of **from_dir()** simply have to be accumulated for this purpose. Another variation of this purpose could be an object that contains an initial goal (in relative coordinates). In this case the results of **from_dir()** have to be subtracted from this relative coordinates to keep track of the remaining steps.

In the conflict resolution part the expression **intended()** (line **(38)**) must be used. The function **intended()** returns a list containing the celladdresses of all objects which want to move to the centre cell. This list[2] is used for the following selection of an object.

With the given explanations the movement specification and conflict resolution part can be interpreted as follows: If a creature exists and its lifetime has not expired a new direction is chosen (lines **(24)** and **(25)**). The if–statement in line **(24)** decides whether this will be a horizontal or a vertical movement (**random(1)** results in 0 or 1). An existing creature is deleted if its lifetime has expired (line **(28)**). If no creature is on the centre cell and this cell is a generator, a new creature is created with a probability of 30% (**random(9)<3**). The attribute of this new creature is then initialised (line **(32)**).

In the conflict resolution phase all cells are inspected that contain a creature that wants to move to the centre cell (line **(38)**–**(42)**). The creature with the smallest remaining lifetime (line **(39)**–**(42)**) is stored in a local variable. If there is at least one creature with direction to the centre cell the previously stored creature is selected (line **(43)**). It must be noted, that the **for**–loop in lines

---

[2] The genuine name of this data type in CDL is **group**. For simplification we refer to it in this context as a list, although it can have more meanings in CDL.

(38)–(42) is not executed at all, if there is no creature with direction towards the centre cell.

3.3 Automatic Transformation

A given CDL++ program is automatically transformed into an equivalent CDL program with two phases. The transformation process involves modifications of the cellstate declaration and replacement of the new CDL++ statements and expressions in the movement and conflict resolution sections.

The transformed sections are combined by an **if** statement. Depending on the current phase (which is indicated either by a global variable or an additionally generated component in the cell state) the code of one or the other section is executed.

Modification of the cell state. The **mob** declaration of each object is changed to a **record** into which additional components are introduced. The proposed algorithm requires two new components of type **celladdress** and two new components of type **boolean**. In order to save memory space the existence flag and the destination direction can be represented by a single enumeration type (**NoObject, Stay, MoveNorth, MoveEast, MoveSouth, MoveWest**). Acceptance and the address of the accepted object can as well be represented by a single enumeration type (**NoObject, Stay, FromNorth, FromEast, FromSouth, FromWest**). To define the enumeration types all **move** statements in the movement section have to be analysed in order to evaluate all possible destinations for an object. The two enumerations are exclusively used each for one or the other phase transition. Thus they can be declared as components of a union to share the same memory space.

Transformation of the Movement Section. The movement section may contain the functions **move, create, delete** and **exists**. Each of these functions is replaced by standard CDL code.

Each **move** function is replaced by an assignment of the value representing the chosen movement direction (**move(*c.creature,[0,1])** equals **MoveNorth**) to the union component of the movement phase. Each **create** or **delete** function is also replaced by an assignment to the union component of the movement phase. The assigned value represents an object that stays at its current location (**Stay**) or represents a non existent object (**NoObject**). Each **exists** function is replaced by a comparison of the union component with all values that represents objects.

Transformation of the Conflict Resolution Section. The three new CDL++ functions **intended, select** and **exists** can occur in the conflict resolution section.

The result of the **intended** function is a group containing the celladdresses of all objects which want to move to the centre cell. Thus this function has to be transformed in one of two different ways depending of its occurrence:

If the resulting group is used as an operand of the **in**–relation to check whether a specific celladdress is contained in the group, the relation is replaced by a check whether the object on the addressed cell wants to move towards the centre cell. This check is equivalent to a comparison of the respective union component of this object with a value representing a direction towards the centre cell.

If the resulting group is used to build an explicit or implicit loop (**for**, **one**, **all**, **num**), the loop has to be reconstructed, so that all possible source directions are scanned. The body of the loop may only be executed, if the addressed cell contains an object with the centre cell as its destination.

The **select** function corresponds to the **move** function in the movement phase. It assigns the corresponding value to the union component of the conflict resolution phase. In addition the user defined part of the cell state is copied. The replacement for the **exists** function is similar to the movement phase.

4 Conclusion

A new two phase model for moving objects was introduced. An object specifies its desired destination in the movement phase. In the conflict resolution phase has to be specified, which one of the possible candidates will be accepted. The implementation of the model uses implicit hidden control states. Due to the two phases, objects can only move with "half speed". Note that half speed appears also in classical CA algorithms for problems where two phases are necessary to resolve the conflict. Therefore half speed is not an overhead of the model for such applications.

CDL was extended to CDL++ allowing to describe such algorithms with moving objects. A pre-compiler was implemented which automatically converts CDL++ to standard CDL. Because of the implicit control states the model increases the state complexity. But it has to be noted that similar control states have explicitly be used if such applications are hand coded in standard CDL. The advantage of CDL++ is, that the problem can be described on a higher abstraction level of moving objects. Control states have not to be declared and managed.

References

[1] Christian Hochberger and Rolf Hoffmann. CDL — a language for cellular processing. In Giacomo R. Sechi, editor, *Proceedings of the Second International Conference on Massively Parallel Computing Systems*, pages 41–46. IEEE, 1996.

[2] Christian Hochberger, Rolf Hoffmann, and Stefan Waldschmidt. Compilation of CDL for different target architecures. In Viktor Malyshkin, editor, *Parallel Computing Technologies*, pages 169–179, Berlin, Heidelberg, 1995. Springer.

[3] Christian Hochberger, Rolf Hoffmann, Klaus-Peter Völkmann, and Jens Steuerwald. The CEPRA-1X cellular processor. In Rainer W. Hartenstein and Viktor K. Prasanna, editors, *Reconfigurable Architectures, High Performance by Configware*. IT Press, Bruchsal, 1997.

[4] Dana J. Eckart. A cellular automata simulation system. *SIGPLAN Notices*, 26(8):80–85, August 1991.

[5] Christian Hochberger. *CDL — Eine Sprache für die Zellularverarbeitung auf verschiedenen Zielplattformen*. PhD thesis, Darmstadt University of Technology, 1999.

Parallel Solution of Large Sparse SPD Linear Systems Based on Overlapping Domain Decomposition

Igor E. Kaporin and Igor N. Konshin

Computing Center RAS, Vavilov str. 40, 117967 Moscow, Russia
kaporin@ccas.ru, horse@ccas.ru

Abstract. We present a parallel iterative solver for large sparse symmetric positive definite (SPD) linear systems based on a new theory describing the convergence of the Preconditioned Conjugate Gradient (PCG) method and a proper combination of advanced preconditioning strategies. Formally, the preconditioning can be interpreted as a special (nearly optimum from the viewpoint of the new PCG theory) version of overlapping domain decomposition with incomplete Cholesky solutions over subdomains. The estimates of parallel efficiency are given as well as the results of numerical experiments for the serial and parallel versions of the solver.

1 The New Theory of the PCG Method Convergence

Consider the PCG method [1] for solving linear algebraic system

$$Ax = b \tag{1}$$

with SPD sparse $n \times n$ matrix A:

$$r_0 = b - Ax_0, \quad p_0 = Hr_0; \quad \text{for } i = 0, 1, \ldots :$$

$$\alpha_i = \frac{r_i^T H r_i}{p_i^T A p_i}, \quad x_{i+1} = x_i + p_i \alpha_i, \quad r_{i+1} = r_i - A p_i \alpha_i,$$

$$\beta_i = \frac{r_{i+1}^T H r_{i+1}}{r_i^T H r_i}, \quad p_{i+1} = H r_{i+1} + p_i \beta_i. \tag{2}$$

The standard upper bound for the iteration number needed for the ε times reduction of the error norm $\sqrt{r_i^T A^{-1} r_i}$ is

$$i_C(\varepsilon) = \frac{1}{2}\sqrt{C} \log \frac{2}{\varepsilon}, \tag{3}$$

where
$$C = C(HA) = \lambda_{\max}(HA)/\lambda_{\min}(HA) \tag{4}$$
is the spectral condition number of the preconditioned matrix HA.

Motivated by the need of a more feasible preconditioning quality criterion, the following theory was developed. It was shown in [5,7] that the number of iterations needed for the ε times reduction of the error norm $\sqrt{r_i^T H r_i}$ can be bounded from above as

$$i_K(\varepsilon) = \log_2 K + \log_2 \frac{1}{\varepsilon}, \tag{5}$$

where

$$K = K(HA) = \left(\frac{1}{n}\mathrm{trace}(HA)\right)^n / \det(HA) \tag{6}$$

is the so-called K-condition number of the preconditioned matrix HA, see [2]. A number of preconditioning strategies were analyzed with respect to a decrease of the K-condition number, see [4,5,7,8]. The preconditioning discussed below is actually based on a proper combination of the Block Incomplete Inverse Cholesky (BIIC) preconditionings [4,6,7] and the robust Incomplete Cholesky 2nd order (IC2) preconditionings [8].

2 A Simple Version of IC2 Factorization

For the sake of convenience, let us assume further that the matrix A is symmetrically scaled to the unit diagonal. The basic relationship determining the IC2 type preconditioning has the form

$$A = U^T U + U^T R + R^T U, \tag{7}$$

where U is a nonsingular upper triangular matrix (an approximation to the exact right Cholesky factor of A), and R is a strictly upper triangular error matrix with "small" elements. The existence and correctness of such decomposition is guaranteed for any SPD matrix A. Some modifications of this approach requiring less computational effort can be found in [8,10].

Very important properties of the IC2 two-side preconditioned matrix

$$M = U^{-T} A U^{-1} \equiv I + RU^{-1} + U^{-T} R^T \tag{8}$$

are as follows:

$$\mathrm{diag}M = I, \qquad K(M) = \det(I + RA^{-1}R^T). \tag{9}$$

The recurrences for the calculation of IC2 factorization can easily be obtained from (7), e.g., when the sparsity patterns of U and R do not have coinciding nonzero positions and their nonzero elements are subjected to the conditions $|U_{i,j}| \geq \tau$ and $|R_{i,j}| < \tau$, respectively, $i < j$. Here $0 < \tau \ll 1$ is the drop tolerance parameter determining the preconditioning quality. In particular, the second equation of (9) easily yields $\log K(M) = O(\|A^{-1}\|\tau^2)$ which should be related to (5). The latter remark explains why this decomposition is referred to as the second order one.

However, the calculation and application of the incomplete Cholesky pre-conditioning cannot be efficiently parallelized for message-passing architectures having relatively large communication overheads. Henceforth, next we consider some special parallel preconditionings which effectively exploit IC2 factorizations of certain set of submatrices of the original coefficient matrix A.

3 Block Explicit Preconditioner

Let us briefly describe the Block Incomplete Inverse Cholesky (BIIC) precondi-tioning algorithm [4, 6, 7]. Let A be reordered and split in the same way as for the Block Jacobi preconditioning, i.e. the t-th diagonal block of the symmetrically reordered matrix has the dimension n_t and $n_1 + \ldots + n_s = n$. Here $t = 1, \ldots, s$, and s is the block dimension of A. For the t-th diagonal block, let us define the "basic" index set as

$$\{k_{t-1} + 1, \ldots, k_t\},$$

where $k_{t-1} = n_1 + \ldots + n_{t-1}$, $k_0 = 0$, $k_s = n$, and introduce the "overlapping" index sets as

$$\{j_t(1), \ldots, j_t(m_t - n_t)), \quad j_t(p) \leq k_{t-1}.$$

For each t, the latter index set typically includes those indices not greater than k_t that are the most "essentially" connected to the basic index set, e.g. in the sense of the sparse matrix graph adjacency relations. Here $m_t \geq n_t$ and, obviously, $m_1 = n_1$, i.e. at least the first overlapping set is empty. The BIIC preconditioner H can be represented in the following additive form:

$$H = \sum_{t=1}^{s} V_t U_t^{-1} (V_t^T E_t E_t^T V_t) U_t^{-T} V_t^T, \tag{10}$$

where V_t and E_t are rectangular matrices composed of unit n-vectors e_j as follows:

$$V_t = [Q_t | E_t], \quad t = 1, \ldots, s,$$

$$Q_t = [e_{j_t(1)} | \ldots | e_{j_t(m_t - n_t)}], \qquad E_t = [e_{k_{t-1}+1} | \ldots | e_{k_t}],$$

(Q_1 is set to an empty matrix), and each upper triangular matrix U_t is the right Cholesky factor of the t-th "extended" diagonal $m_t \times m_t$ submatrix $V_t^T A V_t$, that is,

$$V_t^T A V_t = U_t^T U_t. \tag{11}$$

Remark 1. It was shown in [4, 6, 7] that the BIIC preconditioner H possesses the K-optimality property in the following sense. Let $\mathcal{L}$ be a set of sparse lower triangular matrices which may have nonzero elements only in positions (i, j),

$$j \in \{j_t(1), \dots, j_t(m_t - n_t), k_{t-1} + 1, \dots, i\}, \quad k_{t-1} + 1 \le i \le k_t.$$

Then

$$H = \arg \min_{H = L^T L, L \in \mathcal{L}} K(HA).$$

Another useful property is trace$(HA) = n$.

Remark 2. Note that the Block Jacobi preconditioner (where $m_t = n_t$, $t = 1, \dots, s$, and therefore all Q_t are empty matrices) can be represented using the above notations as

$$H = \sum_{t=1}^{s} E_t (E_t^T A E_t)^{-1} E_t^T,$$

where $E_t^T A E_t$ is exactly the t-th diagonal block of A.

4 Using IC2 Factorizations within the BIIC Preconditioning

For each $t = 1, \dots, s$, let us replace the exact Cholesky factorizations (11) by the corresponding IC2 decompositions of the type (7)

$$V_t^T A V_t = \tilde{U}_t^T \tilde{U}_t + \tilde{U}_t^T R_t + R_t^T \tilde{U}_t. \tag{12}$$

For the sake of simplicity, let also assume that the small element dropping strategy is modified in such a way that the first $m_t - n_t$ diagonal elements of $\tilde{U}_t$ coincide with those of U_t. Using the properties of the IC2 and BIIC decompositions mentioned above, one can see that the ratio of the K-condition numbers for the matrices $\tilde{H}A$ and HA, where

$$\tilde{H} = \sum_{t=1}^{s} V_t \tilde{U}_t^{-1} (V_t^T E_t E_t^T V_t) \tilde{U}_t^{-T} V_t^T, \tag{13}$$

can be estimated as

$$\frac{K(\tilde{H}A)}{K(HA)} = \prod_{t=1}^{s} \det(I + R_t (V_t^T A V_t)^{-1} R_t^T) \le \exp(c_0 \tau^2).$$

The latter inequality follows since R_t are the local IC2 error matrices with $O(\tau)$ elements. Moreover, we expect c_0 to be not very large even for ill-conditioned matrices since usually $\|(V_t^T A V_t)^{-1}\| \ll \|A^{-1}\|$. This yields

$$\log K(\tilde{H}A) \le \log K(HA) + c_0 \tau^2,$$

and the estimate (5),(6) shows that for some reasonably small IC2 dropping tolerance τ such BIIC-IC2 hybrid construction will give nearly the same rate of the PCG convergence as for the K-optimum BIIC preconditioner. At the same time BIIC-IC2 involves essentially smaller costs for the evaluation, storage, and the use of the preconditioner.

5 Parallel Implementation

The above mathematical technologies were implemented in a portable software written in simplified message-passing style using the MPI-like interface to the low-level communication library.

Let us assume that the linear system (1) is solved on a parallel computer having N_{PE} processor elements (PEs) with distributed memory. Let us also assume that $s = N_{PE}$, i.e. the number of processors coincides with the number of blocks to which the original matrix A is split, and the i-th block corresponds to i-th PE, $i = 1, ..., s$.

The proposed algorithm can be implemented as follows. Perform the IC2 factorization (12) of the local submatrix $V_i^T A V_i$ at the local i-th PE. No data exchanges are required at this stage.

The PCG iterations stage (2) involves the following types of operations:

(a) multiplication of the coefficient matrix A by a vector,

(b) multiplication of the preconditioner $\tilde{H}$ by a vector, and

(c) inner product.

Three vector update operations are also needed on each iteration, but they do not require interprocessor communications with our distribution of data, where t-th processor stores the vector components $k_{t-1} + 1, \ldots, k_t$ and the rows of the matrix A with the same numbers as well as the corresponding block of preconditioner.

Matrix by a vector product. The multiplication of matrix by a vector is a well investigated problem. It can be presented as the following three-stage algorithm:

1. for any PE requiring some data which are local for the PE, place the required components of the vector to a local data buffer and send them to PEs which require them;

2. receive the required data from the other PEs;

3. multiply the local matrix coefficient data by the vector gathered.

The resulting components of the vector will be located at the PE which computes them.

Preconditioner by a vector product. The multiplication of preconditioner by a vector can be presented as an analogous algorithm. The differences are the following:

1. the data exchange topology is based on the overlap geometry;

2. the type of operation with the local data (local triangular system solutions instead of the local matrix by vector product);

3. after the first global synchronization, two successive triangular system solutions with U_i^T and U_i are performed, and the second global synchronization operation is required after these local computations.

Inner product. Two inner products are required to perform at each PCG iteration (2). This is one global exchange MPI-like operation consisting from the following local ones:

1. the partial inner product for the local part of the vector is computed at each PE;

2. the scalars obtained are sent to the root PE;

3. the final scalar product is computed on the root PE;

4. the final scalar product is sent from the root PE to the other PEs.

Communication costs. Let us consider a model 3-D problem with standard 7-point stencil matrix operator on a cube, which is split into p^3 cubic subdomains each of the size $m \times m \times m$, i.e. $n = m^3 p^3$ and $N_{PE} = s = p^3$. Let the overlap be of the width of q grid points and the corresponding preconditioner $\tilde{H}$ is two times more dense than the original matrix A (this is a typical preconditioner density used in practice).

The arithmetic and communication costs per one PCG iteration are given in Table 1. It can be easily seen from the Table 1 that the ratio of the total arithmetic costs to the communication costs is approximately equal to $c = 4m/(q+1)$, i.e. it is required to perform c arithmetic operations per one float word exchange between PEs. It should be noted that for 2-D decomposition this ratio is expressed by the same formula, where $m = (n/s)^{1/2}$.

Table 1. The costs per one PCG iteration for the uniform $p \times p \times p$ DD.

Stage	Arithmetic costs	Communication costs
(a) Ax	$7n$	$6m^2 s$
(b) $\tilde{H}x$	$14n$	$6mq(m+2)s$
(c) $y^T x$	$2n$	$4\log_2 s$

Properties of the parallel realization. (1) The total number of global exchange initialization operations does not depend on the number of blocks and the size of the linear system and is equal to 5 per each PCG iteration. (2) After completion of the global data exchange, all the computations can be performed at each PE without any additional synchronizations. (3) There is no serial part in the code implementing the proposed algorithm. (4) The computations are well balanced if the sizes of the local submatrices are approximately equal. (5) The communication costs are not large as compared to the arithmetic costs.

6 Numerical Experiments

We present numerical results obtained on eight-processor SUN 10000 Starfire computer and a cluster of four Pentium II workstations. We have used certain hard-to-solve test matrices arising in finite element analysis of thin shells which were examined in [3] and are available from *MatrixMarket* collection (CYLSHELL set available at URL http://math.nist.gov/MatrixMarket/data/misc/cylshell/cylshell.html). We also present the results obtained for the matrix BIHAR255 resulting from discrete biharmonic operator with 13-point stencil on a 255×255 square grid with Dirichlet type boundary conditions [4, 6, 7].

Table 2. Test matrix properties.

name	mesh	n	nz(A)	$C(A)$
S1RMQ4M1	30×30	5489	281111	$1.8 \cdot 10^6$
S3RMQ4M1	30×30	5489	281111	$1.8 \cdot 10^{10}$
S3DKQ4M2	150×100	90499	4820891	$1.9 \cdot 10^{11}$
S3DKT3M2	150×100	90499	3753461	$3.6 \cdot 10^{11}$
BIHAR255	255×255	65025	840229	$2.2 \cdot 10^8$

Some data on these test matrices are given in Table 2.

Zero initial guess and the relative stopping criterion by the Jacobi scaled residual norm with $\varepsilon = 10^{-9}$ were used for all test problems. For the CYLSHELL set, the right hand side was computed from the test solution $x = [1 \ldots 1]^T$ as in [3], while for BIHAR255 the test solution was obtained from the function $x \sin(\pi x) \sin(\pi y) \exp(xy)$ over the unit square. Block splittings of the matrices were obtained with the use of the public-domain graph partitioning package METIS [9] with the default parameters. The overlap was obtained using sparsity structure of the q-th degree of the coefficient matrix. The preconditioning was constructed using overlap parameter $q = 6$ and IC2 drop tolerance parameter $\tau = 0.003$.

The results on parallel performance are illustrated for BIHAR255 test. The speedups and wall clock times (in seconds) obtained on a SUN 10000 Starfire computer are given in Table 3. The case of 8 PEs is not presented because one node of the computer system was permanently occupied by another process running for a week or even more.

Table 3. Parallel efficiency for BIHAR255 test.

N_{PE}	time	Mflops/N_{PE}	Mults/Sends	Efficiency	Speedup	Actual speedup
1	766.90	16.24	–	100.00	1.00	1.00
2	239.46	16.14	1394.44	97.95	1.96	3.20
3	133.14	15.75	905.54	96.85	2.91	5.76
4	93.67	15.92	612.59	97.51	3.90	8.18
5	69.88	15.92	415.98	95.67	4.78	10.97
6	65.36	15.36	345.35	89.32	5.36	11.73
7	52.55	14.97	294.22	88.39	6.19	14.59

The observed superlinear actual speedup is due to the sharp decrease of the preconditioning costs when passing from the incomplete factorization of the whole matrix to that of its submatrices, which have significantly smaller band-width (see Table 4).

The parallel efficiency obtained on a cluster of four Pentium II 266 MHz workstations connected via an 100 Mbit Ethernet switch was within the 45 to 85% range for the problems of larger sizes.

In Tables 4–6, AC_{prec}, AC_{iter}, and AC_{tot} denote the number of scalar multiplications needed to construct the preconditioner, perform N_{iter} PCG iterations, and the total number of multiplications divided by $nz(A)$, respectively. The "Fill-in" given in percents means the ratio of the space occupied by the preconditioner to the space occupied by the upper triangle of the coefficient matrix.

Table 4. Dependence of operation count and iteration number on the number of blocks for BIHAR255 test.

s	$C(\tilde{H}A)$	N_{iter}	AC_{prec}	AC_{iter}	AC_{tot}	Fill-in,%
1	0.215E+05	408	4934.51	1824.44	6758.95	278.20
2	0.111E+05	313	2250.61	1509.73	3760.35	310.47
3	0.122E+05	328	2143.84	1596.56	3740.40	314.61
4	0.990E+04	314	1547.47	1549.70	3097.17	320.83
5	0.114E+05	315	1246.48	1568.12	2814.59	324.79
6	0.119E+05	336	1165.37	1696.17	2861.54	331.35
7	0.115E+05	328	974.74	1664.06	2638.80	333.66

An important feature of the above described algorithm observed in the course of numerical testing is that its total arithmetic cost grows quite slowly with the increase of the number of subdomains (equal to the number of PEs). This is not the case for the (approximate) Block Jacobi preconditioned CG method, where the number of iterations grows rapidly with the number of subdomains.

In order to compare some other parallel preconditioning to our method, we present iteration data for the diagonal (Jacobi) preconditioning, (approximate) Block Jacobi and the simple "uniform" overlapping with weighting. The same IC2 approximate inversion of blocks were used for the latter two methods. The results obtained with the number of blocks $s = 4$ for the test problem S3DKT3M2 are given in Table 5.

Table 5. Comparison of parallel iterative methods for S3DKQ4M2 test.

Preconditioner	$C(\tilde{H}A)$	N_{iter}	AC_{prec}	AC_{iter}	AC_{tot}	Fill-in,%
Jacobi	0.312E+11	41930	0.00	42272.13	42272.13	0.00
Block Jacobi	0.434E+09	1251	391.59	3530.51	3922.10	158.89
Simple overlap	0.356E+09	1267	755.91	4175.87	4931.78	205.12
BIIC overlap	0.812E+08	643	429.93	1932.18	2362.11	181.22

Further results obtained for the test problems S3DKQ4M2 and S3DKT3M2 are presented in Tables 6 and 7, respectively.

Table 6. Dependence of operation count and iteration number on the number of blocks for S3DKQ4M2 test.

s	$C(\tilde{H}A)$	N_{iter}	AC_{prec}	AC_{iter}	AC_{tot}	Fill-in,%
1	0.323E+08	553	456.48	1446.36	1902.84	147.08
2	0.467E+08	584	474.92	1571.24	2046.16	154.45
3	0.513E+08	579	464.80	1603.54	2068.34	162.19
4	0.532E+08	573	414.62	1582.98	1997.60	161.51
5	0.561E+08	579	422.40	1636.23	2058.63	167.72
6	0.583E+08	569	425.58	1644.81	2070.39	174.06
7	0.597E+08	578	442.12	1671.39	2113.51	174.16
8	0.650E+08	568	403.83	1664.51	2068.34	177.95
10	0.643E+08	557	390.80	1667.49	2058.29	184.14
12	0.704E+08	574	416.56	1749.91	2166.47	189.53
16	0.681E+08	532	365.79	1686.47	2052.26	201.39
20	0.789E+08	564	375.07	1839.39	2214.45	210.37
24	0.876E+08	555	357.88	1844.29	2202.17	216.41
32	0.862E+08	546	363.74	1895.77	2259.51	231.00

As is seen, with the increase of the number of blocks s, the iteration number of the proposed method stays nearly the same, which is important for attaining high speedups on computers with large communication latency. Also, the increase in the storage occupied by the preconditioner is not very substantial as long as the number of subdomains is not large. The reason is that the increase of the overlap is partially compensated by more precise and more sparse incomplete factorizations corresponding to smaller blocks.

7 Conclusions

The experience accumulated by the authors (more than 500 test runs, only small portion of which is presented above) shows that the harder the problem is, the greater the gain in the performance of the proposed method as compared to other commonly used parallel iterative solvers. The parallel properties of the solver appear to be as good as expected from our theoretical considerations.

8 Acknowledgements

The authors would like to acknowledge several useful discussions with V.A.Garanzha and V.N.Konshin concerning algorithmic implementation issues and models of parallel computations.

Table 7. Dependence of operation count and iteration number on the number of blocks for S3DKT3M2 test.

s	$C(\tilde{H}A)$	N_{iter}	AC_{prec}	AC_{iter}	AC_{tot}	Fill-in,%
1	0.398E+08	614	528.23	1738.48	2266.71	164.28
2	0.620E+08	667	518.44	1930.44	2448.88	170.44
3	0.692E+08	666	481.57	1953.73	2435.30	174.27
4	0.776E+08	658	445.01	1967.11	2412.13	179.73
5	0.847E+08	673	445.58	2026.98	2472.56	181.92
6	0.841E+08	682	463.73	2117.29	2581.02	190.96
7	0.906E+08	651	420.54	2000.73	2421.27	187.89
8	0.869E+08	637	424.42	2012.10	2436.52	196.21
10	0.982E+08	666	387.29	2188.58	2575.88	208.65
12	0.107E+09	642	348.71	2082.22	2430.93	204.46
16	0.112E+09	628	326.98	2098.51	2425.48	214.03
20	0.131E+09	658	310.09	2251.29	2561.38	221.84
24	0.137E+09	650	312.75	2278.20	2590.95	229.97
32	0.143E+09	661	288.25	2410.93	2699.18	243.87

References

1. Axelsson, O.: A class of iterative methods for finite element equations. Computer Meth. Appl. Mech. Engrg. **9** (1976) 123–137
2. Axelsson, O.: Iterative solution methods. Cambidge University Press, Cambridge (1994)
3. Benzi, M., Kouhia, R., Tuma, M.: An assessment of some preconditioning techniques in shell problems. Technical Report LA-UR-97-3892, Los Alamos National Laboratory, Los Alamos, NM (1992)
4. Kaporin, I.E.: On preconditioning for the conjugate gradient method when solving discrete analogues of differential problems. Differ. Uravn. **7** (1990) 1225–1236 (in Russian)
5. Kaporin, I.E.: Explicitly preconditioned conjugate gradient method for the solution of unsymmetric linear systems. Int. J. Computer Math. **40** (1992) 169–187
6. Kaporin, I.E.: Spectrum boundary estimation for two-side explicit preconditioning. Vestnik Mosk. Univ., ser. 15, Vychisl. Matem. Kibern. **2** (1993) 28–42 (in Russian)
7. Kaporin, I.E.: New convergence results and preconditioning strategies for the conjugate gradient method. Numer. Linear Algebra Appls., **1** (1994) 179–210
8. Kaporin, I.E.: High quality preconditioning of a general symmetric positive definite matrix based on its $U^T U + U^T R + R^T U$-decomposition. Numer. Linear Algebra Appl., **6** no.2 (1999) (to appear)
9. Karypis, G., Kumar, V.: Multilevel k-way hypergraph partitioning, Technical Report 98-036, Dept. Comp. Sci. Engrg., Army HPC Research Center, Univ. of Minnesota, MN (1998)
10. Tismenetsky, M.: A new preconditioning technique for solving large sparse linear systems. Linear Algebra Appls. 154-156 (1991) 331–353

Restructuring Parallel Programs for On-the-fly Race Detection*

Young-Cheol Kim, and Yong-Kee Jun**

Dept. of Computer Science, Gyeongsang National University
Chinju, 660-701, South Korea
Tel: +82-591-751-5996; Fax: +82-591-762-1944
{yck,jun}@nongae.gsnu.ac.kr

Abstract. Detecting races is important for debugging explicit shared-memory parallel programs, because the races result in unintended non-deterministic executions of the programs. Previous on-the-fly techniques to detect races in parallel programs with inter-thread coordination show serious space overhead in two components of complexity, and can not guarantee that, in an execution instance, the race detected first is not preceded by accesses that also participate in a race. This paper presents a program restructuring technique for on-the-fly race detection, which results in a serializable program preserving the semantics of original program. Monitoring an execution of the restructured program can detect the first races in the original program, eliminating one component of the space complexity.

1 Introduction

It is inherently more difficult to write and debug parallel program than sequential one. Particularly, shared-memory parallel programs may have a special kind of bugs called *data race* or *access anomaly*, in short *race*. A race appears when two instructions in different parallel threads perform accesses to a shared variable without proper synchronization, and when at least one of the accesses is a write to the variable. Detecting races is important for debugging shared-memory parallel programs, because the races result in unintended nondeterministic executions of the program, and then makes debugging the program difficult.

On-the-fly detection [2,4,8] instruments the program to be debugged, and monitors an execution of the program. The monitoring process reports races which occur during the monitored execution. This approach can be a complement to *static analysis* [1,3], because on-the-fly detection can be used to identify feasible (real) races from the potential races reported by static analysis approaches.

---

* University Research Program supported by Ministry of Information and Communication in South Korea.
** In Gyeongsang National University, he is also involved in both Institute of Computer Research and Development, and Information and Communication Research Center, as a research professor.

```
0      parallel do i = 1, N          0      parallel do i = 1, N
1        B₀                          1        B₀
2        if C₀ then wait E           2        if C₀ then goto 100
3        B₁                          3        B₁
4        if C₁ then wait E           4        if C₁ then goto 100
5        B₂                          5        B₂
6      end parallel do               6 100    continue
                                     7      end parallel do
```

$$\text{(a)} \hspace{4cm} \text{(b)}$$

Fig. 1. (a) A parallel loop and (b) its before-wait loop

Although on-the-fly detection may not report as many races as *post-mortem detection* [6, 7], it guarantees to report at least one race for each variable involved in a race. And, for the parallel programs which may have only ordered inter-thread coordination, it guarantees to report the *first races* [4, 8] which are not preceded by accesses that also participate in a race. On-the-fly detection requires less storage space than post-mortem detection, because much of the information collected by the monitoring process can be discarded as an execution progresses, but shows still serious space overhead for parallel programs with inter-thread coordination.

This paper presents a program restructuring technique to detect races on the fly in explicit shared-memory parallel programs that may have general inter-thread coordination. The technique results in a serializable program preserving the semantics of original program. Monitoring an execution of the restructured program can detect the first races in the corresponding execution instance of original program, eliminating one space component out of the two components of its complexity. In the next section, we formulate the problem and objectives of this paper including the related works. In section 3, we describe the main idea and the results of the work. We conclude this paper in section 4.

2 Background

Parallel programs may have two parallel constructs [9]: parallel loop and parallel sections. Although here we use parallel loops as shown in figure 1 due to the restricted space of this paper, our technique also can be applied to parallel sections. In an execution of a parallel loop, multiple threads of control are created at a PARALLEL DO statement and terminated at the corresponding END PARALLEL DO statement. Parallel constructs may be nested inside parallel constructs. Branches are not allowed from within a parallel constructs to outside the parallel constructs or vice versa.

We assume that all synchronization is provided via *event* variables. An event variable is always in one of two states: *clear* or *posted*. The initial value of an event variable is always *clear*. The value of an event variable can be set to *posted* with a POST statement. The value of an event variable can be tested with a WAIT statement. A WAIT statement suspends execution of the thread which executes it until the specified event variable's value is set to *posted*. On the other hand, the posting thread may proceed immediately. A CLEAR statement resets the value of an event variable to *clear*. We assume that there are no CLEAR statements in the programs considered in this paper. A *static block* is a structured block of statements which must not contain any WAIT statement and any external control flow into or out of the static block. Note that a static block may contain POST statements. A *dynamic block* is a sequence of instructions from a static block executed by a single thread. Figure 1(a) shows an example parallel loop considered in this paper, where E is an event variable, B_i is an i-th static block, and C_i is a boolean condition of the logical IF statement which contains a wait operation.

In an execution of parallel program, two accesses to a shared variable are *conflicting* if at least one of them is a write. If two accesses executed concurrently in two different dynamic blocks are conflicting, then these accesses constitute a *race*. On-the-fly race detection instruments additional code into debugged program to monitor and detect races during an execution of the program. In order to detect races on the fly, one needs to determine if a dynamic block's access to a shared variable is logically concurrent with any other previous access to the same variable and then results in a race. This requires *detection protocol* to monitor the dynamic blocks that perform accesses to shared variables and to maintain an *access history* for each shared variable during the execution of the program. Whenever an access to a shared variable occurs, the logical concurrency should be determined between current access and every previous access in the access history of the variable. The logical concurrency between two accesses is determined from the concurrency information on the two dynamic blocks that perform the accesses, which are called *block labels* [2]. The labels are generated on each creation or termination of dynamic blocks, and may be stored in access histories of shared variables.

The on-the-fly analysis, however, has yet large overhead in space. The storage space required consists of two components in its complexity: one is the space to maintain access histories for all shared variables, and the other is the space to maintain block labels of simultaneously active dynamic blocks. For example, the worst-case space complexity of Task Recycling [2] is $O(VT + T^2)$, where V is the number of monitored variables and T is the maximum parallelism of the debugged program. To eliminate one of these two components, our technique resorts to sequential monitoring of the program execution. If an execution contains a race, it can be detected regardless of the thread scheduling, because on-the-fly race detection resorts to checking logical concurrency between two blocks. In this sequential monitoring, the worst-case space complexity of Task Recycling becomes $O(VT)$, because labels are not required to be maintained for simultaneously active dynamic blocks. The sequential execution of the program is *undefined*, if a WAIT statement is executed and the corresponding event variable is not already posted. If a program's sequential execution is defined for all input

```
0       parallel do i = 1, N              8        if C₁ then
1         if C₀ then                      9          wait E
2           wait E                        10         waited = .true.
3           waited = .true.               11       endif
4         endif                           12       if .not. waited then goto 20
5         if .not. waited then goto 10    13       B₂
6         B₁                              14 20     continue
7 10      continue                        15       end parallel do
```

Fig. 2. The after-wait loop of figure 1(a)

data sets, the program is *serializable*. Our primary interest is a technique to restructure parallel programs to serializable programs for sequential monitoring, preserving the semantics of original program.

Previous on-the-fly techniques to detect races in parallel programs with the event synchronization can not guarantee that, in an execution instance, the race detected is the first race. The technique reported in this paper make it possible to use a two-pass on-the-fly algorithm [8] that detects the first races in a special class of parallel programs which may have ordered synchronization. In this kind of synchronization, any pair of the corresponding coordination points are executed on ordered sequence including sequential execution of these points. The first races are important in debugging, because the removal of such races may make other races disappear. It is even possible that all races reported by other on-the-fly algorithms would disappear once the first races are removed. Reporting the first races in two-pass is preferable to previous techniques which might require several iterations of monitoring, because the cost of monitoring a particular execution is still expensive.

3   Restructuring Parallel Programs

In this section, we describe the main idea and the results of the work. We present how to restructure a parallel program which is already instrumented with additional code including the labeling functions for on-the-fly race detection. The main idea of our technique is to restructure one original parallel loop into two serializable loops: the first loop called the *before-wait loop* for all the dynamic blocks executed before the first wait operation in every thread, and the next loop called the *after-wait loop* for all the dynamic blocks executed after the first wait operation in every thread. This technique therefore partitions the set of all dynamic blocks appeared in the execution of original loop into two sets of dynamic blocks which are defined in sequential execution.

In the before-wait loop, each thread is immediately terminated whenever it arrives at the first wait operation of the original loop. The remaining part of the thread continues to execute in the corresponding after-wait loop. For example, consider the before-wait loop shown in figure 1(b) which is constructed directly from the original loop shown in figure 1(a) by replacing each WAIT statement with the predefined special GOTO statement and adding a CONTINUE statement for the GOTOs. This restructuring technique requires every WAIT statement in the original loop to be in one logical IF statement. We resort this to the instrumentation phase that transforms the program to the code in a canonical form. Note that the before-wait loop does not contain any WAIT statement, but may contain POST statements in its static blocks. This means that the before-wait loop does not perform any wait operation, but performs all post operations appeared before the first wait operation in each thread.

In the after-wait loop, each thread is created to continue immediately from the first wait operation of the original loop. For example, consider the after-wait loop shown in figure 2 which is constructed directly from the original loop shown in figure 1(a) by eliminating the first static block and restructuring each WAIT statement to be executed if it is the first wait operation in its thread. The restructured code sets a boolean variable *waited* if the wait operation is the first in the thread, which makes the thread continue to execute the next static block. Otherwise, it performs the predefined special GOTO statement to execute the corresponding CONTINUE statement which is inserted immediately before the next WAIT statement.

Although the partial order of restructured program execution is actually different from that of the original program execution, it shows no problem to monitor the sequential execution for detecting races in the original program. Note that we construct a serializable program by restructuring a parallel program which is already instrumented. The instrumented program is equipped with additional code including the labeling functions for on-the-fly race detection. This approach leads the partitioned loops not to be instrumented for both END PARALLEL DO statement of the before-wait loop and PARALLEL DO statement of the after-wait loop. This implies that the monitored sequential execution of restructured program generates the same block labels that are generated in the monitored parallel execution of original program, preserving the semantics of original program for sequential monitoring. For on-the-fly race detection of the restructured program, therefore, we can apply any existing scheme for not only block labeling but also detection protocol, which makes our technique general.

The technique presented for the parallel programs with one event variable can be extended to the programs with multiple event variables. In case the original program contains more than one event variables, the before-wait loop L_1 performs all the post operations appeared before the first wait operation in each thread. For the case that an event e_j is posted first in a thread only in between the first wait operation for the different events e_i and the first wait operation for e_j, we restructure the after-wait loop L_2 again into two loops: the first loop $L_{2,1}$ for all the dynamic blocks executed between the two first wait operations in every thread, and the next loop $L_{2,2}$ for all the dynamic blocks executed after the first wait operation of e_j in every thread. Then the *before-wait loop* of e_i is L_1, and the *after-wait loop* of e_i is L_2 which is partitioned into $L_{2,1}$ and $L_{2,2}$. The *before-wait loop* of e_j is partitioned into L_1 and $L_{2,1}$, and the *after-wait loop* of e_j is $L_{2,2}$. This technique therefore partitions the set of all dynamic blocks appeared in the execution of the after-wait loop of e_i into two sets of dynamic blocks which are defined in sequential execution. We apply this procedure recursively to the programs with multiple event variables, which partitions one original loop into the multiple loops of which number is proportional to the number of event variables in the original loop.

4 Conclusion

This paper presents a program restructuring technique for on-the-fly race detection, which results in a serializable program preserving the semantics of original program. Previous on-the-fly techniques to detect races in parallel programs with inter-thread coordination show serious space overhead in two components of complexity, and can not guarantee to detect the first race in an execution instance. Monitoring an execution of the restructured program can detect the first races in the original program, eliminating one component of the space complexity. This technique makes on-the-fly race detection more effective and practical in debugging shared-memory parallel programs. We have been implementing our technique in a prototype system called *RaceStand* [5].

References

1. Callahan, D., Kennedy, K., Subhlok, J.: Analysis of Event Synchronization in a Parallel Programming Tool. 2nd Symposium on Principles and Practice of Parallel Programming. ACM (1990) 21-30
2. Dinning, A., Schonberg, E.: An Empirical Comparison of Monitoring Algorithms for Access Anomaly Detection. 2nd Symp. on Principles and Practice of Parallel Programming. ACM (1990) 1-10
3. Grunwald, D., Srinivasan, H.: Efficient Computation of Precedence Information in Parallel Programs. 6th Workshop on Languages and Compilers for Parallel Computing. Springer-Verlag (1993) 602-616
4. Jun, Y., McDowell, C.E.: On-the-fly Detection of the First Races in Programs with Nested Parallelism. 2nd Int'l Conf. on Parallel and Distributed Processing Techniques and Applications. CSREA (1996) 1549-1560
5. Kim, D., Jun, Y.: An Effective Tool for Debugging Races in Parallel Programs. 3rd Intl. Conf. on Parallel and Distributed Processing Techniques and Applications. CSREA (1997) 117-126
6. Netzer, R.H.B., Ghosh, S.: Efficient Race Condition Detection for Shared-Memory Programs with Post/Wait Synchronization. Intl. Conf. on Parallel Processing. Penn. State Univ. (1992) II-242-246
7. Netzer, R.H.B., Miller, B.P.: Improving the Accuracy of Data Race Detection. 3rd Symp. on Principles and Practice of Parallel Programming. ACM (1991) 133-144
8. Park, H., Jun, Y.: Detecting the First Races in Parallel Programs with Ordered Synchronization. 6th Intl. Conf. on Parallel and Distributed Systems. IEEE (1998) 201-208
9. Parallel Computing Forum: PCF Parallel Fortran Extensions. Fortran Forum, Vol. 10(3). ACM (1991)

Solving Initial Value Problems
with a Multiprocessor Code

Dana Petcu

Western University of Timişoara, Computer Science Department
B-dul V.Pârvan 4, RO-1900 Timişoara, Romania,
tel./fax.:++40-56-194002
e-mail: petcu@info.uvt.ro,
home page on web: http://www.info.uvt.ro/~petcu

Abstract. The semidicretization of a time-dependent nonlinear partial differential equation leads to a large-scale initial value problem for ordinary differential equations which often cannot be solved in a reasonable time on a sequential computer. We investigate in what extent can be practically exploited the idea of parallelism across method in the case of such large problems, and using a distributed computational system.

KEYWORDS: mathematical software supporting parallel processing, numerical solutions of large-scale problems, performance analysis, initial values problems for ordinary differential equations.

1 Introduction

We consider the initial value problem (IVP), for a large number of nonlinear ordinary differential equations (ODEs), endowed with a given starting value:

$$y'(t) = f(t, y(t)), \quad t \in [t_0, t_0 + T], \quad y(t_0) = y_0, \tag{1}$$

where $f : [t_0, t_0 + T] \times R^n \to R^n$, $y_0 \in R^n$. The numerical solution of a such generally nonlinear ODE system requires a large amount of computing power. Unfortunately, the actual hardware advancement is not sufficient to meet the requirements as they occur in large-scale problems. A natural approach for giving a positive answer to the need of fast solvers consists in the use of parallel and distributed computer architectures. The main problem is effectively exploiting the computational power of such systems since adequate mathematical software packages, in particular for ODEs, are not yet available. Most of the work to date on the parallel solution of IVPs concentrates on developing potentially useful numerical schemes, rather their effective implementation, comparisons of methods or the development of robust and portable software [1].

We concentrate our study on the class of IVPs which arise in solution methods for time dependent partial differential equations (PDEs). In Section 1 we present some examples.

Parallelism in solving ODEs can be exploited in many ways. For example, if the solutions are needed in real times, if there is a large period of integration, if a parameters fitting is to be performed which requires repeated integration, if the function evaluation is expensive, or if the problem to be solved is stiff and nonlinear. The means of archiving parallelism in IVP solvers can be classified into the following categories [15]:

1. parallelism across the system (across the space) – the possibility of partitioning the system of ODEs by assigning one single equations or a block of them to distinct processors for concurrent integration;
2. parallelism across the method – the possibility of distributing the computational effort of each single integration step, or block of steps, among the various processors;
3. parallelism across the time (across the steps) – the possibility of concurrently executing the integration over a certain number of successive time steps.

We will refer only to the parallelism across method. In Section 2 we present some theoretical considerations about the distribution of the solution computation effort by applying a numerical method on more than one processor.

Using a new software tool, EpODE (ExPert system for ordinary Differential Equations, shortly presented in Section 3) which was constructed according the theory from Section 2, we answer to the following problems:

– in what extent can be used a small number processors of a local network of workstations or of a parallel computer in solving process of a large initial value problem;
– the efficiency of the parallel methods proposed so far for solving ODEs relative to the sequential methods;
– by numerical tests on a wide range of initial value problems, to identify from the class of parallel methods which have been proposed until now those which really take advantage of distributed and parallel computer architecture;
– can be achieved a high level of parallelism when the ODE system is sparse; it is widely believed that only modest gains are possible in the efficiency of the distributed codes since solving IVPs requires frequent data communications.

Section 4 presents the test results and interprets them in order to answer to these four questions.

2 Large-Scale Initial Value Problems – a High-Demanding Computational Problem

Consider the general form of a time-dependent partial differential equation (PDE) in the spatial variable x and the time variable t:

$$u_t = g(x, t, u, u_x, u_{xx}, \ldots),$$

endowed with an initial condition function and a boundary condition

$$h(x) = u(x, t_0), \qquad v(x_b, t, u(x_b, t), u_x(x_b, t), \ldots) = 0.$$

The classical finite-difference or finite-element methods for PDEs are replacing the partial derivatives with algebraic approximations evaluated at some space grid points. In the method of lines (MOL) t is treated as a continuous variable, u_t is keep unmodified, and only u_x, $u_{xx}, \ldots$ are replaced with some algebraic approximations, like the following one:

$$u_{xx}(x_k, t) \leftarrow \frac{u(x_{k+1}, t) - 2u(x_k, t) + u(x_{k-1}, t)}{(x_{k+1} - x_k)^2}.$$

A such discretization lead to an ODE system with t as the independent variable and the kth component being an approximation to $u(x_k, t)$.

Table 1 presents two examples of IVPs generated from PDEs by MOL, and Table 2 enumerates others PDEs defined in one, two and three dimensional space which are considered large-scale ODE generators.

Table 1. Brusselator model of a chemical reaction-diffusion process

PDE system	$u_{1t} = u_1^2 u_2 + a - (b+1)u_1 + \alpha_1 \Delta u_1,$
	$u_{2t} = bu_1 - u_1^2 u_2 + \alpha_2 \Delta u_2$
Interval	$x \in D = [0, 1]^m,\ t \in [0, 10],\ m = 1$ or $m = 2$
Boundary val.	$u_1(x, t) = a(t),\ u_2(x, t) = b(t)/a(t),\ x \in \partial D$
Initial values	$u_1(x, 0) = c(x),\ u_2(x, 0) = b(0)/a(0),\ x \in D$

(a) Case $n = 1$ One dimensional model [7]

Discretization	$x_i = i/(n+1),\ i = 0, \ldots, n+1,\ u_1^{(i)}(t) = u_1(x_i, t)\ u_2^{(i)}(t) = u_2(x_i, t)$
ODE system	$u_{1t}^{(i)} = (u_1^{(i)})^2 u_2^{(i)} + a - (b+1)u_1^{(i)} + (n+1)^2 \alpha [u_1^{(i+1)} - 2u_1^{(i)} + u_1^{(i-1)}]$
	$u_{2t}^{(i)} = bu_1^{(i)} - (u_1^{(i)})^2 u_2^{(i)} + (n+1)^2 \alpha [u_2^{(i+1)} - 2u_2^{(i)} + u_2^{(i-1)}],$
Eqs. number	$2n$
Boundary vals.	$u_1^{(0)}(t) = u_1^{(n+1)}(t) = 1,\ u_2^{(0)}(t) = u_2^{(n+1)}(t) = 3,$
Initial values	$u_1^{(i)}(0) = 1 + \sin(2\pi i/(n+1)),\ u_2^{(i)}(0) = 3$
Constants	$a(t) = 1,\ b(t) = 3,\ c(x) = 1 + \sin(2\pi x),\ \alpha_1 = \alpha_2 = 0.2$

(b) Case $n = 2$ Two-dimensional model [17]

Discretization	$x_{i,j} = 1/(n+1)(i, j),\ i, j = 0, \ldots, n+1,\ u_k^{(i,j)}(t) = u_k(x_i, y_j, t)$
ODE system	$u_{1t}^{(ij)} = (u_1^{(ij)})^2 u_2^{(ij)} + a - (b+1)u_1^{(ij)} + (n+1)^2 \alpha_1 \cdot [u_1^{(i+1\,j)} +$
	$+ u_1^{(i-1\,j)} + u_1^{(i\,j+1)} + u_1^{(i\,j+1)} - 4u_1^{(ij)}]$
	$u_{2t}^{(ij)}) = bu_1^{(ij)}(u_1^{(ij)})^2 u_2^{(ij)} + (n+1)^2 \alpha_2 [u_2^{(i+1\,j)} + u_2^{(i-1\,j)} +$
	$+ u_2^{(i\,j+1)} + u_2^{(i\,j+1)} - 4u_2^{(ij)}],\ i, j = 1, \ldots, n$
Eqs. number	$2n^2$
Boundary val.	$u_1^{(0j)}(t) = u_1^{(n+1\,j)}(t) = u_1^{(i0)}(t) = u_1^{(i\,n+1)}(t) = 2 + \sin(4t)$
	$u_2^{(0j)}(t) = u_2^{(n+1\,j)}(t) = u_2^{(i0)}(t) = u_2^{(i\,n+1)}(t) = 5.45/(2 + \sin(4t))$
Initial values	$u_1^{(ij)}(0) = 2,\ u_2^{(ij)}(0) = 2.725$
Constants	$a(t) = 2 + \sin(4t),\ b(t) = 5.45,\ c(x) = 2,\ \alpha_1 = 0.177,\ \alpha_2 = 0.355$

If we apply the method of lines to solve a nonlinear PDE with a given accuracy, the resulting ODE system has generally a large number of equations, is

Table 2. Other PDE systems which generate large ODE systems by applying MOL

(a) Burgers model illustrating the theory of turbulence [7]	$u_t + (u^2/2)_x = \mu u_{xx}$ $\mu = 0.0003, \qquad 0 \le x \le 1,\ 0 \le t \le 2.5$ $u(0,t) = u(1,t) = 0,\ u(x,0) = \sqrt{[\sin(3\pi x)(1-x)]^3};$
(b) Medical Akzo Nobel problem in the study of the penetration of radio-labelled antibodies into tumorous tissue [10]	$u_{1t} = [(x-1)^4 u_{1xx} + 2(x-1)^3 u_{1x}]/c^2 - k u_1 u_2,$ $u_{2t} = -k u_1 u_2,$ $u_1(x,0) = 0,\ u_2(x,0) = u_0,$ $u_1(0,t) = \varphi(t),\ u_{1x}(1,t) = 0,$ $0 \le x \le 1,\ 0 \le t \le T,$ $T = 20, \quad k = 100,$ $\varphi(t) = \begin{cases} 2, & t \in [0,5] \\ 0, & t \in (5,20] \end{cases}$ $v_0 = 1, \qquad c = 4,$
(c) Cusp problem [7], a combination of a threshold-nerve-impulse mechanism, a cusp catastrophe and the Van der Pol oscillator:	$u_{1t} = -\varepsilon^{-1}(u_1^3 + u_2 u_1 + u_3) + \sigma u_{1xx},$ $u_{2t} = u_3 + cv + \sigma u_{2xx},$ $u_{3t} = (1 - u_2^2)u_3 - u_2 - g u_1 + hv + \sigma u_{3xx},$ where $v = (u_1 - d)(u_1 - e)[(u_1 - d)(u_1 - e) + f]^{-1}$ $u_1(x,0) = 0, u_2(x,0) = -2\cos(2\pi x), u_3(x,0) = 2\sin(2\pi x)$ $u_i(0,t) = u_i(1,t),\ i = 1,2,3,\ \varepsilon = 10^{-4},\ \sigma = 12^{-2},$ $c = 0.07,\ d = 0.7,\ h = 0.035,\ f = 0.1,\ e = 1.3,\ g = 0.4$
(d) Movement of a rectangular plate under the load of a car passing across it – mathematical model described in [7]	$u_{tt} + \omega u_t + \sigma \Delta\Delta u = f(x,y,t),$ $u\big|_{\partial\Omega} = 0,\ \Delta u\big|_{\partial\Omega} = 0,$ $u_t(x,y,0) = 0,$ where $(x,y) \in \Omega = [0,l_x] \times [0,l_y]$ where the load f is the sum of two Gaussian curves with four wheels which move in the x-direction.
(e) Long-range transport of air pollutants in the atmosphere – mathematical model described in [2]	$(c_i)_t = -\sum_{j=1}^{3}(u_j c_i)_{x_j} + \sum_{j=1}^{3}(K_j(c_i)_{x_j})_{x_j} + E_i(x,t) -$ $-(k_{1i} + k_{2i})c_i(x,t) + R_i(c_1,\ldots,c_q),\ i = 1,\ldots,q$ $x \in R^3,\ c_i(x,t)$ is the concentration of the ith pollutant at space point x, $u_j(x,t)$ are wind velocities along the three coordinate axes, $E_i(x,t)$ represents the emission, k_{1i} and k_{2i} are the dry and wet deposition coefficients, $K_j(x,t)$ represents the diffusion coefficients, and R_i describes the chemical reactions.

nonlinear, sparse and stiff, and typically must be solved on a long time scale. As the accuracy requirement increases, the spatial grid needs to be refined. Therefore, if greater accuracy is required for the PDE solution, the ODE system is even larger. The increase ratio of the number of ODEs depends also on the space dimension in which the PDE is defined. In the case of one-dimensional space this dependency is linear, in the case of the two-dimensional space it is quadratic, and in the case of the three-dimensional space it is cubic. The ODE system which results is usually a stiff system, i.e. the explicit methods are generally not suited due to unnatural restrictions on the stepsize, and therefore, implicit methods must be used (which require a large system of nonlinear equations to be solved at each time step). If the model has to be solved over a long time scale, many computations must be done. All the above mentioned remarks motivate why the solution of such ODE systems cannot be obtained on a standard sequential computational system fast enough.

3 Parallelism Across the Method – Exploiting the Method Computation Graph

Parallelism across the method means assigning different parts of the method to different processors. Concurrent evaluations of the entire function f for various values of its argument and the simultaneous solution of distinct (nonlinear) systems of equations are examples of parallelism across method. This form of parallelism is effective for any ODE, whereas parallelism across the problem aims large n values. Therefore parallelism across method seems to have the greatest potential for success on a general-purpose ODE solver using a distributed computing system. More details about the parallelism in solving ODEs can be found in [12].

The parallel numerical methods for ODEs are particular cases of general step-by-step methods which can be described by: (a) an iterative formula,

$$Y_n = AY_{n-1} + h_n\Phi(Y_{n-1}, Y_n, h_{n-1}, t_{n-1}), \quad n \geq 1, \tag{2}$$

where A is a $m \times m$ matrix which is independently on the IVP, and Φ is a function (in most cases a linear one) which is dependently on the IVP; (b) a starting procedure $Y_0 = \phi(h_0)$; (c) an implicit equation solver in the case $(\partial\Phi/\partial Y_n) \not\equiv 0$:

$$\text{solve}(X - AY_{n-1} - h_n\Phi(Y_{n-1}, X, h_{n-1}, t_{n-1}) = 0) \text{ on } X; \tag{3}$$

(d) a validation procedure $Z(t_n, h_n)$ for the approximate values X; (e) an advance formula, i.e. the relationship between Y_n from the left side of (2) at step n and Y_n from the right side of (2) at step $n + 1$:

$$n \leftarrow n + 1, \quad Y_{n-1} \leftarrow X. \tag{4}$$

The computations necessary to advance the solution from one step to another can be expressed by a relation between the values of the dependent variables, and this relation can be represented by a graph.

Since the computation made at each integration step looks like the one made at the preceding steps, the method approach to parallelism explores methods which maximize the concurrency in the graph representing a single-step computation.

We say that directed graph $G = (V, E)$ describes the information flow of the method described by (2-(4)) if the set of vertices is $V = V_1 \cup V_2$, with $V_1 = \{(Y_n)_i, | i = 1, \ldots, m\}$, and $V_2 = \{(Y_{n-1})_i, | i = 1, \ldots, m\}$, whereas $E = E_1 \cup E_2$. V is the set of all values of the dependent variable y which appear in the iterative formulae of the method. A pair $(y_i, y_j) \in E_1$ if $y_j \in V_1$ and its corresponding equation from the set of equations (2), depends on $y_i \in V$, and a pair $(y_i, y_j) \in E_2$ if $y_j \in V_1$, $y_i \in V_2$, and y_j will be play the role of y_i at the step $n + 1$.

Table 3. Partitioning the data-flow graph

(a) The parallel iterated Runge-Kutta method (PDIRK) presented in [15]

$$Y^{(0)} = y_{n-1}e, \ e = (1,1)^T, \ F((t_1,t_2)^T, (y_1,y_2)^T) = (f(t_1,y_1), f(t_2,y_2))^T,$$
$$Y^{(j)} - hDF(t_{n-1} + hc, Y^{(j)}) = y_{n-1}e + h(A-D)F(t_{n-1}e + hc, Y^{(j-1)}), \ 0 < j \le p$$
$$y_n = y_{n-1} + hb^T F(t_{n-1}e + hc, Y^{(p)})$$

based on Radau IIA correctors, i.e.

$$A = \frac{1}{12} \begin{pmatrix} 5 & -1 \\ 9 & 3 \end{pmatrix}, b = \frac{1}{4} \begin{pmatrix} 3 \\ 1 \end{pmatrix}, c = \frac{1}{3} \begin{pmatrix} 1 \\ 3 \end{pmatrix}, \text{ with } D = \frac{1}{30} \begin{pmatrix} 20 - 5\sqrt{6} & 0 \\ 0 & 12 + 3\sqrt{6} \end{pmatrix}$$

is equivalent for $p = 3$ with a six-stages third-order L-stable Runge-Kutta method with the following data-flow graph G:

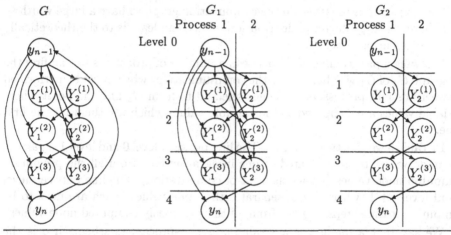

The block predictor-corrector method presented in [14]

$$\begin{pmatrix} y_{n+3/2} \\ y_{n+1} \end{pmatrix} = \begin{pmatrix} y_{n+1/2} \\ y_n \end{pmatrix} + h\frac{1}{18}\left[\begin{pmatrix} 7 & 0 \\ 0 & 3 \end{pmatrix}\begin{pmatrix} f^P_{n+3/2} \\ f^P_{n+1} \end{pmatrix} + \begin{pmatrix} 15 & -4 \\ 12 & 3 \end{pmatrix}\begin{pmatrix} f_{n+1/2} \\ f_n \end{pmatrix}\right],$$
$$\begin{pmatrix} y^P_{n+3/2} \\ y^P_{n+1} \end{pmatrix} = \frac{1}{7}\begin{pmatrix} 3 & 4 \\ -28 & 35 \end{pmatrix}\begin{pmatrix} y_{n+1/2} \\ y_n \end{pmatrix} + h\frac{1}{7}\begin{pmatrix} 15 & -6 \\ 14 & 7 \end{pmatrix}\begin{pmatrix} f_{n+1/2} \\ f_n \end{pmatrix},$$

has the following data-flow graph G:

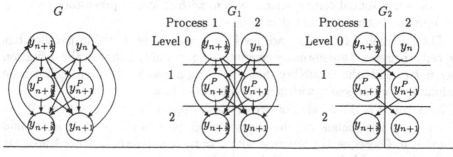

The execution of a graph G follows two steps. The first step consists in computing the output values of each computational node of $G_1 = (V, E_1)$ when all the input values to that node have been computed. When there are cycles in the graph (in the case of implicit methods), computation is not possible until the graph has been modified to break the cycles (using an iterative equation solver). The second step consists in applying (4), i.e. the relation defined by E_2 (in general only assignments).

Distributed execution of a computation graph consists of assigning each node in the graph to a processor. All processors can operate simultaneously only if every processor has nodes which are ready to be evaluated at all times. In order to implement the method on a parallel or distributed computational system, we search for a partitioning on processors and levels of the subgraph $G_1 = (V, E_1)$ of G, in a same manner that it has been theoretical done for internal stages of Runge-Kutta methods in [4] and [8].

Our objective is to structure the computation graph to have a large width so that there is a large degree of distribution, which can lead us to the theoretically shortest execution time.

Knowing a partitioning of G_1 between a number of processors we can find the subgraph G_2 of G_1 which indicates the communications which must be performed between distinct processors. E_1 edges selected to form G_2 link the point where variable values are computed to the variable values which use them for the first time.

In Table 3 we give two examples. The line between level 0 and level 1 separates the node values to be evaluated at one integration step from all the previously computed node values (known as front of computation). The line between level i and level $i + 1$, where $i > 0$, separates the node values which are next to be computed at time-steps j, $j > i$ from all the previously computed node values.

We say that a method is a s-value q-level p-processors scheme if q is the smallest integer for which the s new dependent variable values can be evaluated in q-time-steps and p is the smallest number of processors for which this value of q can be attained.

For an explicit formula each time-step is equal to the time required for a function evaluation plus a little overhead (additions, multiplications, etc.), while for an implicit formula, a time-step can be more expensive, respectively it can be equal to the time required to solve an implicit equation plus a little overhead. Thus on a distributed computational system with at least p processors, one step of the method can be evaluated in q time-steps.

The partition cells within each level are typically evaluated in parallel, but the cells themselves are normally computed sequentially, although the definition does not exclude the possibility that some graph nodes within one cell can be evaluated simultaneously with some graph nodes in another.

Note that s is the number of circles which appear in levels i, with $i > 0$.

For good load balancing, the number of graph nodes in each block should be about q. Consequently, formulas with $s \approx pq$ are preferred. Table 4 presents some examples of balanced parallel methods.

The distributed implementation of each computation graph imposes also adequate data distribution. The best data distribution must minimize the number of interprocess communications (see Table 4.c, variable $k_{n+1}^{(1)}$).

4 Prototype of an ODE Solver

Most of our work in the last two years has been concentrated to create a portable numerical software package with the following properties:

1. to be a tool for computing an approximate solution of an arbitrary large initial value problem, in a reasonable time, using the computational power of one or more processors;
2. to be a tool in which the results of some sequential, parallel and distributed methods can be easily compared; by results we mean not only the approximate solutions which will by produced applying the method to a given problem, but also some statistics like the elapsed computation time, the number of function evaluations or matrix inversions;
3. to be a tool in which the problem, the solving method and the user option for sequential/ parallel/ distributed computations are interpreted as input data in a general solving procedure; the outputs of this procedure are the above mentioned results;
4. to be a tool with which the user can easily describe, respectively select from an extensible database, different initial value problems and methods, and can ask about they degree of parallelism (among other useful information, like the problem type or the method order);
5. to be a tool with a friendly user interface and which acts as an expert system if the user ask for guidance.

A prototype of an ODE solving environment was created which respects these ideas: EpODE (ExPert system for Ordinary Differential Equations). It is designed to be a tool with which a numerical analyst, but also a non-expert in ODEs, can solve an initial value problem of type (1). The problem to be solved will be described in a mathematical form. In order to obtain an approximate solution of the problem, the user can describe an iterative method, can select one from a wide-range data-base, or can let the tool to select a method (a decision tree has been implemented and its crossing depends on the problem and method properties which the tool can detect; for example, some implicit methods will be selected if we solve a stiff IVP). EpODE user interface has been presented in a previous article, in [11]. More details about the concepts beyond EpODE, and about others similar software packages, can be found in [13]. The current version of EpODE can be freely obtained from http://www.info.uvt.ro/~petcu/epode.

The EpODE general procedure which offers the approximate solution of an IVP accepts as inputs the method iterative formula, the advance formula, an item from a list of implicit equation solvers, and $y \in V_1$ which will represent the approximate solution. Based on these information, the graphs G, G_1 and

Table 4. Compucation graphs and partitions of some parallel methods

(a) Predictor-corrector scheme of fourth order [6],
a 4-value, 1-level, 4-processor method:

$$y_{n+4}^{(0)} = y_n^{(3)} + \frac{h}{3}(8f_{n+3}^{(0)} - 4f_{n+2}^{(1)} + 8f_{n+1}^{(2)})$$
$$y_{n+3}^{(1)} = y_n^{(3)} + \frac{h}{8}(3f_{n+3}^{(0)} + 9f_{n+2}^{(1)} + 9f_{n+1}^{(2)} + 3f_n^{(3)})$$
$$y_{n+2}^{(2)} = y_n^{(3)} + \frac{h}{3}(f_{n+2}^{(1)} + 4f_{n+1}^{(2)} + f_n^{(3)})$$
$$y_{n+1}^{(3)} = y_n^{(3)} + \frac{h}{24}(9f_{n+1}^{(2)} + 19f_n^{(3)} - 5f_{n-1}^{(3)} + f_{n-2}^{(3)})$$

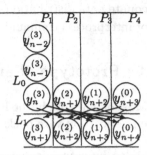

(b) Two-stage explicit block method of fourth order [14],
a 6-value, 2-level, 3-processor method:

$$y_{n+\frac{2}{3}}^P = y_{n+\frac{1}{3}} + \frac{5}{16}hf_{n+\frac{1}{3}}, \quad y_{n+\frac{4}{3}}^P = y_{n+\frac{1}{3}} + 7\frac{h}{32}f_{n+\frac{1}{3}}$$
$$y_{n+1}^P = y_n + \frac{h}{8}f_n$$
$$y_{n+\frac{2}{3}} = y_{n+\frac{1}{3}} + \frac{h}{16}(5f_{n+\frac{5}{3}}^P + 26f_{n+\frac{2}{3}} - 21f_{n+\frac{1}{3}} + 6f_n)$$
$$y_{n+\frac{4}{3}} = y_{n+\frac{1}{3}} + \frac{h}{32}(7f_{n+\frac{4}{3}}^P + 30f_{n+\frac{2}{3}} - 8f_{n+\frac{1}{3}} + 3f_n)$$
$$y_{n+1} = y_n + \frac{h}{8}(f_{n+\frac{5}{3}}^P + 3f_{n+\frac{2}{3}} + 3f_{n+\frac{1}{3}} + f_n)$$

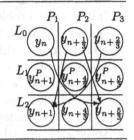

(c) Modified Runge-Kutta method of second order [18],
a 4-value, 2-level, 2-processor method:

$$k_{n+1}^{(1)} = hf(t_{n+1}, y_{n+1}^{(1)})$$
$$y_{n+2}^{(1)} = y_{n+1}^{(1)} + k_{n+1}^{(1)}$$
$$k_n^{(2)} = hf(t_{n+1} + \frac{h}{4}, \frac{1}{2}(y_n^{(1)} + y_n^{(2)}) + \frac{1}{4}k_n^{(1)})$$
$$y_{n+1}^{(2)} = y_n^{(2)} + 2k_n^{(2)} - k_n^{(1)}$$

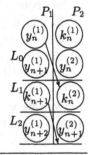

(d) Diagonally implicit Runge-Kutta method,
A-stable, fourth-order [8],
a 5-value, 3-level, 2-processor method:

$$k_1 = f(t_n + \frac{1}{3}h, y_n + \frac{h}{3}k_1)$$
$$k_2 = f(t_n + \frac{2}{3}h, y_n + \frac{h}{3}(k_1 + k_2))$$
$$k_3 = f(t_n + \frac{21+\sqrt{57}}{48}h, y_n + \frac{21+\sqrt{57}}{48}hk_3)$$
$$k_4 = f(t_n + \frac{27-\sqrt{57}}{48}h, y_n + h(\frac{6-2\sqrt{57}}{48}k_3 + \frac{21+\sqrt{57}}{48}k_4))$$
$$y_{n+1} = y_n + h[\frac{9+3\sqrt{57}}{16}(k_1 + k_2) - \frac{1+3\sqrt{57}}{16}(k_3 + k_4)]$$

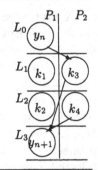

(e) Block diagonally Runge-Kutta method, L-stable
of fourth-order [4], a 5-value, 2-level, 2-processors met.

$$k_1 = f(t_n + \frac{3-\sqrt{6}}{6}h, y_n + \frac{1}{12}h(5k_1 + (1 - 2\sqrt{3})k_2))$$
$$k_2 = f(t_n + \frac{3+\sqrt{6}}{6}h, y_n + \frac{1}{12}h((1 + 2\sqrt{3})k_1 + 5k_2))$$
$$k_3 = f(t_n + \frac{3-\sqrt{6}}{6}h, y_n + \frac{1}{6}h(3k_3 - \sqrt{3}k_2))$$
$$k_4 = f(t_n + \frac{3+\sqrt{6}}{6}h, y_n + \frac{1}{6}h(\sqrt{3}k_1 + 3k_2))$$
$$y_{n+1} = y_n + h[\frac{3}{2}(k_1 + k_2) - (k_3 + k_4)]$$

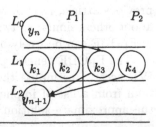

G_2, defined in Section 3, are constructed for each particular inputs. EpODE can detect the graph G_1 which corresponds to the s-value q-level s-processors representation of the method. The graph G_1 is used to establish the order of application of the iterative and advance formulae, in both cases, of sequential or distributed computations. The graph G_2 indicates the communications necessary in the case of distributed computations.

Table 5. Classes of parallel methods and techniques supported by EpODE

Parallelism across:
1. the system:
   1.1. on a large task level: the equation segmentation method   +
   1.2. on a medium task level: by a partitioning of the function evaluations   −
   1.3. on a snall task level: by a partitioning on a basic operator level   −
2. the method:
   2.1. direct methods
      2.1.1. Runge-Kutta methods: the technique based on digraph analysis   +
      2.1.2. modified Runge-Kutta methods: the front-broadening technique   +
      2.1.3. Runge-Kutta methods: the decoupling techniques   −
      2.1.4. extrapolation methods   *
      2.1.5. block methods: by exploiting the data-flow graph   +
      2.1.6. general linear methods: the technique based on digraph analysis   +
   2.2. iterative methods
      2.2.1. predictor-corrector schemes based on multistep formulae   +
      2.2.2. predictor-corrector schemes based on Runge-Kutta correctors   *
      2.2.3. predictor-corrector schemes for block methods with multistep f.   +
      2.2.4. predictor-corrector schemes for block methods with Runge-Kutta c.*
3. the time:
   3.1. waveform relaxation method of Jacobi type   +
   3.2. other methods   −

In Table 5 we have scratched the parallel methods and techniques supported by EpODE. We have denote by '×' a class of methods partially covered, by '+' a class of methods which have been or can be implemented in EpODE, by '−' a class of methods which have not been and cannot be implemented in the current version, and by '*' a class of methods which can be written in a form of some methods from a class denoted by '+'.

In order to apply the parallelism across the system, the initial value problem is analyzed. Using the dependency graph between the problem variables, the tool can detect if the ODE system can be decomposed into some smaller independent subsystems. These subsystems can be integrated in parallel (attaining a high efficiency not only by implementation on a parallel computer, but also on a distributed system). Unfortunately, the equation segmentation method can be applied only to a special class of IVPs.

Table 6. EpODE facilities

	Problem	Method	Solution
User inter- face	Problem variables Differential equations Initial values Integration interval	Method variables Iterative equations Starting procedure Implicit eqs.solver	Error control Select step-size/number Constant/variable stepsize Seq./distrib. computations
Tool faci- lities	Jacobian generator Linearity test Sparsity test Decomposition test Stiffness test Problem classification	Test of implicitness Test: multi-step/stage Test of multiderivative Method order Test A_0-stability Parallelism degree Data flow graph	Select method list accord.IVP Select method accord.req.error Select stepsize accord.method User interuption points Solution in 2D/3D graphics Solution in tabular represent. Time statistics
Data banks	Nonstiff/stiff IVPs Small/large IVPs Linear/nonlinear IVP	Linear one/multistep General linear/nonlinear One/multiderivative Serial/parallel methods	Files with solution values Sessions: IVP+method+sol.

Our numerical tests prove that the parallelism across time cannot be applied to solve large nonlinear ODE systems with similar efficiency results as the parallelism across method, at least when the computations are performed on a distributed system.

The main facilities provided by EpODE are reported in Table 6. The data banks include a wide range of problemes and methods (also those from Tables 1, 2, 3, 4). New problems and methods can be easily added.

5 Numerical Experiments

We present in this selection some examples illustrating the efficiency of parallel methods on distributed computational systems. The initial value problems which were selected for numerical tests are those which can be obatined applying the MOL to the PDEs presented in Tables 1 and 2. We have solve such system of ODEs varying the number of equations from 10 to 400. The numerical solutions and the statistics have been obtained using EpODE facilities. The PVM package (Parallel Virtual Machine [5]) was used for process intercommunication because of his portability on wide range of parallel and distributed computation systems. The studies have been done on a network of Sun and PC workstations. Similar tests on shared memory parallel computers and transputer machines have been reported in [9], respectively in [3].

Table 7 presents the speedups obtained in two distinct cases: applying an explicit and an implicit method on one processor (sequential execution time, T_s) or on two processors (distributed execution time, T_d). Note that the execution

Table 7. Execution times per one step, speedups and efficiency results in the case of one-dimensional Brusselator model presented in Table 1 and two solution methods

No. eqs.	Diagonally implicit Runge-Kutta method presented in Table 4.c					Block predictor-corrector method presented in Table 3.b				
	Seq. times T_s (s)	Distr. times T_d (s)	Comm. over-head	Speedup T_s/T_d	Method efficiency $T_s/(pT_d)$	Seq. times T_s (s)	Distr. times T_d (s)	Comm. over-head	Speedup T_s/T_d	Method efficiency $T_s/(pT_d)$
10	0.294	0.269	23%	1.091	54.6%	0.005	0.581	98%	0.009	0.4%
20	0.875	0.628	13%	1.394	69.7%	0.010	0.605	98%	0.017	0.8%
40	2.820	1.815	9%	1.553	77.7%	0.021	0.625	97%	0.034	1.7%
60	6.239	3.780	8%	1.651	82.5%	0.035	0.639	95%	0.054	2.7%
80	11.66	6.920	7%	1.685	84.3%	0.054	0.651	93%	0.083	4.1%
100	20.21	11.78	7%	1.715	85.8%	0.080	0.675	90%	0.118	5.9%
200	117.3	64.41	7%	1.821	91.0%	0.250	0.775	78%	0.323	16.1%
300	321.0	174.1	6%	1.839	91.9%	0.519	0.864	60%	0.601	30.0%
400	702.3	379.8	6%	1.842	92.1%	0.851	1.016	44%	0.837	41.8%

times are relative to one integration step. Since the effort on different integration steps is similar, and usually the integration interval is very large, the speedup of the distributed code computed on the full integration interval is approximately equal to the speedup of the distributed code computed for one integration step. Whereas for the implicit method we get a good speedup, closest to the ideal value of processor number, for the explicit method the speedup is far to be satisfactory. Since the test problems are stiff ones, the explicit method requires a very small integration step compared with that admitted for the implicit method. The end of integration interval is therefore hardly attained by the explicit method, even through the execution time per one integration step is smaller than that of the implicit method (in the last case an iterative implicit equation solver must be applied, and in the particular case of stiff problems predictor-corrector schemes are inefficient). We have use as implicit equation solver a Newton-like procedure. Note the decrease of the process intercommunication overhead percent with the number of ODEs.

Figure 1 shows the small differences between the speedups reported for different implicit solution methods and the big differences between the efficiency reported for implicit versus explicit methods.

In Table 8 we give more details about the execution times and efficiency measurements reported in Figure 1. Note the small differences between the efficiency of the theree implicit methods with two, three, respectively four levels on one time step.

6 Conclusions

The test results indicate that we can discuss about efficiency of the distributed implementation in the case of implicit methods even if we have a small number

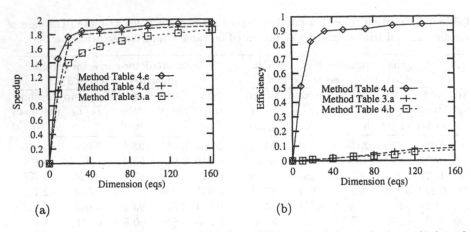

Fig. 1. Speedup and efficiency: (a) for three different implicit methods applied to the IVP produced by the PDE from Table 2.d (b) for three different implicit and explicit methods applied to the IVP produced by the PDE from Table 2.c

of ODEs. In opposite situation is the case of explicit methods when the efficiency attains a reasonable level only for systems of hundred order of ODEs. Therefore a stiff solver for large IVPs is ideally suited for distributed processing, and the theoretical paralleling of explicit method is practically inefficient in the particular case of large-scale sparse ODE systems derived from PDEs.

Table 8. Changing the implicit solution methods for the solution of the two dimensional Brusselator model from Table 1.b

No. eqs.	Diagonally implicit Runge-Kutta method from Table 4.d			Block diagonally Runge-Kutta method from Table 4.e			Diagonally implicit iterated method (g) from Table 3.a		
	Seq.time	Dist.time	Effic.	Seq.time	Dist.time	Effic.	Seq.time	Dist.time	Effic.
20	1.549	0.941	82.3%	1.759	0.996	88.2%	2.125	1.521	69.9%
30	3.055	1.701	89.8%	3.605	1.950	92.4%	4.459	2.909	76.6%
50	6.580	3.630	90.6%	6.895	3.695	93.3%	10.30	6.341	81.3%
70	11.63	6.371	91.3%	11.37	6.035	94.2%	20.10	11.83	84.9%
100	24.03	12.83	93.6%	24.52	12.80	95.8%	38.77	21.97	88.2%
130	48.26	25.52	94.5%	44.49	22.95	96.9%	70.75	39.21	90.2%
160	78.27	41.23	94.9%	78.23	40.24	97.2%	120.7	65.24	92.5%

References

1. Bellen, A.: Introduction, International Conference on Parallel Methods for ODEs. The State of the Art, Grado (Italy), 10-13 September 1991. Appl. Numer. Math. **11** (1983) 3-5.

2. Burrage, K.: Parallel methods for initial value problems, Appl. Num. Math. **11** (1993) 5–45
3. De Meyer, H., Van Daele, M., Vanden Berghe, G.: On the implementation of parallel iterated Runge-Kutta methods on a transputer network. Appl. Numer. Math. **13** (1993) 155–163
4. Iserles, A., Nørsett, S.P.: On the Theory of Parallel Runge-Kutta Methods. IMA J. of Numer. Anal. **10** (1990) 463-488.
5. Geist, A., et al., *PVM: Parallel Virtual Machine. A Users' Guide and Tutorial for Networked Parallel Computing* (1994), MIT Press.
6. Ghoshal, S.K., Gupta, M., Rajaraman, V.: A parallel multistep predictor-corrector algorithm for solving ODEs, J. Par. Distr. Comput. **6** (1989) 630–648
7. Hairer, E., Wanner, G., *Solving Ordinary Differential Equations II, Stiff and Differential-Algebraic Problems* (1991), Springer Verlag.
8. Jackson, K.R., Nørsett, S.P.: The potential for parallelism in Runge-Kutta methods. SIAM J. Numer. Anal. **32** (1995) 49–82
9. Kahaner, D.K., Ng, E., Schiesser, W.E., Thompson, S.: Experiments with an ODE solver in the parallel solution of method of lines problems on a shared-memory parallel computer. J. Comput. & Appl. Math. **38** (1991) 231–253
10. Lioen, W.M., De Swart, J.J.B., Van der Veen, W.A.: Test Set for IVP Solvers, 1996, Report NM-R9615, CWI Amsterdam, http://dbs.cwi.nl:8080/ cwwwi/ owa/ cwwwi.print_reports2?ID=9.
11. Petcu, D.: Implementation of Some Multiprocessor Algorithms for ODEs using PVM, LNCS **1332**: Recent Advances in PVM and MPI, eds. M. Bubak, J. Dongarra, J. Wasniewski, Springer-Verlag, Berlin (1997) 375-383.
12. Petcu, D.: Parallelism in solving ODEs. Mathematical Monographs **64**, Printing House of Western University of Timişoara (1998).
13. Petcu, D., Drăgan, M.: Designing an ODE solving environment. Proceedings of SciTools'98, LNCS (to appear).
14. Tam, H.W.: Two-stage parallel methods for the numerical solution of ODEs, SIAM J. Sci. Stat. Comput. **13** (1992) 1062–1084
15. Van der Houwen, P.J.: Parallel step-by-step methods, Appl. Num. Math. **11** (1983) 69-81.
16. Van der Houwen, P.J., Sommeijer, B.P.: Iterated Runge-Kutta methods on parallel computers. SIAM J. Sci. Stat. Comput. **12** (1991) 1000–1028
17. Vanderwalle, S., Piessens, R.: Numerical experiments with nonlinear waveform relaxation on a parallel processor. Appl. Num. Math. **8** (1991) 149–161
18. Xiao-Qiu, S., De-Gui, L., Zhao-Ding, Y.: Some kinds of parallel Runge-Kutta methods, J. Comput. Math., Suppl. Issue (1992) 79–85.

Parallel Implementation of Constraint Solving *

Alvaro Ruiz-Andino[1], Lourdes Araujo[1], Fernando Sáenz[2], and Jose Ruz[2]

[1] Department of Computer Science
{alvaro, lurdes}@sip.ucm.es

[2] Department of Computer Architecture
{fernan, jjruz}@eucmax.sim.ucm.es

University Complutense of Madrid, SPAIN.

Abstract. Many problems from artificial intelligence can be described as constraint satisfaction problems over finite domains (CSP(FD)), that is, a solution is an assignment of a value to each problem variable such that a set of constraints is satisfied. Arc-consistency algorithms remove inconsistent values from the set of values that can be assigned to a variable (its domain), thus reducing the search space. We have developed a parallelisation scheme of arc-consistency to be run on MIMD multiprocessor. The set of constraints is divided into N partitions, which are executed in parallel on N processors. The parallelisation scheme has been implemented on a CRAY T3E multiprocessor with up to thirty-four processors. Empirical results on speedup and behaviour are reported and discussed.

1 Introduction

Constraint Programming over finite domains (CP(FD)) has been used for specifying and solving complex constraint satisfaction and optimisation problems, such as resource allocation, scheduling and hardware design [8]. Finite domain Constraint Satisfaction Problems (CSP) usually describe NP-complete search problems, but it has been shown that by working locally on constraints and their related variables it is possible to dynamically prune the search space in an efficient way. Techniques following this approach, called arc-consistency (AC) algorithms, eliminate inconsistent values from the solution space. They can be used to reduce the size of the search space both before and while searching. Waltz [9] proposed the first arc-consistency algorithm, and several improved versions are described in the literature: AC-5 [7], and AC-6 [1].

We have developed and tested a parallelisation scheme of arc-consistency for MIMD distributed shared memory multiprocessors. The set of constraints is partitioned into N sets, which are processed in parallel on N processors.

Several parallel processing methods for solving CSP's have been proposed. In [11], a parallel constraint solving technique for a special class of CSP, acyclic constraint networks, is developed. It also presents some results on parallel complexity, generalising results in [3]. In [4], it is concluded that parallel complexity of constraint networks is critically dependent on subtle properties of the network

---

* Supported by project CICYT-TIC98-0445-C03-02/97

which do not influence its sequential complexity. They propose massively parallel processing of arc-consistency with also very simple processing elements.

In [2, 5] Nguyen, Deville and Baudot proposed distributed versions for AC-3, AC-4, and AC-6 for binary CSP's. Instead, our work is focused on AC-5, and, we report empirical data obtained running the parallel arc-consistency algorithms on a CRAY T3E, a distributed shared memory multiprocessor.

1.1 Constraint programming

A constraint satisfaction problem over finite domains may be stated as follows. Given a tuple $\langle \mathcal{V}, \mathcal{D}, \mathcal{C} \rangle$, where

- $\mathcal{V} \equiv \{v_1, \cdots, v_n\}$, is a set of domain variables,
- $\mathcal{D} \equiv \{d_1, \cdots, d_n\}$, is the set of an initial *finite domain* (finite set of values) for each variable,
- $\mathcal{C} \equiv \{c_1, \cdots, c_m\}$, is a set of constraints among the variables in $\mathcal{V}$. A constraint $c \equiv (V_c, R_c)$ is defined by a subset of variables $V_c \subseteq \mathcal{V}$, and a subset of allowed tuples of values $R_c \subseteq \bigotimes_{v_i \in V_c} d_i$, where $\otimes$ denotes Cartesian product.

The goal is to find an assignment for each variable $v_i \in \mathcal{V}$ of a value from each $d_i \in \mathcal{D}$ which satisfies every constraint $c_i \in \mathcal{C}$. Besides the explicit relational constraints, the allowed constraints usually include arithmetic ones as well as some specific symbolic constraints used in classic resource allocation problems like scheduling and packing.

A constraint $c \equiv (V_c, R_c) \in \mathcal{C}$, $V_c \equiv \{v_1, \cdots, v_k\}$, is *arc-consistent* with respect to domains $\{d_1, \cdots, d_k\}$ iff for all $v_i \in V_c$, for all $a \in d_i$, there exists a tuple $(b_1, \cdots, b_{i-1}, a, b_{i+1}, \cdots, b_k) \in R_c$, where $b_j \in d_j$. A CSP is called arc-consistent iff all $c_i \in \mathcal{C}$ are arc-consistent with respect to $\mathcal{D}$.

The starting point of this work is a sequential constraint solver which implements the AC-5 arc-consistency algorithm [7]. AC-5 *revises* constraints removing inconsistent values from the domains of the variables until either a fixed point is reached, or inconsistency is detected. A propagation queue is used to schedule the revision of constraints. As the result of revising a constraint the domain of a variable may be pruned, and in such a case the variable is queued. Termination, correctness, complexity, and properties of the algorithm have been studied extensively in the literature [7]. Correctness is independent of the order of revising the constraints, which constitutes the basis for the correctness of the parallel version of the algorithm.

The rest of the paper is organised as follows. Next section describes the parallel execution scheme. Section 3 reports and discusses the experimental results. Finally, conclusions are drawn in section 4.

2 Parallel Arc-consistency

The arc-consistency algorithm presents an inherent parallelism. Each constraint behaves as a concurrent process which updates the domains of variables, triggered by changes in the domains of other variables. There is an inherent sequentiality, as well, since a constraint must be revised only as the consequence of a previous revision of another constraint. This sequentiality defines a partial order among revising constraints. A constraint is *ready* if any of its variables has been pruned after its last revision. At any time during the execution of the arc-consistency algorithm there will be a set of ready constraints, called the *ready set*. In a sequential version of a consistency algorithm the ready set is stored in a *propagation queue* (updated whenever a variable is modified), assuring a sound execution order of constraints, that is, that a constraint is revised after the pruned variable has been updated. Parallel consistency algorithms simultaneously revise the constraints in the ready set, providing mechanisms to maintain a sound order.

A static partition ensures a sound order of revising constraints, since the parallel algorithm is basically the sequential one, but applied to a subset of the constraints. The only coordination mechanism needed by this scheme comes from the detection of termination, which can be carried out by one of the processors, called the *distinguished* one. The mapping of constraints to processors is generated previously to the execution of arc-consistency. An important factor for the efficiency of this scheme is the criterion for the distribution of constraints among processors, therefore different criteria have been investigated.

Parallelisation of the consistency algorithm requires every processor to have access to a common store for the domains of the variables. Since the presented parallelisation scheme is focused on distributed memory architecture, each processor will maintain a (partial) local copy of the store. Changes in the variables' domains must be communicated to concerned processors in order to maintain coherency among local copies of the domains.

The set of constraints C is partitioned into n disjoint subsets, $C = C_1 \cup \cdots \cup C_n$. This partitioning induces a distribution of the set of domain variables V in n not necessarily disjoint subsets $V_1, \cdots, V_n$ ($V = V_1 \cup \cdots \cup V_n$). For all constraints $c_j \in C_i$, the variables involved in c_j constitute V_i. Partitions $\langle V_i, D_i, C_i \rangle$ are mapped one-to-one to processing elements P_i. Each processing element P_i performs sequential arc-consistency, revising constraints belonging to C_i, and consequently updating local copies of variables in V_i. Since the distribution of the set of variables V is non-disjoint, some variables will be located at several processing elements. Therefore, each processing element P_i must broadcast the prunings of the domain of variable v to every processing element P_j which has been assigned any of those constraints which involve variable v. Upon receiving the notification, processing elements P_j intersect their local copies of the domain with the incoming domain, probably triggering further propagation. Communication among processors is also needed in order to detect termination of the algorithm, either because of reaching the global fixed point, or because of inconsistency detection.

2.1 Parallel Algorithm

The parallel arc-consistency algorithm, as the sequential one, is a fixed point algorithm. Every processor executes a copy of it, maintaining a private propagation queue. The main steps of the algorithm are:

1. Initialize the local propagation queue, as the result of the revision of the local constraints.

2. Repeat the following steps until the global fixed point is reached or inconsistency is detected:
   - Revise local constraints until either the local propagation queue is empty (local fixed point) or inconsistency is detected.
   - Notify local fixed point to the *distinguished* processor, and wait until either:
     - Other processor communicates a change in the domain of a variable, therefore the local fixed point is left and revision of constraints continues.
     - The distinguished processor communicates that the global fixed point has been reached.
     - Other processor communicates inconsistency.

Whenever the revision of a local constraint results in the modification of the domain of a variable v, the processor broadcasts a message to the set of processors that have been assigned any of those constraints which involve variable v. Upon receiving the message these processors either detect inconsistency or properly update their local propagation queue and their local copy of variable v. Whenever a processor detects inconsistency, it broadcasts the failure to the rest of processors. Inconsistency is detected whenever:

- an empty domain results from the revision of a local constraint.
- an empty domain results from the intersection of the local domain of a variable with the domain received from another processor.

The global fixed point is reached when every processor is in a local fixed point and there are no pending messages. The distinguished processor is the only one responsible for the detection of termination. However, it performs local propagation as any other processor. In order to be able to detect the global fixed point, processors must notify to the distinguished one whenever they reach a local fixed point –along with the number of messages they have sent and received– and whenever they leave it due to an incoming message. When termination is detected, the distinguished processor notifies to the rest of processors.

A synchronisation among all processors is needed at the beginning of the algorithm, just after the initialisation of the communication status variables. Another synchronisation is needed if the algorithm finishes with inconsistency detection; otherwise, the global fixed point detection implies a synchronisation among processors.

3 Experimental Results

The presented parallel algorithms have been written in C, and developed and tested on a CRAY T3E multiprocessor with thirty-four 400-MHz DEC Alpha processors, 128 Mb of memory per processor, under UNICOS (UNIX) operating system. Notification of failure, global and local fixed point detection, activity status, and number of messages sent and received, have been implemented using the remote memory write feature of the CRAY T3E multiprocessor (routines from CRAY's shared memory library). Queues of messages are used for receiving domain updates. Messages are broadcasted to queues also using the fast remote memory write feature.

Reported results correspond to the time required to reach the first or all solutions, depending on the benchmark, performing a first fail sequential labelling. Therefore, reported speedup is lower than speedup achieved in a single call to the arc-consistency algorithm, since the search for a solution usually comprises a large number of calls to the arc-consistency algorithm, executed in parallel, interleaved with the selection and assignment of a value to a variable, executed sequentially.

We report the results for two representative benchmarks from the set used to evaluate the performance of the presented parallelisation scheme:

1. *N-Queens* problem consists in placing N queens in an N×N chess board in such a way that no queen attacks each other. The instance presented corresponds to N = 111, size which leads to a significant execution time.
2. *Parametrizable Binary Constraint Satisfaction Problem* (PBCSP). Synthetic parametrizable constraint satisfaction problems allow studying the performance of an arc-consistency algorithm as some significant problem parameters vary. Instances of this problem are randomly generated given four parameters: number of variables (nv), the size of the initial domains (ds), density, and tightness. Figure 1 reports results obtained for an instance of this problem where $nv = 100$, $ds = 20$, $density = 0.75$, and $tightness = 0.85$.

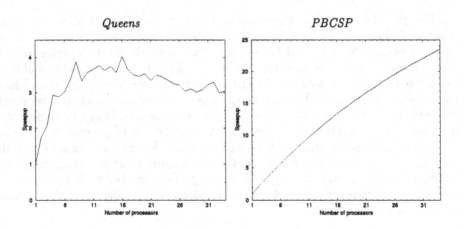

Fig. 1. Speedup curves for selected benchmarks.

Charts in figure 1 show, for each benchmark, the speedup vs. the number of processors. It can be observed that whereas *PBCSP* problems present a nearly linear speedup, the speedup for *Queens* benchmark stops increasing from a certain number of processors. The main factor for this different behaviour are that in *PBCSP* benchmark calls to the arc-consistency algorithm have a larger execution time, and revision of constraints has a larger granularity. Besides, *PBCSP* has a constraint graph with a more uniform topology, leading to a better workload balance. In order to study this factor we have measured the minimum and the maximum number of constraints executed per processor. The difference between minimum and maximum indicates workload balance quality. For *PBCSP* benchmarks, the minimum and maximum values do not differ significantly, indicating a high balanced workload, whereas this is not the case for *Queens* benchmark.

4 Conclusions

We have developed and evaluated a parallelisation scheme of an arc-consistency algorithm for constraint satisfaction problems over finite domains. The scheme has been implemented on a CRAY T3E, a distributed shared memory MIMD multiprocessor, and empirical data are reported for two benchmarks.

The speedup obtained is nearly linear for *PBCSP* benchmarks, whereas for others speedup stops increasing from a problem dependent number of processors. This difference is mainly due to the more uniform constraint graph and larger granularity of *PBCSP* benchmarks, which leads to a better workload balance. In order to study how the performance of the parallel system depends on the characteristics of the constraint satisfaction problem to solve, the parametrizable synthetic benchmark has been tested for different sets of parameters. Results show that the system is better suited for large scale problems with a dense constraint graph.

References

1. Bessiere, D.: Arc-consistency and arc-consistency again. Artificial Intelligence Journal 65 (1994) 179-190.
2. Baudot, B., Deville, Y.: Analysis of Distributed Arc-Consistency Algorithms. Tech. Rep. 97-07. Uni. of Louvain, Belgium (1997).
3. Kasif, S.: On the parallel complexity of discrete relaxation in constraint satisfaction networks. Artificial Intelligence 45 (1990) 275-286.
4. Kasif, S., Delcher, A.L.: Local Consistency in Parallel Constraint-Satisfaction Networks. Artificial Intelligence 69 (1994) 307-327.
5. Nguyen, T., Deville, Y.: A Distributed Arc-Consistency Algorithm. Science of Computer Programming, 30 (1998) 227-250.
6. Ruiz-Andino, A., Araujo, L., Ruz, J.: Parallel constraint satisfaction and optimisation. The PCSO system. Technical Report 71.98. Department of Computer Science. Universidad Complutense de Madrid (1998)
7. Van Hentenryck P., Deville, Y., Teng C.M.: A generic Arc-consistency Algorithm and its Specialisations. Artificial Intelligence 57 (1992) 291-321.
8. Wallace, M.: Constraints in Planning, Scheduling and Placement Problems. Constraint Programming, Springer-Verlag (1994).
9. Waltz, D.: Generating semantic descriptions for drawings of scenes with shadows. Technical Report AI271, MIT, Cambridge, MA. (1972).
10. Yokoo, M.: Asynchronous weak-commitment search for solving distributed constraint satisfaction problems. Principles and Practice of Constraint Programming (1995) 88-102.
11. Zhang, Y., Mackworth, A.K.: Parallel and Distributed Finite Constraint Satisfaction: Complexity, Algorithms and Experiments. Parallel Processing for Artificial Intelligence. Elsevier Science. (1993).

Experiences on Parallelization of Divide and Conquer Algorithms with Parallel Paradigms [*]

Rocco Aversa and Beniamino Di Martino

Dip. di Ingegneria dell' Informazione - 2nd University of Naples - Italy
{aversa,dimartin}@grid.unina.it

Abstract. One of the problems with using Parallel Paradigms to program parallel architectures is the choice of the paradigm which is best suited to the characteristics of the program to be developed/parallelized, and of the target architecture, in terms of performance of the parallel implementation. Another problem arising with parallelization of legacy codes is the attempt to minimize the effort needed for program comprehension, and thus to achieve the minimum restructuring of the sequential code when producing the parallel version. In this paper we address these issues for the *Divide and Conquer* class of algorithms/programs.

1 Introduction

Structured composition [3, 4] of *Parallel Paradigms* [1, 2] has been proposed as a possible programming model for parallel architectures. This approach can help in achieving efficiency, ease of use, reusability and portability in parallel programming. One of the issues arising with this approach is the mapping of the algorithm, or of an already developed sequential program to be parallelized, to a Paradigm which is best suited to the characteristics of the algorithm/program, and of the target architecture, in terms of performance of the parallel implementation. This issue arises especially when trying to use different Paradigms for handling different phases of the algorithm/program, or when trying to compose Paradigms in a hierarchical way. But, even when the algorithm belongs to a well defined algorithmic class, the choice of the mapping Paradigm could depend on minor aspects of the given concrete algorithm, which are nevertheless relevant with respect to performance issues, and thus crucial for the Paradigm's selection. An additional complication is present when parallelizing an already existing sequential program, especially for the so-called "legacy code"; in this case a compelling target, as important as the performance requirements, is the minimum restructuring of the sequential code, in order to minimize the effort required in understanding the code, and in developing the parallel version. In this paper we address this issue for a defined class of algorithms/programs: the *Divide and Conquer* one. We introduce a set of Paradigms suitable to be used for parallelization of divide-and-conquer algorithms, and disentagle the problem

---

[*] This work has been partly supported by MURST, Italy (Project *MOSAICO*) and by the Italian Regional Government (Regione Campania, L. 41/94).

of paradigm's selection. We then show how the paradigm-based strategy is applied to the parallelization of a medium sized N-Body program, which includes a D&C strategy for the construction of an octal tree. We apply the previously described considerations for the selection of the paradigm to be applied to the D&C phase, and we consider in addition the target of minimum restructuring of the sequential code.

2 Parallel Paradigms for Divide and Conquer Algorithms

We consider in the following two parallel Paradigms, which seem particularly amenable to be applied with divide and conquer algorithms/programs. The first Paradigm, frequently called *tree computation*, consists of a set of processes connected by communication channels according to a binary tree structure. Each process receives a problem to be solved, tests for a condition and then either splits the problem into two subproblems that are sent to two child processes, or does some processing and returns a result to its parent. When a process sends over two subproblems, it remains waiting for a reply from each child, then combines these replies and sends back the new result. In practice a number of questions (how deep must be the tree of processes, if processes have to be created dynamically or the entire tree must be instantiated statically, etc.) have to be answered before a working program can be produced out of this Paradigm. However, they do not depend on the particular nature of the computation to be parallelized, but rather they are part of the Paradigm and can be solved once and for all in the context of the Paradigm itself. The second Paradigm, that is usually referred to as a *processor farm*, consists of a *coordinator* process and a set of *worker* processes that act as slaves of the coordinator. In a processor farm, the coordinator decomposes the work to be done in subproblems and assigns a different subproblem to each worker. Upon receipt of a subproblem, each worker solves it and returns a result to the coordinator. Again some details have to be defined before the Paradigm can become a working program, and slightly different organizations can be selected for the processor farm (for instance workers may or may not be allowed to communicate each other). However, even in this case, these issues do pertain to the Paradigm definition and can be entirely dealt with in the Paradigm context. In principle both the tree computation and the processor farm paradigm could be selected for the parallelization of divide and conquer algorithms. In practice, hovever, the choice is driven by minor aspects of the given concrete algorithm, which are nevertheless relevant with respect to performance issues, and thus crucial for the Paradigm's selection. In particular, the computational cost of the split phase of the divide and conquer, and the degree of balancing of the computational workload associated to the split subspaces are characteristics that can play a major role in discriminating between the two Paradigms.

3 Parallelization of an N-body Program with Paradigms

In this section we show how the previously described strategy is applied to the parallelization of a medium sized sequential code. The chosen program solves the well-known N-body problem by computing, during a fixed time interval, the positions of N bodies moving under their mutual attraction. The proposed solution uses a simple approximation: the force on each particle is computed by agglomerating distant particles into groups and using their total mass and centre of mass as a single particle. The sequential algorithm can be summarized using the following pseudo-code:

```
/* main loop */
while (time<end) {
  tree(p,t,N);    /* builds the octal tree */
  forces(p,t,N); /* computes the forces */
  delt=tstep(p,N); /* computes the minimal time step */
  newv(p,N,delt);        newx(p,N,delt);
  /* updates the positions and velocities of the particles */
  time=time+delt; /* updates the simulation time */
}
```

where p is the particle array, t is the octal tree array *octree*, N the total number of particles and delt the time step according to which evolves the algorithm. The algorithm repeats, during the fixed time interval, its three main steps: to build an octal tree (*tree()*) whose nodes represents groups of nearby bodies; to compute the forces aging on each particle through a visit in the octal tree (*forces()*) ; to update the velocities and the positions of the N particles(*newv() and newx()*) . We adopt a step-by-step parallelization strategy, using the MPI programming interface [5], that makes available a great range of point-to-point and collective communication routines, as well as support for process graphs and application topologies. First of all we recognize the force computation stage as a *data-parallel* computation. Each of the N particles, in fact, computes the force acting on it by traversing the *octree* in a completely independent way. Assuming that the tree data structure is replicated on each application process, an immediate parallelization can be obtained by subdividing the particles among the computing nodes of the distributed system. This leads to a linear time reduction (with processor number) of the heaviest step of the algorithm. In the same way we proceed to the parallelizzation of the algorithm steps that update the particles velocities and positions (*newv()* and *newx()*) The sequential code of these phases also performs the same computation on different data (the particles). The updating phase must be followed by a collective communication (*allgather*), so that every process will have an identical fully initialized array "particles", to compute the next time step. In the parallel version the search of the minimum time step can be replaced by a minimum search on the local data followed by a *reduce* operation to obtain the global minimum. The parallelization of the code relative to the construction of the *octree* is not so trivial. At a first glance, the *tree computation* Paradigm appears to be best suited to this step of the algorithm, since the *splitting* phase (a sequence of three sort operations with respect to the three spatial coordinates) is computationally heavy. However, a more accurate analysis of the build tree phase shows a *splitting* step (*quicksort*) characterized by a computational complexity more than linear with the number of the particles in the single tree node($O(NlogN)$), while the time spent for the computation of the total mass and of the coordinates of the center of the mass grows only linearly with the number of particles collected in a tree node. This means that the construction of the first levels of the *octree* is the costliest part of the algorithm but, according to the *tree computation* paradigm, can be performed just by a little portion of the available processes (the first splitting phase, even, by a single node). In this way, the degree of the obtained parallelism is smaller when the algorithm builds the higher levels of the *octree* (the heaviest ones), and exploits all the available computing nodes only when the construction of the tree reaches a level with a number of sons exceeding the processors. On the basis of this consideration it is worth while to parallelize separately the first splitting steps (the *quicksort* routine) until the nodes in the current level of the *octree* exceed in number the computing nodes (*nproc*). We can now distribute the tree nodes among the processes so that each process is responsible for the building of the subtrees assigned to it. This operation can be carried out in parallel and every process is able to fill up its own slice of the complete *octree* data structure. We developed the parallel version of the *quicksort* algorithm using the *tree computation* paradigm applied to a *binomial tree* processes topology that allows to best exploit all the available computing resources. The MPI topology primitives were helpful in writing a library *quicksort* routine that attaches and then detaches, in a transparent way, a given topology structure (in our case a *binomial tree*) to the processes involved in the application.

References

1. P. Brinch Hansen, "Model programs for computational science: a programming methodology for multicomputers", *Concurrency: Practice and Experience*, **5**(5), pp. 407–423, Aug. 1993.
2. M.I. Cole, *Algorithmic Skeletons: Structured Management of Parallel Computation*, MIT Press, Cambridge, MA, 1989.
3. I. Foster and M. Xu, "Libraries for Parallel Paradigm Integration", in *Toward Teraflop Computing and New Grand Challenge Applications*, Nova Science, 1994.
4. J. Darlington, A.J.Field, P.G. Harrison, P.H.J. Kelly, D.W.N. Sharp, Q. Wu and R.L.Whie, "Parallel Programming Using Skeleton Functions", in PARLE'93, LNCS 694, pp. 146-160, Springer-Verlag, 1993.
5. Message Passing Interface Forum. Document for a Standard Message-Passing Interface. Technical Report No. CS-93-214, University of Tennessee, 1994.

Differentiating Message Passing Interface an Bulk Synchronous Parallel Computation Mode

Christophe Cérin

Université de Picardie Jules Verne
LaRIA, Bat Curi, 5 rue du moulin neuf
F-80000 Amiens - France
E-mail: cerin@laria.u-picardie.fr
Ph: (33)[0]322827875, Fax: (33)[0]322827502

Abstract. In this paper we introduce a student exercise that is devoted to compare two parallel languages, namely MPI (Message Passing Interface) and BSP (Bulk Synchronous Parallel language). The work to accomplish is integrated in a "long term project" because questions act as a nest of dolls: answering one opens a new direction.

Keywords: teaching parallel processing, foundations of parallel programming languages, message passing interface (MPI) and bulk synchronous parallel (BSP) models.

1 The Longest Increasing Subsequence Problem

The goal of the exercise is to make progress towards a good understanding of some differences (conceptually) between MPI (Message Passing Interface) and BSP (Bulk Synchronous Parallel computation). The problem is as follows: given a sequence of n distinct positive integers, the goal is to find an increasing subsequence of L. A *longest* increasing subsequence (LIS) is one of maximal length. Finding the length is sequentially performed with time complexity of $\mathcal{O}(n \log n)$. In [1] authors give a linear time solution using a modular linear systolic algorithm for finding both the length and to extract the solution. The student task is to code the previous solution both in MPI and in BSP. The "systolic" algorithm is given to them.

2 The Student Prerequisites

Students have received a course on parallel algorithms on PRAM and, concerning MPI thay have also received information on every aspect of the standard (point to point and collective communication, user defined data types, communicators, virtual process topologies and environmental management). Before the exercise, hey have solved concrete problems, for instance the matrix multiplication to ?serve some problems on caches due to the organization of the computation ? data, prefix like implementations (gather, scatter) and so on.

3SP, the main difference for programmers is that they predict the run length of computation in terms of parameters p, l, g and they can rely on performance to automatically do the task (see for instance [2]).

3 Questions and Expected Answers

We now introduce some part of our "quiz" related to the problem and also some expected remarks:

Defining the solution: in this part, say for the MPI implementation, students concentrate on `send, receive` primitives to implement the systolic algorithm for one cell. It is a strait forward task to do! The difficulty is very low. By contrast, the BSP implementation is more tedious because some cell are supposed not to receive any information for certain tics and the constraint is that programmers should use only remote read/write but no blocked received operation. So, for instance, they have to insert synchronization primitives in the process description for one cell and the number of synchronizations depends on problem size (in the code inserted at the end of the paper, the number of synchronization points is proportional to $n*n$). This observation is the main observation that student should note.

Check the validity of assumptions: in this part, students compare their intuitive reasoning with the experimental results. For instance they report that process 0 never receive but it always send. They should also try to distinguish the bytes received/sent for a synchronization and bytes received/sent due to a "true data exchange".

Design methodology: in this part, students should inform mentor that the design with n processes is unrealistic for large n. Surprisingly, for the input sequence with 54 elements given to them, the execution time is larger than 1 minute because the system need more time to launch processes but students rarely find the explanation corresponding to the observation and they rarely propose to split the problem into chunks of size n/k!

4 Conclusion

In this paper we have introduced a student exercice for the Longest Increasing Subsequence Problem in parallel. Students have to code the solution of finding the length both in MPI and BSP. It turns out that the "linear array solution" forces the MPI programmer to put blocked received instruction to simulate the datum arrival which break the synchronous execution flow; the BSP programmer has to add synchronization primitives to respect the strict SPMD paradigm of the language.

References

1. Christophe Cérin, J.F Myoupo et Catherine Dufourd, *An Efficient Parallel Solution for the Longest Increasing Subsequence Problem*, – 5th International Conference on Computing and Information (ICCI'93), May 27, 29 1993 – Laurentian university, Sudbury, Ontario Canada.
2. R. Miller and J.L. Reed, *The Oxford BSP Library: User's Guide*, Oxford University Computing Laboratory, 1994.

Realization of Complex Arithmetic on Cellular Automata

T. Farid[1], D. Zerbino[2]

[1] Department of Mathematics and Computing Science. Suez Canal University, Ismailia, Egypt.
[2] Lvivska Polytechnica State University, 12 Bandera Str., 290013, Lviv, Ukraine.
E-mail: zerbino@polynet.lviv.ua

Abstract. In this paper we develop a model of cellular automata for massive parallel arithmetic computations with complex numbers on a bit level, show that complex numbers should be represented in the second order negabinary coding system, and suggest a system of automaton rules for evaluating complex arithmetic expressions.

The number of models using massive parallel computations has recently increased. Correctness of synchronous and asynchronous models of the parallel fixed-point computations on cellular automata for multiplication and addition with positive arguments is no longer a problem (see [1]). Using the negabinaries coding systems, we retain principle of its correctness, simultaneously solving the overflow problem. The arithmetic computations with real numbers by using negabinary coding system $(-1)^k 2^k$ has either been investigated (see [2]).

Let us consider the generalized negabinary coding system with the $(-2)^{k/r}$ digit weights, where $k \in [-\infty, +\infty]$ is the integer number of digit and $r > 0$ is the type of negabinary system. Thus, if $r = 1$, we obtain the 1st order negabinary coding system for real numbers. For example, -6.75 in this system is represented like this: $-6.75 = 1001.01 = -8 + 1 + 0.25$. When $r = 2$ we obtain the 2nd order negabinary coding system (c-coding) for representing any complex number. In this case, the weights of digits will be: $\{..., -8, 4c, 4, -2c, -2, c, 1, -0.5c, -0.5, 0.25c, 0.25, ...\}$. Here and in all subsequent expressions $c = (-2)^{1/2}$. For example, the c-coding of the complex number $5.25 - 1.5c$ is: $11011.1001 = 4 - 2c + c + 1 - 0.5c + 0.25$.

The modification of the notion of cellular automata used in this paper is based on the traditional two-dimensional model. Each cell of the cellular space with the coordinates (i, j) can be in one of four stages: $\{0, 1, l, r\}$. Any part of this space can be interpreted as a complex number obtained by evaluating expression of the cell weights. In our case, the cell (i, j) has the weight $(-2)^{(i+j)/2}$. Thus, if $i + j$ is even, the weight of the cell is real. If $i + j$ is odd, the weight of the cell is imaginary.

Other symbols used are: $'l'$ - left assigned input, $'r'$ - right assigned input. Thus we locate the input arguments and output result. The cellular space is divided into two sections: the "working field" and the "register". Each cell in the register can contain one of the four symbols: $\{0, 1, d, s\}$, where $'d','s'$ stand for argument separations.

Fig.1 shows the 8 asynchronous automaton rules, each consisting of two patterns (left and right). The rules can work simultaneously if their left patterns do not overlap in the working field. Otherwise, only one does. The right pattern of the rule is the result of simultaneous substitution of all values in the pattern. The symbols below the patterns belong to the register. The rule is applicable if the condition below the rule is true. The empty cells in fig.1 do not belong to the pattern and can contain any value.

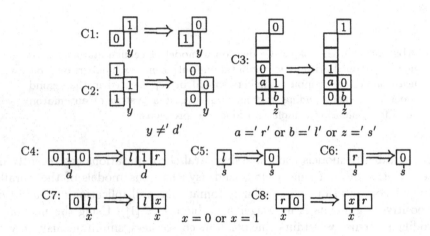

Fig. 1. The system of rules for 2nd order negabinary model.

To obtain the result, it is necessary to input the arguments in certain rows (columns) of the cellular space. The arithmetic operation determines the interlocation of the arguments in the cellular space. After the arguments are assigned, the asynchronous rules start working, and they work in arbitrary order until their proper-pattern combinability exhausts itself. The result of computation is found in the bottom line of the working field.

The model of asynchronous cellular automata is the first step to developing the quantum computer, where cellular patterning would shape asynchronously and spontaneously.

References

1. Bandman O.L., Cellular-Neural Computations. Formal Model and Possible Applications. - Parallel Computing Technologies: Third International Conference, PaCT-95, St. Petersburg, Russia, September 12-25, 1995. pp. 21-35.

2. Valkovskii V.A., Zerbino D.D. The Realization of Arithmetical Computation in Alternative Codes on Cellular Automata. - Problems of Information and Control, No 2, 1997, pp. 49-64. (in Russian).

Parallel Programming System Based on Super Pascal Language

Sergey I. Katkov, Eugeny Y. Ruban

Institute of Informatics Systems of Siberian Division RAS,
Pr. Lavrentjeva, 6, Novosibirsk, 630090, Russia.
e-mail : serj@iis.nsk.su

Abstract. A new parallel programming system based on Super Pascal language is described. The system consists of a converter from Super Pascal language into Turbo Pascal language, a debugger with the visualizer of parallel execution and a static analyzer of parallel conflicts. System is intended for checking parallel algorithms and for learning parallel programming.

1 Introduction

Making and maintaining a library of parallel calculating algorithms suppose an existence of certain publication language. This language should possess sufficiently clear and simple ability to represent parallelism. For this goal Per Brinch Hansen has suggested the parallel programming language Super Pascal [1,2].

Another purpose of the language is approbing and testing parallel algorithms. In this meaning, Super Pascal is considered as a language of detailed and executable specification. Practical application of developed parallel algorithms demands a translation of them into a given industrial parallel programming language for the concrete architecture. At the same time, it is desirable that preliminary checking of the algorithm and obtaining the initial information about its behaviour should be carried out without using high-priced supercomputer resources. Execution of Super Pascal programs on personal computers gives such possibility.

Teaching parallel programming methods is the third purpose of the language. For that matter, Super Pascal seems more perspective.

The specification of Super Pascal can be found in [1].

2 Parallel Programming System and Results

The programming system developed for Super Pascal consists of two main components, one of them performs the functions of a compiler, and the other performs debugging together with visualization of parallel execution. The compiler is developed as a converter from Super Pascal into Turbo Pascal. The converter checks lexical, syntactical and partly semantic correctness of Super Pascal programs. All parallel constructions of Super Pascal are translated by the converter into descriptions simulating Pascal objects or into calls of dynamically support procedures, which imitate a Super Pascal parallelism by the corresponding quasiparallelism. All tools of simulation of Super Pascal parallel constructions are included in a special module written in Turbo Pascal. This module is realized under MS DOS.

A part of the system is a static context-sensitive analyzer detecting possible parallel conflicts on shared data. The analyzer is based on upper approximation of the set of integer expression values by means of finite sets of congruances (polynomials in auxiliary inductive variables), that enables to reveal data dependences typical for the algorithms of computational mathematics. To eliminate data dependences the I test is applied [3]. Now we have been working on the analysis of message passing correctness.

An essential part of every parallel programming system is a debugger, which makes the process of parallel execution comprehensible. The correspondent system component of Super Pascal permits the program to collect up the whole history of its parallel execution and to visualize this saved history. In the history all events connected with parallel execution are represented. The history keeps the whole necessary information about the event. After terminating a program the history of parallel execution can be visualized. Two types of information are defined here: tree of parallel processes and status of channels. A tree of parallel processes represents the hierarchy of existing processes. When visualized, states of processes are displayed by different colours. A status of channels is a list of all channels with information about each one.

The debugger displays, using the history and a source program, the whole information accumulated at the given moment. Thereby, the debugger allows us to get a detailed and demonstrative information about the process of parallel execution. The information about all events (not only parallel) of a executed program can be obtained by standard Turbo Pascal debugger, but of course in terms of Turbo Pascal.

Let's note that we speak about debugging parallel algorithms. The tool for testing of parallel algorithms effectivness is designed at this time.

The considered system gives us necessary facilities to develop and test parallel algorithms. The system is expected to be used in the nearest future in Novosibirsk State University for learning parallel programming. The testing group creates and debugs such parallel algorithms as matrix inversion, sorting, solving of a linear equation system etc. We see further steps of the work on the system in the liquidation of those inconveniences, that will be revealed during its scholastic usage, and in the development of parallel programs construction tools. Making of component for testing of parallel algorithms effectiveness is also our primary task.

References

[1] P.Brinch Hansen. Super Pascal - a publication language for parallel scientific computing. Concurrency Practice and Experience, v.6(5), p. 461 - 483, Aug. 1994.
[2] P.Brinch Hansen. Search for Implicity - Essay in Parallel Programming. Prentice Hall,1997.
[3] Xiangyun Kong, David Klappholtz and Kleanthis Psarris, The I test: An Improved Dependence Test for Automatic Parallelization and Vectorization. IEEE TRANSACTIONS ON PARALLEL AND DISTRIBUTED SYSTEMS, VOL. 2, NO 3, JULY 1991.

Group-Theoretic Methods for Parallel Computation of Convolution

Olga V. Klimova

Institute of Engineering Science
Ural Branch of the Russian Academy of Sciences
91 Pervomayskaya str., Ekaterinburg, 620219, Russia
e-mail: ovs@ imach.uran.ru

1 Introduction

Convolution decomposition allowed creation of fast computation algorithms within the scope of sequential processing [1,2]. However, in one case, the decomposition methods made the algorithm structure redundant, whereas in other case, they imposed restrictions on the decomposition parameters, which need to be mutually prime numbers. Parallel processing requires structural flexibility of algorithms, therefore the decomposition methods primordially characterized by redundancy and restrictions imposed on the parameters are not effective. The methods oriented to parallel processing were created on the basis of the group-theoretic approach to decomposition. The approach is complex in character, that is, it is orientated towards the decomposition of a number of basic functions of digital signal processing — convolution, correlation, discrete Fourier transform (DFT). The objective of this paper is to develop a collection of methods for the parallel computation of convolution by generalizing and extending the results of the group-theoretic decomposition of DFT and convolution [3,4].

2 The Methods for Parallel Computation of Convolution

We represent the method of group-theoretic decomposition of DFT. The method is not connected with the decomposition of the convolution function as it is primordially based on the transforms displaying the cyclic convolution property [1]. Then the main body of computation is connected with the transition to the frequency domain and backwards. The method is based on the realization of this transition over the fast parallel algorithms produced by the group-theoretic decomposition of DFT. The characteristics of the decomposition methods and the corresponding algorithms were described in [4]. The methods presented below are based on group-theoretic decomposition of convolution.

We represent the method of group-theoretic decomposition of signal. The main characteristic feature of the method is the presence of N_1 independent computation processes for the convolutions $C_{j_1}(t)$, when $N = h_1 N_1, j_1 = 0, \ldots,$ $N_1 - 1$. The convolutions $C_{j_1}(t)$ are equivalent on the groups with different structures, but the same order N: $Z_N, Z_{h_1} \times Z_{N_1}, Z_{h_1} \times Z_{N_1}$, due to their independence from the group shift operation [3]. Owing to the structure of the signals defining the functions $C_{j_1}(t)$, fast parallel computational algorithms for $C(t)$ based on different fast orthogonal transforms given on the group $Z_{h_1} \times Z_{N_1}$ have been constructed within the scope of the method.

The following method is based on the group-theoretic decomposition of the convolutions $C_{j_1}(t)$. The corresponding form of representing convolution is

$$C(t) = \sum_{j_1=0}^{N_1-1} C_{j_1}(t) = \sum_{j_1=0}^{N_1-1} \sum_{q_1=0}^{h_1-1} x_{j_1}^*((t_1 - q_1)N_1)y(q_1 N_1 + p_1 - j_1) \ . \tag{1}$$

The fast parallel algorithms of convolution using efficient ways of computation of short convolutions of length h_1 have been developed on the basis of eqn. (1).

Equation (1), hereinafter referred to as group-theoretic (GT-form), is the basis of transforms giving rise to the following method. Its form is almost similar to two-dimensional convolution. The GT - form (1) gives rise to a form different from the two-dimensional one by one position shifts $(q_1 - 1)$ of $(N_1 - 1)$ sequences $y_{-j_1 p_1}(q_1 N_1)$ given on the group Z_{h_1}. The above-mentioned sequences are located at the points $j_1 > p_1$ in the computation of convolution along the coordinate p_1. This form of one-dimensional convolution is referred to as pseudo-two-dimensional form. The corresponding method of parallel computation of convolution allows creation of fast parallel algorithms realizing the computation of two-dimensional convolution and the correction of the values of its samples. The recurrent application of this method makes it possible to use the Walsh transform for the computation of convolution.

3 Conclusion

The methods of parallel computation of convolution illustrate great potentialities of the group-theoretic decomposition approach in the creation of effective parallel algorithms for convolution. The properties of algorithms enable complicated and flexible modern signal processing to be effectively performed in parallel computations.

References

1. McClellan J.H., Rader C.M.: Number Theory in Digital Signal Processing, Prentice-Hall, Englewood Cliffs,N.J.,(1979)
2. Nussbaumer H.J.: Fast Fourier Transform and Convolution Algorithms, Springer-Verlag, Berlin Heidelberg, (1982)
3. Klimova O.V.: Parallel Architecture of the Arbitrary-Length Convolution Processor with the Use of Rader Number Transforms. Izv. AN Tekhn. Kibernet. (Russia). **2** (1994) 183-191
4. Klimova O.V.: Group Theoretical Decomposition and Fast Parallel Algorithms for the Discrete Fourier Transform. Journal of Computer and Systems Sciences International. Vol.36, **5** (1997) 802-806

Knowledge Exploitation for Improved Data Distribution

B. McCollum, P. Milligan and P. H. Corr

School of Computer Science, The Queen's University of Belfast,
Belfast BT7 1NN. N. Ireland
e-mail: p.corr@qub.ac.uk

Abstract. It is generally accepted that the goal of fully automating the process of migrating sequential legacy codes to parallel architectures must remain an unreachable target. Among the systems which have made the greatest advances in this area are those which attempt to utilise the available problem and process related knowledge, making it available explicitly through the use of knowledge based or expert systems. In this paper a novel knowledge model derived from a combination of expert system and neural network techniques is presented.

1   Re-engineering Sequential Codes for Multiprocessor Platforms

It is perhaps pejorative, but nonetheless accurate, to characterise typical users of multiprocessor systems as unskilled in the arts of parallelisation. For such users there is a compelling need for the development of environments which minimise user involvement with the complications of parallelism.

The ideal solution is a fully automatic approach in which a user can simply input a sequential program to the system and receive as output an efficient parallel equivalent. Automatic parallelisation scores high on expression, as programmers are able to use conventional languages, but is problematic in that it requires inherently complex issues such as data dependence analysis, parallel program design, data distribution and load balancing issues to be addressed.

Existing parallelisation systems adopt a range of techniques in an effort to minimise or eliminate the complexity inherent in the fully automated approach. Almost invariably the burden of providing the necessary guidance and expertise lacking in the system falls back on the user. Indeed, existing systems may be classified by the extent to which user interaction is required in the process of code parallelisation. At one end of the spectrum is the purely language based approach in which the user is entirely responsible for determining how parallelism is to be achieved. The other end of the spectrum represents the goal of a fully automatic parallelisation environment, independent of application domain and requiring no user guidance. Between these extremes lie a number of environments which permit the user to interact with the system during execution, with varying degrees of guidance, to choose appropriate program transformations or data partitioning schemes.

2. Knowledge Sources

There are a number of knowledge sources which must be utilised to assist with the parallelisation process. These sources are; the expertise that exists among users; the hierarchical nature of that expertise; the variety of architectural paradigms; the variety of problem domains; the structure of the program code itself and performance profiles gathered during code execution [1,2].

The available knowledge can be regarded as a plethora of partially overlapping and partially conflicting information. To reduce this confusion it is necessary to organise the information in a logical manner. The inherent overlap between the categories, an essential facet of the real world, has to be retained and presented in a logical manner as a 'knowledge pool'. The 'best' information for parallelisation will occur where all knowledge components intersect. To aid migration into this area a neural network has been added to our current expert system based environment [2]. The strengths of the neural network paradigm have been used to assist the expert system extract the knowledge from the code.

Given an input of essential information about a code and an output of the most appropriate parallelisation operations to apply to that code, the 'learned mapping' held by the network effectively encapsulates knowledge which may be brought to bear on the process. The eventual performance of the network in suggesting the most appropriate parallelisation operations is heavily dependent on the quality and accuracy of the original training examples and the characterisation scheme used.

3. Conclusion

The model reported in this paper provides a basis for improving the parallelisation process by enabling a greater volume of information relevant to the re-engineering process to be extracted from a legacy code and utilised. Exploiting this knowledge requires a combination of expert system and neural network techniques, each bringing their own strengths to bear and combining to take full advantage of the knowledge available.

4. References

1 P. F. Leggett, A. T. J. Marsh, S. P. Johnston and M. Cross, Integrating User Knowledge with Information from Parallelisation Tools to Facilitate the Automatic Generation of Efficient Parallel Fortran Code., Parallel Computing, vol. 22, pp259 - 288, 1996.
2 P. J. P. McMullan, P. Milligan, P. P. Sage and P. H. Corr, A Knowledge Based Approach to the Parallelisation, Generation and Evaluation of Code for Execution on Parallel Architectures. IEEE Computer Society Press, ISBN 0-8186-7703-1, pp 58 - 63, 1997

An Expert System Approach to Data Distribution and Distribution Analysis

P. J. P. McMullan, P. Milligan and P. H. Corr

School of Computer Science
The Queen's University of Belfast, Belfast BT7 1NN, N. Ireland
Email: p.p.mcmullan@qub.ac.uk

Abstract. Research into systems aimed at transforming existing legacy programs to an equivalent form for improved execution performance on multiprocessor systems has led to the realisation that the level of parallelization expertise needed is similar to that of a human expert. Data distribution is one of the major obstacles limiting pure automation in parallelization. A system which automatically provides effective data partitioning algorithms can be considered suitable in replacing the human expert [1]. The Fortport project provides a solution to this problem by presenting a suite of tools to apply AI technology in the parallelization of sequential codes. This approach is based on an underlying knowledge model to influence the transformation process.

1. The Fortport System

The Fortport system [2,3] consists of an Input Handler, Transformation stage and Analysis and Generation stage. The input handler feeds an intermediate syntax graph form of the sequential code to the Transformation stage, which restructures the syntax graph and removes data dependencies. Generation and Analysis involves the application of analysis and distribution tools guided by an expert system to produce a parallel equivalent of the input sequential program. Parallel execution results are analysed to determine if refinement or alternative data distribution strategies are required. Feedback is provided to the generation stage via a Feedback Cycle to redefine the parallelization strategy until optimum parallel performance is achieved.

2. Knowledge Sources

The knowledge base used by the expert system is built upon a number of knowledge sources. These sources include; Architecture specific knowledge, Source code characteristics, Expert System parallelization knowledge, Expert User parallelization knowledge, Sequential and Parallel performance statistics and Parallelization strategy records. This knowledge is utilised to emulate the process of parallelization by hand. The expert system bases decisions on the knowledge available. A knowledge base is maintained to record and utilize relevant information obtained from the pool of knowledge sources. This forms the basis to influence the transformation process.

3. Analysis, Evaluation and Data Distribution

A Program Modeler is used to perform a source code analysis of the program in an attempt to model execution behaviour. This information is used to highlight areas of the code for further analysis. The modeler also builds up a database of information in order to help identify suitable parallelization strategies. A Profile Guidance Evaluator uses estimation results from the Program Model Analyser to decide on the best profiling technique to be used in subsequent sequential performance analysis.

The Sequential Performance Analyser identifies sections of the sequential program for which parallelization will be most beneficial. Profiled sequential execution results are used to concentrate parallelization on computationally intensive areas (hotspots).

The Data Distribution Tool is the main parallelization tool within the system, generating processes and distributing work among the processors. Structural and execution analysis influence the parallelization decisions taken. Characterization and Distribution Analysis is performed on the sequential code, and a Strategy Evaluation mechanism builds a list of parallelization strategies. Strategies are chosen from the list based on continuous parallel performance analysis.

The Code Generation Tool creates the parallellized program, used by the Parallel Performance Analyser to identify performance improvements which can be made. A Parallel Code Profiler provides real-time parallel execution performance results. Evaluation can then determine how successful each parallelization strategy has been in achieving a performance improvement. An improvement cycle is implemented to pass control back to the Data Distribution Tool.

4. Conclusion

The Fortport system has been tested for many cases of common program constructs and algorithms with satisfactory performance results. The system has also been tested using an existing scientific problem. This case study has been demonstrated to produce a performance improvement. Therefore the expert system approach within the Fortport system is effective in the problem of intelligent automatic parallelization.

5. References

[1] S. Andel, B. M. Chapman and H. P. Zima, An Expert Advisor for Parallel Programming Environments and its Realization within the Framework of the Vienna Fortran Compilation System, 4th Workshop on Compilers for Parallel Computers, Delft, 1993.
[2] P. J. P. McMullan, P. Milligan, P. P. Sage and P. H. Corr. A Knowledge Based Approach to the Parallelisation, Generation and Evaluation of Code for Execution on Parallel Architectures. IEEE Computer Society Press, ISBN 0-8186-7703-1, pp 58 - 63, 1997.
[3] P. J. P. McMullan, P. Milligan and P. H. Corr. Knowledge Assisted Code Generation and Analysis. Lecture Notes in Computer Science 1225, Springer Verlag, pp 1030-1031, 1997.

Automated Communication Analysis and Code Generation for Non-contiguous Partitions of Two-Dimensional Arrays

P.J. Parsons

High Performance Computing Centre,
University of Reading, Reading, RG6 6AY, U.K.
E-mail: P.J.Parsons@acm.org

Abstract. The effective distribution of data is an important challenge in parallel program development. This paper outlines the process of generating, comparing, selecting and implementing non-contiguous data partitioning approaches for two-dimensional data structures in the SITSS programming system.

1 Introduction

The choice of data distribution strategy can have a significant effect on the performance of a parallel program. Selecting an appropriate strategy and implementing it correctly forms a significant component of the programming effort. For problems involving a large number of different interactions between locations in the data space, evaluating and comparing the effectiveness of a set of partitioning approaches

The implementation of the distributed data space in a program can be entirely the responsibility of the programmer (e.g. MPI [1]), or may be partially implemented by the compiler with some instruction from the programmer (e.g. HPF [2]). In either case the programmer can have a significant impact on the performance of the resulting program by their selection of partitioning approach, and be required to invest significant development time in making the choice of partitioning approach. The automation of the process of selecting an appropriate partitioning approach may therefore be argued to be desirable.

2 Non-contiguous Data Distributions

Two non-contiguous data distributions for two-dimensional arrays have been considered and implemented, called sub-block and cyclic (of which there are two types, regular and reverse).

The sub-block allocation strategy divides the data space in to identically shaped and sized areas, each of which allocates the points it contains to processors using an x by y strategy. A given sub-block strategy is described by four parameters, (a_x, a_y, b_x, b_y), defining the size and internal distribution strategy.

Cyclic allocation strategies assign points in the data space to processes on a rotating basis. Regular cyclic strategies start with the lowest numbered processor and cycle up to the highest numbered processor. Reverse cyclic strategies start with the highest numbered processor and cycle down to the lowest numbered processor. Cyclic allocations are described by two parameters, (c_x, c_y), the first denoting the number of points allocated to each processor along the x axis, and the second the number of lines allocated before the first allocated processor is changed.

The set of all possible partitioning approaches is generated automatically from the dimensions of the data space and the number of processors to be used.

3 Communication Analysis

Any given algorithm contains a defined set of interactions between points in the local data space. Once this set is known, it is possible to calculate the set of inter-process communication produced for each partitioning approach. The analysis techniques described in [3] have been extended for the partitioning approaches considered in this paper. The system determines the inter-process communication produced by every interaction for each partitioning approach to produce a set of abstract communications, and uses knowledge of the mapping of the program on to the physical architecture to determine the actual communication undertaken if each partitioning approach were to be implemented. From knowledge of defined characteristics of the architecture, a cost for each partitioning approach can be calculated, and the partitioning approaches compared to select the one giving the lowest overhead.

4 Generating Code

The code generation strategy used to implement non-contiguous data partitions is an extension of that described in [3]. The data space is implemented as a multi-dimensional array on each process. There is a unique mapping between points the abstract data space and points in the implementation in the code for any pairing of data space and partitioning approach. References in the original algorithm specification are translated automatically by the generated code to ensure communication is implemented correctly. Further work is ongoing to extend these techniques to n-dimensional arrays.

References

1. MPI Forum. *MPI: A Message-Passing Interface Standard*, June 1995.
2. High Performance Fortran Forum. *High Performance Fortran Language Specification*, January 1997.
3. P.J. Parsons and F.A. Rabhi. Generating Parallel Programs from Skeleton Based Specifications. *Journal of Systems Architecture*, 45(4):261–283, December 1998.

WinALT, a Software Tool for Fine-Grain Algorithms and Structures Synthesis and Simulation

D. Beletkov, M. Ostapkevich, S. Piskunov, I. Zhileev

Supercomputer Software Department, ICMMG of SB RAS,
Pr. Lavrentieva, 6, Novosibirsk, 630090, RUSSIA
E-mail: piskunov@ssd.sscc.ru
Tel.: (3832)343994, Fax: (3832)324259

Abstract. The ground of architecture and description of WinALT simulating system are given in the paper. The main purpose of graphical WinALT interface is to visualize the model construction and execution. WinALT language is suitable for representation of versatile classes of fine-grain algorithms and structures. The system has a comprehensive set of tools for user extensions.

1 Introduction

The interest for fine-grain computations grows constantly worldwide. This would be explained by the fact that the mathematical models of fine-grain structures (cellular automata, systolic structures, associative processors, cellular-neural networks, etc) are more and more utilized to solve problems of signal and image processing, mathematical physics and for synthesis of imitational models of processors based upon blocks with 2D and 3D homogeneous structure. Current tendency in the fine-grain models research proves that the results useful for theory or practice cannot be obtained without computational experiments on a computer.

The ground of architecture is done in the paper as well as the description is presented for a software tool for fine-grain structure synthesis and imitation of parallel computation process that takes place in such a structure.

2 The Ground of WinALT System

The proposed tool is intended to be a universal one that covers the needs for all fine-grain parallelism researchers. The existence of such universal tool simplifies a comparison between the results obtained by different users, it also makes it possible for users and developers to cooperate so as to improve the tool itself. Also, fine-grain algorithms and structures may be gathered into libraries, which would be used later as parts of models. The proposed tool is called *a simulating system WinALT*.

The decision to create a single unified tool impose a requirement to the architecture of the system. The architecture must be that of *an open system*, because there are no other architectures that would allow to reflect and meet rapidly changing, constantly growing and versatile requirements of users to tools and services implemented in the system. It is the openness of architecture that is the main difference between WinALT and its ancestor ALT [1,2]. An open system has the following features: extensibility and scalability, interoperability, portability and user friendly interface. The incarnation of these features in the current version of WinALT will be shown below.

3   The Interface of WinALT System

The language and graphical interfaces directly represent properties of parallel computation model named Parallel Substitution Algorithm [3]. This model has shown its efficiency and fitness as the basis for previously created ALT system. The main destination of WinALT graphical interface is the visualization of construction and execution of 3D fine-grain algorithms and structures. A model is composed from its graphical and textual parts. Below the textual part will be referred to as a *simulating program*.

3.1   Graphical User's Interface

The key feature of this interface is that it is user friendly. The principal notion, which is to be represented in concise and convenient form, is a cellular array, which is a graphical image of a data array of no matter what semantics. A 3D cellular array is represented as a stack of layers, one of which is opened (or visible to a user). A layer is shown as a matrix of colored cells. The color denotes current state of its cell. There are two types of arrays. The first type is represented by processed arrays. These arrays are used to keep sources, intermediate data and results of simulation. The second type is constituted by so called templates. The template names are used in the operators of a simulating program, which define the substitutions (their left and right parts).

The interface is aimed to supply a user with the means of easy construction and modification of cellular arrays and to track the changes in these arrays, when they are being transformed by a simulating program. The debugging mode of the visual interface is aimed to give convenient means to examine applicability of operators' templates to processed arrays.

In the process of WinALT development the notion of project was finally forged. A project is the reflection of a model in the system. Thus, a project includes a set of cellular and auxiliary objects, all the sources of simulating programs and all the external libraries, which are used by these programs. Each element of a project may be shown in a window.

In accordance with the chosen GUI metaphor, the tools and services are gathered into menues and toolbars. It has look and feel of a Window95/NT application. In the current version of WinALT the semantic of windows and toolbars in general remains the same as it was described in [4]. A project that implements the well known "parity" cellular algorithm is depicted at Fig. 1. The processed *field* cellular array and *pat* template are in the window (1). The window (2) contains only a set of templates. The windows (3) and (4) bear the two implementations of cellular algorithm. The hierarchy and dependencies of elements in the project are in the left part of the window (1).

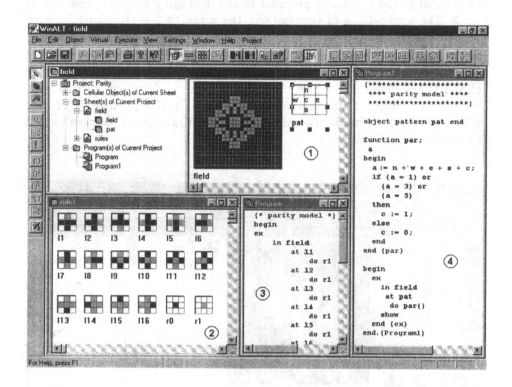

Fig. 1. WinALT main window screenshot

3.2 Language of WinALT System

The language is primarily intended for simulating programs. Its main distinguishing feature is extensibility. It was designed so as the system would be open for users with versatile requirements for means of cellular algorithm and structure models creation. It was taken into consideration that different users have different points of view on how a convenient would look like. Thus, the language was divided into three groups of operators.

The *first* group contains the set of constructions, which is typical for general purpose sequential languages for structured programming.

The *second* group is formed by operators for concise description of parallel spatially distributed computations based on Parallel Substitution Algorithm.

The project depicted at Fig. 1 gives the initial impression about this group of operators. The simulating program, shown in (3), uses only the templates presented in (2). Another implementation of the same algorithm (4) is based upon a functional substitution. Its template *pat* is shown at (1). The substitutional function *par* is shown at (4). The operation of both implementations may be easily understood using the descriptions presented in [1, 3]. An execution of the first variant of the simulating program in the debugging mode is presented at Fig. 2. The applicability of templates in the array *field* is visualized for each single cell assignment.

The *third* part of operators gives means to extend the language and to customize it in accordance with user's demands. The basis for these tools are so called ACL libraries, which give the means to import functions written in C or C++. A number of standard ACLs exists in WinALT package. There are image local filtering, mathematical functions, joystick support, console output functions and some others.

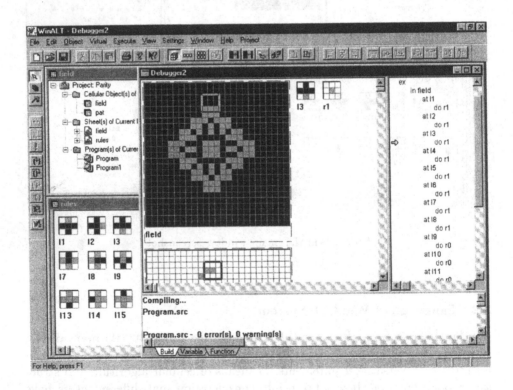

Fig. 2. Debugger window screenshot

A project of cellular diffusion algorithm [5] based upon C program implementation an imported into WinALT is depicted at Fig. 3. Source C language model was written by O.L. Bandman and used here with her permission.

Not only the usage of combination of the three language operator groups gives the mean to define a wide set of parallel-sequential compositions of synchronous cellular array transformations and to implement a functional transformation with a high complexity in a single cell, but also is allows to build the modules of the system itself (e.g. its installator and textual viewer) and to control its execution.

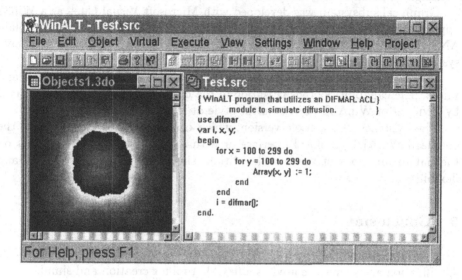

Fig. 3. Diffusion sample screenshot

4   WinALT Architecture and Implementation

There are three definitely visible parts in the system: graphical subsystem, language subsystem and kernel.

Extensibility and scalability of the system is obtained by the modular design that makes it possible to implement most of the system's functions in external libraries. The operations with external libraries are implemented in the kernel.

Events are used as a mean of intermodular communications. Such type of interaction minimizes the number of visible interfaces and gives the possibility to port the system to multiprocessor platforms.

Language subsystem uses the kernel interface for operations with cellular objects and external libraries. The means of language extensibility were described in 3.2. Beside this, the language has capability to be enriched by new operators with the help of event interface implemented in the lexical and syntactic analyzers. The extensibility of graphical interface is understood as the capability to add custom visualization modes for cellular objects.

The interoperability is understood as the capability to use different file formats for cellular array representation, which is primarily intended for input and resulting data exchange with other applications. A user may add support for his own file formats, by the means of so called object drivers, which are some sort of external libraries managed by WinALT kernel.

The portability of WinALT is tightly connected with its implementation. As the user's interface considerably depends on a specific platform and no interplatform standards of graphical interface have yet emerged, the decision was made to design as portable only a console (textual) edition of the system.

Graphical subsystem was developed with Microsoft Visual C++ as a Win32 application. To obtain the portability of kernel and the language subsystem plain ANSI C was used and the developers tried to avoid all the platform specific system calls.

Currently there are implementations of WinALT for Win32 platform and Linux. The capabilities of visualization in the console version are demonstrated by a viewer of WinALT objects in the style of Norton Commander viewers.

The existence of a console version, which can be easily integrated with the standard WinALT graphical interface or with a customized GUI based just on the native functions of the console edition, shows the WinALT mobility and flexibility.

5 Conclusion

The performed tests have shown that WinALT meets main requirements of its specification and it may be used as a flexible tool for creation and simulation of fine-grain algorithms and structures in versatile applications.

References

1. Pogudin, Yu., Bandman, O.: Simulating Cellular Computation with ALT. A Tutorial. Lect. Notes in Comp. Sci. 1277 (1997), pp. 424-435.
2. Markova, V., Pogudin, Yu., Piskunov, S.: Formal Methods and Tools for Design of Cellular Algorithms and Architectures. Programmirovanie 4 (1996), pp. 24-36 (in Russian).
3. Achasova, S., Bandman, O., Markova, V., and Piskunov, S.: Parallel Substitution Algorithm. Theory and Application. World Scientific, Singapore (1994), 180 p.
4. Beletkov, D., Ostapkevich, M., Piskunov, S., Zhileev, I.: Language and User's Interface Tools for a Simulation System with Spatial Parallelism. Proceedings of Sixth International Workshop, Novosibirsk, RAS Sibirian Branch Publisher (1998), pp. 228-232 (in Russian).
5. Malinetsky, G., Stepantsov, M.: Diffusion Processes Simulation by Cellular Automata with Margolus Neighborhood. Journal of Comp. Math. and Math. Physics. 1998. V.38, N6, pp. 1017-1020 (in Russian).

DEALed — A Tool Suite for
Distributed Real-Time Systems Development

Kirill Bolshakov[1], Yuri Karpov[1], Alexei Sintotski[2]

[1]Distributed Computing and Networking Department, Technical Cybernetics School, St.-
Petersburg State Technical University, 195251, Polytechnicheskaya ul. 29, St. Petersburg,
Russian Federation
{karpov, raven}@xjtek.com

[2]Dept. of Computing Science, Eindhoven University of Technology
P.O. Box 513, 5600 MB, Eindhoven, The Netherlands
alexei@win.tue.nl

Abstract. DEALed is a tool suite for development of distributed systems using
DEAL language. DEAL is being developed at Eindhoven University of
Technology as a part of DEDOS project. Area of application of the DEALed is
the development of the distributed real-time safety-critical control systems.

1   Introduction

DEALed is a tool suite targeted to development of distributed real-time control
systems. These systems have the following specific properties:
- Systems are real-time, i.e. control systems have timing requirements. The real-time
  control system should perform any control action within the specified deadlines
  and the developer of such a system should consider its timing requirements;
- Systems are distributed, i.e. they contain concurrent activities and subsystems that
  communicate with each other. Development of a correct distributed control system
  is difficult because the sequential way of the human thinking process;
- Systems are safety-critical, i.e. the cost of potential fault of such systems is very
  high.

The "DEDOS" project established at Eindhoven University of Technology addresses
this class of systems. The goals of DEDOS project are:
- To design the concepts of the dependable distributed operating system, which can
  be execution platform for the distributed real-time safety-critical applications, and
- To design methodology and technology of the development of those applications.

The main concepts of DEDOS operating system are
- DEDOS is the real-time operating system. It is the execution platform for real-time
  applications that satisfies all the requirements to the execution platform from the
  application side;
- DEDOS is the distributed operating system that provides distributed execution
  platform for the distributed application.

The most important from DEAL's point of view concept of the DEDOS operating system is application development model. Development of application consists of two phases:

1. Program development. This phase is platform-independent that means that developer should not consider program execution speed and mapping of the application under development onto computing nodes. In particular, this phase contains
   - Specification of the system under development;
   - Design steps;
   - Formal verification of the application under development with assumption that the execution platform will be capable to execute this application.
2. System generation. The mapping of developed application onto certain execution platform is performed during second phase. This phase contains
   - Feasibility analysis for surety that execution platform is capable to execute developed application;
   - Mapping of the developed application onto the certain execution platform. It may include code generation and per-runtime and/or run-time scheduling of resources.

The "DEAL" project is a subproject of the "DEDOS" project and it concerns the first phase of the two-phase application development model. Along with supporting development for DEAL language, DEALed is aimed at providing the developer with visual specification of behavior, simulation and documentation of the system under development. The following briefly describes main DEAL concepts that are supported by DEALed.

2 DEAL Concepts

The programming language and the design methodology are based on the following concepts:
- Object-orientation as the good and approved method for the maintaining of the design of the complex multicomponent systems;
- Timing annotations as the way to introduce time into the program;
- Formal specification language that allows formal description of components desired behavior;
- Formal verification as the method for the safety-critical systems development;
- End-to-end timing constraints as method for the reusability and simplicity increase.

2.1 Object-Oriented Programming Language

DEAL supports the component object model. Component is the construction unit in the language that may interact with another components. Components may contain another intercommunicating components, which named contained. Such complex components are called compound components, can be distinguished from the elementary components, which does not contain another components, and are distribution units. Thus, the system under development can be represented as the tree, or hierarchy of communicating components, which nodes and leafs are compound and elementary ones respectively.

Component development is class-oriented, i.e. it is possible to specify a class of similar components and use many instances of this class in the system under development.

Components communicate through strictly defined interfaces, provide data and structure hiding. It is not allowed for a component to change state of another component implicitly, without explicit communication act.

The communication mechanism in DEAL is a message passing. It is the asynchronous communication mechanism with infinite FIFO buffers.

2.2 Timing Annotations

Timing annotations is the way for the describing timing constraints in the system under development. Every communication statement of the DEAL program can be annotated. The timing annotation defines the execution moment of the particular statement. Actually timing annotations describe requirements for the program execution speed that should be satisfied after the system generation phase.

Variables in timing annotations are called timing variables. These variables CANNOT be used in the program as the ordinary variables. These variables do not represent states of components. They describe relations between execution times of different statements within the system under development. Therefore, there are two kinds of variables in DEAL programs: ordinary variables that represent the state of components and timing variables that used in timing annotations.

2.3 The Formal Verification

One of the most important features of the DEAL programming language is the formal verification of the system under development. Because DEAL has formally defined compositional semantics and a compositional verification framework, it is possible to perform verification of the system under development on the every design step.

The verification of the system under development is component-based and it is possible to perform verification of the particular component without knowledge of implementations of the contained components. This feature can help with the errors preventing during the first design steps.

2.4 End-to-End Timing Constraints

End-to-end timing constraints concept is the way to increase the design manageability and achieve the high degree of reusability of components. Instead of using constraints, which connect every piece of system and every component, designer can introduce constraints that are vital for the system under development and skip the intermediate ones. It is possible to use end-to-end timing constraints not only within program for one control thread but also to synchronize different components.

For this purpose, the message passing communication mechanism includes possibilities for transfer timing values between components.

End-to-end constraints' benefits are:

- Abstraction from the program's execution speed. For example, the designer abstracts from the program's execution speed and requires only that the deadline should be satisfied in the following DEAL program fragment:

```
read( d1, v )[?t];
x := v + 5;
x := x * x;
write( d2, x )[ < t + d ];
```

There is no information about the execution speed of addition and multiplication in this code fragment but only the requirement that calculations and the result storing should be performed before the particular deadline.

- Abstraction from real-time requirements during functional logic development. The end-to-end timing constraints concept gives logic to developer an abstraction from real-time constraints during phases of the design of functional. Using this feature the design of the complex system with real-time requirements can be performed with the following two steps:
  1. Design of the non real-time (without deadlines in specification) component(s) that performs (perform) useful calculations or logical control.
  2. Design of the required real-time system using non real-time component designed during previous step.

CRealTimeComponent on Fig. 1 is the real-time component under development. To implement this real-time component designer first can develop non real-time component F that implements needed functional behavior. Then, the task of designer will be development of components those implement real-time control. Their parallel composition with the component F should satisfy required real-time specification. Therefore, components A, B and C perform some sort of "translation" of events from real-time to non real-time representation; components X and Y perform reverse "translation".

3 Tool Features

The proposed toolkit provides

- Specification of the system under development and its properties;
- Generation of input files for model checkers and proof checkers for automated and mechanical verification of the system under development;
- Simulation on the with scheduling analysis for resolving of end-to-end timing constraints in the system under development;

Code generation and scheduling analysis for existing real-time operating systems and platforms are under consideration.

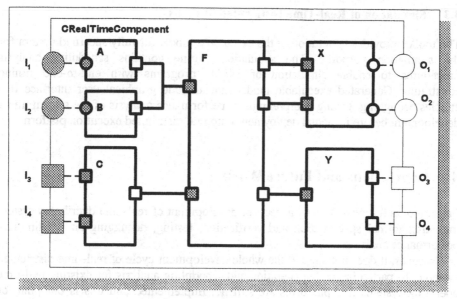

Fig. 1. Real-time system under development.

3.1 Specification Support

The toolkit provides graphical user environment for describing the system under development. Such description consists of two parts:
- Implementation of the system being developed, and
- Formal specification of its properties.

Used formal specification technique is described in [2] and it is based on Hoare triples adopted for real-time reactive systems. Using Message Sequence Charts as a graphical representation of such formal specification is considered.

Implementation of the system under development can be specified in three ways:
- Using textual notation (the DEAL language);
- Using structure charts as a graphical representation of structure of system under development;
- Using state machines as a graphical representation for components behavior.

Two latter types of implementation descriptions are transformed into DEAL constructs. This enables the developer to specify complex behavior in easily understandable graphical form.

3.2 Code Generation for Mechanical Verification Support

The toolkit includes code generators that transform system specification onto verification support systems input languages. Currently only PVS (Prototype Verification System, [4], [5]) interactive proof checker is supported by code generators. Support for real-time model-checkers as SPIN is under consideration.

3.3 Simulation of Real-Time Distributed Systems

The toolkit provides generation of the executable model for fully specified system for the simulation purposes. The simulation engine contains scheduling analysis procedures to enable simulation of DEAL programs with end-to-end timing constraints. Generated executable model may include graphical user interface that enables debugging, testing and preliminary performance analysis of the system under development before its actual deployment onto real distributed execution platform.

4 Conclusions and Future Work

Presented toolkit covers many aspects of development of real-time distributed system including formal specification and verification, testing, debugging and preliminary performance analysis.

However, it does not support the whole development cycle of real-time distributed systems. In particular, code generation and scheduling analysis for existing real-time operating systems and platforms are still not implemented and this is our plan for future work. Using real-time model-checkers for automated programs verification is also under consideration.

5 References

[1]   D.K.Hammer et al., "DEDOS: A Distributed Real-Time Environment", Parallel & Distributed Technology, IEEE Computer Society, pp. 32-46, 1994

[2]   J. Hooman, O. van Roosmalen, "A Programming Language Extension for Distributed Real-Time Systems", Technical report,
       http://www.win.tue.nl/win/cs/tt/hooman/DEALtech.html

[3]   Claus Lewerentz, Thomas Lindner (Editors)Case Study "Production Cell". A Comparative Study in Formal Software Development.FZI-Publication 1/94Karlsruhe University

[4]   A Tutorial Introduction to PVS by Judy Crow, Sam Owre, John Rushby, Natarajan Shankar, and Mandayam Srivas. Presented at WIFT '95: Workshop on Industrial-Strength Formal Specification Techniques, Boca Raton, Florida, April 1995.

[5]   N. Shankar. PVS: Combining Specification, Proof Checking, and Model Checking. Proceedings of FMCAD'96, LNCS 1166

[6]   A.V. Borshchev, Yu.G. Karpov, V.V. Roudakov, A.Yu. Sintotski, A.E. Filippoff, S.I. Fedorenko. "COVERS 3.0 — A C++ Based Graphical Modeling and Simulation Tool". In: V. Malyshkin (Ed.) Parallel Computing Technologies. Proceedings of the 4th International Conference PaCT-97, Lecture Notes in Computer Science No 1277, Springer, 1997, pp. 409-423

[7]   D. Harel. Statecharts: A Visual Formalism for Complex Systems. Science of Computer Programming, Vol. 8, No. 3, June 1987, pp. 231-274

PLATINUM: A Placement Tool Based on Process Initiative

Christophe Lang[1&2], Michel Trehel[1], and Pierre Baptiste[2]

[1] Laboratoire d'Informatique de Besançon, Université de Franche-Comté,
16 route de Gray, 25030 Besançon Cedex, France
{Lang, Trehel}@lib.univ-fcomte.fr
[2] Laboratoire d'Automatique de Besançon, UMR CNRS 6596, Université de
Franche-Comté,
Ecole Nationale Supérieure de Mécanique et des Microtechniques,
25 rue Alain Savary, 25000 Besançon, France
Baptiste@ens2m.fr

Abstract. This paper presents a new load sharing method based on process initiative. The method can be applied either for individual processes in networks of workstations or for parallel computation. We know that the global computing power is most of the time much underutilized. Our goal is to share the load among the different processors. Usually, load sharing algorithms are based on the fact that information and decision of distribution are on the processor. We aim to give processes the ability to decide where they are going to run. This method is based on the independence and the initiative of entities. We have written behavior algorithms for independent processes. We have used them to realize a dynamic placement tool on a network of UNIX workstations : PLATINUM. The aim of this paper is to present our new method through PLATINUM.

1 Introduction

We are in the context of load sharing on distributed systems. It consists in distributing the load between nodes in order to run programs efficiently. For example, in network of workstations, processors remain unused 33 % to 93 % of the time [11] [5].

Our main idea is inspired by the multi-agent systems area. We want to give independence and initiative to processes. For the moment we have developed a dynamic placement tool on UNIX workstations (PLATINUM : PLAcement Tool based on process INitiative in a Unix environMent) which is based on our algorithms.

First, we would like to give an overview of the classical problem in load sharing. Second, we will move on to our contribution to this research area. After that, we will deal with PLATINUM and his main algorithm. Then, we will present experimental results obtained on a network of workstations with PLATINUM. Finally we will conclude and present further work.

2   The Classical Problem

Load sharing gives the ability to distribute the load between all the nodes of a distributed system. So it allows to benefit fully from the available calculation power. When a node becomes overloaded, the algorithm will move one or several processes to an other less loaded node. In the fields of load sharing and load balancing we consider these features : migration or placement, static or dynamic, centralized or distributed ... Most of existing systems are based on the "system's point of view", i.e. it is the processor which decides where processes are going to run. Note that most of the systems are distributed to avoid the bottleneck due to communication between one processor, responsible of distribution, and the others. The distribution is often dynamic to be more efficient.

3   Our Contribution

3.1   Objectives

While load balancing is a global concept to the set of all the processes, we consider the individual problem of a user which has to execute a heavy program. This user does not care about the global balancing but wants its program to run efficiently. He does not have to know where it will run, either on the machine on which it has been started or on one another machine after migration. Nevertheless, this objective, very individualistic, replies to a real problem. Our algorithms have to reflect this individualist aspect.

If we have to make an heavy calculation, each part of this calculation may be associated to an independent process which will move over the network (of workstations or transputers) in order to be executed efficiently. At the end, all the results may be returned to a centralized process which will gather all these results. Our load sharing method iseeasily applied to this situation if processes don't communicate while running.

3.2   Method

We think that if the processes move by themselves over the network, load sharing can be more efficient especially because of the low communication rate. Moreover, the system will be easier to implement since there is no centralized scheduler. Indeed, in this case, we have to deal with synchronization, cooperation and so on. It is not the operating system which will manage the distribution but the processes themselves. The user's program will make its own analyze in order to stay on the processor on which it has been placed or to migrate to one another. In fact, an agent, that runs on behalf of a process, will sequentially move over the network to search a suitable processor. When it finds it, the agent starts the process.

Contrary to other systems like CONDOR [8], our system exploits all the stations of the network. Indeed CONDOR is based on underutilized stations. Thus, our system allows to use fairly loaded stations. The information policy is very important. Since the agents are independent, they are no messages exchanged between them. So, the information policy is reduced to the load indicator.

Then we have to provide an indicator describing the machine state at one particular moment. Usually, we have two load indicator models. The first is based on the length of the processor's queue. The second is based on a program (or daemon) which supervises the system, e.g. it calculates intervals of time separating two accesses to the CPU. We fancy the queue method for several reasons. It seems that, according to previous papers, it is a good indicator, simple to implement. Since there is no centralized scheduler, the system is extensible without modification. Moreover, we can imagine load sharing on WAN of workstations. There is no limitation on the network size.

4 An Intuitive Algorithm

In this paper, we present one of our algorithms : the blind algorithm. An agent, that runs on behalf of a process, will sequentially move over the network to search a suitable processor. When it finds it, the agent starts the process. Of course, the endless quest is the danger of such a method. Therefore, it is necessary to limit the agent's journey. This is one criterion for our performance tests. The agent saves in a file the characteristics of the processors that have been visited. We chose to keep the list of already visited processors in order to avoid going round in circles. In each past database, we can find 2 informations : the name of the station and the load degree. Moreover, when the current station becomes overloaded, the agent will try to find a new suitable station and will migrate the process to it. It is necessary to limit the process'number of migrations.

Each processor has 4 logical neighbors. We eliminate, thanks to the load indicator and the database, the "bad" processors. When the agent has to choose a new station in the neighbors :

- It first chooses non visited processors ,
- if there is no such processors, it chooses the processor which has been visited the first.

If the agent reaches the maximum number of moves, then we can say that the system is rather loaded : the agent migrates the process to the best processor in its past. And then we adapt the threshold depending on the load of the visited processors.

5 PLATINUM

5.1 Implementation

We have worked on a system of 12 heterogeneous workstations under UNIX. These stations are SUN stations : SS4(2 stations), SS5(2), SLC(1), ULTRA1(1), ULTRA5(4), SS1(1), ENTERPRISE2(1). They share their file systems thanks to NFS. The previous load indicator is used in combination with SPEC results (http://www.spec.org) in order to take into account differences between CPU's power.

We have developed two main modules (see figure 1) :

- the agent : it is responsible of the placement of the heavy process. It moves over the network in order to find a suitable station. It records its information in a particular file. It is launched each time it moves to another station. Therefore, there is no real migration for it. It possesses the module which allows the knowledge of the stations load,
- daemons : they are started once for all on stations. Each have got 4 logical neighbors which give the theoretical topology of the system. They receive requests from the agent : processor's neighbors for a new choice, heavy process execution, and so on.

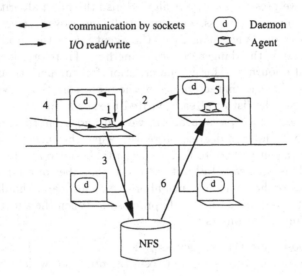

Fig. 1. the PLATINUM prototype

These are the different operations :

1. The agent is started on a station. It gets information from the daemon. It checks the load of the station.
2. If the agent is no satisfied by the station load, it tries to contact another daemon on a neighbor station.
3. The agent records its past on disk.
4. The agent is destroyed on the first station.
5. The chosen station's daemon starts the agent.
6. The agent reads its past from disk and resumes with first operation.

Our algorithms are based on processor's neighbors. We create four virtual neighbors for each processor. Those four neighbors will be given by the daemons launched on each processor. We currently work on allowing the user to modify the number of neighbors and then obtain new topologies like cube, ring and so on...

5.2 Experimental Performances

For good performances, the system must have an heterogeneous load. The heavy program that we have used is a matrices multiplication. The agent that accompanies it has a fixed average threshold. We have made sets of tests. The load of the first station was variable. On the figure 2, the system average load is given in abscissa (obtained with our load indicator). The two curves show the process execution time with our tool and process execution time without our tool (the process has been started on a randomly chosen station).

Due to the fact of the agent mobility, we can note that our prototype presents the evident advantage of not overloading the system with information messages.

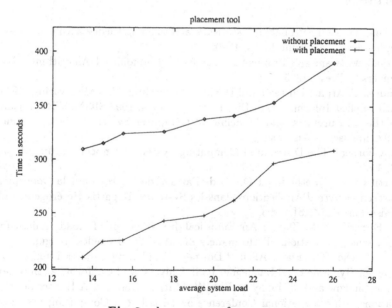

Fig. 2. placement performances

6 Conclusion and Perspectives

Our first algorithm consists in migrations over the system in order to search a suitable station. However, if all stations are overloaded, this technique is not

508

very efficient. This is why we have developed other algorithms based on limited agent travel and information shared between agents. We have chosen to develop intuitive algorithms in order to limit the communication rate.

PLATINUM is simple to install on a UNIX system. We have to start the daemons on each station and then the agent will move over the network. We know that this prototype replies to a real need in universities. We are going to install it on the Franche-Comte University network.

Moreover, since our system is distributed, the user will decide to load share or to load-balance the system with the help of our algorithms. In the first case, only a limited number of processes will move over the network in order to find an underutilized station. If he wants to load balance the system, and that can be the aim of a system administrator, he must launch all processes except system processes with our system. Thus, compared to other load balancing systems, our tool presents the main advantage of being useful for many purposes without any modifications. It's the way you use the system that will determine the load balancing policy.

References

1. Arnold. O Allen : Probability, statistics and queuing theory with computer science applications. Academic Press. 1990.
2. Rajeev Motwani and Prabhakar Raghavan : Randomized Algorithms. Cambridge University Press. 1995.
3. Andrea C. Arpaci-Dusseau and David E. Culler and Alan Mainwaring : Scheduling with Implicit Information in Distributed Systems. 1998 SIGMETRICS Conference on the Measurement and Modeling of Computer Systems, 233-243. June 24-26, 1998. Madison , Wisconsin.,
4. D.J. Farber : The Distributed Computing System. Compcon Spring 73, pages 31-34. 1973.
5. Bertil Folliot : Méthodes et Outils de Partage de Charge pour la Conception et la Mise en Oeuvre d'Applications dans les Systèmes Répartis Hétérogènes. Institute Blaise Pascal, MASI. 1993.
6. D. Ferrari and S. Zhou : An Empirical Investigation of Load Indices for Load Balancing Applications. Performances 87, 515-528. Bruxelles, Belgique.
7. Mor Harchol-Balter and Allen B.Downey : Exploiting Process Lifetime Distributions for Dynamic Load Balancing. ICSI. University of California at Berkeley, 1995.
8. M. J. Litzkow and M. Livny and M. W. Mutka : Condor : A Hunter of Idle Workstations. 8th International Conference on Distributed Computing Systems. IEEE Computer Society Press, 104-111. Washington, D.C., USA, 1988.
9. James S. Plank and Micah Beck and Gerry Kingsley : Libckpt : Transparent Checkpointing under UNIX. USENIX Winter 1995 Technical Conference. New Orleans Louisiana, 1995.
10. Jonathan M. Smith : A Survey of Process Migration Mechanisms. Operating Systems Review, 22(3), pages 28-40. 1988.
11. M. Theimer and K.A. Lantz : Finding Idle Machines in a Workstation-based Distributed System. IEEE Transactions on Software Engineering, 15(11) pages 1444-1458. 1989.

Author Index

Lecture Notes in Computer Science

For information about Vols. 1–1574
please contact your bookseller or Springer-Verlag

Vol. 1613: A. Kuba, M. Šámal, A. Todd-Pokropek (Eds.), Information Processing in Medical Imaging. Proceedings, 1999. XVII, 508 pages. 1999.

Vol. 1614: D.P. Huijsmans, A.W.M. Smeulders (Eds.), Visual Information and Information Systems. Proceedings, 1999. XVII, 827 pages. 1999.

Vol. 1615: C. Polychronopoulos, K. Joe, A. Fukuda, S. Tomita (Eds.), High Performance Computing. Proceedings, 1999. XIV, 408 pages. 1999.

Vol. 1616: P. Cointe (Ed.), Meta-Level Architectures and Reflection. Proceedings, 1999. XI, 273 pages. 1999.

Vol. 1617: N.V. Murray (Ed.), Automated Reasoning with Analytic Tableaux and Related Methods. Proceedings, 1999. X, 325 pages. 1999. (Subseries LNAI).

Vol. 1618: J. Bézivin, P.-A. Muller (Eds.), The Unified Modeling Language. Proceedings, 1998. IX, 443 pages. 1999.

Vol. 1619: M.T. Goodrich, C.C. McGeoch (Eds.), Algorithm Engineering and Experimentation. Proceedings, 1999. VIII, 349 pages. 1999.

Vol. 1620: W. Horn, Y. Shahar, G. Lindberg, S. Andreassen, J. Wyatt (Eds.), Artificial Intelligence in Medicine. Proceedings, 1999. XIII, 454 pages. 1999. (Subseries LNAI).

Vol. 1621: D. Fensel, R. Studer (Eds.), Knowledge Acquisition Modeling and Management. Proceedings, 1999. XI, 404 pages. 1999. (Subseries LNAI).

Vol. 1622: M. González Harbour, J.A. de la Puente (Eds.), Reliable Software Technologies – Ada-Europe'99. Proceedings, 1999. XIII, 451 pages. 1999.

Vol. 1625: B. Reusch (Ed.), Computational Intelligence. Proceedings, 1999. XIV, 710 pages. 1999.

Vol. 1626: M. Jarke, A. Oberweis (Eds.), Advanced Information Systems Engineering. Proceedings, 1999. XIV, 478 pages. 1999.

Vol. 1627: T. Asano, H. Imai, D.T. Lee, S.-i. Nakano, T. Tokuyama (Eds.), Computing and Combinatorics. Proceedings, 1999. XIV, 494 pages. 1999.

Col. 1628: R. Guerraoui (Ed.), ECOOP'99 - Object-Oriented Programming. Proceedings, 1999. XIII, 529 pages. 1999.

Vol. 1629: H. Leopold, N. García (Eds.), Multimedia Applications, Services and Techniques - ECMAST'99. Proceedings, 1999. XV, 574 pages. 1999.

Vol. 1631: P. Narendran, M. Rusinowitch (Eds.), Rewriting Techniques and Applications. Proceedings, 1999. XI, 397 pages. 1999.

Vol. 1632: H. Ganzinger (Ed.), Automated Deduction – Cade-16. Proceedings, 1999. XIV, 429 pages. 1999. (Subseries LNAI).

Vol. 1633: N. Halbwachs, D. Peled (Eds.), Computer Aided Verification. Proceedings, 1999. XII, 506 pages. 1999.

Vol. 1634: S. Džeroski, P. Flach (Eds.), Inductive Logic Programming. Proceedings, 1999. VIII, 303 pages. 1999. (Subseries LNAI).

Vol. 1636: L. Knudsen (Ed.), Fast Software Encryption. Proceedings, 1999. VIII, 317 pages. 1999.

Vol. 1637: J.P. Walser, Integer Optimization by Local Search. XIX, 137 pages. 1999. (Subseries LNAI).

Vol. 1638: A. Hunter, S. Parsons (Eds.), Symbolic and Quantitative Approaches to Reasoning and Uncertainty. Proceedings, 1999. IX, 397 pages. 1999. (Subseries LNAI).

Vol. 1639: S. Donatelli, J. Kleijn (Eds.), Application and Theory of Petri Nets 1999. Proceedings, 1999. VIII, 425 pages. 1999.

Vol. 1640: W. Tepfenhart, W. Cyre (Eds.), Conceptual Structures: Standards and Practices. Proceedings, 1999. XII, 515 pages. 1999. (Subseries LNAI).

Vol. 1642: D.J. Hand, J.N. Kok, M.R. Berthold (Eds.), Advances in Intelligent Data Analysis. Proceedings, 1999. XII, 538 pages. 1999.

Vol. 1643: J. Nešetřil (Ed.), Algorithms – ESA '99. Proceedings, 1999. XII, 552 pages. 1999.

Vol. 1644: J. Wiedermann, P. van Emde Boas, M. Nielsen (Eds.), Automata, Languages, and Programming. Proceedings, 1999. XIV, 720 pages. 1999.

Vol. 1645: M. Crochemore, M. Paterson (Eds.), Combinatorial Pattern Matching. Proceedings, 1999. VIII, 295 pages. 1999.

Vol. 1647: F.J. Garijo, M. Boman (Eds.), Multi-Agent System Engineering. Proceedings, 1999. X, 233 pages. 1999. (Subseries LNAI).

Vol. 1648: M. Franklin (Ed.), Financial Cryptography. Proceedings, 1999. VIII, 269 pages. 1999.

Vol. 1649: R.Y. Pinter, S. Tsur (Eds.), Next Generation Information Technologies and Systems. Proceedings, 1999. IX, 327 pages. 1999.

Vol. 1650: K.-D. Althoff, R. Bergmann, L.K. Branting (Eds.), Case-Based Reasoning Research and Development. Proceedings, 1999. XII, 598 pages. 1999. (Subseries LNAI).

Vol. 1651: R.H. Güting, D. Papadias, F. Lochovsky (Eds.), Advances in Spatial Databases. Proceedings, 1999. XI, 371 pages. 1999.

Vol. 1652: M. Klusch, O.M. Shehory, G. Weiss (Eds.), Cooperative Information Agents III. Proceedings, 1999. XI, 404 pages. 1999. (Subseries LNAI).

Vol. 1653: S. Covaci (Ed.), Active Networks. Proceedings, 1999. XIII, 346 pages. 1999.

Vol. 1654: E.R. Hancock, M. Pelillo (Eds.), Energy Minimization Methods in Computer Vision and Pattern Recognition. Proceedings, 1999. IX, 331 pages. 1999.

Vol. 1661: C. Freksa, D.M. Mark (Eds.), Spatial Information Theory. Proceedings, 1999. XIII, 477 pages. 1999.

Vol. 1662: V. Malyshkin (Ed.), Parallel Computing Technologies. Proceedings, 1999. XIX, 510 pages. 1999.

Vol. 1663: F. Dehne, A. Gupta. J.-R. Sack, R. Tamassia (Eds.), Algorithms and Data Structures. Proceedings, 1999. IX, 366 pages. 1999.

Vol. 1666: M. Wiener (Ed.), Advances in Cryptology – CRYPTO '99. Proceedings, 1999. XII, 639 pages. 1999.

Vol. 1671: D. Hochbaum, K. Jansen, J.D.P. Rolim, A. Sinclair (Eds.), Randomization, Approximation, and Combinatorial Optimization. Proceedings, 1999. IX, 289 pages. 1999.